Mathematics for
Elementary
School Teachers

Mathematics for Elementary School Teachers

Tom Bassarear

Keene State College

HOUGHTON MIFFLIN COMPANY   Boston   New York

This book is dedicated to my wife, Yvette, and to my two children, Emily and Josh, who had to put up with my many absences from the family over the past four years. I'm back!

Sponsoring Editor: *Maureen O'Connor*
Associate Editor: *Karla Paschkis*
Math Development Editor: Lenore Parens
Associate Editor: Dawn Nuttall
Senior Project Editor: *Maria Morelli*
Associate Project Editor: *Tamela Ambush*
Senior Production/Design Coordinator: *Carol Merrigan*
Manufacturing Manager: *Florence Cadran*
Marketing Manager: *Charles Cavaliere*
Cover design: *Stoltze Design*
Photographer: *Y. Takahashi, Photonica*

PHOTO CREDITS

Printed in the U.S.A.

Library of Congress Catalog Card Number: 96-76861

Student Text ISBN: 0-395-66959-6
Exam Copy ISBN: 0-395-84377-4

1 2 3 4 5 6 7 8 9-B-00 99 98 97 96

CONTENTS

6 *Proportional Reasoning*   279

PREFACE

Note: If you haven't read the Explorations Preface, you might want to do that now before reading on. The Explorations Preface sets the overall theme of the course and explains how the two volumes work with each other. This Preface more specifically describes the goals of the course and the features of the textbook.

GOALS OF THE BOOK

Richard Skemp, a noted British mathematics educator, has powerfully articulated the difference between relational understanding (understanding the mathematical structures and connectedness of ideas within and between concepts) and instrumental understanding (simply being able to manipulate formulas). A primary goal of this course is to develop relational understanding. Relational understanding, by definition, can't be "shown." Relational understanding comes out of student exploration and investigation, out of attempts to connect new knowledge to old knowledge. I have seen so many conscientious but frustrated students have tremendous breakthroughs as they began to invest less energy into trying to get it and more energy into trying to make sense of the ideas and problems.

Conceptual Focus

This relates to the two volumes that comprise *Mathematics for Elementary School Teachers* in that I believe that understanding of mathematical procedures and the ability to solve complex problems emerge naturally from focusing on relational understanding. To me this is the heart of the changed focus in the mathematics reform movement, which is partly enunciated in the NCTM Standard on Problem Solving: "Use problem-solving approaches to investigate and understand mathematical content." Thus, in one sense, the book is backwards from many other mathematics books in which concepts are defined and presented and then the examples help the student to better understand the concepts. In the Explorations, a rich question is asked and the concepts emerge from the students' active involvement and from group discussions. In the text, definitions and theorems are often presented after an Investigation. From another perspective, I am seeking to invite and honor all three types of reasoning: deductive, inductive, and intuitive.

For example, rather than presenting the structure for the multiplication procedure, Exploration 3.6, Part 2 has the students grapple with increasingly large multiplication problems. Invariably, the students will invent the distributive principle and be surprised when I give this name to what they have done, for many of them have negative memories of the distributive principle from Algebra 1. In Exploration 5.6, having to order fractions without finding LCM or converting to decimals forces the students to look at relationships between numerator and denominator. In Exploration 9.2, students apply their understanding of transformations and symmetry as they predict which figures will tessellate. They also have to determine what variables—e.g., number of sides, size of angle, regular vs. irregular, concave vs. convex—are relevant. They come to their conclusions in different ways, some more inductively, some more deductively, and some intuitively.

Integrated Big Content Ideas Throughout the Course

So many people think of elementary mathematics as chapter titles, and for a variety of reasons, I have chosen to live within a more traditional partitioning of mathematical content: fractions, decimals, percent, statistics, etc. However, a critically important outcome of this course has to be the students' realization of the underlying connectedness of mathematics. Thus, there are several big ideas that I have tried consciously to weave into the whole textbook.

Functions   Functional relationship, the idea of a unique and predictable relationship between two sets or two variables, is useful in so many areas. Functional relationships thus permeate the book. Students will see that most (all?) mathematical operations are functions. In the operator construct of fractions, they use the fraction as a function machine, and I use function language in Investigation 5.5 (Determining an Appropriate Representation) to solve a fraction problem. Geometric transformations are functions, and geometric relationships—the number of sides and sum of interior angles, the relationship between number of faces, the edges and vertices in polyhedra—embody functions, too. Students will explore the lack of a functional relationship between perimeter and area, and they will find that the act of measuring establishes a functional relationship between an attribute of an object and a number.

Composition-decomposition   The ability to understand most computation algorithms and to do mental arithmetic and estimation relies on the ability to decompose and recompose numbers. For example, 15×12 can be seen as 30×6 or as $15 \times 10 + 15 \times 2$. However, the process composition and decomposition does not stop with numbers. When transforming or measuring geometric figures we decompose and recompose them. Similarly, the problem-solving heuristic of breaking a problem into parts manifests this idea.

Conventions   Many students have no idea that some of the "mathematics" that they "learn" is invariant and some is convention. Making this distinction is an important idea that encourages students to look more carefully at what we ask them to learn and humanizes mathematics. For example, adding from right to left is a convention rather than mathematically required. On the other hand, in our numeration system, the order of numerals in a number is not a convention—$43 \neq 34$. Similarly, there are conventions in graphing and then there are no-nos. For example, in bar graphs, even if a frequency of a value of the independent variable is zero, you cannot just skip it. This has to do with proportional reasoning, as noted below.

Proportional reasoning   Like functions, proportional reasoning shows up in almost every chapter. Proportional reasoning is critical to a deep understanding of fractions, of slope, of probability, of percent, of similarity, and so many other concepts. This idea shows up every year in the Exploration 7.3, Typical Person. As students discuss the graphs they have constructed, they grapple with why some graphs are valid and others are invalid. For example, the width of the bars and the height of the bars is a convention; however, squishing the bars together when the frequency for a value is zero is not allowable.

Unit   We refer to units when developing an understanding of numeration. We refer to unit fractions, and we need to distinguish between units and wholes when working with fractions. When we make a scale for a graph, we are selecting a unit. We need units when making things — for example, we refer to a unit in quilt designs and tessellation patterns. And yes, of course, we talk about units in measurement.

Develop Mathematical Thinking

Whole books have been written on this and while I do not want to oversimplify it, I don't want to avoid it either. I believe mathematical thinking is as much a mindset as it is a constellation of related "skills" and thus, like relational understanding, cannot be directly taught as much as encouraged to develop. When one can think mathematically, one can appropriately use a variety of problem-solving strategies; one can justify one's thinking, which involves being able to communicate; one looks for patterns and can (intuitively, inductively, or deductively) arrive at hypotheses that one can check and revise and then ultimately make generalizations. For instance, in Exploration 4.4 (Star Patterns), as the students make stars they look for patterns, make and check hypotheses, and come to realize that number theory ideas help to explain why different stars have different shapes.

Algebraic thinking   I have chosen to de-emphasize the use of algebraic procedures — but *not* algebraic thinking — for two fundamental reasons. First, like it or not, so many of our students in the course are algebra phobic. I take heart from a statement in *Revitalizing Undergraduate Mathematics Education:* "Teach the students we have, not the ones we wish we had." I clearly think algebra is an important tool, but this course is not the course to pursue this and all the other goals of the course. Second, I try to de-emphasize algebraic solutions to problems in this course and emphasize other solution paths — e.g., guess-check-revise and draw a diagram — because solving equations algebraically is not a tool that elementary school students have, and we clearly want them to develop a wide repertoire of problem-solving tools. I need to note that I do believe that the course encourages the development of algebraic thinking, which is different from emphasizing using formulas to solve problems.

Problem-solving and communication   Problem-solving and communication are such important aspects of mathematical thinking that I want to discuss each of them in a bit more detail. As stated before, I believe that problem-solving is not something we do after the students learn the concepts and procedures. Rather, problem-solving should permeate all of the Investigations and Explorations. Developing a repertoire of problem-solving tools is an important goal in the course, with an emphasis on being able to solve nonroutine and multistep problems. Therefore, this book has fewer exercises that are "just like" the examples. I have come to believe that spending more time on fewer but richer problems results in students developing more mathematical power than doing lots of problems. Alfred North Whitehead's book *The Aims of Education* states this principle more eloquently than I ever could.

One of the most exciting pieces of feedback from instructors who piloted this book is from one who said that for the first time while he had been teaching the course, students were actually talking about mathematical ideas. As a result of the repeated emphasis on active learning, discussing, justifying, and the like, many students come to see the role of definition and notation in mathematics. Many students find explaining and justifying their work and "explaining as if to a friend on the phone" to be very new and frustrating at first, but consistent focus on communication bears rich fruit by the end of the course. As students struggle to explain an idea, a word like "prime" or "vertex" suddenly makes it much easier to describe the relationship they are trying to understand.

In the *Instructor's Resource Manual*, I discuss how learning logs and other devices help students to develop the ability to communicate their ideas and, more importantly, to see the value of being able to communicate mathematically. I have borrowed the notion of "first draft" from my English teacher colleagues. In class I will ask for someone's first draft of a definition or a concept, and throughout the text I encourage students to write and revise as a path to understanding.

ANNOTATED OVERVIEW OF THE COURSE

Let us take a walk through the book to help you get a more tangible (concrete) sense of the book and how the two volumes work together. Because of space limitations, I will highlight aspects of each chapter rather than discuss every section in detail.

Chapter 1: Foundations for Learning Mathematics

This chapter sets the tone for the whole book. The Explorations offer different kinds of problems to grapple with. In the Text, I take some time to explore important strands of mathematical thinking—problem-solving, communication, reasoning, patterns, and connections. I present and discuss the NCTM Standards in more detail.

Chapter 2: Fundamental Concepts

When I first began teaching this course and was still trying to "cover" as much of the book as I could, one day I suddenly realized that what I really wanted from the material on sets and functions was for students to have an appreciation of the need for these ideas. This chapter lays that foundation. Section 2.1 gives students tools to be able to talk of sets and subsets, or to be able to use a Venn diagram when the need arises in other chapters, for example, to understand the relationship between different sets of numbers. Similarly, the notion of function being a certain kind of relationship between two sets or two variables arises throughout the book. Any of the Explorations in Section 2.2 not only will have the students come to an understanding of the notion of functions, but also will get them started on developing mathematical thinking—looking for patterns, making and testing predictions, and making generalizations. The text's Investigations elaborate and refine this idea.

Numeration, discussed in Section 2.3, is a huge concept in elementary school mathematics. Exploration 2.8, Alphabitia, is one of the most powerful I have used. Most of my students report this to be the most significant learning of the semester and/or a turning point in the semester. The Exploration unlocks powerful understandings related to numeration, which the text supports by discussing the evolution of numeration systems over time.

Chapter 3: The Four Fundamental Operations of Arithmetic

These four operations are crucial for elementary school mathematics. Students come to realize that addition, subtraction, multiplication, and division are more than just plus, minus, times, and "gazinta." They see how the concepts of the operations, coupled with an understanding of base 10, enable them to understand how and why the procedures they have done by rote for years actually work. In Exploration 3.6, Part 1, Egyptian duplation piques their interest. The Explorations and Investigations help them to make sense of both standard and nonstandard algorithms.

Chapter 4: Number Theory

Number theory can be one of the most enjoyable chapters in the book. The Star Patterns exploration is one of my favorites because students find so many different patterns and can actually make and check hypotheses. Each of the Explorations in Chapter 4 has students grapple with core concepts of number theory in a connected way, and the text unpacks these concepts by investigating distinct aspects of them.

Chapters 5 and 6: Extending the Number System and Proportional Reasoning

I have chosen an unorthodox organization for Chapters 5 and 6 for conceptual and pedagogical reasons. The sets of integers, fractions, and decimals represent three historically significant extensions to the set of whole numbers. Given the limited time we have with the students, I find it makes more sense to emphasize rational numbers over integers and to connect the development of fraction concepts and operations in Chapter 5. Although the ratio construct is one of four major constructs of rational numbers, I find it to be more powerful to discuss ratio, proportion, and percents together in the context of Proportional Reasoning in Chapter 6.

In Exploration 5.5, students construct fraction manipulatives and then look for rules when ordering fractions, a critically important first step in seeing fractions as more than numerator and denominator. In Exploration 5.11 (Meanings of Operations with Fractions), having students represent problem situations with diagrams requires them to adapt their understanding of the four operations, developed in Chapter 3, to fraction situations. Having first constructed this concept through exploration, the student can approach an Investigation like 5.7 (Ordering Rational Numbers), with a richer understanding of what it really means to say that one rational number is bigger than another.

Exploration 6.5 (Which Ramp Is Steeper?), although challenging, requires students to examine the relationship between length and height to predict steepness; from this they come to see slope as a measure of steepness. They also construct an understanding of proportions that enables them to work much more confidently with percents and pays dividends in most other areas. And, as noted above, the text's focus on the "big idea" of proportional reasoning reaps rewards throughout the book.

Chapter 7: Uncertainty: Data and Chance

This chapter was originally called "Probability and Statistics." However, not only did students find that title intimidating, but I believe "Uncertainty: Data and Chance" more accurately describes what the chapter is actually about. My construction of this chapter was strongly influenced by another book I highly recommend: *On the Shoulders of Giants: New Approaches to Numeracy*, edited by Lynn Arthur Steen. In Exploration 7.1 (Exploring Populations) students make sense of real-life data that has relevance. Exploration 7.3 (Typical Person) is a popular and powerful exploration in which students decide how to collect and then represent data and discuss do's and don'ts of graphing. In Exploration 7.2 they also grapple with centers and spreads in data, two big ideas in statistics. The text focuses on critically interpreting representations others have come up with, and on introducing standard tools of statistical analysis and counting that help us make sense of the world. I am particularly excited that the Investigations with the concepts of mean and standard deviation have been so successful with students—as a result they can express these ideas conceptually instead of simply reporting the procedure.

Chapters 8 and 9: Geometry as Shape and Geometry as Transforming Shapes

I will confess that geometry is my favorite field in mathematics and it pains me to find that so many of my students so dislike it. I have chosen to have three geometry chapters, each focusing on geometry from a different perspective. In Chapter 8, you have the option of introducing geometry through Explorations with Tangrams, geoboards, or pentominoes. This less formal, more concrete introduction allows students with bad memories of geometry to let down their guard, but at the same time do good mathematical explorations. The geometric transformations we explore in Chapter 9 can be one of the most interesting and exciting topics of the course. Quilts and tessellations both spark lots of interest and provoke good mathematical thinking. The text develops concepts and introduces terms that help students to refine understandings that emerge from the Explorations.

Chapter 10: Geometry as Measurement

This chapter addresses measurement from a conceptual framework (i.e., identify the attribute, determine a unit, and determine the amount in terms of the unit) and historical perspective. Both the Explorations and Investigations get the student to make sense of measurement procedures and to grapple with fundamental measurement ideas. Exploration 10.2, Part 2 (How Tall?) generates lots of different solution paths and ideas, and lots of discussion about indirect measurement and precision. Exploration 10.9 (What Does π Mean?) has demystified π in the minds of many of my students and is a wonderful exercise in communication. Exploration 10.13 (Irregular Areas) requires students to apply notions of measuring area to a novel situation; every year students will hypothesize many different strategies, some of which are valid and some of which are not. The text looks at the larger notion of measurement, presents the major formulas in a helpful way, and illustrates different problem-solving paths.

Constructions and LOGO Appendices

Although I love constructions, I find that even in a two-semester course I would prefer to spend more time on concepts that are more critical for elementary teachers to know. Also, the constructions are more straightforward and can more easily be learned on their own. I have placed LOGO as an Appendix for two reasons. First, most teachers I know do not have the means to have students work with LOGO. Second, those teachers who do use LOGO do so in such different ways that it makes sense to present some basics for getting started with LOGO and leave it at that.

Overall Features

Worthwhile mathematical tasks   In developing and selecting Explorations and Investigations, I have searched for ones that will make all students feel challenged and successful. In developing the book, if I found that only some of the students engaged in an Investigation or Exploration, I either modified it or deleted it. One criteria, for me, of a good Investigation or Exploration is that there is more than one way to answer the question or problem that is posed.

Readability   Reviewers of the text and students who have used drafts of the book have praised its readability. I have tried to be informal and engaging and yet not water down the ideas.

Connections   One of the ways to nurture this aspect of mathematics is to integrate it into the textbook as a way of highlighting the interconnected nature of concepts. Brief, boxed inserts called *Connections* appear liberally throughout every text chapter. They have been a popular feature with reviewers and students alike. There are five kinds of connections, each identified with an icon. Browse through the book to get a feel for each kind of connection:

- History—considerations of interesting topics that are related to concepts developed in the text;
- Mathematics—connections between the concept being addressed and other mathematical concepts;
- Language—etymology of terms and/or nuances of terms;
- Beyond the Classroom—applications and uses of mathematical concepts and procedures in the business world, science, and everyday life;
- Children—stories and anecdotes from children's lives that connect to the concept being addressed.

At the same time, connections are interwoven into the chapters in addition to the big ideas mentioned earlier. For example, in Chapter 6, after the ratio model of fractions is developed, we go back and revisit "fraction" problems for which this model provides a new solution path. In Section 7.4, after combinations and permutations are developed, we go back and revisit problems in Section 7.3 for which these concepts may or may not apply. More efficient ways to determine the mean are connected to the idea of repeated addition.

Active learning   As Piaget once said, "To know is to invent." The students have to actively read the text and actively participate in the Explorations. I regularly invite them to "stop and think before reading on." The pencil icon is a visual reminder to do so. In Investigation 6.14, I pose the dilemma of a "fair raise" to introduce the idea of percent increase. The student is encouraged to grapple with the merits of two different "equal" raises. In Investigation 7.20, rather than just presenting the answer to how many combinations of boy/girl are possible among 4 children, the discussion explores different hypotheses that students consistently generate. In Chapter 7, rather than simply giving the definition of a fair game, I encourage it to develop over the course of several Investigations. In Chapter 8, instead of just defining a polyhedron, I ask students to try to extend their knowledge of polygons to see if they can define a polyhedron and the various other terms.

Exercises   To paraphrase a colleague of mine, Neil Davidson, I look for problems that will require thinking. In the exercise sets that follow each section of the text chapters, while I do provide some traditional practice exercises (for which the answers are generally in the back of the book), I have come to believe that grappling with nonroutine, multistep problems produces deeper understanding of mathematical ideas and greater problem-solving skills. I have also sought to include many exercises that are more like problems encountered in everyday life and work settings. You will find a number of problems that friends have reported struggling with or that have come up in my own life.

I need to explicitly mention something this book does not do that many other texts do: identify exercises by type. For example, denoting certain problems as "thinking critically" implies critical thinking is not necessary elsewhere. Labeling certain problems as communication problems implies that communication is only salient sometimes and marginalizes this aspect of mathematical thinking. Denoting certain problems as calculator problems reinforces the traditional role of the teacher deciding when to use and not to use calculators. Finally, "Just for Fun" implies that "real math" is hard work and not fun.

NCTM references   Rather than simply quote from the NCTM Curriculum Standards at the beginning of each chapter, I have sought to integrate the ideas from the Curriculum and Teaching Standards into the fabric of the course. Thus, there is some direct quoting, some paraphrasing, and some illustrating of my use of ideas from the Standards. In the *Instructor's Resource Manual*, I suggest various assessment practices that I believe embody the Assessment Standards more than the traditional daily homework, weekly quiz, and chapter test format.

Features within Each Chapter

What do you think?   These provocative questions may be discussed in class, assigned as journal writings, or given as homework.

Chapter and section introductions   These set the context for the work the students are to begin and connect the new ideas to previous ideas. I try to consistently offer a rationale for each of the topics. See, for example, how the introduction to Chapter 7 focuses on broader concepts of what it means to talk about data and chance.

Investigations   Questions are posed and then the students are asked to "stop, think, and then read on." The pencil icon is a visual reminder to do so. Then there is a Discussion of the investigation, which generally involves several different solution paths. In some cases, the answers are given right there. In some cases, the answer is not given, thus giving you the option of giving the answer after the students have investigated the question, or to use the question as a journal entry or as a homework problem.

Section summaries   I have sought to make these more than simply a restating of what students have learned but rather a looking back at and weaving together of the ideas of the section and putting them in a broader context.

Chapter summary with key terms   Each Chapter Summary begins by summarizing the big ideas of the chapter—those ideas that connect the different sections or connect ideas from this chapter with ideas from earlier chapters. The Chapter Summary also includes a complete list of key terms and basic concepts introduced in the chapter, with page references. Many students find this to be a useful reference.

End-of-Text Features

Four-color insert   This contains actual pages from the Houghton Mifflin K–6 series and enables students to see children interacting with the same concepts that they are now studying.

NCTM curriculum standards   This contains the NCTM's Curriculum Standards for K–4 and Grades 5–8.

Answers to selected exercises   These are provided for student reference. The *Instructor's Resource Manual* contains complete solutions to all end-of-section exercises.

Supplements for Instructor

Instructor's resource manual   This teacher-to-teacher resource manual serves as a guide to building an active, constructivist course. Part I includes four brief chapters. Chapter 1 is an elaboration of the goals of the course and how the Explorations work. Chapter 2 focuses on creating a positive learning environment, including a discussion of the physical environment, expectations and norms, and using cooperative learning. Chapter 3 examines some important differences among students that an instructor needs to think about, e.g., attitudes and beliefs, personal traits, gender, and ethnicity. Chapter 4 discusses assessment, a critical issue in a more innovative course such as this one.

Part 2 includes instructor's notes for each chapter of the Explorations. These notes include a brief chapter overview for the instructor, Intended Outcomes for each Exploration, an indication of time and materials needed, key Issues and Considerations, and discussions that include answers to the Explorations, and more importantly, cover common difficulties/problems students may have, effective opening questions and other tips gleaned from my experience with the Explorations, and examples of students' work.

The *Instructor's Resource Manual* also contains complete solutions to all the end-of-section exercises from the text. As much as possible, I have sought to include different ways that students might solve the problems.

Computerized test generator   The Computerized Test Generator contains more than 1000 test items. This ancillary can also be thought of as a database of additional exercises. These items were carefully written to reflect the philosophy of the text. The emphasis is on understanding concepts rather than symbolic manipulation. Therefore, you will find almost none of the typical multiple-choice type questions. Instead, there are many essay, open-ended, and free-response questions. The first part of the test bank includes questions referenced for each section of the text. The second part includes comprehensive chapter questions for each chapter. The Test Generator is available for the IBM PC and compatible computers and for the Macintosh. DOS and Windows versions provide **on-line testing** and **gradebook** functions.

Printed test bank   The Printed Test Bank is a printout of all items in the Computerized Test Generator. Instructors using the Test Generator can use the test bank to select specific items from the database. Instructors who do not have access to a computer can use the test bank to select items to be included on a test being prepared by hand.

Supplements for student   Apart from the *Student Solutions Manual*, which contains complete solutions to those text exercises that have answers given at the back of the text, there are no student supplements. When I first began writing the book, I intended to write the standard "Student Resource Handbook." However, over the course of the four years of writing the textbook, I have become convinced that such a supplement detracts from the main foci of the book and actually hinders rather than helps the students' development.

ACKNOWLEDGMENTS

It is impossible to completely acknowledge all the people and materials that have influenced the construction of this textbook. I find that several conversations with and writings by Marty Simon, Deborah Schifter, and Deborah Ball have felt, to use an analogy, like a tape loop—ideas or statements that have played over and over and over in my mind. For two years I worked on an NSF project called Mathematics for Tomorrow at Education Development Center. My work and conversations with Ellen Davidson and Jim Hammerman provoked a level of disequilibrium that often felt overwhelming but has been ultimately very helpful.

I highly recommend books and research by the following authors whose writings have enabled my practice to be more deeply connected to frameworks: John Clement, Paul Cobb, Robert Davis, Carol Dweck, Constance Kamii, Robert Karplus, Richard Lesh, Jack Lochhead, and Alan Schoenfeld.

There is not room to cite all the books that I read in preparing for this book. Certain of those books, though, were more influential than others and I particularly recommend them. Over the course of preparing for the book, I paged through the *NCTM Standards* documents many times and found many of the books in the NCTM Addenda series very provocative. Other notable books include: *American Indian Design and Decoration* by Le Roy H. Appleton; *Capitalism & Arithmetic: The New Math of the 15th Century* by Frank Swetz; *From One to Zero: A Universal History of Numbers* by Georges Ifrah; *Introduction to Tessellations* by Dale Seymour & Jill Britton; *Mathematics* by David Bergamini (Ed.); *Metamorphosis: A Source Book of Mathematical Discovery* by Lorraine Mottershead; *Number Words and Number Symbols: A Cultural History of Numbers* by Karl Menninger; *Numbers: Their History and Meaning* by Graham Flegg; *Symmetry: A Unifying Concept* by Istvan & Magdolna Hargiatta; *The History of Arithmetic* by Louis Charles Karpinski; and *The Language of Functions and Graphs* by the Shell Centre for Mathematical Education.

I certainly cannot claim that I invented all of the explorations, investigations, and problems in these two volumes. In many cases, I have made specific acknowledgments; if I missed someone, I apologize in advance. It is my hope that, with the increased amount of collaboration in mathematics education spurred by the NCTM and by advances in technology, teaching and writing will be much less solitary occupations than they have been in the past.

I would like to thank the many reviewers noted below for their thoughtful and helpful comments throughout the development of the book. I would like to particularly thank Nadine S. Bezuk, whose critical comments on an earlier draft of my sections on rational numbers timed nicely with the dissonance I was experiencing at EDC and resulted in a book that is much stronger conceptually than it otherwise would have been. The book also benefits from Doug Cashing's, Clarice Wagner's, and Tad Watanabe's careful attention to accuracy, and from class tests at Henry Ford Community College and the University of Vermont.

Professor Peter Berney, Yavapai College
Professor Nadine S. Bezuk, San Diego State University
Professor Donald A. Buckeye, Eastern Michigan University
Professor Doug Cashing, Saint Bonaventure University
Robert F. Cunningham, Trenton State College
Professor Fred Ettline, College of Charleston
Professor Larry Feldman, Indiana University of Pennsylvania
Professor Merle Friel, Humboldt State University
Professor Robert Hanson, Towson State University
Professor Joseph B. Harkin, SUNY College at Brockport
Professor Susan Herring, Sonoma State University
Professor Karla Karstens, University of Vermont
Professor Mary Ann Byrne Lee, Mankato State University
Professor Lois Linnan, Clarion University

Professor Vena Long, University of Missouri at Kansas City

Professor Vena Long, University of Missouri at Kansas City
Professor Jane Ann McGlaughlin, Trenton State College
Professor Sandra Powers, College of Charleston
Professor James E. Riley, Western Michigan University
Professor Lew Romagnano, Metropolitan State College of Denver
Professor Helen E. Salzberg, Rhode Island College
Professor Connie S. Schrock, Emporia State University
Professor Jean M. Shaw, University of Mississippi
Professor Merriline Smith, California State Polytechnic University
Professor Larry Sowder, San Diego State University
Professor Clarice Wagner, University of South Dakota
Professor Gary Van Velsir, Anne Arundel Community College
Professor Jeanine Vigerust, New Mexico State University
Professor Tad Watanabe, Towson State University
Professor Beverly Witman, Lorain County Community College

Special thanks go to the instructors who participated in the market survey my editors conducted as the book went into its second draft. Their positive reaction to the innovative format was inspiring:

Peter Berney, Yavapai College; Dr. Donald A. Buckeye, Eastern Michigan University; Doug Cashing, St. Bonaventure University; Dr. Forrest Coltharp, Pittsburg State University; Art Daniel, Macomb Community College; Ronald Edwards, Westfield State University; Fred Ettline, College of Charleston; Elise Grabner, Slippery Rock University; William Haigh, Northern State University; J.B. Harkin, SUNY College at Brockport; Susan K. Herring, Sonoma State University; Tess Jackson, Winthrop University; Karla Karstens, University of Vermont; Lois Linnan, Clarion University; John Long, University of Rhode Island; Dr. Jane Ann McLaughlin, Trenton State College; Glenn Prigge, University of North Dakota; Helen Salzberg, Rhode Island College; Dr. Connie S. Schrock, Emporia State University; Jean Simutis, California State University, Hayward; Mary Teagarden, Mesa College; Clare Wagner, University of South Dakota; Tad Watanabe, Towson State University; J. Normon Wells, Georgia State University; and Mary T. Williams, Francis Marion University.

Finally, I would like to thank the many people at Houghton Mifflin who have supported my desire to present to the mathematics community a book that I feel breaks new ground in some important ways. It is not as radical a departure as I had wanted but I understand that a book that looks too different will likely not sell and thus won't effect much change! I would especially like to thank my developmental editor, Karla Paschkis. Over the past four years, Karla learned a lot of math and a lot about the reform movement, and I learned to be a more careful thinker. Having to justify all my ideas was at times frustrating but very helpful.

T.B.

Mathematics for Elementary School Teachers

Foundations for Learning Mathematics

Knowing mathematics means being able to use it in purposeful ways. To learn mathematics, students must be engaged in exploring, conjecturing, and thinking rather than only in rote learning of rules and procedures. Mathematics learning is not a spectator sport. When students construct personal knowledge derived from meaningful experiences, they are much more likely to retain and use what they have learned. This fact underlies [the] teacher s new role in providing experiences that help students make sense of mathematics, to view and use it as a tool for reasoning and problem solving.[1]

NATIONAL COUNCIL OF TEACHERS OF MATHEMATICS

SECTION ◆ 1.1 ◆ **GETTING COMFORTABLE WITH MATHEMATICS**

Were you excited when you signed up for this course? Were you worried? Do you fondly remember your math lessons in elementary school, or have you been trying to forget them for all these years? You are at the beginning of a course in which you will reexamine elementary school mathematics to better understand the underlying concepts and to learn *why* mathematical procedures and formulas actually work. Your approach to this course depends on the attitudes and beliefs you bring to the classroom as a student; in subtle or not-so-subtle ways, you may pass these beliefs along when you enter the classroom as

[1] NCTM, *Curriculum & Evaluation Standards for School Mathematics: Executive Summary* (Reston, VA: NCTM, 1989), p. 5.

a teacher. So before we start working with mathematical concepts, let's look at our current conceptions of mathematics.

Beliefs About and Attitudes Toward Mathematics

This preliminary exercise is designed with two purposes in mind. First, it will help you examine and reflect on your beliefs and attitudes at the beginning of the course. Second, it will help you see a practical use of mathematics.

Rate your attitudes   Six pairs of statements concerning attitudes toward and beliefs about mathematics are given in Table 1.1. Score your beliefs in the following manner:

- If you strongly agree with the statement in column 1, record a 1.
- If you agree with the statement in column 1 more than with the statement in column 2, record a 2.
- If you agree with the statement in column 2 more than with the statement in column 1, record a 3.
- If you strongly agree with the statement in column 2, record a 4.

TABLE 1.1

Column 1	Column 2
1. There will be many problems in this book that I won't be able to solve, even if I try really hard.	1. I believe that if I try really hard, I can solve virtually every problem in this book.
2. There is only one way to solve most "word" problems.	2. There are usually many different ways to solve most "word" problems.
3. The best way to learn is to memorize the different kinds of problems—rate problems, mixture problems, coin problems, etc.—and how to solve them.	3. The best way to learn is to make sure that I understand each step.
4. Some people have mathematical minds and some don't. Nothing they do can *really* make a difference.	4. Some students may have more aptitude for mathematics than others, but everyone can become competent in mathematics.
5. The teacher's job is to show us how to do problems and then give us similar problems to practice.	5. The teacher's job is more like that of a coach or guide—to help us develop the problem-solving tools we need.
6. A good test consists of problems that are just like the ones we have done in class.	6. A good test has problems at a variety of levels of difficulty, including some that are not like the ones in the book.

Adaptive and maladaptive beliefs   We will return to your responses to Table 1.1 soon. Meanwhile, let me say that in over twenty years of teaching mathematics in elementary school, middle school, high school, and college, I have worked with thousands of students. One thing (of many) these students have in common is that their beliefs about mathematics influence how they learn. With respect to their beliefs and attitudes, students generally fall into four basic categories:

- Some students work hard, confident in their problem-solving abilities.
- Some students work hard at memorizing everything the teacher says because they are fearful of getting a wrong answer.
- Some students don't try very hard because they are convinced that mathematics is too difficult for them to understand.
- Some students don't try very hard because they don't think mathematics is relevant or useful.

The first group has what are called adaptive beliefs that help them approach math with a positive and confident attitude. The other three groups have different combinations of maladaptive beliefs that may keep them from thinking of learning as an evolving and enjoyable process. Many students find that they fit into more than one category or that the category they fall into depends upon the teacher and the material.

In Table 1.1, the statements in column 1 indicate maladaptive beliefs and the statements in column 2 indicate the corresponding adaptive beliefs. If you take the arithmetic average, or *mean*, of your scores (by adding up your scores and dividing by 6), you will get a number that we could call your belief index. If your belief index is less than 2, I would say that your beliefs are probably more maladaptive than adaptive. If you encounter difficulties in this course, it may be because some of your beliefs are hindering your ability to learn the material. If you do find this course frustrating, try to discuss your beliefs with your professor, with someone at a math center (if your college has one), or with a friend who is doing well in the course.

Individual attitudes and class attitudes Compare your present beliefs with those of your classmates and then discuss how you could represent what these data tell you—about you as an individual and about the class as a whole.

What did you come up with? Below are several possibilities. If your class does not do this exercise, you can use data (given on page 38) from one of my classes.

If you were to add the belief indexes of every student in your class and divide the total by the number of students, you would get the belief index for the whole class at the beginning of the semester. You could then compare that to the belief index at the end of the semester. You could also compare it to the belief index in other mathematics courses (for example, calculus) or to the belief index of high school freshmen, seventh graders, etc.

You could get the average score for the class for each question. You could represent that score either verbally (for example, the average in our class for the first pair of beliefs was 2.4) or visually (for example, on a bar graph). These are just two possibilities; you and your classmates may come up with others.

If my past experience as a guide, many of you are entering this course with more maladaptive than adaptive beliefs.[2] Yet you just tackled a multistep and nonroutine problem, more of which are appearing in today's elementary textbooks. You figured out how to concretely represent abstract data, and you figured out how to pull together a large group of data into a more easily

[2] It is important to note that I do not want to imply that if you have not done well in mathematics, this is because you have maladaptive beliefs. There are many factors which can affect a student's success in a course. Here we are focusing on changes in students' attitudes and beliefs.

understandable form. You probably also saw that the people in your class approached this problem in a lot of different ways.

Using Mathematics

Let us now turn our attention to how people use mathematics (in everyday situations and in work situations). Take a few minutes to jot down some instances in which you have used mathematics in your life and some instances in which you know that mathematics is used in different careers and work situations. Then read on. . . .

We find that people generally use mathematics for a purpose, for example:

- To persuade a boss that our idea will make money
- To persuade a potential customer that our product will save money
- To predict—tomorrow's weather or who will win the election
- To make a personal decision—whether we can afford to buy a house
- To make a business decision—how much to charge for a new product or whether a new medicine (for example, a cure for AIDS) really works

Solving problems In each of these examples, people are using mathematics as a tool for solving problems. To decide whether you can afford a new car, you have to collect data (on insurance, for example), add decimals, and work with percents (such as sales tax and interest on the loan). The mathematics you will use will help you solve the problem of whether to buy a car.

Think about this situation involving weather forecasters. In 1994 a hurricane brought severe rains to Georgia. Forecasters predicted that the Flint River would crest at 20 feet above flood level; the river actually crested at 13 feet above flood level, much to the relief of many residents. The forecasters probably used decimals and volume formulas or conversions to determine the maximum volume of water that would be flowing. They probably based their final results on computer models of flooding rivers, and the computer models were probably based on data collected on previous flooding.

In Section 1.2, we will focus on developing problem-solving skills that can be used in a wide variety of situations.

SECTION ◆ 1.2 ◆ **PROBLEM-SOLVING AND REASONING**

WHAT DO YOU THINK?

- What problem-solving tools do you bring to this course?
- In addition to verifying your computation, how can you verify your answer to a problem?

When you say *problem-solving* to most people, they think of an image something like Figure 1.1. Many of my students tell me that when they came into the course, their primary learning tool was memorization and their primary problem-solving tool was what they called "trial and error."

But problems need not be a source of dread. If you have done some of the explorations in the *Explorations* volume, you have already discovered some new tools for solving problems. In this section, we will examine some of the tools that are essential for solving multistep and nonroutine problems. Think of problems beyond the walls of the classroom that require mathematics—for example, Exploration 1.2 (Who Owes Whom How Much) and Exploration 1.3 (Budgeting Expenses). Generally, they are not one-step problems (e.g., just divide *a* by *b*), nor are they generally exactly like a problem you have solved before. We do our students a disservice if we lead them to believe that problem-solving is simply memorizing formulas and procedures.

THE FAR SIDE   By GARY LARSON

Hell's library

FIGURE **1.1***

Before we do some problems, stop for a moment. What kinds of problem-solving tools do you bring to this course? Many people will find this exercise more productive if they think of actual problems they have had to solve, such as buying a car, saving for college, or deciding how much food and beverages to buy for a party. Stop and write down your thoughts before reading on. If possible, discuss your ideas with another student also.

Our first problem, though silly, is well known because it nicely illustrates a number of important problem-solving strategies.

INVESTIGATION **1.1** Pigs and Chickens

A farmer has a daughter who needs more practice in mathematics. One morning, the farmer looks out in the barnyard and sees a number of pigs and chickens. The farmer says to her daughter, "I count 24 heads and 80 feet. How many pigs and how many chickens are out there?"

Before reading ahead, work on the problem yourself, or better yet with someone else. Close the book or cover the solution paths while you work on the problem.

When you come up with an answer, compare it to the solution paths below.

DISCUSSION

STRATEGY 1: Use trial and error
One way to solve the problem might look like what you see in Figure 1.2.

$$
\begin{array}{cccccccccc}
12 & 12 & 5 & 19 & 24 & 19 & 5 & 18 & 6 & 16 & 8 \\
\times 4 & \times 2 & \times 4 & \times 2 & \times 4 & \times 4 & \times 2 & \times 4 & \times 2 & \times 4 & \times 2 \\
\hline
48 & 24 & 20 & 38 & 96 & 76 & 10 & 72 & 12 & 64 & 16 \\
\end{array}
$$

$$
\begin{array}{ccccc}
48 & 20 & 76 & 72 & 64 \\
+24 & +38 & +10 & +12 & +16 \\
\hline
72 & 58 & 86 & 84 & 80 \\
\end{array}
$$

FIGURE **1.2**

Unfortunately, trial and error has gotten a bad reputation in schools. Many students come to class believing that it is not a "real" solution to a problem. Also, the words *trial* and *error* do not sound very friendly. However, this strategy is often very appropriate. In fact, many advances in technology have been made by engineers and scientists who were guessing with the help of powerful computers using what-if programs. A what-if program is a logically structured guessing program. Informed trial and error, which I call guess−check−revise, is like a systematic what-if program. Random trial and error, which I call grope-and-hope, is what the student who wrote the solution in Figure 1.2 was doing. In this case, the student finally got the right answer. In many cases though, grope-and-hope does not produce an answer, or if it does produce an answer, the student does not have much confidence that it is correct.

TABLE 1.2

	Number of pigs	Number of chickens	Total number of feet	Difference	Thinking process
First guess	10	14	68		
Second guess	11	13	70	+2	Increasing the number of pigs by 1 adds 2 feet to the total. What if we add 2 more pigs?
Third guess	13	11	74	+4	Increasing the number of pigs by 2 adds 4 feet to the total. Since we need 6 more feet, let's increase the number of pigs by 3 next guess.
Fourth guess	16	8	80		Yes!

STRATEGY 2: Use guess–check–revise (with a table)

One major difference between this strategy and grope-and-hope is that we record our guesses (or hypotheses) in a table and look for patterns in that table. Such a strategy is a powerful new tool for many students because a table often reveals patterns. Look at Table 1.2. A key to "seeing" the patterns is to make a fourth column called "Difference." Do you see how this column helps? We will explore the notion of how seeing patterns can enhance our problem-solving ability in Section 1.3.

It is important to note that the guesses shown in Table 1.2 represent one of many variations of a guess–check–revise strategy.

STRATEGY 3: Make a diagram

Some people think in words, others in numbers, and still others in pictures. Sometimes making a diagram can show one solution to a problem. I stumbled across this approach one day as I was walking around the classroom listening to students work on this problem in small groups. Figure 1.3 shows what one student had done. How do you think she had solved the problem? Write your thoughts before reading on. . . . 🖉

FIGURE **1.3**

I asked her how she had solved the problem. She replied that she had made 24 chickens, which gave her 48 feet. Then she kept turning chickens into pigs (by adding 2 feet each time) until she had 80 feet! I was thrilled, and she was embarrassed. I was thrilled because she had represented the problem visually and she had used reasoning instead of grope-and-hope. She was embarrassed because she felt she had not done it "mathematically." However, she had engaged in what I call mathematical thinking.

Furthermore, this solution connects nicely to an algebraic solution, as we shall see shortly. I have come to believe that for *many* students, the best way to understand the more abstract tools is to first solve problems using more concrete tools and then see the connections between the concrete approach (in this case a drawing or guess–check–revise) and the abstract approach (in this case two equations).

STRATEGY 4: Use algebra

Since the range of abilities present among students taking this course is generally wide, it is likely that some of you fully understand the following algebraic strategy and some of you do not. Furthermore, many students enter this and other college math courses believing that the algebraic strategy is the *right* strategy, or at least the *best* strategy. Let's look at an algebraic solution and then see how it connects to other strategies and to the goals of this course.

Go back and review strategies 1 and 2. They all involved a total of 24 pigs and chickens. Can you explain in words why this is so? Think about this before reading on. . . .

Most students say something like, "Because the total number of animals is 24" or "Well, 24 animals will have 24 heads." Therefore, if we say that

p = the number of pigs

c = the number of chickens

then the *number* of pigs plus the *number* of chickens will be 24. Hence, the first equation is

$p + c = 24$

Many students have difficulty coming up with the second equation. If this applies to you, look back at how we checked our guesses when using Strategy 2, guess–check–revise: We multiplied the number of pigs by 4 and the number of chickens by 2, then added those two numbers to see how close that sum was to 80. In other words, we were doing the following:

(The guess for number of pigs) $\times$ 4 + (the guess for number of chickens) $\times$ 2

$\qquad (p \times 4) \qquad\qquad + \qquad\qquad (c \times 2)$

More conventionally, this would be written as

$4p + 2c$

Using guess–check–revise, we had the right answer when this sum was 80. Thus, the second equation is

$4p + 2c = 80$

If you solve these two equations, using basic algebra, you will discover that $p = 16$ and $c = 8$.

The algebraic strategy in perspective Students who do not do well with equations generally understand this algebraic solution better if they see it *after* they have used guess–check–revise. The reason for this is simple and is grounded in learning theory: *The teacher s explanation (or another student s) is far more meaningful if you can connect it to something you already know.* This is such an important learning principle that I want to elaborate. If I show you how to create the equation before you have attempted the problem on your own, my explanation is not likely to stick. In this case, your knowledge is "Teflon knowledge." The Teflon molecule was specially designed by chemists so that other materials tend not to stick to it. This is a wonderful property for frying pans to have, but not for human brains. To the extent that new ideas and concepts have connections to ideas and knowledge you already have, to that extent you are more likely to retain (that is, to own rather than rent) that new knowledge.

Algebra can be a very effective strategy for many problems. However, I offer the following cautionary notes with respect to the use of algebra in this course. First, the algebraic strategy is not more mathematical than the guess–check–revise strategy; it is simply more abstract. Second, it is better to use guess–check–revise and be confident of the process and of the answer than to use grope-and-hope to come up with an algebraic equation that you hope works out. Furthermore, guess–check–revise is a tool all of your future students should have, regardless of their age, whereas only a small percentage of your future students will have formal algebraic knowledge before grade 8 or 9.

Problem-Solving and Toolboxes

An image of problem-solving I would like to develop in your mind is that of a toolbox. Imagine that your car breaks down and is towed to the garage, where a novice mechanic, right out of training school, is the first to look at it. The novice will probably try a few standard procedures: Insert the key to see what happens, look at the battery connections, look for a loose wire, and so on. If none of those strategies work, the novice mechanic will be stumped and will have to summon the senior mechanic. The senior mechanic may try the same basic procedures and may solve the problem by *interpreting* the results. If this does not solve the problem, the mechanic will have to go to two toolboxes. The first toolbox is a physical one. The second toolbox is a mental one.

At the beginning of this course, many students are like the novice mechanic: When they encounter a problem, they have a limited repertoire of strategies. However, as the course develops, their toolbox grows in two ways. First, the number of tools grows. This is like the novice mechanic's learning to use the garage's diagnostic equipment. Second, their ability to use each tool also grows. This is analogous to the novice mechanic's learning how to use a voltmeter more skillfully.

Looking back   At this point, I want to introduce another process that most successful students have incorporated into their toolbox. They reflect on their work. That is, after solving a problem, they stop and examine their toolbox — what tools they used better and what new tools they used. Take a few minutes now to look at your notes on the strategies we discussed in Investigation 1.1 and then look at "4 Steps for Solving Problems" on the inside front cover of the *Explorations* volume. What tools were used in the various solutions of the pigs-and-chickens problem? What made those tools work better? Then read on. . . . 🖉

My list includes:

1. Draw a diagram — a picture is often worth a thousand words.
2. Guess–check–revise — starting here will help some students to develop the two equations.
3. Make a table — this increases the possibility of seeing more patterns.
4. Look for patterns — extending the table enables certain patterns to become more visible.
5. Develop an equation — a powerful tool, but also surrounded by quicksand for many.

Two final notes about Investigation 1.1:

1. The strategies discussed in Investigation 1.1 do not represent all the different ways in which the pigs-and-chickens problem has been solved. Because of space restrictions, only four were discussed.
2. Many students think that there is only one tool per problem. An important adaptive belief is that there are often several different ways (using different

tools) to solve a problem and that the tools are often used in combination instead of separately.

Polya's Four Steps

Now that we have examined the solving of one problem in detail, let us stop to reflect for a bit. In this textbook, we will examine problem-solving from the perspective of a toolbox—that is, from the perspective of developing tools to help you solve problems. George Polya developed a framework for problem-solving that breaks down problem-solving into four distinguishable steps. In 1945, he outlined these steps in a now-classic book called *How to Solve It.*

When you approach a problem—a math problem, a writing assignment, even a personal problem—if you think that you have to come up with an answer immediately and that there is only one "right" way to reach that answer, a solution may seem to be beyond your grasp. But if you break the problem down and creatively and mindfully approach each *step* of the problem, it generally becomes more manageable. Polya suggests that you first need to make sure you understand the problem. Once you understand the problem and know what you need to find out, you devise a plan for solving the problem. Then you monitor your plan; you check frequently to see whether it is productive or going down a dead-end street. Finally, you look back at your work. This last step involves more than just checking your computation; for example, it includes making sure that your answer makes sense. For each of these four steps, there are specific strategies that we will explore in this chapter and that you will refine throughout this course.

Owning versus renting Instead of just listing Polya's strategies, we are going to discover them by putting them into action. You will notice that I often ask you to stop, think, and write some notes. I really mean it! I have come to distinguish between those students who *own* what they learn and those who simply *rent* what they learn. Many students rent what they have learned just long enough to pass the test. However, within days or weeks of the final exam, it's gone, just like a video that has been returned to the store. Just as with a house, it is much more satisfying to own than to rent. One of the important differences between owners and renters is that those who own the knowledge tend to be *active readers.*

Think and then read on . . . Throughout the book, I will often pose a question and ask you to "think and then read on. . . ." Rather than just look to the next paragraph and see the "answer," you will learn much more if you immediately cover the next paragraph or close the book . . . stop . . . think . . . write down your thoughts . . . and then read on. The phrase "think and read on . . ." is there to remind you to read the book actively rather than passively. An active reader stops and thinks about the material just read and asks questions like: Does this make sense? Have I had experiences like this? When reading an example, the active reader tries to do the example before reading the author's solution. The active reader does the examples with pen or pencil, rather than just reading the author's description. I recommend that you keep a journal (your instructor may give you specific instructions). Keeping a journal has many benefits. Many people find that they learn more by writing down their responses to "think and read on . . ." rather than just stopping for a moment to reflect mentally. Many students find that reading over their journals every week or at the end of each chapter provides new insights into the mathematics and into their own beliefs and attitudes about mathematics.

Using Polya's four steps   On the inside front cover of the *Explorations* volume is an outline of Polya's four steps for successful problem-solving. I encourage you to use that outline in all of the following ways:

1. Use it as a guide when you get stuck.

2. Don't rent it, buy it. Buying it involves paraphrasing my language and adding new strategies that you and your classmates discover. For example, many of my students have added one whole step to help reduce anxiety: first take a deep breath and remind yourself to slow down.

3. Just as we did in Investigation 1.1, after you have successfully solved a problem, stop for a moment and reflect on the tools you used to solve the problem. As the course progresses, you should find that most problems involve the use of several strategies, and you should find that you use the tools more skillfully. For example, using "Make a diagram" skillfully involves deciding how precise your diagram needs to be, checking to see that the diagram illustrates the relevant given information, seeing if the diagram can help you to paraphrase the problem or see it from a new perspective, etc.

Why Emphasize Problem-Solving?

Although Polya described his problem-solving strategies back in 1945, it was quite some time before they had a significant impact on the way mathematics was taught. One of the reasons is that the desired outcomes of mathematics instruction were defined too narrowly. If the stated goal of mathematics classes was to learn and practice the "right" techniques to answer textbook problems, chances are that students rarely saw how math applied to situations outside the classroom.

Another reason for the limited impact of Polya's work is that until recently, "problems" were generally defined too narrowly. For example, many of you learned how to do different kinds of problems—mixture problems, distance problems, percent problems, age problems, coin problems—separately, but have never realized that they have many principles in common. To use language from the NCTM (the National Council of Teachers of Mathematics), there has been too great a focus on single-step problems and routine problems. Consider the examples from the National Assessment of Educational Progress shown in Table 1.3.

TABLE 1.3

Problem	Percent correct Grade 11
1. Here are the ages of six children: 13, 10, 8, 5, 3, 3 What is the average age of these children?	72
2. Edith has an average (mean) score of 80 on five tests. What score does she need on the next test to raise her average to 81?	24

Mary M. Lindquist, ed., *Results from the fourth mathematics assessment of the National Assessment of Educational Programs* (Reston, VA: NCTM, 1989), pp. 30, 32.

To solve the first problem, one only has to remember the procedure for finding an average and then use it:

$$\frac{13 + 10 + 8 + 5 + 3 + 3}{6}$$

However, there is no simple formula for solving the second problem. Try to solve it on your own and then read on. . . .

To solve this one, you have to have a better understanding of what an average means. One approach is to see that if her average for 5 tests is 80, then her total score for the 5 tests is 400. If her average for the 6 tests is to be 81, then her total score for the 6 tests must be 486 (that is, 81 × 6). Since she had a total of 400 points after 5 tests and she needs a total of 486 points after 6 tests, she needs to get an 86 on the sixth test to raise her overall average to 81.

Many students still consider the second question to be a "trick" question unless the teacher has explicitly taught them how to solve that kind of problem. However, many employers note that problems that occur in work situations are rarely *just* like the ones in the book. What employers desperately need is more people who can solve the "trick" problems, because, as one wag put it, "life is a trick problem!"

Many mathematics teachers realized the limitations of the traditional approaches to teaching mathematics, and in 1989 the NCTM published a set of standards (discussed in the Student Preface and in Section 1.6) to guide the learning of mathematics. With respect to problem-solving, the NCTM has urged a turnabout. Traditionally, the teacher "taught" a new concept or skill, and *then* students did *problem-solving*. The NCTM has rejected this separation of teaching and problem-solving. That is, problem-solving involves more than just doing word problems to apply the concepts. In this book, we will investigate a wide variety of problems. By solving these problems, you will discover the meaning of the concepts and how to apply them and come to a much deeper understanding of and appreciation for the formulas or procedures you learn.

Reasoning

There is ample evidence that most students can successfully solve only single-step and routine problems. The trouble is that few real-life[3] problems are single-step or routine; they require thinking and reasoning. They may be similar to other problems, but the solution often requires knowing what features of the previous situation can be applied to the new situation. Examples of this include Exploration 1.2 (Who Owes Whom How Much) and Exploration 1.3 (Budgeting Expenses). Thus, the NCTM has made reasoning one of the centerpieces of a new mathematics curriculum. Mathematical reasoning involves:

- Knowing how and when to use known facts and relationships to explain your thinking

- Being able to justify your answers and solution processes, that is, both being able to explain *how* you solved the problem and being able to justify (or explain) each step

- Becoming comfortable and confident with both inductive and deductive reasoning

The following television commercial illustrates the need for reasoning. The announcer stated, "Rolaids absorbs 47 times its weight in excess

---

[3] I am using the term *real-life* to refer to problem situations "beyond the walls" of the classroom, that is, in everyday life and in business and other work situations. However, the term *real-life* can imply that school mathematics is not "real-life," and that is not the impression that I want to develop. Thus, I will generally try to avoid the term *real-life* and instead use "beyond the classroom."

stomach acid." What is your first response to this statement? Think and read on. . . . 📝

That sounds like a lot. Imagine the weight of one Rolaids tablet, and then imagine 47 times that weight of excess stomach acid being absorbed. However, there is something very important missing in that number—what?

There is no frame of reference or comparative data. For example, it may be that the other leading brands absorb 60 or 75 or 100 times as much. Without being able to compare that number, without a frame of reference, we cannot really say how good the antacid tablet really is.

The NCTM's Reasoning Standard also emphasizes confidence. This is crucial in this course, because if teachers have confidence in themselves, their students are more likely to develop this attitude. As a teacher, I am delighted when students tell me that for the first time in years, math makes sense. For example, there really is a reason why "two negatives make a positive," there really is a reason why the value of π is 3.14 and not 3.02, and these reasons are understandable by regular people, not just "mathematical" people.

When mathematics makes sense, students own what they learn. Students who have only rented what they have learned can generally solve only problems that look just like the ones in the book or the ones done in class. Such students tend to forget much of that learning over the summer, which is one of the reasons so many mathematics classes in grades 2 through college begin each semester reviewing. On the other hand, students who own what they have learned are generally able to apply that learning to solve multistep and nonroutine problems. Such students tend to retain more of that material for longer periods of time.

With these ideas in mind, let us now consider several problems so that you can begin to consciously develop and refine your own problem-solving toolbox.

INVESTIGATION 1.2   How Much Will the Patio Cost?

Let's say you are building a patio in your back yard. You have decided to make the patio 12 feet by 8 feet. The local lumber store sells premade patio blocks, which are 18 inches by 12 inches, for 75¢ each. How much will the patio cost?

Solve this problem on your own, taking time to understand the problem and consider how you might plan to solve it. Then compare your solution and strategies to the ones discussed below. . . . 📝

DISCUSSION

STRATEGY 1: Make a diagram

Let us examine two kinds of diagrams that students often come up with. Since the blocks are $1\frac{1}{2}$ feet long and 1 foot wide, some students find a piece of graph paper and let each square represent 1/2 foot, as shown in Figure 1.4. If you make one x on the grid for each patio block, you can determine the total number. What do you get? 📝

Other students simply sketch the problem on a blank piece of paper as shown in Figure 1.5.

In either case, we can see that we will need 64 blocks, and 64 blocks times 75¢ per block is 4800¢ or $48.

FIGURE **1.4**   FIGURE **1.5**

STRATEGY 2: Divide

There is another way to solve the problem that is quicker, but also requires more thinking at the beginning of the problem. If we divide the total area of the patio by the area of one block, the quotient will tell us how many blocks we need.

The total area of the patio is 12 ft. $\times$ 8 ft. = 96 square feet.

The area of each block is 1.5 ft. $\times$ 1 ft. = 1.5 square feet.

When we divide 96 sq. ft. by 1.5 sq. ft., we get 64 blocks.

Some readers may be kicking themselves for not thinking of this strategy. In Chapter 3, you will find that one of the meanings of division is repeated subtraction. From one perspective, this problem is asking how many times we can subtract 1.5 from 96.

STRATEGY 3: Use dimensional analysis

We can treat the "labels" as algebraic terms. Just as numbers can "cancel," so too can labels. We will investigate canceling further in Chapter 5. Using *dimensional analysis*, we have

$$96 \text{ square feet} \div \frac{1.5 \text{ square feet}}{1 \text{ block}}$$

We can treat this as a division of fractions problem; thus, we need to invert and multiply.

$$= 96 \text{ square feet} \times \frac{1 \text{ block}}{1.5 \text{ square feet}}$$

$$= 64 \text{ blocks}$$

Since square feet "cancel," the meaning of 64 is 64 blocks.

After Investigation 1.1, and also in the *Explorations,* you were asked to take some time to stop and reflect on what you learned from the activity. I have found that most of my best students intuitively do this after every problem that required thinking on their part. I encourage you to do this on your own throughout the book. What problem-solving tools did you learn or refine in this investigation? Write them down before doing the next investigation. If possible, share your insights with another student. 🖋

INVESTIGATION **1.3**   Making Paper Dinosaurs

◆ **A** first-grade teacher is going to have her students make a number of paper dinosaurs for a counting project. She needs one hundred 2 inch by

3 inch rectangles, on which the students will trace and then cut out dinosaurs. How many sheets of paper will she need for this project? Think and then read on. . . .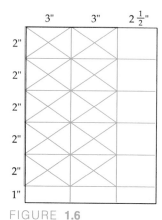

DISCUSSION

The first step is to stop and make sure you understand the problem. Did you realize that we do not have enough information to solve the problem? What else is needed?

We need to know the dimensions of the paper. Let's say she uses standard paper; that is, each sheet is $8\frac{1}{2}$ in. by 11 in.

STRATEGY 1: Divide

This problem may feel similar to the previous one. Let's see if we can use the approach that we learned in the last problem. The total area of one sheet of paper is 8.5 in. × 11 in., or 93.5 square inches. If we divide the total area by the area of one rectangle (6 square inches), we get 15.58 rectangles. According to this strategy, we can get 15.58 rectangles from one sheet of paper. That said, how many sheets will the teacher need in order to make 100 rectangles? Figure it out yourself and read on. . . .

Many students ponder for a while here. Do you divide 100 by 15.58 or by 15? What do you think?

$$100 \div 15.58 = 6.4$$
$$100 \div 15 = 6.7$$

Does this mean that the teacher needs 6 sheets or 7 sheets? If you are wondering about this yourself, one option is to continue to reason it out until it makes more sense. Another option is to try a different strategy. This also can serve as a way of checking your answer. If you get the same answer with a different strategy, the odds are that you are on the right track.

STRATEGY 2: Make a diagram

When we begin to make a diagram, we quickly realize that there are two different ways to lay out the 2 in. by 3 in. rectangles. These are illustrated in the diagrams in Figure 1.6. (Make sure the diagrams make sense to you before reading on.)

FIGURE 1.6

Cutting out the rectangles according to the diagram on the left produces ten 2 in. by 3 in. rectangles; cutting out the rectangles according to the diagram on the right produces twelve 2 in. by 3 in. rectangles.

Actually, we can get more 2 in. × 3 in. cutouts. Do you see how? If not, experiment for a while and then read on. . . .

I must confess that the first draft of this chapter did not contain the layouts shown in Figure 1.7, but rather only those in Figure 1.6. A colleague of mine caught my error. Even professors sometimes get stuck in ruts! This also happens in the business world and is one of the reasons why people work together on teams and have "outside" reviews of their solutions.

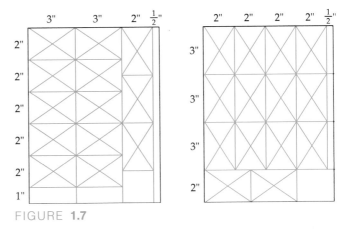

FIGURE **1.7**

We now have a discrepancy between the two methods. When we used division, we got an answer of 15 rectangles. Using the "make a diagram" strategy, we can get at most 14 rectangles. If this were a homework assignment or a quiz, which answer would you turn in? Think and read on. . . .

In this case, the fifteenth rectangle would have to be pieced together from scraps, and so it is more realistic to use 14 rectangles per sheet. If you can get 14 rectangles per page, and you want 100 rectangles, how many sheets will you need? Think before reading on. . . .

If you divide 100 by 14, you get approximately 7.1, and so you will need a bit more than 7 sheets; that is, you will need 8 sheets.

Why didn't the first strategy work here? It is important to note that the "division" strategy was very appropriate for Investigation 1.2, but was inappropriate here. This highlights a belief that many students have about how to go about learning mathematics. Let me explain. If I need to find a file in my computer, I can press the "Find" button and give the name of the file; the computer will search through its memory until it finds that file. Many students use a similar approach when solving problems: Instead of trying to understand the problem, they search their memory for a similar problem. If they find one, they solve the present problem in just the same way. Too often the students do not ask themselves if that strategy is applicable to the new problem. Can you explain *why* the division strategy worked on the patio problem and not on this one? Think and then read on. . . .

In the patio problem, the dimensions of the brick divided the total length and width with no remainder. That is, 12 ÷ 1.5 = 8 and 8 ÷ 1 = 8. In this investigation, we do have a remainder:

$$11 \div 3 = 3\frac{2}{3} \quad \text{and} \quad 8\frac{1}{2} \div 2 = 4\frac{1}{4}$$

Thus, the division strategy works only in some cases. This is true beyond the classroom, too. In businesses and laboratories, workers frequently have to decide whether solutions to old problems are applicable to new ones. In some cases, the solution is directly applicable. In other cases, it is partially applicable. In yet other cases, it is not applicable at all, because there are fundamental differences between the two situations.

Refining the problem In many everyday and work situations, we would still not be finished with the problem. While we have solved the question that was asked, a teacher who is frugal or environmentally sensitive would realize that she can get more rectangles if they don't have to be exactly 3 inches by exactly 2 inches. If the teacher makes the rectangles "a little" smaller, she should be able to get more than 14 per sheet. What would you recommend? Think and then read on. . . .

If you make the length of each rectangle in the left-hand diagram of Figure 1.6 or 1.7 2 5/6 in., you will be able to make 15 rectangles whose dimensions are 2 5/6 in. by 2 in. If you make the length of each rectangle in the right-hand diagram 2 3/4 in., you will be able to make 16 rectangles whose dimensions are 2 3/4 in. by 2 in.

Reflecting on the problem Take a minute to reflect on this problem. What did you learn about problem-solving? What tools did we use on this problem? You may want to refer to the "4 Steps for Solving Problems" on the inside front cover of the *Explorations* volume.

There are two very important points in this investigation. The first is that you need to take care when adapting a strategy from one situation to another. Second, a different kind of thinking happens when we bring real life into problem-solving situations, the computations must be interpreted; we are not finished when we have a number.

LEARNING[4]

A colleague of mine was working through a word problem with her class one day and encouraging the students to think about what they were doing. Suddenly one of the students said, "But you don't need to do all this stuff you are teaching us; you just know the answer." She was stunned, and the ensuing discussion was informative. It turns out that many students believe that the difference between a student and a teacher is that the teacher just knows the answer or automatically knows how to get the answer. That is, teachers don't need such strategies as guess–check–revise, make a table, draw a diagram, look for patterns, etc. The truth is that we do! Virtually all of the most brilliant workers—whether they be engineers, scientists, businesspeople, carpenters, researchers, or entrepreneurs—approach complex problems by using the very tools that are being stressed in this text. Furthermore, even the top people in a field often make hypotheses that seem reasonable (to them and to their colleagues) but that turn out not to be true. So when you are working on these problems, please realize that the tools being discussed in this book are used by people in all kinds of situations.

---

[4] At appropriate places, you will see the arrow icon indicating a specific connection that I will be making—connections called CHILDREN, LEARNING, MATHEMATICS, HISTORY, BEYOND THE CLASSROOM, and LANGUAGE. These notes will help develop the notion of the connectedness of mathematics.

INVESTIGATION **1.4** The Nine Dots Problem

• • •

• • •

• • •

FIGURE **1.8**

Not all problem-solving involves computation and formulas, as this investigation shows.

Without lifting your pencil can you go through all nine dots in Figure 1.8 with only four lines?

DISCUSSION

This is a very famous problem, which some of you may have already encountered because of its moral: This problem is impossible to solve as long as you "stay inside the box." That is, there is no possible way to go through all nine dots with four lines if you stay within the box. In order to solve the problem, you need to go "outside the box." If you haven't solved the problem yet, try to work with this hint. . . .

The solution to the problem can be seen on page 38. This idea of not getting stuck inside the box is crucial to good problem-solving. In many real-life problems, the solution to a problem requires that people think about the problem differently.

Now that you have had some opportunities to examine different problem-solving tools, we will turn to another mathematical tool.

SECTION ◆ 1.3 ◆ PATTERNS

WHAT DO YOU THINK?

- What do patterns have to do with learning mathematics?
- How does the ability to recognize and analyze patterns add to your problem-solving toolbox?

"We encounter patterns every day: in the spoken and written word, in musical forms and video images, in ornamental design and natural geometry, in traffic patterns, and in objects we build. Our ability to recognize, interpret, and create patterns is the key to dealing with the world around us."[5]

Patterns exist virtually everywhere in the world. Look at the floor, the walls, and the ceiling of your classroom, and you are sure to see patterns. Look at the wallpaper display in a store and you will see patterns. Look at Islamic architecture and you will see more patterns than in probably any other kind of architecture because of the decree by Mohammed, the founder of Islam, that there be no statues or paintings of people. There are also patterns in weather that help us to make predictions. In one sense, all patterns can be represented mathematically. This is not as radical a statement as you might think. Look at your television set. Most images on television sets still consist of 512 lines. The image from the transmitting station is coded by establishing a number (symbol) for each point on each of the 512 lines. Your television set then decodes that message and quickly puts the appropriate color in the appropriate spot, creating a picture.

In another landmark book on mathematics education reform, *Everybody Counts*,[6] the authors state, "Mathematics reveals hidden patterns that help us understand the world about us. . . . Mathematics is a science of pattern and order." Many important mathematical ideas have arisen from the recognition of patterns. Recognizing patterns in Exploration 1.1 (The Handshakes Problem) and Exploration 1.4 (How Many Squares?) makes the problems much easier to solve. Patterns also permeate Exploration 1.5 (Magic Squares). Being able to

---

[5] Marjorie Senechal, "Shape," in *On the Shoulders of Giants: New Approaches to Numeracy*, ed. Lynn Steen (Washington, D.C., National Academy Press, 1990), p. 139.

[6] National Research Council, *Everybody Counts: A Report to the Nation on the Future of Mathematics Education* (Washington, D.C., National Academy Press, 1989), p. 31.

understand functions, one of the centerpieces of secondary mathematics and a concept we will explore in Chapter 2, rests upon the student's being comfortable with patterns.

Being able to make use of patterns makes the guess–check–revise strategy much more powerful, as you saw in Investigation 1.1 (Pigs and Chickens). However, as many of you discovered, this is easier said than done. In order to use a pattern, you have to *recognize* it. As we found, making a table increases the likelihood of our recognizing a pattern. Recall also that we did not have just two columns in the pigs-and-chickens problem. *Extending* the table, we created a new column called "Difference" that helped to make the pattern more visible. We then *analyzed* the pattern to see that each time we changed a chicken into a pig, we added two feet. This enabled us to get the solution on the third guess.

Let us now investigate some problems that illustrate the pervasiveness and importance of patterns in mathematics.

INVESTIGATION 1.5 The Sum of the First 100 Numbers

Legend has it that when Carl Gauss (1777–1855), one of the greatest mathematicians of all time, was in first grade, his teacher gave the class the following problem: Find the sum of the first 100 numbers. The teacher then sat down to grade papers, knowing that it would take most of the students a good half hour to do this problem. Gauss came to the teacher's desk in 5 minutes with the answer. He had found a "large" pattern. Work on this problem and then read on. . . .

DISCUSSION

The goal of this investigation isn't to solve the problem as quickly as Gauss did but to understand why patterns are such a remarkable problem-solving tool and to realize that there are many different patterns, depending on how you approach the problem; it is much like seeing an interesting sculpture from different perspectives.

STRATEGY 1: Look for patterns that might make the problem smaller
Suppose we find the sum of the first 10 numbers:

$$1 + 2 + 3 + 4 + 5 + 6 + 7 + 8 + 9 + 10 = 55$$

What is the sum of the second ten numbers?

$$11 + 12 + 13 + 14 + 15 + 16 + 17 + 18 + 19 + 20 = 155$$

What do you think will be the sum of the next 10 numbers?

If you continue this pattern, you will get the answer relatively quickly.

STRATEGY 2: Start with a simpler problem and look for patterns
What if we look at the sums of $1 + 2$, $1 + 2 + 3$, $1 + 2 + 3 + 4$, etc., as shown in Table 1.4, and see what patterns emerge?

Do you see any patterns here? Think and then read on. . . .

Actually, there are many patterns, and a crucial point about patterns and problem-solving is that not all patterns lead directly to a solution. An analogy to paths on a mountain is relevant: All paths lead somewhere; however, some

TABLE 1.4

The sequence	Sum
1 + 2	3
1 + 2 + 3	6
1 + 2 + 3 + 4	10
1 + 2 + 3 + 4 + 5	15

paths are more helpful than others. Let us look at some of the patterns and then analyze one that helps us find the answer to the question.

Looking at differences   When we compare the sums of these sequences, the difference between successive sums increases by 1 each time. For example, the difference between 6 and 3 is 3, the difference between 10 and 6 is 4, the difference between 15 and 10 is 5, etc. Although this is a pattern, it's not very useful at this point because we can't use it to determine the sum of the first 100 numbers without knowing the sums of the first 98 and 99 numbers.

Comparing the number of terms and the sums   Another pattern emerges when, instead of looking at the relationship between numbers in the second column, we look at the problem from a different perspective. For example, what if we compare the number of terms in each sequence to the sum of the sequence (see Table 1.5). What do you see now?

TABLE 1.5

The sequence	Number of terms in the sequence	Sum
1 + 2	2	3
1 + 2 + 3	3	6
1 + 2 + 3 + 4	4	10
1 + 2 + 3 + 4 + 5	5	15

Some students see that when there are 3 terms, the sum is 6, and 6 is $3 \cdot 2$; and when there are 5 terms, the sum is 15, and 15 is $5 \cdot 3$. One guess (or hypothesis) that can be made from this pattern is that when there are 7 terms in the sequence, the sum will be $7 \cdot 4$. Indeed, the sum of the first 7 numbers is 28! But how can we use this pattern to answer the question? Play with this for a bit before reading on. . . .

There are actually a couple of ways to use this pattern. One way is to make a new table and look at what is going on; Table 1.6 illustrates this.

TABLE 1.6

The sequence	Number of terms in the sequence	Sum	What we multiply the second column by to get the sum
1 + 2	2	3	$1\frac{1}{2}$
1 + 2 + 3	3	6	2
1 + 2 + 3 + 4	4	10	$2\frac{1}{2}$
1 + 2 + 3 + 4 + 5	5	15	3
1 + 2 + 3 + 4 + 5 + 6	6	21	$3\frac{1}{2}$
1 + 2 + 3 + 4 + 5 + 6 + 7	7	28	4

Some people can leap from this table to the first 100 numbers and say that we multiply the number of terms in the sequence, 100, by $50\frac{1}{2}$ because when the number of terms is an even number, what you multiply by is simply half of that number plus $\frac{1}{2}$.

LEARNING

Some students are probably shrugging their shoulders and wondering, "How was I supposed to know to do that?" Researchers who looked at differences between "expert" problem-solvers and "novice" problem-solvers found that the experts were more likely to play around with a problem for a while if they didn't feel they had a good problem-solving strategy. There are many instances in which mathematical discoveries and solutions to problems have come from playing around with a problem. This idea of playfulness in mathematics is bizarre to many students. However, I seriously encourage you to think of it as a problem-solving tool; furthermore, this adds a dash of creativity to problem-solving which, in turn, makes it more enjoyable for many students.

Some people don't like fractions and find that if they double the numbers in the second column, they get a table that is easier to work with (see Table 1.7). Some students can make the leap from looking at this table to realizing that the sum of the first 100 numbers will simply be $1/2$ of $100 \cdot 101$. Do you see why this is so?

TABLE 1.7

The sequence	Number of terms in the sequence	Double the sum	The third column decomposed or broken down
$1 + 2$	2	6	$2 \cdot 3$
$1 + 2 + 3$	3	12	$3 \cdot 4$
$1 + 2 + 3 + 4$	4	20	$4 \cdot 5$
$1 + 2 + 3 + 4 + 5$	5	30	$5 \cdot 6$
$1 + 2 + 3 + 4 + 5 + 6$	6	42	$6 \cdot 7$
$1 + 2 + 3 + 4 + 5 + 6 + 7$	7	56	$7 \cdot 8$

At the most general level, we can now say that the sum of the first n numbers is $\frac{1}{2}n(n + 1)$.

STRATEGY 3: Look for patterns in the whole string of numbers

What happens if you add the first and last numbers? What does this lead to? Think and read on. . . .

$$1 + 2 + 3 + 4 + 5 + 6 + \cdots + 95 + 96 + 97 + 98 + 99 + 100$$

If we add $1 + 100$ and then $2 + 99$ and then $3 + 98$ and so on, we always get 101. The question now is, how many pairs adding up to 101 do we have? Once we know that, we can multiply the number of pairs by 101. This is the large pattern that Gauss discovered! The diagram below, in which we connect the pairs of numbers, can help you to understand this strategy better.

$$1 + 2 + 3 + 4 + \cdots + 97 + 98 + 99 + 100$$

STRATEGY 4: Use geometric representation

Some students remember using manipulatives in elementary school, and manipulatives provide concrete models for solving problems. In this case, manipulatives in the form of square tiles can actually change the perspective from which one views the problem. Figure 1.9 shows the sum of the first five numbers represented with tiles. In this case, the student places the tiles on top of each other. If you see this as "half a rectangle," then you can see the connection between this figure and the formula $\frac{1}{2}n(n + 1)$. If you don't see the connection, copy this figure twice (either on paper or with tiles). Put the two copies together to make a rectangle. Since the area of a rectangle is found by multiplying the length times the width, and since each of these "triangles" has half the area of the rectangle, this is another way to solve the problem.

FIGURE **1.9**

LEARNING

A point that I feel cannot be overemphasized is that for many problems from everyday life and business life, there is more than one way to solve the problem, just as there is usually more than one way to get from here to there—whether we are talking about paths up a mountain or routes from New York to Los Angeles. Many students have told me that before they took this course, they had thought that there was just *one right way* to do a problem, and so they never looked for patterns, but instead looked for formulas or procedures. Once the students started looking for patterns, they found them everywhere, and over time they learned how to use their awareness of patterns more powerfully. We can refer to different ways to do a problem as different **solution paths.**

INVESTIGATION 1.6   Pascal's Triangle

HISTORY

As you may have already discovered in other areas, a discovery is not necessarily named after the first person who discovered it. This is true of Pascal's triangle. Figure 1.10 comes from *The Precious Mirror of the Four Elements*, which was written in 1303 by Chu-Shih-chieh, who acknowledged that he had taken the triangle from a book written several hundred years earlier.

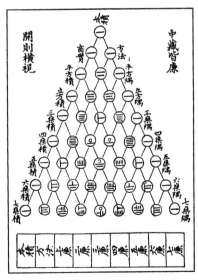

FIGURE 1.10

The pattern shown below is one of the most famous mathematical patterns. It was "discovered" by the mathematician Blaise Pascal (1623–1662).

$$
\begin{array}{ccccccccccccccccc}
&&&&&&&& 1 \\
&&&&&&& 1 && 1 \\
&&&&&& 1 && 2 && 1 \\
&&&&& 1 && 3 && 3 && 1 \\
&&&& 1 && 4 && 6 && 4 && 1 \\
&&& 1 && 5 && 10 && 10 && 5 && 1 \\
&& 1 && 6 && 15 && 20 && 15 && 6 && 1 \\
& 1 && 7 && 21 && 35 && 35 && 21 && 7 && 1 \\
1 && 8 && 28 && 56 && 70 && 56 && 28 && 8 && 1
\end{array}
$$

This pattern occurs in many different fields of mathematics, as you will discover over the course of this book. What patterns do you see?

There are literally hundreds! Examine the triangle, play with it, and describe the patterns you see. You may choose to describe patterns with words, in a table or sequence, or by using mathematical notation.

DISCUSSION

There are many patterns, and there are many ways to describe each pattern. Here are some patterns to get you started:

1. Both top diagonals contain only 1s. Start at the top and go down the left side. You have only 1s.

2. It doesn't matter which way you go. The figure has symmetry such that each diagonal has a twin. For example, look at the second diagonal going down the right: 1, 2, 3, 4, 5, 6, 7, 8, . . . Can you find its twin?

3. Each number (not equal to 1) in the triangle is the sum of the two numbers to its top right and left. Do you understand what I just wrote? Try it out, then read on. . . .

If you don't understand what I just said, look at this visual representation:

Choose any number c (not equal to 1) in the triangle. If we let a and b represent the two numbers immediately above c, then the value of c is equal to the value of $a + b$!

4. Add the numbers in each row in the triangle. What do you get? Do it now and then read on. . . .

The sums of the rows make the following sequence: 1, 2, 4, 8, 16. This sequence can be described as the powers of 2. Can you guess the sum of the numbers in the 10th row? Try it and then read on. . . .

In this case a table is helpful. See Table 1.8 to the left.

In other words, the sum of the numbers in the nth row can be obtained by raising 2 to the $(n - 1)$ power. If you have a calculator with an $\boxed{x^y}$ function, you can determine 2^9 by doing the following: 2 x^y 9 =; 512 will appear.

The Power of Patterns

Some of the greatest mathematicians in history made their mark by discovering and articulating patterns. The wonderful thing about patterns, though, is that they make mathematics more accessible to everyone. This was recognized by the authors of *Everybody Counts*,[7] who wrote:

> Virtually all young children like mathematics. They do mathematics naturally, discovering patterns and making conjectures based on observation. Natural curiosity is a powerful teacher, especially for mathematics. Unfortunately, as children become socialized by school and society, they begin to view mathematics as a rigid system of externally dictated rules governed by standards of accuracy, speed, and memory. Their view of mathematics shifts gradually from enthusiasm to apprehension, from confidence to fear. Eventually, most students leave mathematics under duress, convinced that only geniuses can learn it.

We explored several famous, powerful patterns in this section. You will see many of these patterns again, both in this book and beyond it. But more important, I hope you will see that stepping back from a problem can reveal patterns within it. Sometimes these patterns can help you devise a plan for solving the problem; other times they emerge as you look back on your work.

TABLE 1.8

Row	Sum
1	1
2	2
3	4
4	8
5	16
.	.
.	.
.	.
n	2^{n-1}

MATHEMATICS

When I ask students at the end of my courses what they have learned about mathematics, many of them say that they have come to realize that mathematics is much more connected than they had thought. They saw more connections both among concepts (such as fractions, decimals, and percents) and among problems that they had solved. Do you see connections between Pascal's triangle and other problems in this chapter? Think and read on. . . .

If you didn't, look back at Investigation 1.5 and Exploration 1.1. Those sequences can be found within Pascal's triangle. Can you see them?

SECTION ◆ 1.4

COMMUNICATION

WHAT DO YOU THINK?

■ Why does the NCTM encourage mathematics classrooms to provide numerous opportunities for communication?

There are two distinct kinds of *communication* that you need to be aware of as you work in this course:

1. Communicating with yourself about the problem—that is, being able to make sense of your own strategies and solutions

2. Communicating with other people—sharing your observations and solutions and being able to understand others' observations and solutions

Communication and understanding go hand in hand. Most of the problems we have examined so far, both in the *Explorations* and in the text, were not sim-

[7] National Research Council, *Everybody Counts*: A Report to the Nation on the Future of Mathematics Education (Washington, D.C.: Natonal Academy Press, 1989), pp. 53–54.

ple. Recall the example from the National Assessment of Educational Progress in Table 1.3. To solve the first problem, you simply had to add the numbers and divide by 6. However, to solve the second problem, you had to think about the information. In other words, you had to create a model of the problem in your head that made sense and that connected the relevant information to your mathematical knowledge. Developing the ability to connect the given information to your mathematical knowledge and to your problem-solving toolbox is one of the central objectives of this course. Some students have already developed this ability. However, every year, most of my students enter the course without these tools. Seeing those students' toolboxes develop and seeing their confidence grow is one of the many reasons why I cannot imagine myself being in any other profession!

The NCTM Standards on Communication

Let us now look at what the NCTM Standards say about communication.

The study of mathematics should include numerous opportunities for communication so that students can —

- model situations using oral, written, concrete, pictorial, graphical, and algebraic methods [and] relate [these models] . . . to mathematical ideas;

- relate their everyday language to mathematical language and symbols;

- reflect on and clarify their thinking about mathematical ideas and situations;

- discuss mathematical ideas and make conjectures and convincing arguments;

- realize that representing, discussing, reading, writing, and listening to mathematics are a vital part of learning and using mathematics.

(*Curriculum Standards*, pp. 26, 78)

Look back on the investigations we have already done in this chapter. Do you see that we have been doing these things already? When did we "relate physical materials, pictures, and diagrams to mathematical ideas"? Look back, make your own notes and read on. . . .

I hope you saw that we did this in most of the examples. In most cases, however, the solution involved a two-part process: first, making a diagram and, second, connecting the diagram to the mathematical ideas in the problem. Many of my students report that before this course, their experience was that the teacher did the connecting for them. Since you are to become teachers, this is the place where you develop this ability to make such connections.

When did we "relate [our] everyday language to mathematical language and symbols"? In order to communicate about the patterns in Investigation 1.6 (Pascal's Triangle), we needed mathematical language that made sense: terms like *sum*, *product*, *unit*, and *digit*.

When did we "reflect on and clarify [our] thinking about mathematical ideas and situations"? In Investigation 1.1 (Pigs and Chickens), we found that using guess–check–revise skillfully *requires* reflection. In Investigation 1.3 (Making Paper Dinosaurs), the "real-life" solution came after reflecting on the mathematical solution and then deciding that the rectangles could be a little bit smaller or arranged in different ways.

Being able to communicate clearly is challenging. As you will come to see in this book, one of the reasons for all the mathematical notation that seems to get thrown at you is that *if* you understand the notation, you can reduce confusion and ambiguity in mathematical conversations.

Learning by Communicating

There is another reason for emphasizing communication at the beginning of this course. Few people learn best in isolation. The National Training Laboratories in Bethel, Maine have created the pyramid in Figure 1.11 to represent what we know about learning.

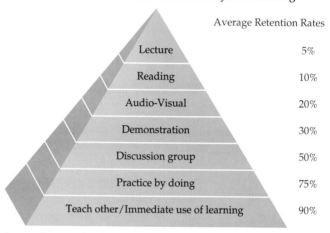

Retention Rates From Different Ways of Learning

Source: Reprinted with permission from NTL Institute from "Retention Rates From Different Ways of Learning."

FIGURE **1.11**

When we bring communication into the learning process—by having students work in small groups, by having students explain how they solved a problem, by having students justify the steps in their solution—the students are more likely to "own" the knowledge they gain.

Let us now examine an aspect of using patterns that was mentioned earlier: being able to describe patterns that you see in such a way that others can understand what you are saying.

INVESTIGATION 1.7 Describing Patterns

FIGURE **1.12**

Suppose a friend of yours misses class and calls you up on the phone to find out what the homework was. You tell her that the teacher had drawn a shape and asked you to write a verbal description of it. "What was the shape?" your friend asks. How would you describe the shape in Figure 1.12? Write down your description, and then read on. . . .

DISCUSSION

Following are three possible descriptions. You may want to sketch the shape following the instructions in each of these, just to see which one seems clearest to you.

DESCRIPTION 1

Draw a horizontal line. Beginning at the left endpoint of that line, draw a vertical line going up that is the same length as the horizontal line. Erase the bottom half of the vertical line. Now draw a (diagonal) line that connects the top of the vertical line to the right endpoint of the horizontal line. Find the middle of the horizontal line and draw a vertical line until you hit the diagonal line. Without lifting your pen, now draw a horizontal line to the left. Keep going after you cross the original vertical line and make the part after you hit the vertical line as long as the part before you hit it. Now connect this point to the original starting point.

DESCRIPTION 2

Make a right isosceles triangle with the right angle at the bottom left corner of the triangle. Draw a square inside that triangle; the length of the sides of the square is one-half the length of the equal sides of the triangle. Erase the left side of the square. Now construct a trapezoid. The bottom base of the trapezoid is also the bottom of the square. To make the top base, begin at the midpoint of the hypotenuse of the original triangle and construct a line that is twice the length of the square.

DESCRIPTION 3

Construct a square. Now construct three right isosceles triangles connected to the east, north, and west sides of the square. First, the east side: The hypotenuse starts at the top of the right side of the square and runs in a southeast direction. Second, the north side: the hypotenuse starts at the same spot (the top of the right side of the square) but runs in a northwest direction. Third, the west side: The hypotenuse starts at the bottom of the left side of the square and runs in a northwest direction. Now you need to erase the left side of the square.

Which description did you like best? The first description involved very little formal language. The second description used several mathematical terms: right isosceles triangle, square, hypotenuse, trapezoid, and midpoint. The third description involved both mathematical terms and lay terms. If your class were to read each of these and select the description they thought was "best," it is likely that each of the three would be seen as the best by some students.

SECTION 1.5 CONNECTIONS

WHAT DO YOU THINK?

- How does making connections add to your toolbox?
- What connections among concepts and problem-solving strategies have you seen thus far in the chapter?

Making *connections* is at the heart of the NCTM Standards. We have already noted connections between Pascal's triangle and Exploration 1.1 (The Handshakes Problem) and Investigation 1.5 (The Sum of the First 100 Numbers). We have also noted that the idea of connections is new to many students. This is addressed in the NCTM Curriculum Standards:

> The mathematics curriculum is generally viewed as consisting of several discrete strands. As a result, computation, geometry, measurement, and problem solving tend to be taught in isolation. It is important that children connect ideas both among and within areas of mathematics. Without such connections, children must learn and remember too many isolated concepts and skills rather than recognizing general principles relevant to several areas.

(*Curriculum Standards*, p. 32)

Let us examine some of the kinds of connections that we would like you to make in this course.

Connecting New Concepts to Old Concepts

One important kind of connection is the connection between new ideas and something that is familiar to you. As we discussed in Section 1.2, if you are not able to make these connections, you may end up with "Teflon knowledge." Consider another example from the NAEP. Students were asked to select the decimal equivalent to 12 percent and then to select the decimal equivalent to .9 percent. The results are given in Table 1.9.

TABLE 1.9

| | Percent Correct | |
	Grade 7	Grade 11
Which decimal is equivalent to 12 percent?	71	90
Which decimal is equivalent to .9 percent?	25	56

Under any circumstances, we would expect a smaller percentage of correct responses for the second question. However, the drop-off is enormous. For seventh graders, the percentage who got the second question correct was barely one-third that for the first question. What connections could have helped these students? Try to answer this question yourself before reading on. . . .

First, they could have connected percents to rational numbers, reasoning that 12 percent means 12/100. Then they could have connected the fraction to a decimal: 12/100 = 0.12. Following this reasoning for the second question, .9 percent means 0.9/100, which converts to 0.009. Alternatively, they could have applied the algorithm, "move the decimal point two places." In other words, .9 becomes .009. Of course, they had to realize that they had to put zeros to the left of .9 in order to be able to move two decimal places! We examine decimals and percents in more detail in Chapters 5 and 6.

Making Connections Among Different Concepts

Many, if not most, students have come to view mathematics as a collection of separate topics. Most mathematicians, however, see mathematics more as a network of *interconnected* concepts, similar to a map of the highways in the United States, with the freeways being equivalent to major connections and surface roads to smaller connections.

Looking at the four basic operations—addition, subtraction, multiplication, and division—we can make the following connections: Addition and subtraction are inverse operations and multiplication can be seen as repeated addition. Likewise, multiplication and division are inverse operations and division can be seen as repeated subtraction. We will investigate these concepts in Chapter 3. In Chapter 6, you will discover or rediscover that percents have close connections to ratios and to equivalent fractions. Many students see algebra and geometry as completely separate, whereas mathematicians see them as very connected.

Connecting Different Models for the Same Concept

In mathematics, many concepts can be represented in different ways. For example, consider the ways of representing 3/4 shown in Figure 1.13. One of them is not a valid representation of what we mean by 3/4. Do you understand why? Can you express that understanding in words?

When you can connect many different representations to the concept underlying all of them, you are well on your way to the kind of mathematical thinking encouraged by the NCTM. Many "good" problem-solvers are good not because they know more than others but because their knowledge is better connected.

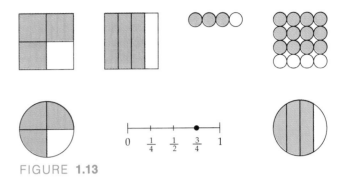

FIGURE **1.13**

Connecting Conceptual and Procedural Knowledge

Most of you have probably learned a variety of standard procedures, also called algorithms. However, fewer of you are likely to know why they work. For example, while you can probably convert a mixed number to an improper fraction—for example, $4\frac{2}{3} = 14/3$—do you know *why* we multiply the whole number by the denominator, add the numerator, and then put the whole thing over the denominator?

Similarly, do you know *why* we "move over" in whole-number multiplication?

$$
\begin{array}{r}
47 \\
35 \\
\hline
235 \\
141 \\
\hline
1645
\end{array}
$$

Coming to understand why these and many other algorithms work will make you a more powerful problem solver and a stronger teacher.

Making Connections Between School Mathematics and "Real Life"

Mathematics enters into some of the most important decisions we make, both as individuals and as a society. Recall the explorations dealing with money. Think about buying tires, buying a house, investing your savings, comparison shopping, deciding how much wallpaper or paint to buy, building a fence, making a budget, figuring out a tip, choosing among credit cards—the list could go on for pages!

Think of how many political issues are connected to mathematics:

- The current and future effects of the federal deficit—How many people realize what a really big number 4 trillion is?

- The issue of income inequality—women earn an average of 70¢ for every dollar men earn, for doing the same job!

- The cost of illiteracy and innumeracy to the United States—In 1990 it was estimated that American employers spent about $40 billion to train their employees in the basic reading, writing, and arithmetic skills they should have learned in school.

Unfortunately, all too many students do not see mathematics as connected. My greatest hope for this course is that it leads you to see that part of your job as a student is to make connections—to make sure that you see how the new concepts and ideas connect to what you already know, to make sure that you see connections between different concepts, and to make sure that you see the connection between the mathematics in this course and mathematics beyond the classroom. If that happens, then our society will begin to be more mathematically literate rather than rank near the bottom internationally in mathematics performance.

The following problem illustrates the importance of making relevant connections when solving problems.

INVESTIGATION 1.8 How Many Pieces of Wire?

A jewelry artisan is making earring hoops. Each hoop requires a piece of wire that is $3\frac{3}{4}$ inches long. If the wire comes in 50 inches coils, how many $3\frac{3}{4}$ inches pieces can be made from one coil, and how much wire is wasted? Solve this problem on your own and then read on. . . .

But before you do, ask yourself, "Do I understand the problem? Does the problem's wording help me devise a plan for solving it? Once I have a solution, can I check it?" Perhaps most important, ask yourself, "What did thinking about *this* problem reveal to me about problem-solving in general?"

DISCUSSION

STRATEGY 1: Divide

Some people quickly realize that you can divide "to get the answer." If you use a calculator, it shows 13.333333 . . . . If you use fractions, you get $13\frac{1}{3}$. Many people interpret these numbers to mean that you can get 13 pieces and you will have 1/3 inch wasted. Unfortunately, that is not correct. If you also got 1/3 inch as wasted, stop! Go back and see if you can figure out why 1/3 inch is not the correct answer and what the correct answer is. Then read on. . . .

One of the reasons why I, like many other math teachers, stress the importance of labels is that they illustrate the meaning of what we are doing. The *meaning* of the quotient $(13\frac{1}{3})$ is 13 whole hoops and $\frac{1}{3}$ of a hoop. That is, 50 inches $\div 3\frac{3}{4}$ inches/hoop $= 13\frac{1}{3}$ hoops. The *meaning* of the fraction $(\frac{1}{3})$ is that what we have left would make $(\frac{1}{3})$ of a hoop. Since one whole piece is $3\frac{3}{4}$ in. long, 1/3 of a piece is 1/3 of $3\frac{3}{4}$; that is, $1\frac{1}{4}$ in. is wasted.

How would we check this answer? Think and then read on. . . .

One way to check would be to multiply $3\frac{3}{4} \times 13$. Do you see why? This would tell us the length of the 13 whole pieces. If this number plus $1\frac{1}{4}$ equals 50, then our answers are correct. In fact, $3\frac{3}{4} \times 13 = 48\frac{3}{4}$ and $48\frac{3}{4} + 1\frac{1}{4} = 50$.

STRATEGY 2: "Act it out"

Some people understand the problem better when they draw a line to represent the 50 in. piece of wire. Draw a picture like that in Figure 1.14 to represent what happens when the artisan cuts off $3\frac{3}{4}$ in. long pieces until the wire is used up.

Number of Inches   0 $3\frac{3}{4}$ $7\frac{1}{2}$ $11\frac{1}{4}$ 15   etc.

Number of Pieces   0   1   2   3   4   5   6   7   8   9   10   11   12   13
FIGURE **1.14**

STRATEGY 3: Make a table

TABLE 1.10

Number of pieces	Number of inches	Thinking process
1	$3\frac{3}{4}$	
2	$7\frac{1}{2}$	
3	$11\frac{1}{4}$	
4	15	Using the concept of ratio and proportion, we can reason that if 4 pieces make 15 inches, then 12 pieces would make 45 inches.
12	45	So 1 more piece works.
13	$48\frac{3}{4}$	

Refer to Table 1.10. The answer to the second part of the question is simply

$$50 - 48\frac{3}{4} = 1\frac{1}{4}$$

What kinds of connections do you see in this problem? Think and then read on. . . .

Connections   Several of the kinds of connections mentioned at the beginning of Section 1.5 are evident in this problem.

- Connecting new concepts to old concepts: If the concept of division of whole numbers (investigated in Chapter 3, Section 2) is well understood, the student can immediately see this as a division problem, but one that involves fractions.

- Connecting different models for the same concept: In Chapter 3, Section 2, you will find that one model for division is repeated subtraction. Drawing the diagram of the wire and marking off $3\frac{3}{4}$ in. segments often triggers the connection between this problem and repeated subtraction, which then produces the insight, "Oh, now I get it; I just have to divide 50 by $3\frac{3}{4}$!"

- Connecting conceptual and procedural knowledge: The procedure for dividing by fractions or decimals is not terribly complex. However, the result of the computation ($13\frac{1}{3}$) is not quite the answer to the question.

Using the NCTM Standards

In this first chapter of the book, we have focused on the first four Curriculum Standards and we have examined several specific aspects of those standards; for example, under Standard 2 (Mathematics as Communication); we examined "reflect on and clarify [students'] thinking about mathematical ideas and situations." As you carry out the various investigations and explorations in this course, I strongly encourage you to stop and reread the NCTM Standards (on the inside back cover of the *Explorations* volume). Are they making more sense? Are you developing the abilities described in the Standards? (I also encourage you to examine the three NCTM documents discussed in the next section.)

Many students find it helpful to keep a reflection notebook, also called a journal or a learning log. In fact, your instructor may make this part of the course. If you do take this time to examine your learning, you will develop mathematical power, and you will be more likely to own rather than rent what you learn.

SECTION 1.6 **PUTTING IT ALL TOGETHER**

Let us now take some time to look at what you have learned in these investigations and discuss what this course is about and what NCTM's vision of school mathematics is about.

The Three NCTM Documents

The NCTM has produced three landmark documents that are dramatically changing the nature of mathematics education in the United States: *Curriculum and Evaluation Standards for School Mathematics* in 1989, *Professional Standards for Teaching Mathematics* in 1991, and *Assessment Standards for School Mathematics* in 1995.

Curriculum and Evaluation Standards for School Mathematics This book articulates why the nature of mathematics instruction in the United States has to change and describes a much larger vision of what students ought to be learning in mathematics in school. The book presents detailed Standards for grades K–4, grades 5–8, and grades 9–12; a synthesis of the elementary and middle school standards can be found in Appendix C. The unifying themes in all three sets of standards are mathematics as problem-solving, mathematics as communication, mathematics as reasoning, and the importance of making connections. *Curriculum and Evaluation Standards* also describes the kinds of topics that should receive increased and decreased attention in school mathematics. A sample of these recommendations is on the inside front and back covers of the textbook.

Professional Standards for Teaching Mathematics Whereas *Curriculum and Evaluation Standards* focuses on what the students should be learning, *Professional Standards for Teaching Mathematics* focuses more on the crucial characteristics of effective classrooms. These characteristics include focusing on worthwhile mathematics tasks, having much more discussion in classes, and making sure that the environment fosters learning in all students. A summary of *Professional Standards for Teaching Mathematics* can be found in Appendix C of the textbook.

Assessment Standards for School Mathematics You should examine and work with *Assessment Standards for School Mathematics* in your methods courses later in your studies. Hopefully, this course will honor these six standards:

1. Assessment should reflect the mathematics that all students need to know and be able to do.

2. Assessment should enhance mathematics learning.

3. Assessment should promote equity.
4. Assessment should be an open process.
5. Assessment should promote valid inferences about mathematics learning.
6. Assessment should be a coherent process.

NCTM's Mathematics Education Goals

Why do we want you to learn about these standards? The NCTM has elaborated many reasons why mathematics education has to change. For one thing, as our society has changed, the educational needs of our society have also changed. Fifty years ago, a much larger proportion of jobs were in agriculture and industry, and the mathematics needed to do those jobs was much simpler. Assembly line workers then had very little need for mathematics beyond simple arithmetic. However, most of today's assembly lines are very different. In many cases, the workers on the line use quality control procedures to perform statistical analyses. Fifty years ago, there were no hand-held calculators. Now they are everywhere; the simplest ones can be bought for less than five dollars in most places.

In *Curriculum and Evaluation Standards for School Mathematics* (pp. 3–4), the NCTM states four fundamental goals for mathematics education in the twenty-first century. These are

1. *Mathematically Literate Workers* A coalition of various United States industries has articulated the kinds of mathematics that "regular" workers need. These include: the ability to use a variety of techniques to approach and work on problems; the ability to see the applicability to mathematical ideas of common and complex problems; and preparation for open problem situations, since most real-world problems are not well formulated.

2. *Lifelong Learning* People can no longer expect to stay in one profession for their entire working life. In fact, the average worker changes careers more than five times. Thus, a flexible work force capable of lifelong learning is crucial for the economic well-being of the country.

3. *Opportunity for All* The belief that only "brighter" students should take mathematics cannot be tolerated anymore. We are virtually the only country in which this belief is pervasive. Students in Japanese trade schools take as much mathematics as our college-prep students do. In this country, women and certain minorities are severely underrepresented in jobs that require higher-level mathematics. The long-term economic future of this country is undermined by this reality.

4. *An Informed Electorate* Many issues raised in political contexts—such as environmental protection, nuclear energy, defense spending, space exploration, and taxation—require a more sophisticated understanding of mathematics than the current "average" citizen possesses.

Implications for School Mathematics

What does all this mean in terms of school mathematics? The NCTM has proposed the following goals. Students should:

1. *Learn to Value Mathematics* Students should have numerous and varied experiences in mathematics classes so that they can appreciate the role of mathematics in our present society and so that they can better understand the relationships between mathematics and "real life." (*Curriculum Standards*, p. 5)

2. *Become Confident in Their Ability to Do Mathematics* When the other four goals are met, such confidence tends to emerge on its own:

> We are convinced that if students are exposed to the kinds of experiences outlined in the [*Curriculum and Evaluation*] *Standards*, they will gain math-ematical power. This term denotes an individual's abilities to explore, conjecture, and reason logically, as well as the ability to use a variety of mathematical methods effectively to solve nonroutine problems. This notion is based on the recognition of mathematics as more than a collection of concepts and skills to be mastered; it includes methods of investigating and reasoning, means of communication, and notions of context. . . . Our premise is that *what* a student learns depends to a great degree on *how* he or she has learned it. . . . This vision sees students studying much of the same mathematics currently taught but with quite a different emphasis.

(Curriculum Standards, p. 6)

3. *Become Mathematical Problem Solvers* "The development of each student's ability to solve problems is essential if he or she is to be a productive citizen" (*Curriculum Standards*, p. 6).

4. *Learn to Communicate Mathematically* This is best accomplished when stu-dents have an opportunity to read, write, and discuss ideas in realistic and relevant problems. (*Curriculum Standards*, p. 6)

5. *Learn to Reason Mathematically* Solving problems in everyday and work situ-ations often involves much more than finding the right formula. Problem-solving in these situations involves reasoning activities such as making conjectures, gathering evidence, and building an argument to support one's hypothesis. (*Curriculum Standards*, p. 6)

The difference between traditional word problems and many real-life prob-lems The NCTM has urged that there be less emphasis on word problems that are one-step problems and that are routine problems. One way to paraphrase these recommendations is to say that we want fewer problems that are "just like" the ones in the book and more problems that *require* thinking on the part of the student.

Table 1.11 contrasts the difference between the word problems generally found in textbooks and real-life problems.

When students undertake what some authors call more authentic prob-lems, they come to realize that mathematics is more than just memorizing and using formulas, and they come to value their own thinking. In doing so, they come to possess what the NCTM refers to as mathematical power:

> Mathematical power includes the ability to explore, conjecture, and reason logically; to solve nonroutine problems; to communicate about and through mathematics; and to connect ideas within mathematics and between mathematics and other intellectual activity. Mathematical power also involves the development of personal self-confidence and a disposition to seek, evaluate, and use quantitative and spatial informa-tion in solving problems and in making decisions. Students' flexibility, perseverance, interest, curiosity, and inventiveness also affect the real-ization of mathematical power.

(Professional Standards, p. 1)

I have seen this growth in many of my own students over the course of my teaching. When the student's focus is on both understanding the mathematical content and developing mathematical tools, when the student's attitudes and beliefs are generally adaptive as opposed to maladaptive, and when the teacher's instructional strategies are focused in the manner suggested above, then the student is more likely to learn the mathematics and to retain that knowledge.

TABLE 1.11

Textbook word problems	Real-Life problems
1. The problem is given.	1. Often, you have to figure out what the problem really is.
2. All the information you need to solve the problem is given.	2. You have to determine the information needed to solve the problem.
3. There is always enough information to solve the problem.	3. Sometimes you will find that there is not enough information to solve the problem.
4. There is no extraneous information.	4. Sometimes there is too much information and you have to decide what information you need and what you don't.
5. The answer is in the back of the book, or the teacher tells you if your answer is correct.	5. You, or your team, decides whether your answer is valid. Your job may depend on how well you can "check" your answer.
6. There is often a right or best way to solve the problem.	6. There are usually many different ways to solve the problem.

EXERCISES

1. A farmer looks out into the barnyard and sees the pigs and the chickens. He says to his daughter, "I count 169 heads and 398 feet. How many pigs and how many chickens are out there?"

2. A Martian farmer looks out into the barnyard and sees tribbles (which have four legs) and chalkas (which have seven legs). She says to her son, "I count 97 heads and 436 feet. How many tribbles and how many chalkas are out there?"

3. How many $3\frac{2}{3}$ oz bottles of perfume can be filled from a jug containing 64 oz? How many ounces of perfume are left over per jug? Determine a jug size that is a whole number and that would produce no waste.

4. Let's say you are building a patio in your back yard. You have decided to make the patio 12 ft by 9 ft. The local building supply store sells bricks that are 6 in. by 4 in. for 25¢ each. How much will the patio cost?

5. Let's say you have decided to make a number of hearts for an activity in your class. Ideally, the hearts would be the size shown. How many sheets of construction paper would you need in order to make 96 hearts that are exactly this size? If it were your class, would it be worth your while to make them slightly larger or slightly smaller? Explain why or why not.

6. Let's say there are 145 students in your class. If each student greeted and shook hands with every student in the class, how many handshakes would there be?

7. Suppose a family of 12 people decides that each person will buy a gift for each member of the family for Christmas. How many gifts will be under the Christmas tree? What if the family had a drawing and each person drew one name but also gave a gift to each parent? How many gifts would now be under the Christmas tree?

8. Alice, Betty, and Carla traded hats and gloves. Alice wore Betty's hat and Carla's gloves. Write a paragraph telling how you know whose hat and gloves Betty and Carla wore.

9. List the next term in each of the sequences below and verbally describe the pattern that enabled you to predict the next term.
   a. □, △, □, □, △
   b. ⌐, ∟, ⌐
   c. 1, 4, 7, 10,
   d. 2, 6, 18, 54,
   e. 1, 4, 9, 16,
   f. 1, 2, 4, 7, 11,
   g. 5, 1, 4, 2, 3, 3,

10. Describe the following figures, as if to someone you were talking to on the phone.

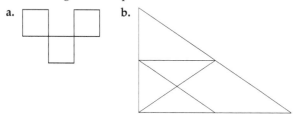

11. Two 2-digit numbers satisfy the following conditions:
    ■ The sum of the digits in each number is 10.
    ■ All four digits are different.
    ■ The sum of the numbers is 155.
    Determine the two numbers.

12. a. On a digital clock, how many times in one day will the numbers be consecutive digits (e.g., 1:23)?
    b. On a digital clock, which digit will appear most often in one day?

13. At a benefit concert, 600 tickets were sold and $1,500 was raised. If there were $2 and $5 tickets, how many of each were sold?

14. For a certain event, 812 tickets were sold, for a total of $1,912. If students paid $2 per ticket and nonstudents paid $3 per ticket, how many student tickets were sold?

15. At the beginning of the month, Jack and Jill had $642 in a checking account. During the month, they wrote checks for $22, $53, and $55. They made a withdrawal of $50 from the automatic teller machine, and they made deposits of $142 and $100. How much money did they have at the end of the month? Solve this problem two different ways.

16. A soft drink manufacturer produces 3,240 cans in an 8 hour day. Cans are packed 24 to a case. How many cases are produced between Monday and Friday?

17. Sarah's diet allows 1,500 calories per day. Thus far, she has had a glass of milk (90 calories), pancakes (150 calories), an apple (75 calories), a salad (150 calories), salad dressing (200 calories), and a piece of cake (350 calories). Can she have a steak (250 calories) and a salad with salad dressing for dinner? If not, what can she have? Solve the problem two different ways.

18. Imagine a jar with a lid that is 6 cm across. The jar is 8 cm high. At the bottom of the jar, there is a caterpillar. Each day the caterpillar crawls up 4 cm. Each night she falls down 2 cm. How long will it take her to touch the lid of the jar?

19. Lisa was born on July 4, 1976. How many days old will she be on January 1, 2000?

20. A sewing machine representative earns $125 a week plus $8 for each deluxe model she sells and $5 for each economy model. How many economy models did she sell in a week in which she made $184 and sold 3 deluxe models?

21. If Sue can eat a small pizza in 6 minutes and Sally can eat one and a half small pizzas in 15 minutes, how long will it take the two of them to eat three small pizzas (assuming they don't get full)?

22. Sally works 40 hours a week and makes $6.85 an hour, but her kids are in child care for 32 hours a week and the day care center charges her $15 per day. If you deduct her child care expenses, how many dollars per hour does she actually make?

23. A worker who smokes spends an average of 2 minutes per hour in getting a cigarette, lighting it, flicking ashes, and so on. How many (work) hours per year does he spend on his habit if he works 40 hours per week for 50 weeks of the year?

24. Martha planted 14 rows of apple trees, and each row had 21 trees. If each tree yielded an average of 250 apples, how many apples grew in her orchard?

25. A farmer needs to fence a rectangular piece of land. She wants the length of the field to be 80 ft longer than the width. If she has 1080 ft of fencing material, what should be the length and the width of the field?

26. Bill is being paid $12 to rake the yard. He raked 2/3 of the yard, and then Jim came by and helped him finish. How much should Bill pay Jim?

27. When Joe wakes up in the morning, the clock is blinking and says 3:30. His watch says 6:45. When did the power go off? What assumption(s) did you make in order to solve the problem?

28. A special rubber ball is dropped from the top of a wall that is 16 meters high. Each time the ball bounces, it rises half as high as the distance it fell. The ball is caught when it bounces 1 meter high. How many times did the ball bounce?

29. Joni is the owner of Red Oak Furniture, which is doing so well that the present staff is overworked. She has two choices: continue to pay overtime or hire a new person. She now has three employees, and they earn time-and-a-half for all time over 40 hours worked in a week. In the past three weeks, they have worked the number of hours shown. Should she hire a new employee?

	Week 1	Week 2	Week 3
Gerald	47	55	42
Nancy	43	51	48
Jose	56	51	42

30. Examine the following pattern of letters: y a b b a d a b b a d o o. If this pattern is repeated over and over, what letter will be in the 275th position?

31. Using four 4s and any operations, make the sums 1–10. For example, $4 + 4 + 4 - 4 = 8$

32. Find the two-digit number that, when added to its reverse, is the closest to 130. (Note: The reverse of 79, for example, is 97.) Show your work. If you got it on the first try, briefly explain your thinking. Otherwise, your successive guesses will suffice.

33. A boatman is to transport a fox, a goose, and a sack of corn across the river. There is room in his boat for only one of the three at a time. Furthermore, if the fox and the goose are left together, the fox will eat the goose. If the goose and the corn are left together, the goose will eat the corn. How can the boatman do the job?

34. The following two jar problems have been around for many years. They are contrived problems to promote reasoning. In these problems, a jar must be filled *completely* and emptied *completely*. For example, you cannot say, "Fill the big jar half full and fill the second jar half full" to get 4 gal.

   a. You are given a 5 gallon and a 3 gallon pail, both of which are unmarked. You are asked to fetch 4 gallons of water from the well in one trip. How?

   b. You have three jugs of capacities 8, 5, and 3 gallons. The largest jug is full of water. The other two are empty. Your task is to redistribute the water so that you wind up with 2 gallons of water in the large jug and 3 gallons of water in each of the other jugs.

35. **a.** In how many different ways can you make change for a quarter?

   b. In how many different ways can you make change for 50 cents?

   c. In how many different ways can you make change for one dollar without using pennies?

36. One of the most famous patterns in mathematics was discovered by the Italian mathematician Leonardo of Pisa (1170–1250), known to us as Fibonacci. He discovered this sequence, which we today call the Fibonacci sequence, while studying the birth rates of rabbits. He posed the following question: Suppose that a pair of rabbits produce a pair of baby rabbits every month, and that rabbits cannot reproduce until they are two months of age. How many pairs of rabbits will you have after one year (assuming, of course, that no rabbits die)? He found that if he listed the number of pairs of rabbits he had after each month, he had a very interesting sequence: 1, 1, 2, 3, 5, 8, 13, 21, 34, 55, 89, 144, 233, . . .

   a. Add the first seven Fibonacci numbers. What do you notice?
   Add the first eight Fibonacci numbers. What do you notice?
   Try to describe this relationship both in words and using notation.

   b. Pick three terms somewhere near the middle. Multiply the first term and the third term. Now add 1 to the square of the middle term. What do you notice? Describe this relationship using notation.

37. There is a connection between the Fibonacci sequence and Pascal's triangle. Can you find it? Let me give you a hint: The Fibonacci sequence can be found in Pascal's triangle.

```
                1
             1     1
          1     2     1
       1     3     3     1
    1     4     6     4     1
  1   5    10    10    5     1
 1   6   15    20   15    6    1
1  7   21   35   35   21   7   1
1  8  28  56  70  56  28  8  1
```

38. **a.** Describe as many patterns as you can find in the triangle below.

   b. Come up with a name for this triangle that connects to what the triangle is about. Briefly explain the reasoning behind your choice for the name.

```
          1
        2   4
      3   6   9
    4   8  12  16
  5  10  15  20  25
```

39. On which day of the year does the one-millionth second occur?

40. When Goodyear Tire Company introduced the Aquatread tire, one of the television commercials stated that the tire displaces over 1 gallon of water per second (at highway speeds); the announcer further stated that this amounts to over 396 gallons per mile. Critique this commercial.

41. **a.** How many different ways can you insert four Xs into a 4 by 4 array so that no row, no column, and no diagonal has more than one X? One solution is given below.

	X		
			X
X			
		X	

   b. Find a solution for a 5 by 5 array using 5 Xs.

42. McDonald's has sold "over 100 billion hamburgers." If we were to stack these hamburgers, how high would the stack be?

43. You are going to visit your grandmother in Buffalo. You had told her that you would be there for dinner, but you are behind schedule. It is now 4:35 p.m. and you are 210 miles from Buffalo. You pull off the freeway and call her to tell her you will be late. What time do you tell her to expect you?

44. How many 3 × 2 rectangles are contained within a 8 × 8 square?

45. How many triangles can you find in the figure below?

46. Make up a 3 × 3 magic square with $5\frac{1}{2}$ in the middle square.

47. One of the more famous magic squares was created by Albrecht Dürer in 1514 in his engraving *Melancholia*. He created a square in which the year appeared in the bottom row of the square.

    a. Describe all the patterns you see in the magic square below.

    b. Describe one of the patterns in words as if you were talking to someone on the phone.

13	3	2	16
8	10	11	5
12	6	7	9
1	15	14	4

48. Make up a 4 × 4 magic square.

49. The following magic figure originated in West Africa.

a. Describe the patterns you see in this magic figure.

b. Describe the relationship between this figure and the first magic square in Exploration 1.5.

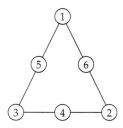

50. Examine the magic triangle below.

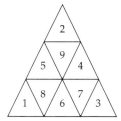

a. Describe all the patterns you notice.

b. Make a new magic triangle with different numbers.

c. What generalizations can you make about magic triangles of order 3, that is, ones in which there are three numbers on each side of the triangle?

d. Make a magic triangle of order 4. Briefly describe the strategies and knowledge that enable you to make the three sums equal.

51. Below is a different kind of magic triangle.

a. Describe the patterns you see in this magic triangle.

b. Create a new magic triangle in which the nine numbers are not consecutive numbers.

52. Leonard Euler, whom many consider to be the greatest mathematician of all time, created this magic square. Describe three patterns that you find in this magic square.

1	48	31	50	33	16	63	18
30	51	46	3	62	19	14	35
47	2	49	32	15	34	17	64
52	29	4	45	20	61	36	13
5	44	25	56	9	40	21	60
28	53	8	41	24	57	12	37
43	6	55	26	39	10	59	22
54	27	42	7	58	23	38	11

53. Benjamin Franklin created this magic square. Describe three patterns that you find in this magic square.

52	61	4	13	20	29	36	45
14	3	62	51	46	35	30	19
53	60	5	12	21	28	37	44
11	6	59	54	43	38	27	22
55	58	7	10	23	26	39	42
9	8	57	56	41	40	25	24
50	63	2	15	18	31	34	47
16	1	64	49	48	33	32	17

CHAPTER SUMMARY

1. One's beliefs about mathematics can powerfully affect one's ability to do mathematics. Many students find that the following big ideas involve a shift in the beliefs that they brought into the course.

2. George Polya's description of the four basic steps in solving problems is a useful framework, but it is the starting point, not the ending point, of your using it.

3. Many problems can be solved in a variety of ways. Some of the more common problem-solving strategies are: guess–check–revise, make a diagram, develop an equation, make a table, look for patterns, connect the problem to a similar problem, break the problem into smaller pieces and act it out.

4. Solving a problem involves more than simply computation. The number is not the answer, and you are not done unless the answer makes sense.

5. Patterns permeate our lives as well as permeating mathematics. Recognizing patterns is the beginning of using them to understand mathematics and solve problems. You should be able to describe, extend, analyze, and create a wide variety of patterns.

6. Communication is an essential aspect of mathematics—being able to communicate with yourself as you learn mathematical ideas and solve problems, and being able to communicate with others. Tools to improve communication include diagrams, vocabulary, and symbols.

7. There are many aspects to being able to develop mathematical connections: Connecting new concepts to old concepts, making connections among different concepts, connecting different models for the same concept, connecting conceptual and procedural knowledge, and making connections between school mathematics and "real life."

8. The NCTM has articulated four fundamental goals for mathematics education in the twenty-first century: mathematically literate workers, lifelong learning, opportunity for all, and an informed electorate.

Basic Concepts

Section 1.1 Getting Comfortable with Mathematics
adaptive beliefs *3*
maladaptive beliefs *3*

Section 1.2 Problem-Solving and Reasoning
problem-solving *4*
what-if program *5*
guess–check–revise *5*
grope-and-hope *5*
connections *7*
own *7*
rent *7*
reflect *8*
Problem-Solving and Toolboxes *8*
toolbox *8*
active readers *9*

Polya's Four Steps
understand the problem *9*
devise a plan *9*
monitor your plan *9*
look back at your work *9*

Sample data for "students' beliefs" exercise, p. 3

	STATEMENT ON LEFT		STATEMENT ON RIGHT	
	Agree strongly	**Agree somewhat**	**Agree somewhat**	**Agree strongly**
Question 1	12	8	6	4
Question 2	8	10	7	3
Question 3	4	11	5	10
Question 4	10	10	9	1
Question 5	10	7	8	5
Question 6	8	15	4	3

Solution to Investigation 1.4, p. 17

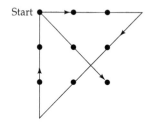

Fundamental Concepts

In this chapter, we will explore three topics that occur throughout elementary school mathematics: sets, functions, and numeration. However, before we explore sets, we will touch on each of these three topics.

When we talk about a herd of deer, a bunch of carrots, an army of ants, a band of jackals, or a pack of lies, we are talking about a *set* of objects that have something in common. In mathematics, we use set language in many situations. For example, we talk about the set of even numbers or the set of common denominators of 20 and 30. Many mathematical concepts and operations are defined in set language, and set language is often useful when talking about mathematical situations.

In many situations, both in daily life and in people's work lives, one set is *functionally* related to another set. The relationship may be simple — for example, the relationship between weight and postage — or it may be complex — for example, the relationship between income and tax.

The base 10 *numeration system*, which most people use without thinking about it, is one of the greatest inventions in human history. The analogy to a guitar is useful. Just as one can learn a few chords and memorize a few songs, one can compute with virtually no understanding of the structure of our numeration system (base, place value). However, a deeper understanding of how the guitar works enables a person to play more complex songs and even to adapt songs. A deeper understanding of our numeration system increases a person's ability to make estimates and to solve more complex problems, to understand connections between whole numbers and decimals, to understand *why* the computation procedures work, and much more.

One of the foundations of the NCTM Standards is the notion that mathematics ought to make sense to more people. (You may be surprised to hear that the idea that mathematics is an esoteric subject that only "smart" people can really understand is held almost solely in the United States.) One part of making sense of mathematics is understanding its vocabulary and symbols. Throughout this book, you will encounter many mathematical words and symbols, some of which will be familiar and some of which will be new to you. It is important that you realize that these words (for example, set, intersection, proportion, and parallelogram) and symbols (e.g., $\cup$, $+$, $\%$, $\neq$, $\frac{a}{b}$) were created to make it easier for people to discuss mathematical ideas. As you encounter new vocabulary and symbols, you might find it helpful to keep the following quote in mind:

> Mathematics is often considered a difficult and mysterious science, because of the numerous symbols which it employs. . . . [T]he technical terms of any profession or trade are incomprehensible to those who have never been trained to use them. But this is not because they are difficult in themselves. On the contrary they have invariably been introduced to make things easy. So in mathematics, granted that we are giving any serious attention to mathematical ideas, the symbolism is invariably an immense simplification.[1]

When you have finished this chapter, it might be useful to look back at the symbols introduced in the chapter. To what extent do the symbols make things easier? Is it important for the average person to know the concepts, or are they needed only by some people in some occupations? What do you think?

S E C T I O N 2.1 **SETS**

WHAT DO YOU THINK?

- How do we use and apply set concepts in everyday life?
- Do we have to use circles to make Venn diagrams?

When mathematics educators discuss how much mathematics a teacher needs to know in order to teach well, there are two extreme positions. Those at one extreme argue that the content of this course should consist only of those concepts that the teachers will actually use with their future students. Those at the other extreme argue that the content of the course should be rigorous so that the teachers will know the mathematics at a much higher level.

My own position is somewhat in the middle. I believe that future teachers will generally be more motivated to learn concepts if they can see that their future students will work with these concepts too. I also feel that the teachers' knowledge needs to be at a higher level than they will teach at, for three reasons. First, if you have a strong understanding of the mathematical ideas, you can be more flexible in your lesson planning and in classroom discussions. Second, you will see more of the connections between concepts. Third, if you have a sense of where your students are headed, you can serve them better. That is, if an elementary teacher knows the concepts that middle school and high school teachers will build on, then the transition from elementary school mathematics to middle and high school mathematics will not be as abrupt as it has been for all too many students.

Sets as a Classification Tool

With this context, let us now look at why you might need to have some knowledge of various set concepts in order to teach more effectively at the elementary

---

[1] *Introduction to Mathematics* (New York, 1911), pp. 59–69, cited in Robert Moritz, *On Mathematics* (New York: Dover Publications, 1914), p. 199.

level. Children use set ideas in everyday life as they look for similarities and differences between sets; for example, they want to know why lions are in the cat family and wolves are in the dog family. Children also look for similarities and differences within sets; for example, they look within a set of blocks for the blocks that they can stack and the blocks that they can't.

Whether we realize it or not, we are classifying many times each day, and our lives are shaped by classifications we and others have made.

INVESTIGATION 2.1   Classifying Quadrilaterals

Without classifying various objects and ideas, it would not be possible to have mathematics. This introductory investigation will help you to connect set language and concepts to other, more concrete mathematical ideas. Look at the eight shapes below. How can you classify these shapes into two groups so that each group has a common characteristic? Give a name to each group if you can. Work and then read on. . . .

DISCUSSION

There are many possible answers to this question. Let us examine some common ones.

One answer:
Those shapes with 4 sides (quadrilaterals)

Those shapes with 5 sides (pentagons)

Another answer:
Those shapes in which all sides are equal

Those shapes in which not all sides are equal

Another answer:

Those shapes with at least one right angle	Those shapes with no right angles

Another answer:

Those shapes in which opposite sides are equal (parallelograms)	Those shapes in which opposite sides are not equal

Defining Sets

In Investigation 2.1, we began with a set, which is a collection of objects, and classified that set into smaller groups (*subsets*) having certain common features. In general, a **subset** is a set that is part of some other set. (A more precise definition will be given later.) Some subsets have names—for example, the subset of the set of shapes in Investigation 2.1 consisting of parallelograms. Other subsets are well defined but have no names; for example, there is no name for the set of geometric figures with at least one right angle.

We speak of individual objects in a given set as members or elements of the set. The symbol ∈ means "is a member of." The symbol ∉ means "is not a member of." For example, if E is the set of even numbers, then $4 \in E$ but $3 \notin E$.

Describing Sets

There are three different ways to describe sets:

1. We can use words.
2. We can make a list.
3. We can use *set-builder notation.*

Words and lists   In many cases, one of these representations is simpler or easier than the others. Let us examine some important mathematical sets and how we can describe them.

The first set of numbers that young children learn is called the set of natural numbers. We can use words to describe this set, or we can describe this set with a list.

N is the set of natural numbers or counting numbers.
$N = \{1, 2, 3, \ldots\}$

We use braces to indicate a set. The three dots are referred to as an "ellipsis" and are used to indicate that the established pattern continues indefinitely.

At some point, children realize that zero is also a number, and this leads to the next set: the set of whole numbers (W), which we can describe with words or with a list:

W is the set of positive whole numbers and zero.
$W = \{0, 1, 2, 3, \ldots\}$

Later, children become aware of negative numbers, and so we have the set of integers (I):

$I = \{\ldots -3, -2, -1, 0, 1, 2, 3, \ldots\}$

Set-builder notation   Another important set is the set of **rational numbers** (*Q*), which we can describe in words:

> *Q* is the set of all numbers that can be represented as the ratio of two integers as long as the denominator is not zero.

We cannot represent this set by making a list. Why is this? . . . 🖉 In this case, and in many other cases, it is actually easier (as long as you understand the notation) to describe the set using what we call set-builder notation:

$$Q = \left\{ \frac{a}{b} \,\middle|\, a \in I \text{ and } b \in I, b \neq 0 \right\}$$

This statement is read in English as "Q is the set of all numbers of the form $\frac{a}{b}$ such that *a* and *b* are both integers, but *b* is not equal to zero."

Set-builder notation always takes the form $\{x \,|\, x$ has a certain property}. Although elementary school students do not use this notation to describe sets, it is helpful occasionally for you to see where your students will go. In high school, when students are working with more complex ideas, this notation makes communication easier.

Let us now apply these different ways of describing sets.

INVESTIGATION **2.2** **Describing Sets**

Consider the following set:

$T = \{10, 20, 30, 40, 50, 60, 70, 80, 90, 100, 110, 120\}$

Try to describe this set with words and with set-builder notation. What do you see as advantages and disadvantages of each of the three ways to describe this set?

If you have difficulty with this question, stop and think what might help. . . . 🖉

You might read the previous section again. You might write down the definitions and examples (or say the important ideas out loud to yourself). Or you might find that discussing this problem with a friend helps. The point here is to develop active learning habits rather than simply reading on to find the answer.

DISCUSSION

Verbal description:

T is the set of all multiples of 10 that are less than 130.

Set-builder notation:

$T = \{x \,|\, x = 10n, 1 \leq n \leq 12, n \in N\}$.

Many students initially have difficulty with set-builder notation. Therefore, let us examine the heart of the description: $x = 10n, 1 \leq n \leq 12, n \in N$.

This notation tells us that we are looking at all numbers that have the form "10n." Since we are not talking about *all* multiples of 10, we have to let the reader know which multiples of 10 are in *T*. The mathematical phrase $1 \leq n \leq 12$ simply tells us that we are looking for multiples of 10 beginning with $10 \cdot 1$ and ending with $10 \cdot 12$. The last part of the description, "$n \in N$," simply lets us know that *n* must be a natural number.

The table below summarizes some of the advantages and disadvantages of each way of describing the set.

	Advantage	Disadvantage
Verbal description	Relatively simple	Subject to misinterpretation; in this case, some readers may not know whether 10 is included
List	No confusion	A bit impractical in some cases
Set-builder notation	Concise, clear	Can be imposing to a novice

Kinds of Sets

Finite and infinite sets　In the course of this book, we will sometimes refer to *finite* and *infinite* sets. If the number of elements in a set is a whole number, that set is said to be **finite**. Some finite sets are small—for example, the set of Nobel Prize winners. Some finite sets are very large—for example, the grains of sand on all the beaches in the world. An **infinite set** has an unlimited number of members.

Consider the following infinite set. Does each way of describing the set make sense?

Verbal description	E is the set of positive even numbers.
List	$E = \{2, 4, 6, 8, \ldots\}$
Set-builder notation	$E = \{x \mid x = 2n, n \in N\}$

Well-defined sets　Thus far, each of the sets we have studied has been a **well-defined set**. That is, there is no ambiguity concerning whether a particular element is a member of the set or not. For example, 1 is not an element of the set of even numbers, and Virginia is not an element of the set called "states in New England." However, in everyday life, many sets are not well defined. For example, "the set of large numbers" is clearly not a well-defined set, whereas "the set of whole numbers greater than one billion" is well defined. Similarly, "the set of wealthy people" is not well defined. We can sharpen the description of this set by saying, for example, "the set of people whose net income is over $100,000." However, tax experts would still not consider this set to be well defined: If a law were enacted that imposed a tax on people whose net income was over $100,000, "net income" would need to be more precisely defined. Over the course of this book, we will frequently encounter problem situations in which part of the problem is that the problem is not well defined; in some cases, the set (of numbers or objects) in the problem is not well defined.

Defining Subsets

The notion of subset is critical because many practical applications of sets involve subsets. What do you think a subset is? Write your current definition of a subset and then read on. . . .

One informal definition of a subset is that a set is a subset of another set if it has fewer elements. While this informal definition of subset makes sense, it presents problems in some situations. Thus, we give a more formal definition of subset:

A set X is a **subset** of a set Y if and only if every member of X is also a member of Y.

The symbol ⊆ means "is a subset of." Thus, we say $X \subseteq Y$. On the other hand, if a set X is not a subset of a set Y, we say $X \not\subseteq Y$.

There is actually another symbol that we can use when talking about subsets. This symbol (⊂) is used when we want to emphasize that the subset is a proper subset. A subset X is a proper subset of set Y if and only if the two sets are not equal *and* every member of X is also a member of Y. In the case of finite sets, this means that the proper subset has fewer elements than the given set.

If and only if   We use the abbreviation **iff** to stand for "if and only if"; iff essentially means that the statement is true "backwards and forwards." For example, the definition of subset is equivalent to *both* statements below.

- If X is a subset of Y, then every member of X is also a member of Y.
- If every member of X is also a member of Y, then X is a subset of Y.

Does this definition of subset make sense to you? If it does, that's great. If it doesn't, you need to find out why and to take steps to understand the definition. One way to do this is to connect it to your original sense of subset, which might be "a smaller piece of the larger set." How would you explain the need for the formal definition of subset?

BEYOND THE CLASSROOM

Sets and subsets occur often in the business world. In fact, "databases" are closely connected to the idea of sets. In my office, I have a collection of articles on teaching mathematics. Let's say one article is entitled "Using Cooperative Learning to Teach Fractions." Physically, I have to store that article in one file folder—the folder called Cooperative Learning or the folder called Fractions or the folder called Elementary Math Methods. This presents a problem, for I wind up losing articles. I could make copies and have a copy in each folder, but that is costly and wasteful. With a database program, I can enter the article in a file and use the following descriptors: cooperative learning, fractions, and elementary math methods. When I want to review my resources on cooperative learning, I give a command to the computer saying, in the language of this section, "Look in the set of teaching resources and find the subset 'cooperative learning.'"

INVESTIGATION 2.3   How Many Subsets?

This investigation serves several purposes. It opens the idea of families of subsets, it shows how subsets might be useful, and it provides an opportunity to develop problem-solving tools.

Let's say that you and your friends decide to go out and get a large pizza. Let T represent the set of toppings that this restaurant offers:

T = {onions, sausage, mushrooms, peppers}

List all the possible different combinations of pizza that you could order, such as a mushroom and onion pizza. Then read on. . . .

DISCUSSION

The text will contain occasional reminders about the process of problem-solving. In this investigation, we focus on understanding the problem and looking back. Before you made your list, did you make sure you understood the question? After you make your list and before reading on, take a few moments to look back: How can you check your solution to make sure you didn't miss any combinations? . . .

STRATEGY 1: List all the combinations systematically

Begin with all combinations that involve onion, from the simplest to the most complex, and then do the same for each of the other toppings (see Table 2.1):

TABLE 2.1

Onion	Sausage	Mushroom	Pepper
o	s	m	p
o, s	s, m	m, p	
o, m	s, p		
o, p	s, m, p		
o, s, m			
o, s, p			
o, m, p			
o, s, m, p			

If you didn't use this strategy, do you understand it? If you cover up the table, can you reconstruct it? If you can't, then chances are you don't really understand this strategy.

There are many patterns within Table 2.1. How many can you see? How would you describe them so that someone who didn't see any patterns could see them from your description?

STRATEGY 2: List all the combinations using another system

Begin with all the ways to have one topping, then all the ways to have two toppings, etc. (see Table 2.2):

TABLE 2.2

One of the four	Two of the four	Three of the four	All of the choices
o	o, s	o, s, m	o, s, m, p
s	o, m	o, s, p	
m	o, p	o, m, p	
p	s, m	s, m, p	
	s, p		
	m, p		

If you didn't use this strategy, do you understand it? If you cover up the table, can you reconstruct it? If you can't, then chances are you don't really understand this strategy.

There are many patterns within Table 2.2. How many can you see? How would you describe them so that someone who didn't see any patterns could see them from your description?

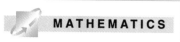

MATHEMATICS

Do you remember Pascal's triangle from Chapter 1? It occurs in Tables 2.1 and 2.2. Can you find it?

One of the common mistakes that students make in such problems is to overlook a combination. There are patterns in both of the tables above that could help you to find all the combinations. Write down all the patterns you see and then read on. . . .

One pattern (in the "Three of the four" column) is that each of the four toppings should be equally represented. Let's say you had somehow omitted the last combination: s, m, p. Looking over the three combinations you had found, you would notice that onion occurred *three* times, but that sausage, mushroom, and pepper each occurred only *two* times. This observation itself names the combination you had missed: sausage, mushroom, and pepper.

Mathematically, there are 16 possible subsets of a set containing four elements. However, if you look at either of the tables above, there are only 15 subsets. What is the missing subset? If you haven't noticed it yet, stop and think before reading on. . . .

The Empty Set

The missing subset is plain pizza. How would we represent this subset using set notation? Recall that the subset called "mushroom pizza" can be represented as {m}, and the pizza with everything on it can be represented as {o, m, p, s}. Write your thoughts before reading on. . . .

One way is to put nothing inside the brackets { }. We also use the following symbol to represent a set that is empty: ∅. We use the terms **empty set** and **null set** interchangeably to mean the set with no elements.

This pizza problem also illustrates two mathematical statements that often baffle students and that will be left as exercises:

- Every set is a subset of itself.
- The empty set is a subset of every set.

Equal and Equivalent Sets

In many situations, the relationship between two sets is important. Let us examine two relationships that will come up occasionally.

Two sets are said to be **equal** iff they contain the same elements. For example, {1, 2, 3, 4, 5} = {5, 4, 3, 2, 1}.

Sometimes two sets are equal even though it may not be obvious at first. For example, if

E = the set of even numbers

D = the set of integers divisible by 2

we say $E = D$. Do you see why?

Two sets are **equivalent** iff they have the same number of elements. More precisely, two sets are equivalent if their elements can be placed in a **one-to-one correspondence**. In such a correspondence, an element of either set is paired with exactly one element in the other set. We use the symbol ~ to designate set equivalence. For example, {United States, Canada, Mexico} ~ {1, 2, 3}.

This definition appears rather formal and intimidating to many students, who exclaim, "Why can't you just say that two sets are equivalent if they have the same number of elements?" The answer is that in most cases, this less formal description of equivalence works.

Equivalence and counting One reason for defining sets in terms of a one-to-one correspondence has to do with the difficulty young children have counting objects accurately. Watch young children trying to count the number of objects in a collection. Initially, they do not realize that each number has to match one and only one object, and so they can count a set several times and arrive at a different number each time! At some point, they realize (and you can see it in their pointing) that there must be a one-to-one correspondence between their words and the physical objects. Thus, although our definition of equivalence appears unnecessarily formal to many students, it reflects what children actually go through in learning to count objects accurately.

Venn Diagrams

Let us now explore applications of set theory. One way to represent sets is to use *Venn diagrams,* which are named after John Venn, the Englishman who invented these diagrams to illustrate ideas in logic. You have probably seen Venn diagrams used in other contexts.

Several years ago, I was teaching a graduate course in cooperative learning. One teacher explained how she had used the Venn diagram in Figure 2.1 to help her students understand the similarities and differences between butterflies and moths. In this Venn diagram, one region represents the set of moths' characteristics, another region represents the set of butterflies' characteristics, and the overlapping region represents the set of characteristics common to both.

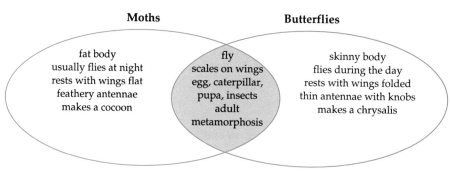

FIGURE **2.1**

Operations on Sets

We will use Venn diagrams as we examine three operations on sets: intersection, union, and complement. Just as a doctor's operation consists of something the doctor does to a patient, a mathematical operation consists of something we do to a set of objects. In Chapter 3, we will examine the mathematical operations of addition, subtraction, multiplication, and division.

When we perform operations on sets of objects, it is often useful to refer to the set that consists of all the elements being considered as the **universal set,** or the **universe,** and to refer to it as *U.* We represent *U* in the Venn diagram with a rectangle.

In the following discussions, we will let *U* be the set of students in a small class:

$$U = \{\text{Amy, Uri, Tia, Eli, Pam, Sue, Tom, Riki}\}$$

We begin with two subsets of U:

$$B = \{\text{students who have at least one brother}\}$$
$$S = \{\text{students who have at least one sister}\}$$

Figure 2.2 represents the students in this hypothetical class.

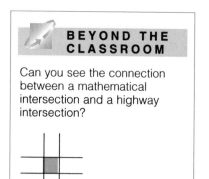

FIGURE **2.2**

BEYOND THE CLASSROOM

Can you see the connection between a mathematical intersection and a highway intersection?

Before we discuss the various operations, does the diagram make sense to you? If you were in the class, where would your name appear? . . .

Intersection We can group this class of eight students into various subsets. How would you describe the subset consisting of Tom and Uri? Think and then read on. . . .

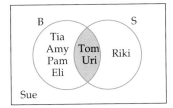

FIGURE **2.3**

One way to describe this subset is, "Those students who have at least one brother and at least one sister."

Mathematically, we call this subset the *intersection* of sets B and S. In mathematical language, we say that the **intersection** of two sets B and S consists of the set of all elements common to both B and S.

We represent the intersection of B and S by shading it (see Figure 2.3).

Using set-builder notation, we write

$$B \cap S = \{x \mid x \in B \text{ and } x \in S\}$$

The symbol $\cap$ is used to denote "intersection."

MATHEMATICS

In Figure 2.1, the characteristics common to both moths and butterflies are listed in the intersection area. Connecting the concept of intersection to previous notation, we can say Tom $\in B \cap S$ (that is, Tom is a member of the set of students who have a brother and a sister), and we can say $(B \cap S) \subset U$ (that is, the set of students who have a brother and a sister is a subset of the entire class).

Union Let us examine another subset of the class: {Tia, Amy, Pam, Eli, Tom, Uri, Riki}.

How would you describe this subset in everyday English? Think and then read on. . . .

There are actually several ways to describe this subset:

- Those students who have at least one brother or sister.
- Those students who have at least one sibling.
- Those students who are not an only child.

Mathematically, we describe this subset as the *union* of sets B and S. In mathematical language, we say that the **union** of two sets B and S consists of the set of all elements that are in set B *or* in set S *or* in both sets B and S.

We represent the union of B and S by shading it (see Figure 2.4).

Symbolically, we write

$$B \cup S = \{x \mid x \in B \text{ and/or } x \in S\}$$

The symbol $\cup$ is used to denote "union."

FIGURE **2.4**

MATHEMATICS

Connecting the concept of union to previous notation, we can say Tom $\in B \cup S$, and we can also say $B \subset (B \cup S)$. Do you see why?

MATHEMATICS

If we denote the universal set as the set of integers, then the complement of the set of even numbers is the set of odd numbers. Do you see why?

Complement Let us examine another subset of the class. Look back to Figure 2.2 and consider this subset of the class: {Tia, Amy, Pam, Eli, Sue}. How would you describe this subset in everyday English? Think and then read on. . . .

One way to describe this subset is, "Those students who have no sisters."

We describe this subset as the *complement* of set S. In mathematical language, the **complement** of set S consists of the set of all elements in U that are *not* in S.

We represent the complement of S by shading it (see Figure 2.5 on page 50).

Symbolically, we write $\overline{S} = \{x \mid x \notin S\}$. We represent the complement of a set by placing a line over the set's letter.

Some people understand complement better if they think of the complement of S as "not S"—that is, all elements that are not in set S.

INVESTIGATION **2.4** **Finding Information from Venn Diagrams**

FIGURE **2.5**

FIGURE **2.6**

FIGURE **2.7**

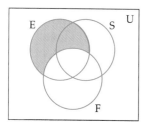

FIGURE **2.8**

The owners of Marksalot (a company that makes all sorts of markers) believe that healthy, happy employees are productive employees, so they had a consultant conduct an anonymous survey about employees' exercise habits, their smoking habits, and one particular aspect of their eating habits. Unfortunately, the consultant quit before the job was done (she got a teaching position). Before quitting, she gave Marksalot a Venn diagram (Figure 2.6) that represents the survey results. Marksalot has asked you to help the company interpret the diagram. Before reading on, take a few minutes to write what conclusions you can make from the information below. . . .

Try to write your conclusions in everyday English. If possible, compare your conclusions with those of a classmate.

U = the employees of Marksalot

E = the set of people who exercise regularly

S = the set of people who do not smoke at all

F = the set of employees who average at least five servings of fruits and vegetables each day, the amount recommended by the Food and Drug Administration

Now try to answer the four questions below on your own and then check your answers. . . .

A. How many employees exercise regularly but don't average five servings of fruits and vegetables? Represent that subset visually and symbolically.

B. Describe the 8 employees who are outside all three circles (see Figure 2.7), first in everyday English and then with symbols.

C. Describe the following subset both in everyday English and visually:

$$(E \cap F) \cup (E \cap S)$$

D. Represent the results of the survey other than with a Venn diagram.

DISCUSSION

A. If we represent the question symbolically, we find that we want to look at the regions that are in E but not in F. There are 15 persons who match the subset "E but not F"—that is, $E \cap \overline{F}$. Symbolically, we have Figure 2.8.

B. In everyday English, these people do not exercise regularly, they do smoke, and they average less than five servings of fruits and vegetables a day.

Symbolically, this set is $\overline{E \cup S \cup F}$: Since $E \cup S \cup F$ describes the subset of employees who fit into one or more of the healthy categories, the complement of this set describes the subset of employees who fit into none of the healthy categories. This is the subset that will probably require a disproportionate amount of medical services over their lifetimes. We will explore the concepts of probability and proportions in Chapters 6 and 7.

C. Many students find themselves intimated by the apparent complexity of this problem. Looking at an analogous arithmetic problem may be useful. What if you were asked to find $(17 \times 34) + (30 \times 76) + (12 \times 56)$? Take a moment to think about how you might solve this problem and how this problem might be connected to finding $(E \cap F) \cup (E \cap S)$. . . . 🖎

Most students have little difficulty with the arithmetic problem. You know that you have to multiply the numbers inside the parentheses before you can add. Many mathematical operations, such as multiplication, are binary operations, operations that can be performed on only two elements at a time. If you had trouble with Question C, can you solve it now? Try to do so before reading on. . . . 🖎

Applying the idea of binary operations, we first find $(E \cap F)$ and $(E \cap S)$, then we find the union of those two sets. See Figure 2.9.

$(E \cap F)$

$(E \cap S)$

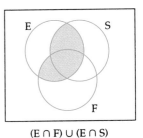

$(E \cap F) \cup (E \cap S)$

FIGURE **12.9**

One description of this set in everyday English is, "Those employees who exercise regularly and who also don't smoke and/or average at least five servings of fruit and vegetables each day."

If this explanation helped and you want to do more problems to see if it does make sense, try some problems in the Exercises for which answers are at the back of the book. One note of caution: Being able to "get the answer" is not the same as "understanding the process." The larger goal of this book is for the mathematical concepts and operations to make sense.

D. Another way to represent the results of the survey is to list the numbers of employees in each of the eight different regions created by the Venn diagram:

- 33 people checked *E*
- 23 people checked *F*
- 26 people checked *S*
- 18 people checked *E* and *F*
- 17 people checked *E* and *S*
- 15 people checked *F* and *S*
- 12 people checked all 3
- 8 people checked none

We could also represent the results with a bar graph. If you don't see this possibility, look at Exercise 24.

Venn Diagrams as a Communication Tool

People other than mathematicians often use Venn diagrams in the same sense that "a picture is worth a thousand words." *Mathematics in Science and Society*, a book for elementary and middle school mathematics teachers, uses Venn diagrams to discuss teaching methodology. In the introduction to one of the

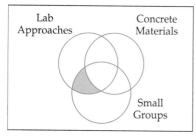

Lab Approaches Concrete Materials Small Groups

FIGURE **2.10**

Source: Mathematics Resource Project, *Mathematics in Science and Society* (Palo Alto, Calif.: Creative Publications, 1977)

chapters in the book, the authors make a teaching point: "This section is devoted to three valuable teacher tools: laboratory approaches, concrete materials and small groups of students. All three of these may—and quite often do—appear in the same lesson." The authors then use Venn diagrams to illustrate the kind of lesson they would be discussing. Try to describe, in everyday English, the kind of lesson represented in Figure 2.10. Then read on. . . . 🖎

They would be describing a lesson in which the students would be doing a math lab in small groups but would not be using concrete materials.

Summary

In this section, we have investigated those concepts from set theory that are most likely to occur in elementary mathematics. Although you are not likely to use these ideas in their formal sense, you will find that you encounter sets and subsets both in elementary school and in everyday life. Most sets in everyday life are finite, but many mathematical sets are infinite. Both in everyday life and in mathematics, there is confusion if a set is not well defined or clearly described. The notion of equivalent sets is one that early childhood educators see young children grapple with as they seek to make sense of relationships. Venn diagrams are used both in elementary school and in other places to describe relationships between various sets. These relationships involve the intersection, union, and complements of sets.

EXERCISES 2.1

1. Rewrite the following statements using mathematical symbols:

   a. 0 is not an element of the null set.

   b. 3 is not an element of set B.

2. Rewrite the following statements using mathematical symbols:

   a. The set D is not a subset of the set E.

   b. The set A is a subset of the set U.

3. Sets can be described in three ways: verbally, by listing the elements, or with set-builder notation. In each of the statements below, a set has been described verbally. Either describe the set in the other two ways or explain why it would be impossible. Then explain which of the three descriptions you think would be most useful and why.

   a. The set of letters in the word "elementary."

   b. The set of countries in Europe.

   c. The set of prime numbers less than 100.

   d. The set of fractions between 0 and 1.

   e. The set of students in your class.

4. Which of the sets in Exercise 3 are not well defined? Redefine those sets so that they are well defined.

5. Let U be the set of all colors and S be the subset {red, orange, yellow, green, blue, violet}.

   For the following questions, place the appropriate symbol in the blank: $\subset, \not\subset, \in, \notin$

   a. S __ U

   b. red __ U

   c. {magenta} __ U

   d. {green, blue} __ S

   Which of the following are true? Briefly explain your answer.

   e. $S \subseteq U$

   f. red $\subseteq U$

   g. gray $\in S$

   h. {green, blue} $\subseteq S$

6. Fill in the most appropriate symbol for each of the following: $\subset, \not\subset, \in, \notin$. *Briefly* justify your choice.

   a. 3 __ {1, 2, 3}

   b. {3} __ {1, 2, 3}

   c. {1} __ {{1}, {2}, {3}}

   d. {a} __ {a, b, c}

   e. {ab} __ {a, b, c, d}

   f. { } __ {1, 2, 3}

7. a. How many subsets does $A = \{p, i, c, k, l, e\}$ have?

   b. Can you make a generalization about the relationship between the number of elements in a set and the number of subsets? *Hint:* Look at Investigation 2.3.

8. Can you apply what you learned in Investigation 2.3 to answer the following question? There are 6 members on the Student Council. A committee consisting of 2 members is to be made. How many different committees are possible?

9. Justify the following statements, as if you were talking to a student who had not read this section.

   a. Every set is a subset of itself.

   b. The empty set is a subset of every set.

10. Make a Venn diagram with four circles. Use a compass or another device to make good circles. How many dis-

tinct regions are there in this diagram? What patterns do you notice in this diagram?

11. Some friends of mine had a young child who was fascinated by fans. It just so happened that every fan he had seen was circular in shape. One year for Christmas, he got a popular toy that is circular in shape. He pulled the string, and a voice said, "Spoon." He happily exclaimed, "Wow, a talking fan." Represent his perception of fans and circular objects with a Venn diagram.

12. Find a Venn diagram from a newspaper, magazine, or elementary school mathematics book. Describe the Venn diagram in words.

13. Let $U = \{x \mid x$ is an American$\}$

$F = \{x \mid x$ is a female$\}$

$S = \{x \mid x$ is a smoker$\}$

$P = \{x \mid x$ has a health problem$\}$

a. Represent the following description with a Venn diagram and with symbols: An American nonsmoking healthy female.

b. Represent $F \cap (S \cup P)$ with a Venn diagram and in everyday English.

c. Represent $(F \cup P) \cap \overline{S}$ with a Venn diagram and in everyday English.

d. Convert the information from the left-hand diagram to everyday English and to symbols.

e. Convert the information from the right-hand diagram to everyday English and to symbols.

 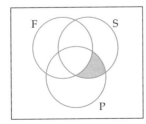

14. In the following Venn diagram,

F = the set of students in the film club

S = the set of students in the science club

C = the set of students in the computer club

For each of the following exercises, briefly explain or justify your solution.

a. Interpret the following sets in English and in symbols.

 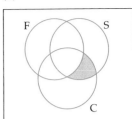

b. Represent the following descriptions in symbolic language and with a Venn diagram.

(i) Those people who are in the science and film clubs but not the computer club.

(ii) Those people who are in none of the three clubs.

15. Use the sets below to answer parts (a) through (f):

$U = \{1, 2, 3, 4, 5, 6, 7, 8, 9, 10, 11, 12, 13, 14, 15, 16, 17, 18, 19, 20\}$

A: the numbers in U that divide 12 with no remainder

B: the numbers in U that divide 15 with no remainder

C: the numbers in U that divide 20 with no remainder

a. Make a *clear* Venn diagram showing the sets U, A, B, and C.

b. Represent the following subset in everyday English and with symbols: $\{7, 8, 9, 11, 13, 14, 16, 17, 18, 19\}$.

c. Represent the following subset in everyday English and with symbols: $\{2, 4\}$.

d. Represent the following subset in everyday English and with a diagram: $\overline{A \cap B}$.

e. Represent the following subset in everyday English and with a diagram: $\overline{A \cup B}$.

f. Represent the following subset with a diagram and with symbols: Those numbers that divide 12 or 15 with no remainder.

16. An elementary teacher has asked her students to place their names in the region that represents their answers to the question, "Which pets live in your home?"

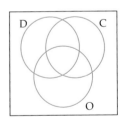

D = the set of students who have at least one dog

C = the set of students who have at least one cat

O = the set of students who have a pet that is not a dog or a cat

Describe the following sets in everyday English and then with a diagram:

a. $C \cap D$ **b.** $\overline{D \cup C}$ **c.** $C \cap O \cap D$

Describe the following sets in symbols and then with a diagram:

d. Students who have dogs but not cats

e. Students who have at least one pet

f. Students who have other pets but neither cats nor dogs

Describe the following sets in everyday English and then with symbols:

g.

h.

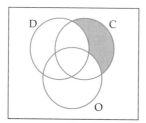

17. Why do you think we use circles instead of squares or triangles or other shapes when we make Venn diagrams? For example, is the representation below equivalent to the standard Venn diagram with three overlapping circles? Explain your answer as if you were talking to a fellow student who does not understand.

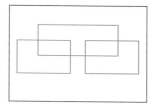

18. Recall the different kinds of sets of numbers described earlier: natural numbers, whole numbers, integers, and rational numbers. Make a Venn diagram to represent how these sets are related.

19. Pollsters often ask people's opinions. Politicians want to know how their position on an issue is viewed by particular constituencies — for example, by young voters, by African Americans, by women, by those who belong to the Sierra Club. Decisions about policies are often made on the basis of this polling information. Let's say that a public opinion survey was conducted to determine how much support there was for the president's policies. People were asked three questions:

Do you support the president's economic policy?

Do you support the president's foreign policy?

Do you support the president's social policy?

Let E, F, and S denote the sets of persons responding yes to the first, second, and third questions, respectively. The results of the survey are shown in the Venn diagram below. The numbers represent the percent of respondents.

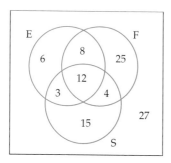

a. What percent agree with his economic policy?

b. What percent agree with just one of his policies?

c. Describe the subset that would be represented by $F \cup (E \cap S)$, either in everyday English or by shading the appropriate portion of the diagram.

d. If the president could make one single region of the Venn diagram larger (that is, have more members), which would it be? Why?

20. In a group of 120 students, 75 know how to use a Macintosh, 65 know how to use an IBM-compatible computer, and 20 do not know how to use either kind.

a. How many students know how to use both kinds of computers?

b. Are the sets in this problem well defined or not? Justify your response.

21. An advertising firm found that a certain ad that ran on both radio and TV was only heard on the radio by 21 percent of the people and was only seen on TV by 33 percent of the people. Just 10 percent of the population both heard the ad on the radio and saw it on TV.

a. What percent of the people in the area has neither seen nor heard the ad?

b. What percent of the people in the area only heard the ad on radio or only saw the ad on TV?

22. Refer back to the discussion about the book *Mathematics in Science and Society* in the last subsection.

a. What would be the focus of the authors' discussion following the Venn diagram below? Describe your answer in everyday English.

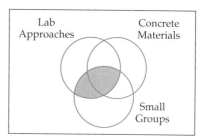

b. The Venn diagram below appeared in the same book. Why do you think the authors used a question mark here?

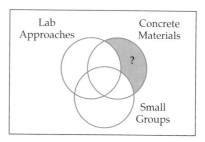

23. Make up a situation for which the following Venn diagram is appropriate.

24. I was curious about the number of high-tech machines that my friends have, so I asked them if they had a VCR, an answering machine, and/or a CD player. I have represented the results of my survey with a Venn diagram and with two different bar graphs.

Number of People Who Own Various Machines

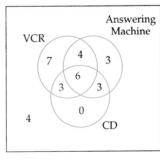

a. Which of the three graphs would you choose as the most useful? Why?

b. Jack thinks that there is a mistake in the bar graph at the top. Assuming that the Venn diagram is accurate, do you agree with Jack? If you do, explain the mistake. If you don't, explain why, as if you were trying to convince Jack.

c. How many friends did I question?

d. From the Venn diagram, what conclusions could you draw concerning the relationship between ownership of the three items?

25. Consider the following two subsets of U, the set of all people:

    I = the set of intelligent people

    S = the set of successful people

a. By yourself, answer the following question: How would you represent these two subsets with a Venn diagram?

b. Discuss your responses with other classmates. What did you learn from this activity? How did the Venn diagram contribute to this learning?

S E C T I O N **2.2** **FUNCTIONS**

WHAT DO YOU THINK?

- What does it mean to say that two sets are functionally related?
- What are some examples of functions in everyday life?
- Can we have functions without numbers?

The NCTM strongly argues that elementary teachers should have sufficient familiarity with the "ideas of algebra"[2] so that their students will explore and develop the concepts and skills that are essential prerequisites for formal algebraic thinking before they enter high school. In many cases, familiarity with the ideas of algebra relates to the NCTM Standard on patterns: recognizing, analyzing, and extending patterns and then applying that understanding in order to determine whether a pattern involves a function and in order to work with that function.

The concept of function is one of the "big ideas" of mathematics. However, many students come to college confusing functions with equations and then find college mathematics very difficult. Success at higher levels of mathematics rests on more than just being able to manipulate equations. In elementary school, children will not investigate functions and other algebraic ideas at a formal level. However, through their investigations, they do need to realize that relationships often exist between different variables—(for example, the area of a rectangle varies according to the length and the width of the rectangle); that patterns and relationships can be represented in various ways (with words, symbols, graphs, and pictures); and that being able to communicate clearly the patterns they see is important.

If students engage in these kinds of investigations during elementary and middle school, then they will see many of the concepts that are developed at the formal level in high school as extensions of what they encountered earlier, not as something that is entirely new and foreign. This section will focus on the concept of function, which is one of the concepts that underlies virtually all algebraic thinking.

I N V E S T I G A T I O N **2.5** **Prelude to Functions: A Geometric Context**

In Exploration 2.5, you worked with **figurate numbers,** a type of number whose name comes from the shape it represents. Figurate numbers present a rich area for investigation: They possess many interesting patterns, they have nice visual representations, so that patterns are readily observable; they are connected to other mathematical ideas; and they can be investigated throughout the elementary curriculum.

Figurate numbers seem to have been invented by the Pythagoreans around the sixth century B.C. The first set of figurate numbers we will explore here is the set of triangular numbers.

Figure 2.11 shows the first four triangular numbers.

FIGURE **2.11**

Write your responses to the following questions. If possible, compare your responses with those of someone else. . . .

A. Assume that a friend who missed the class asks you to describe triangular numbers over the phone. How would you describe them?

[2] Title of the 1988 NCTM yearbook.

B. How many dots are in the fifth triangular number? in the 10th triangular number? in the nth triangular number?

DISCUSSION

A. By having you express the concept of triangular numbers in words, we are emphasizing the development of communication in mathematics. There is no one "correct" description. Chances are that if you gave your description to several people and each of them successfully produced the set of triangular numbers, your description was fine. Many students find that what seems very clear to one person doesn't make sense to another. That is, a description that seems clear to you may make no sense to someone who has no prior experience with the concept. Many teachers, including me, have experienced this phenomenon with our students.

Consider the following description, which makes perfect sense to me, the teacher. Does it make sense to you? What parts of this description might prove difficult for someone who has never heard of triangular numbers? "Let me explain how to draw the fifth triangular number: begin by drawing one dot, then underneath it draw two dots so that, if the single dot dropped down, it would be right in the middle of the two dots. The third row consists of three dots, the fourth row of four dots, and the fifth row of five dots. Each row is staggered so that each dot in a row is above a dot two rows below."

B. Determining how many dots are in the fifth, tenth, and nth triangular numbers is an interesting challenge. Were you able to discover a relationship between each triangular number and how many dots constitute that number? If so, what tools helped? If not, follow the discussion below actively.

There are often many patterns that will lead us to understand and state a relationship in its most general form. It turns out that the difference between successive triangular numbers makes an interesting pattern. Look at Table 2.3. Do you understand what each column represents? Think and then read on. . . .

The column at the far left tells us which triangular number we are looking at. The second column tells us how many dots it takes to make that triangular number. The third column simply notes the difference between the number of dots in the triangular number and the number of dots in the preceding triangular number. The last column shows one way of counting the total number of dots in that triangular number. Extend the table for a few more numbers if you wish. How would you describe what happens to the difference as we go along? Think and then read on. . . .

TABLE 2.3

n	T_n	$T_n - T_{n-1}$	Determining T_n
1	1	—	1
2	3	2	$1 + 2$
3	6	3	$1 + 2 + 3$
4	10	4	$1 + 2 + 3 + 4$
5	15	5	$1 + 2 + 3 + 4 + 5$

One way to describe what happens is that the difference increases by one each time. This is interesting, but it does not lead most students to be able to predict the 10th or the nth triangular number. However, if you noticed the similarity between the sums in the right column and finding the sum of the first 100 numbers (Investigation 1.5), you can find the 10th triangular number and write a rule for determining the *n*th triangular number. Do you see why?

Using the notation introduced in Investigation 1.5, we can say that the *n*th triangular number, T_n, is equal to $\frac{1}{2}n(n + 1)$. For example, to answer the question, how many dots make up the 10th triangular number, we simply take one-half of 10 times 11, and get 55.

Functions

Let us now use this investigation to introduce the concept of function. From our investigation with triangular numbers, we now have a process for determining the exact number of dots it takes to make any triangular number. Furthermore, there is only one answer to the question, "How many dots does it take to make the *n*th triangular number?" When two sets have this kind of relationship, we call that relationship a function.

More formally, we define a function as a relationship between two sets in which each element of the first set is matched with *exactly* one element of the second set.

The first set is called the domain of the function, and the second set is called the range of the function. Look at our work with triangular numbers. Can you identify the domain set and the range set? Do this before reading on. . . .

The first column (*n*) represents the domain and the second column (T_n) represents the range. Technically, what is in these columns is a subset of the domain and a subset of the range.

Explorations 2.5 through 2.7 each uncover functional relationships. In Exploration 2.5, we can predict the number of dots in any triangular or other figurate number; in other words, the number of dots in a figurate number is a function of the figurate number. Similarly, in Exploration 2.6, we can predict the cost of any of the patio rings. We can also predict the period of any pendulum (Exploration 2.7) because a pendulum's period is a function of its length.

It is important to note that not all relationships between two sets are functions. For example, consider the relationship between the set of positive whole numbers and their square roots. In this case, if we ask, "What is the square root of 9?" the answer is +3 *and* −3. That is, each member of the set of positive whole numbers is matched with two square roots.

When we go outside the classroom to look for instances of functions in situations, we find that their value is often the predictability of the relationship. Consider the following questions:

- If I sell 50 computers, what will be my commission?
- If 75 students sign up for a course, how many sections will be offered?
- What are the consequences when you chew gum in Appleby High School?

If Jack sells 50 computers and receives $1000 while Jill sells 50 computers and receives only $700, then there is not a functional relationship between the number of computers sold and the commission.

If one department creates three sections when 75 students preregister while another department creates only two sections, then we say that at that college there is not a functional relationship between the number of students and sections of a course.

If Cindy chews gum in one class and gets detention and chews gum in another class and receives no detention, then there is not a functional relationship between chewing gum and consequences.

INVESTIGATION **2.6**   **Baby-sitting**

Let us extend our understanding of functions by examining a relationship between two variables: hours worked and dollars earned. Let's say Ellen baby-sits and charges $4 per hour. Describe how you would determine how much to pay Ellen. Determine whether the relationship between the two variables—hours and dollars—is a function. Whether you say it is or is not a function, can you justify your response? Then read on. . . .

DISCUSSION

A common response to describing how to pay Ellen is to multiply the number of hours sat by 4. Let us use this situation to introduce several different ways to represent functions, and then we will examine the relationship between time sat and dollars paid more closely.

For purposes of simplicity, let us first look at different representations of this function using only whole-hour amounts.

Tables   We can represent this function with a table in which h represents hours and d represents dollars (see Table 2.4). We can then use the table to determine how much money Ellen will make from baby-sitting.

Equations   We can represent this function with an equation in which h represents hours and d represents dollars:

$$d = 4h$$

Graphs   We can represent this function with a graph (see Figure 2.12).

In some cases, like this one, many people find it more convenient to refer to the input as the **independent variable** and to the output as the **dependent variable.** In this case, we say that the independent variable is the hours baby-sat and the dependent variable is the dollars earned. That is, the number of dollars you earn is dependent on the number of hours you baby-sit.

Ordered pairs   We can represent this function as a set of ordered pairs in which the first element of each ordered pair represents hours and the second element represents dollars:

$$B = \{(1, 4), (2, 8), (3, 12), (4, 16), . . . \}$$

Mappings   Finally, we can represent functions with arrow diagrams. Mathematicians often refer to this representation as a mapping of one set onto another set. We shall soon use this representation when we look at different kinds of functions.

h		d
1	→	4
2	→	8
3	→	12
4	→	16

A closer look at paying the baby-sitter   At first glance, the question of how much to pay the baby-sitter is simple: multiply by 4. However, let us use the problem-solving strategy "act it out" to examine this problem more closely. For example, what if Ellen baby-sat from 7 to 11:10? How much would you pay her? Think before reading on. . . .

Some people say $16. Some say $17—they round to the nearest quarter hour, and they round up. Some people say $18—they round up to the nearest

---

TABLE 2.4

h	d
1	4
2	8
3	12
4	16
5	20
⋮	⋮

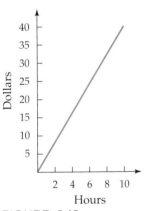

FIGURE **2.12**

HISTORY

René Descartes (1596–1650) invented the Cartesian coordinate system (named after him) to illustrate such relationships on graphs. Legend has it that he got the idea from watching a fly crawl across a ceiling. He realized that a coordinate system could represent the fly's location with one symbol, that is, the ordered pair.

half hour. In actuality, different people have different ways of determining how much to pay a baby-sitter. Let us examine the case of a couple, whom we will call the Alomars, who determine how much to pay their sitter in the following way: They round the time to the nearest half hour. We could now represent the Alomars' process for paying the baby-sitter in each of the ways we have just examined. Is the relationship between time sat and dollars earned a functional relationship in the case of the Alomars? How can you justify your answer? Think and then read on. . . .

Many students find that they need to represent the relationship to help them answer this question. Let us examine one representation more closely. If you were to graph this relationship (using the Alomars' process), what would the graph look like? Try to make your own graph before reading on. . . .

The graph is shown on page 85. Take a look at the graph and see if you can make sense of it before reading on.

If you are having trouble making sense of the graph, let us consider a few examples. Let's say the sitter sits for 2 hours and 50 minutes. Using the Alomars' process, we round this time to 3 hours and pay Ellen $12. As you can see, Ellen will receive $12 for all times between 2 hours and 46 minutes and 3 hours and 14 minutes. So is this a function?

It is, because for any specific time (input), there is exactly one dollar amount (output) associated with that time.

The graph that represents this baby-sitting function is often confusing to students who see it for the first time. However, it is relatively common in real-world mathematics and is a member of the subset of functions called step functions.

Mathematical modeling As you have discovered in this section, and in other mathematics courses, upon closer examination, a problem is often more complicated than it first appears. This is what makes "real-life" problems so challenging. The NCTM has stated that mathematical modeling should be an important part of mathematics education in school. Let us take some time to understand this concept and its importance. We will begin by examining the word *model*. A model of an object is not the object, and is often a scaled-down version of the object. We speak of model airplanes, and architects and engineers build a model of a building or a bridge before constructing the actual object. In one sense, a model is a representation of the original object. There are two important features of many models. First, the model contains many of the properties of the original object. Second, the model can be manipulated and studied to help us better understand the (usually larger and more complex) object. A mathematical model is a mathematical structure that approximates the features of a situation. A mathematical model can be an equation (or a set of equations), a graph, or some other kind of diagram.

In this case, we have seen that the original straight-line graph turns out not to be a useful or accurate model of the baby-sitting situation. The step graph is a more accurate representation. This process of examining a situation and then developing a model that accurately represents that situation is called mathematical modeling. Constructing and interpreting mathematical models is one of the more important uses of mathematics in the real world. Over the course of this book, you will have many opportunities to construct and interpret mathematical models.

Inputs, Outputs, and Function Notation

Many elementary teachers use a game called "What's my rule?" to introduce children to the idea of functions. The students give a number (the *input*), then the teacher performs an operation and gives them the number associated with that input (the *output*). The students then try to guess what the teacher is doing to the inputs. A game of "What's my rule?" is given below.

Teacher: What's my rule?

Student: 3

Teacher: 6

Student: 4

Teacher: 7

Student: I think I know the rule.

Teacher: What is your rule?

Student: You are adding 3. If I give you 10, you will say 13.

Teacher: That's right!

The teacher is adding 3. Algebraically, we would say: $y = x + 3$. We can also use **function notation** to write the rule for adding 3 to any number: $f(x) = x + 3$. This mathematical sentence is read "*f* of *x* equals *x* plus 3." That is, $f(x)$ means "function of *x*."

Function notation is more precise because it emphasizes the relationship between the **input**, which is another name for a member of a function's domain, and the **output**, which is the corresponding member of its range. That is, the output is a function of the input. In this particular case of "What's my rule?" the output $f(x)$ is determined by adding 3 to the input *x*, and so we have

$$f(3) = 3 + 3 = 6$$
$$f(4) = 4 + 3 = 7$$
$$f(10) = 10 + 3 = 13$$

Let's play another round. What is the rule? Think and then read on. . . .

Input	Output
1	4
2	7
3	10

Using everyday English, we could say that the rule (or function) is to triple the input and add 1. Using function notation, we could say that $f(x) = 3x + 1$.

In this game, the domain and range do not have to be sets of numbers. Can you think of an example in which the domain and range are not numbers? Try to do so before reading on. . . .

Here is one example, from Margie Hoey, a second grade teacher with whom I worked. One student placed some students in one group and some students in another group. The determining factor was whether the student was wearing blue or not. That is, the domain set consisted of the set of students in the class. The range set had two elements: "is wearing blue" and "is not wearing blue." For example,

Input	Output
Anastasia ⟶	Is wearing blue
Benito ⟶	
Cecilia	
Damon	
Emilia ⟶	Is not wearing blue

HISTORY

Although the concept of function can be traced back to the Babylonians about four thousand years ago, the notation we use to represent functions has been widespread only since the late 1800s. Many famous mathematicians contributed to the evolution of our current notation, including René Descartes and Gottfried von Leibnitz in the 1600s, Johann Bernoulli and Leonard Euler in the 1700s, and Joseph Lagrange and Jean Fourier in the 1800s.

Do you see why this student's "rule" represents a function? Try to make up more rules that do not involve numbers.

INVESTIGATION 2.7   Choosing Between Functions

Jackie has been promoted to chief salesperson of Southside Computers. She has two choices as to how she will be paid. She can receive $50 for every computer system she sells, or she can receive $250 a week plus $25 for every computer system she sells. Looking at the past year, she finds that she has averaged 9.3 sales per week, and she figures that she can do a little better this year. What would you recommend? Work on this problem for a bit and then read on. . . .

DISCUSSION

You may want to start by plugging in a few numbers—that is, using guess–check–revise. Do you see that if Jackie sells only a *few* computers, she will be better off with the second plan, but that the first plan is better if she sells a *lot* of computers? This realization leads to a specific mathematical question: At what point will the two plans give her the same money? Once she can answer that question, she can base her decision on whether she believes she will sell more or less than that amount. Below we see three very different strategies for solving this subproblem: guess–check–revise, use algebra, and make a graph. If you already solved the problem using one strategy, try to use the other strategies now and then read on. . . .

STRATEGY 1: Guess, check, and revise
This strategy is illustrated in Table 2.5.

TABLE 2.5

Sales	Plan A	Plan B	Reflection/Analysis
0	0	250	
2	100	300	Plan A goes up 100; plan B goes up 50. Plan A is still $200 below plan B. Since it takes eight 25s to make 200, increase the number of computers sold by 8. Do you see why?
10	500	500	

What does the last row mean? Think and read on. . . .

It means that Jackie makes the same amount under both plans when she sells 10 computers a month. If she thinks she will sell more than 10, then plan A is better for her.

STRATEGY 2: Use algebra
Let y = Jackie's weekly salary.
Let x = the number of computer systems she sells.

The equation that represents plan A is:

$$y = 50x$$

The equation that represents plan B is:

$$y = 250 + 25x$$

Do you understand how both of these equations were constructed? We have two equations in two unknowns that we can solve:

$$50x = 250 + 25x$$
$$25x = 250$$
$$x = 10$$

STRATEGY 3: Make a graph

Where the two lines cross will show the point at which her earnings under both plans will be equal.

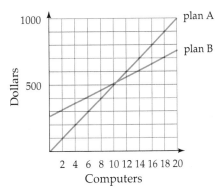

FIGURE **2.13**

The two lines cross at the point (10, 500) (see Figure 2.13). In other words, the ordered pair (10, 500) is an element of both graphs.

More on Mapping Functions

Most of the functions we encounter outside the classroom lend themselves to graphic representation. However, there are many useful functions that better lend themselves to mappings. Recall the "What's my rule?" example in which the input set was the students and the output set was {wearing blue, not wearing blue}.

Many mathematical functions are nicely represented by mappings such as determining whether a number is divisible by 3. Do you understand the following mapping, which represents a functional relationship between the sum of the digits in a number and whether the number is divisible by 3. Do you see why it is a function? Think and read on. . . .

The sum of the digits in a number is divisible by 3	$\rightarrow$	The number is divisible by 3
The sum of the digits in a number is not divisible by 3	$\rightarrow$	The number is not divisible by 3

The input set consists of the set of whole numbers. The output set consists of two elements: "divisible by 3" and "not divisible by 3." Since it is true that every element of the input set is matched with exactly one element of the output set, this mapping represents a function.

Now look back through the investigations and explorations you have done in Chapters 1 and 2. Which ones involved functions? Think and then read on. . . .

There is a functional relationship in many cases. We will discuss one example here; others will be left as exercises.

In Investigation 1.1, the relationship between the number of pigs and chickens and the number of feet is a function. Do you see why? How can such a function be mapped?

The relationship is a function because if you know the number of pigs and the number of chickens, then you can determine exactly the total number of feet. More formally, we would say that if the domain set consists of ordered pairs in which the first number represents pigs and the second number represents chickens, and the range consists of a subset of the set of whole numbers, then for every input, there is exactly one output. For example, 16 pigs and 8 chickens will have 80 feet.

I N V E S T I G A T I O N 2.8 Interpreting Graphs of Functions

FIGURE 2.14

We see graphs of functional relationships every day in newspapers and magazines. The purpose of this investigation is to examine some of the nuances involved in interpreting graphs.

The graph in Figure 2.14 shows the value of the stock of a company over the course of a year.

Write your responses to the following questions. . . .

A. Approximately when was the value of the stock $110?

B. In which month did the stock's value show the biggest decline?

C. How much did the value of the stock decrease during the third quarter?

DISCUSSION

Frequently, interpretations of graphs require us to examine the question and the graph carefully. What problem-solving tools did you use in this problem?

A. The value of the stock first reaches $110 just to the right of the M, standing for March. Many students are not sure whether the line above the M represents the beginning of March or the end of March. If this applies to you, what could you do to make sense of the graph? Think and then read on. . . .

If we look at the left side of the graph, we can see that the beginning of the year (January 1) is at the beginning of the graph, and so the first vertical line represents the beginning of January; the second vertical line therefore represents the beginning of February, and so on. Therefore, the value of the stock first reaches $110 just after the beginning of March. The graph is not large enough or marked precisely enough for us to determine the exact date on which the stock's value was $110. However, we can be more precise than simply saying "sometime in March." What do you think?

A rough estimate is that the value reaches $110 about $\frac{1}{4}$ to $\frac{1}{3}$ of the way from March 1 to April 1. So we could say "early March" or "somewhere in the second week of March."

Did you see that the value of the stock actually hits $110 twice during the year? The second time occurs in the last week of September.

B. We can determine the month with the greatest decline by finding all months that show a decline, estimating the value of the stock at the beginning and ending of these months, and determining which month has the biggest difference. Another way to determine the biggest decline is to recall the algebraic concept of slope. From this perspective, we can focus on those months during which the stock's value declined and find the month with the steepest slope.

September shows the biggest decline, although August is a close second.

C. Students often encounter two problems with this question. The first is not knowing what is meant by the third quarter. If you didn't know this term, what did you do in order to find out (rather than just reading ahead)? This is important because resourcefulness is an important quality of good problem-solvers and good teachers.

The other problem is that once we find out that the third quarter means from the end of June to the end of September (or, equivalently, the first of July to the first of October), we must make sure that we locate those points correctly on the graph. The value of the stock at the end of June is about $127 or $128, and the value of the stock at the end of September is about $107 or $108. Thus, the value of the stock declined about $20. Do you see why we say about $20?

If we take the biggest possible difference $(128 - 107)$, we get 21. If we take the smallest possible difference, $(127 - 108)$, we get 19. Alternatively, we could also say that the value of the stock declined between $19 and $21 during this period; this response tells the reader that the graph (the data available to us) is not precise enough for us to give an exact answer.

Summary

Let us take an active look back at this section. First, close the book and think for a few moments. What did you learn in this section? What seems important? Write down your thoughts. . . . 📖

Now look back over the text and your notes. Do you need to revise or elaborate on what you wrote? . . . 📖

The big idea of this section is the concept of function. One of the most useful aspects of functions is that when we determine that there is a functional relationship between two sets, we can use this knowledge to make predictions, whether of the length of a pendulum (Exploration 2.7) or the cost of a patio (Exploration 2.6). We learned that terms like *domain, range, independent variable, dependent variable, input,* and *output,* can make it easier to describe and discuss functions. We have learned that domain, independent variable, and input are related terms. Similarly, range, dependent variable, and output are related terms.

We have learned that there are many different ways to describe functions: tables, graphs, equations, words, ordered pairs, mappings, and function notation. Many students are surprised to find that we do not need numbers to have a function. We also learned that not all relationships are functions. We also examined practical applications of functions: interpreting stock market graphs and selecting salary options.

If you can describe what a function is both in everyday English and in mathematical terms, and if you can give examples of functions in real life, then you have learned quite a bit in this section. Many textbooks require students only to find values of functions. In this section, there has been an emphasis on different ways of representing functions and an emphasis on interpreting functions.

Finally, we have learned that we can use mathematical tools to create a mathematical model of a situation and that we need to think carefully to see if our model fits the situation. Recall Investigation 2.6.

EXERCISES 2.2

1. Look back to Investigation 1.8, in which we examined how many small pieces of wire could be cut from one long piece. Is the relationship between the length of the long wire and the number of small pieces a function or not? Please justify your response.

2. The table below shows the process by which a college department determines the number of sections of a course to offer.

Number of students	Number of sections
Less than 6	Course not offered this semester
6–29	1
30–59	2
60–89	3
90–119	4

   a. Make a graph to represent this process.

   b. Is the relationship between the number of students and the number of sections a function? Justify your answer.

3. Let's say you have children, you hire a baby-sitter frequently, and you pay the baby-sitter $4 per hour. Describe how *you* would pay the baby-sitter, first in words, then with a graph. In order to receive full credit, the reader must be able to pay the baby-sitter the same amount that *you* would pay, based on your descriptions.

4. Let's say the entire freshmen class of Wannago High School is going on a field trip. The number of buses needed is a function of the number of people going. To keep matters simple, let's say that the school bus company has buses that can hold 36 passengers and that there will be two adults per bus.

   a. How many buses will be needed for 232 students?

   b. Represent this function graphically.

5. At the time this book was written, the postage on a letter was determined by the following set of rules:

   The first ounce costs 32¢.

   Each additional ounce, or fraction thereof, costs 23¢.

   a. How much would it cost to mail a letter weighing 6.3 ounces?

   b. Draw a graph of this function.

6. Archaeologists can estimate a person's height from the length of the femur (thigh bone). The formula for doing so is

   $$H = 2.3L + 61.4$$

   where all measurements are in centimeters. Let's say an archaeologist has found a femur of a human and the bone is 45 centimeters long. How tall do we think the person was at the time of death?

7. In Investigation 2.3 in Section 2.1, we found that a set containing 4 elements has a total of 16 subsets.

   a. Fill in the blanks in the chart below.

   b. Describe in words the relationship between the number of elements in a set and the number of subsets. Refer to the table below.

   c. Describe the relationship with an equation.

Number of elements in the set	Number of subsets
1	?
2	?
3	?
4	16
5	?

8. We can make up other figurate numbers. For example, look at the L numbers.

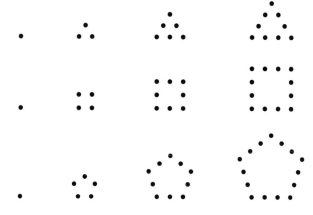

   a. Describe the set of L numbers in everyday English.

   b. Describe the set of L numbers in relation to one or more of the other sets of figurate numbers.

   c. Represent the relationship between the nth L number and the number of dots that constitute the nth L number with a graph.

   d. Represent the relationship between the nth L number and the number of dots that constitute the nth L number with a formula.

   e. Is the relationship between the domain (the nth L number) and the range (the number of dots in the nth L number) a function? Justify your response.

   f. Joshua claims that if you can represent the relationship between two variables with a formula, it must be a function. What do you think about his hypothesis? Defend your response.

9. The set of figurate numbers can be extended to different kinds of numbers. The diagrams below show the first four trinumbers, quadrinumbers, and pentinumbers respectively.

a. What is the value of the fifth trinumber? the 10th trinumber? the *n*th trinumber?

b. What is the value of the fifth quadrinumber? the 10th quadrinumber? the *n*th quadrinumber?

c. What is the value of the fifth pentinumber? the 10th pentinumber? the *n*th pentinumber?

d. With respect to part (a), describe how you could use what you learned about triangular numbers to help you answer that question.

10. Describe another relationship from Chapter 1 that involves a functional relationship between two sets.

11. John says that Investigation 1.1 (Pigs and Chickens) does not represent a function because two different inputs can have the same output. For example, (7, 17) and (0, 31) both map to the same number of feet. Do you agree with John? Why or why not?

12. Is it mathematically correct to say that one's grade is a function of the amount of time one spends on the course? Justify your response.

13. There is a relationship between the successive squares of triangular numbers. This relationship can be expressed in everyday English as, "Select any triangular number and square it. Then take the previous triangular number and square it. Now take the difference between the two numbers."

a. Express this relationship in notation.

b. Is this relationship a function? Justify your response.

14. Jack and Jill run a catering business. Their fee for catering banquets is $150 plus $4 per person.

a. Express this relationship with a table.

b. Express this relationship with an equation.

c. Express this relationship with a graph. What would be a realistic domain for the graph?

d. Jack and Jill catered a banquet for which they charged $462. How many people attended?

e. Their goal is to gross $2,000 a month. How many jobs do they need to average in order to make their goal? (There is no single right answer.)

15. My parents live in Park Rapids, Minnesota. When I visit them, I fly to Minneapolis and rent a car. It is about 160 miles to Park Rapids. The last time I visited them, I spent three days with them, counting my arrival and departure days. The car rental agency offered two options: $45 a day plus 30¢ per mile or $185 for the week. Which do you recommend?

16. Let's say you have a choice between two checking plans. With the first plan, you will be charged $2 per month plus 15¢ per check. With the second plan, you will be charged $5 per month regardless of how many checks you write. If you write only a few checks, the first plan is clearly cheaper. Similarly, if you write 200 checks a month, the second plan is clearly cheaper.

a. Determine the number *x* that will enable you to make the following statement: If you write 1 to *x* checks per month, choose the first plan. If you write more than *x* checks per month, choose the second plan.

b. Determine the number *x* using a method different from the one you used in part (a).

c. Which of the plans are functions: both, only one, or neither? Justify your response.

17. There is a functional relationship between the frequency of cricket chirps and the temperature. The rule is to count the number of chirps in one minute, divide by 4, and add 40.

a. What temperature does 50 chirps per minute correspond to?

b. Without calculating, will 100 chirps per minute correspond to twice the temperature of 50 chirps per minute? That is, does chirping at twice the rate mean that the temperature is twice as high? Explain your reasoning.

c. Translate the rule into an equation.

d. Draw a graph to represent this relationship.

18. Consider the graph below, which shows the depreciation of a copy machine over five years.

a. What is the value of the machine when it is two years old?

b. By how much does the machine decrease in value in one year?

c. Predict when the value of the copy machine will be zero.

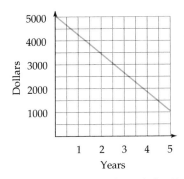

19. The graph below shows the value of the Dow Jones Industrial Average over the course of a year.

a. Approximately when was the Dow Jones average 2100?

b. Which month showed the biggest decline?

c. How much did the Dow Jones average gain during the second quarter (from the end of March to the end of June)?

20. There is a mathematical relationship between motivation and perceived chance of success. Carnival operators use this relationship masterfully. Think of the ring toss, in which you toss rings at bottles. If your ring lands on one of the bottles, you win a prize. If the bottles are too close, a high percentage of people win and the carnival loses money. However, if the bottles are too far away, virtually no one will participate. Therefore, the ideal distance (from the carnival owner's perspective) is determined by a maximization function—that is, the distance for which the value of total ticket sales minus cost of prizes is the greatest.

    The graph below accompanied a research paper that reported the authors' investigation of motivation. Translate this graph to words. In other words, briefly describe what the graph is saying.

21. I can recall trying to explain to my children that thunder is the sound that lightning makes. It took some time for them to understand this because there is often a delay of many seconds between seeing the lightning and hearing the thunder. Lightning travels at 186,000 miles per second, whereas thunder travels at the rate of approximately 750 miles per hour.

    a. Let's say that you see a flash of lightning and 5 seconds later you hear the thunder. How far away did the lightning strike?

    b. The relationship between the time (from seeing the flash to hearing the sound) and the distance (between the lightning and you) can be more easily expressed if we translate the speed of sound to the same units as the speed of lightning, that is, to miles per second. What is the speed of sound in miles per second?

    c. Write a formula to express this relationship.

22. When driving a car, a general rule of thumb to avoid tailgating is to maintain a distance of one car length for every 10 miles per hour. Let's say that you wanted to gather more precise information about the relationship between the speed of a car and the time it takes the car to stop. There are two parts to the time it takes to stop. The first part is the reaction time of the driver—for example, the time lapse between the instant the driver thinks "hit the brake" and the time that the driver's foot actually hits the brake pedal. The second part is the time

it takes the car to stop.

    a. Develop an experimental procedure to determine a person's reaction time. The experiment cannot actually use a car.

    b. Collect the data.

    c. If a car was going 65 miles per hour, how far would the car travel between the instant when a person thought to hit the brake and the instant when the brake was hit?

    d. What hypotheses do you have about braking distances for different kinds of cars? For example, do you think more expensive cars will have shorter or longer braking distances?

    e. What is your prediction as to the shape of the graph?

    f. Do you think the relationship between speed and time to stop is a function or not? Defend your response.

23. I usually have a cup of tea by my side in my office at school and in my office at home. For years, I kept my tea in plastic cups with lids so that the tea would cool down more slowly than it would in ceramic mugs. However, it still cooled down, and the plastic mugs are not as pretty as the ceramic mugs. Several years ago, my wife gave me a cup warmer so that my tea would not cool down. I was very grateful. This gift, however, led me to wonder about how well different containers insulate liquids. Let's say that you have two different cups and you want to know which one will keep your tea or coffee hotter longer.

    a. Design an experiment to answer this question.

    b. Predict what the graph might look like.

    c. Carry out the experiment.

    d. Report your results. How might you compare the efficiency of the two containers?

24. Find a graph from a newspaper or magazine that repre-

sents a functional relationship between two variables.

a. Explain why the relationship is functional.

b. Describe the relationship in words, as if you were talking on the phone to someone who cannot see the graph.

c. Make up and answer one question based on data in the graph.

25. Describe a real-life scenario involving a functional relationship between two variables.

NUMERATION

"Through and through the world is infested with quantity: to talk sense is to talk quantities. It is no use saying the nation is large—how large? It is no use saying that radium is scarce—how scarce? You cannot evade quantity. You may fly to poetry and music, and quantity and number will face you in your rhythms and your octaves."[3]

Numbers permeate our everyday lives. In Chapter 3, we will examine how we operate with numbers (addition, subtraction, multiplication, and division) and how we use exact numbers and estimates. In this section, we will lay the foundation for that work by examining the numeration system we use. Most adults don't think twice about our numeration system. Yet it represents one of the greatest advances in human history, and its widespread use is surprisingly recent—less than 500 years. If you look at Standard 6 in the list of Standards for Grades K–4, you can see that the NCTM stresses the importance of students not just understanding how to count but also understanding how our numeration system works. Rather than read about why our numeration system is so powerful and so much "better" than other systems, you will appreciate our system and understand its properties better if you participate in the reenactment of the invention of numeration systems, which is the aim of Exploration 2.8: Alphabitia.

Origins of Numbers and Counting

History   Did you know that the base 10 numeration system you use every day is called the Hindu-Arabic numeration system because it was invented by the Hindus and transmitted to the West by the Arabs? Did you know that this system has been in widespread use in the West for only 500 years? Did you know that people had to invent counting?

The earliest systems must have been quite simple, probably tallies. The oldest archaeological evidence of such thinking is a wolf bone, over 30,000 years old, discovered in the former Czechoslovakia (see Figure 2.15). On the bone are 55 notches in two rows, divided into groups of five. We can only guess what the notches represent—how many animals the hunter had killed or how many people there were in the tribe.

FIGURE **2.15**

Anthropologists have discovered several tribes in the twentieth century that did not have any counting systems! Other anthropologists have discovered

---

[3]Alfred North Whitehead, cited in Julian Weissglass, *Exploring Elementary Mathematics* (Dubuque, Iowa: Kendall Hunt Publishing, 1990), p. 100.

how shepherds, throughout the ages, have been able to keep track of their sheep without using numbers to count them. Each morning as the sheep left the pen, the shepherds made a notch on a piece of wood or on some other object. In the evening, when the sheep returned, they would again make a notch for each sheep. Looking at the two tallies, they could quickly see if any sheep were missing.

The beginnings of what we call civilization were laid when humans made the transition from being hunter-gatherers to being farmers—that is, from a nomadic life to a settled life. Archaeologists generally agree that this transition took place almost simultaneously in many parts of the world some ten to twelve thousand years ago. It was probably during this transition that the need for more sophisticated numeration systems developed. For example, a tribe need kill only a few animals, but one crop of corn will yield many hundreds of ears of corn.

The invention of numeration systems was not as simple as you might think. We have evidence that humans originally distinguished between only one of something and two of something; after that it was "many." The ancient Sumerian words for one, two, and three were the words for man, woman, and many. The Aranda tribe in Australia used the word *ninta* for one and *tara* for two. Their words for three and four were *tara-ma-ninta* and *tara-ma-tara*.

Requirements for counting   In order to have a counting system, people first needed to realize that the number of objects is independent of the objects themselves. Look at Figure 2.16. What do you see?

FIGURE **2.16**

There are three objects in each of the sets. However, the number three is an abstraction that represents an amount. Archaeologists have found that people didn't always understand this. For example, the Thimshians, a tribe in British Columbia, had seven sets of words in their language for each number they knew, depending on whether the word referred to (1) animals and flat objects, (2) time and round objects, (3) humans, (4) trees and long objects, (5) canoes, (6) measures, and (7) miscellaneous objects. Whereas we would say three people, three beavers, three days, and so on, they would use a different word for "three" in each case. There is evidence in some of our own words of such origins. For example, we have many different nouns denoting two: a pair, a couple, a brace (of pheasants), a span (of horses), a duet.

Having a counting system also requires that we recognize a one-to-one correspondence between two equivalent sets: the set of objects we are counting and the set of numbers we are using to count them. (Notice the use of set language as we develop the concepts related to counting.) I watched both of my children miscount objects for some time, either counting too many or too few, because they had not yet realized that they needed to say the next number each time they touched the next object. It took some time to realize that each object represented the next number, as shown in Figure 2.17—that is, that there is a one-to-one correspondence between the set of objects, and the set of numbers.

FIGURE **2.17**

There is another aspect of counting that needs to be noted also. Most people think of numbers in terms of counting discrete objects. However, this is only one of the two major contexts in which numbers occur. For example, in Figure 2.18, there are 3 balls, there are 3 ounces of water in the jar, and the length of the line is 3 centimeters. In the first case, the 3 tells us how many objects we have. However, in the two latter cases, the number tells how many of the units we have. In this example, the units are ounces and centimeters.

FIGURE **2.18**

Working with numbers that represent discrete sets is more concrete than working with numbers that represent measures. Recall the Thimshian language. Virtually all of the seven categories involved discrete sets. Ascribing numbers to continuous objects or events, such as length, time, or area, is more abstract.

Note that we distinguish between number, which refers to the amount (being counted or measured), and numeral, which refers to the symbol(s) used to designate the amount.

Patterns in Counting

As humans developed names for numbers larger than the number of fingers on one or two hands, the names for the larger numbers were often combinations of names for smaller numbers. Can you see the patterns and fill in the blanks for the three systems in Table 2.6 on page 72? What patterns did you see? Did you find any surprises after you checked your answers on page 85?

People who have investigated the development of numeration systems, from prehistoric tallies to the Hindu-Arabic system, have discovered that many of the numeration systems had patterns, both in the symbols and in the words, around the amounts we call 5 and 10. However, a surprising number of systems also show patterns around 2, 20, and 60 (the French word for eighty, *quatre-vingts*, literally means "four twenties").

As time went on, people developed increasingly elaborate numeration systems so that they could have words and symbols for larger amounts of objects. We will examine three different numeration systems—Egyptian, Roman, and Babylonian—before we examine our own base 10 system. Essentially, though, all numeration systems are simply a set of rules used with a set of symbols so that each amount can be represented by a unique element or combination of elements from that set of symbols! Do you see the connection to functions?

TABLE 2.6

Number	Greenland Eskimos	Aztecs	Luo of Kenya
1	atauseq	ce	achiel
2	machdlug	ome	ariyo
3	pinasut	yey	adek
4	sisasmat	naui	angwen
5	tadlimat	maculli	abich
6	achfineq-atauseq (other hand one)	chica-ce	ab-chiel
7	achfineq-machdlug	chic-ome	ab-ariyo
8	— — — — — — — — — — — — — — —	chicu-ey	— — — — — — — — — — — — — —
9	achfineq-sisasmat	chic-naui	— — — — — — — — — — — — — —
10	qulit (first foot)	matlacti	apar
11	achqaneq-atauseq (first foot one)	matlacti-on-ce	apar-achiel
12	— — — — — — — — — — — —	— — — — — — — — — — — — —	apar-ariyo
13			
15	achfechsaneq (other foot)	caxtulli	— — — — — — — — — — — — — —
16	— — — — — — — — — — — —	— — — — — — — — — — — — —	
20	inuk navdlucho (a man ended)	cem-poualli	piero-ariyo

The Egyptian Numeration System

The earliest known written numbers are from Egypt about 5,000 years ago. The Egyptians made their "paper" from a water plant called papyrus that grew in the marshes. They found that if they cut this plant into thin strips, placed the strips very close together, then placed another layer crosswise, and finally let it dry, they could write on the substance that resulted. Our word *paper* derives from their word for papyrus.

Symbols in the Egyptian system   The Egyptians developed a numeration system that combined picture symbols (hieroglyphics) with tally marks to represent numbers. Table 2.7 gives the primary symbols in the Egyptian system.

TABLE 2.7

1,000,000	100,000	10,000	1,000	100	10	1
Astonished person	Polliwog or burbot fish	Pointing finger	Lotus flower	Scroll	Heelbone	Staff, stroke

The Egyptians could represent amounts using combinations of these basic numerals. To deepen your understanding of how the Egyptian system worked, use it to answer the following questions. Check your answers on page 85.

What is the value of each of the following numbers?

1. ꜩ ꝯꝯꝯ∩∩||| 2. ꜣ ꝰꝰꝰꝰꝰ ꜩꜩꜩ ∩∩||

How would the Egyptians represent the following amounts?

3. 1,202   **4.** 304

Working with the Egyptian system   Take a few minutes to think about the following questions. Write your thoughts before reading on. If possible, compare your responses with those of a classmate. . . .

1. What do you notice about the Egyptian system? Do you see any patterns?

2. Do you see similarities between this and the more primitive systems we have discussed?

3. Do you see any limitations or disadvantages of this system?

4. Try to describe the rules for this system, as if you were talking to someone on the phone.

The Egyptian numeration system resembles many earlier counting systems in that it uses tallies and pictures. In this sense, it is called an *additive system*. Do you see why?

Look at the way this system represents the amount 2,312. In one sense, the Egyptians saw this amount as $1,000 + 1,000 + 100 + 100 + 100 + 10 + 1 + 1$ and wrote it as ꜰꜰꜹꜹꜹꞈ||. In an **additive system**, the value of a number is literally the sum of the numerals.

However, this system represents a powerful advance: They created a new numeral for every *power of 10*. Do you understand this?

They had a numeral for the amount 1. To represent amounts between 1 and 10, they simply repeated the numeral. For the amount 10, they created a new numeral. All amounts between 10 and 100 can now be expressed using combinations of these two numerals. For the amount 100, they created a new numeral, and so on.

These amounts for which they created numerals are called **powers of ten**.

1	10	10·10	10·10·10	10·10·10·10	10·10·10·10·10	10·10·10·10·10·10
1	10	100	1000	10,000	100,000	1,000,000

We can express $10 \cdot 10$ as 10^2. If you recall your work with exponents from algebra, you can express 10 as 10^1 and 1 as 10^0. Thus, we can express the value of each of the Egyptian numerals as a power of 10:

$$10^0 \quad 10^1 \quad 10^2 \quad 10^3 \quad 10^4 \quad 10^5 \quad 10^6$$

The Egyptian system was not a full-blown base 10 system, as we shall find out, but it was a remarkable achievement for its time. Egyptian rulers could represent very large numbers. One of the primary limitations of this system, as we shall see in Chapter 3, was that computation in this system was extremely cumbersome. It was so difficult, in fact, that the few who could compute had very high status in the society.

The Roman Numeration System

The Roman system is of historical importance because it was the numeration system used in Europe from the time of the Roman Empire until after the Renaissance. In fact, several remote areas of Europe continued to use it well into the twentieth century. Some film makers still list the copyright year of their films in Roman numerals

Symbols in the Roman system Table 2.8 on page 74 gives the primary symbols used by early Romans and later Romans.

Again, to deepen your understanding of how the Roman system worked, use it to answer the following questions. Check your answers on page 85.

What is the value of each of the following numbers (using the numerals of the Later Roman system)?

1. MXI   **2.** MDXCVII

The X precedes the C in MDXCVII above. Notice how this placement affects the value. We will discuss this aspect of the Roman system later.

Amount	Early Roman	Later Roman
1	I	I
5	V or Λ	V
10	X	X
50	↓	L
100	⊙	C
500	� and ▷	D
1000	⊕ or ∞	M

How do you think the Romans would represent the following amounts?

3. 1,102   **4.** 319

Working with the Roman system   Take a few minutes to think about the following questions. Write your thoughts before reading on. If possible, compare your responses with those of a classmate. . . . 🖉

1. What do you notice about the Roman system? Do you see any patterns?
2. Do you see similarities between this system and the Egyptian system?
3. Do you see any limitations or disadvantages of this system?
4. Try to describe the rules for the Roman system, as if you were talking to someone on the phone.

Like the Egyptians, the Romans created new numerals with each power of 10, that is, 1, 10, 100, 1,000, etc. However, the Romans also created new numerals at "halfway" amounts, that is, 5, 50, 500, etc. Why do you think they did this? Think and then read on. . . . 🖉

This invention reduced some of the repetitiveness that encumbered the Egyptian system. For example, 55 is not XXXXXIIIII, but rather LV.

Basically, the Roman system was an additive system. However, the Later Roman system introduced a *subtractive* aspect. For example, IV can be seen as "one before five." This invention further reduced the length of many large numbers. For example, when writing the amount 444, users of the Later Roman system no longer had to write CCCCXXXXIIII, but rather could write . . . well, what do you think? 🖉

Check your answer on page 85.

Though the Roman system has additive aspects like the Egyptian system (for example, XXX = 30), we consider the Roman system to be a positional system because the value of a numeral (often) depends on its position. For example, IV = 4 but VI = 6.

As in the Egyptian system, computation in the Roman system was complicated and cumbersome, and neither system had anything resembling our zero.

The Babylonian Numeration System

The Babylonian numeration system is a refinement of a system developed by the Sumerians several thousand years ago. Both the Sumerian and Babylonian empires were located in the region occupied by modern Iraq. The Sumerians did not have papyrus, but clay was abundant. Thus, they kept records by writing on clay tablets with a pointed stick called a stylus. Thousands of clay tablets with their writing and numbers have survived to the present time; the earliest of these tablets were written almost five thousand years ago.

Symbols in the Babylonian system Because they had to make their numbers by pressing into clay instead of writing on papyrus, their symbols could not be as "fancy" as the Egyptian symbols. In fact, this physical constraint was probably the impetus for the advances that their system represents. They had only two symbols, an upright wedge that symbolized "one" and a sideways wedge that symbolized "ten." In fact, the Babylonian writing system is called **cuneiform,** meaning wedge-shaped.

Amount	Symbol
1	❚
10	❮

Amounts could be expressed using combinations of these numerals; for example, 23 was written as ❮❮❚❚❚

However, being restricted to only two numerals creates a problem with large amounts. The Babylonians' solution to this problem was to choose the amount 60 as an important number. Unlike the Egyptians and the Romans, they did not create a new numeral for this amount. Rather, they agreed (amongst themselves) that they would have a new *place*. For example, the amount 73 was represented as ❚ ❮❚❚❚. That is, the ❚ at the left represented 60 and the ❮❚❚❚ to the right represented 13. In other words, they "saw" 73 as 60 + 13.

Similarly, ❚❚❚ ❮❚❚ was seen as six 60s plus 12, or 372.
 ❚❚❚

As with the other two systems, use the following questions to better understand their system. Check your answers on page 85.

What is the value of each of the following numbers?

1. ❚❚ ❮❚❚   2. ❚❚❚ ❮❮❮❚❚   3. ❚ ❮❚ ❮❮❚
             ❚❚ ❮

How do you think the Babylonians would represent the following amounts?

4. 1,202   5. 304

Working with the Babylonian system Take a few minutes to think about the following questions. Write your thoughts before reading on. If possible, compare your responses with those of a classmate. . . .

1. What do you notice about the Babylonian system? Do you see any patterns?

2. Do you see similarities between this system and the Egyptian and Roman systems?

3. Do you see any limitations or disadvantages of the Babylonian system?

4. Try to describe the rules for this system, as if you were talking to someone on the phone.

Place value All three systems have vestiges of tallies for the first four numbers: IIII, ❘❘❘❘, ❚❚❚❚. The Romans invented a new numeral for 5. The Egyptians and Babylonians waited until 10 to create a new numeral. To represent larger amounts, the Babylonians invented the idea of the value of a numeral being a function of its place in the number. This is the earliest occurrence of the concept of **place value** in recorded history. With this idea of place value, they could represent any amount using only two numerals.

We can understand the value of their system by examining their numbers with expanded notation. Look at the following Babylonian number:

$$\text{▼▼ ◀◀▼▼▼ ◀◀▼}$$

Since the ◀◀▼ occurs in the first (or rightmost) place, its value is simply the sum of the values of the numerals—that is, $10 + 10 + 1 = 21$. However, the value of the ◀◀▼▼▼ in the second place is determined by multiplying the face value of the numerals by 60—that is, $60 \cdot 23$. The value of the ▼▼ in the third place is determined by multiplying the face value of the numerals by 60^2—that is, $60^2 \cdot 2$.

The value of this amount is:

$$60^2 \cdot 2 + 60 \cdot 23 + 21 = 7{,}200 + 1{,}380 + 21 = 8{,}601$$

Thus, in order to understand the Babylonian system, you have to look at the face value of the numerals *and* the place of the numerals in the number. Therefore, although the Babylonian system still has additive aspects (e.g., $5 = $ ▼▼▼▼▼), the value of a number is no longer determined simply by adding the values of the numerals. One must take into account the place of each numeral in the number.

This later Babylonian system is thus considered by many scholars to be the first place-value system[4] because the value of every symbol depends on its place in the number and there is a symbol to designate when a place is empty. Exercise 10 looks at another very different place-value numeration system that was developed by the Mayas in Central America between 300 and 900 A.D.

The Babylonian system is more sophisticated than the Egyptian and Roman systems.[5] However, there were some "glitches" associated with this invention. Before you read on, imagine that you were a Babylonian. What problems could you see with this new idea of place value?

What if there were nothing in a place? For example, how could the Babylonians represent the amount 3,624? Try this and then read on. . . . 🖎

The need for a zero If we represent this amount from the Babylonian perspective, we note that $60^2 = 3{,}600$. Thus, the Babylonians saw 3,624 as $3{,}600 + 24$. They would use ▼ in the third place to represent 3,600, and they would use ◀◀▼▼▼▼ in the first place to represent 24, but the second place is empty. Thus, if they wrote ▼ ◀◀▼▼▼▼, how was the reader to know that this is not $60 + 24 = 84$? Again, try to imagine yourself as a Babylonian. How might you solve this problem? Think and read on. . . . If possible, compare your ideas with those of a classmate. 🖎

Archaeologists have found evidence that later Babylonian writers experimented with several different notations to represent an empty place. A Babylonian mathematical table from about 300 B.C. contains a new symbol ◥◣ that acts like a zero. Using this convention, they could thus represent 3,624 as

$$\text{▼▼ ◥◣ ◀◀▼▼}$$
$$\text{▼▼}$$

[4] Georges Ifrah, *From One to Zero: A Universal History of Numbers*, p. 373. Translated from the French 1985.

[5] Ifrah, p. xiv.

The slightly sideways wedges indicate that the second place is empty, and thus we can unambiguously interpret this numeral as representing

$$2 \cdot 60^2 + 0 + 24 = 3{,}624$$

In the exercises, you will find that the Mayans also created a numeration system with a zero. As you may have discovered in your work as an Alphabitian in Exploration 2.8, creating a system with a base and with a symbol to act as a place holder is not a simple task. This is why it took humans so long to create such systems.

The Development of Base 10: The Hindu–Arabic System

We have now seen how the Egyptian and Roman systems represented important advances over tallying, allowing people to count and represent large amounts with numerals. We have seen how the Babylonians struggled with the concept of the value of a numeral depending on its place in the number. You are now in a position to better understand and appreciate the structure of the base 10 numeration system we use today—the Hindu-Arabic system.

We can still only guess at early stages of this system because we have no early archaeological evidence, as we have for the Egyptian and Babylonian systems. However, at some point, someone or some group discovered that all numbers could be represented using combinations of just ten symbols. One of these symbols, zero, constituted a tremendous leap in abstraction, because it both represented nothing and also represented an empty place. You have seen how the Babylonians struggled with this dilemma for many hundreds of years.

Archaeologists tell us that the Hindu numeration system emerged around 600 A.D. and that the earliest known zero is found inscribed on the wall of a temple in central India dated at 870 A.D. By 800 A.D., news of this system came to Baghdad, which had been founded in 762 A.D. by followers of Mohammed. Leonardo of Pisa, whom you encountered in Chapter 1, traveled throughout the Mediterranean and the Middle East, where he first heard of the new system. In his book *Liber Abaci* (translated as *Book of Computations*), published in 1202, he argued the merits of this new system, but it took some time for the Hindu-Arabic system to replace the Roman system that almost everyone in Europe used. In fact, a thirteenth-century law forbade bankers of Florence to use these Hindu–Arabic numerals, because it was felt that forgeries were easier in the new system than in the Roman system. However (as you will discover in Chapter 3), one of the biggest advantages of this new system was ease of computation, and it was not long before the merchants realized how much easier computing was in this new system.

Figure 2.19 on page 78 traces the development of the ten numerals that make up our numeration system.[6] Just as the ancient Egyptians used papyrus and the Sumerians used clay tablets, the people in ancient India used dried palm leaves to write with. Some historians believe that the Indians could have joined up these strokes, so that $=$ became z and $\equiv$ became Z.

The development of numeration systems from the most primitive (tally) to the most efficient (base 10) has taken tens of thousands of years. Although the base 10 system is the one you grew up with, it is also the most abstract of the systems and possibly the most difficult (initially) for children. The next section describes the essential mathematical structure of the Hindu-Arabic numeration system. However, rather than just reading this section, stop first and reflect on what you have learned thus far in your own investigations. Imagine describing

---

[6] Karl Menninger, *Number Words and Number Symbols: A Cultural History of Number,* trans. Paul Broneer (Cambridge, Mass., MIT Press, 1969), p. 418.

this system to a Babylonian, Egyptian, or Roman who has suddenly been transported into our time. Imagine that this person can understand English and has a counting table like Table 2.9 but is still struggling to make sense of this system. How would you describe the essential features of this system to that person? Do so before reading on. . . .

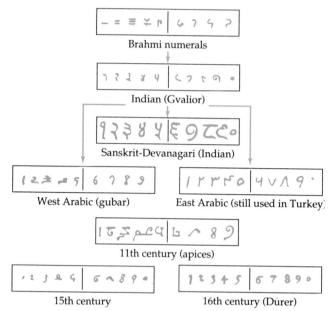

Brahmi numerals

Indian (Gvalior)

Sanskrit-Devanagari (Indian)

West Arabic (gubar)   East Arabic (still used in Turkey)

11th century (apices)

15th century   16th century (Dürer)

Source: Karl Menninger, *Number Words and Number Symbols: A Cultural History of Numbers*, 1969, p. 418. Reprinted by permission of MIT Press.

FIGURE **2.19**

TABLE 2.9

Egyptian	Roman	Babylonian	Hindu-Arabic
I	I	▼	1
II	II	▼▼	2
III	III	▼▼▼	3
IIII	IV	▼▼▼▼	4
IIIII	V	▼▼▼▼▼	5
IIIIII	VI	▼▼▼▼▼▼	6
IIIIIII	VII	▼▼▼▼▼▼▼	7
IIIIIIII	VIII	▼▼▼▼▼▼▼▼	8
IIIIIIIII	IX	▼▼▼▼▼▼▼▼▼	9
∩	X	❮	10
∩∩	XX	❮❮	20
∩∩∩∩∩	L	❮❮❮❮❮	50
∩∩∩∩∩∩	LX	▼	60
⌒	C	▼❮❮❮❮	100

Advantages of Base 10

Our base 10 numeration system has several characteristics that make it so powerful.

No tallies   The base 10 system has no vestiges of tallies. Any amount can be expressed using only 10 digits: 0, 1, 2, 3, 4, 5, 6, 7, 8, and 9. In fact, the word *digit* literally means finger.

Decimal system   The base 10 system is a decimal system, because it is based on groupings (powers) of 10. The value of each successive place to the left is 10 times the value of the previous place:

100,000   10,000   1,000   100   10   1

Ten ones make one ten.

Ten tens make one hundred.

Ten hundreds make one thousand.

Ten thousands make ten thousand.

Expanded form   When we represent a number by decomposing it into the sum of the values from each place, we are using expanded form. There are different variations of expanded form. For example, each of the expressions below emphasizes the structure of the number, 234—some more simply and some using exponents.
We can also use exponents to represent whole numbers.

$$200 + 30 + 4$$
$$= 2 \cdot 100 + 3 \cdot 10 + 4 \cdot 1$$
$$= 2 \cdot 10^2 + 3 \cdot 10^1 + 4 \cdot 10^0$$

Note: $10^1 = 10$ and $10^0 = 1$.

Expanded form is an important tool for two reasons. First, it is one of the many tools that mathematicians use to represent the process of decomposing numbers into smaller amounts to help us better understand the concepts and procedures that we use. Second, in Chapter 3, we will use expanded form to understand why the procedures we use to add, subtract, multiply, and divide actually work.

The concept of zero   The fourth reason that the base 10 system is powerful is the invention of the concept of zero, represented by the symbol 0. "The invention of zero marks one of the most important developments in the whole history of mathematics."[7] This is the feature that moves us beyond the Babylonian system. Recall the Babylonians' attempts to deal with the confusion when a place was empty. It was the genius of some person or persons in ancient India to fully develop this idea, which made for the most efficient system of representing amounts and also made computation much, much easier. One of the most difficult aspects of this system is that the symbol 0 has two related meanings: in one sense, it works just like any other digit (it can be seen as the number 0), and at the same time, it also acts as a place holder. It takes young schoolchildren several years to fully understand and accept this. I recall my five-year-old daughter saying that zero meant "nothing" and insisting that it was not a number!

Do you understand these four aspects of our numeration system? When you were exploring the Alphabitian system in Exploration 2.8, did you struggle with one or more of these concepts? Do you recall having difficulties with any of these yourself in elementary school? Exploration 2.10 is a game that helps people to understand more deeply this idea of place value.

Connecting Geometric and Numerical Representations

Let me now ask a question that will help you to assess your understanding of these concepts and to extend your understanding: What do you think the fifth

---

[7] H.A. Freebury, *A History of Mathematics* (New York: The Macmillan Co., 1958), p. 170.

place in our **base 10 manipulatives** looks like? I ask this question of my students, and many are baffled by the question and need a hint. If you find yourself baffled, read the following.

If you mentally step back and look at this system, you will notice that the first place is represented by a unit, which we will call a "small cube"; the second place is represented by a long; the third place is represented by a flat; and the fourth place is represented by a block (a "big cube"). If you were to draw a picture of the fifth place, what would it look like? Think about this and read on. . . . 🖎

Rather than give a direct answer to the question, we will lead up to it. As we look at each place, we see some amazing patterns. Let us start at the beginning, with units.

- Ten ones make one ten. In a physical sense, ten units become one long.
- Then ten tens become one hundred. In a physical sense, ten longs become one flat.
- Then ten hundreds become one thousand. In a physical sense, ten flats become a "big cube."

Continuing this pattern, we see that ten thousands become one ten-thousand. In a physical sense, we can represent ten thousands as a "big long." There are other representations; for example, we could have represented 10,000 as a pile of ten "big cubes," as shown in Figure 2.20.

1,000   10,000   10,000

FIGURE **2.20**

Both representations show a value of 10,000. Mathematically, we say that the former representation is more powerful because it makes a better connection. One of the reasons it makes a better connection is that it fits a larger pattern that you will soon see.

If we continue the pattern in this way, we can represent ten 10,000s (big longs) as one 100,000, which we can represent visually as a "big flat," as shown in Figure 2.21.

1,000   10,000   100,000

FIGURE **2.21**

Table 2.10 on page 81 shows the name of each place, the amount it represents, and its shape.

Do you see now why the representation of 10,000 as a "big long" is more powerful than the other representations?

Think about the terms, look at the physical shape of each place, and look at the way we write numbers. All three representations are closely connected.

Shape:	Huge cube	Big flat	Big long	Big cube	Flat	Long	Cube	etc.
Name:	One million	Hundred thousand	Ten thousand	One thousand	Hundred	Ten	One	etc.

TABLE 2.10

Million	Hundred thousand	Ten thousand	Thousand	Hundred	Ten	One
1,000,000 huge cube	100,000 big flat	10,000 big long	1,000 big cube	100 flat	10 long	1 small cube

- The name changes every three terms—thousand, million, billion, etc.
- The shape changes every three terms—cube, long, flat.
- We place commas after every three terms, e.g., 345,234,186.

Is this a coincidence, or is this the reason why we separate large numbers by groups of three?

Summary

Almost certainly, base 10 has become the universal counting system today because we have 10 fingers on both hands. We also could have selected base 5—fingers on one hand—or base 20—digits on fingers and toes, not an uncommon choice when we look at historical records. (As you will find out in Chapter 3, computation would be much easier for most people if our species had one more finger on each hand, in which case we would have used base 12.)

We have explored different counting systems to give you an appreciation of the significance of base 10 and its abstractness—it took humans many thousands of years to finally invent such a powerful numeration system. In the course of the *Explorations*, you have come to appreciate the importance of mathematical vocabulary, including the terms *digit* and *place* (ones place, tens place, etc.). You have realized that with the concepts of base and place value, and a symbol to represent "nothing," we can represent any amount using only a few digits (in base 10, we use 0, 1, 2, 3, 4, 5, 6, 7, 8, and 9). You have been introduced, through expanded form, to the tool of decomposing a number into its constituent parts. This notion of breaking an object or idea into its component parts is an essential tool in all scientific disciplines.

In this section, you have probably gained a deeper appreciation of both the power and the abstractness of our base 10 numeration system. To use an old phrase, I wish I had a dollar for every student who has said something like, "Wow, no wonder it's hard for little kids to learn how to count; I never thought of it [our system] that way before." In Chapter 3, we will first examine the meanings of the four basic operations of addition, subtraction, multiplication, and division. In that chapter, you will come to better understand the value of expanded form. Then we will learn how the algorithms, which most adults take for granted, really work. By the end of Chapter 3, your appreciation of the Hindu-Arabic system should be even greater!

EXERCISES 2.3

1. **a.** Fill in the blanks in these counting systems.

   b. What patterns do you see in these systems?

   c. Describe the "rules" of this system as if you were talking on the phone to a friend who missed the class when this system was discussed.

Base 10	Maya	Luli of Paraguay	South American
1	hun	alapea	tey
2	ca	tamop	cayupa
3	ox	tamlip	toazumba
4	can	lokep	cajesa
5	ho	lokep moile alapea (four and one) or is alapea (one hand)	teente
6	uac	lokep moile tamep	teyentetey
7	uuc	?	teyente-cayapa
8	uaxac	lokep moile lokep	?
9	bolon	lokep moile lokep alapea	teyente-cajesa
10	lahun	is yaoum (both hands)	caya-ente
11	buluc	is yaoum moile alapea (hands and one)	caya-ente-tey
12	lah-ca	is yaoum moile tamep	?
13	ox-lahun	?	?
15	ho-lahun	?	toazumba-ente
16	?	?	?
20	hunkal	is eln yaoum (hands, feet)	?
21	?	?	?
22	?	?	?

2. Find the base 10 equivalent of each of these numerals.

   a. 𒈦𒈦𒈦∩∩∩| **b.** 𓏲𓏲𓏲////∩||

   c. MDCLXVI   **d.** MDXIX

   e. CIX   **f.** ⟨⟨❮ ❮❮ ❮❮

   g. ❮❮ ⟨❮❮❮   **h.** ⟨⟨⟨❮❮❮

3. Represent the base 10 amounts in Egyptian, Roman, and Babylonian symbols.

   a. 312   **b.** 1,206   **c.** 6,000

   d. 10,000   **e.** 123,456

4. An amusing exercise is to convert English words to Roman values. For example, the English word LID would be worth 50 + 1 + 500 = 551.

   a. What is the value of MIX?

   b. What is the most valuable English word made up only of letters in the Roman numeration system?

   c. What is the most valuable English word that you can find, if we allow any English word, but determine its value by adding only those letters that have values in the Roman system?

5. Represent the following base 10 numbers by sketching the base 10 manipulatives.

   a. 345   **b.** 2,001

6. Represent the following base 10 numbers in expanded form.

   a. 345   **b.** 2,001   **c.** 10,101

7. Rewrite each of the following in standard form.

   a. $4 \cdot 10^3 + 8 \cdot 10^2 + 5 \cdot 10 + 9$

   b. $3 \cdot 10^4 + 2 \cdot 10^2 + 4 \cdot 10$

   c. $7 \cdot 10^5 + 5 \cdot 10^4 + 3$

8. The symbols developed by the ancient Greeks are visually quite fascinating and remind me of the children's game called hangman. The basic symbols for amounts up to 10,000 are given below.

1	5	10	50	100	500	1,000	5,000	10,000
I	Γ	Δ	⌐	H	⌐	X	⌐	M

   Translate the following Greek numbers to base 10:

   a. ⌐ΔΔΓII   **b.** H ⌐ΔΔΓI

   Translate the following base 10 numbers to Greek:

   c. 347   **d.** 5,555

9. An ancient Chinese mathematician named Sun-Tsu who lived in the first century A.D. described the use of calculating rods (made of bamboo) for representing numbers. The digits for 1 to 9 are represented as follows:

   However, when the digits from 1 to 9 appear in the tens column, they are represented as follows:

1	2	3	4	5	6	7	8	9
—	=	≡	≣	≣	⊥	⊥	⊥	⊥

   Thereafter, every time you move over one place, you change from one form to the other.

   Thus, the number 4,763 would be represented as: ≣ ⊤ ⊥ III and the amount 8,888 would be represented as: ⊤ ⊥ ⊤ ⊥

   Translate the following numbers into base 10:

   a. III — IIII ⊥   **b.** ⊤ ≡ ⊤

   Represent the following numbers in the Chinese system:

   c. 346   **d.** 12,345

10. One of the most impressive of the ancient numeration systems comes from the Mayans of Central America. Their numeration system was developed around 400 or 300 B.C. They used only three symbols: dot, line, and oval. The oval functions in a manner very similar to our zero. They also wrote their numbers vertically.

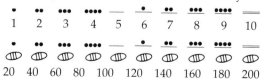

Many mathematics historians credit the Mayans with being the first civilization to develop a numeration system with a fully functioning zero. At first, the Mayan system seems to be a base 20 system. If this were the case, however, the values of their places would be 1, 20, 20^2, 20^3, 20^4, etc. Instead, however, the value of their places is 1, 20, 360, 360 × 20, 360 × 20^2, 360 × 20^3, etc. We are fairly certain that their choice of this system has to do with the fact that at the time of its creation, they thought that the length of a year was 360 days. Below are three base 10 numbers and how they would be written in the Mayan system.

$46 =$ $300 =$ $407 =$
$(2 × 20)$ $(15 × 20)$ $(1 × 360)$
$+ 6$ $+ 0$ $+ (2 × 20)$
                     $+ 7$

Translate the following Mayan numbers to base 10:

a.   b.   c.

Write the following base 10 numbers in Mayan:

d. 245   **e.** 500   **f.** 3600

In Exercises 11 through 22, recall your examination of different bases in the *Explorations*.

11. What comes after:

a. 34_5 b. 1011_2 c. 99_{12} d. $9E_{12}$
e. 101_2 f. 111_{12} g. 124_5 h. 405_6

12. What comes before:

a. 1010_5 b. 340_5 c. 100_{12} d. $TE0_{12}$
e. 1010_2 f. 110_{12} g. 120_4 h. 60_7

13. Convert the following numbers to base 10.

a. 41_5 b. 55_6 c. 210_5 d. 2104_5
e. 101_5 f. 1111_6 g. 303_4 h. 606_7
i. 1101_2 j. 10001_2 k. 99_{12} l. $90E_{12}$

14. Convert the following numbers from base 10 to the designated base.

a. $44_{10} = ?_5$ b. $152_{10} = ?_5$ c. $92_{10} = ?_2$
d. $206_{10} = ?_2$ e. $72_{10} = ?_{12}$ f. $402_{10} = ?_{12}$
g. $44_{10} = ?_6$ h. $1252_{10} = ?_6$ i. $144_{10} = ?_{12}$
j. $100_{10} = ?_5$ k. $99_{10} = ?_{12}$ l. $1052_{10} = ?_5$
m. $2,500,000_{10} = ?_5$ n. $2,500,000_{10} = ?_2$

15. In what base does 25 + 25 = 51?

16. What base makes the following statement true: $23_{10} = 25_x$

17. What value of x in the tens place makes the following statement true: $5x2_{10} = 734_{10}$

18. If $44_x = 28_{10}$, how many base x candy bars will fit into a box holding 110_5 candy bars?

19. Convert 222_3 into base 6 directly, as though you had never heard of base 10. A diagram is helpful but not required. In order to receive credit, there must be a writ-

ten explanation of how you converted from the given base 3 number to the base 6 number.

20. Convert $204_6 = ?_3$ directly, without going through base 10.

21. Explain the following conversion problems as if you were talking to a struggling student.

a. $234_{10} = ?_5$ b. $405_8 = ?_{10}$

22. One common mistake that young children make when counting is illustrated below: twenty-six, twenty-seven, twenty-eight, twenty-nine, twenty-ten, twenty-eleven, etc.

Can you describe the nature of the child's mistake? That is, what is the child not understanding or what misconception of counting causes the mistake? Do you see this mistake differently now than you would have before this course? If so, please explain.

23. Another common mistake that young children make when counting is illustrated below: twenty-six, twenty-seven, twenty-eight, twenty-nine, thirty-one, thirty-two, etc.

Can you describe the nature of the child's mistake? That is, what is the child not understanding or what misconception of counting causes the mistake? Do you see this mistake differently now than you would have before this course? If so, please explain.

24. We speak of so many children having little or no understanding of place value. What does "place value" mean to you? Define the concept in your own words. This involves giving some meaningful explanation of what "place value" means mathematically.

25. We have discussed the development of more sophisticated numeration systems in class, culminating in the Hindu-Arabic base 10 system that we currently use. Describe the advantages of the Hindu-Arabic system over the Roman system.

26. In addition to a better understanding of place value, what else have you learned about base 10 by working in other bases in the *Explorations*?

27. This book was published in 1997, which is in the twentieth century, not the nineteenth century. Can you explain why?

28. When we write large numbers, why do we put a comma between every three numbers instead of between every two or four numbers?

29. You are Zirkle, from Zordon, and you have just finished your trip to the solar system. Your planet has managed to develop interplanetary travel without ever developing a sophisticated number system. You have examined three different bases (base 2, base 5, and base 6), and you are preparing your recommendations for your home planet. Summarize the pros and cons of each base, and then tell which base you recommend your planet adopt. *Note:* Your species has no fingers, only paws. Therefore, none of the bases has an advantage with respect to your anatomy.

a. Summarize the pros and cons of each base in a table like the one below. *Note:* Entries in the cells need to demonstrate that you understand the advantage or disadvantage/limitation. That is, an entry should state *what* the advantage or disadvantage is and also give a brief *explanation* of the advantage or disadvantage.

Base	+	−
2		
5		
6		

b. Write your final recommendation: an essay of at least one paragraph, that is, more than two sentences. You may refer to your chart, so that you don't have to be redundant.

30. Balance scales usually come with a variety of weights. The balance scale below works in the following manner:

You put the object you want to weigh in one pan, and you place weights in the other pan until the arrow points straight down.

Let's say that the scale below comes with the following weights: 1 gram, 2 grams, 2 grams, 5 grams, 10 grams, 10 grams, 20 grams, 50 grams.

Thus, using only these eight weights, the heaviest object we can weigh is 100 grams. Suppose you could choose whatever weights you wanted. If you were restricted to only eight weights, is there a different combination that would enable you to weigh objects heavier than 100 grams, but still weigh any object to the nearest gram?

CHAPTER SUMMARY

1. Many mathematical concepts and problems involve various kinds of sets and subsets of those sets.

2. When two sets or variables are said to be functionally related, this tells us that the relationship between those two sets or variables is such that knowing an element of one set (or the value of the independent variable) enables us to make predictions.

3. Our current (Hindu-Arabic) numeration system evolved over thousands of years, and people from many cultures developed ideas that contributed to our system.

4. Our numeration system has four characteristics:

   a. Any amount can be expressed using only the basic 10 digits.

   b. It is based on groupings (powers) of 10.

   c. The value of any digit depends on its place.

   d. Zero can represent both a value and an empty place.

Basic Concepts

Section 2.1 Sets
set *40*
subset *44*
Venn diagrams *48*
binary operations *51*
member, element *42*
proper subset *45*
universal set, or the universe *48*

Ways to describe sets
words, list *42*
set-builder notation *43*

Important mathematical sets
natural numbers (*N*) *42*
whole numbers (*W*) *42*
integers (*I*) *42*
rational numbers (*Q*) *43*

Kinds of sets
finite and infinite sets *44*
well-defined set *44*
empty set, null set *47*

Relationships between sets
equal *47*
equivalent *47*
one-to-one correspondence *47*

Operations on sets
intersection *49*   union *49*
complement *49*

Section 2.2 Functions
figure numbers *56*   function *58*
domain, range *58*   mathematical model
independent variable,   *60*
  dependent variable *59*   function notation *61*
input, output *61*

Ways to represent functions:
table *59*   graph *59*
ordered pairs *59*   equation *59*
mapping *59*

Section 2.3 Numeration
Origins of numbers and counting *69*

Answers to questions in text:

Paying the baby-sitter: graph, p. 60

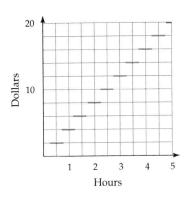

Patterns in counting: missing words in Table 2.6, p. 72

Number	Greenland Eskimos	Aztec	Luo of Kenya
8	achfineq-pinasut		ab-adek
9			ab-angwen
12	achqaneq-machdlug	matlacti-on-ome	
13	achqaneq-pinasut	matlacti-on-yey	apar-adek
15			apar-abich
16	achfechsaneq-atauseq	caxtulli-on-ce	apar-ab-chiel

The Egyptian numeration system: symbols, p. 72

1. 1,323　　**2.** 143,022　　**3.** 𓏲𓎉𓎉𓏼𓏼　　**4.** 𓎉𓎉𓎉𓏼𓏼𓏼𓏼

The Roman numeration system: symbols, p. 74

1. 1,011　　**2.** 1,597　　**3.** MCCII　　**4.** CCCXIX

Working with the system

The later Roman symbol for 444 was CDXLIV

The Babylonian numeration system: places, p. 75

1. 120 + 12 = 132
2. 5 × 60 + 42 = 342
3. 1 × 60² + 11 × 60 + 21 = 3,600 + 660 + 21 = 4,281
4. 1,202 would be seen as 20 × 60 + 2 = ❮❮ ❚❚
5. 304 would be seen as five 60s plus 4 or ❚❚❚ ❚❚❚ ❚❚ ❚

3

The Four Fundamental Operations of Arithmetic

In this chapter, we will examine what are called the four fundamental operations of arithmetic: addition, subtraction, multiplication, and division. Understanding these four operations "is central to knowing mathematics" (*Curriculum Standards*, p. 41). This is a critical chapter because so many seemingly different problem situations can be represented by a single operation. Also, in many real-life situations, a problem may require multiple operations, and it is not always obvious which operation is needed. For example, if a hospital has 35 ounces of medicine and each dose requires 2/3 of an ounce, how many doses does the hospital have? In this case, do we multiply or divide? Do you know why? In the course of the text and the explorations, we will "develop meaning for the operations by modeling and discussing a rich variety of problem situations" (*Curriculum Standards*, p. 41) so that you can understand at a deep level how these four operations are related to one another.

In the first two sections, we will explore addition, subtraction, multiplication, and division. You will come to understand that each operation has multiple meanings, that there are several different ways to represent these operations, and that this has implications for problem-solving. Our exploration of patterns and properties not only will give you important tools for solving problems, but will also enable you to better understand the procedures, called algorithms, that we use in computation and will make you a more powerful problem solver. The third section will focus on developing a repertoire of strategies for

HISTORY

I cannot overemphasize how recent most of our everyday mathematics actually is. During the Middle Ages, many authors considered an operation to be any mathematical technique or procedure that the author considered important. In fact, especially when the Hindu-Arabic numeration system was still new in Europe, many authors considered numeration to be an operation. It has only been in the last century that mathematicians have linked the concept of operation to the concept of function.[1]

estimating, because much (if not most) of the computation done in daily life involves estimation rather than determining exact answers. In the course of investigating these concepts in the text and the *Explorations* volume, your "operation sense" and "number sense" will become stronger. These are two crucial components to being able to use these four operations skillfully.

A Nonroutine, Multistep Problem

Before examining each of the operations separately, let us explore a real-life problem that requires several of the operations — that is, a nonroutine, multistep problem. As mentioned earlier, much research indicates that many of our students can do routine problems (that is, problems "just like" the ones the teacher did or the ones shown in the book) and single-step problems; however, most of our students perform poorly when the problems are not routine and when they require several steps and/or computations. However, *this* is what most problems outside the classroom are like! In order to become successful at these kinds of problems, one must have a deeper understanding of fundamental mathematical concepts and procedures. As you do the problem, do you feel confident about which operation to use? Do you see more than one way to arrive at the answer?

It is the beginning of the month, and Annie wants to buy a bicycle for $300. She has $173 in the bank, and she just got a birthday check for $40 from her grandparents. Her source of income is baby-sitting, for which she charges $4 an hour. How many hours of baby-sitting will she need to do if she wants to be able to buy the bicycle at the end of the month? She also figures that she will spend about $25 this month on recreation.

In order to do this problem, most people perform several mathematical operations, and not everyone does it the same way. Some students add Annie's resources ($173 + 40 = 213$), subtract her expenses ($213 - 25 = 188$), and then see how much she needs (that is, how far 188 is from 300). Other students note that $40 - 25$ is a net difference of 15, add this to 173 to get 188, and now find the difference between 188 and 300. Still other students determine how much money she needs by adding or subtracting the numbers in the order in which they occur: $300 - 173 - 40 + 25 = 112$.

Now we need to divide $112 by $4 per hour, and we find that she will achieve her goal if she baby-sits 28 hours this month.

What does this problem have to do with operations on whole numbers? In one sense, it serves as what is called an advance organizer for this chapter. Most real-life problems involve more than one operation (they are not what the NCTM calls routine one-step problems). In this problem, there are many different ways to arrive at the solution, not just one "right" way. In order to solve the problem, you first have to make sense of it in order to determine what operations to do and in what order.

SECTION 3.1 ## UNDERSTANDING ADDITION AND SUBTRACTION

If you did Explorations 3.1 through 3.3, you probably found that trying to add and subtract in Alphabitia threw you back into the kind of confusion that young children often encounter when they try to make sense of adding and subtracting in base 10. Now that you have a deeper understanding of numera-

[1] Frank J. Swetz, *Capitalism and Arithmetic: The New Math of the 15th Century* (La Salle, Ill.: Open Court, 1987), p. 181.

tion, we will develop a deeper understanding of addition and subtraction. The understanding of numeration and these operations will enable you to understand why the various computation procedures actually work. Without this understanding, your "mathematical power" is significantly lessened.

Addition

Children encounter addition even before they have mastered counting. They naturally combine objects and want to know how many. For example, there are 4 people in our family, and 2 guests have come for dinner. How many people will be eating?

Examine the following addition problems and then write your responses to the following questions in your own words. Pretend that you are a young child who has not yet learned addition.

■ How might you solve these problems?

■ In what ways are the problems different? In what ways are they similar?

■ What does addition mean?

Four addition problems

1. Andy has 3 marbles, and his older sister Bella gives him 5 more. How many does he have now?

2. Betty and Joe each drank 6 ounces of orange juice. How much juice did they drink in all?

3. Sally has 4 feet of yellow ribbon and 3 feet of red ribbon. How many feet of ribbon does she have?

4. Josh has 4 red trucks and 2 blue trucks. How many trucks does he have altogether?

There are several classical stages in children's understanding of addition. At the most basic level, the child counts the sum. For example, in the first problem, many young children would answer the question by putting the marbles on the floor and then counting the two groups. The traditional definition of addition is in set language, and children intuitively begin with this model (see Figure 3.1).

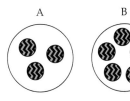

FIGURE **3.1**

Let A = the set of Andy's marbles and B = the set of Bella's marbles.

Then $n(A) = a$, the number of marbles Andy has, and $n(B) = b$, the number of marbles Bella has.

We then define **addition** in the following way:

> If A and B are disjoint sets, containing a and b elements, respectively, then $a + b = n(A \cup B)$.

In other words, the **sum** of a and b is equal to the number of elements in the union of the two sets. Do you see why the sets have to be disjoint?

The numbers a and b are called **addends.**

In the next stage of development, the child "counts on." That is, the child begins with the first number and counts however many more the second number represents. A child solving Problem 1 in this manner would say, "4, 5, 6, 7, 8," probably keeping track of the second addend (5) with fingers. At the next level, the child realizes that it is possible to begin with the larger number (3 + 5 = 5 + 3) and counts, "6, 7, 8." Finally, the child simply knows that 3 + 5 = 8.

Contexts for Addition

Problems 1 and 4 are easier for most children, because the child can see the actual marbles and trucks, and count 1, 2, 3, 4, 5, 6, 7, 8 marbles. Problems 2 and 3 are more abstract in that the child cannot actually see 6 ounces or 4 feet. The child might represent the problem with concrete objects, such as 4 buttons for the yellow ribbon and 3 buttons for the red ribbon. These problems represent two basic contexts in which we operate on numbers. Some numbers represent discrete amounts, and some numbers represent measured (continuous) amounts.

A Pictorial Model for Addition

One of the themes of this book is the power of "multiple representations," that there is generally more than one way in which we can represent most mathematical concepts and problems. If we draw diagrams to represent the four addition problems, they seem on the surface to be quite different, except for the marbles and trucks problems (see Figure 3.2).

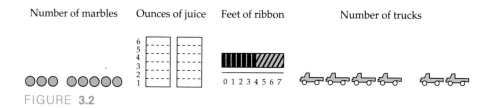

FIGURE **3.2**

In each of these cases, however, we are joining two sets or we are increasing a set. We can highlight the similarities among the problems with the representations in Figure 3.3.

FIGURE **3.3**

In general, we can represent any addition problem $a + b = c$ as shown in Figure 3.4.

FIGURE **3.4**

Do you see any advantages of this general model over having no model at all? If you do, what advantages do you see? Think and then read on. . . .

1. This model captures the way in which *all* addition problems are similar — that is, joining and combining two amounts to make a larger amount.

2. This model also relates to the notion of parts and wholes, an abstraction that is important in the development of whole-number ideas and also in understanding other mathematical ideas, like fractions.

3. This model also works well whether the elements to be combined are discrete objects or measurements.

4. Perhaps the most important advantage of the pictorial model is that we can define all four operations in this context, as we shall soon see. This reveals the essential connectedness of the four operations. When students see this connectedness and the connection between numbers and place value, they are likely to be more successful with nonroutine and multistep problems.

Did your list include these advantages? The same ideas in different words? Other advantages?

One researcher who has worked extensively with young children and looked at how children come to make sense of numbers and operations on numbers tells us that "(p)robably the major conceptual achievement of the early school years is the interpretation of numbers in terms of part and whole relationships."[2] It is important to note that understanding part-whole relationships with whole numbers allows numbers to be interpreted simultaneously as positions on the mental number line and as compositions of other numbers. For example, 18 is the number after 17 and before 19, but 18 can also be seen as $10 + 8, 9 + 9, 20 - 2$, and so on. Understanding that a number can be composed (put together) and decomposed (broken into parts) is essential for being able to work confidently with the four operations. This notion of composing and decomposing is one of the big ideas of elementary mathematics, and we will come back to it repeatedly throughout the text.

Number Lines: An Addition Model

The number line plays an important role throughout arithmetic, but research shows that American schoolchildren tend to have a hard time understanding and using this model. Therefore, we will take a little time to further investigate the number line as a tool for representing (and solving) addition problems. We will come back to the number line when we examine the other operations. Before you read on, try to think of physical examples of number lines in everyday life.

Number lines are found on rulers, clocks, graphs, and thermometers. A number line can be constructed by taking a line (not necessarily a straight line) and marking off two points: zero (the origin) and one. The distance from 0 to the point 1 is called the unit segment, and the distance between all consecutive whole numbers is the same. Although number lines are most commonly used to represent length, they may be used to model all kinds of problems. For example, we could use a number line to indicate time, with each unit representing one unit of time — day, minute, year, etc.

How could we have represented the ribbon problem with a number line? Write down your thoughts before reading on. . . .

In the diagram at the left in Figure 3.5 on page 92, we first draw an arrow (in this case representing the length of the ribbon) 4 units long. We draw

[2] Lauren Resnick, "A Developmental Theory of Number Understanding," in *The Development of Mathematical Thinking,* ed. Herbert Ginsburg (New York: Academic Press, 1983), p. 114.

another arrow 3 units long and connect the two arrows. The arrow at the top represents the combined length of the two shorter arrows.

In the diagram at the right, we start at the point on the line representing the length of the first ribbon and then draw an arrow 3 units long (representing the second ribbon). The location where the arrow ends tells us the combined length of the two ribbons.

Both diagrams represent 4 + 3 on the number line, although the one on the left more closely resembles the actual laying of the two ribbons end to end.

FIGURE **3.5**

Properties of Addition

Another aspect of mathematical power comes from understanding the properties of the various operations. As usual, this is best grasped by some exploration rather than presentation. Look at Table 3.1, the addition table for base 10.

Sometimes students in this course forget how new addition is to young children. Recall how strange the Alphabitian system was to you. Think back to your work with Alphabitia: What observations made adding more comfortable for you? Can you think of analogous observations that might make the learning of base 10 addition facts easier for young children?

When young children start to learn about adding, Table 3.1 has been the traditional method of representing the 100 "addition facts" that they have to

TABLE 3.1

	0	1	2	3	4	5	6	7	8	9
0	0	1	2	3	4	5	6	7	8	9
1	1	2	3	4	5	6	7	8	9	10
2	2	3	4	5	6	7	8	9	10	11
3	3	4	5	6	7	8	9	10	11	12
4	4	5	6	7	8	9	10	11	12	13
5	5	6	7	8	9	10	11	12	13	14
6	6	7	8	9	10	11	12	13	14	15
7	7	8	9	10	11	12	13	14	15	16
8	8	9	10	11	12	13	14	15	16	17
9	9	10	11	12	13	14	15	16	17	18

learn. It can look imposing to some children! However, understanding some properties of addition and base 10 can unlock its potential as a learning tool. Take a few moments to think about what addition means and to look at the addition table. What do you observe (insights or patterns) that might make learning the addition facts easier for children? Think before reading on. . . .

One observation (in children's language) is that "adding zero doesn't change your answer." Mathematicians call this the identity property of addition. It is represented symbolically as

$$a + 0 = 0 + a = a$$

Children discover that when you add 1 to any number, you get the next number from counting. In other words, they connect addition and counting. Did you make this connection when doing the Alphabitian explorations?

We also find that when we add any two numbers, we get the same sum regardless of the order in which we added; that is,

$$a + b = b + a$$

This property is known as the commutative property of addition and is one that all children come to recognize. I have been fortunate enough to be with a few children when they made this discovery. They were as excited as Edison probably was when he finally invented the light bulb. Their faces just shone when they shared with me the discovery that you get the same number either way!

This discovery occurs in different ways. Some students, more naturally curious than others, simply wonder whether the order matters; they discover that it doesn't. For other students, the discovery is of a visual nature. That is, if we draw a diagonal line from the top left corner to the bottom right corner of Table 3.1 and then fold the table in half along that line, we find that the two halves of the table are identical. Mathematically, we speak of the symmetric nature of the addition table.

There is another discovery that makes learning addition easier, called "bridging with 10." For example, if you ask a child, "what is 7 + 5?" and then ask how the child got the answer, many children will say something like, "7 + 3 is 10 and 2 more is 12." What happens is that students quickly learn the combinations that make a long (that is, 10) when using base 10 manipulatives. Many will intuitively decompose 7 + 5 into 7 + 3 + 2.

This leads to a third property, called the associative property of addition. For example, 7 + (3 + 2) = (7 + 3) + 2. Formally, we say

$$(a + b) + c = a + (b + c)$$

There is one last property of addition that often seems almost trivially obvious, called the closure property of addition. Stated in everyday language, the closure property means that the sum of any two whole numbers is a unique whole number. There are two parts to this property: (1) uniqueness (the sum will always be the same number) and (2) existence (the sum will always be a whole number).

For most college students, this property evokes one of two reactions: either "so what" or "here we go again, making something obvious look complicated." Let me turn the tables on you. How might this property relate to a question a child might actually ask? Think and read on. . . .

Children will literally ask closure questions: "Will *any* two numbers make a whole number?"

From a more formal perspective, not all sets are closed under addition. For example, consider the set of odd whole numbers {1, 3, 5, . . .}. The sum of two odd numbers is not in the set of odd numbers; thus, we say that the set of odd numbers is not closed under addition. What about the set of even numbers? In higher mathematics, there are many different kinds of sets, and it is often important to know whether the set is closed under the various operations.

INVESTIGATION **3.1**   A Pattern in the Addition Table

As you will come to appreciate by the end of this course, patterns can help make the learning of mathematics easier and more interesting. Exploration 3.2 revealed patterns in the Alphabitian addition table. Let us investigate one of many patterns in adding in base 10. In the addition table, if you look at any 2 × 2 matrix (that is, a rectangular array of numbers or other symbols), the sum of the numbers in each diagonal is equal. For example, in the matrix below, 6 + 8 = 7 + 7. Can you justify this pattern mathematically? Work on it and then read on. . . .

6	7
7	8

DISCUSSION

Description 1

At a verbal level, one could justify this pattern by saying that in any 2 × 2 matrix in the table, the two numbers in one diagonal are always identical and the other two numbers are always one less and one more than this number. Therefore, the sum of the two other numbers will "cancel out," so that you get the "same" sum in either case. If you had a hard time following the previous two sentences, you are not alone, although I have heard second graders explain this pattern in language as elaborate as that above.

Description 2

We can use some notation to make the description less ambiguous. Noting that the value of each number increases by 1 each time that we move across (or down) the table, we can let x represent the number in the top left corner of the diagonal. Thus, in relation to x, the values of the other three numbers are

x	$x + 1$
$x + 1$	$x + 2$

It is now a simple algebraic exercise to demonstrate that the sum of each diagonal is $2x + 2$.

Description 3

Yet other students will say that the sums of the diagonals are equal because "it's the same numbers in both cases." What do you think such a student might be seeing? Think before reading on. . . .

Let's say that we are looking at the matrix formed by the intersection of the 2 row and 3 row and the 4 column and the 5 column. The numbers are 6, 7 and 7, 8. However, if we represent the numbers by their origin, we have

2 + 4	3 + 4
2 + 5	3 + 5

The sum of the top-left-to-bottom-right diagonal is $(2 + 4) + (3 + 5)$. However, because of the commutative and associative properties, this sum is equal to $(2 + 5) + (3 + 4)$. In other words, we are indeed using the same numbers!

We can now generalize this cell by saying that the matrix formed by the intersection of the a row and the b row and the c column and the d column is

$a + c$	$b + c$
$a + d$	$b + d$

and

$$a + c + b + d = a + d + b + c$$

 MATHEMATICS

We have defined addition in the context of whole numbers. In later chapters, we will examine how to extend/modify this definition so that it will fit other numbers, for example,

$$\frac{3}{4} + \frac{2}{5} \qquad {}^-4 + {}^-5$$

$$4.342 + 5.6 \qquad x + 22 = 37$$

Can you see that the simplistic notion of addition as joining and combining doesn't fit all of these situations? As we examine extensions of the number line, we will examine how our definition of addition (and other operations) must be refined.

Let us now examine how addition with larger numbers is performed.

Algorithms

If our only goal was to master computation, we could simply do it by rote with lots of practice. However, if our goal is to be able to solve problems, then we need to understand how addition procedures work. While it is true that calculators (and computers) can do the tedious computations for us, the calculator cannot do the thinking. Remember Investigation 1.8 about dividing the wire into segments and having to find how much wire was wasted? The computation was relatively easy, but interpreting the computation was difficult for many students. In this section, we will examine the meaning of the procedures for adding and subtracting that you have learned. It is critical that, as future teachers, you know not simply how to compute but why these established procedures work. The word algorithm simply means a standardized procedure, that is, one that can be described in step-by-step terms.

HISTORY

An Arabic scholar named Al-Khowarizmi wrote many books on mathematics and astronomy. In 825 A.D., he published a book that explained the use of the Hindu numerals, including the standard procedures for the fundamental operations such as multiplying and dividing. The Latin translation of his name is *Algorismus*. This is where our word *algorithm* comes from. He also wrote another book, the short title of which is *Al Jabr*, which is translated as "the science of reduction and cancellations." This is the origin of our word *algebra*.

The NCTM Curriculum Standards emphasize the importance of connecting what we call "procedural understanding" to "conceptual understanding." In less formal language, they are saying that teachers and students must not only know how to do the procedures but also understand their structure, that is, why they work. Specifically, "It is important to tie these conceptual ideas to more abstract procedures . . . [so that] children will not perceive of mathematics as an arbitrary set of rules; [they] will not need to learn or memorize as many procedures; and [they] will have the foundation to apply, re-create, and invent new ones when needed" (*Curriculum Standards*, p. 32).

With these thoughts in mind, let us investigate the problem of adding larger numbers efficiently. At the end of the discussion, you will understand why different addition algorithms work.

Adding Without Base 10

Imagine that you were a Roman. How might you add these two numbers? As you found in Section 2.3, Romans couldn't just add the VII to the VI and "carry" the III.

$$\begin{array}{r} XXXVII \\ + \quad XLVI \\ \hline \end{array}$$

We are not certain how the Romans actually added. There is evidence that the Babylonians did calculations in the sand with pebbles and inscribed the results on clay tablets. In fact, our word *calculate* comes from *calculus,* meaning "small stone." This pebble method is very possibly a precursor of the abacus, which has been used extensively in the Orient. The term *carrying* may have also come from carrying the pebbles from one column to the next. We do know that computation was rather cumbersome and that few people in those days could do what we call basic arithmetic. They were accorded high status in the society because of their knowledge!

LEARNING

The National Assessment of Education Progress (NAEP) has found that third graders' success in computation decreases considerably when they move from two-digit problems to three-digit problems. Further research indicates that many students are memorizing rather than understanding the process.

Investigating Addition Algorithms in Base 10

Let us look at one of the more difficult of the three-digit addition problems, one in which we encounter zeros. Many of my students find that, even though procedurally we treat zero "just like any other number," they feel just a bit uncomfortable when they run into zeros. Therefore, an analysis of such a problem is often helpful.

Add 267 + 133 as you normally would. Can you explain the "whys" of each step? Try to do so before reading on. You may or may not wish to use base 10 blocks.

In the context of our base 10 numeration system, we are combining 2 hundreds, 6 tens, and 7 ones with 1 hundred, 3 tens, and 3 ones. If the student understands the process of combining and regrouping, then this problem is *not* substantially more difficult than one with smaller numbers, only longer.

Using Manipulatives	**Using Words**

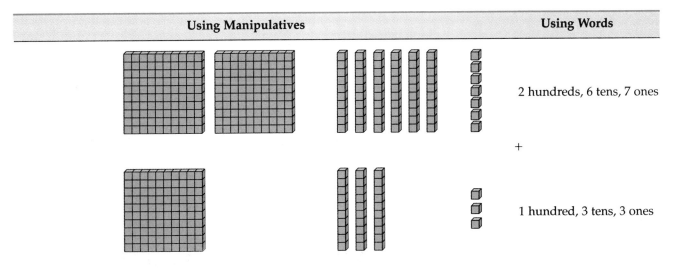

2 hundreds, 6 tens, 7 ones

+

1 hundred, 3 tens, 3 ones

Recalling what addition means, when we literally combine the two sets, we have 3 hundreds, 9 tens, and 10 ones.

3 hundreds, 9 tens, 10 ones

However, this is not a valid answer. Thus, we have to regroup. After we "trade" the 10 ones for 1 ten, we now have 3 hundreds, 10 tens, and 0 ones.

3 hundreds, 10 tens, 0 ones

Since we now have 10 tens (once again not a valid representation in base 10), we trade them for another hundred, giving us 4 hundreds, no tens, and no ones, that is, 400.

4 hundreds, 0 tens, 0 ones

A commonly used algorithm Now look at one common algorithm for addition (the one you probably learned in grade school). Using this algorithm, we go from right to left (that is, we begin with the ones place).

7 + 3 = 10; place the 0 in the ones place and put the 1 above the tens place.

$$\begin{array}{r} {}^{1} \\ 267 \\ \underline{133} \\ 0 \end{array}$$

$1 + 6 + 3 = 10$; place the 0 in the tens place and put the 1 above the hundreds place.

```
 1 1
267
133
─────
  00
```

$1 + 2 + 1 = 4$; place the 4 in the hundreds place. The sum is 400.

```
 1 1
267
133
─────
 400
```

Can you explain the *whys* behind the *hows* of this algorithm? That is, in the language of the NCTM Standards, how can you justify this procedure? Think about this before reading on. . . .

There are two levels of justification of this algorithm. First, let us focus on justifying the actual procedure. Then, at a more formal level, we will examine the properties that underlie the procedure.

Focusing on the procedure, when we add 7 ones and 3 ones, we have 10 ones, but in our numeration system, we can have at most 9 (of any unit) in a place. Therefore, we must regroup; in this case, 10 ones become 1 ten and 0 ones. Therefore, we place the numeral 0 in the ones place and the numeral 1 in the tens place. Looking at the tens place, we find that we now have 1 ten plus 6 tens plus 3 tens, making 10 tens. As before, this is not allowed in our numeration system, and so we regroup the 10 tens as 1 hundred and 0 tens. As before, we place the numeral 0 in the tens place and the numeral 1 in the hundreds place. Looking at the hundreds place, we find that we have 1 hundred plus 2 hundreds plus 1 hundred, giving us 4 hundreds. Reading our sum, we have 4 hundreds, 0 tens, and 0 ones, that is, 400. Do you see the relationship between this justification and what we did physically with the base 10 blocks?

We can also examine this procedure from a more formal perspective. Representing the problem in expanded form enables us to understand why it works. Knowing that addition can be seen as combining, we can represent our problem in the following way.

Statement	Justification
$267 + 133$	
$= (2 \cdot 100 + 6 \cdot 10 + 7) + (1 \cdot 100 + 3 \cdot 10 + 3)$	Expanded form
$= (2 \cdot 100 + 1 \cdot 100) + (6 \cdot 10 + 3 \cdot 10) + (7 + 3)$	Commutative and associative properties
$= (2 + 1)100 + (6 + 3)10 + (7 + 3)$	Distributive property
$= 3(100) + 9(10) + 10$	Addition
$= 3(100) + (9 + 1)10$	Distributive property
$= 3(100) + 10(10)$	Addition
$= 3(100) + 100$	Multiplication
$= (3 + 1)100$	Distributive property
$= 4(100)$	Addition
$= 400$	Multiplication

Seeing how numbers can be *composed* and *decomposed* makes it possible to deeply understand the algorithm. To understand the addition algorithm, we **decompose** the number using expanded form; we can then see how those different parts can be reconfigured — **composed** — to make our new whole, that is, the sum. When you were challenged to add amounts in Alphabitia in Exploration 3.1, at first you may have found that the manipulatives were essential, both because their concreteness made you more comfortable (for example, BAC was B flats, A longs, and C units) and because you could "see" the addition process actually happening. In one sense, the manipulatives let you see the parts (expanded form) and the whole at the same time.

Other Addition Algorithms

It is important to note that the algorithm just described is only one of many possible algorithms for adding two numbers. Many mathematics educators and schoolteachers report that schoolchildren often invent other algorithms that make just as much sense as this one. In fact, the algorithms that you grew up with are not universal throughout the world even today. After the base 10 system was developed, many different algorithms for doing computation were invented.

The calculation on the left below shows how 564 + 378 is computed by most people in the United States today. The calculation on the right shows how 564 + 378 was computed by some people in the Middle Ages. Advocates of this method argued for putting the sum at the top. The first step was simply to write the ones digit when adding each column. In the second step, if the actual sum of the column to the right was greater than ten, the number was crossed out and increased by one. This method is possibly the origin of the phrase "**adding up**."

$$
\begin{array}{r}
{\scriptstyle 1\ 1} \\
564 \\
\underline{378} \\
942
\end{array}
\qquad
\begin{array}{r}
{\scriptstyle 9\ 4} \\
\cancel{832} \\
564 \\
378
\end{array}
$$

The Partial Sums Algorithm

An algorithm developed in India more than 1,000 years ago called the **partial sums** method works like this: You first find the sum of the digits in each place and make sure to put them in the correct place. The calculation at the left shows one variation; the calculation at the right shows the same problem with lines, which were more often used by the Arabs. Try to explain why it works before reading on. . . . 🖊

$$
\begin{array}{r}
3\ 6\ 9 \\
4\ 7\ 8 \\
\hline
1\ 7 \\
1\ 3 \\
7 \\
\hline
8\ 4\ 7
\end{array}
\qquad
\begin{array}{c}
3\,|\,6\,|\,9 \\
4\,|\,7\,|\,8 \\
\hline
\ \ \,|\,1\,|\,7 \\
1\,|\,3\,| \\
7\,|\ \ \,| \\
\hline
8\ 4\ 7
\end{array}
$$

Why does it work?   The 9 and the 8 represent 9 ones plus 8 ones, which makes 17 ones, which is equivalent to 1 ten and 7 ones. Thus, the 1 goes in the tens place and the 7 goes in the ones place. The 6 and the 7 represent 6 tens plus 7 tens, which makes 13 tens, which is equivalent to 1 hundred and 3 tens. Thus, the 1 goes in the hundreds place and the 3 goes in the tens place. The 3 and the

LEARNING

A friend of mine, David Sobel, was talking about mathematics with his six-year-old daughter, Tara. They were doing double-digit addition. David had just shown Tara that 20 + 20 = 40. Tara thought for a moment and then proudly announced that 50 + 50 must be 70. When David asked how she had got that answer, she said, "when you add the same numbers that have a zero at the end, you just skip ten!" In so many mathematical situations, there are many ways to interpret the data. It takes time and practice to improve your ability to analyze and interpret patterns. It is important to note that both David and I were encouraged, not discouraged, by Tara's thinking. Why was this?

4 represent 3 hundreds plus 4 hundreds, which makes 7 hundreds, which obviously goes in the hundreds place. It is possible that this algorithm was popular because many people had trouble "carrying" the extra numbers in their heads.

Subtraction

Now let us investigate the operation of subtraction, which presents some interesting issues for young children. We will connect the pictorial model developed for addition to subtraction, but first let's look at some questions to make sure you are actively involved.

Assume that you are a young child who has not yet learned subtraction. How might you solve these problems—using manipulatives or diagrams, or in your head using common sense and other mathematical knowledge? Purposely "forgetting" what you already know about subtraction will probably clear the way for you to see beyond the mechanics of the operation to its underlying meaning—and that's what this investigation is about. Note your thoughts before reading on. . . .

Five subtraction problems

1. Joe had 7 marbles. He lost 2 in a game. How many does he have left?
2. Billy has 23 marbles and Yaka has 32. How many more does Yaka have?
3. At the beginning of the week, the hospital had 32 ounces of insulin, and at the end of the week, it had 14 ounces. How much insulin was used during the week?
4. Alicia was 45 inches tall at the **beginning** of the first grade and 53 inches at the end of the third grade. How many inches did she grow during this time?
5. The Jones farm has 35 pigs and 18 chickens. How many more pigs are there than chickens?

Now go back to these five problems and answer the following questions:

- In what ways are the problems different? In what ways are they similar?

- What does subtraction mean? For example, what words come to mind when you think of subtraction?

Contexts for Subtraction

One way in which the problems are different is connected to the two contexts we discussed for addition—that is, whether we are subtracting discrete sets or measured amounts.

Problems 1, 2, and 5 are discrete problems—we can represent the problems directly with pictures.

Problems 3 and 4 are measurement (continuous) problems—ounces and inches are measured amounts, representing how many of a certain unit we are talking about.

These problems differ in another way, and this difference is connected to the idea of parts and wholes that we find in all four operations. In "take-away" problems, a part is taken away from a whole. In "comparison" problems, two amounts are being compared. In some cases, the comparison is between two subsets of a large set (two parts of a whole); in other cases, the comparison is between two sets (wholes). Can you determine which of the five problems above are take-away and which are comparison? Think and then read on. . . .

Children often have trouble seeing the comparison model as subtraction. Do you see why? Think before reading on. . . .

Part of the reason is that many students will determine the answer by counting up from the smaller number. For example, when determining how many inches Alicia grew, many children see this as "45 plus what makes 53?"—that is, 45 + ? = 53. For this reason, some teachers refer to the comparison model as the **missing addend model.**

Even with larger numbers, many children prefer to count up rather than to subtract. They will subtract if they are forced to, but it frequently does not jibe with their common sense. Recall that one of the lines in Standard 3 is that students should believe that mathematics makes sense.

CHILDREN

I recall reading a paper about children with mathematical learning disabilities, several years ago, that speaks to the need for learners to see the connectedness of mathematical ideas. The author was called in to diagnose a third grader who was having difficulties with mathematics. The author discovered that the child did not see addition and subtraction as related, was not able to see the operations as parts and wholes, and was not able to use the commutative property of addition. That is, she saw the four number sentences on the right as four unrelated number sentences. It was no wonder that she was having difficulty remembering her addition and subtraction facts!

Problems 1 and 3 are take-away problems, whereas the other three problems fit the comparison model. Figure 3.6 shows the subtraction problem $7 - 2$ in the two contexts.

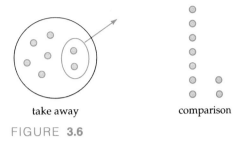

take away   comparison

FIGURE **3.6**

A Pictorial Model for Subtraction

Now look at all five subtraction problems, and put aside the categories (discrete measurement, take away, and comparison). Is it possible, as we did with addition, to represent all of these problems with a single model? Write your thoughts and then read on. . . .

One way to express the commonality is that in all cases, we have a large amount and two smaller amounts whose sum is equal to the larger number. Recall the pictorial model for addition: If we invert that diagram, we have a pictorial representation of a general model for subtraction (see Figure 3.7).

FIGURE **3.7**

It is important to note that "whole" and "part" refer to the numerical values rather than the contexts. For example, in Problem 2, we are comparing two wholes and saying that one whole contains 9 more marbles than the other.

We define **subtraction** formally in the following manner:

$$c - b = a \text{ iff } a + b = c$$

That is,

The difference between two numbers c and b is a if and only if c is the sum of a and b.

In mathematical language, c is called the **minuend,** b the **subtrahend,** and a the **difference.**

This model also highlights the connections between addition and subtraction problems (see Figure 3.8):

$3 + 5 = 8$
$5 + 3 = 8$
$8 - 3 = 5$
$8 - 5 = 3$

8	
3	5

FIGURE **3.8**

Referring to the composition and decomposition notion, we can join 3 and 5 to make 8, and we can decompose 8 into 5 and 3. We will use this awareness of the ability to break amounts into convenient parts when we examine mental computation and estimation in Section 3.3.

Subtraction with Number Lines

Many measurement situations naturally lend themselves to a number line representation, for example, time and distance. Let's use an example to explore this model. Joanne had 8 feet of rope and used 3 feet to stake a tent. How much rope does she have left? Try to represent this problem with a number line and then read on. . . .

As with addition, we can use a number line to solve the problem in either of two ways (see Figure 3.9).

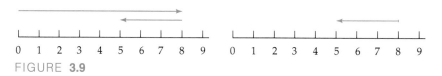

FIGURE **3.9**

Do both ways make sense? Does one way feel more comfortable to you? As with the addition number lines, the left diagram more closely resembles the physical representation of the problem.

Properties of Subtraction

Think back to the properties of addition—identity, commutativity, associativity, and closure. Do those same properties hold for subtraction? Think and then read on. . . .

Some students think that subtraction has an identity property, since if we take away zero from a number, its value does not change; that is, $a - 0 = a$. This is true; however, if we reverse the order, the result is not true—that is, $0 - a \neq a$. Therefore, we generally say that the operation of subtraction does not have an identity property. In higher mathematics, we say that the operation of subtraction has a right-identity but not a left-identity. After examining a few cases, you can see that the operation of subtraction does not possess the commutative property or the associative property. The commutative property is not immediately understood by children. I recall one first grader arguing that $3 - 5$ was 0 because "you can't have less than nothing" and another arguing that it was 2 because "you just turn them around." Finally, the operation of subtraction is not closed for the set of natural numbers because the difference of two numbers can be a negative number.

INVESTIGATION 3.2 How Far Is It?

This problem, which actually happened to me, provides a good opportunity for you to apply your developing problem-solving tools and your understanding of subtraction and number line models to a real problem. I had to go to a meeting one day in Concord, New Hampshire. Since it was a business meeting, I would be reimbursed for my mileage. When I left Keene, I noted that my odometer read 26,688. Unfortunately, I forgot to check my odometer in Concord. However, on the way home, I saw a sign that said I was 36 miles from Keene. At that point, my odometer said 26,768. I now had enough information to determine the round-trip distance between Keene and Concord. What did I come up with? Try to solve this problem on your own before reading on. If you get stuck, what problem-solving tools might be useful?

DISCUSSION

Of course, I could have waited until I had gotten home, taken the mileage then, and subtracted 26,688 from that number. However, that would not be a challenging problem, and I did this actual problem because I was aware that there was a reasonable probability that I would forget to note my mileage when I got home!

This problem practically begs for a number line diagram. However, as many of my students have told me, creating good diagrams is easier said than done. To make this point more concrete, many students tell me that when they see a good diagram, it often makes sense, but that they don't know how to create the diagram themselves. In this problem, a useful diagram often emerges in two stages. For example, students respond in different ways to the diagram in Figure 3.10. Some students don't immediately understand the diagram, others understand it but don't find that it leads to the answer, whereas still others see it and "eureka," the solution to the problem literally appears right before their eyes. If you find that this diagram is not a eureka experience, what might be added to the diagram or how it could be modified? Please try to modify it yourself before reading on. . . . ✐

FIGURE **3.10**

There are different ways in which students find this diagram useful. For some students, the diagram points to a further step in the problem. For example, they now know what to do with 26,688 and 26,768. For other students, the diagram tells them that they have enough information to find the round trip distance. Yet other students use algebraic notation and see two equations. Depending on how you see the problem, your modified diagram might look like either of the ones in Figure 3.11. Using either of these diagrams, or one of your own making, can you solve the problem now? Try to do so before reading on. . . . ✐

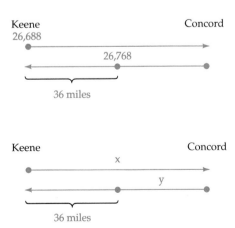

FIGURE **3.11**

One key to this problem is to use given information to produce more information. If we subtract 26,688 from 26,768, we get 80; what does that tell us? It tells us that I had traveled 80 miles at that point; adding this 80 to 36, we know the round-trip distance. A student using algebra would have an equation, $x + y = 80$, and would come to the same realization: The round trip distance is 116 miles.

BEYOND THE CLASSROOM

In Investigation 3.2, we found the mathematical solution to the problem. Had I remembered to check my odometer in Concord or in Keene, however, it very well might not have shown that I drove 58 miles to Concord or 116 miles round trip. Do you see why? Think and then read on. . . .

The 36-mile sign does not mean that I am 36 miles away from my house. It means that I am 36 miles from Keene. But that begs the question, "36 miles from *where* in Keene?" For example, think of a sign telling you that you are 36 miles from New York City. What does that mean? Does it mean 36 miles to the center of New York City or to the city limits? In general, it means that you are 36 miles from what the map makers consider to be the geographical center of the city, not the city limits. Do you see why mileage signs are made this way? How they determine the center is another question. What do you think is the center of the town closest to you?

Understanding Subtraction in Base 10

Let us now examine some standard and non-standard algorithms for subtraction. Again, recall the Alphabitian problems; for a child, subtracting $32 - 14$ can be as overwhelming and confusing as many students originally found DA − BC in the Alphabitian system.

> When nothing remains, put down a small circle so that the place be not empty, but the circle must occupy it, so that the number of places will not be diminished when the place is empty and the second be mistaken for the first.[3]

This quote comes from a text written by Al-Khowarizmi in 825 A.D. as he tried to explain the procedure for subtracting in the new (Hindu) numeration system. Do you understand what he is saying? What function does the circle serve?

Researchers have found that when subtraction problems have zeros, the success rate for most third graders goes down drastically. However, this need not be so. Let us examine the following problem: $300 - 148$. Although there is no single procedure that all students use to solve this problem (unless they are forced to by their teacher), we will examine here how this problem might be solved going from left to right.

Using Manipulatives	Using Words	Using Symbols
	We need to regroup 300 so that we can "take away" 148.	$\begin{array}{r} 3\,0\,0 \\ -\,1\,4\,8 \\ \hline \end{array}$

---

[3] Karl Menninger, *Number Words and Number Symbols: A Cultural History of Numbers* (Cambridge, Mass.: MIT Press, 1969), p. 413.

Using Manipulatives		Using Words	Using Symbols
		We can trade one of the three hundreds for 10 tens, giving us 2 hundreds and 10 tens, which has the same value as 3 hundreds.	$\begin{array}{r} 2\ 1 \\ \cancel{3}\ 0\ 0 \\ -\ 1\ 4\ 8 \\ \hline \end{array}$
		Next, we can trade one of the tens for 10 ones. We now have 2 hundreds, 9 tens, and 10 ones, which still has the same value as 3 hundreds.	$\begin{array}{r} 2\ 9\ 1 \\ \cancel{3}\ \cancel{0}\ 0 \\ -\ 1\ 4\ 8 \\ \hline \end{array}$
		Now we can take away 1 hundred, 4 tens, and 8 ones.	$\begin{array}{r} 2\ 9\ 1 \\ \cancel{3}\ \cancel{0}\ 0 \\ -\ 1\ 4\ 8 \\ \hline 1\ 5\ 2 \end{array}$

Justifying the Standard Algorithm

It is beyond the scope of this book to formally prove every algorithm, procedure, and theorem. What is essential is that elementary students and teachers understand the algorithms that they use, that is, that they understand the whys of the algorithm. Does the explanation above help you to understand the left-to-right subtraction procedure? If not, please read it again or refer to your notes from the Alphabitia explorations, or work with a friend so that it does make sense.

Some students find that representing the problem in expanded form is helpful. A key to understanding this algorithm is to understand the equivalence of 3 hundreds and 2 hundreds, 9 tens, and 10 ones. Although they look different, and the numerals are different (300 versus 29^{1}0), the amounts are equal. Another key to understanding this algorithm is to know why we needed to do the regrouping. This is easier to see at the physical level; without these regroupings, we literally cannot "take away" 1 flat, 4 longs, and 8 units.

3 hundreds + 0 tens + 0 ones →	2 hundreds + 10 tens + 0 ones →	2 hundreds + 9 tens + 10 ones
−1 hundred + 4 tens + 8 ones	−1 hundred + 4 tens + 8 ones	−1 hundred + 4 tens + 8 ones
Cannot subtract the tens or the ones	Cannot subtract the ones	Subtraction possible

An Alternative Algorithm

It is important to note that the standard algorithm (in the discussion above) is more closely connected to the take-away context for subtraction than to the comparison or missing addend context. For example, consider the problem 802 −248 in a missing addend context: Joan wants to buy a computer for $802; if she has $248, how much more does she need? If we are solving this problem in the missing addend context, we are asking what number combined with 248 gives us 802. One possible algorithm would begin with the smaller amount and adding to it beginning with the hundreds place and finishing with the ones place. Both of my children invented this procedure when I asked them to tell me how they determined the difference before they were taught the standard algorithm.

WHAT IS THOUGHT	WHAT IS WRITTEN	
	"Answer" column	"Working" column
How many hundreds can we add to 238 without going over 802?	500	738
We can add 500, which brings us to 738.		
Now, how many tens can we add to 738 without going over 802?	60	798
We can add 60, which brings us to 798.		
How many ones do we need to add to 798 to get to 802?	4	802
We need 4 ones.		

The answer of 564 is obtained by adding the numbers in the answer column. Though many college students find this algorithm initially awkward, when elementary children are encouraged to develop their own means for answering subtraction problems, we see algorithms like this one much more often than we do the more standard ones that many textbooks contain. As you will find in this section, the standard algorithm is one of many possible algorithms and is not necessarily the one that children find easiest to understand.

As with addition, the composition and decomposition of numbers enables us to better understand both the standard subtraction algorithms and other algorithms for subtraction. When you explored subtraction in Alphabitia in Exploration 3.3, you may have found that not all students subtracted in the same way; some went left to right, some went right to left, and for some it depended on whether or not there were zeros in the subtrahend. Regardless of the procedure, subtracting with confidence requires that we be comfortable with the idea of decomposing and recomposing the number.

"Carrying" and "Borrowing"

Traditionally, elementary teachers have tended to use the word *carry* when regrouping for addition and *borrow* when regrouping for subtraction. Many current elementary teachers do not use these words. Can you guess why? Think and then read on. . . . 🖉

One problem is that the term *borrow* is misleading. When I borrow an egg from a neighbor or when I borrow a tissue, that is different from "borrowing" a ten.

Another problem with carry and borrow is that the terms connote two different processes, when in fact the same process is involved: trading (regrouping). We trade up when carrying, and we trade down when borrowing. For example, consider the related addition and subtraction problems 36 + 28 = 64 and $64 - 36 = 28$. When we add the digits in the ones place, we trade in 10 of the ones for 1 ten, and so 14 ones becomes 1 ten and 4 ones. In the subtraction problem, we go the other way: We trade a ten for 10 ones, and so 1 ten and 4 ones become 14 ones.

$$(14 \text{ ones} \rightarrow 1 \text{ ten and 4 ones}) \quad (1 \text{ ten and 4 ones} \rightarrow 14 \text{ ones})$$

$$
\begin{array}{r}
1 \\
3\ 6 \\
+2\ 8 \\
\hline
6\ 4
\end{array}
\qquad
\begin{array}{r}
5\ 1 \\
\not{6}\ 4 \\
-\ 3\ 6 \\
\hline
2\ 8
\end{array}
$$

Many adults do not realize that these processes are virtually identical; they have never stopped to think about it. When learning the algorithms for the first time, young children find it much easier if there is a reason for what they do. The connection between these two processes is further explored in Exploration 3.3.

INVESTIGATION 3.3   Another Subtraction Algorithm

When children are allowed to invent their own methods for subtracting, many children will invent left to right algorithms. I recall being sick in the second grade. I missed a lot of school and had a very hard time with subtraction. I could not make sense of the method that was taught, and I invented a left to right method, because that was how it made sense to me. To this day, if I subtract from right to left when multiple regroupings are required, I have to think carefully.

In 1986, I was helping a friend from New Zealand with some mathematics, and I was stunned to find how he subtracted. Since then, I discovered that this New Zealand algorithm is the "standard" algorithm in many different countries. Look at the process. Can you figure it out? Why does it work?

$$
\begin{array}{r}
9\ 8\ 4 \\
-3\ 6\ 8 \\
\hline
\end{array}
\qquad
\begin{array}{r}
9\ 8\ {}^1 4 \\
-3\ {}^7\!\not{6}\ 8 \\
\hline
6\ 1\ 6
\end{array}
$$

DISCUSSION

Faced with this problem, many children will say, "You can't take 8 from 4." In the United States, we regroup 984 as 9 hundreds, 7 tens, and 14 ones. In New Zealand, they increase both subtrahend and minuend by 10, so that subtraction is possible in the ones column and the difference between the two is still the same. That is, the difference between 984 and 368 (original problem) is equal to the difference between 994 (which is equivalent to 98^14) and 378.

I am always amazed when people tell me that they like other subjects better than mathematics because there is no room for creativity in mathematics. When I look at all the different algorithms that have been created over thousands of years, I see so much creativity!

Summary

In this section, we have examined the operations of addition and subtraction. You now know that addition can mean to combine or join two sets; it can also mean to increase a set by a certain amount. You know that subtraction can mean to take away an amount from a set, it can mean to ask how much bigger one set is than another, and it can also mean to ask how much a set must increase in order to get to a certain amount (missing addend model). Especially in the case of subtraction, you have seen that these meanings are not always obvious to children.

Addition and subtraction problems arise from discrete or measurement (continuous) contexts. We can represent these problems in various ways: with circles, with part-whole rectangles, or with number lines. The choice of model sometimes depends on personal preference and sometimes depends on the nature of the problem being solved.

These representations help us to see connections between addition and subtraction. In one sense, addition consists of adding two parts to make a whole. In one sense, subtraction consists of having a whole and a part and needing to find the value of the other part. You are becoming more comfortable with the idea of composition and decomposition, which appears repeatedly throughout mathematics. In one sense, addition is an act of composition, putting together two parts to make a new whole. In one sense, subtraction is an act of decomposition, breaking a whole into a given part and a part we need to find.

We have examined patterns in the addition table. Recognizing these patterns helps children to become more comfortable with adding. We have seen that describing the patterns that we see requires some thinking and that mathematical vocabulary and definitions, developed over the centuries, can make communication easier and reduce ambiguity.

You have learned that there are certain properties that hold for addition of whole numbers but not for subtraction: identity, commutativity, associativity, and closure. The identity property may seem obvious now, but it will be seen as an important part of the whole set of properties in Section 3.2.

Finally, we have examined both standard and alternative algorithms for whole number addition and subtraction. You have learned that the algorithms we currently use in the United States are not the only possible procedures for computing. The ability not only to compute with these algorithms but also to be able to explain why they work is a crucial part of developing mathematical power.

In Section 3.2, we will do a similar examination of multiplication and division, and then we will examine the relationships among all four operations.

EXERCISES 3.1

1. Refer to the base 10 addition table. If we look at any of the diagonals going in a top-left-to-lower-right direction, the value of each successive term increases by 2 each time. Explain this pattern.

2. In many textbooks, students are encouraged to learn their fact families. This is the fact family for 10: $1 + 9$, $2 + 8, 3 + 7, 4 + 6, 5 + 5, 6 + 4, 7 + 3, 8 + 2, 9 + 1$. Transform each fact pair to an ordered pair and graph the pairs on graph paper. Why does the line look the way it does?

3. Below is an addition algorithm from an old text. Explain why it works.

$$
\begin{array}{r}
3\ 6 \\
+\ 4\ 8 \\
\hline
1\ 4 \\
7 \\
\hline
8\ 4
\end{array}
$$

4. A subtraction algorithm that was popular in India many centuries ago is called the reverse method. It has similarities to the standard algorithm in use in the United States in that it involves a "borrowing" step and a "paying back" step. Examine the algorithm in action in the example below.

Step 1	Step 2	Step 3
$\begin{array}{r} 6\ 3\ 2 \\ -2\ 1\ 4 \\ \hline 4\ 2 \end{array}$	$\begin{array}{r} 4\ 3\ {}^{1}2 \\ -2\ 1\ 4 \\ \hline 4\ 2 \end{array}$	$\begin{array}{r} 4\ 3\ {}^{1}2 \\ -2\ 1\ 4 \\ \hline 4\ 2\!\!\!/\ 8 \\ {}_{1} \end{array}$

   a. Solve the following problems using this algorithm.

$$
\begin{array}{r} 5\ 4\ 3 \\ -3\ 1\ 7 \\ \hline \end{array}
\qquad
\begin{array}{r} 6\ 3\ 5 \\ -2\ 7\ 3 \\ \hline \end{array}
\qquad
\begin{array}{r} 6\ 1\ 2 \\ -2\ 5\ 8 \\ \hline \end{array}
\qquad
\begin{array}{r} 7\ 0\ 0 \\ -3\ 7\ 4 \\ \hline \end{array}
$$

   b. Explain how and why this algorithm works.

5. As you may remember from working with Alphabitia, understanding how to add large numbers is not simple. Many young children encounter many difficulties when

they do addition where regrouping is needed — one has to understand place value in order to know where to place the digits, and what seems simple to an adult is not simple to many children. The invention of the lattice method, popular during the Middle Ages, addressed this problem. Look at the example below.

a. Take a few minutes on your own to figure out how this method works. You may wish to make up some other problems. Then write down instructions for how it works as if you were talking to a friend who missed class and hasn't a clue.

b. One of the advantages of this algorithm is more apparent when adding long rows of figures. For example, use this algorithm to add the following numbers: 638 + 746 + 65 + 824.

6. Solve the following addition problems with the lattice algorithm:

   a. $5,568_{10}$
      $+2,745_{10}$

   b. 322_5
      $+234_5$

   c. 764_8
      $+215_8$

7. Pretend you are a young child again. Which algorithm do you think would be easiest to learn first: the standard algorithm, the partial sums algorithm, or the lattice algorithm? Explain your reasoning.

8. Finish the following addition problem, which has been done in expanded form.

   $345 = 3$ hundreds $+ 4$ tens $+ 5$ ones
   $+268 = 2$ hundreds $+ 6$ tens $+ 8$ ones

9. Identify and explain the errors in each of the problems below, all of which have occurred in real classrooms.

   a. 36
      +28
      ___
       91

   b. 36
      + 28
      ____
      514

   c. 365
      +287
      ____
      742

10. Place the digits 1, 2, 3, 6, 7, and 8 in the boxes to obtain

    a. The greatest sum

    b. The least sum

11. Choose among the digits 1, 2, 3, 4, 5, 6, 7, 8, and 9 to make the sum equal 500. You can use each digit only once. How many different ways can you make 500?

12. Determine the values of N and P that make this a true statement. Explain how you arrived at the answer.

    N
    N
    N
    $+ P$
    ___
    PN

13. How many different ways can you make this a true statement, using each of the whole numbers 1 through 9 only once?

    For example, 152
                  368
                  479
                  ___

14. Make up a subtraction story problem for each of the following contexts. Briefly *explain* why the story problem is an example of the particular model.

    a. Take-away

    b. Missing addend

    c. Comparison

15. a. Explain why the operation of subtraction is not commutative.

    b. Explain why the operation of subtraction is not associative.

16. A student's work on a subtraction problem is shown here. Explain the numerals in the top row, 3, 9, 10, as if you were talking to a third grader who is having difficulty with the process.

    3 9 1
    4̸ 0̸ 0
    −1 3 5
    _____
    2 6 5

17. Examine the problem at the right.

    a. Explain, in mathematical terms, what the student did wrong. Where are the problems in the student's thinking?

       3 1 1
       4̸ 0̸ 0̸
       −2 3 6
       _____
       1 7 4

    b. How would you help the student if the quote below represents her explanation:

       "You can't take 6 from 0 and you can't take 3 from 0, so you have to borrow from the four. Cross out 4 and write 3, cross out the zeros and write 10."

18. This is a true story. A second grade teacher asked her students to explain how they had solved the problem below. One student said the following: "If you take 6 away from 2, you get minus four. When you take 50 from 70, you get 20. Then minus 4 plus 20 is 16." What do you think of this student's thinking? Was he just lucky on this problem, or could it qualify as an algorithm?

    72
    −56
    ___
    ⁻4
    20
    ___
    16

19. Identify and explain the errors in each of the problems below, all of which have occurred in real classrooms.

    a. 76
       −48
       ___
        32

    b. 76
       −48
       ___
        22

    c. 76
       −48
       ___
        38

d. $\begin{array}{r} 70 \\ -48 \\ \hline 38 \end{array}$ e. $\begin{array}{r} 70 \\ -48 \\ \hline 32 \end{array}$ f. $\begin{array}{r} 700 \\ -482 \\ \hline 228 \end{array}$

20. Place the digits 1, 2, 3, 6, 7, and 8 in the boxes to obtain

    a. The greatest difference

    b. The least difference

21. Choose among the digits 1, 2, 3, 4, 5, 6, 7, 8, and 9 to make the difference 234. You can use each digit only once. How many different ways can you make 234?

22. For each number line problem below, identify the computation it models and briefly justify your answer.

    a.

    b.

    c.

    d.

    e.

    f.

23. Represent the following problems on a number line. Explain each problem as if you were talking to someone who was not taking this class.

a. 5 + 4

b. 8 − 3

24. Respond to the following as if you were talking to a principal who is familiar with the NCTM Standards. You want to convince the principal to hire you. The principal has just said that she has only recently realized that the words *borrowing* and *carrying* are no longer used by effective math teachers. Rather, they use alternative terms like *renaming* or *regrouping*. The principal asks if you agree with the change in language and why.

25. With three boys on a large scale, it read 170 pounds. When Adam stepped off, the scale read 115 pounds. When Ben stepped off, the scale read 65 pounds. What is the weight of each boy?

26. A mule and a horse were carrying some bales of cloth. The mule said to the horse, "If you give me one of your bales, I shall carry as many as you." "If you give me one of yours," replied the horse, "I will be carrying twice as many as you." How many bales was each animal carrying?

27. Place the numbers 1 through 8 in the circles so that no two consecutive numbers are in circles that are adjacent to each other (that is, directly connected).

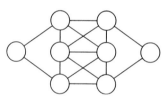

S E C T I O N   **3.2**   **UNDERSTANDING MULTIPLICATION AND DIVISION**

Do you remember learning about multiplication and division in elementary school? If so, what do you remember? When I ask my own students this question, most of their answers have to do with trying to learn the multiplication table and with the frustration of learning the long division procedure. Admittedly, multiplication and division are more complex concepts than addition and subtraction. However, students who develop a good understanding of the structures of multiplication and division and their connections with each other and with addition and subtraction report being amazed to find that multiplication and division can actually make sense!

As in Section 3.1, we will first examine the multiple meanings of each operation and models for representing them. Examination of patterns and properties will lay the groundwork for understanding how the algorithms work. Then we will examine the connections among the various operations. This, in turn, paves the way for a strong operation sense, which enables you to solve the nonroutine and multistep problem situations that pervade everyday and work settings.

Multiplication

Many elementary methods textbooks group addition and subtraction in one chapter and then multiplication and division in another chapter. This is not

CHILDREN

Many young children encounter the concept of multiplication even before school; for example, if the tooth fairy gives me fifty cents for each tooth, how much will I get for all my teeth?

simply because children learn addition and subtraction first, but also because multiplication and division are more complex and abstract concepts. In fact, many of my students report that while they learned *more* about addition and subtraction in this course, they learned quite a bit of *new* material about multiplication and division. Mathematics starts to crumble for many students when they get to multiplication, especially learning (or memorizing) the multiplication tables. In fact, many adults do not know all the single-digit multiplication facts, e.g. 8×7. Given how available calculators are, this is not a huge problem, although it is sometimes embarrassing. However, more problematic is the fact that few adults understand the different meanings of multiplication, and this lack of knowledge limits their ability to solve real-world problems. One of the goals of the following examination of multiplication is for you to understand the different meanings of multiplication and why it is useful to know these different meanings.

Assume that you are a young child who has not yet learned multiplication. How might you solve these problems—using manipulatives or diagrams, or using common sense and other mathematical knowledge? Note your thoughts before reading on. . . .

Four multiplication problems

1. One piece of candy costs 4¢. How much would 3 pieces cost?
2. If Jackie walks at 4 mph for 3 hours, how far will she have walked?
3. A carpet is 4 feet by 3 feet. What is the area of the carpet?
4. Carla has 4 blouses and 3 skirts. How many combinations can she wear? (Assume that all possible combinations go together!)

Contexts for Multiplication

Now go back to these four problems and answer the following questions:

- In what ways are the problems different? In what ways are they similar?
- What does multiplication mean? For example, what words come to mind when you think of multiplication?

If we represent the four problems with diagrams, as in Figure 3.12, the differences appear to be tremendous, although all four problems are solved as 4 times 3.

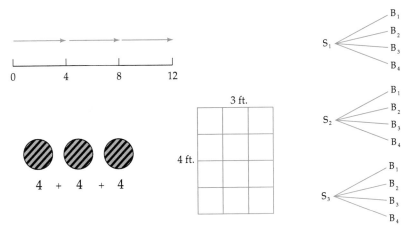

FIGURE **3.12**

Problem 1 is like the discrete sets we encountered with addition and subtraction. It is also literally **repeated addition**, that is, solved by adding $4 + 4 + 4$.

Problem 2 involves a certain number of measured units and can be represented with a number line that shows repeated addition of the measures.

Problem 3 involves measures, but it involves repeated addition less than it involves counting the number of new units. This problem illustrates the area context of multiplication.

Problem 4 involves discrete objects, but it relies on repeated addition less than it relies on putting combinations in an array. In set language, what we did in this problem was to examine two sets and look at all possible ways of pairing the elements of those sets. We will see later in this section that we can represent this context with the *Cartesian product model of multiplication*.

A General Model for Multiplication

As you can see, multiplication is a more complex concept than addition and subtraction, and it is more than simply repeated addition. Can you describe the four problems in such a way that they all have something in common, as we did for addition and subtraction? Work on this question and then read on. . . .

Our general model for addition can be extended to multiplication. Figure 3.13 shows one diagram for $4 \cdot 3$. Do you see the resemblance between the addition and multiplication models? As with addition and subtraction, the *general model of multiplication* can be cast in part-whole language: The product (the whole) is built from parts that are equal in size or amount.

Traditionally, multiplication is represented as

$$n \text{ times } a = \overbrace{a + a + a + \cdots + a}^{n \text{ times}}$$

We generally use a dot to denote multiplication (since x is used in algebra to denote a variable). If $n \cdot a = b$, then n is called the **multiplier**, a is called the **multiplicand**, and b is called the **product**. Furthermore, n and a can be said to be **factors** of b; b is a **multiple** of both n and a.

Using boxes, we can represent a **general model for multiplication** (Figure 3.14):

n times a = the amount a added n times

That is, a is the value of whatever is in each box.

FIGURE **3.14**

The general model shown in Figure 3.14 works well for Problems 1 and 2. However, the last two problems do not really fit the model. We can force-fit them, but repeated addition is not the essence of those models. Therefore, we look for other models that can represent these contexts better.

The need for this is not readily apparent when working with whole numbers. Thus, a sneak preview: In Chapter 5, we will see that the repeated addition model of multiplication just doesn't work well for 3/4 times 2/3, that is, adding three-fourths two-thirds of a time simply doesn't make sense as repeated addition. Let us now examine more closely the area model and Cartesian product models of multiplication.

FIGURE **3.13**

FIGURE **3.15**

FIGURE **3.16**

Area Model for Multiplication

The **area model for multiplication** is an important one that we will see throughout the book. Figure 3.15 is a discrete representation for $4 \cdot 3$.

If we can change each dot to a square, as in Figure 3.16, many students can better see the connection between the repeated addition model and the area model.

As you may recall, the formula for the area of a rectangle is length times width. Thus, any multiplication problem $a \cdot b$ can be represented as a rectangle whose length is a units and whose width is b units. We will use this context in the next section when we examine the multiplication algorithm and in Chapter 5 when we examine multiplication of fractions and decimals.

Cartesian Product Model for Multiplication

As we saw in Problem 4, the Cartesian product of any two sets A and B is the set consisting of *all* possible ways of combining elements of the first set with elements of the second set. Using more formal language, we say that the Cartesian product of any two sets A and B consists of all possible ordered pairs such that the first element is from set A and the second element is from set B. In mathematical notation, we write

$$A \times B = \{(a, b) \mid a \in A \text{ and } b \in B\}$$

In Problem 4, the Cartesian product of the set S of skirts and the set B of blouses is

$$\{(S_1, B_1), (S_1, B_2), (S_1, B_3), (S_1, B_4), (S_2, B_1), (S_2, B_2), (S_2, B_3), (S_2, B_4),$$
$$(S_3, B_1), (S_3, B_2), (S_3, B_3), (S_3, B_4)\}$$

The definition of multiplication as Cartesian product is similar to our definition of addition using set language:

> If $n(A) = a$ represents the number of elements in set A, and if $n(B) = b$ represents the number of elements in set B, then the number of elements in the Cartesian product of sets A and B is equal to the product of a and b.

In notation,

$$a \cdot b = n(A \times B)$$

That is, the value of a times b is equal to the number of elements in the Cartesian product of set A and set B.

There are many real-life situations in which the Cartesian product is a useful problem-solving tool. In Chapter 7, we will find that this concept can help us examine probability situations.

Properties of Multiplication

Which of the properties that hold for addition also hold for multiplication? Write your thoughts and then read on. . . .

When adding, we found that "zero doesn't do anything." However, when we multiply any number by zero, the product is zero. This property of multiplication, which is not intuitively obvious to many children, is known as the **zero property of multiplication**

$$a \cdot 0 = 0 \cdot a = 0$$

Many children are either intrigued or confused by the fact that when adding, "zero doesn't change your answer," but that when multiplying, "one doesn't change your answer." Stated in everyday language, "when we multiply any number by 1, we get the same number." This is called the identity property of multiplication

$$a \cdot 1 = 1 \cdot a = a$$

Just as with addition, when we multiply any two numbers, we get the same product regardless of the order; that is, $a \cdot b = b \cdot a$. This property is known as the **commutative property of multiplication.**

Just as with addition, grouping doesn't matter when we multiply several numbers. For example, $(5 \cdot 4) \cdot 7 = 5 \cdot (4 \cdot 7) = 140$, although the problem is much easier to do mentally in the first way. Why is this? This grouping property is known as the **associative property of multiplication**

$$(a \cdot b) \cdot c = a \cdot (b \cdot c)$$

MATHEMATICS

The distributive property is a powerful one that we will encounter later in this chapter when we learn why the multiplication algorithm works. We will also see it in Chapter 5 when we examine multiplication with fractions and decimals, and it occurs throughout algebra. It is also widely misunderstood; hence many students do not have this property in their toolbox. This is like a mechanic's toolbox not containing a crescent wrench!

There is another property, called the **distributive property,** that connects multiplication to the operations of addition and subtraction. Consider the following problem given to third grade students: How many cans of soda are in three 24-can cases? When students are given freedom to invent their own solutions to these problems rather than "discover" the teacher's way, they will solve this problem in a variety of ways, three of which are discussed below.

Some will simply add $24 + 24 + 24$.

Others will represent the problem with base 10 blocks, as in Figure 3.17. They will count 6 tens and 12 ones, convert to 7 tens and 2 ones, and give the answer of 72.

FIGURE **3.17**

In this case, the students are using the **distributive property of multiplication over addition:**

$$a(b + c) = ab + ac$$

These students have transformed $3 \cdot 24$ into $3 \cdot (20 + 4) = 3 \cdot 20 + 3 \cdot 4 = 60 + 12 = 72$. That is, 3 groups of 24 can be decomposed by breaking the 24 into 2 tens and 4 ones, which is equivalent to 3 groups of 20 and 3 groups of 4 (see Figure 3.18).

$3(20 + 4)$ $3 \cdot 20$ + $3 \cdot 4$

FIGURE **3.18**

Others will solve the problem with money: 24¢ is one penny less than a quarter; do this three times and you will have 3 quarters take away 3 pennies, that is, $75 - 3 = 72$. In this case, the students are using the **distributive property of multiplication over subtraction:**

$$a(b - c) = ab - ac$$

The students have transformed $3 \cdot 24$ into $3 \cdot (25 - 1) = 3 \cdot 25 - 3 \cdot 1 = 75 - 3 = 72$

The Multiplication Table

We discussed patterns in the multiplication table in Exploration 3.5. Let us further examine the multiplication table to see how patterns can help children learn the table's 100 "multiplication facts." What patterns do you see in Table 3.2? Write your observations and then read on. . . . 🖎

TABLE 3.2

	1	2	3	4	5	6	7	8	9	10
1	1	2	3	4	5	6	7	8	9	10
2	2	4	6	8	10	12	14	16	18	20
3	3	6	9	12	15	18	21	24	27	30
4	4	8	12	16	20	24	28	32	36	40
5	5	10	15	20	25	30	35	40	45	50
6	6	12	18	24	30	36	42	48	54	60
7	7	14	21	28	35	42	49	56	63	70
8	8	16	24	32	40	48	56	64	72	80
9	9	18	27	36	45	54	63	72	81	90
10	10	20	30	40	50	60	70	80	90	100

INVESTIGATION 3.4 A Pattern in the Multiplication Table

Let us examine one pattern. A student noted that every odd number in the table is "surrounded" by even numbers, but that the reverse is not the case. Let us investigate the first observation. Why do you think every odd number in the table is surrounded by even numbers? Work on this problem before reading on. . . . 🖎

DISCUSSION

A key to unlocking this mystery comes from the following generalizations: The product of two even numbers is always an even number, the product of two odd numbers is always an odd number, and the product of an odd number and an even number is always an even number. We will explore odd and even numbers further in Chapter 4. If you didn't make much progress on this question before, try to use this information and see if you can explain this phenomenon now. Then read on. . . . 🖎

Let us look first at a specific case and then a general case. The diagram below shows 35 (from 7 · 5) and the numbers that surround it in the table.

		6	7	8
		.	.	.
		.	.	.
		.	.	.
4	. . .	24	28	32
5	. . .	30	35	40
6	. . .	36	42	48

More generally, we can write

		Even	Odd	Even
		.	.	.
		.	.	.
		.	.	.
Even	. . .	Even	Even	Even
Odd	. . .	Even	Odd	Even
Even	. . .	Even	Even	Even

Thus, we see that each of the eight numbers surrounding an odd number in a multiplication table is either the product of two even numbers or the product of an odd number and an even number. Thus none of them can be an odd number.

Looking back   Because of space constraints, we cannot "look back" at every problem-solving situation in the textbook. However, we do so occasionally to illustrate the value of this step. Stop for a moment to reflect on the following questions: What did you learn from exploring this pattern? How might this investigation help one with multiplication facts? Why aren't even numbers surrounded by odd numbers? 🖎

Some students find that Investigation 3.4 illustrates several problem-solving strategies: breaking a problem into smaller parts and looking for other ways to represent a problem. Some students highlight the odd numbers on a multiplication table and "see" the pattern in a new way as a result of the highlighting.

Using this pattern   I will present two ways in which this knowledge can help with multiplication facts. First, a brief reflection on Investigation 3.4 yields the deduction that 3/4 of the multiplication facts are even numbers; that is, only one in four multiplication facts is an odd number. Second, nowhere in the multiplication table do we have two odd numbers in a row. Thus, for example, if I know that 7 · 7 is 49, then 8 · 7 can't be 55 or 57. The generalizations about the products of odd and even numbers would help, for example, a student who wasn't sure whether 7 · 7 was 48 or 49.

Ultimately, the most important outcome of looking for and examining patterns is that the student comes to see that mathematics is more than just a bunch of facts and rules and that these "relationships" not only are sometimes intriguing but also make us more mathematically powerful.

Changes in Units

There is an important difference between multiplication and addition (or subtraction). When we add or subtract two amounts, the labels do not change: oranges plus oranges = oranges. However, this is not true with multiplication. Look back to the four multiplication problems presented at the beginning of this section. Do you see this? ✐

- We are multiplying 3 *pieces* by 4 *cents per piece* and getting 12 *cents.*
- We are multiplying 4 *miles per hour* by 3 *hours* and getting 12 *miles.*
- We are multiplying 4 *feet* by 3 *feet* and getting 12 *square feet.*
- We are multiplying 4 *blouses* by 3 *skirts* and getting 12 *outfits.*

This matter of changing units is a crucial one and will develop over the course of the book. Recall Exploration 1.3, where you multiplied dollars per gallon by gallons to get the total cost of gasoline.

Now let us apply some of this knowledge about multiplication to a real-life setting.

INVESTIGATION 3.5   Using Various Strategies in a Real-Life Multiplication Situation

A warehouse has 50 bays (places to stack pallets). Four pallets can be stacked in each bay, each pallet can hold 24 cartons, and each carton holds 12 boxes. How many boxes can the warehouse contain? If each box sells for $4, what is the value of the merchandise in a full warehouse? Work on this problem yourself before reading on. . . . ✐

DISCUSSION

As with many of our problems, there are several strategies that will lead to a solution. Many of my students tell me that they can understand the problem when they read my solutions, but that they have trouble coming up with a strategy on their own. Therefore, I urge you not to read the discussions of the investigations until after you have attempted the problem (on your own or with a friend), and when you do read the discussion, read "actively."

STRATEGY 1: Draw a diagram

There are many possible ways to represent this problem with a diagram. The diagram in Figure 3.19 is not "the right diagram," but rather an example of a useful diagram. If you didn't solve the problem or if you didn't solve it with a diagram, take a few moments to look at this diagram. Does it help? How? Does it connect to or stimulate your thinking about what operation(s) might be involved? ✐

Bay

pallet	pallet
pallet	pallet

FIGURE **3.19**

STRATEGY 2: Use smaller numbers

What if there were 3 bays, 4 pallets in each bay, 2 cartons in each pallet, and 5 boxes in each carton?

Many researchers have found that if they give two problems that are mathematically identical, but with one having big or messy numbers, the success rate can be dramatically different. Do the smaller numbers help you to see the problem more clearly so that you can deduce what operation(s) to use? Some students find that this strategy makes it easier to draw a diagram that helps them figure out what to do.

STRATEGY 3: Use dimensional analysis

Recall this tool, which was introduced in Investigation 1.2 (How Much Will the Patio Cost?). Using dimensional analysis, you cancel the larger units to concentrate on the aspect of the problem you want to solve. In this problem, we have 50 bays. However, we don't want to know the amount in terms of bays, we want to know it in terms of a smaller unit—boxes.

We can multiply 50 bays by 4 pallets per bay. Using dimensional analysis, this looks like

$$50 \, \text{bays} \cdot \frac{4 \, \text{pallets}}{\text{bay}} = 200 \, \text{pallets}$$

That is, if we use pallets as our unit of measurement, we have 200 pallets. Recall the *Changes in Units* discussion on p. 117. Since we do not want the answer in terms of pallets, we continue to change units:

$$200 \, \text{pallets} \cdot \frac{24 \, \text{cartons}}{\text{pallet}} = 4{,}800 \, \text{cartons}$$

Translating to an even smaller unit:

$$4{,}800 \, \text{cartons} \cdot \frac{12 \, \text{boxes}}{\text{carton}} = 57{,}600 \, \text{boxes}$$

The value of the merchandise is

$$57{,}600 \, \text{boxes} \cdot \frac{\$4}{\text{box}} = \$230{,}400$$

A student more confident with using dimensional analysis can do the entire problem in one step:

$$50 \, \text{bays} \cdot \frac{4 \, \text{pallets}}{\text{bay}} \cdot \frac{24 \, \text{cartons}}{\text{pallet}} \cdot \frac{12 \, \text{boxes}}{\text{carton}} \cdot \frac{\$4}{\text{box}} = \$230{,}400$$

I recall being shown this tool in a high school chemistry class, and I have used it in all kinds of school and nonschool problems since then. If this tool is new to you, does dimensional analysis make sense to you now? If it does not, you might want to work on this with a classmate or with your instructor. You might do Exercise 42 at the end of this section to see if you can use this tool on your own.

The Multiplication Algorithm in Base 10

From this section and Explorations 3.4 and 3.6, you now have a better understanding of different models of multiplication and an understanding of the importance of the distributive property. We will now examine the standard multiplication algorithm, which is perhaps the most difficult of the algorithms to understand at the conceptual level. It rests upon an understanding that any multiplication problem can be represented as a rectangle and an understanding of the distributive property. We will examine this algorithm with 56 · 34.

The rectangular model of the product Without base 10, we are left with an imposing problem! Figure 3.20 shows 34 rows of 56 units. The answer is there, but who wants to count them all?

FIGURE **3.20**

However, if we apply our knowledge of base 10, we can find alternatives to counting each single unit.

Using base 10 to model the product One first step is to see what the problem would look like if we represented it using our knowledge of base 10 (see Figure 3.21). That is, we would have 56 (5 tens and 6 ones) 34 times. This makes our job only slightly easier. Who wants to add 56 thirty-four times?

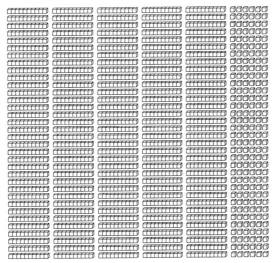

FIGURE **3.21**

Once again, our knowledge of base 10 can make the counting process less tedious.

Using our knowledge that 10 ones make a ten, and that 10 tens make a hundred, we can turn units into longs and longs into flats (see Figure 3.22). Do you see the connection between these processes and the diagram below? Do you see that this diagram is another representation of 56 × 34? Do you see connections between this diagram and how you would compute 56 × 34?

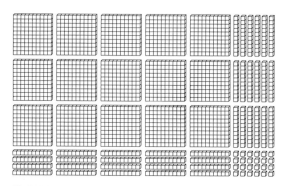

FIGURE **3.22**

Counting the new groups When we represent the problem using the rectangular model of multiplication, we see that the standard algorithm systematically does the regrouping for us. Let us first look at how we can quickly count the amount in each of the four regions in Figure 3.22. Can you use your knowledge of multiplication to do so? Try to do this on your own before reading on. . . .

- The flats region consists of 5 · 3 = 15 flats, which have a value of 1,500.
- The longs region above the units region consists of 6 · 3 = 18 longs, which have a value of 180.
- The longs region to the left of the units region consists of 5 · 4 = 20 longs, which have a value of 200.
- The units region consists of 6 · 4 = 24.

Adding these four regions, we have

$$
\begin{array}{r}
1,500 \\
180 \\
200 \\
\underline{24} \\
1,904
\end{array}
$$

Thus, when we use the algorithm to determine the product 56 · 34, we determine four products (in this case, 6 · 4, 5 · 4, 6 · 3, and 5 · 3), and we know what to do with the products. These products are called **partial products.**

Do you see how the four regions in Figure 3.22, the four sums in the addition problem above, and the four partial products relate to one another?

When we represent the problem in expanded form, we can see how the four partial products connect to the algorithm.

$$
\begin{array}{r}
50 + 6 \\
\times\ 30 + 4 \\
\hline
200 + 24 \\
1500 + 180 \\
\hline
\end{array}
$$

The standard multiplication algorithm Now look at the algorithm in its most concise form. Can you justify each step of this algorithm?

$$
\begin{array}{r}
56 \\
\times\ 34 \\
\hline
224 \\
1680 \\
\hline
1904
\end{array}
$$

When we move up to larger multiplication problems, the manipulatives and visual representations become more cumbersome. However, if the students understand the process, they can apply that understanding to the larger problems. This understanding also lays the foundation for estimation strategies, which we shall explore in Section 3.3. For example, when we represent 324 times 6 in expanded form, we have three partial products. The value of the partial product $3 \cdot 6$ (which represents 300 times 6) is much larger than the value of the other two partial products (120 and 24). Therefore, 300 times 6 (1,800) is a quick and reasonable estimate for this problem.

$$
\begin{array}{r}
324 \\
\times\ \ 6 \\
\hline
\end{array}
\qquad
\begin{array}{r}
300 + 20 + 4 \\
\times \qquad\qquad\ 6 \\
\hline
1,800 + 120 + 24
\end{array}
$$

As with addition and subtraction, we come to understand the algorithm by decomposing the numbers (using expanded form) and looking at how the ideas of base and place value help us to determine the total product. Recall again the statement by Lauren Resnick, "(p)robably the major conceptual achievement of the early school years is the interpretation of numbers in terms of part and whole relationships." When one understands what the operations mean and has the tools (expanded form, place value, and so forth), then one can make full sense of the operations, and that forms the basis for what the NCTM Standards has called "mathematical power."

The Lattice Algorithm for Multiplication

Just as there was a lattice algorithm for addition (see Exercise 5 in Section 3.1), so too is there one for multiplication. See if you can figure out how this algorithm works for $45 \cdot 28$ (see Figure 3.23). Play with it for a while before reading on. . . .

FIGURE **3.23**

Just as the standard algorithm produces four partial products, so too does the lattice algorithm. The partial products 8, 10, 32, and 40 are in the four boxes. The key to the lattice algorithm is to see the diagonals (or chutes) going like this: ∠. If you add the numbers in each chute and regroup to the next chute when you get more than 9, you can get the answer.

Try some other problems using the lattice algorithm: for example, $46 \cdot 32$ or $345 \cdot 68$. Can you explain why it works? What are some of the advantages and disadvantages of this algorithm? These questions will be left as an Exercise. One of my grandmothers told me that this was how she learned multiplication when she was a young girl. Many of my students believe that this algorithm might help children learn multiplication better, serving much like training wheels when children are learning how to ride a bicycle.

Division

Division is probably the least understood of the four basic operations. In workshops with elementary teachers, I have found that while most of them can perform division computations, many of them find word problems requiring division to be baffling. Many of the classic difficulties people have with division—understanding the long division algorithm, knowing how to deal with remainders, and knowing when to divide and when to use other operations—go back to a lack of understanding of what division means. To develop that understanding, I ask you to examine the following division problems and then answer the following questions in your own words.

Contexts for Division

Assume that you are a young child who has not yet learned division. How might you solve these problems, using manipulatives or diagrams, or using common sense and other mathematical knowledge? Note your thoughts before reading on. . . .

Four division problems

1. Applewood Elementary School has just bought 24 Apple computers for its 4 fifth grade classes. How many computers will each classroom get?
2. Jeannie is making popsicles. If she has 24 ounces of juice and each popsicle takes 4 ounces, how many popsicles can she make?
3. Melissa, Vanessa, Corissa, and Valerie bought a bolt of cloth that is 24 yards long. If they share it equally, how many yards of cloth does each person get?
4. Andy has 24 apples with which to make apple pies. If it takes 4 apples per pie, how many pies can he bake?

   Now go back to these four problems and answer the following questions:

■ In what ways are the problems different? In what ways are they similar?

■ What does division mean? For example, what words come to mind when you think of division?

   As with the other operations, some of these problems involve discrete objects (Problems 1 and 4), whereas other problems involve measured (continuous) amounts (Problems 2 and 3).

   Another difference emerges when we solve these problems as young children do. Left to themselves, most children will solve Problems 1 and 3 in a way that is very different from the way they will solve Problems 2 and 4. Do you see why?

Models for Division

Let us solve Problems 1 and 4 simultaneously to understand two different models of division.

To solve the first problem, most children will give one computer to each class, dealing them out one by one: one for our class, one for your class, and so on. Some students use multiplication facts or guess and check and start out bigger: two for our class, two for your class, and so on. They then keep dealing until all the computers have been distributed.

To solve the fourth problem, most children do something very different. They make groups of 4 (each representing one pie) until there are no more apples left.

Visually, we have   Visually, we have

Each classroom gets 6 Apple computers.

This model is called the **partitioning model** because we solve the problem by first setting up the appropriate number of groups (partitions), which we then fill.

We have enough apples to make 6 pies.

This model is called the **repeated subtraction model** because we repeatedly subtract the given amount until we can do so no more. Some books call this the measurement model of division.

Now let us look at how the models are related. First we need some terminology.

Division terminology   In both cases, the problem would be written as

$$24 \div 4 = 6 \text{ or as } 4\overline{)24}^{\,6}$$

The division of the number b by the nonzero number n is formally defined as

$$b \div n = a \text{ iff } a \cdot n = b$$

The number b is called the **dividend**, n is called the **divisor**, and a is called the **quotient**.

Comparing the two division models   With this terminology, we can compare the two models in Table 3.3. What patterns or connections do you notice between the two models? Think and then read on. . . .

TABLE 3.3

	Dividend		**Divisor**	**Quotient**
Partitioning	24 computers	divided into	4 classes yields	6 computers per class
Repeated subtraction	24 apples	divided into	4 apples per pie yields	6 pies

We can also represent both division contexts with the general part-whole box model we have developed for the other three operations. At the most general level, we have

	Dividend	**Divisor**	**Quotient**
Partitioning	Whole	Number of parts (groups)	Number in each part (group)
Repeated subtraction	Whole	Number in each part (group)	Number of parts (groups)

Stop for a moment to reflect on these models. Does this representation connect with the problems we have done here and the problems you did in your explorations? How are these two models of division alike and different?

We can represent the models visually:

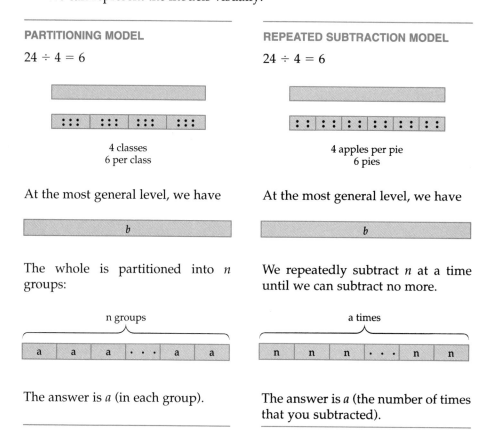

PARTITIONING MODEL

$24 \div 4 = 6$

4 classes
6 per class

At the most general level, we have

b

The whole is partitioned into n groups:

n groups

| a | a | a | $\cdots$ | a | a |

The answer is a (in each group).

REPEATED SUBTRACTION MODEL

$24 \div 4 = 6$

4 apples per pie
6 pies

At the most general level, we have

b

We repeatedly subtract n at a time until we can subtract no more.

a times

| n | n | n | $\cdots$ | n | n |

The answer is a (the number of times that you subtracted).

As with the other operations, we can "see" division in part-whole language: We begin with a whole that is divided into equal parts. There are two different ways in which we can divide the whole: by making partitions of equal size or by repeatedly subtracting parts of equal size. In both cases, we have a whole that we are decomposing in different ways.

The Missing Factor Model of Division

Going back to the formal definition of division, $b \div n = a$ iff $a \cdot n = b$, we can understand another model for division.

Just as some children interpret and solve some subtraction problems by finding the missing addend, some children interpret and solve some division problems by finding the missing factor. For example, consider the two problems we have just analyzed. Some children will solve either or both of these problems by asking themselves: 4 times what is equal to 24?

This model for division, called the missing factor model for division, gives us another tool for working with division, one that we will use often in this and future chapters.

Division and Number Lines

Although the number line is not commonly used to represent division problems, it can be used. What problem is represented in the number line in Figure 3.24? Does the number line fit both models or just one model? Think and then read on. . . .

FIGURE **3.24**

The problem is $15 \div 5 = 3$. The number line fits only the repeated subtraction model. In other words, we cannot use the number line to model a partitioning problem. Why is this?

Properties of Division

Of the properties we have investigated for the other operations, identity, commutativity, associativity, and closure, which do you think hold for division? Think and then read on. . . .

If you have been making connections among the operations, you probably have realized that addition and multiplication are alike in that each operation has an identity and that the commutative and associative properties hold for those operations. You saw that those properties did not hold for subtraction, although subtraction does have a right-identity. Therefore, you might be inclined to say the same for division. Division does have a right-identity; that is, $a \div 1 = a$ for all numbers. The commutative and associative properties do not hold for division. Similarly, the set of natural numbers is not closed under division. Why is this?

Division by Zero

Our definition for division implies that "you can't divide by zero." Can you explain why? Think about this and then read on. . . .

There are several ways in which we can investigate this problem. We can use inductive reasoning: making a table and look for patterns. Do you understand Table 3.4? What pattern do you see that can help you to explain why "you can't divide by zero"?

TABLE 3.4

Computation	Dividend	Divisor	Quotient
$5 \div 1$	5	1	5
$5 \div 0.1$	5	0.1	50
$5 \div 0.01$	5	0.01	500
$5 \div 0.001$	5	0.001	5,000
$5 \div 0.00000001$	5	0.00000001	?

HISTORY

Many people do not realize how recent much of our mathematical notation is. The symbols we use for addition and subtraction, + and − , first appeared in Germany in the late 1400s. Historical records indicate that these symbols were first used to indicate sacks that were surplus or minus in weight. Michael Stiffe was the first person to use + and − as symbols of operation as well as of abbreviation. He did this in the mid-1500s. In 1631, William Oughtred first used the letter x to represent multiplication (as in $3 \times 4 = 12$). Italian merchants introduced the symbol for division (÷) in the 1400s to indicate a half. For example, they wrote $4\div$ to indicate $4\frac{1}{2}$. The equal sign first appeared in the late 1500s in a book by Robert Recorde: "I will setteas I doe often in woorke vse, a pair of paralleles, or . . . lines of one lengthe, thus: =, bicause noe .2. thynges can be moare equalle."[4] It was more than 100 years later that the use of this sign became widespread.

We can also approach the problem of dividing by zero by seeing if either context fits the model. What if we had 24 computers and we wanted to distribute them to zero classrooms? How many computers would each classroom get? That doesn't make much sense. Let's try repeated subtraction. What if we had 24 apples and each pie took zero apples? How many pies could we bake? This doesn't make sense either. From a practical (contextual) level, division by zero just doesn't make sense. Thus, we say that division by zero is undefined.

A third approach to this problem is to assume that it is possible; this is called **indirect proof.** If division by zero were possible, then x divided by zero would be equal to some number k (that is, $x \div 0 = k$). However, if this is true, then according to our definition of division, $k \cdot 0 = x$, but this is not possible because we know that $k \cdot 0 = 0$.

Division Algorithms

At the beginning of each course, I ask my students to write math autobiographies in which I ask them to tell me math-related memories from early childhood though high school, both positive and negative, that stand out. A common sentence in these autobiographies goes something like, "I liked mathematics until long division." To this day, many adults think that understanding why the standard division algorithm works is like understanding the structure of quantum physics — that is, something beyond the ability of "ordinary people." They know what to do, but not why. For example, faced with 252 divided by 4, most people say something like "4 gazinta 25 6 times," but "gazinta" is a mystery. The purpose of Investigations 3.6 and 3.7 is to convince you that "gazinta" is not as esoteric as quantum physics.

INVESTIGATION 3.6   Understanding Division Algorithms

Solve the two division problems as if you didn't know any algorithms; you may use manipulatives or draw diagrams or use reasoning. Then read on. . . .

A. Warren has 252 guests coming to his wedding. Each table holds 4 guests. How many tables will he need?

B. Mickey has 252 marbles that he wants to distribute equally into 4 piles. How many marbles are in each pile?

DISCUSSION

A. If you represent these problems with base 10 blocks, you may have found that they weren't very useful for Problem A because it essentially asks how many groups of 4 there are in 252. Some students solve this problem by using the missing factor model: 4 times what makes 252?

---

[4] H. A. Freebury, *A History of Mathematics* (New York: Macmillan, 1961), p. 89.

Guess	Result	Thinking
50 tables	200 people	Too low, try a bigger number, let's say 60 tables
60 tables	240 people	We need 3 more tables for the 12 remaining people.
63 tables	252 people	

B. The base 10 blocks are more useful for Problem B. Recall the janitor trying to determine how many desks went into each room in Exploration 3.9. In this case, Mickey's problem is to divide (distribute) 252 into four groups equally. Using base 10 manipulatives, he can figure out how to do this most efficiently. Since he cannot give 100 to each person, he has to trade the two hundreds (flats) for 20 longs. He still has 252, but physically, he has 25 longs and 2 units.

Now he can place 6 longs in each group.

He is left with 1 long and 2 units, representing 12; thus he trades the long for ten units. This lets him place 3 ones in each group.

INVESTIGATION **3.7**   **Understanding Long Division at the Symbolic Level**

Since the long division algorithm is intimidating to many people, let us examine another division problem. What is $432 \div 3$? First, try to do this yourself, justifying each step. Then read on. . . .

DISCUSSION
We want to divide 432 into 3 equal groups.

At the physical level, we have

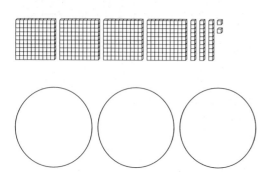

Dividing flats   We can place one flat (hundred) into each group. Then we have to change the remaining hundred into 10 tens. We have 132 left.

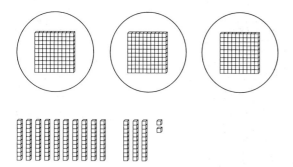

Dividing longs   We can place 4 longs (tens) in each pile. The remaining ten is converted into ones. We have 12 ones left.

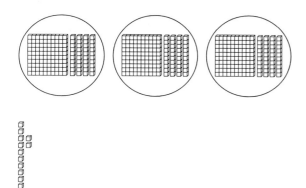

Dividing units   We can place 4 units (ones) into each pile. We are finished.

At the symbolic level, we have

$$3\overline{)432}$$

Dividing in the hundreds column   4 divided by 3 is 1, and 1 times 3 tells us how much has been distributed.

We place the 1, representing 1 hundred, in the hundreds column.

We then subtract 3 from 4 to find out how many hundreds we have left to distribute (1).

Last, we "bring down" the next number (representing 3 tens). We now interpret the "13" as 13 tens.

$$
\begin{array}{r}
1 \\
3\overline{)432} \\
\underline{3} \\
13
\end{array}
$$

Dividing the tens column   13 divided by 4 is 3 and 4 times 3 tells us how much has been distributed.

We place the 4, representing 4 tens, in the tens column.

We subtract the 12 tens from the 13 tens to find out how many tens we have left to distribute (1).

We bring down the 2 ones. We interpret the 12 as 12 ones.

$$
\begin{array}{r}
14 \\
3\overline{)432} \\
\underline{3} \\
13 \\
\underline{12} \\
12
\end{array}
$$

Dividing in the ones column   When we divide 12 ones by 3, we get 4 ones with no remainder.

$$
\begin{array}{r}
144 \\
3\overline{)432} \\
\underline{3} \\
13 \\
\underline{12} \\
12 \\
\underline{12}
\end{array}
$$

Looking back   Having examined long division problems in these two investigations, write your response to the following questions before reading on. . . .

1. What is happening when we say "gazinta"?

2. What is happening when we multiply?

3. What is happening when we subtract after we multiply?

4. What is happening when we bring down the next number?

Let us look at the answers to these questions.

1. When we say "gazinta," we are simply determining the first step in distributing the amount in the dividend into equal groups. For example, in the problem $36\overline{)864}$, when we say that 36 "doesn't go into 8," mathematically, this means that when we divide 864 into 36 equal groups, we do not have enough to have 1 hundred in each group, and therefore we have to look at the next place. When we say that 36 "goes into 86 two times," mathematically this means that when we distribute 86 tens into 36 groups of equal size, we have enough for 2 tens in each group, and thus we place the 2 over the 6, that is, in the tens place.

2. When we multiply, we determine how much has been distributed, or, in other words, how much of our original amount has been used up. In the case of $36\overline{)864}$, we find that we have used up 720.

3. We subtract after we multiply so that we can find out how much of the dividend is left after the first distribution. In this case, we have 14 tens left over. That is, these tens cannot be distributed equally into 36 equal-size groups, and so they have to be traded in for ones.

4. When we bring down the next number, we are determining how much we have to distribute. In this case, we have the 14 tens and the 4 ones that we bring down — that is, a total of 144 — to distribute equally into 36 groups.

As with the three other operations, a deep understanding of this division algorithm requires one to be comfortable with the ideas of base and place value and also to be comfortable with the ways in which a number can be decomposed into various parts.

It is important to emphasize that although our numeration system was invented over one thousand years ago, the division algorithm that you learned in elementary school is only one of many algorithms for division that were invented over this time. The following discussion has you explore an algorithm that was popular in the Middle Ages, and Exploration 3.9 had you explore an alternative algorithm (called the **scaffolding algorithm**) that many people find easier than the standard one.

The Galley Algorithm

A method of long division, popular in Europe in the Middle Ages, is called the galley method and is a modification of an algorithm that traces back to eighth-century India. It was called the galley method because the scratches caused the diagram to resemble a sail, and a galley is a kind of ship. The example below shows how this method would be used to divide 1,750 by 14.

---

[5] Louis Charles Karpinski, *The History of Arithmetic* (New York: Russell & Russel, Inc., 1965), p. 81.

Computation	Explanation
1750 14	The problem begins by dividing 17 by 14.
3 ~1~750 1 ~14~ 14	The quotient of 1 is placed at the right. The difference is placed above the 7. Then the 17 and the 14 are crossed out and the divisor (14) is moved one place to the right, but is written diagonally (probably to save space — paper was very expensive in those days!)
3 ~1~750 12 ~14~ 14	Then 35 is divided by 14, giving a quotient of 2, which is placed to the right of the 1.
3 7 ~1~7~50 12 ~14~ ~14~ 14	The 35 is replaced by the remainder of 7. The 14 is crossed out and moved over 1 place.
~3~ 7 ~17~50 125 ~14~ ~14~ ~14~	Then 70 is divided by 14, giving a quotient of 5.

Can you understand how and why the algorithm works? Connecting this algorithm to the standard long division algorithm will be left as an exercise.

INVESTIGATION **3.8** **Missing Digits**

Determine the three missing digits:

4□□2 ÷ 8□ = 48

How can you apply your understanding of multiplication and division to solve this problem? What problem-solving strategies seem more helpful? Work on this yourself and then read on. . . .

DISCUSSION

One of the key themes in this book is the idea of multiple representations, which is like looking at an object from different perspectives — from above, from below, at ground level, from the side, and so on. Sometimes, one representation sheds more light on a problem than another. If you were stuck, look at the following representation of the problem. Does this help?

$$\frac{4\square\square2}{8\square} = 48$$

If you are still stuck, try using a multiplication representation:

$8\square \cdot 48 = 4\square\square 2$

What does this tell you now about the ones digit of the first number? Think and then read on. . . . 🖉

It must be a 4 or a 9. Do you see why? Test your intuition—which one do you think it is? 🖉

Now you can finish the problem. When you have come up with a solution, don't forget to look back at your work. What did this investigation tell you about operations? How did your problem-solving toolbox—looking for patterns, working backwards, multiple representations, and so on—grow as a result of doing this problem?

INVESTIGATION 3.9 Connecting Algorithms to Contexts and Models

Consider the four computations below, which illustrate the standard algorithms.

$$
\begin{array}{cccc}
\overset{1}{463} & \overset{6\ \ 9}{\cancel{7}\ \cancel{0}\ ^{13}} & \begin{array}{r}46 \\ \times 87 \\ \hline 322 \\ 368 \\ \hline 4002\end{array} & \begin{array}{r}875 \\ 3\overline{)2625} \\ 24 \\ \hline 22 \\ 21 \\ \hline 15 \\ 15\end{array} \\
+\ 854 & -4\ 7\ 6 & & \\
\hline
1317 & 2\ 2\ 7 & &
\end{array}
$$

How does each algorithm relate to a context or model for an operation? Write your ideas and then read on. . . . 🖉

DISCUSSION

The standard addition algorithm connects nicely to both joining and increasing contexts. The standard subtraction algorithm, however, is an enactment (acting out) of the take-away context. The standard multiplication algorithm represents the area model. The standard division algorithm connects to both the partitioning and repeated subtraction models; in this text, we have demonstrated the connection to the partitioning model.

Algorithms and the Hindu-Arabic Numeration System

We have just examined connections between algorithms and specific operations. Let us look at another important connection—between algorithms and our numeration system. These algorithms could not be used with Roman or Egyptian numerals. Do you see why? How does each of these algorithms use base 10 concepts? In each of the algorithms, we encounter rules that tell us where to place the number in question, whether it be a regrouped amount in addition and subtraction, a partial product in multiplication, or a number in the quotient in division. Each of these algorithms represents the culmination of years of efforts on the part of people to find more and more effective ways to combine the brilliance of the Hindu-Arabic numeration system with the essential concepts of the four operations. As noted before, these are not the only algorithms for the operations (and not everyone agrees that they are the easiest to learn or use). Rather, they are the ones that are most commonly used in the United States at the current time.

Operation Sense

Now that we have examined each of the four operations, let us explore some problems in which we can apply our knowledge. Someone who knows which operation to perform in a problem is said to have good operation sense, a term that represents an important skill but is hard to define. Operation sense is more than just knowing what operation to use in what situation. If we want mathematics problems to model real-life problems, then, as you have seen in this book, many problems will not be routine, one-step problems. In the context of solving more complex problems, students with good operation sense have the following "knowledge":

- They can see the relationships among the operations—for example, multiplication is the inverse of division.

- They can apply their understanding of the properties of the operations—for example, they can use the distributive property.

- The diagrams that they draw connect the problem to the models of the operations.

- They have a sense of the effects of each operation—for example, when dividing, the larger the divisor the smaller the quotient.

One of the goals of Investigation 3.10 and Explorations 3.11 and 3.12 is for you to come to appreciate the need for operation sense and to develop this ability. That is, the successful completion of these problems requires you to see and use various connections between these four operations.

INVESTIGATION 3.10 Applying Models to a Real-Life Situation

A teacher is going to do a project with the two fifth grade classes in the school. One class has 21 students, and the other has 15 students. She has decided that all of these students will be divided into 12 groups and that each group will need 72 inches of string. She has a roll of string that is 882 inches long. Does she have enough string, or will she need to buy more? Do this problem yourself without using a calculator before reading on. . . .

DISCUSSION

You can use either multiplication or division to solve this problem. Using multiplication, $72 \cdot 12 = 864$ tells you that you will have enough string for each group, with 18 inches of string to spare. If you use division, the problem can be interpreted either as a partitioning problem or as a repeated subtraction problem. Do you see why?

- If you divide 882 inches by 72 inches per group, this says that you are seeing the problem in terms of repeated subtraction. What does your answer of 12 with a remainder of 18 tell you?

- If you divide 882 inches by 12 groups, this says that you are seeing the problem in terms of partitioning. What does your answer of 73 with a remainder of 6 tell you?

In the repeated subtraction model, the 12 says that if you repeatedly cut 72 inches, you can do this 12 times, and you will have 18 inches of string left over. In the partitioning model, the 73 says that if each group is to have an equal amount of string, you have enough string to make 12 pieces that are each 73 inches long and you will have 6 inches left over. In either case, you have to understand what your quotient means, and you have to think about what the remainder means.

There are two other aspects of this problem that are worthy of emphasis.

First, although the mathematical answer is that the teacher has enough string, the teacher might actually conclude from her computations that she needs more string. Why is this?

What if the students make mistakes? Since $72 \cdot 12 = 864$, the teacher has only 18 inches of string in reserve. Thus, although the mathematical answer is that the teacher has enough string, the real-life answer would depend on the nature of the project. For example, if the students were to cut the pieces into specified lengths and I was confident that some groups would mismeasure the lengths, I would not feel confident that I had enough string.

Second, compare this question to the following problem: A teacher is going to have her students do a project in which each group of students will need 72 inches of string. If the teacher has 882 inches of string, how many groups can she have in her class?

This problem is a one-step, routine problem, the kind the NCTM says should be deemphasized. The student simply has to decide whether to add, subtract, multiply, or divide; if the student just guesses, there is a 25 percent chance of being right. This is what many students do. Larry Sowder[6] examined children's strategies for solving word problems and reported these kinds of strategies: "Look at the numbers; they will tell you which operation to use. Try all the operations and choose the most reasonable answer. Look for key words or phrases to tell which operation to use."

Furthermore, the actual problem has been sanitized so that the student simply has to use the numbers given. In the first version of the problem, the number of students in each class (21 and 15) is *irrelevant to the question being asked.* These numbers were given not to try to trick you, but because in real-life settings, we generally have lots of information. The first part of the problem is to decide if we have enough information to solve the problem and to decide what information is relevant to the question we are asking.

Order of Operations

Complex computations that use more than one operation pose a potential problem. To see what I mean, do this problem with pencil and paper and then on your calculator: $3 \cdot 4 - 8 \div 2$. What did you come up with? Stop, think, and then read on. . . .

Unless you have a very inexpensive or antique calculator, you will get 8. However, if you do each operation in the order in which it appears in the problem, you will get 2. Why did the calculator give a different answer?

The fact that we can get two different answers from the same problem has led to rules called the order of operations. These rules tell you the order in which to perform operations so that each expression can have only one value. Most calculators are programmed to obey the order of operations.

What did the calculator actually do to get 8? Write the process in words and see if a friend can see how to get 8. Then read on. . . .

[6] Larry Sowder, "Children's Solutions of Story Problems," *Journal of Mathematical Behavior,* 7 (1988), pp. 227–228.

In the absence of parentheses, multiply 3 times 4 to get 12, then divide 8 by 2 to get 4. Now subtract 4 from 12 to get 8. You may remember order of operations from school as "Please Excuse My Dear Aunt Sally," which is a mnemonic to remind you of the order in which a computation is done: start inside the *p*arentheses, then do *m*ultiplication and *d*ivision as they occur from left to right, and finally do *a*ddition and *s*ubtraction as they occur from left to right. (The *e* from "Excuse" refers to exponents, which we will discuss in Chapter 5.)

If we insert parentheses so that more people would understand this problem, it would read as: $(3 \cdot 4) - (8 \div 2)$. How many different answers can you get depending on different placements of parentheses?

Operations and Functions

Each of the operations in this chapter is a function because for each input (an ordered pair of two numbers), there is one and only one output. For example, the input (6, 2) produces a sum of 8, a difference of 4, a product of 12, and a quotient of 3. Although awareness of this connection between operations and functions does not necessarily make you a stronger problem solver, it is important in addressing the realization that mathematics is much more like a road map or a connected network than like a set of unrelated formulas and procedures, an image many adults have of mathematics.

Summary

There are actually two parts to this section, first our examination of multiplication and division, and then our examination of the connections among all four operations.

We have found that multiplication can be represented as repeated addition, as the area enclosed by the multiplier and the multiplicand, or as the number of combinations (Cartesian product). Similarly, division problems can be seen as partitioning, repeated subtraction, or as a missing factor. Being able to interpret and represent a problem goes a long way toward being able to solve problems.

Visual models help us to see connections between multiplication and division. In one sense, multiplication consists of adding two or more equal-size parts to make a whole. Similarly, division can be seen in one way as decomposing a whole into parts that are all the same size.

You have learned that there are certain properties that hold for multiplication of whole numbers but not for division: commutativity, associativity, and closure. Just as we have the zero property of addition, we have the identity property of multiplication. Thus, the numbers 0 and 1 hold a certain importance, and they also have a rich history, as you will find in Chapter 4. We also learned of a property that connects operations: the distributive property. This property is a key to understanding how the multiplication algorithm works.

We have seen that the multiplication and division algorithms we currently use in the United States are not the only possible procedures for computing. Your ability not only to compute with these algorithms but also to be able to explain why they work is a crucial part of developing mathematical power.

We have also examined the various connections among the four operations, including order of operations, and applied our understanding of those connections so that our operation sense becomes more powerful.

A key goal of this section is for you to better understand how these four operations are related to one another. What similarities do you see among the operations? What connections do you see among them? Take a few minutes to draw a diagram that shows the relationships among the four operations. Then read on. . . .

Addition and subtraction are inverse operations. Multiplication and division are inverse operations.

One model of multiplication is repeated addition, and one model of division is repeated subtraction. We have a missing addend model for subtraction, and we have a missing factor model for division.

The operations of addition and multiplication are closed under the set of whole numbers; subtraction and division are not. The commutative and associative properties hold for addition and multiplication, but not for subtraction and division. We have identity properties for addition and multiplication; because subtraction and division are not commutative, we have only right-identities for these operations. We can speak of the distributive property of multiplication over addition and of the distributive property of multiplication over subtraction.

With addition and subtraction, the units in each part are always identical; for example, 3 *sheep* plus 5 *sheep* equals 8 *sheep*. However, with multiplication and division, the units are different; for example, 3 *miles per hour* times 4 *hours* yields a product of 12 *miles*.

In many addition and multiplication situations, we are joining or combining parts to make a whole. In many subtraction and division situations, we are taking a whole apart.

These statements represent a verbal description of the operations' similarities and connections. One of many visual representations of the similarities and connections is shown in Figure 3.25.

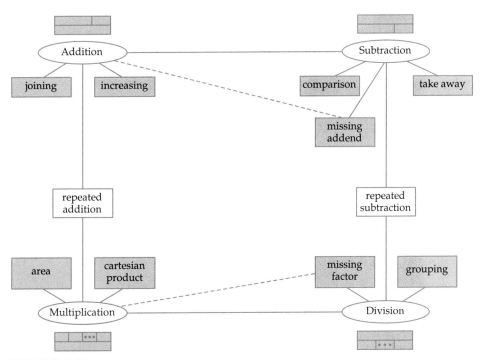

FIGURE **3.25**

We have seen that the standard algorithms are related to some of the operations' contexts and models. These algorithms rely on our base 10 system. Again, it is important to reemphasize that these standard algorithms are not the only ones, nor necessarily the best ones. You have also seen other algorithms, some of which are currently used in other parts of the world.

A statement from the beginning of the chapter is worth repeating: Understanding these four operations is central to knowing mathematics. Many of my students have been amazed to find that a solid understanding of these operations enabled them to solve multistep and nonroutine problems that initially seemed very imposing and complex. In Chapter 5, when we examine three extensions of the number line—integers, fractions, and decimals—you will find that you will have to modify your understanding of these operations to accommodate the problems that arise with those kinds of numbers.

EXERCISES 3.2

1. Make up story problems and diagrams to illustrate $5 \cdot 3$ in the four different contexts described in this section.

2. Write a realistic story to represent each problem below.
   a. $12 \cdot 4$ **b.** $35 \cdot 3$ **c.** $5 \cdot (3 + 7)$

3. $V = \{a, e, i, o\}$ and $E = \{a, b, c, d, e\}$.
   a. Name one element of $V \times E$.
   b. Name one element of $E \times V$.
   c. How many elements are in $V \times E$?

4. $A = \{p, l, a, y\}$ and $B = \{b, a, l\}$.
   a. How many elements are in $A \times B$?
   b. Is $(p, a) \in A \times B$?

5. If $A = \{1, 2, 3\}$ and $B = \{a, b\}$, find $A \times B$.

6. If $A \times B = \{(6, x), (6, y), (6, z), (7, x), (7, y), (7, z)\}$, find A and B.

7. There are 12 elements in $E \times F$. Four of them are $(1, 6)$, $(3, 2)$, $(4, 2)$ and $(5, 5)$. List the rest.

8. Do you think we could speak of a distributive property of addition over multiplication? How would you determine whether it held or not?

9. For each of the following questions, refer to the base 10 multiplication table.
   a. The top-left-to-lower-right diagonal divides the table into three sets: diagonal, upper part, and lower part. What do you notice about the upper part and the lower part? What property is illustrated here?
   b. Look at the top-right-to-lower-left diagonal. Describe the patterns you see. Justify the patterns.
   c. The products of the diagonals of any 2 by 2 matrix are equal. Explain why.
   d. In any row, the sum of the xth number and the yth number is equal to the $(x + y)$th number. Suppose someone did not understand this terminology. Express this pattern in another way. Explain why the pattern occurs.
   e. Look at the 9s column in the multiplication table. The sum of the digits is always 9. Can you explain why?
   f. Look at the 9s column in the multiplication table. As we go down the column, the ones digit decreases by 1 each time and the tens digit increases by 1 each time. Can you explain why?

10. Let's say you forgot what $9 \cdot 7$ is. How would you figure out the product, using other multiplication facts?

There are many, many different ways! Explain why your alternative is equal to $9 \cdot 7$.

11. Fingers are a set of manipulatives that most people have, and they can be used to help students remember their multiplication facts for nine. This is how the method works. Suppose you want to know $9 \cdot 7$. Bend down finger number seven. The number of fingers to the left of the bent finger gives you the value of the tens place of the product, and the number of fingers to the right of the bent finger gives you the value of the ones place of the product. Why does this work?

12. Before the Russian Revolution in 1917, most of the people in Russian villages did not use base 10 but still used the Roman system. The Egyptian method of multiplication had somehow become transformed into a different process, known today as the Russian peasant algorithm. It works by simultaneously doubling one of the numbers and halving the other. Fractions are simply disregarded; for example, half of 19 is $9\frac{1}{2}$—drop the $\frac{1}{2}$. We find the product by first looking in the "Halve" column. Whenever you see an odd number in that column, circle that row. To find the answer, add the circled numbers in the "Double" column. The example below shows how it works.

Problem: $25 \cdot 19$.

Double		Halve
25	·	19
50	·	9
100	·	4
200	·	2
400	·	1

Circling the appropriate numbers, we add:

25
50
400
―――
475

Solve the following problems using the Russian peasant algorithm.
a. $25 \cdot 17$ **b.** $48 \cdot 39$ **c.** $120 \cdot 42$
d. Explain why this algorithm works.

13. Another ancient method of multiplication is shown below with the problem 102 · 96.

    Find the average: 99

    Take half the difference of the numbers: 3

    Look up the square of 99: 9,801

    Look up the square of 3: 9

    Subtract and you have your answer: 9,792

    a. Use this method to determine the product of 36 and 54.

    b. Explain why it works.

14. Draw a diagram to represent 34 · 28. Explain how to obtain the product from the diagram.

15. Look at this multiplication problem, solved using the standard algorithm:

    ```
         42
       ×36
        252
        126
       1512
    ```

    a. In this problem, we multiply 2 · 6 and carry the 1. What is it that we are carrying? What is the mathematical meaning of this carrying?

    b. Before we do the second set of multiplications (that is, 3 · 2 and then 3 · 4), we move over. Why do we move over instead of just putting the product (126) directly below the previous product (256)?

16. When we multiply larger numbers, we are used to moving over one column each time we move through the process. Why do we move over?

    ```
          645
        ×324
         2580
         1290
         1935
       208980
    ```

17. a. Write directions for multiplying 46 · 37 using the lattice algorithm.

    b. Explain why this method works.

    c. What mathematics do you have to know in order to be able to use this method?

    d. Discuss some advantages and disadvantages of this algorithm.

18. Below is the start of the solution of a multiplication problem using a new algorithm. Explain the meaning of the numbers 20, 15, 8, and 6. Then finish the problem, showing and explaining your work. *Note:* You need to explain *why* the four numbers are placed where they are and then explain *why* the algorithm works. You may, but are not required to, use a diagram in your explanation.

    ```
         4    3
       ×2    5
        20   15
        8    6
    ```

19. Identify and explain the errors in the problems below, all of which have occurred in real classrooms.

a.	b.	c.	d.
46	46	46	46
×28	×28	×28	×28
404	3248	368	92
101	812	92	368
1414	4060	460	3772

20. Place the digits 0, 1, 3, 5, 7 in the boxes below to obtain

    a. The greatest product   b. The least product

21. Place the numbers 2, 3, 5 and 7 in the boxes at the bottom to make the largest product at the top. The figure at the left shows one possibility that has been started.

22. Let's say you have an inexpensive calculator that has only an eight-digit or nine-digit display, and thus you cannot get the answers to these computations directly from your calculator. Determine the products by a means other than doing them out longhand, assuming that you have only these resources: your knowledge of multiplication and base 10 and a calculator with an eight- or nine-digit display. Justify your method; that is, why will it give you the desired product?

    a. 999,999,999 · 56

    b. 987,654,321 · 9

    c. 11,111,111,111 · 45

    d. 34,000 · 56,000

23. Select any two-digit number and multiply it by 99. Repeat this process for two or more two-digit numbers. Look for patterns that would enable you to compute the product of any two-digit number and 99 in your head.

    a. Describe how you can determine the product of any two-digit number and 99.

    b. Describe how you can determine the product of any two-digit number and 999.

24. Take your house number or room number and double it, add 5, multiply by 50, add your age, and subtract 250. What do you get? Can you explain why this trick works?

25. Four children want to share 168 jelly beans. How many does each get? Which model of division is operative here? Model the problem with a diagram.

26. a. Make up a division story problem for the partitioning model. Make a diagram and explain why this problem is an example of the partitioning model.

    b. Make up a division story problem for the repeated subtraction model. Make a diagram and explain why this problem is an example of the repeated subtraction model.

27. For each number line problem below, identify the computation it models and briefly justify your answer.

a.   b.

28. Represent the following problems on a number line. Explain each problem as if you were talking to someone who was not taking this class.

   a. 6 · 3   b. 12 ÷ 3

29. You are teaching fifth grade and you are "reviewing" division. Let's say that Lionel has a hard time with division and uses the scaffolding method, but he forgot to write the answer. What is the answer? Explain Lionel's method.

```
            7
           10
           60
          100
          400
     12)6924
          4800

          2124
          1200

           924
           720

           204
           120

            84
            84

             0
```

30. Identify and explain the errors in the problems below, all of which have occurred in real classrooms.

   a.
   ```
         54
      7)3528
        35

        28
        28
   ```
   b.
   ```
        540
      7)3528
        35

        28
        28
   ```
   c.
   ```
        79 R26
      8)658
        56

        98
        72
   ```

31. Place the digits 2, 4, 7, and 9 in the boxes below to obtain:

   a. The greatest quotient   b. The least quotient

   □)□□□

32. If you divide a number that is larger than 75 by a number that is less than 3, what can you tell about the relative value of the quotient? Explain your choice.

   a. It must be greater than 25.

   b. It must be less than 25.

   c. It will be between 3 and 75.

   d. There is not enough information to conclude any of the above.

33. When 96 is divided by x, a quotient of $y \neq 1$ and a remainder of 5 results. Find x and y.

34. a. How many buses are needed if each bus can take 25 passengers and there are 334 students?

   b. How many buses are needed if we also place two adults on each bus?

35. Wei is having a party. She is expecting 120 people and wants enough juice so that each person can have two glasses. If the juice comes in 32-ounce containers, how many cans of juice should she buy? If each can costs 89 cents, how much will it cost?

36. Telephone directories are now available on CD-ROMs, which can hold an enormous amount of information. Let's say that there was a master directory that contained the names and addresses of 250 million people, roughly the population of the United States. If we were to print the names and addresses of all these people on paper, how many pages would that require? First, you will need to determine how many names will fit on one page.

37. Joe had planned to sell 10 pencils at 20¢ each. However, his little brother broke two of the pencils. If he wants to make the same amount of money, how much should he charge for the pencils now?

38. Orange soda comes in six-packs that are packed four to a carton. To make sure that each of the 247 students in the sixth grade will have a soda for the class picnic, how many cartons should we order? How could you figure this out mentally?

39. Janice has decided to buy a computer for her son. So far, she has $450 in the bank. The computer costs $1,234. If she can afford $15 per week, when will she have the money?

40. Melanie recorded a tape of her guitar playing. It cost her $1,200 to record the master tape, and it costs $2.50 to make each copy. If she sells the tapes for $10 each, how many tapes must she sell to break even?

41. Your elementary school is having a fund-raiser. The school has a deal with a company from which it buys wrapping paper at the following rate: 100 rolls for $150. The school plans to sell the paper in packs of 4 for $9. How many rolls should the school buy to make a profit of $500?

42. A factory can make 250 gizmos every hour. If the factory operates 24 hours per day, how many gizmos can they make in one year?

43. This problem is over two thousand years old! A dog is chasing a rabbit that has a 150-foot head start. If the dog runs 9 feet for every 7 feet jumped by the rabbit, in how many leaps will the dog catch up with the rabbit?

44. Mathematics abounds in children's literature. Consider this age-old children's rhyme:

   As I was going to St. Ives

   I met a man with seven wives.

   Every wife had seven sacks;

   Every sack had seven cats;

Every cat had seven kits.

Kits, cats, sacks, and wives:

How many were going to St. Ives?

45. Examine the following pattern of letters:

yabbadabbadoo yabbadabbadoo yabbadabbadoo yabbadabbadoo

If this pattern keeps repeating, what letter will be in the 275th position?

46. **a.** How many cubes would it take to make a staircase like the one on the left if the last stair was 99 cubes high?

   b. How many cubes would it take to make a staircase like the one on the right if the last stair was 99 cubes high?

47. A 5 by 5 grid has 16 squares on the border.

   a. How many squares will be on the border of a 10 by 10 grid?

   b. How many squares will be on the border of an n by n grid?

48. Using a calculator, Ralph multiplied by 10 when he should have divided by 10. The display read 300. What should the correct answer be?

49. Determine the numbers in the empty boxes

   a.

a	b	$a + b$	$a \cdot b$
65		131	
234		1,000	
	72		86976

   b.

a	b	$a + b$	$a \div b$
153			17
		20	19

   c.

a	b	$a - b$	$a \cdot b$
		20	1,056

   d.

a	b	$a \cdot b$	$a \div b$
		20	5
	37		925

50. Find the missing digits below

   a. $74 \cdot 8\square = 6,\square\square4$

   b. $\square\square4 \cdot 64\square = 489,346$

   c. $18 \cdot (\square\square4 + 29\square) = 10,116$

   d. $(\square3) \cdot (\square) \cdot (\square7) = 1,547$

   e. $1,530 = \square\square \cdot 48 + 42$

51. In the following puzzle, each letter has a value between 0 and 9. Find the value of each symbol so that the following computations are all accurate.

$$
\begin{array}{cc}
A \\
+A \\
\hline
B
\end{array}
\quad
\begin{array}{cc}
C \\
+C \\
\hline
DE
\end{array}
\quad
\begin{array}{cc}
B \\
-E \\
\hline
B
\end{array}
\quad
\begin{array}{cc}
F \\
\times D \\
\hline
F
\end{array}
\quad
\begin{array}{cc}
A \\
\times A \\
\hline
G
\end{array}
\quad
\begin{array}{cc}
B \\
\times F \\
\hline
HF
\end{array}
$$

$$
\begin{array}{cc}
C \\
\times A \\
\hline
DC
\end{array}
\qquad
H\overline{)DB}^{\;J}
\qquad
A\overline{)HD}^{\;K}
$$

52. For each of the following, determine possible whole numbers a, b, and c for which the statement is true.

   a. $(a \div b) \div c = a \div (b \div c)$

   b. $a(b - c) = ab - ac$

   c. $(a - b) - c = a - (b - c)$

53. Find the 5-digit number that has the following pattern: If you put a 1 after it, the number is three times as large as it would be if you had put a 1 before it.

54. The square on the left is a multiplication magic square. How is a multiplication magic square similar to and different from an addition magic square? Can you make another multiplication magic square?

14	39	6	74
111	4	26	21
26	21	111	4
6	74	14	39

55. Place the numbers 1 through 9 in the boxes below so that all three equations work. You cannot use any number twice.

   $\square + \square = \square$

   $\square - \square = \square$

   $\square \div \square = \square$

56. You are Zirkle, from Zordon, and you have just finished your trip to the solar system. Your planet has managed to develop interplanetary travel without ever developing a sophisticated number system. You have examined three different bases; in the United States, these bases would be called base 5, base 10, and base 12. You are now preparing your recommendations for your home planet. Summarize the pros and cons of each base, and then tell which base you recommend your planet adopt.

Note: Your species has no fingers, only paws.

57. For your most important learning with respect to one of the four operations, describe what it was that you learned and why this is the most important learning.

For example, "I never realized that multiplication can be represented as a rectangle. This has helped me to understand the multiplication algorithm better. For example, 14×5 can be seen as 1 ten and 4 ones 5 times."

S E C T I O N   ◆ **3.3** ◆   **MENTAL ARITHMETIC AND ESTIMATION**

WHAT DO YOU THINK?

■ With the prevalence of calculators, why is mental computation still important?

■ Why might people use rounded numbers rather than exact numbers?

■ What numbers on the front page of today's newspaper are really estimates?

The availability of inexpensive calculators has profoundly changed the way we compute. Most people now rely on calculators when exact answers are needed. However, estimating skills are still very important in cases where an exact answer is not needed and to check the reasonableness of results obtained on the calculator. Estimation, in turn, requires good mental arithmetic skills, which come from an understanding of the nature of the operations, a firm understanding of place value, and the ability to use various properties (for example, the associative and distributive properties).

▲ The NCTM Standards not only emphasize the need for students to understand how to estimate but reinforce the importance of students being more actively involved in the construction of knowledge, as opposed to simply receiving procedures from teachers. Thus, the Standards note that students need to "develop, analyze, and explain procedures for computation and techniques for estimation" (*Curriculum Standards*, p. 94).

Estimation

When are numbers estimates and not exact numbers?   Before we examine some methods of estimation, we need to understand when numbers represent estimates and when they represent exact numbers. All of the following numbers are estimates. What ways can you see to group them according to why they are estimates? For example, the age of a dinosaur bone is an estimate because present dating methods do not allow us to get an exact number; in other words, the exact age is unknown.

■ A certain dinosaur bone is 65 million years old.

■ The population of the United States is 270,000,000.

■ The number of hungry children in the United States is 12 million.

■ The area of the Sahara Desert is 3,320,000 square miles.

■ The mean July temperature in Tucson, Arizona, is 86 degrees.

■ Jane lives 55 miles from the nearest airport.

■ My office is 12 feet by 9 feet.

Numbers are estimates when:

1. The exact value is unknown—for example, predictions and numbers that are too large or difficult to determine.

2. The value is not constant—for example, population and barometric air pressure.

3. There are limitations in measurement—for example, the length of a desk and the area of a pond.

Note that these are not the only instances when a number is actually an estimate, but rather three common categories. The purpose here is not to memorize categories, but to realize that many numbers we see around us are actually estimates.

Rounding Just as many numbers in everyday life are estimates rather than exact numbers, many numbers are rounded. For example:

- It took Jackie 10 hours to get from Boston to Buffalo.
- Anna gets 34 miles per gallon with her new car.
- Rosie put 2,100 miles on her car last month.
- Fred paid $12,000 for his new car.
- The population of Sacramento, California, is 370,000.

The preceding examples bring another question to mind: Why do we round? Stop for a minute to think of your own response. Then read on. . . .

Below are two of many possible reasons:

1. Rounding makes comprehension easier. Which of the following sentences would you prefer to read in a newspaper? Why?

   The school budget for the 34,168 students was $153,167,458.

   The school budget for the 34,000 students was $153 million.

2. Rounding makes computation easier. Let's say you were trying to determine the cost of buying new textbooks for your fifth grade class. There are 23 students, and the textbooks cost $19.75. If you wanted to get a sense of the cost, you would probably round 19.75 to 20 and multiply 23 by 20.

When do we use estimation and when do we do we use exact computation?
Before you read this section, close the book and write down your thoughts about this question. Then read on. . . .

Following are several examples of when people generally estimate:

- Making a budget—cost of college, cost of food per month
- Determining the cost of a trip or vacation—ski trip, camping trip, trip to Europe
- Deciding which to buy—whether to buy a new car or a used car
- Determining time—how long to get to . . .
- Determining if we have enough money—being at the grocery store when short on cash
- Deciding how much the tip should be (at a restaurant)
- Determining how long the paper or project will take

Estimation methods As you will find in this chapter, we do not estimate in the same way in all situations. The method(s) we use to estimate depend partly on how close the estimate has to be and on whether we deliberately want to over- or underestimate (for example, underestimating when budgeting can cause serious problems). Finally, people usually prefer certain methods to other methods. In many cases, different methods will produce estimates that are nearly identical, and in other cases, certain methods are easier than other methods.

Before we develop our estimation toolbox, we will first develop our ability to compute exact answers mentally. This may surprise you, but the development of mental math skills will result in your coming to a deeper understanding of the four operations and will, in turn, make your estimation tools stronger.

LEARNING

Every year in my middle school mathematics methods course, my students develop a series of questions about a topic, and then they go into the schools and ask actual students these questions in order to learn more about what the students know and don't know. Every year my students make up estimation problems, and every year my students are quite stunned to find that many of the middle school students have few or no estimation and mental math strategies in their repertoire. This is all the more amazing since we find that in their everyday lives, people require estimates more often than exact answers.

Mental Arithmetic

Occasionally, I will note some ways in which the philosophy of this book and that of traditional instruction differ. In a more traditional setting, this book (and your teacher) would "teach" you the "best" mental arithmetic strategies, probably by demonstration, and then have you practice those strategies. A more progressive approach would be to "teach" you the "best" strategies but have you actively involved in understanding and making sense of each strategy. If you have done Exploration 3.15, you have experienced a teaching approach consistent with a philosophy called constructivism. That is, rather than receive the teacher's best strategies, you construct your own strategies by connecting knowledge and information you already know and by explaining your ideas and listening to others. This section enables you to examine strategies that you might have heard but only partially understand or strategies that did not come up in your class or group. If you have not done the explorations—or even if you have!—I encourage you to read this section actively.

Mental Addition Strategies

Do the following ten computations in your head. Briefly note the strategies you used, and try to give names to them.

Note: One mental tool all students have is being able to visualize the standard algorithm in their heads. For example, for the first problem, you could say: "9 + 7 = 16, carry the one, then 5 + 3 = 8 + the carried 1 makes 9; the answer is 96." However, since you already know that method, I ask you not to use it here, but to try others. There are actually quicker ways to do this problem in your head than using the traditional algorithm. See if you can discover any of them.

1.	39 +57	2.	38 +46	3.	68 +35	4.	66 +19	5.	686 +140
6.	545 +228	7.	186 +125	8.	4,265 +436	9.	245 +138	10.	580 +423

The right answer to each of these sums isn't really what's at issue. Rather, the hope is that you will use these strategies as a jumping-off point for understanding mental addition more clearly. Now that you have done the computations on your own, let us examine several strategies. How are they different from, or similar to, the strategies you used?

Leading digit One strategy that works nicely with most addition problems is **leading-digit.** Some people refer to it as **front-end** since we add the "front" of the numbers first. For example, we can look at Problem 1 as 80 + 16 = 96; that is, we add the numbers in the tens column (3 + 5), add the numbers in the one's column (9 + 7), and then add 80 + 16 to get 96.

This strategy can be used with larger numbers. For example, try this strategy with Problem 6 and then read on. . . . 🖎

700 + 60 + 13, or 773

The leading-digit method is new to most students, and some find it awkward at first. However, in the long run, it is generally faster than doing the algorithm in your head. For example, doing Problem 6 in your head using the standard algorithm looks like this: 5 + 8 = 13, carry the one; 4 + 2 + the carried 1 is seven, so that's 73; 5 + 2 = 7, so it's 773.

Try some of the other problems using the leading-digit method. Make up problems for additional practice (with a partner if possible). It is important that you become familiar with this strategy because it is commonly used in estimating.

Compensation Another powerful mental math strategy is called compensation. Look at Problem 1 to see how this strategy works. Instead of trying to add 39 + 57, we could have added 40 + 56. Do you see how we transform 39 + 57 into 40 + 56?

By adding 1 to the first number and subtracting 1 from the second number, we have created a new problem that is much easier to solve mentally. Why is this? Mathematically, we used the following transformation:

$$39 + 57 = (40 - 1) + 57 = 40 + (57 - 1) = 40 + 56$$

Which other problems lend themselves to this strategy?

Break and bridge We can use the break and bridge strategy in Problem 3. To add 68 + 35, break 35 into 30 + 5 and do the following:

$$(68 + 30) + 5 = 98 + 5 = 103$$

Which other problems lend themselves to this strategy?

Compatible numbers Another powerful strategy is creating compatible numbers. This often involves seeing pairs of digits whose sum is 10. Just as children quickly learn the pairs of digits whose sum makes a long (for example, 1 and 9, 2 and 8), most people can sense which combinations of numbers will make multiples of 100. Thus, in Problem 7, 186 + 125, we can see that the 180 and the 120 combine to make 300, and then we have 11 (6 + 5) more.

Do you see how place value and base 10 are used in this strategy? If you can see Problem 7 as 18 tens and 12 tens, then you have 30 tens, that is 300. Look at Problems 3 and 10. What ways can you see to get multiples of 10 and 100 in those problems?

The compatible numbers strategy is especially useful when adding several numbers mentally. Try it with the following problem and then read on: 16 + 35 + 28 + 15.

We can obtain the exact sum by adding the 35 and 15 together and the 28 and 16 together. Next, we add the results:

$$50 + 44 = 94$$

Choosing a strategy Which strategy you use is often a matter of preference. For example, Problem 3 (68 + 35) may be done mentally in at least four different ways, each of which is the "best" way for some students. While in general no one way is inherently superior to another, it is better to be proficient at several methods than at just one.

Leading digit:	$68 + 35 = 60 + 30 + 8 + 5$
Compensation:	$68 + 35 = 70 + 33$
Break and bridge:	$68 + 35 = 68 + 30 + 5$
Compatible numbers:	$68 + 35 = 65 + 35 + 3$

Justifying strategies How do these strategies use base 10, expanded form, and the commutative and associative properties? Think and then read on. . . .

Let's look at the compatible numbers strategy for Problem 3 in detail:

The action	Justification
68 + 35 = (65 + 3) + 35	Substitution
= 65 + (3 + 35)	Associative
= 65 + (35 + 3)	Commutative
= (65 + 35) + 3	Associative
= 100 + 3	Addition
= 103	Addition

Estimation Strategies for Addition

Explorations 3.16 and 3.17 challenged you to apply your understanding of base 10 and your mental math abilities to determine estimates in two settings outside the classroom. Here we will analyze some estimation problems to better understand the application of base 10 concepts and mental math strategies.

INVESTIGATION **3.11**   **What Was the Total Attendance?**

In each of the following estimation problems, first obtain a rough estimate (5–10 seconds), then obtain the best estimate you can and then read on. Use mental arithmetic strategies in your estimates.

A. Approximately what was the total attendance for the following three football games at Foxborough Stadium?   75,145   34,135   55,124

DISCUSSION

Remember that one of the main goals of the investigations is for you to develop a repertoire of strategies. Check your estimates against the ones obtained below with different strategies. Do you find you like certain strategies better than others? Are there any that you find you have a hard time understanding? In this situation, there are several estimation strategies that work well:

Leading digit: 7 + 3 + 5 = 15; that is, 150,000
The leading-digit method will always give you an estimate that is lower than the actual sum. Why is this?

Refined leading digit: 150,000 + (5 + 4 + 5 = 14—that is, 14,000)
= 150,000 + 14,000 = 164,000

Rounding: 80,000 + 30,000 + 60,000 = 170,000

Compatible numbers: 75 + 35 + 55 = 110 + 55 = 165, which represents 165,000

B. Approximately what was the total attendance for three baseball games at Wrigley Field in Chicago? Make your own rough estimate and then a refined estimate before reading on. . . .

32,425   31,456   34,234

DISCUSSION

Are you getting quicker at estimating? Are you finding that you are applying the mental addition techniques? Each of the four methods above could have been used here. You may well have come up with another strategy called **clustering,** since all three numbers are relatively close together. In this case, a very quick, rough estimate would be

$$30,000 \times 3 = 90,000$$

What strategy or combination of strategies would yield an estimate that was closer to the exact attendance? If we use, for example, a refined leading-digit strategy, we can get 90,000 + 7,000, and looking at the 425, 456, and 234, we can see that this is about 1,000. Thus, a more refined estimate is about 98,000.

Looking back In this investigation, how close were your rough estimates to your best estimates? Can you make up a situation in which someone would need only a rough estimate? How about a situation in which someone would want an estimate that was more refined?

There are two points to keep in mind when estimating and doing mental mathematics:

1. The method you use is often partially determined by the problem itself. If you want only a rough estimate, you might use leading-digit or rounding. If you want a more refined estimate, you might use compatible numbers. If you want to make sure you have enough money, you might round everything up so that the estimated sum is definitely greater than the actual sum.

2. It is not so much a matter of there being right or wrong ways to estimate or better or poorer methods. There is a certain amount of latitude for preferences, just as some tennis players will like a certain type of racket and others will like another type of racket. However, if you have a large repertoire of estimating and mental math techniques in your toolbox, you will be more skillful.

A Refined Technique for Rounding

Most textbooks offer the following guidelines for rounding:

> If the appropriate digit is less than 5, round down. Otherwise round up.

For example, if we estimate 35 + 57, we round to 40 + 60 = 100. There is a problem with this method, though. Suppose we want to estimate the sum of the following numbers:

Problem	Traditional rounding
35	40
42	40
76	80
45	50
35	40
85	90

If we have a problem in which many of the numbers end in a 5, this method will give an estimate that is too high.

A more refined set of guidelines for rounding makes the following modification:

If the digit to the left of the 5 is odd, round up.

If the digit to the left of the 5 is even, round down.

When we encounter problems with columns of addition, it is likely that the number of evens and odds will be close, thus canceling each other out. Let us see how this affects the estimate with the preceding problem:

Problem	Standard rounding	Refined rounding
35	40	40
42	40	40
76	80	80
45	50	40
35	40	40
85	90	80
318	340	320

If we use this refined method, our estimate will generally be closer to the actual amount. Why won't it always be closer?

INVESTIGATION 3.12 Estimating by Making Compatible Numbers

Using compatible numbers is an effective strategy to estimate the following sums. Try this on your own and then check below. . . .

A. 38
    72
    89
    65
    27

B. 23
    359
    177
    675
    162
    315

DISCUSSION

A. In this case, a quick glance shows us that 38 and 65 will make a sum close to 100, and so will 72 + 27. If we see this, our estimate of 200 + 89 = 289 is quite close to the actual answer of 291.

```
      38
      72
100 <  89
      65  > 100
      27
```

B. Using compatible numbers, we can estimate 200 + 500 + 1,000 = 1,700.

```
        23
200 <   359
        177  > 500
        675
        162  > 1,000
        315
```

INVESTIGATION 3.13 How Much Money Did Sandy Spend?

Sandy wrote checks for the following amounts. Approximately how much did she just spend?

$173	Credit card
$97	Electricity
$63	Gas credit card
$212	Insurance
$4	Parking ticket
$36	Phone

A. As before, first make a very quick, rough estimate.

B. See how close you can get to the exact answer, but without using pencil-and-paper or a calculator.

DISCUSSION

A. To find a rough estimate, we could use the leading-digit method; this would give us 3 hundreds, but then we would have to remember the 3 hundreds while adding the tens. A quicker way to make a rough estimate is to use compatible numbers: 173 + 212 make about 400; 97 and 4 make another 100, and then 63 + 36 make another 100. Our rough estimate is $600.

B. There are many ways to obtain a more accurate estimate. One way might begin by rounding:

$$170 + 100 + 60 + 210 + 40$$

Then we could add these rounded numbers to obtain an estimate of $580.

Again, it is not a matter of which strategies are better or right, but of having a sense of how accurate an estimate we need and then being able to employ a strategy that can get us close to the actual answer.

What would be a scenario in which Sandy would be satisfied with a rough estimate? What would be a scenario in which Sandy would want her estimate to be "pretty" close to the actual amount?

Looking back Before we move on to subtraction, take a few moments to look back over the strategies for mental addition and estimation that we have explored. Do you find that you prefer some over others? Do you see that some strategies work better with some numbers than with others? Try to create scenarios for which some estimation strategies would be more appropriate than others. Identify those places in which these strategies use properties of addition or important base 10 structures.

Mental Subtraction Strategies

Not surprisingly, fewer people estimate confidently when subtracting than when adding. In fact, one of the ways that I assess how well a student understands the various models for subtraction and the relationship between addition and subtraction is by seeing the extent to which a student can develop a repertoire of mental strategies for subtraction.

Do the following computations in your head. Briefly note the strategies you used, and try to give names to them.

Note: One mental tool all students have is being able to visualize the standard algorithm in their heads. For example, for the first problem, you could say: "cross out the 6, and now subtract 15 − 8 = 7 and then 5 − 2 = 3; the answer is 37." However, since you already know that method, I ask you not to use it here, but to try others.

1. $\quad 65$	**2.** $\quad 62$	**3.** $\quad 184$	**4.** $\quad 132$	**5.** $1,000$
$\underline{-28}$	$\underline{-29}$	$\underline{-125}$	$\underline{-36}$	$\underline{-648}$

As with addition, there are a variety of subtraction strategies. As you read the discussion below, reflect on the strategies. Do they make sense to you? If not, ask yourself why. Is it because you don't understand how the strategy works? Is it because you don't feel your mental subtraction skills are strong enough to use it? Again, it's not so much a matter of right or better strategies as it is of having a repertoire. Almost all of the strategies work better with certain kinds of numbers than with others.

In Problem 1, one alternative is to **add up**—that is, to ask how we get from 28 to 65. One student's actual thinking could look like this: "28 + 40 = 68, that's 3 too much, so 40 − 3 = 37."

Another alternative for Problem 1 is to find the nearest ten and add up: "28 + 2 = 30, then we need 35 more to get to 65. 35 + 2 = 37."

Some students understand this problem better with a **number line**, as in Figure 3.26. In one sense, we are going from 28 to 30 to 65.

FIGURE **3.26**

In Problem 2, compensate: Add 1 to both numbers. This transforms the difficult 62 − 29 to the relatively simple 63 − 30. This strategy is related to the algorithm for subtraction that my New Zealand friend used in Investigation 3.3. Do you see how?

Some students better understand the compensation strategy by using a number line (see Figure 3.27). On a number line, 62 − 29 can be interpreted as how far apart the two numbers are. In other words, how long is the road from 29 to 62? If we move the beginning and the ending of the road one unit, we haven't changed the length of the road.

Thus 62 − 29 and 63 − 30 have the same difference.

FIGURE **3.27**

In Problem 3, add up: 125 + **60** = 185, then take off **1**. The answer is 60 − 1 = 59.

In Problem 4, try the compensation strategy: 132 − 36 is close to 136 − 36 = **100**, but we must take away **4** to get 96. In other words, we added 4 to 132, but then had to remember to take it off again.

Problem 4 can also be solved by using compatible numbers: 36 + **64** = 100, and then **32** more to get to 132, so the answer is 64 + 32 = 96.

In Problem 5, use compatible numbers: 48 and 52 are compatible numbers; that is, their sum is 100. Therefore, 648 + **52** makes 700. Then we add **300** to get to 1,000. The answer is 352.

Problem 5 can also be solved by adding up: 648 + **300** = 948. We need **52** more. The difference is 300 + 52 = 352.

Do you understand all of the strategies discussed here? Try to make a problem in which one strategy would be more appropriate than another. Most students find that they retain these strategies if they make up some problems on their own and practice.

INVESTIGATION 3.14 Mental Subtraction in Various Contexts

Do these two problems on your own before reading on. . . .

A. Mental math with money: How much change do you get if you give a $10 bill when the cashier tells you $4.76? How would you do this problem mentally? Try it and then read on. . . .

B. Mental math with non-base 10 numbers: You left home at 3:25 and got to the meeting at 6:15. How long did it take you to get to the meeting? Try it and then read on. . . .

DISCUSSION

A. Before we had electronic cash registers, cashiers had to determine the change, and most could do it mentally. What strategy does the following language imply: "4.76, 4.80, 5 dollars, 10 dollars"? The cashier is adapting the add-up strategy: 4 pennies, 2 dimes, and 5 dollars makes $5.24.

B. Even when using non-base 10 numbers, adding up is an effective strategy: 3:25 + 35 minutes makes 4 o'clock, 2 more hours gets you to 6 o'clock, and then 15 more minutes. In other words you are adding 2 hours + 35 minutes + 15 minutes = 2 hours + 50 minutes.

Once again a number line is instructive (see Figure 3.28).

FIGURE **3.28**

Alternatively, you might reason that 3:25 to 6:25 is 3 hours and you need to "back off" 10 minutes, that is, the answer is 2 hours and 50 minutes.

INVESTIGATION 3.15 Rough and Best Estimates with Subtraction

Now let us apply these skills to problems where we are likely to estimate with subtraction. Remembering that one of the main goals of the investigations is to develop a repertoire of strategies, check your estimates against the ones discussed below. In each of the problems below, first obtain a rough estimate (5 to 10 seconds), then obtain the best estimate you can. Do you find that you like certain strategies better than others? Are there any that you find you have a hard time understanding?

A. In 1995, Acstead State College had an enrollment of 4,234, whereas Milburn College had an enrollment of 3,475. How many more students did Acstead have than Milburn?

4,234
−3,475

B. The attendance at the Yankees game was 73,468, whereas the attendance at the Mets game was 46,743. How much greater was the attendance at the Yankees game?

$$73,468$$
$$-46,743$$

DISCUSSION

A. You can get a quick estimate by rounding: $4,200 - 3,500 = 700$

To get a more accurate estimate, you could use adding up:

$3,475 + \mathbf{800} = 4,275$, then back off **40** to get 4,235. The estimate is $800 - 40 = 760$.

Do these strategies make sense to you? Did you do something different? How would you describe a scenario in which someone would be satisfied with a rough estimate? How would you describe a scenario in which someone would want the estimate to be pretty close to the actual amount?

B. Leading digit: $7 - 4 = 3$, giving an estimate of about 30,000.

Rounding: $70,000 - 50,000 = 20,000$.

Rounding and adding up: $47,000 + 3,000$ makes 50,000. Adding up to 73,000 gives 23,000. Our estimate is $3,000 + 23,000 = 26,000$.

Looking back   Before we move on to multiplication, take a few moments to look back over the strategies for mental subtraction and estimation that we have explored. Do you find that you prefer some over others? Can you connect these strategies to different models or contexts of subtraction—for example, take-away, comparison, missing addend, number line? Can you explain which strategies make powerful use of structures of our base 10 numeration system—for example, the leading-digit strategy? Do you see that some strategies work with some numbers better than with others? Can you create scenarios for which some estimation strategies would be more appropriate than others?

Mental Multiplication

Many of my students are surprised to find that with some thought and practice, they can do many more multiplication problems mentally than they would have thought possible. Doing so successfully generally requires us to apply the various properties of multiplication, often creatively!

Do the following computations in your head. Briefly note the strategies you used, and try to give names to them.

1.	2.	3.	4.	5.	6.
64	16	35	849	60	65
× 5	×25	×12	× 2	×30	×24

As you read these strategies, once again monitor your own thinking. Do you understand how the strategies work? If not, do you simply need to reread the discussion, or would it be helpful to make up and do some similar problems, or would it be more helpful to practice with a friend?

In Problem 1, use **multiples of 10** as a reference point:

$$64 \times 5 = \tfrac{1}{2} \text{ of } 64 \times 10 = \tfrac{1}{2} \text{ of } 640 = 320$$

In Problem 2, the **halve and double** method gives

$$16 \times 25 = 8 \times 50 = 400$$

Do you see the use of the commutative and associative properties here?

For Problem 3, try the distributive property: 35×12 can be seen as twelve 35s, which can be broken apart to ten 35s + two 35s, or

$$(10 \times 35) + (2 \times 35) = 350 + 70 = 420$$

In Problem 4, try compatible numbers in conjunction with the distributive property:

$$849 \times 2 = (850 - 1) \times 2 = 1{,}700 - 2 = 1{,}698$$

For Problem 5, use multiples of 10:

$$60 \times 30 = 6 \times 3 \times 10 \times 10 = 18 \times 100$$

What people often think in this case is "18 with two zeros," or 1,800.

In Problem 6, try using **expanded notation** and then determining the four **partial products:**

```
     65              60  +  5
    ×24              20  +  4
    ___             _____
                    240 +  20
            1,200 + 100
```

Adding the four partial products, starting from left to right, one might say: 1,200 + 100 is 1,300, then add 240 to get 1,540, then add 20 to get 1,560.

Since looking back or reflecting is such an important learning tool, and since so few students bring that tool into this course, I am risking overemphasizing it. Now that you have examined various mental multiplication strategies, do you see advantages and limitations of the various strategies? Do you understand the names given to the strategies, or can you come up with names that you like better?

INVESTIGATION 3.16 Developing Estimation Strategies for Multiplication

In each of the problems below, first obtain a rough estimate, then obtain the best estimate you can before reading on. Can you describe a scenario in which the rough estimate would be appropriate? Can you describe a scenario in which a more refined estimate would be appropriate?

A. Chip rode 78 miles last week. At this rate, how many miles will he ride this year?

DISCUSSION

STRATEGY 1: Find a *lower* and *upper bound* for the answer

Since we want to estimate the product of 78 and 52, if we round both numbers down to the nearest 10, we have $70 \times 50 = 3{,}500$. Similarly, if we round both numbers up to the nearest 10, we have $80 \times 60 = 4{,}800$. The actual product of 78 and 52 lies between these two numbers. The estimate from rounding down is called a **lower bound,** and the estimate from rounding up is called an **upper bound.** Using this technique, we can quickly say that Chip will ride between 3,500 and 4,800 miles this year.

STRATEGY 2: Round one number up and round the other number down
Thus 78×52 becomes $80 \times 50 = 4{,}000$.

STRATEGY 3: Use expanded form and estimate the sum of the four partial products

$$
\begin{array}{r}
70 + 8 \\
50 + 2 \\
\hline
140 + 16 \\
3{,}500 + 400
\end{array}
$$

One thought process might go like this: "$70 \times 50 = 3{,}500$, 50×8 is 400, and 70×2 is more than 100. So the answer will be $3{,}500$ plus more than 500, let's say $4{,}050$."

Determine the actual answer. How close were the different estimates?

> **B.** Jane plans to start graduate school in September. She figures that she can save \$345 per month for the next 9 months. How much will she have saved? Work on this and then read on. . . .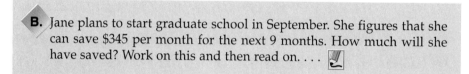

DISCUSSION
Use the distributive property:

$$345 \times 9 = (345 \times 10) - (345 \times 1) = 3{,}450 - 345 \approx 3{,}100$$

> **C.** There were 47,752 Americans killed or missing in Vietnam. The number of Americans killed or missing in World War II was about 6 times that number. Approximately how many Americans were killed or missing in World War II? Work on this and then read on. . . .
>
> $$
> \begin{array}{r}
> 47{,}752 \\
> \times \quad 6 \\
> \hline
> \end{array}
> $$

DISCUSSION
We can get a rough estimate using rounding:

$$50{,}000 \times 6 = 300{,}000$$

We can get a more refined estimate by rounding and using mental math (double and halve):

$$48 \times 6 = 96 \times 3 = 288, \text{ or } 288{,}000$$

Looking back Before we move on to division, take a few moments to look back over the strategies for mental multiplication and estimation that we have explored. Do you find that you prefer some over others? Can you identify those places in which these strategies use properties of multiplication (for example, the distributive property)? Can you see which strategies make use of the multiplication algorithm (for example, partial products)? Can you see which strategies make use of base 10 structures (for example, expanded notation)? Do you see that some strategies work with some numbers better than with others? Can you create scenarios for which some estimation strategies would be more appropriate than others?

Mental Division Strategies

Mental division is new territory for almost all of my students. Even the division idea of canceling zeros is one that many students feel apprehensive about before this course. Therefore, examine each of the problems below carefully. How might you determine the exact answer, applying what you know about division? Briefly note the strategies you used, and try to give names to them.

1. $20\overline{)6000}$ 2. $400\overline{)20,000}$ 3. $8\overline{)152}$ 4. $5\overline{)345}$

In Problem 1, we will examine two different ways to use canceling.

One method of canceling transforms the problem from 6,000/20 to 60 · 100/20, which can then be simplified to 3 · 100 or 60 · 5, since 20 divides both 60 and 100 without remainder.

$$\frac{6,000}{20} \rightarrow \frac{60 \cdot 100}{20} \begin{array}{c} \nearrow 3 \cdot 100 \\ \searrow 60 \cdot 5 \end{array}$$

Another way to cancel in Problem 1 is to transform it from 6,000/20 to 600/2, which is equal to 300.

In this case, we are actually applying the idea of equivalent fractions, which we will examine in Chapter 5. That is, we are dividing both numerator and denominator by the same amount, 10.

Can you use either of these strategies to solve Problem 2? If so, which?

Problem 3 lends itself to compatible numbers; for example, 160 ÷ 8 = 20. We can use the distributive property to get an exact answer, since

$$\frac{152}{8} = \frac{160 - 8}{8} = 20 - 1 = 19$$

We can use compatible numbers in Problem 4: 350 ÷ 5 = 70.
We can also use the distributive property in Problem 4:

$$\frac{345}{5} = \frac{350 - 5}{5} = 70 - 1 = 69$$

In Problem 4, we can also use the idea of equivalent fractions, and multiply both numerator and denominator by 2. The resulting fraction 690/10 easily simplifies to 69.

INVESTIGATION 3.17 Estimates with Division

Now let us apply these mental division skills to problems in which we are likely to use division to estimate. In each of the problems below, obtain an estimate before reading on. . . .

Do you find that you like certain strategies better than others? Are there any that you have a hard time understanding? Can you describe a scenario in which a rough estimate would be adequate? A scenario in which a more refined estimate would be more appropriate?

A. Mr. & Mrs. Smith pay $9,100 a year for their son's college. Translate this into a monthly payment that they can put into their budget.

DISCUSSION

Using the **missing factor model**, ask yourself, "12 times what is closest to 91?" $12 \times 7 = 84$, $12 \times 8 = 96$. Since 91 is just about in the middle (of 84 and 96), it is reasonable to conclude that $12 \times 7\frac{1}{2}$ will be close to 91, and so our estimate is $7\frac{1}{2}$ hundred a month, or, more conventionally, $750 per month.

> **B.** Pierre just bought a new van, and he wants to see what kind of mileage he gets. He filled up with gas after going 489 miles, and the car took 19 gallons of gas. Estimate the mileage.

DISCUSSION

One strategy is to round both the divisor and the dividend up.

$\frac{489}{19}$ will be close to $\frac{500}{20}$, and this is equivalent to $\frac{50}{2}$, and so he is getting about 25 mpg.

This strategy is interesting because it is not identical to the one used in multiplication, where we get more accurate estimates if we round one number up and the other down. In the case of division, we obtain more accurate estimates if we round both numbers up or both numbers down to manageable numbers. Can you explain why? Work on this for a while and then read on. . . .

Hint: It will be helpful to make up some problems and check this out. For example, try 3,750 ÷ 13. Decrease both: to 3,600 and 12, which are compatible numbers. Increase both: to 3,900 and 13. Then decrease one and increase the other—for example, 3,750 to 4,000 and 13 to 10. Compare the results. Make up some other problems. Can you use ideas developed thus far to help you?

> **C.** A large business ran 5,432 copies in the last 7 business days. How many copies is it averaging per day?

DISCUSSION

A rough estimate could be gotten by making compatible numbers, increasing both, and solving the problem. For example, 5,600 ÷ 7 gives an estimate of 800.

A more refined strategy would be to use multiplication:

$$7 \times 700 = 4,900$$
$$7 \times 800 = 5,600$$

Since 5,432 is closer to 5,600 than it is to 4,900, a rough estimate would be just under 800.

Do any of these strategies reflect the work you did in Exploration 3.17 with the risograph machine?

> **D.** Employees put 25¢ in a can for each cup of coffee they drink. Last week the can contained $29.50. How many cups of coffee were drunk?

DISCUSSION

STRATEGY 1: Solve the problem in dollars
That is, 25¢ per cup means 4 cups per dollar.

You can estimate 30×4 cups per dollar $= 120$ cups.

Using this strategy, you could actually use mental math and get the exact answer in two ways:

$$29.50 \times 4 = (29 \times 4) + \left(\frac{1}{2} \times 4\right) = 116 + 2 = 118$$

or

$$29.50 \times 4 = (30 \times 4) - \left(\frac{1}{2} \times 4\right) = 120 - 2 = 118$$

STRATEGY 2: Solve the problem in cents

That is, $29.50 is about $30, which is equivalent to 3,000¢.

$$\frac{3,000}{25} = \frac{2,500 + 500}{25} = 100 + 20 = 120$$

Looking back   Take a few moments to look back over the strategies for mental division and estimation that we have explored. Have you added to your repertoire? Do you understand how the distributive property and expanded notation are applied? Do you see that some strategies work with some numbers better than with others? Can you connect these strategies to different models or contexts of division—for example, missing factor or repeated subtraction?

Summary

Take a few moments to look back upon this section and your notes. In this section and its *Explorations*, we have applied many of the ideas that were developed in the previous three sections, that is, base 10 and place value from Chapter 2, Section 3 and the concepts and procedures for adding, subtracting, multiplying, and dividing from the first two sections of this chapter. In one sense, your ability to do mental arithmetic and estimation depends on how well you understand the ideas of numeration and of the four operations. Many of the mental arithmetic and estimation strategies make use of place value and of expanded form. Many of these strategies are directly connected to certain models and properties of the operations: for example, subtraction can be interpreted as the distance between two numbers. We frequently used properties of the operations, especially the distributive property. Many of the strategies in this section apply aspects of the algorithms in Sections 3.1 and 3.2—partial sums and partial products, for example.

As stated throughout this chapter, it is crucial to recognize numbers as compositions of parts and be able to decompose numbers according to the needs of the problem. When we examine fractions in Chapter 5, this composition and decomposition will be essential if you are to understand what fractions mean and to be able to understand the connection between procedures for computing with whole numbers and with fractions.

In this section and its *Explorations*, we explored more real-life problems than we have elsewhere. To see why, look at the front page of any newspaper and examine the numbers in each of the stories. Which numbers are exact numbers and which are not? Which of the nonexact numbers are estimates and which are rounded? How can you tell? Why do you think the writer or editor chose to estimate or round?

This last question is another way of assessing the extent to which the ideas of this section are owned as opposed to rented: If someone asked you why we need to learn mental math and estimation when a calculator is generally nearby, what would you say?

EXERCISES 3.3

Note: In all of the exercises, briefly explain your reasoning.

1. Determine the following sums mentally. Briefly describe how you obtained the sum.

   a. 47
      +55

   b. 69
      +77

   c. 88
      +77

   d. 56
      +19

   e. 577
      +126

   f. 735
      +248

   g. 269
      + 87

   h. 75
      36
      187
      65

   i. 24
      53
      387

   j. 583
      +423

2. Estimate the following sums. Briefly describe how you obtained your estimate.

   a. 473
      345
      +355

   b. 6,963
      3,286
      +7,147

   c. 88,865
      32,565
      +23,784

   d. 536,455
      94,352
      +659,346

   e. 473
      345
      134
      565
      943
      +355

   f. 69,655
      32,438
      90,432
      24,684
      79,833
      +71,347

   g. 234,345,343
      325,345,689
      587,247,678
      56,345,865
      +234,764,874

3. From each of the following lists, select 3 numbers whose sum will be closest to the target sum. Briefly explain your reasoning--how did you determine those three numbers?

	Numbers			Target
a. 37	83	56	74	150
b. 73	32	94	53	200
c. 24	39	47	97	170
d. 115	175	164	153	400
e. 185	372	153	274	650
f. 352	423	439	583	1,200

4. Determine the following differences mentally. Briefly describe how you obtained your estimate.

   a. 87
      −29

   b. 70
      −23

   c. 82
      −34

   d. 500
      −134

   e. 502
      −206

   f. 473
      −258

   g. 625
      −475

   h. 808
      −707

   i. 506
      − 29

   j. 4,000
      − 555

5. Estimate the following differences. Briefly describe how you obtained the difference.

   a. 4,473
      −2,355

   b. 65,963
      −29,147

   c. 73,463
      −28,543

   d. 43,433
      −16,328

   e. 413,082
      −285,876

   f. 320,283
      −184,438

   g. 3,133,543
      −1,903,253

   h. 71,234,033
      −32,753,962

6. From each of the following lists, select 2 numbers whose difference will be closest to the target difference.

	Numbers		Target
a. 315	475	764	300
b. 185	372	953	650
c. 382	723	793	350

7. Determine the products mentally.

   a. 16
      ×16

   b. 16
      ×25

   c. 66
      × 5

   d. 849
      × 2

   e. 60
      ×30

   f. 450
      × 20

   g. 35
      ×12

   h. 65
      ×42

   i. 736
      × 4

   j. 35
      ×16

   k. 632
      × 4

8. Estimate as closely as you can.

   a. 41×68 b. 56×74 c. 62×83

   d. 57×38 e. $34,345 \times 48$ f. 417×23

9. By estimating, determine which of the following is wrong. Explain your reasoning.

   a. $3,312 \times 13 = 43,056$

   b. $23 \times 874 = 30,102$

   c. $563 \times 86 = 48,418$

10. Which two numbers will have a product closest to 2,000?

    43   34   65   83   111

11. Which of the following might represent the cube of 156?

    a. 3,796,416   c. 3,944,312

    b. 4,251,528   d. 3,581,577

12. Determine the quotients mentally.

    a. $\dfrac{6,000}{20}$ b. $\dfrac{4,800}{60}$ c. $\dfrac{10,000}{200}$

    d. $\dfrac{9,000}{30}$ e. $\dfrac{3,600}{90}$ f. $\dfrac{20,000}{400}$

13. Estimate as closely as you can.

    a. $8\overline{)5,432}$ b. $7\overline{)29,123}$ c. $20\overline{)342,354}$

14. By estimating, determine which of the following is wrong.

    a. $75,296 \div 16 = 4,706$

    b. $34,272 \div 48 = 714$

    c. $38,844 \div 498 = 780$

15. In each of the following, use the information from the computed problem to mentally compute the other problems.

    a.
       587
       ×345
       2935
       23480
       176100
       202,515

       $587 \times 40 = ?$
       $587 \times 45 = ?$
       $587 \times 305 = ?$
       $87 \times 45 = ?$
       $870 \times 45 = ?$
       $587 \times 300 = ?$

b.

$$
\begin{array}{r}
742 \\
36\overline{)26{,}712} \\
25{,}200 \\
\hline
1{,}510 \\
1{,}440 \\
\hline
72 \\
72 \\
\hline
\end{array}
$$

$36 \times 400 = ?$

$742 \times 36 = ?$

$25{,}200 \div 360 = ?$

$742 \times 30 = ?$

$26{,}712 - 1{,}510 = ?$

In Exercises 16–22, determine the answer mentally.

16. Peter bought a house for $116,000 and sold it for $145,000. How much profit did he make?

17. I left my house at 3:34 P.M. and arrived at 6:15 P.M. How long did it take me?

18. Washington College has 4,132 full-time students, whereas Lincoln College has 2,824 students. How much larger is Washington than Lincoln?

19. A concert hall has 36 seats in a row, and there are 25 rows. How many people can be seated?

20. A fund-raiser has a goal of $55,000. So far, $34,854 has been collected. How much more is needed?

21. A camping show rents booth space for $1.50 per square foot. How much would it cost to rent a 10-foot by 15-foot space?

22. I went shopping for socks. Assuming that the two brands were of comparable quality, which is the better deal: 9 pairs for $6.99 or 4 pairs for $3.49?

In Exercises 23–42, do each of the following. First, determine a rough estimate in 5 to 10 seconds. Then determine your best estimate. "Best estimate" means no pencil and paper and less than 30 seconds or so. Otherwise, we defeat the purpose of estimating! Then determine the exact answer.

23. Several years ago, the flat roof over my kitchen was leaking. My friend at the hardware store told me of a new product that would fix my roof. Each can of roof sealant would cover 100 square feet and cost $26. My roof was 23 feet 8 inches long and 15 feet 6 inches wide. How many cans of roof sealant did I need to buy?

24. Mindy rode her bike 3 times last week. At the beginning of the week, the odometer read 302.4, and at the end of the week it read 315.2. At this rate, how many miles will she ride this year?

25. Mr. and Mrs. Smith will pay $8,400 this year for their daughter's college tuition. Approximately how much is this per month?

26. Jackie Adams bought a piece of property for $28,543 and sold it for $73,463. Approximately how much profit did she make?

27. a. It is 450 miles to home. How long will it take at 55 mph?

    b. It is 450 miles to home. How long will it take at 65 mph?

28. A traveling saleswoman is adding up her miles this week. How many miles did she travel?

    165
    78
    57
    345
    142

29. Sandy wants to get an idea of the cost of lumber for a project. She has determined that she needs a total of about 450 feet of boards, and the cost is 23¢ per foot. Approximately, how much will they cost?

30. Two college students are riding across the United States on bicycles. They are averaging 112 miles per day.

    a. If it is 2,987 miles from San Francisco to New York, will they complete the trip in one month?

    b. Approximately how far would they travel in 30 days if they average 167 miles per day?

31. In driving to Peterborough, it took me 27 minutes to go 18 miles. What was my average speed?

32. When someone turns 21, how many days old is that person?

33. A soft drink manufacturer produces 3,240 cans in an 8-hour day. Cans are packaged 24 to a case. How many cases are produced each week? each month?

34. We bought a new van in June 1990. In December 1991, we had logged 18,345 miles. Our plan was to keep the van until 100,000 miles. At the rate at which we were putting miles on the van, approximately when would the van hit 100,000 miles?

35. Julie is working out on a computerized ski machine. She will exercise for 30 minutes, and her goal is to burn 400 calories. She starts at 12:07, the machine says that she has burned 148 calories. At this rate, will she reach her goal?

36. It takes the average person 6 seconds to read this sentence. In that time, 24 people will be born on the Earth. At this rate, how many people are born each year? How long will it take to equal the number of people in your state?

37. A student lives in Hanover, which is 62 miles from her school. How many miles per semester does she travel if she drives to school twice a week? How much does she spend for gas? Assume a 15-week semester.

38. A fund-raiser has a goal of raising $55,000 in one month. After five days, the amount raised is $9,345. Are they on track?

39. The Alvarez family has decided that camping will be more fun if they buy the following items. Approximately how much will the family spend?

Lantern	$35.95
New stove	$59.99
Four new air mattresses at	$14.95 each

A screen house to put over
the picnic table $57.50

A new set of camping pots
and pans $24.95

40. If a dripping faucet wastes water at the rate of 75 ounces per day, how many gallons would this be per year?

41. Take your pulse for 15 seconds. Based on this measurement, how many times would you say it beat since you got up this morning? This week? Since you were born?

42. Given the increasingly fast advances in technology, it is not far-fetched to think that someday, every person in the United States could have an Internet account. Imagine that 250 million Americans each had an Internet account and that an Internet directory was available. If we printed that directory, how many pages would it contain?

43. How many people are listed in the phone book in the town or city in which your college or university is located? First, describe and justify your plan for answering this question.

44. Determine which number goes where: 7 90 20

   An adult dolphin is about ___ feet long and has ____ teeth. Dolphins live to about ___ years.

45. A student of a teacher with whom I was working made up the following problem.

   Determine which number goes where: 30 48 1961 20 20,000

   The Berlin wall was set up in ____. The wall was approximately ___ miles long or ____ kilometers long. More than ____ people fled before the wall was erected. The wall was about ____ feet tall.

46. Make up your own problem similar to the one above.

47. In 1993, a newspaper reported that nearly 3,000,000 crimes occur each year in U.S. schools. What do you think was meant by crimes? Do you believe this figure? Do you think it is too small? too big? Why?

48. A newspaper story said that 7 percent of all Americans eat at McDonald's each day. Is this true or another case of journalistic exaggeration? Write your report. One fact: There are approximately 9,000 McDonald's restaurants.

49. How many Cheerios are in a box? First, define the problem better. Devise a strategy to estimate the number, then devise another strategy. Are your results close? Which strategy do you think is more accurate?

50. What base 10 concepts and/or properties are we making use of when we employ the leading-digit method of estimation?

51. An article in the January 1995 issue of *Teaching Children Mathematics* (p. 269) reported the following statistic: Every 57 minutes an under-age drinker is involved in a traffic fatality.

   a. Estimate the number in one year.

   b. What additional information would you like to have to clarify the question?

52. Find an article from a newspaper or magazine that demands from the reader knowledge of numeration, basic operations, or estimation. Describe the mathematical knowledge you used in analyzing the article.

53. Develop a question for which you will need to gather data. For example, how much water do you use when taking a shower? How much time do you spend studying? What percent of the students on your campus smoke?

   a. Write down the question.

   b. Write down the numbers that you will need to find or estimate in order to answer the question.

   c. Write down any assumptions you are making in order to determine the estimate.

   d. Find or estimate the numbers, do the computations, and give the answer to your question. Show your work.

54. A computer company has 3,765 copies of a hot selling program and wants to ship the same number to each of its 18 distributors. Approximately how many programs does each distributor get? Francie estimated this way: She rounded 3,765 to 4,000 and 18 to 20, and then divided 4,000 by 20 in her head; her estimate was 200. However, Nadine says that this way of estimating isn't good because, if you are going to round, you should round one number up and one number down. Nadine rounded 18 up to 20 and 3,765 down to 3,600, and so her estimate is $3,600 \div 20 = 180$. Francie responds that although the latter method works for multiplication (round one number up and one number down), it doesn't work for division. With whom do you agree? Why?

CHAPTER SUMMARY

1. Many students have said that really understanding base 10 and the four operations was the beginning of a new attitude toward mathematics. We will continue to examine new and important mathematical ideas throughout this book, but the foundation for much of elementary mathematics has now been laid.

2. Each operation has multiple meanings.

3. Many algorithms have been developed to enable us to compute more efficiently.

4. The standard algorithm for each operation does not connect equally well to each meaning of the operation.

5. Being able to make sense of algorithms requires:

   ■ The ability to apply base 10 and place value concepts

   ■ The ability to compose and decompose the numbers (for example, to use expanded form)

6. Patterns enable us to understand the operations more deeply.

7. In many real-life problems, the answer depends on knowing how to interpret one's computation.

8. Being able to perform mental math and to estimate requires:

   ■ The ability to apply base 10 and place value concepts

   ■ The ability to compose and decompose the numbers (for example, to use expanded form)

   ■ The ability to apply properties of the operations, especially the commutative, associative, and distributive properties

9. Numbers in real-life settings are sometimes exact, sometimes rounded, and sometimes estimates.

10. In real-life problem-solving, one needs to know when to find an exact answer and when to find an estimate.

11. Real-life problem solvers need to know whether their estimates are reasonable.

12. People may use rounded numbers rather than exact numbers for a variety of reasons.

Basic Concepts

Section 3.1 Understanding Addition and Subtraction

Addition terminology:
sum *89*   addends *89*
addition *89*

Addition contexts:
discrete *90*
continuous *90*

Addition models:
pictorial *90*   number line *91*
tables *92*

Addition properties:
identity *93*   commutativity *93*
associativity *93*   closure *93*

Algorithms for addition:
common *97*   partial sums *99*
lattice *109*

Subtraction contexts:
take away *100*   comparison *100*
missing addend *101*

Subtraction terminology:
minuend *101*   subtrahend *101*
difference *101*

Subtraction models:
pictorial *101*   number lines *102*

Algorithms for subtraction:
standard *105*   New Zealand *107*
adding up *99*

Other terminology:
matrix *94*   addition *89*
algorithm *95*   decompose *99*
compose *99*   subtraction *101*

Section 3.2 Understanding Multiplication and Division

Multiplication contexts and models:
repeated addition *112*   area *113*
general *112*   Cartesian product *113*

Multiplication terminology:
multiplier *112*   multiplicand *112*
product *112*   factor *112*
multiple *112*

Multiplication properties:
zero *113*   identity *114*
commutativity *114* associativity *114*
distributivity *114*
distributive property of multiplication over addition *114*
distributive property of multiplication over subtraction *114*

Algorithms for multiplication:
standard *120*   lattice *121*
partial products *120*

Division contexts and models:
partitioning *123*   missing factor *125*
repeated subtraction *123*

Division terminology:
dividend *123*   divisor *123*
quotient *123*

Division concepts:
division by zero *125*

Algorithms for division:
galley *129*   scaffolding *129*

Other terminology:

indirect proof *126*   operation sense *132*
order of operations *133*   multiplication *110*
division *121*

Section 3.3 Mental Math and Estimation

Strategies for mental computation and estimation:
(Note that some of these strategies can be used both for mental computation and for estimation, some strategies are applicable to more than one operation, and some are alternative ways to solve the same problem.)

rounding *141*   compensation *143*
mental addition *142*   break and bridge *143*
leading-digit   compatible numbers
   (front end) *142*   *143*

clustering *145*
add up *148*
number line *148*
multiples of 10 *150*
halve and double *151*
expanded notation
   151
partial products *151*

lower bound *151*
upper bound *151*
canceling zeros *153*
canceling *153*
equivalent fractions
   153
missing factor model
   154

Number Theory

Somewhere around the fourth century B.C. in Greece, a profound shift in the focus of mathematics took place—a shift from simply wanting to know *how* to wanting to know *why*. Until that time, numbers were primarily used for practical purposes. Probably the most recognizable example of this changed focus is the Pythagorean theorem: $a^2 + b^2 = c^2$. Long before the Pythagoreans, other people had known of this relationship. However, the Pythagoreans and other early Greek mathematicians were not content to know that this relationship held for certain right triangles; they proved that it must hold for *any* right triangle. The field of number theory was born during this time.

 Number theory is a branch of mathematics that focuses primarily on natural numbers and their relationships.[2] "Number theory offers many rich opportunities for explorations that are interesting, enjoyable, and useful. These explorations have payoffs in problem-solving, in understanding and developing other mathematical concepts, [and] in illustrating the beauty of mathematics, and understanding the human aspects of the historical development of numbers" (*Curriculum Standards*, p. 91).

A curious reader might ask why future elementary teachers should study number theory. There are several reasons. Many number theory concepts, including factors and multiples, prime and composite numbers, and divisibility relationships, are firmly embedded in the elementary school curriculum. If elementary students understand these concepts, they can more easily compose and decompose mathematical expressions. This, in turn, makes the transition to high school mathematics less difficult.

Many students at all levels find numbers and number patterns fascinating. Being able to see patterns and to make and test generalizations is an important

[1] Cited in Lancelot Hogben, *Mathematics for the Millions* (New York: W. W. Norton & Co., 1937), p. 190.

[2] Technically, number theory deals with the larger set of integers; recall our discussion in Chapter 2 of various sets of numbers: natural numbers (*N*), whole numbers (*W*), and intergers (*I*). Pedagogically, however, it works better to focus our investigations on the set of natural numbers, which is also called the set of counting numbers.

part of mathematical thinking, making number theory fertile ground for mathematically rich investigations. For thousands of years, people throughout the world have been fascinated by patterns in numbers and relationships between different sets of numbers. In this chapter, we will explore some of the more interesting and famous ones. Remember Carl Gauss, from Chapter 1, who found a way to add the first 100 natural numbers so quickly? As an adult, he once said, "Mathematics is the queen of the sciences, and arithmetic is the queen of mathematics." By arithmetic he meant number theory.

Number theory connects with other mathematical concepts and fields. Some of the topics that number theory relates to include fractions (least common multiple and greatest common factor), probability (patterns in counting different combinations), decimals (patterns in repeating as opposed to nonrepeating decimals), algebra (modular arithmetic), and geometry (string art, star patterns).

SECTION ◆ 4.1   DIVISIBILITY AND RELATED CONCEPTS

WHAT DO YOU THINK?

- What do "odd" and "even" mean?
- How can you tell if one number is divisible by another without dividing?
- What connections do you see between divisibility and decomposition?

In this section, we will investigate the basic concepts that will help you to understand the various structures of natural numbers. In Chapter 3, we examined two different ways in which numbers can be decomposed: additive and multiplicative. For example, 12 can be decomposed into $8 + 4$, and it can be decomposed into $4 \cdot 3$. Depending on circumstances, either decomposition might be relevant. In this chapter, we will explore multiplicative decompositions of natural numbers. As you will discover, being able to decompose numbers and knowing which decomposition is relevant is a theme that recurs throughout elementary mathematics.

INVESTIGATION 4.1   Interesting Dates

We will begin our investigations with a playful question. Many mathematics teachers and mathematicians would smile when writing down December 8, 1996. Do you see why? Think before reading on. . . . 📝

If we were to write this date in shorthand, we would write 12/8/96.

A. Describe the relationship among these three numbers in words.

B. Determine how many instances of this pattern occurred in the years 1900–1919.

DISCUSSION

A. One way of describing the relationship among the three numbers is to say that the third number is the product of the first two: 96 is the product of 12 and 8.

There are several mathematical concepts and terms that come out of this relationship: factor, multiple, divisible, divisor, and divides. These terms are all related. Therefore, we will define one term formally and state how the other terms relate to it.

If a and b are two natural numbers and there is a third natural number c such that $a \cdot c = b$, then we say that a divides b, and we write $a \mid b$.

When one number does not divide another number, we write $a \nmid b$.

■ If $a \mid b$, then a is a factor of b.

■ If $a \mid b$, then b is a multiple of a.

■ If $a \mid b$, then b is divisible by a.

■ If $a \mid b$, then a is a divisor of b.

B. Let us now explore the second question. There are no such dates in 1900. In 1901, there is only one such date: 1/1/01. Before you look at the table below, make your own table and then read on. . . .

STRATEGY 1: Make a table

Table 4.1 is not the only possible table and is not necessarily the best table.

TABLE 4.1

1/1/01					
1/2/02	2/1/02				
1/3/03	3/1/03				
1/4/04	2/2/04	4/1/04			
1/5/05	5/1/05				
1/6/06	2/3/06	3/2/06	6/1/06		
1/7/07	7/1/07				
1/8/08	2/4/08	4/2/08	8/1/08		
1/9/09	3/3/09	9/1/09			
1/10/10	2/5/10	5/2/10	10/1/10		
1/11/11	11/1/11				
1/12/12	2/6/12	3/4/12	4/3/12	6/2/12	12/1/12
1/13/13					
1/14/14	2/7/14	7/2/14			
1/15/15	3/5/15	5/3/15			
1/16/16	2/8/16	4/4/16	8/2/16		
1/17/17					
1/18/18	2/9/18	3/6/18	6/3/18	9/2/18	
1/19/19					

In one sense, we are done—we have found all 53 possible dates. However, there is still a lot of interesting mathematics to be gleaned from looking for and examining patterns and relationships. Take a few minutes to examine the table above. What patterns and relationships do you observe in the table?

STRATEGY 2: Make a table with a different organization

Before we discuss the patterns and relationships in Table 4.1, let us take a look at another representation of our data. As you may recall, one of the themes of this book is that different representations of information and data often enable us to see patterns that we did not see before, in the same way that a sculpture will look different as you walk around it. Look at Table 4.2. It presents the same 53 dates as Table 4.1 but is organized differently. Note any new insights, patterns, or observations before reading on. . . .

TABLE 4.2

1/1/01						
1/2/02	2/1/02					
1/3/03	3/1/03					
1/4/04	4/1/04					2/2/04
1/5/05	5/1/05					
1/6/06	6/1/06	2/3/06	3/2/06			
1/7/07	7/1/07					
1/8/08	8/1/08	2/4/08	4/2/08			
1/9/09	9/1/09					3/3/09
1/10/10	10/1/10	2/5/10	5/2/10			
1/11/11	11/1/11					
1/12/12	12/1/12	2/6/12	6/2/12	3/4/12	4/3/12	
1/13/13						
1/14/14		2/7/14	7/2/14			
1/15/15				3/5/15	5/3/15	
1/16/16		2/8/16	8/2/16			4/4/16
1/17/17						
1/18/18		2/9/18	9/2/18	3/6/18	6/3/18	
1/19/19						

One pattern is that many dates have a twin. For example, the dates in the first and second columns, the dates in the third and fourth columns, and the dates in the fifth and sixth columns are twins. Someone who sees this connection early can finish the problem more quickly — sort of a "2 for 1" deal. Mathematically, we can talk about symmetry in our set.

We can also see that some dates do not have twins. For example, 1/7/07 has a twin, but 1/13/13 doesn't. Why not?

If we stop for a moment, we realize that 13/1/13 is not a valid date.

Some valid dates have no twins: 2/2/04, 3/3/09, 4/4/16. In this case, the numbers 4, 9, and 16 are square numbers.

Odd and Even Numbers

One of the first ways in which children encounter number theory is with **odd** and **even numbers**. Let me introduce this discussion with a story. One morning my five-year-old son, Josh, asked me at the breakfast table if 44 was an odd or an even number; at that time, my 45th birthday was a few days away. I asked him what he thought, and he said he thought it was even. I asked him what he thought an even number was. Before you read his response, think about this question yourself. Then read on. . . .

Josh's response was that even numbers were fair. I asked him what he meant by fair. His response was, "Well, it's fair if two teams can get the same amount."

Take a few moments to write your own definition of odd and even. Given our explorations in Alphabitia, can you make a definition that will work for that system too?

Below are several different ways in which even numbers have been defined. Note that the notion of *even* is closely tied to the notion of decomposition. That is, if a number can be decomposed in the following way, then it is even.

A number is an even number if and only if:

- It has 2 as a factor.
- It is divisible by 2.
- Its ones digit ends in 2, 4, 6, 8, or 0; (this one is not true for all bases; do you see why?).
- It can be represented as the sum of two equal numbers.

A natural number x is even if there exists another natural number a such that $x = 2a$.

Take a minute to write the analogous ways in which odd numbers can be defined.

Please don't skip over this. You will use this thinking in the next investigation.

CHILDREN

It is important to emphasize that most concepts in the elementary school curriculum can be represented concretely and that most, but not all, students need to experience these concepts concretely in order to understand them deeply. This is true with the concepts of factor, multiple, and divisible.

Cuisenaire rods are a commonly used manipulative in elementary schools that work nicely with many elementary mathematics concepts. They come in ten different lengths, each length being a different color (see Figure 4.1). The length of each of the rods is a multiple of the length of the shortest rod.

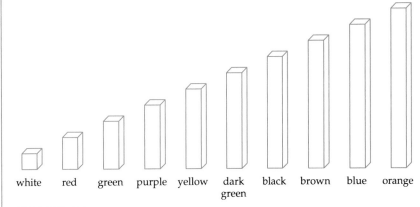

white   red   green   purple   yellow   dark green   black   brown   blue   orange

FIGURE **4.1**

Children will spontaneously build "trains" with Cuisenaire rods. To see if one number is a factor of another number, we can begin by making a large train using Cuisenaire rods of only one color. For example, consider a 20 train (two orange rods). A child can readily test whether 4 is a factor of 20 by seeing if the large train can be made using only purple (4) rods (see Figure 4.2).

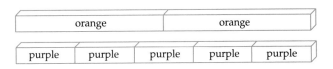

FIGURE **4.2**

INVESTIGATION **4.2** **Patterns in Odd and Even Numbers**

In this investigation, we will examine and discover some of the many patterns that emerge when odd and even numbers are combined. There are several reasons for investigating odd and even numbers. One is that many people find it fun; I have seen the excitement on young children's faces as they discover these patterns. Another reason is that in order to see and then explain these patterns, one has to look more closely at the concepts; thus, we come out of the investigation with a deeper understanding of odd and even numbers and other mathematical ideas and tools. Finally, this and many other investigations in this book focus on going from noticing a pattern that seems to be true to being able to prove that it is true everywhere. Once again, this ability to prove the "*why* behind the *what*," a habit of mind that we first see in the early Greeks more than 2,000 years ago, represents one of the great advances in human thinking.

Let us begin the investigation by thinking about the following questions and noting your responses before reading on. . . .

A. What do you notice about adding two odd numbers? two even numbers? an odd and an even number?

B. Can you explain the pattern you see in the sum of two odd numbers?

DISCUSSION

A. The patterns for adding odd and even numbers can most succinctly be represented as

odd + odd = even

even + even = even

odd + even = odd

B. Now that we have seen *what* the pattern is, how might we explain *why* it holds for all odd and even numbers? What tools do you have that might enable you to show *why* this is true?

STRATEGY 1: Make a drawing

Let us begin by examining the question from a geometrical perspective. See Figure 4.3, which represents any odd number. Why is this figure a valid representation of any odd number?

FIGURE **4.3**

Think of two Cuisenaire rods, one of which is one unit longer than the other. Any odd number can be represented in this manner. Can you connect any of your definitions to this diagram? How?

If we think of *even* as meaning able to be separated into two groups that have the same amount, then *odd* must mean that we can't do that; in other words, one of the piles will be one unit longer. What if we combine two different odd numbers? Draw that diagram. What do you see? At this point, make another attempt to explain why the sum of two odd numbers must be an even number. You may find that you can refine or extend your ideas from your first explanations, or you may find that the picture and explanation above is different from what you had written.

When we build a concrete model to show the combination of two odd numbers, the first odd number has one unit left over and the second odd number has one unit left over, as in Figure 4.4. When we combine the two numbers, the two units become a pair.

FIGURE **4.4**

There are two ways in which this model connects with our idea of *even*. Some students might say that now there are no units left over, and thus we have an even number. Other students might refer to Figure 4.4 and, using language from our work with base 10 blocks, say that when we combine the two numbers, we have two sticks of equal length; thus, it is an even number.

STRATEGY 2: Use algebra

Let us now examine an algebraic explanation for why the sum of two odd numbers must be an even number. Since one of the characteristics of *all* even numbers is that they are divisible by 2, we can say that $2n$ represents *any* even number as long as n represents a natural number. Since one of the characteristics of *all* odd numbers is that they are not divisible by 2, we can say that $2n + 1$ represents any odd number. Why is this? Try to use these ideas to show with symbols why the sum of any two odd numbers is an even number. Then read on. . . .

Statement	Reason
$(2n + 1) + (2m + 1)$	This represents the sum of *any* two odd numbers, where m and n represent *any* natural numbers.
$= 2n + 2m + 2$	We can change the original expression to this expression because of the associative and commutative properties.
$= 2(n + m + 1)$	We can change the previous expression to this expression because of the distributive property.

However, this form means that this number, $2(n + m + 1)$, has to be an even number. Why is this?

See if you can prove the other two statements (even + even = even and odd + even = odd) in a similar fashion.

In Chapter 2, we stated that many relationships between two sets in mathematics are functional relationships. Is this relationship we have just examined (that is, whether the sum of two numbers will be odd or even) a functional relationship? Why or why not? Think and read on. . . .

Function language If we cast this notion of the sum of two numbers being odd or even in function language, we can see that the input set consists of all ordered pairs of natural numbers; that is,

Input set $= \{(a, b) \mid a, b \in N\}$

Similarly, the output set consists of two elements, even and odd; that is,

Output set = {even, odd}

We can illustrate this with a mapping diagram (Figure 4.5):

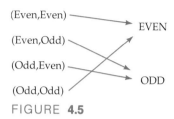

FIGURE **4.5**

We see that every element of the input set is connected to exactly one element of the output set, for example, even + even always produces an even number. Therefore, this relationship is a functional one.

INVESTIGATION **4.3**   **Understanding Divisibility Relationships**

There are a host of theorems that concern divisibility. We will examine two here, partly because we will need them later in the section, and partly because this investigation provides practice in the kind of mathematical thinking originally developed by the early Greeks, that is, advancing from demonstrating that a statement is true in a particular case to proving that the statement is true for all numbers—what we call proving the general case.

A. We know that $6 \mid 42$ and $6 \mid 72$. Does it necessarily follow that 6 divides their sum—that is, does 6 divide $(42 + 72)$? Before doing any computation, what do you think?

DISCUSSION

In this particular case, it is true; 6 does divide $42 + 72$, because $6 \cdot 19 = 114$.

B. In fact, pick any three natural numbers a, b, and c for which $a \mid b$ and $a \mid c$. Then $a \mid (b + c)$. Can you prove this?

Let me restate this general question in English and in mathematical notation:

English: If a number divides two numbers, will it necessarily divide their sum?

Notation: If $a \mid b$ and $a \mid c$, is it always true that $a \mid (b + c)$?

How might we prove this? Work on this question and then read on. . . .

DISCUSSION

One proof uses the definition of divisibility and looks like this:

If $a \mid b$, then there is a natural number x such that $ax = b$.

Similarly, if $a \mid c$, then there is a natural number y such that $ay = c$.

BEYOND THE CLASSROOM

The question in Investigation 4.3 may seem to be silly to some people, but science is full of examples of products or medicines or mathematical principles that worked in many test cases, but were later found not to work in all cases. In some instances, it was a matter of, "Aw, shucks, we were wrong," but in other cases, it was a matter of lives being lost. Therefore, this ability to be able to prove that a hypothesis either is true in only some cases or is true in all cases is an important ability in many areas of life.

The proof consists of transforming $b + c$ to show that it must be divisible by a:

$$b + c = ax + ay \quad \text{Here we are substituting } ax \text{ for } b \text{ and } ay \text{ for } c.$$
$$= a(x + y) \quad \text{This is true because of the distributive property.}$$

We now have a valid proof. Do you see why? Think and then read on. . . . 🖉

We have proved the general case, because if $b + c$ can be expressed as the product of a and some natural number, then by definition $(b + c)$ is divisible by a. Therefore, we have proved that if $a \mid b$ and $a \mid c$, then $a \mid (b + c)$.

INVESTIGATION **4.4** Determining the Truth of an Inverse Statement

Suppose we turn things around and consider the inverse statement: What if a number a divides neither of two larger numbers? Can we say that it will never divide the sum of those two numbers? Think and then read on. . . . 🖉

This question can be stated in English and in notation as:

English: If a does not divide b and a does not divide c, then will a divide their sum?

Notation: If $a \nmid b$ and $a \nmid c$, then $a \nmid (b + c)$?

DISCUSSION

Although this hypothesis seems reasonable, we can show that it is invalid by using a **counterexample,** an example that proves a hypothesis to be false.

For example, consider $a = 3$, $b = 7$, and $c = 2$.

Although $3 \nmid 7$ and $3 \nmid 2$, $3 \mid (7 + 2)$.

Thus, it is not true that if $a \nmid b$ and $a \nmid c$, then $a \nmid (b + c)$.

Note: A mathematical statement is considered to be true only if it is true 100 percent of the time. If there is even one exception (a counterexample), then the statement is considered to be mathematically false.

Deductive Reasoning

Although this text de-emphasizes the more formal aspects of mathematics, there are rules of logic that are more prominent in secondary and college mathematics. These rules provide the foundation for what we call deductive reasoning. There are a few such terms that we need to discuss, if only briefly.

Most hypotheses and theorems can be stated in "if-then" language: for example, if $a \mid b$ and $a \mid c$, then $a \mid (b + c)$. Many everyday statements can also be expressed in this language:

If you do your chores, then you can go outside and play.

If you want to drive a car, then you must obtain a driver's license.

Such statements are called **conditional statements.** That is, if the condition(s) in the first part of the statement are met, then the second part of the statement will happen. In mathematics, the "if" part of such statements is called the **hypothesis** and the "then" part is called the **conclusion**.

As you just found, when we prove a conditional statement to be true, its inverse is not necessarily true. When we make a conditional statement, there are actually three related statements:

Statement:	If X, then Y.
Contrapositive:	If not Y, then not X.
Converse:	If Y, then X.
Inverse:	If not X, then not Y.

It turns out that a statement and its contrapositive are logically equivalent. That is, if one is true, then the other must be true. Similarly, the converse and the inverse are logically equivalent.

Let us first consider an everyday example. A friend of mine was riding in the country with her two-year-old daughter. The daughter saw her first cow and said, "Mommy, look at that big dog!" She had equated the statement "If it is a dog, then it has four legs," with its converse, which, of course, was not true.

Statement:	If it is a dog, then it has four legs.
Contrapositive:	If it doesn't have four legs, then it is not a dog.
Converse:	If it has four legs, then it is a dog.
Inverse:	If it is not a dog, then it doesn't have four legs.

Another aspect of mathematical logic concerns the case in which a statement and its converse are both true. We call such statements **biconditional statements,** and we can express this relationship most succinctly by using the phrase "if and only if," or "iff." As you may recall from Chapter 2, many mathematical definitions are written using this language.

Let us now examine the classical divisibility rules. In the course of our examination, we will look at why they are true (as we did for rules about evens and odds), and we will also examine how we can make and test our own predictions.

Divisibility Rules

Before the widespread use of calculators, knowing divisibility rules was quite useful. For example, simplifying $42/54$ is much easier for a student who immediately sees that both numbers are divisible by 6. In the context of the NCTM Standards, the usefulness of the concept of divisibility is not so much in knowing the rules as it is in the opportunity for investigations with this concept to deepen your understanding of whole-number relationships and to develop your problem-solving toolbox.

Think back to Investigation 4.1. Are there any dates in the year 1996 that fit that pattern? Work on this and then read on. . . .

There are several ways to answer this question. One is simply random guess–check–revise. Another way is to be systematic: $1 \cdot ? = 96$, $2 \cdot ? = 96$, $3 \cdot ? = 96$, and so forth. Another way is to first find all the factors of 96. We will explore the second strategy now and the third strategy in the next section.

It turns out that there are four dates in 1996 that fit the pattern: 4/24/96, 6/16/96, 8/12/96, and 12/8/96. If we use a systematic approach, we are essentially asking, in each case, does this number divide 96 and, if so, is the result a valid date? For example, does 3 divide 96? You can answer this by dividing. However, if you know the divisibility rule for 3, you immediately know that 3 does indeed divide 96.

Before we consider some of the common divisibility rules, let me ask you a question: What rules do you remember from grade school? If you don't remember any of them, take a few minutes to see if you can *discover* any of the rules. In other words, just by looking at a large number, such as 96 or 142, can you tell whether it is divisible by 2 without dividing by 2, or if it is divisible by 3 without dividing by 3, and so on? Play around for a while and see how many divisibility rules you can remember and/or construct before reading on. . . .

Since one of the themes of this book is the connectedness of mathematics, you may not be surprised to hear that many of the divisibility rules are related to one another. We will discuss them from this perspective. Several of the divisibility rules are quite simple. Let us examine them first.

Divisibility by 2   When will a number be divisible by 2? Another way of asking this question is: If you think of (the set of) all numbers that are divisible by 2, what do they have in common? What they have in common is that they are all even numbers. Thus, the divisibility rule for 2 is

> A number is divisible by 2 iff it is an even number.

An equivalent statement is

> A number is divisible by 2 iff its ones digit is a 0, 2, 4, 6, or 8.

Note that this statement holds for base 10. Divisibility rules in other bases will be left as exercises.

Divisibility by 5   This rule is simple in base 10:

> A number is divisible by 5 iff its ones digit is a 0 or a 5.

Do you see why this rule is so easy in base 10? Think and then read on. . . .

Think back to base 10 manipulatives. When we count by 5s, we are counting by half longs.

Divisibility by 10   A number is divisible by 10 iff the ones digit is 0.

These three divisibility rules are generally the easiest to remember. Do you think it is a coincidence that 2 and 5 both divide 10?

Divisibility by 3   Make up several numbers and determine whether or not they are divisible by 3. Look at the numbers that are divisible by 3. Can you see any patterns that would enable you to determine that a number is or is not divisible by 3 without having to divide? If you don't, consider this statement: "divisible by 3" is analogous to an exclusive club. That is, every number that is divisible by 3 has some characteristic that every number not divisible by 3 does not have. Look again at your two sets of numbers (those that are divisible by 3 and those that are not); make up more numbers and place them in the appropriate set, for this is a great chance to develop the part of the problem-solving toolbox dealing with looking for patterns. Then read on. . . .

INVESTIGATION 4.5   Understanding Why the Divisibility Rule for 3 Works

Formally, we say that

> A number is divisible by 3 iff the sum of the digits of the number is divisible by 3.

For example, $3 \mid 567$ because $3 \mid (5 + 6 + 7)$. Let us use the divisibility relationships that we explored earlier to explain *why* the divisibility rule for 3 works. Recall that one of the main purposes of this course is to learn not just the whats of mathematics but also the whys.

Pick a few numbers that are divisible by 3 and see if you can see what the sum of the digits has to do with divisibility by 3. For example, 243 is divisible by 3. Why? Explore this for a while and then read on....

DISCUSSION

Begin with manipulatives   We will first work through a concrete representation and then move to the more general case. If we represent 243 with base 10 manipulatives, we have Figure 4.6.

FIGURE 4.6

In one sense, we can look at this representation as three distinct groups: flats, longs, and units. The key to understanding why this rule works lies in the fact that if $a \mid b$ and $a \mid c$, then $a \mid (b + c)$. We will use an unproved extension of that theorem: If $a \mid b$, $a \mid c$, and $a \mid d$, then $a \mid (b + c + d)$ for all natural numbers a, b, c, and d. Do you see what this theorem has to do with showing why 243 is divisible by 3? Think and then read on....

If we can break down our number into various components so that each component is divisible by 3, then the natural number will be divisible by 3. What can we do to the flats and the longs to make them divisible by 3? Think and then read on....

If we cut one unit from each flat and each long, we still have the same amount, that is, 243 (see Figure 4.7). But now the 99 blocks and the 9 blocks are divisible by 3.

FIGURE 4.7

We simply move the "extra" units created in cutting the flats and longs and put them with the original 3 units (see Figure 4.8). Now we have 9 ones, and 9 is divisible by 3.

FIGURE **4.8**

Now use expanded notation   We can use expanded notation now to show what we have done and to better understand why the divisibility rule for 3 works.

Statement	Reason
$243 = 200 + 40 + 3$	We have rewritten the amount using expanded notation.
$= (100 + 100) + (10 + 10 + 10 + 10) + 3$	We have substituted equivalent amounts (for example, $100 + 100$ for 200).
$= (99 + 1 + 99 + 1) + (9 + 1 + 9 + 1 + 9 + 1 + 9 + 1) + 3$	100 and 10 are not divisible by 3, but if we take one away from each 100 and each 10, what remains *is* divisible by 3.
$= 2(99) + 4(9) + (2 + 4 + 3)$	We have used the commutative and associative properties to rearrange what we had.

Finally, use the theorem   We can now use the theorem, If $a \mid b$, $a \mid c$, and $a \mid d$, then $a \mid (b + c + d)$. That is, if we can show that 3 divides each of the three expressions above [$2(99)$, $4(9)$, and $(2 + 4 + 3)$], then 3 must divide the sum 243; that is, 243 is divisible by 3! Let us examine each of the three expressions in turn.

We know that $3 \mid 2(99)$ because $3 \mid 99$. This knowledge comes from another (unproved) theorem that states that if $a \mid b$, then $a \mid bc$ for all natural numbers a, b, and c. This can be stated in English as: If a number divides another number, then it divides any multiple of that number.

Similarly, $3 \mid 4(9)$ because $3 \mid 9$.

Therefore, demonstrating that $3 \mid 243$ rests upon knowing that $3 \mid (2 + 4 + 3)$. However, $2 + 4 + 3$ is simply the sum of the digits of 243!

Generalizing the justification   This does not constitute a proof of the divisibility rule for 3, but rather is an examination into the structure of the rule. You may want to do the above kind of analysis with a few other numbers to better understand why it works. If we had represented 243 as *abc*, we would have a proof of the divisibility rule for 3 for any three-digit number. That is,

$$abc = 100a + 10b + c = 99a + a + 9b + b + c = 99a + 9b + (a + b + c).$$

Divisibility by 9   As you discovered when you worked with the multiplication table in Explorations 3.3 and 3.4, the 3 family and the 9 family are related. So too are their divisibility rules. Before reading the rule below, see if you can guess what it is. You could approach this task in two different ways. Choose several numbers and multiply them by 9 or make up a bunch of numbers and divide them by 9. The first approach creates one set while the second approach creates two sets, divisible by 9 and not divisible by 9. Here is another chance to apply your problem-solving skills (looking for patterns) and content knowledge (looking to see if you can adapt the divisibility rule for 3). In either case, see what you can come up with before reading on. . . . 🖎

A number is divisible by 9 iff the sum of its digits is divisible by 9.

The justification of this rule is left as an exercise.

INVESTIGATION 4.6   Divisibility by 4 and 8

Just as the divisibility rules for 3 and 9 are similar, so too are the divisibility rules for 2, 4, and 8.

A. As before, choose several numbers and determine which are divisible by 4. Then find patterns that will lead you to be able to predict whether a number is divisible by 4 without dividing. Then read on. . . . 🖎

B. Choose several numbers and determine which are divisible by 8. Find patterns to help you predict whether a number is divisible by 8. Then read on. . . . 🖎

DISCUSSION

A. The divisibility rule for 4 is not terribly obvious. However, rather than just presenting it, let me give you a couple of examples and see if you can figure out the rule from the examples, that is, by using **inductive reasoning**.

Consider the number 532. The test for divisibility by 4 centers on whether $4 \mid 32$. Similarly, with the number 123,456, the test for divisibility by 4 centers on whether $4 \mid 56$.

Now try to express this rule in English as if you were explaining it to someone on the phone. Then read on. . . . 🖎

There are many valid ways to express the rule. One looks like this:

A number is divisible by 4 iff the number represented by the last two digits is divisible by 4.

By the last two digits, I mean the ones digit and the tens digit.

Before we examine why this rule works, you may want to try it with a few numbers.

The key to understanding how this rule works is to realize that no matter how many hundreds we have, *that* part of the number will always be divisible by 4. This is true because $4 \mid 100$, and therefore any multiple of 100 will also be divisible by 4.

Proof for three-digit numbers:

Statement	Reason
$xyz = 100x + 10y + z$	Rewrite using expanded form.
$4 \mid 100x$	Because $4 \mid 100$, $4 \mid 100a$.
If $4 \mid (10y + z)$, then $4 \mid xyz$	Because of the theorem, if $a \mid b$ and $a \mid c$, then $a \mid (b + c)$

B. Before stating the rule for divisibility by 8, let me give you a hint and see if you can figure it out. The rule for 8 is similar to the rule for 4. Think and then read on . . . .

To help you understand the rule rather than just memorizing it, consider the number 2,346 and whether it is divisible by 8. This is another case in which expanded notation can be helpful:

$$2,328 = 2,000 + 300 + 20 + 8$$

Will any of the parts be divisible by 8? Think and read on. . . .

Since $8 \mid 1000$, any multiple of 1,000 will be divisible by 8, and so $8 \mid 2,000$. However, since 8 does not divide 100, we need to look at the last *three* digits to determine divisibility by 8. That is, if $8 \mid 328$, then the original number 2,346 will be divisible by 8.

The divisibility rule for 8 uses language similar to the rule for 4:

A number is divisible by 8 iff the number represented by the last three digits is divisible by 8.

Some students have noted that although 8 does not divide 100, 8 does divide any even multiple of 100. In other words, $8 \mid 200$, $8 \mid 400$, and so forth. Thus, we can say that if the digit representing the hundreds place is even, we have to look at only the last two digits. This led me to believe that if the digit representing the hundreds place is odd, there might be a pattern that might enable us to determine divisibility by 8 by looking at only the last two digits. What do you think? This question will be left as an exercise.

Divisibility by 6 The divisibility rule for 6 has a different flavor from the other rules. How might you determine whether a large number was divisible by 6 without actually dividing? Think and then read on. . . .

A number n is divisible by 6 iff n is divisible by 2 and by 3.

This can also be stated as

$6 \mid n$ iff $2 \mid n$ and $3 \mid n$

Why do you think this rule must be true?

Let us now investigate how we might apply this divisibility rule to a larger number.

INVESTIGATION 4.7 Creating a Divisibility Rule for 12

What about a divisibility rule for 12? Can we use what we know, or do we just have to divide (longhand or with a calculator)? Think and then read on. . . .

DISCUSSION

When I have asked my classes this, I generally get different hypotheses. Let us examine two of them. Some students say that if a number is divisible by 2 and by 6, then it must be divisible by 12. Other students say that if a number is divisible by 3 and by 4, then it must be divisible by 12. Is this one of those cases in which both answers are correct, or is only one correct? Think and then read on. . . .

In this case, the first hypothesis is not always true. Can you see why? For example, 2 | 18 and 6 | 18 but 12 ∤ 18. If you thought this first hypothesis was correct, can you now see why it isn't? If you knew that it wasn't correct, can you explain why? In either case, take a few minutes to think about how you would explain to someone why this hypothesis is not true. Then read on. . . .

This hypothesis doesn't work because "divisible by 2" is a redundant condition. If a number is divisible by 6, then it *must* be divisible by 2. Thus, saying that a number is divisible by 2 and divisible by 6 is mathematically equivalent to simply saying that it is divisible by 6.

Revisiting Venn diagrams   The preceding sentence makes great sense to some students and absolutely no sense to others. If you are in the latter set, the old adage that a picture is worth a thousand words may be relevant. Let us examine some Venn diagrams (pictures) and see how they can contribute to our understanding of divisibility rules.

If a number is divisible by 6, it must be divisible by 2, means that the set of numbers divisible by 6 is a subset of the set of numbers divisible by 2, as shown in the figure at the left in Figure 4.9. When we look at divisibility by 3 and by 4, however, we see that they are not disjoint sets (like the sets of even and odd numbers), but rather overlapping sets. Thus, the diagram at the right in Figure 4.9 illustrates the relationship between the numbers divisible by 3 and the numbers divisible by 4. The intersection of these two sets is the set of numbers divisible by 12.

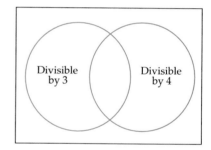

FIGURE **4.9**

We can say that a number is divisible by 12 iff it is divisible by 3 and by 4.

Summary

The ideas of divisibility, divides, factor, and multiple are highly interconnected. As we examined patterns in dates and patterns in even and odd numbers, we saw how the concepts of factor, multiple, and divisibility enabled us to better understand the problems we were investigating. Which term we use often depends on our perspective. For example, we might say that 6 divides 24, that 24 is divisible by 6, that 6 is a factor of 24, that 24 is a multiple of 6, or that 6 is a divisor of 24. This notion of divisibility is useful because the relationship between two numbers is often important in explaining patterns and making predictions. We also used divisibility ideas to develop and explain the various divisibility rules. In Exploration 4.4, for example, when the number of points in the stars is divisible by the number denoting how to connect the dots, a polygon is formed. We also found that in order to understand why divisibility rules work, it was helpful to understand some basic principles and terminology of deductive reasoning: the inverse, converse, and contrapositive of a statement.

The notion of divisibility is highly connected to another important idea that you have seen several times in this book already: decomposition. Just as an understanding of computation algorithms in Chapter 3 depended on decomposing the numbers, so too does an understanding of divisibility require that one be comfortable with taking numbers apart and putting them together—that is, decomposing and composing them. As we saw in Chapter 3, we can decompose numbers additively or multiplicatively; for example, we can see 6 as $3 + 3$ or as $2 \cdot 3$. In this section, we found that divisibility relates to multiplicative decompositions.

EXERCISES 4.1

1. Write at least two different definitions of "odd number." When would it be preferable to use each definition?

2. Earlier in this section, we examined the relationships between adding odd and even numbers. This question asks you to examine the relationships between multiplying odd and even numbers.

   a. Explain why the product of an odd number and an odd number is an odd number. *Hint:* Look at the discussion of why the sum of an even number of odd numbers is an even number.

   b. How would you describe the rule for determining whether the product of many natural numbers is even or odd? For example, is $2 \cdot 3 \cdot 4 \cdot 5 \cdot 6$ an odd number or an even number?

3. a. Find four different odd numbers whose sum is 20.

   b. How many combinations of four different odd numbers whose sum is 30 can you find? Describe your strategies.

4. What can you say about two numbers if their sum is even and their product is odd? Justify your answer.

5. The sum of three numbers is even. Must the product of the three numbers be even or odd, or are both possible? Justify your answer.

6. The game of darts is mathematically rich with respect to number theory.

   a. If you throw five darts, in how many ways can you get a score of 21 if we assume that every dart hits the dartboard? Write your solution and summarize your strategy.

   b. In how many different ways can you get a score of 22?

   c. Make a list of all possible scores from throwing five darts. Describe your strategy for finding *all possible scores*. If you were stumped on part (b), does this exercise shed any light?

7. a. In how many different ways can one make a score of 22 with 6 darts?

   b. What if we take away the restriction that all darts must hit the board? Now how many possibilities for a score of 22 are there?

   c. Why do all combinations with missed darts include 2 misses?

8. There are some interesting connections between the set of odd and even numbers and the sets of figurate numbers you encountered in Exploration 2.5.

   a. The table below is generated by finding the sum of consecutive odd numbers. Can you explain why the sum of consecutive odd numbers generates the set S of square numbers, $S = \{1, 4, 9, 16, 25, 36, \ldots\}$?

   $$1$$
   $$1 + 3 = 4$$
   $$1 + 3 + 5 = 9$$
   $$1 + 3 + 5 + 7 = 16$$

   b. There is another way to generate the set of square numbers, shown below. Can you explain how the following sequence leads to the set of square numbers?

   $$1$$
   $$1 + 2 + 1$$
   $$1 + 2 + 3 + 2 + 1$$
   $$1 + 2 + 3 + 4 + 3 + 2 + 1$$
   $$1 + 2 + 3 + 4 + 5 + 4 + 3 + 2 + 1$$

9. Look at the following three examples:

   $$2 \cdot 4 = 3^2 - 1^2$$
   $$4 \cdot 6 = 5^2 - 1^2$$
   $$6 \cdot 8 = 7^2 - 1^2$$

   a. Describe what you see.

   b. Predict what the next row will look like.

   c. Describe the nth row and justify your description.

10. a. Describe the following sequence:

   $$1 \cdot 8 + 1 = 9$$
   $$12 \cdot 8 + 2 = 98$$
   $$123 \cdot 8 + 3 = 987$$
   $$1234 \cdot 8 + 4 = 9876$$

b. What will be the ninth row in this sequence?

c. Does the pattern break after that, does it continue, or is it modified?

11. I'm thinking of two numbers. Determine the numbers if:

   a. Their sum is 45 and their difference is 15.

   b. Their sum is 48 and their quotient is 3.

   c. Their sum is 61, but if the digits in each of the numbers are reversed, their sum is 115.

12. Begin a sequence by selecting any two numbers between 1 and 9. To continue the sequence, add the two numbers and record the digit that appears in the ones place. For example, 5, 7, 2, 9, 1. You will note that eventually the pattern repeats. Try this with a variety of starting numbers: $5 + 7 = \mathbf{12}, 7 + 2 = \mathbf{9}, 2 + 9 = \mathbf{11}$

   a. What is the shortest sequence you can find?

   b. What is the longest sequence you can find?

   c. How many different number sequences can you generate?

   d. What other patterns do you notice?

13. a. Find the following products: $37 \cdot 3$ and then $37 \cdot 6$. What do you predict will be the product of $37 \cdot 9$? Describe, in words, the pattern that you see.

   b. Now predict how long you think the pattern will continue and explain your prediction.

   c. Some students believe that the pattern breaks when we get to $37 \cdot 30$, and others don't. What do you think? Why?

14. In Investigation 4.1, we explored one set of dates.

   a. Consider the following dates: 2/3/45 and 6/7/89. First, write a general description for all dates that will be members of this set. Second, determine how many instances of this pattern will occur in this century.

   b. Create your own set of dates that have a number theory connection. First, write a general description for all dates that will be members of this set. Second, determine how many instances of this pattern will occur in this century.

15. This problem has been around for many years. Can you determine the ages of Alfie's children from analyzing the following conversation?

   Alfie: Can you guess the ages of my three children? The product of their ages is 36.

   Bernice: That's not enough information. Give me another hint.

   Alfie: The sum of their ages is the same as our street address.

   Bernice: That's still not enough information. Give me another hint.

   Alfie: My oldest child is a girl.

   Bernice: Now I can figure it out.

   Note: Problems 16 and 17 can consist of a rote practice of the divisibility rules or they can be a wonderful opportunity for thinking. *Before* checking each number

for the specific divisibility rule, try to predict the answer. For example, does 123,456 "feel" like the sum of the digits will be divisible by 3? Or in Exercise 17(b), before checking to see if 4|98, does it "feel" like it will or it won't? If your intuition is often right, can you explain why? In many cases, what is behind a good intuition is a sense of patterns.

16. Use divisibility rules to answer the following. Briefly explain how you arrived at your conclusion. Simply dividing the larger number by the smaller is not acceptable.

   a. Is the number 123,456 divisible by 3? Why or why not?

   b. Is the number 123,456 divisible by 6? Why or why not?

   c. Is the number 123,456 divisible by 8? Why or why not?

   d. Is the number 2,345,678 divisible by 4? Why or why not?

   e. Is the number 2,345,678 divisible by 6? Why or why not?

   f. Is the number 2,345,678 divisible by 9? Why or why not?

17. Test the numbers below for divisibility by 2, 3, 4, 5, 6, 8, 9, and 12.

   a. 222,444   b. 213,498   c. 987,987,987

18. Write a definition for "divides" in your own words. Then have someone who is not in this course read your definition and explain to you what "divides" means, based on your definition.

19. In the following number there are two missing digits: 467,__2. You are told that this number is divisible by 144. What is the number? Explain how you found it.

20. One aspect of parenting that has nearly driven me crazy is that kids lose things. My children are still young and love to play card games. However, they lose cards, and consequently, we have several decks of cards, none of which is complete. This situation reminded me of a problem that I have seen in many guises. I offer it to you now in the context of card games. We have assembled quite a pile of cards and are playing a game in which all the cards are dealt out before playing. We have made the following amazing discovery:

   If two people are playing, one card will be left over.

   If three people are playing, two cards will be left over.

   If four people are playing, three cards will be left over.

   If five people are playing, four cards will be left over.

   If six people are playing, five cards will be left over.

   If seven people are playing, no cards will be left over.

   How many cards are in this deck?

21. This is a variation on the card game problem. If two, three, four, five, or six people are playing, one card will be left over (in each case). If seven people are playing, no cards will be left over. How many cards are in the deck?

22. Joe wrote the divisibility rule for 4 in the following way: A number is divisible by 4 if the last two digits are divisible by 4. Is his expression accurate? Is it clear? If you like it, explain why. If you think it is not accurate or not clear, explain what is inaccurate or vague.

23. We learned earlier that if the digit representing the hundreds place is even, then a number is divisible by 8 iff the number represented by the last two digits is divisible by 8. Finish and justify the second part of this modification of the divisibility rule for 8: If the digit representing the hundreds place is an odd number, then a number is divisible by 8 if _____.

24. Prove the divisibility rule for 9 for any three-digit number.

25. Some textbooks present two other divisibility rules. Examine each of the rules below to make sure you can use them. Then explain why they work.

    a. A number is divisible by 7 if the number obtained by subtracting double the ones digit from the number represented by the remaining digits is divisible by 7.

    b. A whole number is divisible by 11 if the sum of the digits representing even powers of 10 minus the sum of the digits representing odd powers of ten is also divisible by 11.

26. Devise and justify a divisibility rule for

    a. 18

    b. 24

    c. 25

    d. 4 in base 5

    e. 3 in base 12

27. Classify each of the following as true or false, assuming that a, b, and c are integers. If the statement is true, briefly explain why it is true. If the statement is false, give a counterexample, and then rewrite it so that it is true.

    a. If $a \mid b$ and $a \nmid c$, then $a \mid bc$

    b. If a number is divisible by 3, then every digit of that number is divisible by 3.

    c. If $c \mid ab$, then $c \mid a$ or $c \mid b$.

    d. If $4 \mid a$ and $6 \mid a$, then $24 \mid a$.

    e. If $12 \mid a$, then $6 \mid a$.

    f. If $d \mid a$, then $d \mid a^2$

28. Each of the conjectures below is either true or false. For each, if you think it is true, try to prove that it is true or justify why you think it is true. If you think it is false, provide a counterexample.

    a. The sum of 3 consecutive numbers is divisible by 3.

    b. The product of any 3 consecutive numbers is divisible by 6.

    c. The product of any 4 consecutive numbers is divisible by 24.

    d. The square of any odd number can be represented in the form $8n + 1$, where $n \in W$.

29. a. What can you say about the divisibility of the sum of three consecutive numbers? In other words, are there any numbers that will always divide this sum, regardless of the three numbers?

    b. What about the sum of any four consecutive numbers?

    c. What about the sum of any five consecutive numbers?

30. For 6 consecutive years, Joan's age was divisible by her granddaughter's age. What were their ages during that period?

31. a. Let's say you have a bunch of 6¢ and 5¢ stamps and a package for which the postage is $1.93. Can you make $1.93 with only 5¢ and 6¢ stamps?

    b. What if you have only 5¢ stamps and 6¢ stamps and the postage is $1.80? How many different ways can you make the postage?

32. a. What is the units digit of 3^{900}? *Hint:* make a table and look for a pattern.

    b. What is the remainder when 3^{123} is divided by 5?

    c. What is the remainder when 3^{900} is divided by 2?

33. Look at the following:

    $17 \mid 10^2 - 7^2$

    $35 \mid 30^2 - 5^2$

    a. Create another example that fits this pattern.

    b. Can you generalize this pattern? That is, can you express the relationship in such a way that someone else could use your directions to create more examples?

    c. Can you prove your generalization?

34. At the end of this section, we used Venn diagrams to represent some divisibility relationships.

    a. Represent the relationship between the set of numbers divisible by 4 and the set of numbers divisible by 8 with a Venn diagram.

    b. Represent the relationship between the set of numbers divisible by 3 and the set of numbers divisible by 9 with a Venn diagram.

    c. Represent the relationship between the set of numbers divisible by 5 and the set of numbers divisible by 10 with a Venn diagram.

    d. Represent the relationship between the set of numbers divisible by 5 and the set of numbers divisible by 25 with a Venn diagram.

    e. Represent the relationship between the set of numbers divisible by 2, the set of numbers divisible by 4, the set of numbers divisible by 8, and the set of numbers divisible by 16 with a Venn diagram.

35. Can you tell if the following sum will be an odd or an even number without actually adding the numbers? Play with some other examples and then summarize and justify whatever hypotheses/rules you come up with.

    $21 + 56 + 37 + 23 + 49 + 20 + 73 + 34$

SECTION ◆ **4.2** PRIME AND COMPOSITE NUMBERS

Over the centuries, many famous mathematicians have been fascinated by prime numbers. The Greeks are believed to have discovered prime numbers and were also fascinated by them. The prime numbers were considered to be the building blocks of all natural numbers greater than 1. Children are often intrigued by prime numbers. Recall the statement from Chapter 3 that "(p)robably the major conceptual achievement of the early school years is the interpretation of numbers in terms of part and whole relationships." As in the previous section, we will again be focusing on multiplicative compositions and decompositions of natural numbers.

Let us begin our examination of prime and composite numbers by first revisiting Investigation 4.1. Are there any dates in the year 1997 that fit that pattern? Work on this and then read on. . . . 🖎

It turns out that there are no such dates, because 97 is a prime number. That is, it has only two factors: 1 and itself.

> A natural number is a **prime** number iff it has exactly two factors: 1 and itself.

A natural number that has more than two factors is called a **composite** number. Note the relationship between the words *composite* and *decomposition*, a term we have encountered several times already in this course.

The number 1 doesn't fit into either of the sets above, and so we say that 1 is neither a prime number nor a composite number.

Over the years, I have found that my strongest students are the ones who not only know facts and procedures, but also have good number sense. One of the ways to develop this number sense in elementary children is through investigations that deal with prime numbers.

Determining Whether a Number Is Prime or Composite

A question that has fascinated both ancient and modern mathematicians concerns being able to determine whether a large number is a prime number or a composite number. We don't need a large number for this question to be difficult. For example, is the number 103 prime or composite? Work on this question for a minute or so and then read on. . . . 🖎

Immediately, we can see that no even number will divide 103. However, without sophisticated techniques, in order to determine if 103 is prime, we must check to see if it is divisible by each odd number up to 51. Thus, we would have to check: 3, 5, 7, 9, 11, 13, 15, 17, 19, 21, 23, 25, 27, 29, 31, 33, 35, 37, 39, 41, 43, 45, 47, 49, 51. Do you see why we can stop at 51?

There is a very elegant shortcut that saves us from having to test all these numbers. This shortcut was discovered over 2,000 years ago and emerges from the following investigation.

INVESTIGATION **4.8** The Sieve of Eratosthenes

◆ **T**he **sieve of Eratosthenes** was developed by the Greek mathematician Eratosthenes, who lived about 230 B.C., as a tool for determining all prime numbers less than a given number. Our demonstrating the sieve here has several purposes. First, it will uncover a more efficient way to determine if a large number is prime or not. Second, it will further develop your ability to see and to extend patterns. As usual, you will get far more from the following activity if you do it with pencil and paper rather than just read.

TABLE 4.3

1	2	3	4	5	6	7	8	9	10
11	12	13	14	15	16	17	18	19	20
21	22	23	24	25	26	27	28	29	30
31	32	33	34	35	36	37	38	39	40
41	42	43	44	45	46	47	48	49	50
51	52	53	54	55	56	57	58	59	60
61	62	63	64	65	66	67	68	69	70
71	72	73	74	75	76	77	78	79	80
81	82	83	84	85	86	87	88	89	90
91	92	93	94	95	96	97	98	99	100
101	102	103	104	105	106	107	108	109	110
111	112	113	114	115	116	117	118	119	120
121	122	123	124	125	126	127	128	129	130
131	132	133	134	135	136	137	138	139	140
141	142	143	144	145	146	147	148	149	150

In Table 4.3, cross out 1, which is neither composite nor prime.

Circle 2, which is the first prime number. Now cross out all multiples of 2.

Circle the next unmarked number (3), which must be prime, and cross out all multiples of 3. Did you make use of any patterns to help you cross out multiples of 3?

Circle the next unmarked number (5), and then cross out all multiples of 5.

Circle the next unmarked number (7) and stop. Based on the crossing out that you have already done, what do you predict will be the first multiple of 7 that you will have to cross out? Think and then cross out all multiples of 7 and then read on. . . .

You found that the first multiple of 7 that wasn't already crossed out was 49; that is, 7 · 7. The other multiples of 7 that you had to cross out were 7 · 11, 7 · 13, and 7 · 17.

Now circle the next prime number, 11, and stop. Before you cross out all multiples of 11, what do you predict will be the first multiple of 11 that you will have to cross out? Think and then cross out all multiples of 11 and then read on. . . .

You found that the first multiple of 11 that wasn't already crossed out was 121; that is 11 · 11. Now circle all the numbers in the table that have not yet been crossed out. What do you think these numbers have in common? Think and then read on. . . .

DISCUSSION

If your intuition said that these are all prime numbers, you are right. Can you explain *why* all these numbers *must* be prime numbers? For example, can you explain why 149, for example, cannot be a multiple of 7, 11, 13, 17, 19, or any other prime number less than 149? Work on this question and then read on.

One way of demonstrating why all the remaining numbers must be prime involves **indirect reasoning**, which is a method of logic in which we prove that something is false by assuming that it is true and then showing that this assumption leads to a contradiction.

Let us assume that one of the circled numbers in the sieve, for example 149, is not prime.

- 149 is clearly not a multiple of 2, because it's an odd number.
- 149 cannot be a multiple of 3, because it would have been crossed out with the multiples of 3.
- 149 cannot be a multiple of 5, because it would have been crossed out with the multiples of 5.
- 149 cannot be a multiple of 7, because it would have been crossed out with the multiples of 7.
- 149 cannot be a multiple of 11, because it would have been crossed out with the multiples of 11.
- 149 cannot be a multiple of 13, because we know from our investigation with the sieve that the first possible multiple of 13 that hasn't already been crossed out would be 13 · 13, which is 169.

In similar fashion, we can show that 149 cannot be a multiple of any other number. This disproves the initial assumption that 149 was not prime. Therefore, it is impossible that 149 is a composite number, and therefore, it must be a prime number.

Actually, once we know that 13 is not a factor of 149, we are finished. Do you see why?

If we begin to cross out multiples of 13, we find that all the multiples of 13 from 1 · 13 to 12 · 13 had already been crossed out. Therefore, the first multiple of 13 that we needed to cross out is 13 · 13. But 13 · 13 is 169, which is greater than 149, and so we know that 13 cannot be a factor of 149. Similarly, all numbers greater than 13 (which must have squares that are greater than 13^2) cannot be factors of 149. We can turn this observation into a generalization: If the square of a number is greater than the number we are testing for, we can stop.

This very powerful generalization, in turn, can be stated as a rule:

> **Test for determining if a number is prime:**
> To determine whether a natural number n is a prime number, list all the prime numbers p that satisfy the equation $p \leq \sqrt{n}$. If none of those prime numbers divides n, then n is a prime number.

Prime Factorization

Recall the question about possible dates in 1996 in which the product of the day and month will be 96. We mentioned that another strategy would be to find all the factors of 96. One tool for finding all the factors of a number is to determine the prime factorization of that number—that is, to represent that number as the product of numbers, each of which is prime.

The prime factorization of 96 is $2 \cdot 2 \cdot 2 \cdot 2 \cdot 2 \cdot 3$. Do you see how this representation can help us to determine all the factors of 96? Think and then read on. . . .

We simply check to see if our number can be constructed from the prime factorization. Clearly, 2 and 3 are factors of 96.

- 4 is a factor because $4 = 2 \cdot 2$.
- 5 is not a factor of 96 because 5 is not in this set.
- 6 is a factor because $6 = 2 \cdot 3$.
- 7 is not a factor of 96 because 7 is not in this set.
- 8 is a factor because $8 = 2 \cdot 2 \cdot 2$.
- 9 is not a factor of 96 because $3 \cdot 3$ is not in this set.
- 10 is not a factor of 96 because $2 \cdot 5$ is not in this set.
- 11 is not a factor of 96 because 11 is not in this set.
- 12 is a factor because $12 = 2 \cdot 2 \cdot 3$.

Since $8 \cdot 12 = 96$, we don't have to look any further. Do you see why?

Recall the first investigation, in which we saw that many dates came in pairs. In this case, each factor up to 12 is part of a pair: $1 \cdot 96$, $2 \cdot 48$, $3 \cdot 32$, $4 \cdot 24$, $6 \cdot 16$, and $8 \cdot 12$.

Thus, the factors of 96 are: 1, 2, 3, 4, 6, 8, 12, 16, 24, 32, 48, and 96.

Now it is simply a matter of determining which possibilities are valid dates; for example, 1/96/96 is not a valid date, nor is 2/48/96.

Determining the prime factorization of a number is not an easy task for many students, and there are many different methods. Take a few minutes to determine the prime factorization of 36 and 84. Then read the following discussion.

Tree diagrams and prime factorization   One technique for determining the prime factorization of a number that appeals to many students is to use a tree diagram. The top of the tree is the original number. Each number is equal to the product of the two numbers immediately below it. Below are two tree diagrams that produce the prime factorization for 36, that is, $2 \cdot 2 \cdot 3 \cdot 3$.

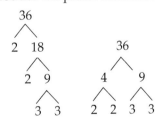

Division and prime factorization   Other students prefer a technique that looks like long division that goes up instead of down. The division is done mentally. Some students like to do it "in order"; that is, they divide by 2 until they can do it no more, then go to bigger and bigger prime numbers. When they do this, their final answer is already in order from smallest to largest.

[3] David Wells, *The Penguin Dictionary of Curious and Interesting Numbers* (New York: Penguin Books, 1986), p. 30.

[4] Ibid., p. 30.

$$\begin{array}{r} 7 \\ 3\overline{)21} \\ 2\overline{)42} \\ 2\overline{)84} \end{array} \qquad 84 = 2 \cdot 2 \cdot 3 \cdot 7$$

The Fundamental Theorem of Arithmetic

If you compare the two tree diagrams above, you can see that we got the same prime factorization for 36 regardless of how we started. It turns out that this is true in all cases. This seemingly obvious statement actually has quite a formal name, the **Fundamental Theorem of Arithmetic**. It states that every natural number greater than 1 has one unique way of being represented as a product of its prime factors.

Let us use the number 60 to illustrate this theorem. As you can see, it doesn't matter which path we take. When we get to the end, all the factors are prime, and we find that $60 = 2 \cdot 2 \cdot 3 \cdot 5$.

$$60 = 2 \cdot 30 = 2 \cdot (6 \cdot 5) = 2 \cdot [(3 \cdot 2) \cdot 5] = 2 \cdot 3 \cdot 2 \cdot 5 = 2 \cdot 2 \cdot 3 \cdot 5$$
$$60 = 10 \cdot 6 = (2 \cdot 5) \cdot (2 \cdot 3) = 2 \cdot 5 \cdot 2 \cdot 3 = 2 \cdot 2 \cdot 3 \cdot 5$$

A Largest Prime Number?

"And the boy in Winnetka, Illinois, who wanted to know: Is there a train so long you can't count the cars? Is there a blackboard so long it will hold all the numbers?" (Carl Sandburg).

This quote brings to mind a related question: Is there a largest prime number? Do you think there is one or not? What arguments could be made either way? 🖉

The Fundamental Theorem of Arithmetic enables us to answer this question. It turns out that there is no largest prime number; there are infinitely many. The first proof of this conjecture occurs in Euclid's *Elements*. The proof uses indirect reasoning, in which we begin by assuming that there is a largest prime number, which we will call P.

Let us now create a number X, in the following way:

$$X = (2 \cdot 3 \cdot 4 \cdots P) + 1$$

Since we have assumed that P is the largest *prime* number, X must therefore be a *composite* number; that is, it must have at least one factor other than 1 and itself.

Let F represent the smallest *prime factor* of X. Since F is a prime number and since P is the largest prime number, F must be a prime number less than P; that is, it must be one of the numbers 2, 3, 4, . . . up to P.

However, it cannot be one of these numbers. Do you see why? Think before reading on. . . . 🖉

We constructed our number X in such a way that it is not divisible by 2, 3, 4, or any number up to P. That is equivalent to saying that 2 is not a factor of X, 3 is not a factor, and so forth. Thus, the smallest possible prime factor of X is greater than P, which is supposed to be the largest prime number. This contradiction shows that the assumption that there is a largest prime number cannot be true.

BEYOND THE CLASSROOM

The invention of radio earlier in this century had many ramifications for people's lives. During World War II, the ability to communicate by radio enabled commanders to be more effective both before and during battles. However, the other side was able to receive the messages too, as long as they knew the radio frequency on which the messages were transmitted. Therefore, important messages were sent in code. Functions were created to encode messages. One very simple coding function is to replace each letter with the next letter in the alphabet. Using this code, what is the following message: I B Q Q Z C J S U I E B Z? The answer is at the end of the next paragraph. As time went on, each side became better at cracking the other side's codes. A team of British analysts developed a machine to crack German codes, which became known as the German Enigma cipher machine.

More recently, several MIT scientists have developed what is called a safe coding system. The process involves selecting two very large prime numbers. The coding key is the product of these two numbers. Since it is very difficult to factor extremely large numbers, it is virtually impossible to crack such codes. Answer to coded message: happy birthday!

INVESTIGATION **4.9** **Numbers with Personalities: Perfect and Other Numbers**

Some of the names that have been given to certain kinds of numbers convey human characteristics: for example, perfect, amicable, sociable, weird, narcissistic, and irrational. We will examine some of these numbers, because they provide rich ground for developing mathematical thinking; they are also good "rainy-day activities" when you teach.

A. A number *n* is a **perfect** number iff the sum of its *proper divisors* is equal to *n*. A **proper divisor** of a number is a divisor that is less than the number. Do you see why 6 is the first perfect number?

DISCUSSION

Six is the first perfect number because 1, 2, and 3 are the proper divisors of 6 and their sum is 6.

B. Perfect numbers lead to two other kinds of numbers, which are called abundant and deficient. Before looking at the definitions of these terms, try to define them yourself....

A number *n* is an **abundant** number iff the sum of its proper divisors is greater than *n*.

A number *n* is a **deficient** number iff the sum of its proper divisors is less than *n*.

Make a table listing the first 30 natural numbers. Put an A next to ones you think will be abundant, a D next to ones you think will be deficient, and a ? next to ones you feel could go either way. Try to articulate the reasoning behind your predictions. Then read on....

DISCUSSION

All prime numbers are deficient by definition. Do you see why? Since the only proper factor of a prime number is 1, the sum of the proper factors of a prime number is 1. Of the nonprime numbers less than 30, the deficient numbers are: 4, 8, 9, 10, 14, 15, 16, 21, 22, 25, 26, 27.

Does this list shed light on any other relationships? What does it show?

Notice that the subset of the square numbers in the above set {4, 9, 16, 25} has only deficient numbers. Also, except for 3, any doubles of members of the set of prime numbers less than 30 {2, 3, 5, 7, 11, 13, 17, 19, 23, 29} will also be deficient. Why is this?

The following numbers are abundant: 12, 18, 20, 24, and 30. What do you notice about this set?

One pattern that students often observe that leads to a hypothesis is that all of these numbers are even. Is this just coincidence, or is it true that all abundant numbers are even numbers? What do you think? This question will be left unanswered for you to solve on your own.

The active reader will have noticed that we overlooked 28 in our lists of deficient and abundant numbers. Why?

Summary

In this section, we have examined another way of classifying natural numbers: prime and composite (and, of course, 1, which is neither prime nor composite). The Sieve of Eratosthenes not only gave us a tool to determine if a number is prime but also helped us to develop and refine other problem-solving tools. We have also found that each number has a unique prime factorization, which is another kind of decomposition (funny how this idea keeps coming up!). It is critically important to note that the decomposition of composite numbers into their prime factors is a multiplicative decomposition; this is one of many places where seeing a number in additive or multiplicative terms is not a matter of preference but a matter of structure.

We have explored several strategies that enable us to determine the prime factorization of a natural number. When you teach children, you will find that the Fundamental Theorem of Arithmetic, like the commutative property, is not immediately obvious to children, and in both cases, an understanding of these ideas makes work with mathematics much easier. Determining the prime factorization is like looking through a microscope to see the atomic structure of a molecule. In one sense, prime numbers are the building blocks for whole numbers. We have also seen that the concept of prime and composite numbers has applications outside the classroom.

The notions of prime and composite enable us to better understand Explorations 4.1 through 4.5. Think back to the ones that you did. How does this section add to your understanding of those explorations? Then read on. . . . 📖

In Exploration 4.1 (Taxman), we realize that the first move is to select the largest prime number. We realize that numbers with many factors (like 24) are better left for the end of the game. Do you see why? In Exploration 4.2 (Factors), we found that although all prime numbers have only two factors, the set of composite numbers is not so simple. Although most composite numbers have an even number of factors, not all do, and some composite numbers have many factors. Some have so many factors that we call them abundant numbers!

EXERCISES 4.2

1. Find the prime factorization of the numbers below:

   a. 92   **b.** 144   **c.** 196

   d. 504   **e.** 756   **f.** 14,586

2. In each case below, determine whether the number is prime or composite. You will probably want to use a combination of divisibility tests, common sense, and concepts from our work with prime numbers to answer this question.

   a. 223   **b.** 347   **c.** 437

   d. 961   **e.** 3,437

3. Which of the numbers between 511 and 525 are prime? Briefly explain your reason for denoting each number as either composite or prime.

4. Consider the numbers representing the second half of the twentieth century. Which of those numbers are prime?

5. To determine whether 617 is a prime number, it suffices to check that no prime number less than ___ is a factor of it. Explain your answer.

6. A **superprime** is defined in the following way: It is a number such that when each time a digit is removed (one at a time), starting at the right side, the remaining number is still prime. For example, 2,391 is a super prime because 239 is a prime and 23 is a prime and 2 is a prime. Find three three-digit superprime numbers. Describe strategies that helped your search.

7. There is an all-star team of abundant numbers called **superabundant** numbers. Here are the membership criteria for inclusion to this exclusive club:

   Take the sum of all its divisors, including itself. Divide by this sum by the number itself.

   If this quotient is greater than the quotient for any natural number less than this number, then the number is called superabundant.

   a. Design and run a spreadsheet to determine which of the first 50 natural numbers are superabundant, and then write directions for your program so that others may use it.

   b. Describe any new patterns or observations about characteristics of superabundant numbers that you found in making and analyzing this table.

   c. Make a line graph of the first 50 natural numbers in which the horizontal axis consists of successive natural numbers and the vertical axis represents the value of the quotient used to determine whether the number is superabundant. What new observations come from the graph?

   d. Predict the next superabundant number and explain the reasoning behind your prediction.

8. Construct a number that has exactly 5 divisors.

9. **a.** Find the smallest natural number that is divisible by the first ten counting numbers.

   b. How else could this question have been worded?

10. **a.** What is the smallest four-digit number that has exactly 3 factors? Justify your answer and explain how you arrived at your solution.

    b. What is the largest three-digit number that has exactly 4 factors? Justify your answer and explain how you arrived at your solution.

11. What is the smallest composite number that is divisible by none of the primes 2, 3, 5, and 7? Briefly explain your answer.

12. Here are partial directions for creating five consecutive composite numbers. First, begin with $2 \cdot 3 \cdot 4 \cdot 5 \cdot 6$. Then use the divisibility theorem from the previous section; that is, if $a \mid b$ and $a \mid c$, then $a \mid (b + c)$. Can you use these hints to create five consecutive composite numbers?

13. An organization with 100 people will be divided into smaller committees.

    a. What are the possible committee sizes if every committee must be the same size?

    b. What are the possible committee sizes if the organization wants to have some large committees (each the same size) and some smaller committees (each the same size), and the larger committees must be at least twice the size of the smaller ones?

    c. Create at least one more restriction on part (b) that would lead to fewer possible answers.

14. **a.** If 21 divides m, what else must divide m?

    b. If 36 divides m, what else must divide m?

15. If you examine all the prime numbers less than 100, some of them are "next-door neighbors"—for example, 11 and 13, 17 and 19, 71 and 73. Mathematicians call these twin primes or prime twins. What about prime triplets? Only one set of prime triplets exists: 3, 5, 7. Prove that there cannot be another set of prime triplets.

16. This is a famous problem in mathematics education. Suppose you lined up 1,000 dolls in a row, all facing up. Then suppose you walked down the line and turned over every other doll. Now, one-half of the dolls would be facing up (those representing odd numbers) and one-half of the dolls would be facing down. Now suppose you walked down the line again, and this time turned over every third doll. That is, if it was facing up, you would turn it so that it was facing down; if it was facing down, you would turn it so that it was facing up. Continue in this manner 1,000 times. At this point, which dolls will be facing up and which dolls will be facing down?

The following suggestions may help you with the problem: Some students find it helpful to make the problem smaller—for example, 50 dolls or 25 dolls. Some students find it helpful to model the problem. What other objects could you use to represent the dolls? Most students find it helpful to make a table to represent their findings.

17. **a.** Describe the patterns you find in the following figure.

    b. Explain how to make the figure as if you were talking on the phone to someone.

    c. Find a shortcut for finding the sum of any hexagon.

    d. Find a shortcut for finding the sum of any row.

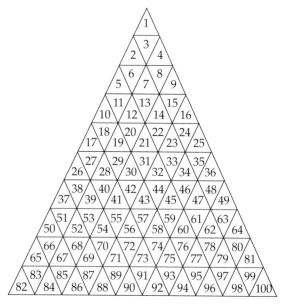

18. The following questions have come from students over the years. Explore these questions with a partner. After your exploration, summarize and justify your findings.

a. Of the first 100 numbers, 25 are prime. How many of the second hundred numbers will be prime? Will the frequency (density) of prime numbers increase, decrease, or stay at about 25 percent as the numbers get larger and larger?

b. Can you predict when twin primes will occur? How many are there in the first 100 numbers? Will there be the same number of twin primes in the next 100 numbers?

c. The largest difference between two prime numbers less than 100 is 8—that is, between 89 and 97. What is the largest difference you can find between any two prime numbers?

d. Are there more primes with a 1, 3, 7, or 9 in the ones place?

19. These are some famous conjectures, some of which have yet to be proved or disproved! Explore these conjectures with a partner. Then explain why you think the conjecture is true.

a. Any prime greater than 3 is within 1 unit of a multiple of 6.

b. Every even number can be expressed as the difference of two primes.

c. This conjecture comes from Fermat: Any prime number of the form $p = 4n + 1$, $n \in N$, can be expressed as the sum of two squares in only one way.

d. This conjecture is called Goldbach's conjecture after Christian Goldbach (1690–1764): Any even number greater than 2 can be expressed as the sum of two primes. To this day, no one has found a counterexample or proved this conjecture.

e. Another conjecture made by Goldbach: Any odd number greater than 5 can be expressed as the sum of three prime numbers.

f. Every triangular number can be represented as the sum of a square number and two triangular numbers.

SECTION   4.3

GREATEST COMMON FACTOR AND LEAST COMMON MULTIPLE

WHAT DO YOU THINK?

- What does it mean to say that the GCF and the LCM let us decompose composite numbers?

- How are the GCF and the LCM related to each other?

One of the many decisions I had to make when writing this book was where to place the section on the greatest common factor (GCF) and least common multiple (LCM). In elementary school, these concepts are used primarily when adding and simplifying fractions, and so this section could be placed in Chapter 5. However, these concepts have applications beyond fractions problems, and one of the goals of this book is to get students to see that mathematics is more than just procedures and that many mathematical ideas are connected to other mathematical ideas. Therefore, we will first examine these concepts in this chapter and then apply them to fraction ideas in Chapter 5.

The following problem is similar to Investigation 1.3, in which the teacher wanted to cut out squares for her students to use in making paper dinosaurs. Let's say that a teacher has a rectangular sheet of cardboard 420 centimeters long and 378 centimeters wide, and that he wants to cut that sheet into many squares, all of the same size. What are the dimensions of the largest possible square (whose length is a whole number) that will create no waste? Think about this problem and then read on. . . .

DISCUSSION

STRATEGY 1: Use guess–check–revise

Looking at the numbers, we can see that they are both divisible by 2. So we could make 2 by 2 squares. Using the divisibility rule for 3, we can see that they are also divisible by 3, and so we can make 3 by 3 squares. We can proceed in this manner, checking for divisibility by 4, 5, 6, and so on, until we find that we can go no further.

STRATEGY 2: Use prime factorization

What if we found the prime factorization of both numbers? How might that help us? Think about this before reading on. . . .

$$378 = 2 \cdot 3 \cdot 3 \cdot 3 \cdot 7$$
$$420 = 2 \cdot 2 \cdot 3 \cdot 5 \cdot 7$$

Since we are looking for a number that divides *both* 378 and 420, an equivalent statement is that we are looking for a number that is a factor of both. In fact, we are looking for the largest such common factor. By looking at the prime factorization of both numbers, we can see that they have in common a 2, a 3, and a 7. How does this help? Some students say, "Add the three numbers, and that will be the largest square, that is, 12 by 12." Some students say, "Multiply the three numbers, and that will be the largest square, that is, 42 by 42." What do you think? Why?

When we examine factors, we are looking at numbers from a *multiplicative* perspective, and thus adding them is not connected to this question. In fact, 12 does not divide 378; do you see why? However, 42 does divide both 378 and 420. Do you see why?

In fact, 42 is the *greatest* number that divides both 378 and 420. If we express this conclusion using the term *factor* instead of *divides*, we can say that 42 is the greatest factor that 378 and 420 have in common. A more concise way to say this is that 42 is the *greatest common factor* of 378 and 420.

The Greatest Common Factor

Whenever we examine two natural numbers, we can create a set of numbers called their common factors. In some cases, the only common factor is 1; for example, examine 7 and 10. However, in many cases, the numbers have several common factors. The greatest of these common factors is called the greatest common factor (GCF). We use the notation **GCF**(a, b) to express the GCF of two natural numbers a and b.

Note: In a similar fashion, we can speak of the GCF of three or more numbers. This will be explored in the exercises.

Exploring the greatest common factor concept Before we examine techniques for finding the GCF of two or more numbers, let us take some time to explore the concept. This is analogous to the work we did in Chapter 3 when we explored the concepts of addition and subtraction to better understand the algorithms, and then explored the concepts of multiplication and division to better understand those algorithms. What can we say about the size of the GCF of *any* two numbers *a* and *b*? For example, will it always be smaller than the two numbers? Can it be in between two numbers? What do you think? One student compared this question to thinking of the qualifications for a job; for example, what qualities would you expect in an excellent elementary teacher: likes children, has eyes in the back of the head, doesn't require much sleep? Take a few moments to think about this before reading on. . . .

The GCF of two numbers is generally smaller than either of them, since it has to be a factor of each. However, there are some cases in which the GCF of two numbers is *not* smaller than either of them. Can you think of such a case? Think and then read on. . . .

Although the GCF can never be larger than either of the numbers, it can be equal to the smaller of the two numbers. For example, the GCF of 4 and 8 is 4.

In a manner similar to a detective story, we can make predictions about the GCF if we know just a little bit about the two numbers. For example, if you know that two numbers are prime, what can you say about their GCF? Think and then read on. . . .

Prime numbers have only two factors, and one of them is 1. Since the other factor will be the number itself, we can conclude that if the two numbers are prime, their GCF is 1.

What can you say about the GCF of two even numbers? Think and then read on. . . .

Their GCF will be at least 2. Why is this?

What about the GCF of two odd numbers? Think and then read on. . . .

This clue alone is not enough to say much, except that the GCF will be an odd number also. Why is this?

INVESTIGATION 4.11 Methods for Finding the GCF

Let us now investigate how we might determine the GCF of two numbers. Rather than give an efficient procedure right away, we will take some time to build the foundation of this procedure, much like taking care while constructing the foundation of a house.

Using only the definition of GCF, how would you determine GCF(45, 60)? Work on this any way you want to. My only recommendation is that you think about the meaning of whatever you do, as opposed to "grope-and-hope." Think and then read on. . . .

DISCUSSION

STRATEGY 1: Use factorization

We could, as we just saw, determine all the factors of each number and then find the largest of the common factors:

> Factors of 45 = {1, 3, 5, 9, 15, 45}
>
> Factors of 60 = {1, 2, 3, 4, 5, 6, 10, 12, 15, 20, 30, 60}
>
> Common factors = {1, 3, 5, 15}

We see from this list that 15 is the GCF of 45 and 60.

STRATEGY 2: Use intuition or number sense

A student who is highly intuitive and has good number sense might just know that 15 divides both these numbers. The fact that 15 divides both numbers simply means that 15 is a common factor. How might you reason that, in fact, 15 is the GCF? Think before reading on. . . . 🖉

Let us represent the results of dividing each number by 5 (which we know is not the GCF) and by 15. What do you notice?

$$45 = 5 \cdot 9 \qquad 45 = 15 \cdot 3$$
$$60 = 5 \cdot 12 \qquad 60 = 15 \cdot 4$$

When we divide 45 and 60 by 5, we are left with 9 and 12. When we divide 45 and 60 by 15, we are left with 3 and 4. One difference between the factors 9 and 12 and the factors 3 and 4 is that 3 and 4 have no common factors.

When two numbers have no factors in common, they are said to be **relatively prime.** One of my students came up with an interesting paraphrase of this concept: If two numbers are relatively prime, they are prime to each other.

Since 3 and 4 are relatively prime, 15 is the GCF of 45 and 60. Do you see why?

STRATEGY 3: Repeatedly divide by prime numbers

What about people who did not have the intuition and number sense to see this? Is their only recourse the long way we saw above? Another procedure involves an adaptation of the long division algorithm. The problem below illustrates a systematic application in that we begin with the smallest prime divisor and then move up. That is, we first divide both numbers by 3. At this point, we move up to 5 because 15 and 20 are both divisible by 5. The resulting quotients, 3 and 4, have no factors in common. The GCF of 45 and 60 is the product of their common factors: $3 \cdot 5 = 15$.

$$
\begin{array}{r}
3, \ 4 \\
5{\overline{\smash{\big)}\,15, \ 20}} \\
3{\overline{\smash{\big)}\,45, \ 60}}
\end{array}
$$

STRATEGY 4: Use prime factorization

This strategy uses the Fundamental Theorem of Arithmetic, which we explored in Section 4.2. We first determine the prime factorization of each number and then look for common factors. If we look at the prime factorizations of 45 and 60 and circle the factors that the two numbers have in common, we have the following:

$$45 = 3 \cdot \boxed{3 \cdot 5}$$
$$60 = 2 \cdot 2 \cdot \boxed{3 \cdot 5}$$

We can further refine this procedure by using exponents:

$$45 = 3^2 \cdot 5^1$$
$$60 = 2^2 \cdot 3^1 \cdot 5^1$$

The GCF is determined by examining those factors that both numbers have in common and then taking the *smallest* exponent in each case. The common factors of 45 and 60 are 3 and 5. The smallest exponent of 3 is 1, and the smaller exponent of 5 is 1. Thus $3 \cdot 5$ is the GCF.

CHILDREN

Using Cuisenaire rods, how many different ways can you make a 12 train and an 8 train using the same colors?

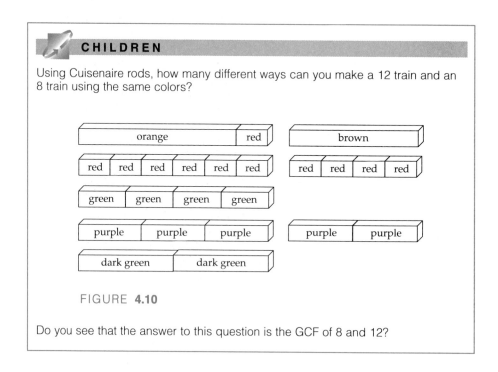

FIGURE **4.10**

Do you see that the answer to this question is the GCF of 8 and 12?

Least Common Multiple

Let us begin our investigation of the least common multiple (LCM) by having you think about the following question before reading on: What do you think "least common multiple" means? Write a definition in your own language.

Let us examine this concept word by word, using a specific example. Suppose we wanted to find the least common multiple of 8 and 12. At the most basic level, we can generate the set of multiples of 8 and 12, and then find the smallest number that the two sets have in common.

Multiples of 8 = {8, 16, 24, 32, 40, 48, 56, 64, 72, 80, 88, 96, 104, . . .}
Multiples of 12 = {12, 24, 36, 48, 60, 72, 84, 96, 108, 120, 132, . . .}

What multiples do the two numbers have in common?

These two numbers have many common multiples: {24, 48, 72, 96, . . .}. Since the least of the common multiples is 24, we say that LCM(8, 12) = 24.

Whenever we examine two natural numbers, we can create a set of numbers called their common multiples. The least of these common multiples is called the **least common multiple** (LCM). We use the notation **LCM(*a*, *b*)** to express the LCM of two natural numbers, *a* and *b*.

Note: In a similar fashion, we can speak of the LCM of three or more numbers. This will be explored in the exercises.

Exploring the least common multiple concept The active reader might think at this point, "Yes, this will work, but what if the numbers are larger? This approach could get tedious pretty fast!" This is true. However, as we did with the greatest common factor, let us extend that definition to learn more about the general attributes of the LCM. What can we say about the size of the LCM of *any* two numbers *a* and *b*? For example, will it always be greater than the two numbers? Can it be in between the two numbers? What do you think? Take a few moments to think about this before reading on. . . .

The LCM of two numbers is generally greater than either of them, since it has to be a multiple of each. However, there are some cases in which the LCM of two numbers is *not* greater than either of them. Can you think of such a case? Think and then read on. . . .

When one number is a multiple of the other, the LCM will be equal to the larger number; for example, LCM(5, 10) = 10. Why is this?

Now let me give you two more numbers. Without doing any computation, what can you tell me about the LCM of 18 and 40? Think and read on. . . .

Several possible responses include:

- It is greater than 40.
- It is less than or equal to $18 \cdot 40$, or 720.
- It will be a multiple of both numbers.
- It ends in a zero, since all multiples of 40 end in 0.

Strategies for Finding the LCM

Now let us examine how we might find the actual LCM of 18 and 40. Again, there are many ways to determine the LCM of two numbers. We will examine several ways.

One way of determining the LCM of 18 and 40 is to construct the LCM by beginning with one of the numbers and applying our understanding of LCM. This process is illustrated in the following discussion:

Reasoning	**The work**
The LCM *must* contain all the factors of 18.	$18 = 2 \cdot 3 \cdot 3$, LCM(18, 40) must contain: $2 \cdot 3 \cdot 3$
Now, in order to *also* be a multiple of 40, the LCM will have to contain all the factors in the prime factorization of 40.	$40 = 2 \cdot 2 \cdot 2 \cdot 5$
Looking now at the factors of 18, what factors of 40 are we missing? Think and then read on. . . .	
We need to put two more 2s and one 5 into our prime factorization of LCM(18, 40).	LCM(18, 40) must contain: **2** $\cdot$ **2** $\cdot$ 2 $\cdot$ 3 $\cdot$ 3 $\cdot$ **5** That is, LCM(18, 40) = 360.

Reasoning	The work
Another way of illustrating this process is to note the prime factorizations of each number and realize that the Least Common Multiple must contain all the factors in either number with no redundancies. That is, the LCM needs to contain three 2s, two 3s, and one 5.	$2 \cdot 3 \cdot 3$ $2 \cdot 2 \cdot 2 \cdot \quad \cdot 5$

Using Prime Factorization and Exponents to Find the LCM

There is a more formal way to find the LCM, and this is connected to one of the ways in which we found the GCF. This method comes from representing the prime factorization of each number in exponential form:

$$18 = 2 \cdot 3 \cdot 3 \qquad = 2^1 \cdot 3^2$$
$$40 = 2 \cdot 2 \cdot 2 \cdot 5 \qquad = 2^3 \cdot 5^1$$

When finding the GCF, we took the smaller exponent of all common factors. What do you think we will do when finding the LCM? Think and read on. . . . 📖

In order for a number to be the LCM, it must contain all the factors in either number. For example, since the prime factorization of 18 contains a 2, the LCM must contain a 2. However, since the prime factorization of 40 contains three 2s, the LCM must contain three 2s. Thus, when we examine the prime factorization of each number, whenever there is a common factor, we must take the greater exponent.

Using this method, we find that LCM(18, 40) = $2^3 \cdot 3^2 \cdot 5^1$. Do you see why? 📖

The only factor that 18 and 40 have in common is 2, and the greatest exponent above 2 is 3 (meaning that $2 \cdot 2 \cdot 2$ is a factor of 40). Therefore, the prime factorization of the LCM must contain 2^3. The non-common factors are 3 and 5, and so 3^2 and 5^1 are also placed in the prime factorization of the LCM.

Note: This procedure with exponents makes sense to some students and not to others. The point is not that everyone should use this procedure because it is the *best* procedure. Rather, the point is that this is a very efficient procedure *if* you feel comfortable with it. If you don't feel comfortable with this procedure, then you can work with it until it makes more sense or you can use another procedure.

The concepts of GCF and LCM are two essential number theory concepts. Investigation 4.10 (Cutting Squares) demonstrates one real-life application. If you did Exploration 4.5, you found that these terms enabled you to predict orbits and paths in star patterns. The most direct application of these concepts in the elementary school curriculum has to do with fractions. We need to find the GCF when we are simplifying fractions, and we need to find the LCM when we are adding fractions with unlike denominators. In the remainder of this section, we will develop and explore relationships between GCF and LCM.

from two regions, the GCF consists of numbers from the common region, and the LCM consists of numbers from all three regions.

LEARNING

For some mathematicians, the unorthodox use of Venn diagrams is heresy. However, for many mathematics educators, there is much value in having students invent (sometimes unorthodox) procedures and algorithms. This is alluded to in several places in the NCTM Standards. They speak of increasing attention to "creating algorithms and procedures" (*Curriculum Standards*, p. 70). In the

Professional Standards, they speak of "invented and conventional terms and symbols" among Tools for Enhancing Discourse (*Professional Standards*, p. 52). One of the cornerstone assumptions of the NCTM Standards is the belief in the value of "conjecturing, inventing, and problem solving—away from an emphasis on mechanistic answer-finding" (*Professional Standards*, p. 3).

Yet Another Way to Find the LCM

This relationship between the GCF and the LCM has a very practical application. It yields another way to find the LCM of two numbers. Do you see how? Think and then read on. . . .

Consider, for example, finding LCM(40, 72). The equation in Investigation 4.12 is an algebraic equation, and thus we can use the rules of algebra to solve the equation for LCM(a, b). Doing so, we have

$$\text{LCM}(a, b) = \frac{a \cdot b}{\text{GCF}(a, b)}$$

As you may have already discovered, finding the GCF of two numbers is generally much easier than finding the LCM. Thus, to find LCM(40, 72), we have only to find GCF(40, 72) and then solve the equation. Since GCF(40, 72) = 8, we have

$$\text{LCM}(40, 72) = \frac{40 \cdot 72}{8}$$

If you pause for a few seconds, you should be able to see how you can determine this computation in your head. Do so and then read on. . . .

If you first divide the 72 by 8, you then have the relatively simple multiplication problem $40 \cdot 9$, which is 360.

INVESTIGATION **4.13** Going Deeper into the GCF and the LCM

The following problem provides an opportunity to develop your problem-solving toolbox while applying your understanding of GCF, LCM, and their relationship.

If the GCF of 45 and x is 9, and the LCM of 45 and x is 135, find x.

Take a few minutes to work on this problem on your own and then read on. . . .

DISCUSSION

There are several different ways to solve this problem. I want to take this time to emphasize the value of thinking *before* jumping into a problem. Think about the characteristics of x. What do we know about x from the given information? First, let's look at the other two numbers.

$$45 = 3 \cdot 3 \cdot 5$$
$$135 = 3 \cdot 3 \cdot 3 \cdot 5$$

If 9 is the GCF of 45 and x, that means x is a multiple of 9. Do you see why? If the LCM of 45 and x is 135, that means that the prime factorization of x has to have at least three 3s. Do you see why?

Using this line of reasoning, our first candidate for the answer is a multiple of 9 that has three 3s: $3 \cdot 3 \cdot 3 = 27$

It also turns out, not surprisingly, that 27 is the correct answer. The value of doing a bit of qualitative thinking at the beginning of the problem recalls the old proverb, "A stitch in time saves nine!"

Relationships of Operations on the Set of Natural Numbers

One of the more important goals of elementary school mathematics is for students to be able not only to compute but to understand the relatedness of various mathematical concepts and procedures. There is much evidence, from the National Assessment of Educational Progress and elsewhere, that this is not happening for many students. This represents an ironic twist. As mentioned at the beginning of the chapter, the Pythagoreans were fascinated by the properties of and relationships among natural numbers. They called the study of natural numbers *arithmetic* to distinguish it from *logistic*, by which they meant the practical art of computing with numbers. Thus, what they called logistics, and felt was beneath arithmetic, is what we have come to call arithmetic! The Pythagoreans are also credited with developing the word *mathematics*, by which they meant the following four subjects: geometry, arithmetic, music, and astronomy.

One of the important "big ideas" that the Pythagoreans meant by arithmetic is the part-whole aspect of numbers—what some people refer to as understanding how numbers are decomposed and composed. In the lower elementary grades, the primary focus is on additive decompositions. For example, a student who understands the various ways in which 10 can be decomposed—9 + 1, 8 + 2, 7 + 3, 6 + 4, 5 + 5, and so on—knows more than just "number facts." This decomposition is a critical part of knowing how to add and subtract when regrouping and is a critical part of good mental arithmetic and estimating. In the upper elementary grades, understanding multiplicative decompositions is introduced and developed. For example, 12 can be decomposed in many ways—$12 \cdot 1$, $6 \cdot 2$, and $4 \cdot 3$, as well as its prime decomposition, $2 \cdot 2 \cdot 3$.

Additive and multiplicative decomposition are "big ideas" that occur repeatedly throughout mathematics. Understanding additive and multiplicative relationships enables us to compare amounts in two different ways. For example, if an item costs $10 in one store and $15 in another store, we can compare the two prices in additive terms—it costs $5 more in the second store—or we can compare the two prices in multiplicative terms—it costs $1\frac{1}{2}$ times as much or it costs 50 percent more in the second store. These comparisons have to do with how we choose to decompose the amounts: 15 as 10 + 5 or 15 as $3 \cdot 5$ and 10 as $2 \cdot 5$. These two different ways of comparing amounts will be developed in Chapter 5 and Chapter 6.

Being aware of the relationships among these mathematical ideas (divisibility, decomposition, and additive versus multiplicative comparisons) is a key to developing what the NCTM has called mathematical power. Therefore, it is worth repeating. Because people learn and perceive ideas in different ways, I also offer the diagram in Figure 4.13, which illustrates the relationships among these three ideas. The figure shows that when we examine the way two numbers are related, we can decompose them additively or multiplicatively. In the former case, relating two numbers often leads to statements that use the words *more than* or *less than*. In the latter case, relating two numbers often leads to statements involving concepts and terms such as *divisibility, ratio, percent more,* or *percent increase.* This is only a partial map of how these three concepts are related, but it addresses the often-asked question: Am I ever going to need this stuff?

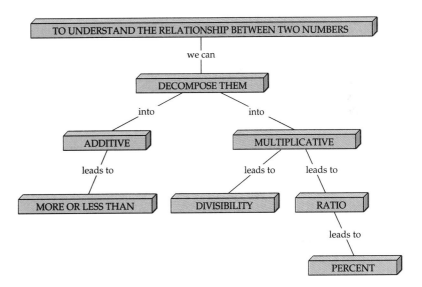

FIGURE **4.13**

Summary

In this section, we have investigated the concepts of the greatest common factor and the least common multiple. In developing more efficient strategies for determining the GCF or the LCM of two or more numbers, we used concepts from the first two sections of the chapter (divisibility, prime, and prime factorization), and we again used the idea of decomposition. In this case, the additive decompositions were not relevant; rather, the multiplicative decompositions enabled us to determine the GCF and LCM and to better understand how these two ideas are related.

These ideas of GCF, LCM, and relatively prime shed new light on our understanding of the subtler star patterns in Explorations 4.4 and 4.5. Some star patterns are polygons (triangles, squares, pentagons, and so on), and some star patterns look like stars. If we consider the relationship between x and n in star (x, n) and if x is a multiple of n (but not double n) then a polygon is created. Otherwise, a star is created. If x and n are relatively prime, then the star will have one orbit.

EXERCISES 4.3

1. Find the following:
   a. GCF(30, 75)
   b. GCF(45, 54)
   c. GCF(12, 35)
   d. GCF(27, 189)
   e. GCF(75, 144)
   f. GCF(105, 132)
   g. GCF(156, 910)
   h. GCF(630, 1,848)

2. Find the following:
   a. GCF(12, 30, 75)
   b. GCF(12, 333, 8,415)

3. Find the following:
   a. LCM(12, 20)
   b. LCM(30, 75)
   c. LCM(44, 66)
   d. LCM(462, 630)

4. Find the following:
   a. LCM(12, 30, 75)
   b. LCM(20, 30, 40)

5. a. Find two numbers such that their GCF = 2.
   b. Find two numbers, both greater than 100, such that their GCF = 2.
   c. Find two numbers such that their GCF = 6.
   d. Find two numbers, both greater than 100, such that their GCF = 6.

6. Find the GCF and the LCM of the following pairs of numbers:
   a. 25, 40
   b. 72, 108
   c. 252, 420
   d. 3,780, 3,960

7. The GCF of two numbers is 18. Their LCM is 630. What are the two numbers?

8. The GCF of 66 and x is 11; the LCM of 66 and x is 858. Find x.

9. The GCF of two numbers m and n is 12, their LCM is 600, and both m and n are less than 500. Find m and n.

10. A child has a large supply of dominoes, each of which measures 32 millimeters by 56 millimeters. She wants to lay them out to form a solid square, and she wants them all to be laid out horizontally. What will be the dimensions of the smallest square that she can form, and how many dominoes will it require?

11. George vacuums the rugs every 18 days, mows the grass every 12 days, and pays the bills every 15 days. Today he did all three. How long will it be before he has another day like today?

12. In each of the following, explain your answer.
    a. What is the relationship between a and b if GCF(a, b) = a?
    b. GCF(a, a) = ?
    c. If GCF(a, b) = b, then LCM (a, b) = ?

13. Classify each of the following as true or false, assuming that a, b, and c are integers. If a statement is true, justify it. If it is false, give a counterexample, and then revise the statement to make it a true statement.
    a. If a and b are different and prime, then GCF(a, b) = 1.
    b. If a and b are relatively prime, then LCM(a, b) = ab.
    c. If a and b are different and are both even, then GCF(a, b) = 2.
    d. If GCF(a, b) = 2, then a and b are both even.
    e. LCM(a, b) | ab.

14. Ann and Bob are cycling on a track. Ann completes one lap every 12 seconds, and Bob completes one lap every 15 seconds. When will Ann lap Bob, assuming that they started together?

15. A manufacturer sells widgets, each of which is packaged in a box whose dimensions are 4 centimeters by 6 centimeters by 10 centimeters. Design the dimensions of a box to ship widgets. Your box must hold at least 1,000 widgets.

16. I am thinking of a 2-digit number in which the sum of the digits is 9 and the number is even. These clues alone do not create one answer. Add one more clue so that there is only one answer.

CHAPTER SUMMARY

1. Prime numbers are the building blocks for the set of natural numbers.

2. Divisibility, GCF, and LCM enable us to decompose composite numbers. If elementary students understand these concepts, they can more easily compose and decompose mathematical expressions.

3. These decompositions are multiplicative rather than additive.

4. These mathematical concepts and a good problem-solving toolbox are essential to being able to see patterns that lead to hypotheses, which are then tested and either confirmed or revised.

5. Number theory connects with other mathematical concepts and fields.

6. Exploring numbers and number patterns can be fascinating and enjoyable.

Basic Concepts

Section 4.1 Divisibility and Related Concepts

divides *162*

factor *163*

multiple *163*

divisible *163*

divisor *163*

odd and even numbers *164*

Divisibility relationships:

If $a \mid b$ and $a \mid c$, then $a \mid (b + c)$. *168*

If $a \mid b$, then $a \mid kb$. *173*

Divisibility Rules:

Divisibility by 2 *171*

Divisibility by 5 *171*

Divisibility by 10 *171*

Divisibility by 3 *171*

deductive reasoning: hypothesis, conclusion.

Statement: If X, then Y. *170*

Contrapositive: If not Y, then not X. *170*

Converse: If Y, then X. *170*

Inverse: If not X, then not Y. *170*

counterexample *169*

conditional statements *169*

hypothesis *170*

conclusion *170*

biconditional statements *170*

inductive reasoning *174*

Section 4.2 Prime and Composite Numbers

prime *180*

composite *180*

sieve of Eratosthenes *180*

indirect reasoning *182*

test for determining if a number is prime *182*

prime factorization *183*

the Fundamental Theorem of Arithmetic *184*

perfect numbers, proper divisor, abundant numbers, deficient numbers *185*

Section 4.3 Greatest Common Factor and Least Common Multiple

greatest common factor (GCF) *189*

Methods for determining the GCF

listing all factors of each number, using prime factorization and reasoning, using factor trees, using intuition, repeated division by prime numbers, using prime factorization and exponential notation

least common multiple (LCM) *192*

Methods for finding the LCM

listing a sufficient number of multiples of each number, using factor trees, using prime factorization and reasoning, using prime factorization and exponential notation

$$LCM(a, b) = \frac{a \cdot b}{GCF(a, b)}$$ *197*

relatively prime *191*

Extending the Number System

For many thousands of years, positive whole numbers were adequate for most people's needs. However, the limitations of positive whole numbers became more and more problematic as time went on. In this chapter, we will examine four extensions of the set of positive whole numbers: negative numbers, fractions, decimals, and irrational numbers.[1] Most people do not realize how recent the invention of these kinds of numbers is and that these sets of numbers represent significant and important leaps in the development of mathematics. In this chapter, it is important that you come to appreciate the significance of each of these sets of numbers and that you understand how they are related to one another. In Chapter 3, we examined the various meanings of the four basic operations and how various algorithms enable us to compute quickly. In this chapter, we will examine what each of these new sets of numbers means. Knowing what they mean and understanding the four operations will then enable you to make sense of the computation algorithms that we use for integers, fractions, and decimals. As before, knowing why as well as how increases one's mathematical power:

> ◤ Teachers [of all grades] should be able to extend the number systems from the whole numbers to fractions and integers, then rationals and real numbers, including a discussion of the extension of the operations, properties, and ordering. Notions of fractions, decimals, percents, ratio, and proportion should be developed through problems with an applied flavor.
>
> (*Professional Standards*, p. 136)

[1] Although there are still numbers beyond irrational numbers, we will limit ourselves to the sets of numbers mentioned here because these are the sets that we focus on in K–8 mathematics.

SECTION 5.1 **INTEGERS**

- Why is it that the sum of two negative numbers is a negative number, but the product of two negative numbers is a positive number?

- How do operations with integers connect with whole-number operations? How do they differ?

Our first extension of the set of whole numbers is the set of **integers**, which is simply the union of the set of positive whole numbers, the set of **negative whole numbers,** and zero. Although most of people's everyday use of mathematics involves positive whole numbers, we encounter negative numbers in various ways. One of the major goals of this section is for you to understand how the procedures for computing with positive whole numbers relate to computing when one or more of the numbers is negative.

Integer Connections

Before we examine operations with integers, let us take a little time to see how integers connect to the set of whole numbers we have been working with up to now.

- We began our study of numbers with the set of natural numbers

    N: $\{1, 2, 3, 4, \ldots\}$

- With the invention of zero, we have the set of whole numbers

    W: $\{0, 1, 2, 3, 4, \ldots\}$

- With the invention of negative numbers, we have the set of integers

    I: $\{\ldots {}^-4, {}^-3, {}^-2, {}^-1, 0, 1, 2, 3, 4, \ldots\}$

Figure 5.1 shows a Venn diagram illustrating the notion of extending our set of numbers as our ancestors invented new kinds of numbers. Each set of numbers contains the previous set. We will extend this diagram as we discuss fractions, decimals, and irrational numbers.

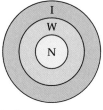

FIGURE **5.1**

HISTORY

Like our base 10 numeration system, the set of integers was developed relatively recently. Negative numbers were either ignored or dismissed as absurd by most of the ancients. We find the earliest mention of negative numbers and how we might compute with them in the works of Brahmagupta (628 A.D.) in India. Other early work with the concept of negative numbers is found in the writings of al-Khwarizmi (825 A.D.) in Persia and Chu Shi-Ku (1300 A.D.) in China. The first modern mathematician to treat negative numbers seriously was Cardan in 1545. He accepted negative numbers as solutions of equations and, like the three authors above, stated the rules for computing with them. However, he referred to them as "false" numbers. Descartes, who developed the coordinate system, still referred to negative numbers as false numbers.

Integers in our world When do we use negative numbers? Stop to reflect on where you have encountered negative numbers before reading on. . . .

People use negative numbers both on and off the job. For instance:

- Businesses use negative numbers to indicate a business deficit, or "negative profit."

- We often use negative numbers when describing change. For example, graphs often have negative numbers.

- We use negative numbers to indicate temperatures below zero.

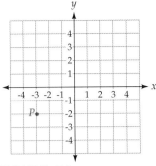

FIGURE 5.2

- Locations below sea level are often represented with negative numbers.
- A golfer uses negative numbers to indicate a score below par.
- Physicists use negative numbers to indicate negatively charged particles.
- We use a coordinate system to indicate the position of an object in space. For example, the location of point P in Figure 5.2 is ($^-3$, $^-2$).

Representing Integers

There are many models for representing integers. We will focus on the number line model because it is the model to which most real-life applications connect.

Number lines can be represented horizontally or vertically, as shown in Figure 5.3.

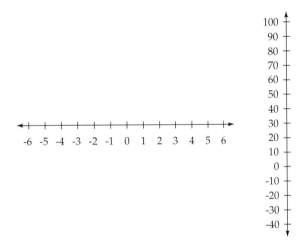

FIGURE 5.3

Some other models commonly used to represent integers and their applications include black and red chips, positively and negatively charged particles, and money (assets and liabilities). If you did Exploration 5.1, you used black and white dots to represent integers. The discrete model is a representation of integers that generally makes more sense to young children than the number line model.

Operations with Integers

In this section, we will examine the four operations with negative numbers. As you recall from Chapter 3, we developed models for each of the operations:

- addition: combine, increase
- subtraction: take away, comparison, missing addend
- multiplication: repeated addition, rectangular array, Cartesian product
- division: partitioning, repeated subtraction, missing factor

As we strive to develop ways to operate *meaningfully* with negative numbers, we will also examine which of these models for the operations work and which do not.

Many textbooks present the students with various algorithms (that is, rules) for adding, subtracting, multiplying, and dividing with negative numbers. There are several problems with this approach. First, students remember the rules only as long as they use them. I call this rented or Teflon knowledge; that is, after a few months, the rules are gone. If the students do not have a strong understanding of where the rules came from, then they have nothing to show for all that work. Second, in many real-life situations, the most difficult part of the problem is figuring out how best to approach it. Most real-life problems lend themselves to different solution strategies, not one "right" way that everyone "should" use. Thus, rather than present you with rules, we will investigate how we obtain sums, differences, products, and quotients with negative numbers. If you first solve, or at least attempt to solve, each problem *on your own*, you will find that not only will you be able to compute confidently with negative numbers, but also your problem-solving toolbox will be fuller. Furthermore, even if you forget the rules one year from now, you will be able to use your knowledge to re-create them.

Understanding Addition with Integers

We will use a problem-solving tool from higher mathematics to develop algorithms for adding integers: We will examine all possible combinations (cases) and then look for patterns. The four cases are represented below:

	a	*b*	Example
Case 1: Both numbers are positive.	+	+	3 + 4
Case 2: One number is positive, one number is negative, and the magnitude of the negative number is greater than the magnitude of the positive number.	+	−	3 + $^-$4
Case 3: One number is positive, one number is negative, and the magnitude of the positive number is greater than the magnitude of the negative number.	−	+	$^-$3 + 4
Case 4: Both numbers are negative.	−	−	$^-$3 + $^-$4

Language You may have noticed that sometimes the + and − signs have been raised (superscripted) and sometimes not. This convention allows us to avoid meaningless sentences. For example, we will read the problem $^-6 - {}^-8$ as "*negative 6 minus negative 8*" instead of "minus 6 minus minus 8."

The words *plus* and *minus* will be used to refer to the *operations* of addition and subtraction. The words *positive* and *negative* will be used to refer to the *value* of the number.

For practice, translate each of the equations below into English. Check your translations with the sentences at the right.

$$^-5 + {}^-4 = {}^-9 \qquad \text{Negative 5 plus negative 4 is equal to negative 9.}$$
$$32 + {}^-48 = {}^-16 \qquad \text{32 plus negative 48 is equal to negative 16.}$$

Let us now examine the first two cases.

Case 1

Both numbers are positive. We explored this case in depth in Chapter 3.

Case 2

One number is positive, one number is negative, and the magnitude of the negative number is greater than the magnitude of the positive number.

Do several other examples and then try to express a rule that would apply to any addition problem in which the magnitude of the negative number is greater than the magnitude of the positive number. Then read on. . . . 🖎

We will examine a specific problem in detail and then look at generalizations. How would you represent the problem 3 + ⁻4?

Number line model From our work with number lines in Chapter 3, we learned that the problem 3 + 4 can be represented as shown at the left in Figure 5.4. That is, we begin at zero and move 3 units to the right, then we move 4 more units to the right; thus, we find that 3 + 4 = 7. If a positive number is represented by an arrow pointing to the right (the positive direction), then a negative number is represented by an arrow pointing to the left (the negative direction). Thus, the problem 3 + ⁻4 can be represented as shown at the right in Figure 5.4. That is, we begin at zero and move 3 units to the right and then move 4 units to the left; thus, we find that 3 + ⁻4 = ⁻1. As you may have already found, sometimes the sum of a positive number and a negative number is positive (for example, 12 + ⁻5 = ⁺7) and sometimes it is negative, as in Figure 5.4.

FIGURE **5.4**

If you do a number of problems, you realize that the procedure for adding a positive number and a negative number feels a lot like subtraction. In fact, one description of a general rule is: Disregard the signs and subtract the *smaller* number from the *larger* number; the sign of the sum is the same as the sign of the *larger* number.

Absolute Value

There is a mathematical way to say "disregard the sign in front of the number," and that is to use the term *absolute value.* Let us first define this concept and then use it to state the rule for adding a positive number and a negative number more precisely.

One way to illustrate the concept of absolute value is to consider how far the number is from zero (the origin). The **absolute value** tells us the distance of the number from zero. For example, the numbers ⁺5 and ⁻5 are both the same distance from zero, and so they both have the same absolute value, which is 5 (see Figure 5.5).

FIGURE **5.5**

With notation, we say: |⁻5| = 5. Similarly, |⁺5| = 5.

In English, we say that the absolute value of negative 5 is 5, and the absolute value of positive 5 is also 5.

We can also use a balance scale (a common manipulative used in elementary schools) to illustrate the concept of absolute value. If we place a weight under ⁻5 and an equal weight under ⁺5, the scale will balance (see Figure 5.6).

FIGURE **5.6**

There is also language for referring to pairs of numbers whose absolute values are equal: We say they are opposites or negatives of each other. Thus, the **opposite** of ⁺6 is ⁻6 and the opposite of ⁻6 is ⁺6. Using another meaning of **negative,** we say that the negative of ⁺6 is ⁻6 and the negative of ⁻6 is ⁺6.

As you can readily see, when we add any integer and its opposite, the result is zero; that is:

$$a + \bar{}a = 0$$

Thus, we can say that every integer has an additive inverse.

In this text, we will use the term **additive inverse** instead of *negative* for two reasons. First, the term *negative* often creates a false impression. For example, if $x = \bar{}6$, then $\bar{}x = \bar{}^{+}6$. In other words, when working with variables, the value of $\bar{}x$ is often positive. Second, when working with fractions, we will develop a similar concept with a similar term: the *multiplicative inverse*.

The concept of absolute value lets us now state the rule for adding a positive number and a negative number more precisely: We first find the difference of the absolute values of the two numbers; the sign of the sum is the sign of the number with the larger absolute value.

MATHEMATICS

With one exception, all the properties of addition, subtraction, multiplication, and division that we developed in Chapter 3 hold *for all numbers.* That exception is the closure property. Whether or not a set is closed under an operation depends on the nature of the set. This concept will be pursued in an exercise.

The Other Two Cases of Integer Addition

Case 3   One number is positive, one number is negative, and the magnitude of the positive number is greater than the magnitude of the negative number (e.g., $4 + \bar{}3$).

When we look carefully at all integer addition problems that fit in this case, we find that the generalization stated in the preceding paragraph applies to this case too. In other words, the similarity between Case 2 problems ($3 + \bar{}4$, $2 + \bar{}8$, $\bar{}7 + 3$, $\bar{}9 + 4$) and Case 3 problems ($4 + \bar{}3$, $7 + \bar{}2$, $\bar{}6 + 9$, $\bar{}1 + 5$) is that one number is positive and one number is negative. Regardless of which number has the larger magnitude, we can use the same procedure to determine the answer.

This discussion connects to NCTM Curriculum Standard 3 (Mathematics as Reasoning), to sets language and to NCTM Curriculum Standard 4 (Mathematical Connections). When we first examine all the possibilities when adding integers, we have four distinct subsets. However, when we look closely as two of these subsets, their similarity (one positive, one negative) outweighs their difference (which number has the greater absolute value).

Case 4   In case 4, both numbers are negative. Let us examine a specific problem in detail and then look for generalizations. Figure 5.7 shows a representation of $\bar{}3 + \bar{}4$ on a number line. Do several other examples and then try to express a rule that would apply to any addition problem in which both numbers are negative. Many students find that they can do this more easily if they have a context. For example, Jeremy borrowed 3 dollars from Annie and then borrowed 4 more dollars. How much does he owe her? Then read on. . . . 📝

FIGURE **5.7**

With the concept of absolute value, we can state the rule for adding two negative numbers precisely: To find the sum of two negative numbers, we first find the sum of the absolute values of the two numbers and then place a negative sign in front of this sum.

Understanding Subtraction with Integers

In Exploration 5.2, you examined integer subtraction with the take-away model and the comparison model. In the text, we focus on connecting whole-number subtraction to integer subtraction.

INVESTIGATION **5.1**   Subtraction with Integers

> **D**o the following subtraction problems yourself before reading on. As you work, check to make sure that you are using your understanding of integers and whole numbers rather than just guessing.
>
> **1.** $14 - {}^{-}25 =$ **2.** ${}^{-}5 - 17 =$ **3.** ${}^{-}6 - {}^{-}8 =$ **4.** ${}^{-}12 - 5 =$

DISCUSSION

If you found that you did better with adding negative numbers than with subtracting negative numbers, I have good news: We define subtraction of negative numbers in terms of addition, which most people understand more easily.

To make the connection stronger, let us examine how we might use what we know about subtraction to determine the answer to $4 - 6$. In one sense, we cannot "take away" 6. However, if we think in terms of a checking account, if we take away 6 from 4, we will have a deficit of 2, that is, ${}^{-}2$. We could apply our work with subtraction and number lines from Chapter 3: When we subtract one number from another, we move to the left. When we begin at the point 4 and move 6 units to the left, we end up at the point negative 2, as shown in Figure 5.8.

-2 -1 0 1 2 3 4

FIGURE **5.8**

Thus, we can conclude that $4 - 6 = {}^{-}2$.

However, this is similar to the addition problem $4 + {}^{-}6 = {}^{-}2$.

We use this knowledge to formally define subtraction of integers in terms of addition:

$$a - b = a + {}^{-}b$$

That is, subtracting is equivalent to adding the additive inverse.

This definition works with the set of natural numbers ($5 - 2 = 5 + {}^{-}2$), but it also enables us to operate when the numbers are not both positive and when b is larger than a.

Connecting Whole-Number Subtraction to Integer Subtraction

In Chapter 3, we examined different models for the four operations and different algorithms. In order for your knowledge of mathematics to be as connected as possible, it is important that you see how we apply these models to each new set of numbers.

Go back to Chapter 3 and examine how we defined subtraction there. In what ways are the two definitions of subtraction the same (that is, equivalent)? In what ways are they different? Why did we define subtraction differently there from the way we define it here? Think and then read on. . . .

Let us compare the two definitions:

Chapter 3: $a - b = c$ iff there is a number c such that $c + b = a$

Chapter 5: $a - b = a + {}^{-}b$

If you examine the actual problems involved in subtracting a positive number from a positive number, you find that we are not adding the opposite as much as we are taking away a positive amount or comparing the size of two sets (each with positive values). Therefore, although the definition given in this chapter seems simpler and more practical (to most of my students), it doesn't connect as well to subtraction with two positive whole numbers. Therefore, I chose to defer this definition until this chapter so that the work in Chapter 3 was more focused on the context in which subtraction occurs when all three of the numbers (minuend, subtrahend, and difference) are positive numbers.

Connecting Subtraction Contexts to Algorithms

One essential component of what it means to understand an operation is recognizing conditions in real-world situations that indicate that the operation would be useful in those situations.

(*Curriculum Standards,* p. 41)

We have now developed efficient procedures for integer addition and subtraction. However, as you have discovered, in many real-life settings, translating words into a mathematical sentence is not always simple. Therefore, we will examine a few such settings to apply our knowledge.

Problem 1   Denine realized that she had overdrawn her checking account by $60, and she was fined $15 for a returned check. What is her present balance? Work on this problem and then read on. . . .

If we translate this problem to mathematical language, we find that we need to take away $15 from negative $60. Thus, the problem is $^-60 - 15$. Using our understanding of subtraction, we translate this subtraction problem to the following addition problem: $^-60 + {}^-15$. Applying our understanding of integer addition, we have an answer of $^-75$; that is, her present balance is negative $75 (or she is $75 in the red).

Problem 2   On one day the high temperature in Nome, Alaska, was $^-6$ degrees. On that same day, the high temperature at the North Pole was $^-64$ degrees. How much warmer was Nome than the North Pole? Work on this problem and then read on. . . .

If we translate this problem to mathematical language, we find that we are using the comparison model of subtraction. Thus, the problem is $^-6 - {}^-64$, which we can translate as $-6 + {}^+64$, and the answer is 58; that is, it was 58 degrees warmer in Nome.

We could also have interpreted this as a missing addend problem: $^-64 + x = {}^-6$.

Using algebra, $x = {}^-6 - {}^-64 = 58$.

Understanding Multiplication with Integers

There are very few simple real-world problems in which we multiply and divide integers. Most cases of integer multiplication and division occur in solving equations. Because the ability to work confidently with algebraic language is critical in high school and college, understanding the procedures is important. Recall one of the sentences in Standard 3 (Mathematics as Reasoning): "The study of mathematics should emphasize reasoning so that students can believe that mathematics makes sense" (*Curriculum Standards*, p. 29). If you did Exploration 5.3, you realized that although the rules for integer multiplication are simple, justifying them is more difficult.

INVESTIGATION **5.2** **The Product of a Positive and a Negative Number**

Consider the following problem: 5 · ⁻3. Can we apply our understanding of multiplication with positive numbers to determine the product? Think and read on. . . .

DISCUSSION

Applying the repeated addition model of multiplication, 5 · ⁻3 literally means to add ⁻3 five times, that is, ⁻3 + ⁻3 + ⁻3 + ⁻3 + ⁻3. We know from integer addition that the sum must be ⁻15. That is, we can deduce that 5 · ⁻3 = ⁻15.

What about ⁻3 · 5? Think and read on. . . .

Trying to apply repeated addition here is problematical; that is, we add 5 *negative 3 times*. However, the commutative property makes the task easier: ⁻3 · 5 = 5 · ⁻3 = ⁻15.

From this discussion, we can recall the rule that you may have memorized in school: The product of a positive number and a negative number is a negative number.

Two negative numbers What about ⁻3 · ⁻5? None of the models for positive whole-number multiplication adapt nicely to this problem, and the commutative property does us no good here. However, we can use our knowledge that a positive times a negative is a negative and make use of patterns:

We know that   4 · ⁻3 = ⁻12
Thus,   3 · ⁻3 = ⁻9
Similarly,   2 · ⁻3 = ⁻6
And so,   1 · ⁻3 = ⁻3
                    0 · ⁻3 = 0   Recall the zero property of
                                      multiplication from Chapter 3.
                   ⁻1 · ⁻3 = ?

What does ⁻1 · ⁻3 have to equal if the pattern is to continue? Think and then read on. . . .

As the number line in Figure 5.9 illustrates, in this case, each product is 3 more than the previous product, and 3 more than 0 is ⁺3.

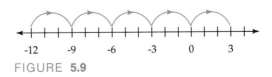

FIGURE **5.9**

From this discussion, we can recall the rule that you may have memorized in school: The product of two negative numbers is a positive number.

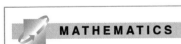

MATHEMATICS

Leonard Euler (1770) produced one of the earliest proofs that ⁻1 · ⁻1 = 1. However, many great mathematicians thought that the idea of a negative number times a negative number was absurd. Many eighteenth-century algebra textbooks rejected multiplication of negative numbers because this was not a problem that they saw as having any real-life relevance.

Understanding Division with Integers

Just as we interpreted integer subtraction by applying our knowledge of the relationship between subtraction and addition, we can now understand integer division by applying our knowledge of the relationship between division and multiplication. From an intuitive perspective, you may sense that the multiplication rules translate quite directly to division; that is,

- The quotient of a positive and a negative number is a negative number.
- The quotient of two negative numbers is a positive number.

We can apply the missing factor model of division ($y \div n = x$ iff $x \cdot n = y$) to verify these rules.

For example, consider the problem $^-12 \div 4$. There is little doubt that the quotient is either $^-3$ or $^+3$. Many students simply guess, but we can apply this model to help us find the correct answer. Applying our definition of division, we can say that

$$^-12 \div 4 = x \quad \text{iff} \quad x \cdot 4 = ^-12$$

What number times 4 is equal to negative 12? We know from multiplication that that number must be $^-3$. Therefore, $^-12 \div 4$ must equal $^-3$.

Similarly, consider $^-15 \div ^-3$. Applying our definition of division, we can say that

$$^-15 \div ^-3 = x \quad \text{iff} \quad x \cdot ^-3 = ^-15$$

We know from multiplication that that number must be $^-5$. Therefore, $^-15 \div ^-3$ must equal 5.

Summary

In this section, we have learned that the set of integers includes both the set of positive and negative numbers and zero. Many people mistakenly equate the set of integers with the set of negative numbers; however, the latter is a subset of the former. We have discovered that there are many ways to represent integers, and we have explored two models for representing integers: number lines in the text and dots in Explorations 5.1–5.3. We have adapted our understanding of the four basic operations, learned in Chapter 3, so that the algorithms for adding, subtracting, multiplying, and dividing integers make sense. In the course of exploring these operations, it became important to understand several new terms: absolute value, opposite, negative, and additive inverse.

In seeking to make sense of integer operations, we find that we cannot rely solely on common sense and manipulatives, as we did with operations with the set of natural numbers. For example, $^-20 \div ^-4$ does not readily lend itself to a concrete, real-life problem or to a division as partitioning representation. At some point in the study of mathematics, the students must metaphorically "leap from the nest" and be able to use more analytic methods of reasoning to construct new understandings on the foundations of old ones.

Although operations with integers are not generally introduced until middle school, this section is important for several reasons. First, teachers need to have a sense of what lies beyond the concepts their students are learning at the present time. Even if you teach younger students, it is important that you know how the more sophisticated sets of numbers connect to the set of natural numbers and that the four basic operations, which students first learn in the context of natural numbers, will need to make sense with these more sophisticated kinds of numbers. Second, many students have trouble with algebra because there are too many rules to memorize. However, as you have seen in this section, we can apply our understanding of the meaning of the four operations and the properties of the four operations to understand the procedures for operating with integers. Third, you are likely to encounter gifted students. I happened to be visiting a second grade teacher one day when one of her students invented the procedure for integer subtraction on the spot. The teacher was explaining how to subtract with regrouping with the problem $72 - 58$. She said, "You can't take 8 from 2." He replied, "Yes, you can; you get minus 6; then you take 50 from 70, which is 20, and 20 minus 6 is 14!"

EXERCISES 5.1

1. Perform the computations:

   a. $^-356 - {}^-138$

   b. $\dfrac{{}^-36 + 48}{{}^-6}$

   c. $16 - (^-3)$

   d. $^-217 + 139$

   e. $^-2(3 - 10)$

   f. $^-3 \cdot 5 + (^-6 \div 2)$

   g. $16 - (^-3)^2$

   h. $^-6 + (24 \div {}^-3)$

   i. $^-124 - {}^-345$

   j. $(47 + {}^-11)/({}^-6)$

2. Find the missing number:

   a. $^-65 + \square = 173$

   b. $36 - \square = 83$

   c. $331 + \square = {}^-86$

   d. $^-812 + \square = {}^-223$

   e. $^-342 + \square = {}^-129$

   f. $^-12,348 - \square = {}^-348$

3. Show two different ways to determine the following sum:

   $$^-19 + {}^-6 + {}^-22 + 8 + {}^-4 + 7 + 1$$

4. The origin of our symbols for $+$ and $-$ can be traced back to the practice of merchants in the Middle Ages, who used the signs p for *piu* (more) and m for *meno* (less) to indicate how much above or below a standard weight each sack was. Thus, if the standard weight was 100 pounds, a sack weighing 96 pounds would have m4 written on it. How much overweight or underweight is the following shipment? Describe at least two different ways you could have solved this problem.

5. The formula for converting from Fahrenheit to Celsius is given by $C = \dfrac{5(F - 32)}{9}$. If the temperature outside is 23° Fahrenheit, what would the temperature be in Celsius?

6. At what temperature would the Fahrenheit and Celsius temperatures be equal?

7. Here are the low (Fahrenheit) temperatures for one week in Minneapolis, Minnesota: $^-19, {}^-6, {}^-22, 8, {}^-4, 7, 1$. What was the mean (average) low temperature for the week?

8. The Crabby Apple restaurant lost $2,500 in January. If its net worth at the end of the month was $^-\$400$, what was its net worth at the beginning of the month?

9. Jacob opens a savings account on January 1 with a deposit of $250. He has "direct deposit," in which $25 is deposited every other week. The bank also charges a $3 monthly processing fee. How much money will he have at the end of the year?

10. Have you ever been on an airplane and heard the pilot say that the plane would be a little late because it would be flying into a strong headwind or to hear that even though the plane was taking off a bit late, you would be making up time because you would be flying with a tailwind? This problem asks you to analyze such a situation. You have the following data: A plane flying at its maximum speed can go 200 miles per hour with a tailwind or 160 miles per hour into a headwind.

    a. What is the wind speed?

    b. What would be the maximum speed of the plane if there were no wind?

11. If you were flying to a city 800 miles away, what will be the difference in flight time between flying into a 40 mph headwind and with a 40 mph tailwind if the plane's maximum speed with no wind is 160 mph?

12. Let's say the countdown for a space shuttle launch has begun. At "T minus 27 hours" (that is, twenty-seven hours before launch), a problem occurs. If the technicians have not fixed the problem by T minus 8 hours, the launch will have to be scratched. How much time do the technicians have to correct the problem?

13. John had $123 in the bank but wrote a check for $56 and another check for $86. What is his current balance?

14. Many Americans do not realize that our calendar is not universal. For example, the copyright date for this textbook is 1997. However, this year would be reported as 5758 in the Jewish calendar. According to the standard calendar, when was the world created?

15. In Chapter 1, we investigated magic squares, in which each row, column, and diagonal had the same sum. The

magic square below is a subtraction magic square. Why is this?

15	7	8
5	4	1
10	3	7

a. Make another subtraction magic square.

b. Make a subtraction magic square in which all the numbers are negative numbers.

c. Make a subtraction magic square in which four of the numbers are positive, four are negative, and one number is zero.

d. Write instructions explaining to someone how to make a subtraction magic square that works for any number.

16. The graph below shows the United States trade balance (the difference between exports and imports) from 1970 to 1992.[2]

   a. When was the lowest balance? Approximately what was it?

   b. What was the net change from 1980 to 1990?

   c. What was the year of the biggest decline? How much was the decline?

U.S. Trade Balance (billions of dollars)

[2] *The American Almanac 1993–1994: Statistical Abstract of the United States* (Austin, Tex.: The Reference Press), No. 1344, p. 808.

17. Below are the low and high temperatures on a winter day in several cities. Make up and answer two questions from the chart.

	Low	High
Anchorage	$^-28$	$^-7$
Minneapolis	$^-12$	5
Honolulu	68	73
Miami Beach	68	87
Portland	26	46

18. Examine some daily newspapers or weekly magazines to find articles that require some knowledge of negative numbers. Either make up a story problem that might come out of the article or explain how a knowledge of negative numbers is needed in order to understand the article. For example, recall Exercise 16 about the U.S. trade balance.

19. Consider the positive and negative values of the integers from 1 to 9:

$$\pm 1 \quad \pm 2 \quad \pm 3 \quad \pm 4 \quad \pm 5 \quad \pm 6 \quad \pm 7 \quad \pm 8 \quad \pm 9$$

The sum of the nine positive integers is $^+45$, and the sum of the nine negative integers is $^-45$. How many numbers between $^-45$ and $^+45$ can be made by adding and using each number or its opposite exactly once? For example, here is one combination whose sum is $^-3$.

$$1 + 2 + 3 + 4 + 5 + 6 + {}^-7 + {}^-8 + {}^-9 = {}^-3$$

20. Let x and y represent any positive whole numbers, $x \neq y$. For each of the operations below, tell whether the result will be always positive, will be always negative, or might be one or the other. Explain your reasoning.

   a. $|x - y|$

   b. $x^2 - y^2$

   c. $x^2 - xy + y^2$

   d. $x^2 + 2xy - y^2$

21. Let x and y represent *any* integers, $x \neq y$. For each of the operations below, tell whether the result will be always positive, will be always negative, or might be one or the other. Explain your reasoning.

   a. $|x - y|$

   b. $x^2 - y^2$

   c. $x^2 - xy + y^2$

   d. $x^2 + 2xy - y^2$

22. Sam was told by the doctor that he had to lose about 40 pounds. Six weeks ago he weighed 185 pounds. Below is his weekly record of his progress. How much does he weigh now? Do this problem at least two different ways.

Week	1	2	3	4	5	6
Change	$^-3$	$^-2$	$^+1$	$^-6$	$^+3$	$^-2$

23. The set of integers is closed under which of the four fundamental operations?

24. The term *wind chill factor* is an important concept for people living in or visiting a cold climate in winter. Most body heat is lost through the skin, and the wind can accelerate this cooling process. For example, if the air temperature is 20°F and there is a 30 mph wind, the wind chill temperature is ⁻2°F. That is, you are losing body heat at the same rate as if it were 2 degrees below zero on a calm day! Examine the wind chill table below.

a. If the air temperature is ⁻20°F and there is a 15 mph wind, what is the wind chill temperature?

b. Describe two observations from the chart.

Wind Chill Temperature (°F)

Air temperature (°F)	0	5	10	15	20	25	30	35	40
32	34	32	27	24	21	17	14	12	10
28	30	28	23	19	15	12	9	6	4
24	26	24	19	14	10	7	3	0	−3
20	23	20	14	9	5	1	−2	−6	−9
16	19	16	10	5	0	−4	−8	−12	−17
12	15	12	6	0	−5	−10	−15	−19	−24
8	11	8	1	−5	−11	−16	−21	−26	−32
4	7	4	−3	−10	−16	−22	−28	−34	−40
0	3	0	−7	−15	−22	−28	−35	−42	−49
−4	−1	−4	−12	−20	−28	−35	−42	−50	−58
−8	−4	−8	−16	−25	−33	−41	−50	−59	−67
−12	−8	−12	−21	−30	−39	−48	−58	−68	
−16	−12	−16	−26	−36	−45	−55	−66		
−20	−16	−20	−30	−41	−52	−63			
−24	−20	−24	−35	−47	−58				
−28	−24	−28	−39	−52	−65				
−32	−27	−32	−44	−58					
−36	−31	−36	−49	−64					
−40	−35	−40	−54	−69					

Source: R.G. Steadman, "Indices of Windchill of Clothed Persons." *Journal of Applied Meteorology,* vol. 10, August 1971. Reprinted with permissions from the American Meteorological Society.

SECTION 5.2 FRACTIONS AND RATIONAL NUMBERS

WHAT DO YOU THINK?

- What does a fraction represent?
- Why is 1/5 less than 1/3?
- What is the difference between the whole and the unit?

The concept of rational numbers is one of the "big ideas" of elementary mathematics, and it is also one of the more abstract and difficult. Because of this, we will spend some time investigating rational numbers. As you will soon discover, fractions are more than just numbers, and the numerator and denominator are more than just the top and bottom numbers.

In this chapter, we will build on the part-whole relationships developed in Chapter 2, and we will continue to use composition and decomposition (first seen with expanded form in Chapter 2) to probe more deeply into the whys of elementary mathematics.

In this section, we will introduce the four interpretations of fractions. We will explore the fraction as a measure interpretation in different settings and with different models so that it makes sense. We will also come to understand what it means to say that two fractions are equivalent and what simplest form, commonly called reducing fractions, means.

Although the concept of fractions may be almost as old as mathematical thinking, operations with fractions are a relatively recent part of the history of mathematics. In Section 5.1, we discovered that the set of integers simply involves an extension of the number system. Fractions, on the other hand, are different from counting numbers and integers in a very significant way: *Two numbers are needed to represent one amount!* From another perspective, when we work with rational numbers, we change the question from *how many?* to *how much?* I hope that by the end of this section, you will see what a difference this makes!

CHILDREN

Children encounter the notion of rational numbers and fractions even before they enter school through the notion of sharing between two people. That is, when one whole is divided into two equal parts, each person has one half.

Two Different Sets

Before we begin, it is necessary to make a distinction between *fraction* and *rational number*.

A **rational number** is a number whose value can be expressed as the quotient or ratio of two *integers* a and b, represented as $\frac{a}{b}$, where $b \neq 0$.

A **fraction** is a number whose value can be expressed as the quotient or ratio of *any two numbers* a and b, represented as $\frac{a}{b}$, where $b \neq 0$. For example, $\sqrt{2}/3$ is a fraction but not a rational number.

In either case, a is called the **numerator** and b is called the **denominator**.

Technically, the set of rational numbers is a subset of the set of fractions, which can include amounts like $\sqrt{2}/2$ and $\pi/6$. In elementary school, children work with fractions that are rational numbers, and that will be our primary focus in this chapter. Therefore, we will generally use the term *fraction*.

Fractions in History

The notion of 3/4 may make sense to you now, but it is not easy for many children, and it is such an abstraction that it is relatively recent in human history.

The Egyptians expressed all fractions (with the exception of 2/3) as unit fractions, that is, fractions whose numerator is 1. They used the symbol ⬯, which they placed above a numeral to indicate a fraction. Thus, 1/12 was written as ⬯∩∥. The Egyptians' decision to represent fractions with unit fractions only was a consequence of their difficulty with using two numbers to represent a single amount.

As we saw earlier, the idea of representing all amounts with whole numbers was very appealing to many of the ancient Greeks, and so they did not even consider the concept of a part of a whole. Rather, they worked with ratios. For example, instead of saying that 2/5 of the students at a college are male, they would say that the ratio of males to females is 2 to 3. (We will examine ratios more closely in Chapter 6.)

The Romans also avoided fractions as much as possible. We live with the effects of one of their ways of avoiding fractions: Rather than dealing with parts of a unit, they created smaller units. Their word for twelfth was *unica*, which is where our words *ounce* and *inch* come from.

Our present method of writing fractions (for example, $\frac{2}{3}$) was probably invented by the Hindus. Brahmagupta (628 A.D.) wrote $\frac{2}{3}$. The bar seems to have been introduced by the Arabs, but just as the base 10 system took many years to be accepted, it was some time before most writers used the bar when expressing fractions. Part of the problem seems to have been caused by printing difficulties, and even today few word processors are able to express fractions vertically; instead they write 2/3.

LANGUAGE

The origin of the word *fraction* is also interesting; it is derived from the Latin word *fractio*, which comes from the Latin word *frangere*, meaning "to break." In early American arithmetic books, the term *broken numbers* was often used instead of the word *fraction*. The first known mention of the actual word *fraction* was by Chaucer in 1321.[3]

INVESTIGATION **5.3**   **Rational Number Contexts: What Does 3/4 Mean?**

This investigation uncovers the different meanings of fractions. Thus, although the following situations each involve the fraction 3/4, they represent 3/4 in different contexts. One of the goals of our work with rational numbers is for you to understand the similarities and differences among these contexts. Thus, think carefully as you work.

Represent each of the following situations with a diagram. Then read on. . . . 📝

---

[3] Louis Karpinski, *The History of Arithmetic* (New York: Russell & Russell, 1965), p. 127.

> **A.** Joey grew 3/4 of an inch last month.
>
> **B.** Four children want to share 3 pies equally. How much pie does each person get?
>
> **C.** At a recent meeting, 3/4 of the participants were women. If there were 12 people at the meeting, how many were women?
>
> **D.** At a college, 3/4 of the students are women.

DISCUSSION

Do you see how the pictures in Figure 5.10 connect to the verbal descriptions?

FIGURE **5.10**

Each of the situations embodies one of the four major contexts in which we use rational numbers.

A. The first situation illustrates **rational number as a measure.** To measure the appropriate location of 3/4 , we must divide (partition) the unit length (1 inch) into 4 equal lengths. The length of 3 of those equal lengths shows how much Joey grew.

When we are dealing with the fraction a/b in the context of measuring, we have some amount or object that has been divided into b equal amounts, and we are considering a of those pieces. In this sense, $1/b$ is a unit of measure.

B. The second situation illustrates **rational number as a quotient.** The initial problem situation is 3 (pies) divided among 4 (people). The answer of 3/4 pie per person represents the value of each person's share; that is, the denominator once again is in relation to the unit (1 pie). If we divide 1 pie into 4 pieces, each person's share is 3 of those pieces.

When we are dealing with a fraction in the context of a quotient of whole numbers, an amount a needs to be shared or divided equally into b groups; in this context, a/b means that the amount a is to be distributed (or put) into b parts. Note that in this case, a represents pies and b represents people.

C. The third situation embodies **rational number as an operator.** In this case, 3/4 acts as a function machine (recall "What's my rule?" from Chapter 2) by operating on the whole (in this case, 12 people). In this example, the input is 12 people, and 3/4 is the rule that tells us what to do—that is, take 3 of every 4 people in the whole. The output is thus 9 people.

The operator context can be thought of as a stretching or shrinking process; a/b is a function machine that tells us the extent to which the given object or amount is to be stretched or shrunk. This context has also been called "the most algebraic of the basic ideas."[4]

D. The fourth situation illustrates **rational number as a ratio.** That is, if 3/4 of the students are women, then if we count all the men as 1 group, then the number of women would be equal to 3 of those groups. In this case, we can represent this statement in fraction language—3/4 of the students are women—or

---

[4] Thomas E. Kieran, quoted in *Understanding Rational Numbers and Proportions,* Frances R. Curio and Nadine S. Bezuk. Reston (VA.: NCTM, 1994), p. 3.

we can represent the statement in ratio language — the ratio of women to men is 3 to 1, that is, 3:1.

A ratio is a relationship between 2 quantities. Ratios can involve comparisons between parts and parts (for example, women:men = 3:1), comparisons between parts and wholes (women: total = 3:4), or comparisons between two different wholes (when we say that a car averages 30 miles per gallon, we are comparing the number of miles traveled to the number of gallons consumed).

We will examine the measure context in this section, the quotient and operator contexts in Section 5.3, and the ratio context in Chapter 6. However, we shall soon find that they are highly interconnected and that many problems can be interpreted in more than one context. See Exploration 5.11 (Meanings of Operations with Fractions).

What do these contexts have in common? There are certain important ideas that abide in all the contexts:

- Each case can be interpreted in part-whole relationships.
- Something is to be partitioned into parts of equal size (value). The something can have a value of 1, in which case the unit = the whole. The something can have a value ≠ 1, in which case the unit ≠ the whole.
- The numerator and denominator are like codes that tell us about the relative sizes of the parts and the unit, and the code is multiplicative in nature. For example, when we say 1/2, it is not the difference between the two numbers that contains the key to the value; rather, it is the fact that the value of the denominator is twice the value of the numerator that contains the key. Thus, 1/2 has the same value as 4/8, not 7/8.

It is also important to note that the diagrams in Figure 5.10 on page 217 also illustrate three basic ways in which we can represent rational numbers: **length models** (e.g., number lines and Cuisenaire rods), **area models** (e.g., squares, circles, Geoboards, Pattern Blocks™), and **set models** (e.g., discrete circles and egg cartons). These are not the only representations (for example, we can speak of volume models), but these three have been found useful in helping people to understand fraction concepts and useful in terms of representing problems visually.

The unit and the whole are not always the same! Equating the unit with the whole is one of the most common misconceptions that people have about working with fractions. Let us revisit the four problems posed on page 217. In each case, what is the whole? What is the unit? What do we mean by whole and by unit? Think and then read on. . . . 🖎

In the first case, the whole is 3/4 inch — that is how much Joey grew; the unit is 1 inch. In the second case, the whole is 3 pies; the unit is 1 pie. In the third case, the whole is 12 people; the unit is 1 person. In the fourth case, the whole is the number of students at the college; the unit is 1 person.

The whole is the given object or amount. The unit is that amount to which we give a value of 1:1 inch, 1 pie, 1 person. In some cases, the whole and the unit are coincident (the same). For example, if Lisa gets 1/2 of a pizza and Liam gets 1/3 of the pizza, the whole is 1 pizza and the unit is also 1 pizza. However, if Ramon buys $2\frac{1}{2}$ gallons of gas and his brother takes 1/2 gallon, the whole is $2\frac{1}{2}$ gallons and the unit is 1 gallon. The need to think about wholes and units comes up in several explorations (5.7, 5.10, 5.11, and 5.12) and throughout this chapter.

Let us now investigate the context of rational number as measure.

INVESTIGATION **5.4** **Fractions as Measure**

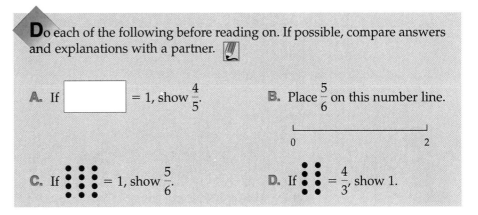

Do each of the following before reading on. If possible, compare answers and explanations with a partner.

A. If [ ] = 1, show $\frac{4}{5}$.

B. Place $\frac{5}{6}$ on this number line.

0   2

C. If [dots] = 1, show $\frac{5}{6}$.

D. If [dots] = $\frac{4}{3}$, show 1.

DISCUSSION

A. This question is relatively straightforward: divide the rectangle into 5 equal regions, shade in 4 of them [Figure 5.11(a)].

B. This question requires you to grapple with the difference between the unit and the whole.

In this case, the whole and the unit are not the same. This is important, because the meaning of the denominator is in relation to the unit. That is, to find the location of 5/6, we do not take the whole line and divide it into 6 equal lengths. Rather, we first must determine the unit (length) and then divide that length into 6 equal lengths. Recall the wire problem (Investigation 1.8). In that problem, the unit is 1 inch but the whole is 50 inches. This difference between the whole and the unit cannot be overemphasized [Figure 5.11(b)].

C. To make sense of this question, we must partition the dots into 6 equal-size groups. Recall the partitioning model of whole-number division. We then take 5 of those groups to show 5/6 [Figure 5.11(c)].

D. For many students, this question is the most difficult. There are different ways to make sense of this situation and answer the question. For example, we can focus on the numerator, which indicates that we have 4 equal parts. When we then focus on the denominator, we find that three of these equal parts represent the unit (that is, three of those parts have a value of 1).

On the other hand, we can interpret this statement from a ratio context. For example, if 8 dots have a value of 4/3, then 4 dots will have a value of 2/3, and so 2 dots will have a value of 1/3. Many people feel more confident once they get to a unit fraction; they reason that if 2 dots have a value of 1/3, then 6 dots will have a value of 3/3—that is, 1 [Figure 5.11(d)].

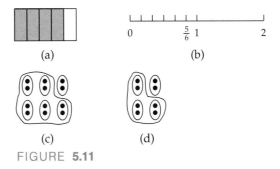

(a)

0          $\frac{5}{6}$ 1   2

(b)

(c)   (d)

FIGURE **5.11**

Let us work with another problem to develop these fraction ideas further.

INVESTIGATION **5.5** *Determining an Appropriate Representation*

Jose paid $6 for a 3/4-pound box of chocolates (see Figure 5.12). What is the price of 1 pound (at this rate)? Work on this and then read on. . . .

FIGURE **5.12**

DISCUSSION

An area model is an appropriate representation, since boxes of chocolates are often rectangular in shape. If we look at the box in terms of weight, we have 3/4 of a pound. If we look at the box in terms of money, it costs $6. In one sense, we are saying that 3/4 of a pound is equivalent to $6. That is, there is a functional relationship between 3/4 (box) and 6 (dollars). There are many strategies for transforming this information into an answer.

FIGURE **5.13**

STRATEGY 1: "See" the multiplication in the question

Thinking of the problem as "we have 3 parts, which are equivalent to $6" invites the question, "What number do we add three times to get 6?" In other words, "3 times what is 6?"

From this perspective, we realize that each part (that is, each quarter pound) has a value of $2 (see Figure 5.13), and so one pound will cost $8.

STRATEGY 2: Apply the function concept

Input	Output	Reasoning
$\frac{3}{4}$ pound	$6	Essentially, we now have the rule (recall "What's my rule?").
$1\frac{1}{2}$ pounds	$12	We are using the idea of proportional reasoning, which we will explore in more detail in Chapter 6. If we double the amount, we must double the price.
3 pounds	$24	We double the amount again. Why do we do this?
1 pound	$8	Most people work more confidently with whole numbers and can now confidently reason that if 3 pounds cost $24, then 1 pound costs $8.

It is important to note that there is no one "right" way to use the function concept. We could also have reasoned that if 3/4 pound costs $6, then 1/4 pound must cost $2, and therefore 1 pound must cost $8.

Let us continue our investigation of the meaning of fractions with a story problem.

INVESTIGATION **5.6** *How Many Blue Balloons?*

Josh goes through a large bag of balloons containing red and blue balloons. He finds that 1/8 of them are blue. He also notes that there are 120 more red balloons than blue balloons. How many blue balloons are in the bag? Work on this and then read on. . . .

DISCUSSION

Balloons are discrete amounts, and so we could represent this problem with a discrete model. However, this would be tedious; drawing 120 more red balloons would take some time! In this case, even though the actual problem involves discrete objects, a more appropriate model to represent the problem is an area model.

This idea of appropriate representations of a problem situation is one that has been neglected in school mathematics and one that the NCTM and other educational bodies (for example, the National Science Teachers Association) are encouraging teachers to emphasize more. Do you understand Figure 5.14? If you were unable to solve this problem, before reading on, try to solve the problem using Figure 5.14 and then read on. . . . 🖊

FIGURE **5.14**

STRATEGY 1: Use reasoning

If we now try to connect the problem to Figure 5.14, *one* way (of many) to verbalize this would be to say that the blue balloons are represented by 1 box, and the red balloons are represented by 7 boxes. We unlock the secret to the solution when we connect the figure to the other piece of given information: There are 120 *more* red balloons than blue balloons. This means that 6 boxes must represent 120 balloons. Why is this? From this, we can conclude that 1 box represents 20 balloons. Thus, there are 20 blue balloons and $7 \cdot 20 = 140$ red balloons.

Check this solution with the original problem. Does this answer work?

If there are 20 blue balloons and 140 red balloons, then there are 160 balloons in all. Since 20 is 1/8 of 160 and 140 is 120 more than 20, our solution fits the given information.

STRATEGY 2: Use algebra

Those students who are fluent algebraically may have wondered why we didn't use algebra. In this case, if you are comfortable with algebra, it certainly is quicker. However, there are several ways to do the algebra. Try to solve this problem algebraically and then read on. . . . 🖊

One algebraic solution path:

■ We can let $x =$ the number of blue balloons.

■ We can then represent the number of red balloons as $x + 120$.

■ This means that $x + (x + 120)$ — that is, $2x + 120$ — represents the total number of balloons.

■ Since 1/8 of them are blue, we can say that $x = \frac{1}{8}(2x + 120)$.

■ It is important to note that we can connect language nicely to the equation; that is, the number of blue balloons is 1/8 the total number of balloons.

■ When we solve this equation for x, we find that $x = 20$.

Another algebraic solution path:

■ If 1/8 of the balloons are blue, that means that 7/8 of them are red.

■ If we let $x =$ the number of balloons in all, we have the following equation:

$$\frac{7}{8}x - \frac{1}{8}x = 120$$

■ As before, we can connect language nicely to the equation; that is, the difference between the number of red and blue balloons is 120.

■ Solving this equation for x, we get $x = 160$, and 1/8 of 160 is 20.

Not only are there different ways to solve this problem algebraically, it is important to note that x did not represent the same thing in every case. This is another reason for taking the time on your paper to make sure that you (and the reader) know what the x refers to.

Equivalent Fractions

Let us now examine the concept of equivalent fractions.

> Two fractions are **equivalent fractions** if they have the same value.

When you made your own manipulatives in Exploration 5.5, you could literally see the equivalence of certain fractions as you developed strategies to cut the unit squares or circles into pieces. However, it is not always obvious that two fractions do indeed have the same value.

Almost all of the essential fraction ideas surface in the concept of equivalent fractions, and this concept permeates many of the fraction problems that we encounter. One of the biggest challenges in approaching this section is that you already know the procedures for finding equivalent fractions. For example, you know that 3/4 and 6/8 are equivalent fractions because you can multiply 3/4 by 2/2.

$$\frac{3}{4} = \frac{3}{4} \cdot \frac{2}{2} = \frac{6}{8}$$

As we have stressed repeatedly in this book, mathematical power and number sense come from not just knowing procedures but also knowing why these procedures work and how they connect to other mathematical ideas. Therefore, we will do some work to make sense of the procedures for determining equivalent fractions. To the extent possible, try to assume that you don't know the procedure when answering the questions.

Equivalence   Please address the two questions before reading on. . . .

- What does "equivalent" mean?
- Where else have you encountered the notion of equivalence in mathematics and in life outside school?

One way of looking at "equivalent" comes from taking apart the actual word: *equi-valent*, or equal value. We needed the notion of equivalence when we added and subtracted whole numbers with regrouping; for example, 1 ten and 2 ones is equivalent to 12 ones. We use equivalence with money every day; for example, one quarter is equivalent to 25 pennies.

Using models   Similarly, two fractions are equivalent if they have the same value. Using this notion, can you illustrate the equivalence of 3/4 and 6/8 using one or more of the fraction models we have discussed: area, length, or set? Do this before reading on. . . .

We can use the set model to illustrate equivalence. For example, consider a set of 8 dots [Figure 5.15(a)]. If we take 6 of them, we literally have 6/8 [Figure 5.15(b)]. However, we can also partition this set into 4 equal groups of 2 dots; if we then take three of these four equal groups, we have, by definition, taken 3/4 of the set [Figure 5.15(c)].

(a)   (b)   (c)

FIGURE **5.15**

However, we could also have used an area model. For example, consider a rectangle representing 1 [Figure 5.16(a)]. We can partition the rectangle into 4 equal regions and shade in 3 of them to represent 3/4 [Figure 5.16(b)]. However, if we draw a horizontal line through the middle of the rectangle, the rectangle has now been partitioned into 8 equal regions. Since 6 of those regions have been shaded in, we have, by definition, 6/8 of the rectangle [Figure 5.16(c)].

(a)

(b)

(c)

FIGURE **5.16**

Patterns and Order: Approaches to Procedures

Patterns in a sequence   As stated before in this book, mathematics has been referred to as "a science of pattern and order." Let us examine equivalent fractions from the perspective of pattern and order. Look at the sequence of equivalent fractions below. What "patterns" and "order" do you notice? What is the next fraction in the sequence? Why?

$$\frac{3}{4} = \frac{6}{8} = \frac{9}{12} = \frac{12}{16} \cdots$$

Some of the many aspects of pattern and order include:

1. As we move from one fraction to another, the numerator increases by 3 and the denominator increases by 4. In this sense, the 3/4 acts as a "function machine."

2. The numerator of each of the fractions is a multiple of 3, and the denominator of each of the fractions is the same multiple of 4.

3. All the denominators are even numbers, while every other numerator is an even number.

We can translate the first statement into notation:

Specific example: $\dfrac{3}{4} = \dfrac{3 + 3}{4 + 4} = \dfrac{6}{8}$

More general case: $\dfrac{a}{b} = \dfrac{\overbrace{a + a + \cdots + a}^{n \text{ times}}}{\underbrace{b + b + \cdots + b}_{n \text{ times}}} = \dfrac{an}{bn}$

We can also translate the second statement into notation:

Specific example: $\dfrac{3}{4} = \dfrac{3 \cdot 2}{4 \cdot 2} = \dfrac{6}{8}$

More general case: $\dfrac{a}{b} = \dfrac{a \cdot n}{b \cdot n} = \dfrac{an}{bn}$

Another pattern   Another aspect of equivalent fractions is used extensively in algebra. Look at the following pairs of equivalent fractions. What can you say about each pair?

$$\frac{3}{4} = \frac{6}{8} \qquad \frac{5}{6} = \frac{10}{12} \qquad \frac{3}{8} = \frac{9}{24}$$

In each case, the product of the first numerator and the second denominator is equal to the product of the second numerator and the first denominator. This relationship (often referred to as cross multiplication) is used (often incorrectly) as a shortcut in solving equations. It is expressed most abstractly as:

$$\frac{a}{b} = \frac{c}{d} \quad \text{iff} \quad ad = bc$$

Addressing a Common Difficulty in Language

When trying to explain why 3/4 and 6/8 are equivalent, many students use the word *divide*—for example, "We divided the rectangle in half, and now there were 8 equal regions compared to 4 before." This choice of words is interesting and points to a problem that many children have in trying to understand equivalent fractions at a conceptual level. When we look at why fractions are equivalent, we commonly encounter this word *divide*. However, in the procedure for creating equivalent fractions, we *multiply* the top and bottom by the same number! If we physically divide, why do we mathematically multiply? Think about this and then read on. . . .

There is no simple answer to this question. It has to do with the reciprocal relationship between multiplication and division. Figure 5.17(a) shows 3/4. If we divide each of the regions by 2, we are also multiplying the total number of regions by 2 [Figure 5.17(b)]. We now have 6 out of 8 regions shaded, that is 6/8. Starting with 3/4, we could have divided each region into 3 smaller pieces. By dividing each region into 3 smaller pieces, we are multiplying the number of pieces by 3, and we can name this shaded amount 9/12 [Figure 5.17(c)].

(a) (b) (c)

FIGURE **5.17**

Simplest Form

A fraction is in simplest form if the numerator and the denominator are relatively prime numbers. The notion of simplifying fractions is clearly connected to the concept of equivalent fractions, and we will discuss it here. One important connection is that when we are simplifying fractions, we are essentially finding an equivalent fraction in which the numerator and denominator are smaller (and thus simpler) numbers. For example,

$$\frac{15}{20} = \frac{15 \div 5}{20 \div 5} = \frac{3}{4}$$

As has been true for other procedures, there are many strategies for simplifying fractions. Before we discuss them, simplify the following fractions yourself: 24/40, 42/60, and 63/105.

One strategy is to use guess–test–revise. For example, you might divide both numerator and denominator by 4, which produces 6/10. A quick glance reveals that this can be simplified further to 3/5.

$$\frac{24}{40} = \frac{24 \div 4}{40 \div 4} = \frac{6}{10} = \frac{6 \div 2}{10 \div 2} = \frac{3}{5}$$

Another strategy is to determine the prime factorization of each number and then either cross out the common factors or select the "uncommon" factors.

$$24 = 2 \cdot 2 \cdot 2 \cdot 3$$
$$40 = 2 \cdot 2 \cdot 2 \cdot 5$$

Let us examine more closely what happens when we are able to simplify the fraction in one step, as we did above to simplify 15/20. What is the relationship between the divisor and the original numerator and denominator in each of the three fractions given above (24/40, 42/60, and 63/105)?

$$\frac{24 \div 8}{40 \div 8} \qquad \frac{42 \div 6}{60 \div 6} \qquad \frac{63 \div 21}{105 \div 21}$$

In each case, to simplify the fraction in one step, we divide both the numerator and the denominator by their GCF. By doing so, we ensure that the resulting numerator and denominator will have no factors in common. In other words, a fraction is in simplest terms when the numerator and the denominator are relatively prime.

Developing fraction sense The purpose of this work and Exploration 5.8 is to develop "fraction sense." Number sense simply cannot be directly taught; rather, it emerges from being aware of the connectedness of and subtle relationships between various concepts and procedures. We see this awareness all the time when we watch experts at work: the dancer who can "feel" the subtle rhythms in a new piece of music, the electrician who rewired my house who could tell so much about the wiring problems from so little evidence, the mechanic who can look at a nut and know that he needs a 5/16-inch wrench.

As you are coming to realize, the set of fractions is in many ways very different from the set of whole numbers. Another important difference between fractions and whole numbers is that the whole numbers are evenly spaced on the number line. This is not true for fractions.

INVESTIGATION **5.7** Ordering Rational Numbers

Arrange these fractions from smallest to largest without converting to equivalent fractions or converting to decimals—that is, by focusing on fraction concepts and reasoning tools. Think and then read on. . . .

$$\frac{3}{4} \qquad \frac{2}{5} \qquad \frac{5}{6}$$

DISCUSSION
One of the reasons for Exploration 5.5 is to increase the chance that all students will develop a sense of the relative size of fractions through hands-on work with fractions with different denominators. There are a variety of ways in which students can validly answer the question. We will explore several of these ways with the intention of refining or expanding your "fraction sense" toolbox.

Some people start by looking for the largest or the smallest, whereas others start by picking two whose order they know. In this example, let us start that way. We know that $\frac{2}{5} < \frac{3}{4}$. An area diagram would readily show this.

However, we can use another tool, which we will use in many other situations, to conclude that $\frac{2}{5} < \frac{3}{4}$. This tool uses the fraction $\frac{1}{2}$ as a reference point.

We know that $\frac{3}{4}$ is greater than $\frac{1}{2}$ because 3 is more than $\frac{1}{2}$ of 4; similarly, we know that $\frac{2}{5}$ is less than $\frac{1}{2}$ because 2 is less than $\frac{1}{2}$ of 5. Thus, we can conclude that $\frac{2}{5} < \frac{3}{4}$.

The next debate concerns $\frac{5}{6}$ and $\frac{3}{4}$. How would you explain which is larger? Think and then read on. . . .

Looking at the two fractions, we see that they are both one piece away from 1. Since sixths are smaller than fourths, we can reason that $\frac{5}{6}$ must be greater than $\frac{3}{4}$ because the distance between $\frac{5}{6}$ and 1 is $\frac{1}{6}$, whereas the distance between $\frac{3}{4}$ and 1 is $\frac{1}{4}$.

The Denseness of the Set of Rational Numbers

This kind of activity brings up a question that youngsters often ask: Can we name *any* point on the number line with a rational number? What do you think?

For example, name a rational number between 1/2 and 3/4. If we did this with a whole class, we would get a number of correct responses, although 2/3 might be the most common.

Can you name another rational number between 1/2 and 3/4? How many can you name?

In fact, we can say that between any two rational numbers, there are an infinite number of rational numbers. Mathematicians refer to this property by saying that rational numbers are **dense.** Think of naming every point on a number line, knowing that no matter how close two rational numbers are, we can find an infinite number of rational numbers between those two rational numbers.

At the same time, there are points on the number line that cannot be named by rational numbers! Can you think of any such points? Think and then read on. . . .

Such points, for example, $\sqrt{2}$ and π, are called **irrational numbers;** these numbers cannot be expressed as a ratio between two integers. We will explore such numbers in Section 5.4.

Summary

This section and Explorations 5.5 to 5.8 lay the groundwork for understanding operations with fractions. In this section, we have seen that there are four major interpretations of fractions—as measures, as quotients, as operators, and as ratios. We have seen that we need to pay attention when we work with fractions because the fraction concept is not at all a simple one.

You have learned that a fraction is not simply a number; rather, a fraction expresses a relationship between two quantities. The numerator and denominator can be seen as a code that tells us the relative size of the fraction.

In order to work effectively with fractions as measures, we need a strong understanding of several basic ideas:

- We are dealing with part-whole relationships.
- Something is to be partitioned into parts.

■ All of the parts must have the same value.

■ We need to take care not to confuse the unit with the whole, which are the same in some situations but not in others.

■ We can use various models to represent fractions and fraction situations. In this book, we emphasize number line, area, and discrete models.

We then applied these ideas in order to more fully understand the notions of equivalent fraction and simplifying fractions. A deeper understanding of rational numbers enables us to sense their relative size; this fraction sense is useful in estimating and problem-solving.

If you look back over the investigations in this section and Explorations 5.5 to 5.8, you will find that to the extent that you could apply these ideas, you were able to develop strategies that would enable you to confidently solve the problems. These ideas will continue to be important as we explore other fraction ideas and algorithms in the next section.

EXERCISES 5.2

1. Let's say that Amy made 15 out of 21 free throws and Jane made 8 out of 12. Which student had a better rate of success? Explain your answer.

2. Two elementary school principals are comparing their schools' attendance.

	Total enrollment	Absent
Wheelock	264	32
Fuller	402	58

Which school had the larger fraction of students absent? Justify your answer.

3. In each of the questions below, justify your answer.

a. If [ ] has a value of 4/5, draw and shade in the amount that would have a value of 1. Justify your answer.

b. If [ ] = 1 1/3, then shade in the amount equal to 1. Justify your answer.

c. If ⋮⋮⋮ = $\frac{3}{4}$, show 1.

d. If ⋰⋰ = $\frac{5}{4}$, show 1.

e. On the number line below, mark the approximate location of 1. Explain your reasoning.

f. On the number line below, approximate the value of x. Explain your reasoning.

g. Name a fraction between 2/3 and 3/4.

h. Name a fraction between 1/4 and 1/5.

i. Name a fraction closer to 1 than to 7/8.

j. Name a fraction between 1/4 and 1/2 that has a denominator of 11.

4. Let's say you are making rulers for your students to help them learn fractions. You have decided to have a ruler marking every 1/6-inch and every 1/8-inch. How many different marks will there be per inch?

5. Draw three diagrams to represent each of the following fractions. Justify your diagrams.

	Length	Area	Discrete
$\frac{3}{5}$	0 ———•—— 1		
$1\frac{2}{3}$			
$\frac{9}{4}$			

6. Look at the sequence below and look at the multiplication table in Chapter 3. Do you see a connection? Can you explain the connection, or is it just coincidence?

$$\frac{2}{3} = \frac{4}{6} = \frac{6}{9} = \frac{8}{12} = \frac{10}{15} = \cdots$$

7. Simplify the following fractions.

a. $\frac{25}{40}$ b. $\frac{32}{48}$ c. $\frac{54}{60}$ d. $\frac{26}{65}$

e. $\frac{168}{216}$ f. $\frac{84}{132}$ g. $\frac{493}{510}$ h. $\frac{101010}{505050}$

8. Arrange the following fractions in order from least in value to greatest in value without converting to decimals or finding the LCM. Explain your reasoning.

   a. $\dfrac{3}{4}$ $\dfrac{4}{5}$ $\dfrac{5}{15}$

   b. $\dfrac{6}{7}$ $\dfrac{5}{11}$ $\dfrac{2}{3}$

   c. $\dfrac{1}{3}$ $\dfrac{2}{5}$ $\dfrac{5}{8}$ $\dfrac{3}{4}$ $\dfrac{3}{50}$

   d. $\dfrac{2}{5}$ $\dfrac{5}{6}$ $\dfrac{4}{7}$ $\dfrac{7}{8}$ $\dfrac{3}{10}$

9. Is 10/13 closer to 1/2 or to 1? Justify your choice.

10. Which of the following fractions is the farthest from 1? Explain why.

    2/3   3/4   5/6   6/7   7/8

11. In the following exercise, $0 < a < b < c$. For the following pairs, tell which is larger and explain why, or explain why you cannot be sure which is larger. Try to answer the questions using only reasoning rather than plugging in numbers. You may then substitute actual numbers to check your reasoning.

    a. $\dfrac{a}{b}$ or $\dfrac{a}{c}$ b. $\dfrac{a}{b}$ or $\dfrac{b}{c}$ c. $\dfrac{a}{c}$ or $\dfrac{b}{c}$

12. The fraction of Fortune 1000 companies that employed undercover security agents in 1974 was 1/10. In 1985 it was 1/2. Compare the two numbers.

13. Let's say you decide to give blood at a blood drive. The body of an average adult contains about 5 quarts of blood. If you donate one pint of blood, what fraction of your blood do you give?

14. You are driving to Memphis, 115 miles away. You have 24 miles to go. Approximately, what fraction of the trip is left? Justify your choice of fraction.

15. You have from 10 to 11:30 P.M. to do a project.

    a. At 11, what fraction of the time remains?

    b. At 11:20, what fraction of the time remains?

16. In 1950 the annual per capita consumption of eggs was 395; that is, the average person ate 395 eggs per year. In 1990 the per capita consumption had dropped to 236. Fill in the blank with a fraction: In 1990 the average person eats ____ as many eggs as the average person did in 1950.

17. Below are the median prices of homes sold in 1991, by region of the country:

South	$88,200
Northeast	$136,700
Midwest	$76,800
West	$147,600

    The median selling price of a home in the South is approximately what fraction of the median selling price of a home in the West?

18. PhonesRUs did a survey to determine telephone usage at a college. On the day the survey was done, a total of 5,243 calls were made.

    a. If 1,371 calls were made to directory assistance, approximately what fraction of the total calls were made to directory assistance? Justify your choice.

    b. The three pizza restaurants that delivered pizza received 737 calls. Approximately what fraction of the total calls were for pizza? Justify your choice.

19. In 1991 the average salary for beginning public school teachers was $22,700, and the average salary for all public school teachers was $32,900. The average salary for beginning public school teachers is approximately what fraction of the average salary for all public school teachers?

20. The data below show the area (in square miles) of several states and some of the Great Lakes:

Lake Superior	31,800
Lake Huron	23,010
All five Great Lakes	94,710
New Hampshire	9,279
California	158,706
Tennessee	42,104
Rhode Island	1,212

    For each of the questions below, using mental arithmetic and estimation, find a fraction with a small, "friendly" denominator (2, 3, 4, 5, 6, 8, 10, or 12) that most closely approximates the actual fraction. Justify your reasoning.

    a. Lake Huron is approximately what fraction of the size of Lake Superior?

    b. New Hampshire is approximately what fraction of the size of Lake Superior?

    c. Lake Superior is approximately what fraction of the size of Tennessee?

    d. The area of all five Great Lakes is approximately what fraction of the size of California?

21. There are approximately 4,800,000,000 people in the world. Using mental math and estimation, find a fraction to represent the fraction of the world's population that belongs to each of the following religions. Justify your reasoning.

Christianity	1,548,500,000
Islam	817,000,000
Hinduism	645,500,000
Buddhism	295,600,000
Judaism	17,800,000
Total	3,324,400,000

22. Each year the Weather Channel displays a map to indicate those portions of the country that will be celebrating a "white Christmas." If the shaded areas represent those regions that will have snow on the ground on Christmas Day, approximately what fraction of the con-

tiguous United States will have a white Christmas? Explain your answer.

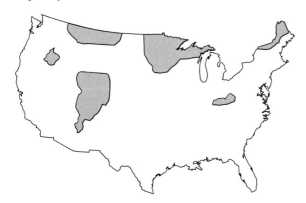

23. Give approximate values of this function for the given values of *x*:

$$f(x) = \frac{2x - 1}{3x + 7}$$

   a. $x = 3$
   b. $x = 10$
   c. $x = 100$
   d. What do you observe about the change in the value of the function as *x* gets larger and larger?

24. Write a fraction to represent the shaded portion. Justify your response.

25. If the numerator and the denominator of a fraction are increased by the same amount, is the new fraction greater than, equal to, or less than the original fraction? Justify your answer. Read this problem carefully; it is not a trick problem, but you need to make sure you interpret the wording correctly.

26. The music teacher would like to have the same number of girls and boys in the chorus. She finds that 5/8 of the chorus are girls, but that if she can get 12 more boys, the chorus will have the same number of boys and girls.
   a. How many students are in the chorus?
   b. If there are 216 children in the school, which unit fraction would you select to represent the fraction of students in the present chorus?

27. Darcy loves tomatoes, but she lives in Minnesota, where the growing season is shorter than in most of the country. Therefore, she begins her tomato plants inside. However, she tells her friend that there were some casualties this spring. One-third of the plants were destroyed by her cat. Furthermore, one-fourth of the

remaining plants were destroyed by a disease. What fraction survived?

28. I recall a teacher asking for fractions that were equivalent to 3/4 and one student replying $\frac{1\frac{1}{2}}{2}$. How would you respond to this answer? Justify your response.

29. We have seen that there are two formulas for converting between the Celsius and Fahrenheit temperatures:

$$C = \frac{5(F - 32)}{9} \qquad F = \frac{9C}{5} + 32$$

Fill in the blank in the following sentence: One Celsius degree is ____ of a Fahrenheit degree. Write a short paragraph to justify your choice.

30. Let us reinterpret the way gold is classified in terms of fractions. Pure gold is designated as 24-karat gold. Pure gold is very expensive and very soft; therefore, gold is often mixed with other metals such as copper or zinc to make it stronger.
   a. Represent 14-karat gold in terms of a fraction.
   b. If 1 ounce of pure gold costs $750, approximately how much would 1 ounce of 14-karat gold cost? Estimate your answer first.
   c. If you wanted to give a real-life answer to part (b), should you also know whether the other metal was copper or zinc? Why or why not?
   d. Find out why the number 24 was picked to designate pure gold; for example, why wasn't 10 or 100 selected?

31. I have a 35 mm camera and am a very amateur photographer. However, I do know that I need to set the camera speed for 1/60 of a second indoors and that 1/250 of a second is a good outdoor speed. When I decide to take a picture, I see on my camera a dial like the one below. The numbers 1000, 500, 250, and so forth represent the fractions 1/1000, 1/500, and so forth. The numbers continue to decrease until they get to 1 and then they increase again.
   a. Compare the shutter speeds of 1/125 and 1/500. Do this using whole sentences. Can you do this in more than one way?
   b. Explain the meaning of the following part of the dial: 8, 4, 2, 1, 2, 4.
   c. Find out the history of the shutter speeds. That is, why were these speeds chosen and not, for example, 1/10 of a second or 1/100 of a second. Why 1/15 instead of 1/16?

SECTION 5.3 **UNDERSTANDING OPERATIONS WITH FRACTIONS**

One of the sentences in the NCTM Standards that has burned in my head is that students should "believe that mathematics makes sense." My earliest memories of teaching (tutoring while in college) are of surprise that this field, which was so much fun for me, made almost no sense to many other people. There are many algorithms that enable us to manipulate fractions quickly: algorithms for adding, subtracting, multiplying, and dividing, and algorithms for translating improper fractions into mixed numbers and vice versa. However, as I have stressed in this book so far, it is simply not enough for an elementary teacher to know how to compute. It is crucial that the teacher also knows the *whys* behind the *whats*. If you only know the *whats*, your ability to apply that knowledge to nonroutine and multistep problems will be limited. After all, most real-life problems are nonroutine and multistep! Therefore, please take care in this section not to just skip over, saying "I know how to do that," but please ask yourself the questions that are posed. Can you really get into the *why*? I have seen many elementary teachers have wonderful discussions when students asked why and the teacher knew what to do with that question!

Addition of Rational Numbers

Addition of fractions is one of those situations that mathematics is famous for—The procedure goes against what most people's common sense tells them to do. When we add fractions, we do not add the numerators and the denominators; on the other hand, when we multiply fractions, we *do* multiply the numerators and the denominators.

$$\frac{1}{2} + \frac{1}{3} \neq \frac{2}{5} \quad \text{but} \quad \frac{2}{3} \times \frac{4}{5} = \frac{8}{15}$$

Can you explain *why* we need to find a common denominator before we can add fractions with different denominators? Write (a first draft) in your notebook and then read on. . . .

INVESTIGATION 5.8 Using Fraction Models to Understand Addition of Fractions

Using either the area model, length model, or the set model, determine the sum of $\frac{1}{2} + \frac{1}{3}$ and then try to explain *why* we need to find a common denominator in order to add fractions. This is your "second draft" for justifying the need for a common denominator. Then read on. . . .

DISCUSSION

This is an excellent place to demonstrate the role of manipulatives and that different manipulatives do different things.

Although children bring to school a primitive understanding of fractions, schools often teach procedures at the expense of understanding. The NCTM Standards encourages teachers to use "physical materials, diagrams, and real-world situations in conjunction with ongoing efforts to relate [the students'] learning experiences to oral language and symbols. . . [Such efforts] will reduce the amount of time currently spent in the upper grades in correcting students' misconceptions and procedural difficulties" (*Curriculum Standards*, p. 57).

Using Pattern Blocks   In Exploration 5.5, you worked with two kinds of area manipulatives: squares and circles. Let us now consider Pattern Blocks (see Figure 5.18). How might you use Pattern Blocks to add 1/2 and 1/3?

FIGURE **5.18**

If we let the (yellow) hexagon represent 1, then the trapezoid is 1/2, the parallelogram is 1/3, and the triangle is 1/6 . Using the notion of addition as combining, we can combine the two and we have 1/2 + 1/3 = .

We could be humorous and say that parallelogram + trapezoid = baby carriage! The key question, though, is to determine the numerical value of this amount. The solution lies in realizing that to name an amount with a fraction, we must have equal-size parts. If you are familiar with Pattern Blocks, you realize that an equivalent representation is to cover this amount with 5 triangles, as in Figure 5.19.

FIGURE **5.19**

Since the value of each triangle is 1/6, we can now say that $\frac{1}{2} + \frac{1}{3} = \frac{5}{6}$.

Using Cuisenaire rods   This is a very different question with Cuisenaire rods. There is no "natural" choice for 1. Thus, you have to think of a color for which you can represent 1/2 of that color and 1/3 of that color. If students have worked with Cuisenaire rods in previous contexts (recall the discussion of GCF and LCM in Chapter 4), they will be familiar with the relationships among the various rods. One of many different solutions is to choose the dark green rod to have a value of 1. The red rod now has a value of 1/3, and the green rod has a value of 1/2. See Figure 5.20(a). As with Pattern Blocks, when we combine these two parts, in order to name the amount, we have to find a way to represent this length with equal-size pieces, and 5 white rods have the same length. Since 6 white rods have the same length as the dark green rod, each of the white rods has a value of 1/6, and therefore 5 of them have a value of 5/6. See Figure 5.20(b).

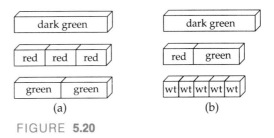

FIGURE **5.20**

Looking back   An important outcome of working with manipulatives is for the students to see that, for example, the yellow Pattern Block is not 6, but rather can be assigned any value, and the value of the other pieces is determined by their relationship to this block. So too with the Cuisenaire rods. Recall your work with the different models in Exploration 5.7.

Connecting Concepts to a Procedure for Adding Fractions

Let us now connect this work to the general procedure for adding fractions. Look at the addition problem below. Try to explain this procedure meaningfully, that is, to *justify* each step. Do this before reading on. . . . 🖊

$$\frac{2}{3} + \frac{1}{4} = \frac{8}{12} + \frac{3}{12} = \frac{11}{12}$$

In order to add two fractions that have different denominators, we determine the least common multiple of those two numbers, in this case 12. When working with fractions, we often refer to the LCM as the **lowest common denominator**. We now determine an equivalent fraction (with denominator 12) for each of the addends. We do this because all of the parts have to be the same size. We know that 2/3 is equivalent to 8/12 and 1/4 is equivalent to 3/12. Now that both fractions have the same denominator (that is, all pieces are the same size), we can combine them. We find that we have 8 + 3 = 11 pieces, each of which has a value of 1/12. Thus, the answer is 11/12.

You may remember and use the algebraic shortcut that is presented below without proof:

$$\frac{a}{b} + \frac{c}{d} = \frac{ad + bc}{bd}$$

If this doesn't make sense, try it for the numbers above; that is, substitute 2 for a, 3 for b, and so forth.

Which method will be faster when the least common multiple is not the product of the two denominators? For example, $\frac{7}{8} + \frac{5}{6} = $? You might try it both ways to see which method you prefer.

Mixed Numbers and Improper Fractions

Up to this point, all of the addition problems have involved only **proper fractions**—that is, fractions whose value is between 0 and 1. Why do you think these fractions are called proper fractions? In many real-life situations, we encounter mixed numbers (for example, $5\frac{1}{4}$) and improper fractions (for example, 21/4). Take a couple of minutes to write down your own definitions of these two terms and then read on. . . . 🖊

An **improper fraction** is one in which the numerator is at least as large as the denominator.

A **mixed number** is a number that has a whole-number component and a proper fraction component.

The language we use to describe mixed numbers is important. How do you say $5\frac{1}{4}$ in English? Just as we found the value of expanded form helpful with whole numbers, there is an expanded form for mixed numbers. How do you think we would represent $5\frac{1}{4}$ in expanded form?

A recent National Assessment of Educational Progress contained the following item:

$5\frac{1}{4}$ is the same as:

(a) 5 + 1/4   (b) 5 − 1/4   (c) 5 × 1/4   (d) 5 ÷ 1/4   (e) I don't know

Only 47 percent of the seventh graders chose the correct response, (a). Even more startling, an even smaller percentage of eleventh graders chose the correct response—only 44 percent. This lack of connectedness between concepts and procedures is one of the reasons why students do so much worse on algebraic equations with fractions than on algebraic equations with whole numbers. In this case, the problem is not the algebra so much as it is the arithmetic!

INVESTIGATION 5.9 Connecting Improper Fractions and Mixed Numbers

Most of you remember the procedure for converting a mixed number to an improper fraction.

For example, to convert $3\frac{1}{4}$ to an improper fraction, we do the following:

$$3\frac{1}{4} = \frac{3 \cdot 4 + 1}{4}$$

However, did you ever stop to think about what this might feel like to a youngster? On the surface, this procedure is as far from common sense as almost any in mathematics: We multiply the *whole number* by the *denominator* and then we add the *numerator*, and then we put this number on top of the *original denominator.* This sounds a lot like "gazinta" and "bring down" from division.

How would you explain the why of this procedure to, let's say, a fifth grade student? Record your first attempt and then read on. . . .

DISCUSSION

As is often the case, concrete representations are most helpful to most students. Figure 5.21 shows some concrete representations of $3\frac{1}{4}$.

FIGURE **5.21**

With these in mind, now make a second attempt to explain the why of the procedure. Then read on. . . .

In each of the representations, we see that the process is similar to the kinds of regrouping we did with whole numbers. In converting from the mixed number to the improper fraction, we need to convert all the units to fourths because in order for the improper fraction, 13/4, to have meaning, all the pieces must be the same size, that is, they must be fourths. We can convert each 1 to four fourths and then add all the fourths to get 13/4. However, since one context for multiplication is repeated addition, we see that we are adding three 4's; hence $3 \cdot 4$. When we add these 12 fourths to the 1 fourth we already had, we have a total of 13 fourths.

$$3\frac{1}{4} = 1 + 1 + 1 + \frac{1}{4}$$

$$3\frac{1}{4} = \frac{4}{4} + \frac{4}{4} + \frac{4}{4} + \frac{1}{4}$$

$$3\frac{1}{4} = \frac{3 \cdot 4}{4} + \frac{1}{4}$$

$$3\frac{1}{4} = \frac{3 \cdot 4 + 1}{4}$$

$$3\frac{1}{4} = \frac{13}{4}$$

Understanding Subtraction of Rational Numbers

For the most part, subtraction of fractions involves essentially the same processes as does addition. However, many students encounter difficulty in situations that involve regrouping. Therefore, it is important to examine this process also. Consider the following problem: $23\frac{2}{5} - 17\frac{4}{5}$. First do it on your own, writing down your justification of each step. Then read on. . . .

$$23\frac{2}{5} = 22\frac{7}{5}$$

$$-17\frac{4}{5} = 17\frac{4}{5}$$

$$5\frac{3}{5}$$

Let us discuss the transformation from $23\frac{2}{5}$ to $22\frac{7}{5}$, because this is difficult for many children. How would you explain this, as if you were talking to someone who does not understand it?

We must do some renaming because we cannot subtract 4/5 from 2/5. With fractions, instead of converting 1 ten into 10 ones (as we did with whole numbers), we convert 1 into five fifths (or six sixths, or ten tenths, depending on the common denominator). Once again, expanded form will help to illustrate the process and justify the equivalence of $23\frac{2}{5}$ and $22\frac{7}{5}$.

$$23\frac{2}{5} = 23 + \frac{2}{5} = (22 + 1) + \frac{2}{5} = 22 + \left(\frac{5}{5} + \frac{2}{5}\right) = 22 + \frac{7}{5} = 22\frac{7}{5}$$

Estimation and Mental Arithmetic:
INVESTIGATION 5.10 **Sums and Differences of Fractions**

As was the case with whole numbers, many everyday situations requiring computations with fractions do not require exact answers, but rather estimates. Think of circumstances in which you or other people might need to find the sum of fractions or the difference between fractions. Try to come up with realistic problem situations. In which of those situations do you need an exact answer? In which of those situations do you need an estimate, a ballpark answer?

When I have done this exercise with students and teachers, we find that more often than not, an estimate rather than an exact answer is needed. Thus, it is important to examine strategies for estimating. As we have seen before with whole numbers, this also involves examining mental arithmetic. Because there are many strategies, we will examine them using a process similar to the one we used when developing estimation and mental math strategies with whole numbers.

Part 1: Mental addition and subtraction with fractions

In each of the following problems, try to find the sum or the difference entirely in your head.

Briefly describe your strategies. Then read the discussion below.

A. $\quad 2\frac{1}{2}$ B. $\quad 3\frac{4}{5}$ C. $\quad 7\frac{3}{4}$ D. $\quad 7$ E. $\quad 9\frac{1}{4}$

$\quad +5\frac{3}{4}$ $\quad +1\frac{2}{3}$ $\quad 5\frac{1}{8}$ $\quad -2\frac{5}{8}$ $\quad -3\frac{5}{8}$

$\qquad\qquad\qquad\qquad +2\frac{1}{2}$

DISCUSSION

Keep the following points in mind for each problem:

- Deciding which strategy is better is often not as helpful as knowing which strategy works best for you.

- Other useful strategies have not been included here because too many strategies (and 1,500-page books) can overwhelm students!

A. $2\frac{1}{2} + 5\frac{3}{4}$

STRATEGY 1: Represent the sum with expanded form and use the commutative and associative properties

$$2\frac{1}{2} + 5\frac{3}{4} = 2 + \frac{1}{2} + 5 + \frac{3}{4} = 2 + 5 + \frac{1}{2} + \frac{3}{4} = 7 + \frac{1}{2} + \frac{3}{4}$$

That is, we quickly transform the problem into $7 + \frac{1}{2} + \frac{3}{4}$.
Decomposing $\frac{3}{4}$ into $\frac{1}{2} + \frac{1}{4}$, we then have $7 + \frac{1}{2} + \frac{1}{2} + \frac{1}{4} = 8\frac{1}{4}$.

STRATEGY 2: Add up and break into parts

$$\left(2\frac{1}{2} + 5\right) + \frac{3}{4} = 7\frac{1}{2} + \frac{3}{4} = 7\frac{1}{2} + \frac{1}{2} + \frac{1}{4} = 8 + \frac{1}{4} = 8\frac{1}{4}$$

B. $3\frac{4}{5} + 1\frac{2}{3}$

Use the shortcut

$$\frac{4}{5} + \frac{2}{3} = \frac{4 \cdot 3 + 5 \cdot 2}{15} = \frac{22}{15} = 1\frac{7}{15}$$

Add this to the sum obtained from the whole numbers and we have $4 + 1\frac{7}{15} = 5\frac{7}{15}$.

C. $7\frac{3}{4} + 5\frac{1}{8} + 2\frac{1}{2}$

STRATEGY 1: Look for compatible numbers

$\frac{3}{4}$ and $\frac{1}{2}$ can be added mentally to get $1\frac{1}{4}$; then add $1\frac{1}{4} + \frac{1}{8} = 1\frac{2}{8} + \frac{1}{8} = 1\frac{3}{8}$. Add this to the 14, and we have $15\frac{3}{8}$. *Note:* I find it easier to add $\frac{3}{4}$ and $\frac{1}{2}$ first rather than adding $\frac{3}{4}$ and $\frac{1}{8}$ and then $\frac{1}{2}$. Do you see why? Which would be easier for you?

STRATEGY 2: Convert to common denominator

Since the common denominator is relatively small and the conversions to eighths are relatively easy, some students find it easier to add all three at once, thinking something like this: "6 + 1 + 4 = 11, that means 11 eighths, which is 8 eighths (1) + 3 eighths. Add this to the 14 and we have $15\frac{3}{8}$ as the answer."

D. $7 - 2\frac{5}{8}$

STRATEGY 1: Break into parts and subtract

First, $7 - 2 = 5$; now take $\frac{5}{8}$ from 5 to get $4\frac{3}{8}$.

STRATEGY 2: Add up

$2\frac{5}{8} + 4 = 6\frac{5}{8}$. How much more do we need to get to 7? We need $\frac{3}{8}$ more. The answer is $4\frac{3}{8}$.

E. $9\frac{1}{4} - 3\frac{5}{8}$

Add up:

$3\frac{5}{8}$ plus 5 equals $8\frac{5}{8}$ plus $\frac{3}{8}$ equals 9 plus $\frac{2}{8} = 9\frac{1}{4}$. What you have to remember to add now is $5 + \frac{3}{8} + \frac{2}{8} = 5\frac{5}{8}$.

A number line helps some students to better understand the process (see Figure 5.22).

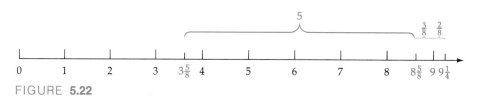

FIGURE **5.22**

This is one place where many students find the explorations paying rich dividends. Making the manipulatives (Exploration 5.5), grappling with relative sizes of fractions (Exploration 5.6), and developing fraction sense (Exploration 5.8) all focus on understanding the relationships involved in fractions. Having a good understanding of these relationships enables the student to more confidently decompose and then recompose the various fractions. Again we find the composition and decomposition of numbers in this chapter.

We can now apply these strategies to problems with a story.

Part 2: Estimating sums and differences with fractions

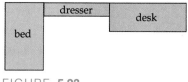

FIGURE **5.23**

> **A.** In their retirement, the parents of a close friend of mine have created a dollhouse to represent their dream house. They are shopping, and they see some miniature furniture that might fit in one of the bedrooms. The bed is 7/8 inch wide; the dresser is $1\frac{1}{2}$ inches long, and the desk is $1\frac{3}{4}$ inches long. If the three articles are placed as shown in Figure 5.23, will they fit into the dollhouse bedroom, which is 4 inches wide? Try to add the three lengths in your head, then read on. . . .

DISCUSSION

STRATEGY 1: Make a quick estimate
A quick estimation reveals that it will be close:

$$1 + 1\frac{1}{2} + 1\frac{1}{2} = 4$$

STRATEGY 2: Add the two easier numbers

$$1\frac{1}{2} + 1\frac{3}{4} = 1\frac{1}{2} + 1\frac{1}{2} + \frac{1}{4} = 3\frac{1}{4}$$

Thus, we need a more careful estimate.

We can use number sense here; that is, we know that $3\frac{1}{4} + \frac{3}{4} = 4$, and since $\frac{7}{8} > \frac{3}{4}$, we can conclude that the furniture is too big.

> **B.** It rained almost every day this past week. Here are the amounts per day. How much rain fell during the week? First, make a rough estimate. Then make a refined estimate. Then read on. . . .

Monday	$1\frac{3}{4}$ inches	Friday	0 inches
Tuesday	$\frac{1}{2}$ inch	Saturday	$3\frac{3}{4}$ inches
Wednesday	$\frac{5}{8}$ inch	Sunday	$1\frac{5}{16}$ inches
Thursday	$\frac{7}{8}$ inch		

DISCUSSION

STRATEGY 1: Make a rough estimate

One way to get a rough estimate is to round each fraction to the nearest $\frac{1}{2}$ inch and keep a cumulative total:

$$1\frac{1}{2} + \frac{1}{2} = 2;\ 2 \text{ plus } \frac{1}{2} = 2\frac{1}{2};\ 2\frac{1}{2} \text{ plus } 1 = 3\frac{1}{2};\ 3\frac{1}{2} \text{ plus } 3\frac{1}{2} = 7;\ 7 \text{ plus } 1\frac{1}{2} = 8\frac{1}{2}$$

STRATEGY 2: Look for compatible numbers

One way to get a closer estimate is to look for compatible numbers — numbers whose sum is close to one or numbers that you can quickly add mentally.

$$\left(1\frac{3}{4} + 3\frac{3}{4}\right) + \frac{1}{2} \qquad + \left(\frac{5}{8} + 1\frac{5}{16}\right) + \frac{7}{8} =$$

$$5\frac{1}{2} \qquad + \frac{1}{2} \qquad + \text{ just under } 2 + \text{ just under } 1 = \text{ just under } 9$$

Before we move on, take a few moments to reflect on the mental math and estimation strategies that you used and that were discussed here. What strategies have been adapted from ones we developed with whole numbers, such as compatible numbers? What strategies are new, such as the algebra shortcut?

INVESTIGATION 5.11   Understanding Multiplication of Rational Numbers

CHILDREN

There is another difference between multiplying whole numbers and multiplying fractions that bears noting, for it often baffles children when they encounter fraction computations for the first time. One notion of multiplication that many people (often unconsciously) make from working with whole numbers is that "multiplication makes bigger and division makes smaller," but just the opposite is true when we multiply proper fractions!

The following multiplication problems have several purposes. First, they will enable you to connect the meaning of multiplication, which we developed with whole numbers, to fraction situations. Second, they will enable you to connect the meaning of fractions to fraction multiplication. Third, your ability to apply this knowledge to nonroutine and multistep problems should increase. Finally, you will be able to understand and explain things that teachers need to know — for example, why $3\frac{1}{2} \cdot 2\frac{1}{4} \neq 6\frac{1}{8}$.

For each of the following problems, represent the situation with a diagram and determine the answer from the diagram. As you are doing this, think back to the models we developed for whole-number multiplication. Which problems connect well to repeated addition? to a rectangular array? to the Cartesian product? Which problems do not connect well? Why don't they?

A. Julio runs four times a week. His route is 2 1/4 miles long. How many miles does he run each week?

DISCUSSION

This connects nicely to multiplication as repeated addition: 4 times 2 1/4.

We can represent this problem on a number line, as in Figure 5.24.

FIGURE **5.24**

> **B.** A group of investors purchased a rectangular parcel of land that is 3/4 of a mile long and 2/3 of a mile wide. How many square miles did they buy?

DISCUSSION

This problem is definitely not repeated addition, but it does connect to the area model of multiplication. Here we can say that we want 2/3 of 3/4 (of 1 square mile).

However, getting the answer by applying our knowledge of multiplication and fractions is not terribly easy. If the large square in Figure 5.25 represents 1 mile by 1 mile, the shaded region represents the area of the land that the investors bought: 3/4 of a mile by 2/3 of a mile. But how do we give a name to this amount? Try to do this yourself and then read on. . . .

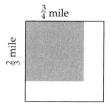

FIGURE **5.25**

Just as we decomposed and recomposed numbers in working with whole numbers (when regrouping, for example), we need to decompose this amount in such a way that we can recompose the amount as a set of equal-size pieces.

We can create equal-size pieces (needed to name a fraction) by first dividing the square into fourths (with vertical lines) and then into thirds (with horizontal lines). If we put the two diagrams together and shade in the area enclosed by 3/4 times 2/3, we have the figure on the right in Figure 5.26. Can you determine the answer now from the diagram? Can you justify that answer?

FIGURE **5.26**

Since our unit (1 square mile) has been divided into 12 equal-size regions, each region has a value of 1/12 square mile. The plot of land covers 6 of these rectangles, thus its value is 6/12 or 1/2 square mile.

 C. If 2/3 of the class went on a field trip and there are 24 students in the class, how many students went on the field trip?

DISCUSSION

Problems like this one illustrate the third fraction context that we mentioned in Section 5.2: fraction as operator. The operator context can be thought of as a stretching or a shrinking process. In this case, we have a whole (24 students), and we are shrinking that whole—that is, we are considering a part (2/3) of that whole. When students memorize "of means multiply," they are memorizing a procedure but not understanding this interpretation of fractions.

Let us now see how we can apply our knowledge of fractions and operations to solve this problem. Figure 5.27(a) represents the problem using a set model, with each dot representing one person. Since we have 2/3 of the people, the 2/3 tells us that we have to partition this amount into 3 equal groups and then take 2 of those groups. Figure 5.27(b) represents the problem using an area model. The whole rectangle represents the whole class. We have shaded in 2/3 of the rectangle. If the whole class represents 24 students, then when we divide the class into 3 equal regions, each region must represent 8 students (that is, $8 + 8 + 8 = 24$ or $3 \cdot 8 = 24$).

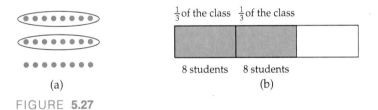

(a)   (b)

FIGURE **5.27**

Connecting Multiplication of Fractions to the Multiplication Algorithm

As we did with multiplication of whole numbers, we will develop the algorithm with the rectangular model. Let us do so with the problem

$$\frac{3}{4} \cdot 2\frac{1}{2}$$

Let us first represent the problem with a diagram, determine the answer from that diagram, and then look to connect this solution to the algorithm. First, check to make sure that you understand that Figure 5.28 represents $\frac{3}{4} \cdot 2\frac{1}{2}$. Then determine the answer from the diagram before reading on. . . .

FIGURE **5.28**

As we know, all the parts must be the same size in order to name the amount with a fraction. We can readily see (from Figure 5.29) that the numerator of our product must be 15 (that is, there are 15 parts). But what is the denominator? Please resist the temptation to answer this question by doing the algorithm. In my own class, this question is actually a method I use to assess how deeply my students understand the meaning of denominator. Then read on. . . .

$$2\frac{1}{2}$$

$$\frac{3}{4}$$

FIGURE **5.29**

I usually get three different responses for the denominator: 24 because there are 24 parts in the "whole" diagram, 15 because there are 5 times 3 parts in the $2\frac{1}{2}$, and 8 because it takes 8 parts to make a 1 by 1 square (the unit).

The correct answer is 8. Why is this? Recall that the value of the denominator is determined by its relationship to the unit. That is, the denominator shows how many pieces it takes to have a value of 1, rather than how many pieces are in the whole.

Therefore, we have determined that

$$\frac{3}{4} \cdot 2\frac{1}{2} = \frac{15}{8} = 1\frac{7}{8}$$

Now let us examine the algorithm and look for connections between the algorithm and the concepts. We must first convert $2\frac{1}{2}$ to an improper fraction, and then we simply find the product of the numerators and the product of the denominators:

$$\frac{3}{4} \cdot 2\frac{1}{2} = \frac{3}{4} \cdot \frac{5}{2} = \frac{3 \cdot 5}{4 \cdot 2} = \frac{15}{8}$$

Can you justify this procedure? Can you explain the *whys* behind these *whats*? Think. Look back to Figure 5.29. Then read on. . . .

If we look at the shaded region in Figure 5.29, we have 3 rows, each containing 5 regions; that is, we have 3 times 5 regions. Just as we found that the whole-number multiplication algorithm automatically regrouped for us, so too the fraction multiplication algorithm automatically creates equal-sized pieces. Similarly, we have $4 \cdot 2$ pieces in each unit.

Because of the space limitations of a textbook, I cannot present further examples here. However, I recommend that you do several problems on your own to ensure that you own rather than rent this connection between the rectangular model and the algorithm.

Justifying the Equality of Equivalent Fractions

In Section 5.2, we examined equivalent fractions. We can now justify the procedure we used mathematically. The process is shown at the left for a specific case and at the right for the general case.

Specific case	Justification	General case
$\dfrac{3}{4} = \dfrac{3}{4} \cdot 1$	Multiplicative identify	$\dfrac{a}{b} = \dfrac{a}{b} \cdot 1$
$= \dfrac{3}{4} \cdot \dfrac{2}{2}$	Substitution	$= \dfrac{a}{b} \cdot \dfrac{c}{c}$
$= \dfrac{3 \cdot 2}{4 \cdot 2}$	Definition of multiplication of fractions	$= \dfrac{a \cdot c}{b \cdot c}$
$= \dfrac{6}{8}$		

The general case also emphasizes that the numerator and denominator of the new fraction are simply multiples of the numerator and denominator of the original fraction.

INVESTIGATION 5.12 Division of Rational Numbers

HISTORY

The Hindu mathematician Mahavira (850 A.D.) first stated a rule for dividing fractions: "After making the denominator of the divisor its numerator and vice versa, the operations to be conducted then is as in the multiplication [of fractions]." It was not until the sixteenth century that this procedure was "discovered" in Europe.[5]

As with most concepts being considered in this course, you probably remember the procedure. This recalls a famous saying of unknown origin: "Ours is not to reason why, just invert and multiply."

$$\frac{3}{4} \div \frac{5}{6} = \frac{3}{4} \times \frac{6}{5} = \frac{18}{20} = \frac{9}{10}$$

Now, though, ours *is* to reason why. If you did Exploration 5.12, Part 1, you examined why the invert and multiply algorithm works; Exploration 5.12, Part 2 examined an alternative algorithm first invented by another Indian mathematician, Brahmagupta, more than one thousand years ago. Let us begin our investigation of the fraction division algorithm by first examining fraction division problems in context.

Recall the two contexts for division with whole numbers: partitioning and repeated subtraction.

Make up a story for each of the two division problems below.

First, solve the problem using what you know about division and fractions.

Then respond to the following questions: Which of your stories were from the partitioning model, and which were from the repeated subtraction model? If you made up a story connected to one model, could you make up another story for the same problem using the other model?

A. The divisor is a whole number: 3 ÷ 4

B. The divisor is a proper fraction: 3 ÷ 2/5

DISCUSSION

A. Most people make up a story for 3 ÷ 4 using the partitioning model, and most of the stories involve sharing. In fact, for many (if not most) children, the first experience with fractions has to do with sharing; for example, you each get 1/2 of the candy bar. Children seldom need to be taught a central fraction concept: The parts must be equal!

[5] Louis Karpinski, *The History of Arithmetic* (New York: Russell & Russell, 1965), p. 128.

Let us consider one such story and examine a solution: Basil has 3 quarts of ice cream that he wants to share equally with three friends, that is, among 4 people. How much is each person's share?

Figure 5.30 shows a partitioning (dealing) solution. That is, if we divide each quart into 4 equal parts, each person gets one part per quart. Each person's share thus consists of 3 parts, each of which is 1/4 quart. Therefore, each person's share is 3/4 of a quart.

There are two aspects of this problem that bear noting.

First, $3 \div 4 = \frac{3}{4}$. As mentioned at the beginning of Section 5.2, fraction as division is another of the rational number contexts. That is, the division problem $a \div b$ and the fraction a/b are equivalent. This relationship between fractions and division is often problematic for children, and many do not realize that this is not a commutative relationship. For example, research has shown that many middle school children cannot accurately translate $5 \div 6$ into 5/6 and vice versa.

Second, some people literally interpret this problem as a multiplication problem. If we are dividing the ice cream among 4 people, then each person gets 1/4 of the ice cream. This connection between the two operations produces the following equality: $3 \div 4 = 3 \cdot \frac{1}{4}$ which we just mentioned. We will return to this relationship between multiplication and division shortly. However, first let us examine a story for the other problem.

B. Story for $3 \div 2/5$: Jake is stranded in the middle of the desert. He has 3 quarts of water, and he figures that he will drink 2/5 of a quart each day. How many days' supply does he have?

Solve the problem using only your knowledge of fractions and your knowledge of division. Then read on. . . .

This is a repeated subtraction problem because we have an amount (3 quarts) and we are specifying the size of the group (2/5 of a quart) to be repeatedly subtracted. The answer will be the number of groups we have. Virtually all stories for this problem involve repeated subtraction. In fact, I cannot make up a realistic story for this problem using the partitioning model of division. Do you see why?

I have chosen to represent this problem with a number line, although an area or set model could also have been used. Each day Jake uses 2/5 of a quart. We see from Figure 5.31 that he is able to drink 2/5 of a quart each day for 7 days. However, we have a small problem: We have repeatedly subtracted 2/5 of a quart, but we have 1/5 of a quart left over. Does this answer contradict the answer that comes from using the algorithm, which tells us that $3 \div \frac{2}{5} = 7\frac{1}{2}$? How do we reconcile the difference between the answer from the diagram and from the algorithm? Think and then read on. . . .

FIGURE **5.31**

It turns out that both answers are correct — they represent different ways of describing the remainder; recall the remainder discussion in Chapter 3 and Exploration 5.13. The 1/5 tells us that the remainder is 1/5 of a quart; thus, we can say that at the end of 7 days, he will have 1/5 of a quart left. The $7\frac{1}{2}$ tells us that the remainder is equivalent to 1/2 day's water. This underscores the point made in Investigation 1.8 (How Many Pieces of Wire?) that often the key to a problem is knowing what the computation means.

FIGURE **5.30**

Making Sense of the Standard Division Algorithm

Although using the invert and multiply algorithm is rather straightforward, understanding why it works is another matter. It does not lend itself to a diagrammatic representation as most of the other algorithms we have examined. Therefore, we will begin to build our understanding of it by examining the similarities between how division and multiplication are connected and how subtraction and addition are connected.

We need to examine one new concept to do so. Just as we discovered in the first section of this chapter that every integer has an additive inverse, every rational number has a multiplicative inverse. These parallel concepts are shown side by side below:

^-a is the additive inverse of a	$\dfrac{1}{a}$ is the *multiplicative inverse* of a (if $a \neq 0$)
$a + {}^-a = 0$ for any integer a	$a \cdot \dfrac{1}{a} = 1$ for any rational number $a \neq 0$

Let us now recall the way in which we defined integer subtraction in terms of addition, and then we will define fraction division in terms of fraction multiplication.

$a - b = a + {}^-b$;	$a \div b = a \cdot \dfrac{1}{b}$;
that is, to subtract b, we add the (additive) inverse of b.	that is, to divide by b, we multiply by the (multiplicative) inverse of b
In other words, one way to interpret **subtraction** is to **add** the **additive inverse** of the second number.	In other words, one way to interpret **division** is to **multiply** by the **multiplicative inverse** of the second number.

Revisiting properties The properties that we developed in Chapter 3 extend to operations with fractions. That is, the commutative and associative properties hold for addition and multiplication but not for subtraction and division. The distributive properties hold for fractions. Both identity properties hold: 0 is the identity for addition and 1 for multiplication. The zero property of multiplication holds. We still have additive inverses, and we have now acquired the multiplicative inverse for all numbers except 0. With this in mind, let's investigate the four operations with fractions.

INVESTIGATION 5.13 Estimating Products and Quotients

As you discovered in our discussion of adding and multiplying fractions, many everyday situations that ask us to compute with fractions require estimates rather than exact answers. Let us now examine some estimation strategies for multiplication and division.

> In each of the problems below, do the following: first obtain a rough estimate (5 to 10 seconds), then try to get as close as you can to the actual answer—either a refined estimate or, in some cases, an exact answer (computed mentally).
>
> **A.** Anastasia walks at a pace of 3 1/2 miles per hour for 2 hours and 15 minutes. How far does she walk during this time?

DISCUSSION

Note: We first need to convert the time to fractional form; that is, we are estimating $3\frac{1}{2} \cdot 2\frac{1}{4}$.

STRATEGY 1: Bound the answer

One kind of estimating involves bounding the answer. For example, the answer will be at least 6. We get this by focusing only on the whole numbers. We call 6 a lower bound.

An upper bound can be obtained by rounding both numbers to the next highest whole number. The upper bound is thus $4 \cdot 3 = 12$.

STRATEGY 2: Get rid of one of the proper fractions (that is, rounding)

Another method of making a rough estimate involves getting rid of one of the proper fractions. We can more easily determine $3\frac{1}{2} \cdot 2 = 7$ or $3 \cdot 2\frac{1}{4} = 6\frac{3}{4}$.

STRATEGY 3: Use partial products

We can estimate the four partial products:

$$3\frac{1}{2} \times 2\frac{1}{4} = \left(3 + \frac{1}{2}\right) \times \left(2 + \frac{1}{4}\right) = (3 \times 2) + \left(3 \times \frac{1}{4}\right) + \left(2 \times \frac{1}{2}\right) + \left(\frac{1}{2} \times \frac{1}{4}\right)$$
$$\approx \quad 6 \quad + \quad 1 \quad + \quad 1 \quad + \quad 0 \quad \approx 8$$

> **B.** The Jones family finds that they spend about 2/3 of their income on food and rent. If their monthly income is $1,635, how much is their monthly food and rent bill?

DISCUSSION

Rough estimate (using compatible numbers):

$$2/3 \times 1,500 = 1,000$$

More refined estimate (using compatible numbers):

$$2/3 \times 1,650 = 2/3 \quad (1,500 + 150) = 1,000 + 100 = 1,100$$

> **C.** Marvin has 23 yards of cloth with which to make costumes for the play. Each costume requires $3\frac{1}{4}$ yards of material. How many costumes can he make?

DISCUSSION

Rough estimate (using bounding):

$$23 \div 3 = 7 \ 2/3$$
$$23 \div 4 = 5 \ 3/4$$

The estimate is about 6 or 7 costumes.
Refined estimate (using repeated addition):

$$3 \ 1/4 \times 2 = 6 \ 1/2, \text{ so}$$
$$3 \ 1/4 \times 4 = 13, \text{ so}$$
$$3 \ 1/4 \times 8 = 26$$

Since $26 - 3 = 23$, this estimate yields 7 costumes.

> **D.** Shelly has 25 pounds of dog food, and each day she feeds her dog 3/4 pound. How many days' worth of food does she have?

DISCUSSION

Rough estimate (using bounding):

$$25 \div 1 = 25 \quad \text{and} \quad 25 \div 1/2 = 50$$

Thus she has enough for more than 25 days and less than 50 days.
Refined estimate (using the algorithm and the commutative and associative properties):

$$25 \div 3/4 = 25 \times 4/3 = 100/3 = 33 \ 1/3$$

which is the actual quotient. Thus, she has 33 days' worth of dog food.

Applying Fraction Understandings to Nonroutine Problems

We have carefully examined the different meanings that fractions can have, and we have examined the four operations in terms of fractions. In the following nonroutine problems, you will need to determine which computation(s) to do and how to interpret the computation(s).

INVESTIGATION 5.14 When Did He Run Out of Gas?

> **J**eremy started on a trip from Mobile, Alabama, to New Orleans, approximately 120 miles away. His car ran out of gas after he had gone one-third of the second half of the trip. How far is Jeremy from New Orleans? Work on this problem yourself and then read on. . . .

DISCUSSION

This is a case in which a good diagram practically solves the problem by itself (see Figure 5.32).

FIGURE **5.32**

If 1/2 of the trip is equal to 60 miles, then each of the "thirds of the second half" is equal to 20 miles. X marks the spot of "one-third of the second half of the trip." So Jeremy is still 40 miles from New Orleans.

INVESTIGATION **5.15** Will She Be Late?

Can you help Jenny? She thinks she is going to be late to school, which starts at 8:15. She is not sure exactly how long it takes her to walk from home to school. However, she looked at her watch when she passed the video store at 7:50, and then she looked at her watch when she passed the convenience store at 7:57. It just so happens that the video store is one-third of the way from home to school, and the convenience store is exactly halfway. If she continues walking at this rate, will she be on time? Work on this problem and then read on. . . .

DISCUSSION

Not surprisingly, this problem is much more easily represented with a number line than with any other model. Figure 5.33 shows a beginning representation. What else can we add to the diagram so that it will tell us the answer? Think and read on. . . .

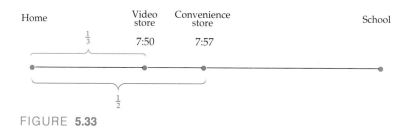

FIGURE **5.33**

A key to the solution is to observe that it took her 7 minutes to go from 1/3 of the way to 1/2 of the way. If you recall from Chapter 3 that distance between two numbers is a subtraction problem, you can see that $1/2 - 1/3 = 1/6$ and that it takes her 7 minutes to go 1/6 of the distance. This means that it would take her 42 minutes to go the whole way, but that in itself doesn't do us any good because we don't know when she started. However, if it takes her 42 minutes to go the whole distance, it takes her 21 minutes to go halfway, and 21 minutes after 7:57 is 8:18. Yes, she had better run!

INVESTIGATION **5.16** They've Lost Their Faculty!

Suppose you are reading the newspaper and you see that American State College has had to reduce its faculty by one-sixth because of an economic crisis in the state. The article says that American State College now has 350 faculty members. A curious reader might ask, "How many did they have before the cut?" Think about this problem before reading on. . . .

DISCUSSION

STRATEGY 1: Represent the situation with a diagram
The large rectangle in Figure 5.34 represents the original faculty.

FIGURE **5.34**

If the college lost one-sixth of its faculty, then we can divide that rectangle into 6 equal pieces and take away one piece, which represents one-sixth of the faculty. Thus the 5 remaining boxes represent the remaining 5/6 of the faculty.

Since we know that there are 350 faculty members now, the value of those 5 boxes is 350. But if the value of 5 boxes is 350, then the value of one box is 70. Now we can answer the problem. Do you see why?

Since the value of the original faculty was represented by 6 boxes, there were $6 \times 70 = 420$ faculty.

STRATEGY 2: Use algebra

Can you find an algebraic solution? Work on it and then read on. . . .

One algebraic solution comes from letting $x =$ the number of the faculty before the cut. Since the remaining faculty represents 5/6 of the original, 350 is 5/6 of x; that is, $\frac{5}{6}x = 350$.

We solve the equation by multiplying both sides by $\frac{6}{5}$:

$$\left(\frac{6}{5}\right)\frac{5}{6}x = \left(\frac{6}{5}\right)350 \qquad \text{and} \qquad x = 420$$

Summary

Let us take a few moments to look back on this section. What have you learned? What fraction ideas make more sense now than they did before? What fraction ideas still feel difficult?

In this section, we have focused on connecting conceptual knowledge to procedural knowledge—on understanding the whys behind the whats of the algorithms for operations with fractions. In order to be successful in the explorations, your focus should be more on understanding relationships among ideas and connecting ideas to one another than on solving "word problems" that have answers. Ultimately, we want you to become competent and confident when you encounter word problems in your everyday and work life. However, success in problem-solving first requires you to grapple with relationships within and between the mathematical ideas.

We have found that the contexts in which we first studied these four operations in Chapter 3 do not all apply when working with fractions; for example, the partitioning model of division does not apply when the divisor is not a whole number. In making sense of algorithms, we need to pay attention to the very fraction ideas that we developed in Section 5.2: that the parts in a fraction have the same value, that working with fractions involves parts and wholes, and that we have to pay attention to units and wholes (they are not always the same). We also found that we have to make sure that what we are doing makes sense; recall Investigation 5.11C, concerning the students on the field trip.

When we explored mental arithmetic and estimation with fractions, we found that many of the strategies developed in Chapter 3 applied directly to computing with fractions—for example, the commutative and associative properties, compatible numbers, adding up, partial products, and expanded form.

When we applied our knowledge of operations to nonroutine and multi-step problems, we found that we needed to think about how we might represent the problem. We also had to make sure that we kept basic fraction ideas in mind—for example, the distinction between the unit and the whole.

Now that we have a deeper understanding of fractions, we are ready for our next extension of the number system—to decimals and real numbers.

EXERCISES 5.3

1. Perform the following computations.

   a. $23\frac{7}{8}$
      $+56\frac{5}{6}$

   b. $-3\frac{5}{12}$
      $+1\frac{9}{40}$

   c. $7\frac{3}{4}$
      $8\frac{3}{5}$
      $+7\frac{3}{10}$

   d. 213
      $-21\frac{5}{16}$

   e. $9\frac{1}{4}$
      $-12\frac{5}{6}$

   f. $12\frac{1}{3} \times 5\frac{3}{8}$

   g. $6\frac{3}{4} \times 14\frac{2}{3}$

   h. $36 \times 3\frac{3}{4}$

   i. $\frac{3}{10} \times 45$

2. Determine each of the following mentally, and briefly explain your solution.

   a. $5\frac{3}{4}$
      $+7\frac{5}{8}$

   b. $8\frac{4}{5}$
      $+6\frac{2}{3}$

   c. $16\frac{3}{4}$
      $15\frac{1}{2}$
      $+7\frac{1}{4}$

   d. 26
      $-6\frac{3}{5}$

   e. $7\frac{1}{3}$
      $-3\frac{1}{2}$

   f. $8\frac{2}{3} + 7\frac{5}{6} + 4\frac{2}{3} + 2\frac{2}{3}$

   g. $3\frac{2}{3} \cdot 12$

   h. $2\frac{1}{2} \cdot 3\frac{1}{4}$

3. For each of the following, determine which of the choices represents the better estimate. Then explain your choice.

   a. $5\frac{5}{8} + 4\frac{3}{32}$ Greater than 10 or less than 10?

   b. $\frac{7}{8} + \frac{3}{4} + \frac{1}{16}$ Greater than 2 or less than 2?

   c. $\frac{1}{4} + 1\frac{9}{10}$ Greater than 2 or less than 2?

   d. $8\frac{1}{2} - 2\frac{2}{3}$ Between which two numbers: 5 and 5 1/2 or 5 1/2 and 6?

   e. $8\frac{3}{4} \times 2\frac{7}{8}$ Greater or less than 20?

   f. $4\frac{7}{8} \div 8\frac{7}{8}$ Greater or less than 1/2?

For Exercises 4 to 13, first estimate the answer, then explain your estimate, then determine the "exact" answer. Then explain whether the "exact" answer is an exact number or still an estimate.

4. Sunflower seeds are sold in packages that weigh $3\frac{1}{4}$ ounces. If there is a supply of 66 ounces of sunflower seeds, how many packages of seed can be made? How many ounces of seeds will be left over?

5. What is the weight (in ounces) of a $4\frac{1}{2}$-inch by $7\frac{3}{4}$-inch rectangle of sheet metal, if one square inch weighs 1/8 ounce?

6. Betty is stacking boxes at a factory. Each box is $13\frac{3}{4}$ inches high. The ceiling is 16 feet. How many boxes can she stack in one pile?

7. Javier is 2/3 as tall as his dad. Javier is 49 inches tall. How tall is his dad?

8. A recent survey concluded that 3/4 of the teachers in a certain school district had at least 10 years of teaching experience. If there are 152 teachers in the district, approximately how many have at least 10 years of teaching experience?

9. We find from the *Unofficial U.S. Census* that more than 136,800,000 Americans admit to doodling. Of the doodlers, slightly less than 2/3 said they doodle while talking on the telephone. Approximately how many Americans doodle while talking on the telephone?

10. Below is a picture of the gas gauge in Jackie's car. If Jackie figures that her car averages 34 miles per gallon and her car has a 12-gallon tank, about how many miles

does she have left on this tank before she runs out of gas?

11. John is making a bookcase. If the bookcase is $72\frac{3}{8}$ inches tall and he wants 5 shelves, equally spaced, tell him where to drill the holes on the side. Each shelf is 3/8 inch thick. Your solution needs to contain a description that is clear enough so that he could understand it.

12. Julianna has $22\frac{1}{2}$ yards of material. If it takes 3/4 yard of material to make a pair of shorts, can she make enough shorts for 30 children?

13. Johanna is making a chest of drawers. She has decided for aesthetic reasons that the base bar will be 2 1/2 inches above the ground, and the top will be beveled and will be 3 inches in height. She decides to have the four boards that support the drawers be $1\frac{3}{4}$ inches thick. How much space should she leave for each drawer? The chest of drawers will be 48 inches tall. [*Note:* The diagram is not drawn to scale.]

14. An analysis of freshmen at a college revealed that 1/4 of the freshmen women were from homes where both parents were professionals. Of these, 3/5 were interested in the same profession as one or both of their parents. If this latter group is made up of 18 students, how many freshmen women are there?

15. A small office purchases bottled drinking water. The water comes in containers that hold 5 gallons. Two-thirds of the office container was drained last week to put out a fire in the wastebasket.
    a. How much water (in ounces) is left in the container?
    b. How many 12-ounce glasses can be filled with the water that remains in the container?

16. Let's say that a certain antibiotic kills approximately 1/2 of the germs on the first day, 1/2 of the remaining on the second day, and so on.
    a. After 10 days, what fraction of the germs remain?
    b. If you had 20 million germs in your body at the beginning, how many of them will be alive at the end of the tenth day?

17. A fruit juice drink is 5/7 water and 1/6 fruit juice (by weight). Other additives (primarily sugar) make up what fraction of its weight?

18. In a certain town, 2/3 of the women are married and only 1/2 of the men are married. What fraction of the community is single? What assumptions do you make in order to solve the problem?

19. The Jacksons just bought some land in the country. Their deed shows that they bought $4\frac{1}{2}$ acres, and that there is a $1\frac{1}{3}$-acre pond on their land. The pond covers approximately what fraction of their property?

20. Four people order a pizza, which is cut into four pieces. Afterwards, three of the people are still hungry and order another pizza, which is also cut into 4 pieces. One person decides to eat only 1 piece, and the other two share what remains. What fraction of the total (two pizzas) does each person eat?

21. A manufacturing company finds that approximately 3 out of every 1,000 spark plugs it produces are defective. Last year the company produced 186,000 spark plugs. Approximately how many were defective?

22. In 1991, 207,610 rapes were reported to police. Estimates of the fraction of rape victims who report the rape range from 1/2 to 1/6. If 1/2 of all rape victims reported the rape to police, approximately how many women were raped in 1991? If only 1/6 of all rape victims reported the rape to police, approximately how many women were raped in 1991?

23. This is the kind of problem that really does happen—some data are lost, but other data can be used to retrieve them. Here are the employment data for a state:
    - 5/8 of the population is urban, 3/8 is rural.
    - 1/10 of the urban population is unemployed, and 1/6 of the rural population is unemployed.

    What fraction of the work force is unemployed? Illustrate this problem and solution with a diagram.

24. The Petersons have an apple-pressing machine that they use to make apple juice. The first pressing gets about 1/3 of the total juice in the apples. Each succeeding pressing extracts about 1/3 of the remaining juice in the apples. How many pressings will it take to get at least 3/4 of the apples' juice? How many pressings to get at least 9/10 of the juice?

25. Make up a realistic story problem for $2\frac{1}{2} \div 3/4$ and solve the problem using the meaning of fractions and division (that is, without the algorithm).

26. Make up a realistic story problem for the following multiplication of fraction contexts:
    a. A proper fraction times a proper fraction
    b. A proper fraction times a whole number
    c. A proper fraction times a mixed number
    d. A mixed number times a mixed number

27. Find the difference: $\dfrac{bc}{a} - \dfrac{bd}{ac}$

28. **a.** How would you figure $26 \times 11/12$ on a calculator? Show two ways.

    b. How would you figure $26 \div 11/12$ on a calculator?

29. Ginger has $8\frac{1}{3}$ yards of silk cloth from India. She has decided to divide the cloth equally into 3 parts, one for each of her siblings. How much cloth does each person get? *Do this problem without using an algorithm*, that is, using reasoning. You may want to use a diagram, but you are not required to do so.

30. Use a number line model or a set model to find $\frac{2}{3} + \frac{1}{4}$. Justify each step in the process.

31. When we convert $13/5$ to $2\frac{3}{5}$, which model of division do we use? Explain your answer.

32. Irene has discovered a rule that works for some addition problems. For example, consider $1/5 + 1/2$. The rule is this: The numerator of the answer is equal to the sum of the denominators of the two fractions, and the denominator of the answer is equal to the product of the denominators of the two fractions. What do you think of her rule? Describe the set of fractions for which this rule works. Can you modify her rule so that it works for a larger set of problems?

33. A student says that she has found a quick way to divide fractions. She demonstrates her method as follows:

    $$9\frac{1}{4} \div 3\frac{3}{4} = 3\frac{1}{3}, \text{ since } 9 \div 3 = 3 \text{ and } \frac{1}{4} \div \frac{3}{4} = \frac{1}{3}$$

    $$20\frac{3}{5} \div 4\frac{3}{5} = 5\frac{1}{1}, \text{ since } 20 \div 4 = 5 \text{ and } \frac{3}{5} \div \frac{3}{5} = 1$$

    Unfortunately, her idea is not correct. Where is the conceptual error?

34. Demonstrate how to obtain the following product two different ways, neither of which can be the standard algorithm: $3\frac{1}{3} \times 2\frac{1}{2}$. Then explain why $6\frac{1}{6}$ is not the correct answer, as if you were talking to a student for whom $6\frac{1}{6}$ is the obvious answer.

35. What is wrong with the students' work in these problems?

    a. $\dfrac{3}{5} + \dfrac{2}{5} = \dfrac{5}{10}$

    b. $\dfrac{1}{5} + \dfrac{2}{3} = \dfrac{3}{8} + \dfrac{10}{8} = \dfrac{13}{8} = 1\frac{3}{8}$

    c. $\dfrac{2}{3} \cdot \dfrac{3}{8} = \dfrac{9}{16}$

    d. $8\frac{1}{2} \div 2\frac{1}{4} = 4\frac{1}{4}$

36. Can you explain the following mistake?

    $$\begin{aligned} 7\frac{1}{8} &= 6\frac{11}{8} \\ -\ 3\frac{5}{8} &= 3\frac{5}{8} \\ \hline 3\frac{6}{8} &= 3\frac{3}{4} \end{aligned}$$

37. Locate and explain the error in the following:

    $$\frac{ab + c}{a} = \frac{\cancel{a}b + c}{\cancel{a}} = b + c$$

38. Selecting among the numbers 1 through 9 and repeating none of them, fill in the boxes below to make the sum as close as possible to 1, but not equal to 1.

39. Use each of these numbers exactly once to make the following equation true: 1, 2, 3, 5, 11, 15.

40. Selecting among the numbers 1 through 9 and repeating none of them, fill in the boxes below to make the smallest possible difference greater than zero.

41. Selecting among the numbers 1 through 9 and repeating none of them, make the following equation true.

    $$\frac{\square}{\square} \times \frac{\square}{\square} = \frac{1}{2}$$

42. Selecting among the numbers 1 through 9 and repeating none of them, make the largest possible quotient.

    $$\frac{\square}{\square} \div \frac{\square}{\square}$$

43. Selecting among the numbers 1 through 9 and repeating none of them, make the quotient closest to one-half.

    $$\frac{\square}{\square} \div \frac{\square}{\square}$$

44. Can you make a magic triangle consisting only of unit fractions so that no fraction occurs more than once?

    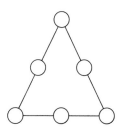

BEYOND INTEGERS AND FRACTIONS: DECIMALS, EXPONENTS, AND REAL NUMBERS

WHAT DO YOU THINK?

- What would Alphabitian decimals look like?
- Why is there no "oneths" place?

In this section, we will extend the system of numbers yet again—to decimals and to irrational numbers (that is, numbers that cannot be expressed as the quotient of two integers, such as $\sqrt{2}$ and π). There is a name for the set of numbers that includes both rational and irrational numbers: the set of real numbers (an interesting choice for this set!). There are many sets of numbers beyond the real numbers, but they are not considered until high school.

Decimals

Technically, the set of decimals is not an extension of the set of fractions. Rather, our use of decimal numbers comes out of an alternate way of representing fractions, using the advantages of our base 10 system. In fact, the word decimal comes from the Latin word *decem,* which means ten. Thus, decimal numbers are any numbers that are written in terms of our base 10 place value. Conventionally, we refer to decimals as fractions that have been written using a decimal point.

The history of decimals   If you stop to think about it, decimals could not have been invented before our base 10 system. Credit for bringing decimals into everyday life goes to Simon Stevin, who was the first to try to explain them. His book *The Art of Tenths or Decimal Arithmetic* was first published in 1585.

> We will speak freely of the great utility of this invention . . . for the astronomer knows the difficult multiplication and divisions which proceed from the progression with degrees, minutes, seconds, and thirds. . . . This discovery . . . teaches (to tell much in one word) to compute easily, without fractions, all computations which are encountered in the affairs of human beings, in such a way that the four principles of arithmetic which are called addition, subtraction, multiplication, and division . . . are able to achieve this end." He went on to say that this work treats of "something so simple that it hardly merits the name of invention."[6]

The use of decimals was spurred primarily by a desire to make computation easier. For example, which computation would be easier to do: $24\frac{7}{8} \times 6\frac{4}{5}$ or 24.875×6.8? You may want to do both. How much faster was the decimal computation?

Even today there is not one universal notation. For example:

United States	England	Continental Europe
54.23	54·23	54,23

No decimals?   Imagine our world without decimals! As you discovered earlier in this course, the base 10 numeration system has been in widespread use for less than 500 years. The widespread use of decimals is even more recent.

[6] Louis Karpinski, *The History of Arithmetic* (New York: Russell & Russell, 1965), p. 131.

What would life in the United States be like if no one had invented decimals—that is, if we expressed amounts using only whole numbers and fractions? Would things just look different (for example, 43 dollars and 26 cents instead of $43.26), or would some things be impossible?

You might find it helpful to look at cases in which we use decimals and to explore alternatives, as shown above for $43.26. Spend some time writing your answers to these questions before reading on. . . .

As you may have realized as you thought about these questions, much of our use of decimals involves measurement:

■ We measure mass: for example, the package weighs 2.4 ounces.

■ We measure distance: for example, Joan lives 3.7 miles from school.

■ We measure time: for example, the world record for the 100-yard dash is 9.89 seconds.

Decimals are used in many aspects of daily life to communicate. For example,

■ The U.S. birth rate is 16.3 per 1,000 population.

■ The average life expectancy in the United States is 71.8 years.

■ The average interest rate on CDs (certificates of deposit) on June 1, 1994, was 3.23 percent.

■ The new city budget is $3.48 million.

Developing decimals The next twelve Investigations look at decimals from several perspectives: examining different characteristics of the decimal system, why the algorithms work, rounding, scientific notation, and many kinds of problem-solving. Using your increasing problem-solving, communicating, and reasoning abilities and your increasingly better connected network of mathematical concepts, you will be able to strengthen your own understanding of these concepts.

> When children possess a sound understanding of fraction and decimal concepts, they can use this knowledge to describe real-world phenomena and apply it to problems involving measurement, probability, and statistics. . . It is critical in grades K–4 to develop concepts and relationships that will serve as a foundation for more advanced concepts and skills.
>
> (*Curriculum Standards*, p. 57)

Connecting decimals to integers and fractions I have found that many students who plan to teach elementary school do not feel that investigations with decimals are relevant because they believe that they will never teach decimals. In fact, although formal work with decimals is generally taught in middle school, informal work with decimals is part of the elementary school curriculum. What the NCTM is stressing is that in order to prepare elementary students best for the decimal instruction they will receive in middle school, the elementary teacher needs to understand the conceptual relationships between decimals and whole numbers and between decimals and fractions.

The set of decimals has important connections to both the set of fractions and the set of integers. Much research indicates that these connections are not understood by a majority of students, and with severe consequences—limitations in ability to solve nonroutine problems and work confidently in higher mathematics. The following investigations will help you to understand both similarities and differences between decimals and these other two sets.

Connecting Decimals and Integers

There are many important similarities and differences between the set of decimals and the set of integers. Before reading on, stop to think about the two sets of numbers. What similarities and differences can you see?

From one perspective, the set of decimals can be seen as an extension of base 10 counting numbers. Exploration 5.14 helps to develop your decimal sense so that you develop a better "feel" for the relative size of tenths, hundredths, thousandths, and so on.

... thousands	hundreds	tens	ones	tenths	hundredths	thousandths ...
10^3	10^2	10^1	10^0	10^{-1}	10^{-2}	10^{-3}
1,000	100	10	1	0.1	0.01	0.001

Several similarities are worth noting. First, the system of decimals and the system of integers are both base 10 place value systems. That is, the value of each digit depends on its place, and the value of each place to the right is one-tenth the value of the previous place. Rather than state the differences, we will let them emerge through investigation.

INVESTIGATION 5.17   Base 10 Blocks and Decimals

One of the themes of this book has been the importance of multiple representations for understanding mathematical concepts. In order to develop your understanding of decimals, we will investigate two representations: base 10 blocks (see Exploration 5.14 for more work on this model) and number line models (after Investigation 5.20). Each representation highlights different aspects of decimals and their relationship to other systems.

Let's say that a sample of gold weighs 3.6 ounces. How would you use base 10 blocks (shown in Figure 5.35) to represent this amount? Note that the "small cube" was formerly called a "unit." Work on this and read on. . . .

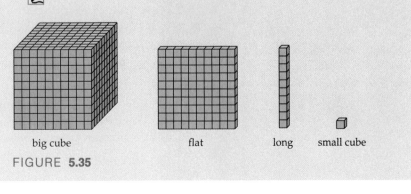

big cube   flat   long   small cube

FIGURE **5.35**

DISCUSSION

Any solution requires us to designate one of the pieces as the unit. For example, if we designate the block as having a value of 1, then we would show 3.6 ounces as in Figure 5.36. Do you see why?

FIGURE **5.36**

However, we could also have selected the flat to be the unit. If we had, then we would show 3.6 ounces as in Figure 5.37.

FIGURE **5.37**

Zero and Decimals

We will examine the role of zero in decimals in the following two investigations.

INVESTIGATION **5.18** **When Two Decimals Are Equal**

What if we added one or two zeros at the end of 0.2? Would that change its value? That is, do 0.2, 0.20, and 0.200 have the same value? Many sixth and seventh graders (and a surprising number of adults) believe that 0.2, 0.20, and 0.200 not only look different, but also have different values because of the added zeros. How would you convince such a person that the value is not changed? Recall that, in the context of the NCTM Standards, this involves justifying the reason — that is, explaining the *why*. Work on this and then read on. . . .

DISCUSSION

There are several ways to justify the equality. We will consider two below.

STRATEGY 1: Connect decimals to fractions

- 0.2 is equivalent to the fraction 2/10.
- 0.20 is equivalent to the fraction 20/100, which can be shown to be equivalent to 2/10.
- 0.200 is equivalent to the fraction 200/1,000, which can be shown to be equivalent to 2/10.

This strategy uses an important mathematical property. The transitive property is stated below for any three numbers, a, b, and c.

Transitive property of equality:

If $a = b$ and $b = c$, then $a = c$.

Transitive property of inequality:

If $a < b$ and $b < c$, then $a < c$.

Using the transitive property of equality, since 0.2, 0.20, and 0.200 are all equal to 2/10, they are equal to each other.

STRATEGY 2: Use manipulatives
In this case, let a square represent a value of 1. Such manipulatives are sold commercially as Decimal Squares©. We can divide this square into 10 equal pieces, 100 equal pieces, or 1,000 equal pieces, as in Figure 5.38.

Shade in 0.2 of the first square, 0.20 of the second square, and 0.200 of the third square.

FIGURE **5.38**

We find that in each case, the same area is shaded. Connecting to the area model of fractions, we conclude that 0.2, 0.20, and 0.200 are all equivalent decimals.

INVESTIGATION **5.19** When Is the Zero Necessary and When Is It Optional?

An important difference between decimals and whole numbers has do with our old friend zero. Examine each number below. In each case, explain whether you think the zero in the number is necessary, optional, or incorrect. If you think it is necessary, explain why. If you think it is optional, explain why the zero doesn't matter. If you think the use of the zero is incorrect, explain why the zero should not be there.

A. 2.08　　**B.** 0.56　　**C.** .507　　**D.** 20.6　　**E.** 3.60

DISCUSSION
A. With 2.08, the zero is necessary; 2 wholes, 0 tenths, and 8 hundredths.

B. With 0.56, the use of the zero is optional; it is more of a convention, like shaking hands with the right hand.

C. With .507, the zero is necessary: 5 tenths, 0 hundredths, and 7 thousandths.

D. With 20.6, the zero is necessary: 2 tens, 0 ones, and 6 tenths.

E. In one sense, the zero here is optional. Mathematically, 3.6 = 3.60, as was seen in Investigation 5.18. However, in another sense, it depends on how the number is being used. For example, if we ask how long the room is, what is the difference between a response of 3.6 meters and a response of 3.60 meters?

A response of 3.6 meters implies that the room has been measured to the nearest tenth of a meter, that is, the length of the room is closer to 3.6 meters than to 3.5 or 3.7 meters. If the person doing the measuring has only this amount of accuracy but reports the length as 3.60, I call this an example of pseudo-precision.

Some differences between decimals and integers This investigation illustrates some important differences between decimals and integers. With decimals, when we add a zero at the right end of the number, the value is unchanged; for example, 48.6 = 48.60. As you know, this is not true with integers; for example 48 ≠ 480. There are two other differences between the two systems that are worth noting. One has to do with language: With whole numbers, the suffix for each place is *-s*; with decimals, it is *-ths* — for example, the hundreds place versus the hundredths place. Another difference is that there is a ones place but not a oneths place; this lack of symmetry has been noted by more than one youngster. How would you explain it?

INVESTIGATION 5.20 Connecting Decimals and Fractions

As stated before, each decimal can be translated to a fraction. You may be familiar with common translations between decimals and fractions: 0.5 = 1/2, 0.25 = 1/4, and so on.

Many problem-solving situations require us to convert a fraction to decimal form or vice versa.

A. How many of the following common fractions can you convert to decimals immediately? How can you determine the decimal equivalent of others without using a calculator?

1/2   1/3   1/4   1/5   1/6   1/8   1/10   1/16
1/50   1/100   1/1,000

DISCUSSION

Either by hand or with a calculator, all but 1/3 and 1/6 can be readily converted to decimal form. When we convert 1/6 to a decimal (by dividing 1 by 6), we find that it "repeats"; that is, the value is 0.1666666. . . . There are two ways to write repeating decimals. We can write 1/6 in decimal form as 0.166... or as $0.1\overline{6}$. The bar shows the part that repeats. For example, we would write 348/999 as 0.348484848... or as $0.\overline{348}$.

Exploration 5.15 explores the relationship between decimals that repeat and decimals that terminate.

B. Now let us examine translating decimals to fractions. Translate the decimals 0.1, 0.007, and $0.\overline{18}$ to fractions before reading on. . . .

DISCUSSION

Most people have no trouble with the first two: 1/10 and 7/1000. The last decimal is equivalent to 2/11. Someone (unknown to history) discovered the process that enables us to conclude that there is a unique fraction associated with every repeating decimal. The process works like this:

Let $x = 0.18181818...$, (that is, $0.\overline{18}$).

Now multiply both sides by 100, so that we have:

$100x = 18.\overline{18}$

Do you see how these two equations allow us to determine the exact value of $0.\overline{18}$? Think and then read on. . . .

The key is to subtract the first equation from the second one. The repeating part drops out, and we have $99x = 18$. When we solve the equation for x and simplify the fraction, we find that 0.181818... is simply 2/11 in disguise! You can check this by doing the division $2 \div 11$.

Decimals, Fractions, and Precision

We have used number lines as a model to represent whole numbers and fractions. The number line can also be used to represent decimals, using the analogy of a zoom lens. Suppose you had never heard of decimals and had to determine the length of the wire in Figure 5.39 as accurately as you could. Do this and then read on. . . .

FIGURE **5.39**

A visual inspection of Figure 5.39 shows that the wire appears to be closer to 4 1/3 inches than to 4 1/4 inches. With decimals, we do not look at the most appropriate unit fraction; instead, we look at the fractional length in terms of tenths, hundredths, thousandths, and so forth. Now imagine using a zoom lens (see Figure 5.40). To the nearest tenth of an inch, how long is the wire?

FIGURE **5.40**

Since the length is closer to 4.3 inches than to 4.4 inches, we say that the length is 4.3 inches. If we want more precision, we can keep zooming in, in which case we move more decimal places to the right. Theoretically, we can continue this magnification process indefinitely. Realistically, electron microscopes are able to measure distances of one ten-millionth of an inch, or 0.0000001 inch.

Exploration 5.16 provides another opportunity for exploring decimals and precision.

INVESTIGATION **5.21** **Ordering Decimals**

Just as young children need time to develop proper ordering relationships with whole numbers (for example, that 30, not 31, comes after 29), older children need time to develop ordering relationships with fractions and with decimals. Exploration 5.14 provides more decimals to order.

Order the following decimals, from smallest to largest: 0.39, 0.046, and 0.4. Justify your solution. There are several different strategies. If you answer the question using one strategy, go back and try to use a different strategy. Do this before reading on. . . .

DISCUSSION

STRATEGY 1: Use equivalent fractions

$$0.39 = \frac{39}{100} = \frac{390}{1,000}$$

$$0.046 = \frac{46}{1,000}$$

$$0.4 = \frac{4}{10} = \frac{400}{1,000}$$

Thus, the order is 0.046, 0.39, 0.4.

STRATEGY 2: Line up the decimal points

0.39 = 0.390

0.046 = 0.046

0.4 = 0.400

STRATEGY 3: Represent them on a number line

INVESTIGATION 5.22 Rounding with Decimals

If you stop and think about it, rounding of decimals occurs frequently. For example, the rate I am charged for electricity is 9.746 cents per kilowatt-hour. If someone asked me what the electric rate is, however, I would say about 10 cents per kWh. When doing tax forms, the IRS allows people to round some amounts to the nearest dollar. Thus, I might record postage expenses as $75 instead of $74.68.

The process of rounding with decimals is very similar to the process of rounding with whole numbers. In fact, if you *really* understand place value, then rounding with decimals is very straightforward. As you may have found with the Right Bucket game (Exploration 5.18), being able to round decimals is important when estimating.

Round each of the numbers to the nearest hundredth and to the nearest tenth:

A. 3.623   **B.** 76.199   **C.** 36.215   **D.** 2.0368

E. As you work on these, take mental stock of your confidence level. If you do not feel 100 percent confident, what models (discussed earlier) might you use to increase your confidence?

DISCUSSION

A. 3.623 to the nearest hundredth is 3.62, and to the nearest tenth is 3.6.

B. 76.199 to the nearest hundredth is 76.20, and to the nearest tenth is 76.2.

C. 36.215 to the nearest hundredth is 36.22, and to the nearest tenth is 36.2.

D. 2.0368 to the nearest hundredth is 2.04, and to the nearest tenth is 2.0.

E. Some students find the number line or physical models useful in determining how to round. One other common strategy looks like this: Look at 76.199. If we look at only two decimal places, we have 76.19. Therefore, the question can be seen as: Is 76.199 closer to 76.19 or 76.20?

If we insert zeros so that all three decimals are given in thousandths, we have

> 76.200
>
> 76.199
>
> 76.190

Do you see how this strategy helps?

The number 36.215 requires us to deal with a 5 in the relevant place. To the nearest hundredth, this question becomes a decision between 36.21 and 36.22. Remember that with whole numbers, the decision was not to always round up when encountering a 5, but rather to round so that the last nonzero digit is an even number. We will apply that rule here. Thus, we round 36.215 up to 36.22, but we round 36.245 down to 36.24.

Many students round confidently except when they encounter a zero. For example, many students feel comfortable stating that 2.0368 to the nearest hundredth rounds to 2.04 but do not feel comfortable stating that 2.0368 to the nearest tenth rounds to 2.0. If you feel this discomfort, I suggest using a number line, the base 10 blocks, or the strategy mentioned at the beginning of this discussion so that your understanding of rounding is more owned than rented.

INVESTIGATION 5.23 Decimals and Language

> **I** saw the following line in a newspaper: "The School Board has proposed a budget of $24.06 million." Express the School Board's proposed budget as a whole number. Do this before reading on. . . .

DISCUSSION

I have received many different answers from students in my own class, including the following:

> 24 million 600 thousand dollars
>
> 24 million 60 thousand dollars
>
> 24 million 6 hundred dollars
>
> 24 million and 6 dollars
>
> 24 million dollars and 6 cents

Let us look at several strategies that students have used to determine the correct answer.

STRATEGY 1: Connect decimals to fractions

Some students who have successfully used this strategy did not know how to represent 24.06 million at first, and so they began with decimal/fraction connections that they did know.

24.5 million	= 24,500,000	since 0.5 = 1/2
24.25 million	= 24,250,000	since 0.25 = 1/4
24.1 million	= 24,100,000	since 0.1 = 1/10 [This is often a hard place for many students to *start*, but it makes sense now, in light of the first two steps.]
24.06 million	= 24,060,000	because it must be less than 24,100,000

STRATEGY 2: Connect decimals to expanded form

Some students who have successfully used this strategy did not know how to represent 24.06 million at first, and found the solution by analyzing the meaning of 0.06 million.

24.06 million means 24 whole millions and six hundredths of another million.

Now we have to find the value of six hundredths of a million.
Using a calculator or computing by hand,

$$0.06 \times 1,000,000 = 60,000$$

Thus, applying our knowledge of expanded form,

$$24.06 \text{ million} = 24,000,000 + 60,000 = 24,060,000$$

Once again we come back to the importance of being able to compose and decompose numbers: whole numbers, integers, fractions, and now decimals.

STRATEGY 3: Connect decimals to place value

If your understanding of place value is powerful, you know that the *places* of the digits will not change. Thus, when we represent 24.06 million as a whole number, we simply "add zeros" and we have 24,060,000. The *place* of the 6 does not change.

Operations with Decimals: Addition and Subtraction

With the widespread use of calculators, it is not common for most people to do decimal computations longhand any more. However, it is crucial to understand why the basic algorithms work because it is often necessary to interpret what the calculator displays; recall Investigation 1.8; the "answer" on the calculator display didn't indicate how much wire was wasted.

Few people make mistakes when adding or subtracting decimals if all the numbers have the same number of places, such as 3.24 + 5.56. However, a majority of middle school students have difficulty with a problem like the following: 7.8 + 0.46. Can you explain how to determine the sum and justify each step? You may recall being taught to "line up the decimal places," but why does that rule work?

We can justify the lining up of decimal places in terms of both whole-number computation and fraction computation. When adding whole numbers, we begin with the ones place and move to the left, regrouping as necessary. Adapting this procedure to decimals, we begin with the smallest place, in this

LANGUAGE

The language we use when we write checks is connected to place value. How would you write this amount: $206.45?

It would be incorrect to say "two hundred and six dollars and 45 cents." Can you see why? To reduce confusion, the convention is to use *and* only once—just before giving the cents. Thus, the conventional way to write $206.45 is "two hundred six dollars and 45 cents."

case, the hundredths place. We have 6 hundredths. Moving to the tenths place, we have 12 tenths (regrouped to 1 and 2 tenths). Moving to the ones place, we have 7 plus the regrouped 1, giving us a sum of 8 ones, 2 tenths, and 6 hundredths, that is, 8.26.

From the perspective of fractions, we need common denominators. Thus, representing the decimals in expanded form and applying the commutative and associative properties, we have

$$7.8 + 0.46$$

$$= \left(7 + \frac{8}{10}\right) + \left(\frac{4}{10} + \frac{6}{100}\right)$$

$$= 7 + \frac{12}{10} + \frac{6}{100}$$

$$= 7 + 1 + \frac{2}{10} + \frac{6}{100}$$

$$= 8 + \frac{20}{100} + \frac{6}{100}$$

$$= 8 + \frac{26}{100}$$

$$= 8.26$$

Multiplication with Decimals

Children often find multiplication with decimals confusing. Let us examine two problems that arise:

- How do we know where to put the decimal point?
- How can you multiply tenths by tenths and get hundredths — for example, $3.2 \times 2.6 = 8.32$?

Note: There are three ways to represent multiplication: 3.2×2.6, $3.2 \cdot 2.6$, and $(3.2)(2.6)$. The dot, which we use to represent whole-number multiplication, can be confusing when showing decimal multiplication, and so we shall use the $\times$ or parentheses.

Let us examine the problem $(3.2)(2.6)$. Stop and look at the precision in this problem. We multiply two numbers that are accurate to the tenths place, but our answer includes a number in the hundredths place. For example, let's say the dimensions of a room are 3.2 meters by 2.6 meters, but its area is 8.32 square meters. If both the multiplier and multiplicand are in tenths, why isn't the product in tenths also?

We look to a diagram for the explanation. We know from Chapter 3 that any multiplication problem can be represented by a rectangle; that is, the product of the two numbers is equal to the enclosed area. In this case, let us make a rectangle that is 3.2 meters long and 2.6 meters wide [Figure 5.41(a)].

Before reading on, please work on the following questions:

- How can you determine the area of the rectangle directly from the diagram?
- What are the connections between the diagram and the standard algorithm for multiplying decimals?

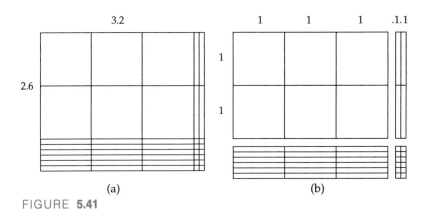

FIGURE **5.41**

In this diagram, we have four distinct regions that correspond to the four partial products [see Figure 5.41(b)]. The top left region consists of 6 squares (each of which measures 1 meter by 1 meter). Thus, the top left region has a value of 6 square meters.

The top right region consists of 4 longs, each of which measures 1 meter by 0.1 meter. Thus each longs has a value of 0.1 square meter. Thus the value of the top right region is 0.4 square meter.

The bottom left region consists of $3 \times 6 = 18$ longs and has a value of 1.8 square meters.

The bottom right region consists of 12 little squares, each of which is 0.1 meter by 0.1 meter. Thus the value of each square is 0.1×0.1, or 0.01 square meter. Therefore, the value of this region is 0.12 square meter, since we have $2 \times 6 = 12$ of these little squares.

Adding up the value of the four regions, we have $6 + 0.4 + 1.8 + 0.12 = 8.32$ square meters.

The calculation at the left below shows the sums of the four regions, and the calculation at the right shows the standard multiplication procedure. Do you see the connections?

$$
\begin{array}{r}
3.2 \\
\times 2.6 \\
\hline
1.8 \\
.12 \\
6 \\
.4 \\
\hline
8.32
\end{array}
\qquad
\begin{array}{r}
3.2 \\
\times 2.6 \\
\hline
192 \\
64 \\
\hline
8.32
\end{array}
$$

We are still applying the distributive property. Going back to the meaning of whole-number multiplication, the multiplication algorithm simply tells us the sums of the four regions. The first row of the algorithm (the digits 192) tells us the product of 3.2×0.6, and the second row (64) tells us the product of 3.2×2. The beauty of the procedure is more evident when we realize that $3.2 \times 6 = 1.92$ and $3.2 \times 2 = 6.4$ don't "line up." However, when we move 64 over one place, the two partial sums now line up just right. We are not generally aware of this lining up; we just remember how many decimal places to move over in the answer column.

Division with Decimals

Most of you know the procedure for dividing with decimals. For example, let us say that you travel 247.9 miles on 7.4 gallons of gas. To determine the miles per gallon, you divide 247.9 by 7.4. If you don't have a calculator, you know to move the decimal points over one place; you also know that the answer is 33.5 because you move the decimal point in the dividend straight up. This procedure is illustrated below. Can you provide a mathematical justification for moving the decimal point? Think and then read on. . . .

$$
7.4\overline{)247.9} \quad \longrightarrow \quad
\begin{array}{r}
33.5 \\
74\overline{)2479.0} \\
\underline{222} \\
259 \\
\underline{222} \\
370 \\
370
\end{array}
$$

One key is the idea of multiple representations, which has been presented many times. We can also represent this division problem in the following form: 247.9/7.4. This form connects to the idea of equivalent fractions. If we multiply this decimal fraction by 10/10, we have

$$
\frac{247.9}{7.4} \times \frac{10}{10} = \frac{2479}{74}
$$

In other words, 247.9/7.4 has the same value as 2479/74. By moving the decimal point over, we create an equivalent computation in which the divisor (denominator) is a whole number.

INVESTIGATION 5.24   Decimal Sense: Grocery Store Estimates

An understanding of how the algorithms work increases one's ability to estimate, as you may have found in Exploration 5.14. As we have stressed throughout this book, the development of number sense is crucial if people are to be able to apply their knowledge to solve multistep and non-routine problems. In this and the next investigation, we will examine some estimation problems. We will pay attention to adapting estimation strategies developed with whole numbers and fractions and to using properties developed in Chapter 3 when appropriate.

In doing math outside the classroom, we generally find that we are more likely to solve decimal problems by estimating than by doing pencil-and-paper mathematics. Let's say that it is Friday afternoon. You drop by the supermarket to get a few items. Suddenly you realize that you didn't go to the bank, and you find that you have only $7.45. The milk is $1.95. The ice cream is $1.87. Grapes are 89¢ a pound, and you have just over a pound. The bag of potato chips is $1.69. The loaf of bread is $1.29. Do you have enough money? How would you estimate this amount in your head? Try it and then read on. . . .

DISCUSSION

STRATEGY 1: Use leading digit and compatible numbers
Looking at the "dollars column" (that is, the ones column), we have 4.
Next, we look at the "dimes" (tenths) column.

This is what that strategy sounds like:

■ 8 (dimes) + 2 (dimes) is one dollar.

■ 9 (dimes) + 6 (dimes) is a dollar fifty, so that's two fifty.

■ 8 (dimes) more makes three thirty, plus the 4 (dollars). That's seven thirty plus the cents. Nope, don't have enough money!

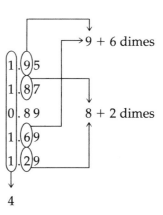

STRATEGY 2: **Round up and use compatible numbers**

> $1.95 is almost **$2**
>
> $1.70 + 1.30 = **$3**
>
> $.89 + $1.87 ≈ $.90 + $1.90 = **$2.80**

Thus, we need almost $7.80, and we know that the actual sum is lower than this estimate. In situations like this, people often intentionally over-estimate because they don't want to find out at the checkout counter that they don't have enough money.

One key point in this investigation is that there are many ways to estimate. The focus should not be on "getting" the "right" way, but rather on developing ways that make sense to you and that are reasonably sophisticated.

This next investigation offers several ways to apply ideas from different concepts we have studied.

INVESTIGATION 5.25 Decimal Sense: How Much Will the Project Cost?

Let's say a contractor needs 308 sheets of plywood for a project. He can get them for $7.55 each at one store. He could also get them for $7.39 at another store, but he doesn't particularly like the owners, and more paperwork would be required. How much money would he save if he went to the second store? Estimate the answer as closely as you can without using a calculator or pencil and paper. Then read on. . . .

DISCUSSION

We could try to estimate 308 × 7.55 and 308 × 7.39, but this would be quite tedious. With a bit of reflection, we realize that what we need to know is not the approximate total cost, but rather the difference. Since the difference is 16¢ or $.16 per sheet, we find that we really have to estimate 308 × $.16 or 308 × 16¢.

STRATEGY 1: **Convert to fractions**

$$0.16 \times 308 \approx \frac{1}{6} \times 300 = \$50$$

STRATEGY 2: **Use substitution and the associative property**

$$0.16 \times 308 \approx 0.16 \times (100 \times 3)$$
$$= (0.16 \times 100) \times 3$$
$$= 16 \times 3$$
$$= \$48$$

INVESTIGATION **5.26** How Much Did They Pay for Their Home?

Now that we have explored the mechanics of estimation, let us examine estimation in contexts. This adds the dimension of deciding what operation to use, deciding how to interpret the result, and the like.

The Hill family is moving. The value of their home is two and a half times what they paid for it, and it is now worth $123,250. Approximately how much did they pay for it?

DISCUSSION

Before we can estimate, we have to translate the problem into a form that enables us to estimate.

We can translate this problem as

Buying price × 2.5 = $123,250

This is a division (missing factor) problem, and the answer will be 123,250/2.5.

STRATEGY 1: Guess–check–revise

What number times 2.5 is equal to $123,250?

First guess: 40,000; check: 40,000 × 2.5 = 100,000; revise.

Second guess: 50,000; check: 50,000 × 2.5 = 125,000.

The Hills paid about $50,000 for their house.

STRATEGY 2: Use compable numbers

$$\frac{120,000}{2} = 60,000 \qquad \frac{120,000}{3} = 40,000, \quad \text{so} \quad \frac{120,000}{2.5} \approx 50,000$$

LEARNING

As stated throughout the book, there is considerable evidence that many of our children enter high school with little ability to apply their mathematical knowledge to nonroutine problems. Consider the following examples from the National Assessment of Educational Progress. Students were given the following problem and asked to circle the correct product among five choices.

Select the correct answer to 3.04 × 5.3.

Many of you might say, "Well, 72 percent of all eleventh graders is not that bad (see Table 5.1). After all, a lot of eleventh graders don't go on to college, and a lot of eleventh graders aren't taking any math and may be a bit rusty." But now look at a very similar problem, which actually should have been easier because the students were asked only to estimate the product.

TABLE 5.1

PERCENT CORRECT	
Grade 7	**Grade 11**
57	72

Which of the following is the best estimate of 3.04 × 5.3?

As Table 5.2 shows, barely one out of five seventh graders was able to see that 16 is the best estimate of 3.04 × 5.3! In fact, more seventh graders chose 1.6, probably because it was the only answer that had a decimal point. Barely one out of three eleventh graders recognized that 16 is the best estimate of 3.04 × 5.3!

TABLE 5.2

PERCENT RESPONDING		
	Grade 7	Grade 11
1.6	28	21
16	21	37
160	18	17
1,600	22	11
I don't know	9	12

INVESTIGATION 5.27 How Long Will She Run?

A runner is running at 7.6 meters per second. At this rate, about how long will it take her to run 100 meters?

DISCUSSION

This problem is a classic example of how decimals can obscure simple relationships. The problem-solving strategy of using simpler numbers is powerful here. For example, suppose the runner was running at 5 meters per second. How long would it take her to run 100 meters? With these simpler numbers, it is almost immediately apparent that it will take 20 seconds; that is, divide 100 by 5. We can now apply this understanding to this problem and see that it will take her 100/7.6, or about 100/8 seconds, which is about 12 or 13 seconds. Over my teaching career, I have seen many students be very intimidated by "ugly" numbers.

INVESTIGATION 5.28 Exponents: Bacteria

With the development of negative numbers and decimals, we are now poised to better understand the operation of exponentiation, which is an operation that we have already referred to in the book (for example, in describing place value relationships) and that we will use in future investigations.

If a kind of bacteria doubles every hour, how many bacteria will there be after 24 hours if we begin with 1 bacterium? Think and then read on. . . .

DISCUSSION

There are several ways to address this problem. For example, we can make a table to represent the growth. The third column simply represents the number of bacteria, using exponents.

Does this help you? Using exponents, how would you represent the number of bacteria after 24 hours?

Number of hours	Number of bacteria	Number of bacteria
0	1	
1	2	
2	4	2^2
3	8	2^3
4	16	2^4
5	32	2^5

The number of bacteria after 24 hours will be 2 to the 24th power.

Exponents and multiplication   Just as multiplication can be seen as repeated addition, exponentiation can be seen as repeated multiplication, as in Figure 5.42.

$$b^x = \overbrace{b \cdot b \cdot b \cdot b \cdots b \cdot b \cdot b}^{b \text{ occurs } x \text{ times}}$$

FIGURE **5.42**

In mathematical language, b is called the **base** and x is called the **exponent**. We say:

$b^2 = b$ **squared**

$b^3 = b$ **cubed**

$b^4 = b$ to the fourth power

$b^x = b$ to the xth power

Computing exponents   This then brings us to another problem: How do you determine the value of 2^{24}? What do you think? If you remember anything about exponents, explore alternatives for a while before reading on. If you don't recall anything about exponents, read the following discussion first and then try. . . . 🖉

In one sense, we want to know how to make the following computation less tedious:

$$2 \cdot 2$$

One (of several) possibilities is to translate this computation to an equivalent computation, using the associative property of multiplication:

$$(2 \cdot 2 \cdot 2 \cdot 2) \cdot (2 \cdot 2 \cdot 2 \cdot 2) \cdot (2 \cdot 2 \cdot 2 \cdot 2) \cdot (2 \cdot 2 \cdot 2 \cdot 2) \cdot (2 \cdot 2 \cdot 2 \cdot 2) \cdot (2 \cdot 2 \cdot 2 \cdot 2)$$

That is, it is much quicker to press $16 \cdot 16 \cdot 16 \cdot 16 \cdot 16 \cdot 16$ on a calculator than to press 2 twenty-four times.

If you have a scientific calculator, pressing the following entries yields the answer:

$$2 \boxed{y^x} \ 24 \ = 16777216, \text{ that is, } 16{,}777{,}216.$$

Negative exponents   When the exponent is 2 or greater, we can interpret it as repeated multiplication. However, what if the exponent is less than 2? For example, what are the meanings and value of the following amounts: $2^1, 2^0, 2^{-1}, 2^{-2}$?

One way to understand the meaning and value of such exponents is to look at the connections among all exponents. For example, what is happening to the value of the expression each time we decrease the exponent? Try to verbalize this and then read on. . . .

$$2^4 = 16$$
$$2^3 = 8$$
$$2^2 = 4$$
$$2^1 = ?$$
$$2^0 = ?$$
$$2^{-1} = ?$$

One way to verbalize the pattern is to say that each time the exponent decreases, the value of the expression is divided by 2. It is reasonable to assume that this pattern will continue, and thus it is reasonable to conclude that the value of 2^1 is $4 \div 2 = 2$. This line of reasoning enables us to continue the progression. In this manner, we deduce that the value of 2^0 is $2 \div 2 = 1$.

Continuing this pattern, $2^{-1} = 1 \div 2 = 1/2$, and so $2^{-2} = 1/2 \div 2 = 1/4$.

Can you verbalize the pattern now so that you can give the value of 2^{-n}? Work on it and then read on. . . .

Once again, we rely on multiple representations. We can represent 2^{-2} as $1/4$, or we can represent 2^{-2} as $1/2^2$, since $4 = 2^2$. This now leads us to the generalization that

$$2^{-n} = \frac{1}{2^n}$$

HISTORY

In the 1500s, Francois Viete and Michael Stifel introduced symbols for unknowns and powers, for example, x and x^2. Before this time, writing algebraic expressions was very tedious. For example, the expression we write as $x^2 + 2x - 8$ would have been written as Zp 2Rm 8 in the 1500s.[7] To decipher the sixteenth-century code, you need to know that they let R represent the unknown amount; however, to represent the square of the unknown amount, they chose a different letter, Z (for zensus or census); then they used p for plus and m for minus. With this code, we can now translate Zp 2Rm 8 as "some unknown to the second power plus 2 of those unknowns minus 8." Can you imagine solving equations or factoring in the sixteenth century? With this primitive notation, it was very cumbersome.

INVESTIGATION 5.29   Scientific Notation: How Far Is a Light-Year?

One of the ways in which we use exponents is to express very small and very large numbers. In many cases, the numbers that we use are so large or so small that computation becomes very cumbersome. For example, the U.S. federal deficit at the time of the writing of this book was $5.12 trillion, which is 5,120,000,000,000. The wavelength of red light is 0.00000000000000586 meter. The following situation is a good introduction to the need for an alternative notation, which we call *scientific notation*.

[7] H.A. Freebury, *A History of Mathematics* (N.Y.: The Macmillan Co., 1961), p. 92.

The size of the universe is so huge that it is almost beyond the ability of the human mind to comprehend. One way in which astronomers address this hugeness is to measure astronomical distances not in miles or kilometers but rather in a unit called "light-years," that is, the distance light travels in one year. The speed of light is 186,000 miles per second. Determine the length of a light-year. Work on this yourself before reading on. . . .

DISCUSSION

In this problem, dimensional analysis can greatly simplify the computations.

$$1 \text{ light-year} = \frac{186,000 \text{ miles}}{1 \text{ second}} \times \frac{60 \text{ seconds}}{1 \text{ minute}} \times \frac{60 \text{ minutes}}{1 \text{ hour}} \times \frac{24 \text{ hours}}{1 \text{ day}} \times \frac{365.25 \text{ days}}{1 \text{ year}}$$

If you have a very inexpensive calculator, you probably got a big E, representing "Error."

Most of you will have something like this:

5.8697 12   or   5.8697136 12

The more sophisticated calculators represent the computation in scientific notation, which allows us to represent very large or very small numbers without having to count all the zeros. The 5.8697 12 is the calculator's code for 5.8697×10^{12}.

Let's work with smaller and simpler numbers to ensure that you can understand how scientific notation works. Consider the number 34,000. One way to represent this amount that connects to place value comes from the realization that this number means 34 thousands. Symbolically, we can thus say:

$34,000 = 34 \times 1000$

We could also represent 34 as 3.4×10. Substituting 3.4×10 for 34, we now have

$3.4 \times 10 \times 1,000$

We can now simplify this as

$3.4 \times 10,000$

Now we can substitute 10^5 for 10,000, and we have

3.4×10^5

Formally, we say that a number is in scientific notation if it is in the form $a \times 10^b$ where a is a number between 1 and 10 and b is an integer.

The reasoning behind restricting a to a number between 1 and 10 is based on convention rather than mathematical structure. This convention makes it easier for us to compare amounts. For example, if we have 6.4×10^7 and 5.6×10^8, we immediately know that the second amount is larger. However, if we have 0.64×10^8 and 56×10^7, it is not as quickly evident that the second amount is larger.

Now let us return to our problem of representing the length of a light-year. Translate this amount to a whole number and then read on. . . .

One strategy is to write the decimal, add "a bunch of zeros," and then move the decimal point 12 times:

5.869700000000000000

When we erase all the extra zeros and insert the commas, we have 5,869,700,000,000. How would you say this amount?

We would say 5.9 trillion miles.

Irrational Numbers

Thus far, our investigation of numbers has proceeded from counting numbers to whole numbers to integers to fractions and to decimals. There is one more set of numbers that we shall consider in this course. The discovery of this set of numbers is also one of the more dramatic stories in the history of mathematics. Many important contributions to mathematics came from a group of people who called themselves Pythagoreans, whom you first encountered in Chapter 4. As you may recall, one of their core beliefs was that all the laws of the universe could be represented using only whole numbers and ratios of whole numbers. Now recall the Pythagorean theorem (for any right triangle with legs a and b and hypotenuse c, $a^2 + b^2 = c^2$) and our mention that the Greeks were the first people to prove this relationship. Ironically, this proof was part of the undoing of the Pythagoreans. Here is how it happened.

Consider a right triangle in which the length of each of the two sides is one inch, as shown in Figure 5.43.

1 in.

1 in.

FIGURE **5.43**

If we call the hypotenuse x and apply the Pythagorean theorem, we have

$$1^2 + 1^2 = x^2$$
$$x^2 = 2$$

That is, x is the number that, when multiplied by itself, equals 2.

This problem was perplexing to the Pythagoreans, because, try as they might, they could not find a rational number that, when multiplied by itself, came to *exactly* 2.

Using modern notation and base 10 arithmetic, we know that we can get *very* close:

$$1.4 \times 1.4 = 1.96$$
$$1.41421 \times 1.41421 = 1.9999899$$

However, there is no rational number (that is, a number that can be expressed as the quotient of two integers) that will produce a product of exactly 2. In modern language, we say $x = \sqrt{2}$.

Finally, one member of the sect proved that there is no rational number that would solve this problem. This discovery was like a child finding out that Santa Claus is not real or an adult finding out that there really are people from other planets. What it meant for the Pythagoreans was that one of their cornerstone beliefs — that all the laws of the universe could be represented as whole numbers and ratios of whole numbers — was not true.

What happened to the person who discovered the proof? Legend has it that he was set out to sea in a leaky rowboat! This is possibly the source of the saying, "Don't kill the messenger who bears the bad news." It is also interesting to note that the word *irrational*, even in our present time, means "contrary to reason."

INVESTIGATION **5.30** Square Roots

Since students in elementary school may come upon situations in which they will encounter square roots that are not rational numbers, it is important to briefly investigate square roots. Technically, any positive number has two square roots. For example, the square roots of 81 are $^+9$ and $^-9$. Why is this? Since, in elementary school, square roots are explored only in the context of measurement, and since all lengths are positive, we will focus our explorations with the positive square roots of numbers, also called the **principal square root.**

Before the development of hand-held calculators, schoolchildren had to learn an algorithm for approximating the square root of a number. This algorithm was a standardized procedure that was taught and practiced in much the same way that long division was taught and practiced.

Without using the square root button on your calculator, determine the square root of 800 to the nearest hundredth. As you do so, use the tools that seem most appropriate. Then read on. . . .

DISCUSSION

To determine $\sqrt{800}$, a little estimating and mental math helps. For example,

$$30 \times 30 = 900$$

Therefore, a reasonable starting point would be 29. However, if you apply the mental math skills developed in Chapter 3, you realize that 29^2 is still too high. Can you mentally compute 29×29?

We can represent 29×29 as $(30 - 1)(30 - 1)$ and apply the distributive property. In any case, since we know that $30^2 = 900$ and $29^2 = 841$, a reasonable first guess is 28. If you want to actively follow the discussion below, please cover the table and think about *your* next guess and your reasoning before reading on. . . .

Guess	Result	Analysis
28	784	Too low. Since 800 is closer to 784 than to 841, the next guess should be closer to 28 than to 29.
28.4	806.56	Not bad! Let's try 28.3
28.3	800.89	Clearly 28.2 will be too small. Next guess? 28.29? 28.28? Why?
28.29	800.3241	
28.28	799.7584	

Clearly $28.28 < \sqrt{800} < 28.29$. Without getting out your calculator or pencil and paper, which is closer? How did you figure it out?

The Real Number System

With the set of irrational numbers, we can now extend our system of numbers to the set of **real numbers,** which is defined as the union of the sets of rational and irrational numbers. This is as far as we will go with number systems in this course. The next major expansion, which students encounter in high school, is imaginary and complex numbers—for example, the square root of ⁻1.

Let us look back at the numbers we have examined in this course with respect to how they are related to each other. We began our study of numbers with the set of natural numbers, which is the first set of numbers young children encounter. Our first extension of the number line was to add zero. The union of the set of natural numbers and zero is called the set of whole numbers. We then examined two kinds of numbers that children will encounter in elementary school: integers and rational numbers. Finally, we encountered numbers that cannot be represented as the ratio of two whole numbers—that is, irrational numbers. If you were to represent the relationships among these number systems visually, what kind of a diagram might you draw? Do this before reading on. . . .

Look at Figure 5.44. Could you explain this chart to someone who was familiar with the terms but not the relationships? Try to do so before reading on. . . .

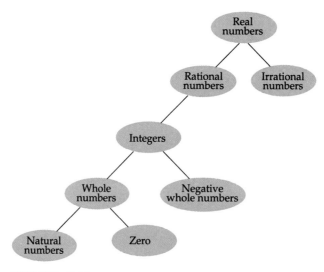

FIGURE **5.44**

Properties of Real Numbers

As we have explored each of these sets of numbers, we have examined the properties of these number systems. These properties are not simply "technical stuff" that children should memorize because their teachers say so. When students understand and own these properties, their ability to successfully work with higher mathematics in general and algebraic concepts in particular greatly increases. We have used these properties to understand algorithms, and we have used these properties when estimating.

Now that we have finished our investigations of different sets of numbers, it is worthwhile to stop and reflect on what we have learned.

I hope you will witness students discovering some of these properties (for example, "It doesn't matter whether you add 6 and 7 or 7 and 6, you get the same thing"), and that your students will be curious enough in your class to ask you questions like, "Will you always get a number when you divide?" Which property is this student asking about?

This question connects to the closure property. The operations of addition, subtraction, and multiplication are closed for real numbers. That is, for any two real numbers, a and b:

$a + b$ is a real number, $a - b$ is a real number, and $a \cdot b$ is a real number.

Why do we not say that division is closed for real numbers?

If we were to say that division is closed, we would have to make one qualification. If we say that for any two real numbers a and b, a/b is a real number, we would simply have to note that b cannot equal zero.

Recall also that the closure properties for the four operations do not hold for all the number systems we have encountered. For example, the set of natural numbers is closed for addition and multiplication only. Do you remember why? The absence of closure with the natural numbers, whole numbers, and integers can be disturbing for youngsters. Do you see why the following two questions have to do with the closure property?

- "What if you subtract a big number from a little number?"
- "How can you divide 10 cookies among three people?"

Another property that is important for you to know about has to do with the density property of rational numbers, which represents a qualitative difference between the set of rational numbers and the three previous sets. However, as dense as the rational numbers were, we found that the number line was not yet complete, because there are points on the real number line that have no rational name. When we add the set of irrational numbers to the set of rational numbers, our number line is now complete. That is, there is a name for every single point on the line. This is known as the **completeness property**:

There is a real number name for the length of any line segment.

Expressed in the context of measurement, we can say that we can now give the exact length of any line.

Summary

To understand decimals, we explored their relationship both to the set of integers and to the set of rational numbers. In doing so, we examined different ways to represent decimals, including base 10 blocks and number lines.

When examining connections with integers, we found that zero presents special issues, just as zero did with integers. When representing an amount with a decimal, sometimes the placement of a zero is necessary and sometimes the placement is optional (a convention).

When examining connections with fractions, we found that some decimals terminate ($1/2 = 0.5$) but some do not ($1/3 = 0.333...$). Exploration 5.15 examines the whys of this phenomenon.

Understanding decimal computations relied on the connections with whole numbers and with fractions. When adding and subtracting, we must add digits that represent the same place value, just as we did with whole numbers. To understand why we put the decimal in a particular place when multiplying, we needed to examine decimal multiplication in the context of an area model, just as we did with multiplication of whole numbers. To justify the movement of the decimal when dividing, however, we made use of the relationship between decimals and fractions.

The operation of exponentiation was introduced as repeated multiplication. Exponentiation enables us to understand an important use of decimals in many fields: scientific notation, which is used to represent very large and very small numbers.

Finally, we examined one more extension of the number system, irrational numbers, thus completing our journey through number systems in this course. Although the set of rational numbers is dense, the set of real numbers is complete and sufficient for most everyday and business uses of elementary mathematics.

EXERCISES 5.4

1. Express each of the following as directed.

   a. 3/40 as a decimal

   b. 4/5 as a decimal

   c. 3/100 as a decimal

   d. 0.36 as a fraction in simplest form

   e. 0.005 as a fraction in simplest form

   f. 1.6 as a mixed number

2. Using grid paper, represent each of the problems below and explain how to determine the product by interpreting the grid.

   a. 0.3×0.2 b. 1.2×0.4 c. 3.4×2.6

3. Circle the smaller of the pairs of numbers:

   a. 0.4   0.42

   b. 1.03   0.98899

   c. 0.05   0.058

   d. 0.302   0.087

4. Order the following decimals from smallest (at the left) to largest (at the right).

   a. 0.56, 0.058, 0.0084, 0.6

   b. 1.04, 0.065, 0.0086, 0.9

5. a. Name a decimal between 0.999 and 1.

   b. Name a fraction between 3.44 and 3.45.

6. Place the following numbers on the number line below:

   a. 3.2, 3.8, 2.9, 3.04

   b. 2.43, 2.4325, 2.4396, 2.441

   c. 0.004, 0.00397, 0.00394

7. Recall the question about the proposed school board budget in Investigation 5.23. What if the superintendent recommended adding $380,000 to the proposed budget of $24.06 million? How much would the new budget be, both in whole-number form and in decimal form?

8. Recall the discussion of reporting of innings pitched in baseball on page 256. Why do you think this is reported in a way that is mathematically inaccurate?

9. Our system of money is not a pure decimal system. Why not? Actually, this question has two parts:

   a. What aspects of our money system are not aspects of a pure decimal system?

   b. Why don't we use a pure decimal system?

10. Estimate each of the following, then briefly explain and justify your estimate.

    a. $19.4 + 136 + 4.825$

    b. $23.4 + 24.6 + 5.7 + 34.4$

    c. $23.34 - 22.56$

    d. $\$10.00 - \$4.34$

    e. 12.5×0.034

    f. 2.3×6.7

    g. 34.2×0.007

    h. $7.8 \div 3.12$

11. Represent the following numbers in scientific notation:

    a. 123,456,789

    b. 3,000,000,000,000,000

    c. 0.00000000056

    d. 0.000000302

12. Perform the following computations using scientific notation:

    a. $123,000,000,000 \times 34,000,000$

    b. $123,552,000,000 \div 23,400,000$

    c. $0.0000000034 \times 0.0000000045$

    d. $(0.00043)^3$

13. The width of a certain cell is 3×10^{-6} cm. If we placed 250 of these cells side by side, how long would that line be? Express this length without using scientific notation.

14. a. Explain how you would determine the length of a light-year if you had a calculator that did not "know" scientific notation—that is, that just displayed an E sign for answers that were too big. Justify your work. What properties developed in Chapter 3 did you use?

    b. Determine the following product with such a calculator:

       $14,000 \times 3,356,000 \times 7,890,000$

15. a. Suppose a particular bacterium can divide into two bacteria every 45 minutes. If this process continues for 48 hours, how many bacteria will there be? Express your answer in scientific notation.

    b. What if we had started with 100 bacteria instead of 1? Predict the answer without doing any pencil-and-paper or calculator computation. Justify your reasoning.

    c. What if we had started with 1 bacteria that doubled every 16 minutes. How many would there be after 48 hours?

16. Sherry is a hard-working student who is suffering from fatigue. The doctor says that she is not getting enough sleep. Below are her bedtimes for one work week. What is her average bedtime?

    10:30 P.M.   11:15 P.M.   11:45 P.M.   1:15 A.M.   11:00 P.M.

17. People frequently mispunch the calculator when doing problems.

a. Let's say you were multiplying 24 boards @ $4.50 per board and got $1,080. What is the right answer? What did you punch?

b. Let's say you are adding $3.45 + $12.45 + $16.23 + $34.45 + $23.45. You have just entered the last number and hit the = sign, and you realize that you punched $3.45 for the last number. What could you do with the number that now appears on the calculator rather than starting all over?

c. Let's say you are finding the cost of 12 boards @ $3.45 per board. You have just multiplied 12 × $3.45 to get $41.40. Now you decide that you want to buy 14 boards. There are several alternatives to multiplying 14 × $3.45. Can you find them?

18. The national debt at the time of the writing of this book was just over $5.12 trillion. How could we represent this amount in a way that people could relate to?

19. Earlier in the chapter, we discussed the misuse of decimals with respect to baseball. When I was reading *Innumeracy* by John Paulos, I came across another misuse of decimals that astonished me. Most people know that "normal body temperature" is 98.6° Fahrenheit. How do you think this number was determined?

Paulos tells us that the number was determined in the following manner. Many years ago (he doesn't say when), researchers kept track of the "normal" body temperature of many people. The temperatures were recorded in Celsius rather than Fahrenheit. The researchers determined that the "normal" body temperature varies between 36.2 and 37.5. That is, some people's normal body temperature is as low as 36.2°C, whereas other people's normal body temperature is as high as 37.5°C. However, most people want an exact number for normal body temperature, not a range. Let's say you were an American who wanted to represent normal body temperature in degrees Fahrenheit, and you wanted one number rather than a range.

a. If you had been given this task, what would be your answer for normal body temperature in Fahrenheit? Justify your decision.

b. Can you give a plausible explanation for how someone came up with 98.6?

20. Let's say a company receives medicine in 1-gallon (128-ounce) jars and then sells the medicine in vials that hold 1.25 ounces. If we were to ask how many vials can be made from 1 gallon, we would divide 128 by 1.25 and obtain 102.4. What does the 102 mean? What does the .4 mean?

21. Without doing any computation, which is bigger, $(0.8)^3$ or $(0.8)^2$? Briefly explain how you arrived at your decision.

22. Think back to the Alphabitian system that we developed in Chapters 2 and 3. Answer each of the following questions without translating the amounts to base 10. That is, answer them as if you were an Alphabitian and that was the only numeration system you knew.

a. Draw a picture to represent the value of 0.A.

b. Add A.B + C.D.

23. The telephone rates between Los Angeles and Tokyo are $9.50 for the first 3 minutes and $1.85 for each additional minute. What would be the cost of a 20-minute phone call?

24. Judy recently took a trip in her car. The trip took 11 hours, including a lunch break of 1/2 hour. She filled the gasoline tank (11.3 gallons) and noted that the odometer read 38329.8. At the end of the trip, she refilled the tank (12.4 gallons), and the odometer read 38735.4. She paid 1.46\frac{9}{10}$ per gallon.

a. How many miles per gallon did the car get on the trip (to the nearest tenth of a mile per gallon)?

b. What was the cost of the gas ?

c. What was her average speed?

25. Most gasoline stations price gasoline out to 9/10 of a cent—that is 1.46\frac{9}{10}$ per gallon rather than just $1.46 per gallon. How much extra money per day might a gasoline station expect to make from this extra 9/10 cent per gallon?

26. A manufacturing plant used 4.2 centimeters of wire on each item. If 3,549 cm of wire are used in a day, how many items were manufactured? If the cost of the wire is 3.4¢ per meter, what is the cost per day of the wire?

27. A group of students held a car wash to raise money. They charged $2.50 for regular cars and $4.00 for trucks. They washed 150 cars and 68 trucks. If they spent $15 on soap, sponges, and other supplies, how much profit did they make?

28. In the *Guinness Book of World Records*, the record for dominoes toppling was 281,581 in 12 minutes 57.3 seconds. How many dominoes fell per minute? per second?

29. In the *Guinness Book of World Records*, the greatest distance a baby carriage was pushed in 24 hours was 342.25 miles. What was the average speed of the baby carriage? What was the average time per mile to the nearest second?

30. Let's say your electric rate is 9.23¢/kWh, and you have 5 different 100-watt lights in the house that run from 5 P.M. until 11 P.M. (1 in the kitchen, 2 in the living room, 1 in the dining room, and 1 in the bedroom). How much do you pay per day for running these lights?

31. Oil companies argue that using super unleaded rather than regular unleaded pays for itself because you get better mileage. If this were the only benefit from using super unleaded and you get 20 miles per gallon with regular unleaded that costs $1.09 per gallon, how many miles per gallon would you need to get with super unleaded at $1.29 per gallon?

32. You have decided to open a checking account with Xanadu County Savings and Loan. They offer you two options: (a) pay a flat $5.00 per month fee, (b) pay a monthly fee of $2 and 10¢ per check.

a. If you figure that you will write about 15 checks per month, which option is cheaper?

b. How many checks per month would give you the same fee in both cases?

33. The length of the tropical year is 365.24220 days, as compared to the length of 365.2425 days used by the Gregorian calendar.

   a. What is the difference (in seconds) between the tropical year and the Gregorian calendar year?

   b. How many years will it take for this difference to amount to one day?

34. A laser printer prints characters at a density of 300 dots per inch, both horizontally and vertically.

   a. How many dots can be printed across the 8.5-inch width of a standard piece of paper?

   b. If every dot on a standard 8.5 × 11 inch piece of paper was printed, how many dots would that be? Express your answer in scientific notation.

35. Your school has just purchased a new high-tech mimeograph machine called a risograph. The accountant has determined that the school pays 5¢ per copy using the copier machine but only 2¢ per copy on the risograph. The school has kept track of the usage of the risograph for a week and has found the average number of copies per day is 1,375. How much money per year will the school save with the purchase of the new machine? What assumptions did you make in order to solve this problem?

36. Betty has arrived! She just traded in her compact car for a midsized sedan. The payments on her old car were $135.45 per month, it averaged 34 miles per gallon, and car insurance was $450 per year. The payments on her new car are $234.67 per month, it averages 25 miles per gallon, and car insurance will be $675 per year. How much will her monthly car expenses increase? Assume that she drives 12,500 miles per year and pays $1.24 per gallon for gas.

37. Henry is currently working at a job that pays $9.45 per hour, and he regularly works 40 hours per week. Another company has offered to pay him an annual salary of $24,000. How does this offer compare to his present yearly income? What assumptions did you make in order to solve this problem?

38. Let's say the cost of gas just went up by 5¢ per gallon. Approximately how much will this affect the average citizen?

39. Let's say you were on vacation, traveling through a small town, and you saw that the temperature was 21°C but you were not familiar enough with Celsius to know offhand what this meant. However, you knew that the conversion from Celsius to Fahrenheit is $F = 1.8C + 32$.

   a. Estimate the Fahrenheit equivalent of 21°C in your head and explain your reasoning. What properties and/or estimation strategies developed in Chapter 3 did you use?

   b. Estimate the Fahrenheit equivalent of 28°C in your head and explain your reasoning.

   c. Determine the Celsius temperature, to the nearest degree, that would be closest to 100°F.

CHAPTER SUMMARY

1. The set of integers is simply an extension of the set of whole numbers.

2. Operations with positive whole numbers can be adapted to work with integers.

3. A fraction is not simply a number; rather, a fraction expresses a relationship between two quantities. The numerator and denominator can be seen as a code that tells us the relative size of the fraction.

4. Fractions can be interpreted in four ways: as measure, as quotient, as operator, and as ratio.

5. Certain important ideas abide in all the rational number contexts:

   ▪ Something is to be partitioned into parts of equal size (value).

   ▪ The something can have a value of 1, in which case the unit = the whole.

   ▪ The something can have a value ≠ 1, in which case the unit ≠ the whole.

6. The set of decimals has important connections with the set of integers and with the set of rational numbers.

7. All the sets of numbers that children will study in elementary school are subsets of the set of real numbers.

Basic Concepts

Section 5.1 Integers
integers *204*
negative whole numbers *204*
absolute value *207*   opposite *207*
negative *207*   additive inverse *208*
$a - b = a + {}^-b$ *209*

Section 5.2 Fractions and Rational Numbers
rational number *216*
fraction *216*
numerator *216*
denominator *216*
rational number as a measure, as a quotient, as an operator, as a ratio *217*
models to represent rational numbers:
   length models, area models, set models *218*

6

Proportional Reasoning

I n one respect, this chapter represents the culmination of the first five chapters. Over the course of the first five chapters, we have explored fundamental mathematical concepts and we have investigated applications of those concepts in real-life settings. In this chapter, we will focus explicitly on the idea of proportional reasoning. This is not a new idea—it was introduced by the concept of multiplication—but it has remained implicit up to now. The concept of proportional reasoning is a powerful one. In fact, some have said that proportional reasoning is both the capstone of [children's] elementary [school] arithmetic and the cornerstone of all that is to follow.[1] The NCTM asserts that "the ability to reason proportionally develops in students throughout grades 5–8. It is of such great importance that it merits whatever time and effort must be expended to assure its careful development" (*Curriculum Standards*, p. 82). Let us examine why.

Additive Versus Multiplicative Comparisons

Much of our use of mathematics involves comparisons (How much more does this car cost than that one?) and change (How has the standard of living changed in the past 20 years?). To compare amounts and express change, we can use the mathematical tools called ratio, proportion, and percent. We shall see that these tools involve *multiplicative comparisons* between amounts.

In this chapter, we will examine two fundamentally different ways in which we can compare amounts and describe changes. For example, let's say we are comparing the cost of two cars, one of which costs $10,000 and the other $15,000.

[1] Richard Lesh, Thomas Post, and Merylyn Behr, "Proportional Reasoning," in *Number Concepts and Operations in the Middle Grades,* ed. James Hiebert and Merylyn Behr (Reston, Va.: NCTM, 1988), p. 94.

We can say that the second car costs $5,000 *more than* the first car, that it costs 1 1/2 *times as much as* the first car, or that it costs 50% *more than* the first car.

The first and third descriptions both use the word *more*, but the first expresses the relationship in *additive* terms, and the second and third express the relationship in *multiplicative* terms. The equations below illustrate why we use the terms additive and multiplicative to contrast the two ways to compare the amounts. To make the mathematics more visible, let b = the cost of the second car and a = the cost of the first car.

There are many ways to express this relationship, using addition, subtraction, multiplication, division, and ratios (see the equations below). However, the first two are equivalent, and we call them both **additive comparisons**. The last three representations are equivalent, and we call them **multiplicative comparisons**.

$$b = a + 5,000 \qquad b - a = 5,000$$

$$b = 1\frac{1}{2}a \qquad \frac{b}{a} = \frac{3}{2} \qquad b:a = 3:2$$

We tend to use multiplicative comparisons more than additive ones. For example, we hear on television that a paper towel absorbs "50% more liquid than the leading brand." If you did Exploration 6.2, did you use additive or multiplicative comparisons in Step 2?

In the first section, we will develop the concepts of ratio and proportion and investigate real-life applications. Many real-life problems involving whole numbers or fractions actually have to do with ratios and proportions. In the second section, we will develop the concept of percent, the use of which pervades virtually everyone's daily life. The concept of percents rests firmly on the concept of ratio and proportion. Therefore, understanding how ratios and proportions operate is very important.

SECTION ◆ 6.1 ◆ RATIO AND PROPORTION

The Unit Concept Matures

WHAT DO YOU THINK?

- Are all ratios fractions? Are all fractions ratios? Why or why not?
- What do we mean by proportional reasoning?
- How do the concepts of ratio and proportion give us tools for making comparisons?

A noted educator and scientist once wrote that "it seems odd to refer to a relationship as a quantity."[2] For example, if we say that there are 25 students in a class, we can see or visualize them. Similarly, if we say that a "large" drink is 20 ounces, we can see or visualize that amount using our knowledge of measurement. We might use 1 ounce as our referent unit, or we might use a standard 12-ounce can as our referent unit; that is, "20 ounces is not quite 2 cans of soda." However, it is much harder to "see" rates—for example, this car gets 35 miles per gallon. That is, when we say "35 miles per gallon," the 35 actually expresses a *relationship* between two amounts (miles traveled and gallons consumed). Yet, as Schwartz notes, we "refer to [this] relationship as a quantity." However, 35 miles per gallon is much more abstract than 35 ounces or 35 people.

In the primary grades, children mostly work with whole numbers and with the operations of addition and subtraction. As their understanding of mathematical ideas grows, they move from counting physical objects to counting numbers themselves. In both cases, however, the unit is still a single whole entity (for example, 1 ounce or 1 person). With the introduction of multiplica-

---

[2] Judah Schwartz, "Intensive Quantity and Referent Transforming Arithmetic Operations," in *Number Concepts and Operations in the Middle Grades,* ed. James Hiebert and Merylyn Behr (Reston, VA.: NCTM, 1988), p. 43.

tion and division and then the introduction of rational numbers, both operations and numbers become more complex, as you saw in Chapters 3 and 5.

"Underneath all of the surface level changes is a fundamental change with far-reaching ramifications: a change in the nature of the unit. It is difficult to overestimate the significance of this basic shift. Many of the important differences in the subject matter between the primary and middle grades can be traced back to a change in the nature of the unit. Given the difficulty of mastering the concept of unit in whole number situations, it is not surprising that changes in the nature of the unit in the middle grades bring new cognitive demands and renewed difficulties for students."[3] In the example above, we talked about 35 miles per gallon. In this case, our unit is 1 mile per gallon—a more complex unit than 1 ounce or 1 student. As noted in Chapter 5, one reason that multiplication and division problems are generally more difficult than addition and subtraction problems is that they involve a more complex unit.

These observations point out that in this and the next section, it is crucial that we ask ourselves questions about the unit as we solve problems and answer questions.

Ratios, Rates, and Proportions

A **ratio** is a relationship between two amounts or quantities. It can be expressed in the following equivalent ways: $a:b$, a/b, or $\frac{a}{b}$.

When the two amounts in a ratio represent different quantities, we often refer to such ratios as **rates**—for example, 30 miles/gallon or 55 miles/hour.

When we set two ratios equal to each other, we have a **proportion**. That is, $a:b = c:d$ iff $\frac{a}{b} = \frac{c}{d}$ and $b \neq 0$, $d \neq 0$.

Ratios, Rates, and Proportions in Mathematics and Real Life

Ratios and rates pervade mathematics. When two fractions are equivalent, we have a proportion. Ratio is inherent in the concept of place value: The ratio of the value of each place to the value of the place to its right is $10:1$. When we convert one unit to another, such as kilometers to miles, we use proportions. The concept of similarity involves equal ratios. When we make graphs, we use proportions. When we make scale drawings and scale models, we obey proportions. The essence of probability involves ratios. These are a few of the many aspects of ratio and proportion in mathematics.

Ratios, rates, and proportions show up in all kinds of real-world contexts, including:

- *Banking:* When I applied for a mortgage, the bank applied a ratio called the 28% rule: If the ratio of fixed monthly payments (mortgage, property tax, car payments, and so forth) to monthly income is more than $28:100$, the bank is not likely to make the loan.

- *Botany:* If we represent the number of complete turns made around the stem by t and represent the number of leaves between the two points as n, the fraction t/n is called a divergency constant for that species (see Figure 6.1). Table 6.1 gives divergency constants for a number of different trees. The numerators and denominators are all Fibonacci numbers (see Exercise 36 in Chapter 1). This divergency constant, which can be expressed as a fraction, is actually a ratio. Do you see why?

Source: Excerpted from *Symmetry: A Unifying Concept* © 1994 by Istvan and Magdolna Hargittai. Reprinted by permission.

FIGURE 6.1

[3]James Hiebert and Merylyn Behr, "Introduction: Capturing the Major Themes," in *Number Concepts and Operations in the Middle Grades,* ed. James Hiebert and Merylyn Behr (Reston, Va.: NCTM, 1988), p. 2.

TABLE 6.1	
Tree	**Divergency constant**
Elm	1/2
Beech, hazel	1/3
Apple, oak, apricot, poplar	2/5
Pear, weeping willow	3/8
Willow, almond, pussy willow	5/13

- *Commerce:* Many companies use rates to determine how much to charge for their goods or services. For example, Allied Shipping Company charges $7 for every 100 pounds of goods shipped.

- *Cooking:* If you want to make more than the amount given in the recipe, all the ingredients must be increased in the correct proportion.

- *Education:* One of the criteria used to determine the "quality" of a college is the student:teacher ratio.

- *Shopping:* If you get 250 tablets of generic aspirin for $2.49 and 100 tablets of name-brand aspirin for $3.89, how much cheaper is the generic aspirin?

- *Sports:* Football writers and announcers talk about the "turnover ratio," determined by subtracting the number of times a football team has lost the ball because of a fumble or interception from the number of times it has recovered the ball because of a fumble or interception. If a team has caused a total of 30 fumbles and interceptions and lost the ball 25 times because of fumbles and interceptions, the team is said to have a +5 ratio. Unfortunately, this is not a valid use of the term *ratio.* Can you explain why not? Would you recommend that these writers and announcers convert the numbers to a ratio or use the same numbers but invent a different term?

In many instances, quantities "should be" but are not proportional. Try to think of a few before reading on. . . .

Airline rates are often not proportional. Longer flights are often proportionally cheaper than short flights, and flights between major cities tend to be proportionally cheaper than flights between small cities. Phone rates are often not proportional in similar ways.

The affirmative action debate for the past 30 years has been based on a belief that many people hold: that the ratio of a minority in society and the ratio of that minority in the work force or the schools should be equal. For example, the ratio of women:men is approximately 1:1, but the ratio of female college presidents to male college presidents is not 1:1, and so we say that a disproportionate number of college presidents are men.

Delving Further into Ratios

Look at the following ratio statements. If the statement can be expressed as a fraction statement, do so. If it cannot, try to explain why. Then read on. . . .

1. The ratio of males to females at Mountain State College is 3:2.

2. In order to get a stain out of a shirt, Lisa made a mixture of bleach and water in the ratio 3 parts water to 1 part bleach.

3. In the rectangle in Figure 6.2, the ratio of the width to the length is 2:3.

6"

9"

FIGURE **6.2**

4. Fred's car gets 25 miles per gallon.

Statement 1: We can say 3/5 of the students are male and that 2/5 of the students are female.

Statement 2: The stain mixture Lisa made was a 1/4 bleach solution. [Note: Many people would be more likely to call this a 25% bleach solution.]

Statement 3: There are two ways in which we can translate this statement into fraction language. We can say that the width is 2/3 as long as the length. Alternatively, we can say that the length is $1\frac{1}{2}$ times as long as the width.

Statement 4: There is no way to translate this statement into fraction language. Do you see why? In Statement 3, the two amounts (parts) had the same unit: length. In this statement, the two amounts are measured with different units: miles and gallons.

Table 6.2 summarizes some of these points:

TABLE 6.2

Statement	Diagram	Whole?	Can be expressed as fraction statement?
1	Males / Females	The student body	Yes
2	Bleach / Water / Water / Water	The mixture	Yes
3	6" × 9"	Either number can be seen as the whole	The whole length is 9 inches, and 6 is 2/3 of 9. The whole width is 6 inches, and 9 is $1\frac{1}{2}$ times 6
4	Miles: 25, 50, 75 / Gallons: 1, 2, 3	No whole	No

When Are Ratios Like and Unlike Fractions?

Before we move on to problem-solving situations, let us summarize the ways in which ratios are like fractions and the ways in which they are unlike fractions.

Ratios are like fractions in that they can be expressed as an ordered pair of numbers representing two sets or two amounts. Ratios are different from fractions in that fractions are restricted to part/whole relationships, whereas ratios are not.

Let us illustrate this difference by returning to the example of the water-bleach mixture.

The ratio of water:bleach is 3:1. However, there are actually several possible ratios:

3 water : 1 bleach	1 bleach : 3 water	3 water : 4 total	1 bleach : 4 total
part : part	part : part	part : whole	part : whole

Since a part/whole relationship exists, the water-bleach mixture can be expressed as a fraction.

In the case of the miles per gallon, we cannot make a fraction statement. However, the ratio is 24 miles : 1 gallon, which is a whole : whole relationship even though the two amounts are measures of different units; namely, miles and gallons.

Note also that some ratios represent discrete amounts, such as students, whereas others represent measured amounts, such as bleach, water, length of a side, miles, or gallons.

Let us now examine these various concepts and ideas that underlie what we call *proportional reasoning*. This first investigation represents a classical problem with a history to it.

INVESTIGATION 6.1   Unit Pricing—Is Bigger Always Cheaper?

Let's say you want to buy some laundry detergent. The small jug costs $2.99 for 36 fluid ounces and the large jug costs $3.79 for 48 fluid ounces. Which is the better buy?

DISCUSSION

STRATEGY 1: Use fractions

In this case, the additive comparison is not the one that is useful. That is, we get 12 more ounces for 80 more cents. However, we can use this information to make a valid multiplicative comparison.

Since the larger size gives you 1/3 more detergent, if it costs 1/3 more, then the value of both sizes will be the same. Does the larger jug cost 1/3 more? Since 1/3 of $2.99 is $1.00, the two sizes will be the same value if the large size costs $4. Note that here we are rounding $2.99 to $3.00. Since $3.79 is less than $4, we conclude that the larger size is a better buy. Why is this?

Perhaps you used this strategy in Exploration 6.1 to determine which box of pancake mix was the better buy. This strategy, used intuitively by many students,[4] is called the **factor of change method**. In this case, the factor of change was 1/3. That is, if we multiply the 36 ounces and the 299 cents by the same factor, we produce an equivalent ratio. The idea of equivalent fractions helps us to understand why this method works.

$$\frac{299 \text{ cents}}{36 \text{ ounces}} \times \frac{1\frac{1}{3}}{1\frac{1}{3}} = \frac{400 \text{ cents}}{48 \text{ ounces}}$$

STRATEGY 2: Use ratios and a calculator

$$\frac{\$2.99}{36 \text{ ounces}} = 0.0830556$$

$$\frac{\$3.79}{48 \text{ ounces}} = 0.0789583$$

---

[4] Kathleen Cramer, Thomas Post, and Sarah Currier, "Learning and Teaching Ratio and Proportion: Research Implications," in *Research Ideas for the Classroom: Middle Grades Mathematics,* ed. Douglas T. Owens (New York: Macmillan, 1993), pp. 159–178.

I have deliberately not placed labels on the two amounts. What do the two decimals mean? Think and read on. . . . 🖉

The meaning of 0.083 is $.083 per ounce or 8.3 cents per ounce. From a meaningful interpretation of these ratios, we see that the larger size is a better buy because its unit price is less, that is, $.079 per ounce is less than $.083 per ounce.

This strategy, also intuitively used by many students, is known as the unit-rate method. That is, we determine the cost of 1 unit (in this case 1 ounce).

STRATEGY 3: Another way to express the ratios?

Maria says she used the previous strategy but "upside down." What do these ratios mean? What do you think of her idea? Is this a variation of the unit-rate method?

$$\frac{36 \text{ ounces}}{\$2.99} \qquad \frac{48 \text{ ounces}}{\$3.79}$$

In this case, we have 12.0 ounces per dollar versus 12.7 ounces per dollar. This is a variation of the unit-rate method. In this case, the unit is 1 dollar instead of 1 ounce; that is, the ratios tell us how much detergent we get for a unit of money. Had we selected cents as our unit, we would have had the ratios 0.120 ounce per cent versus 0.127 ounce per cent.

STRATEGY 4: Solve a proportion

We can let x represent how much a 48-ounce jug of equivalent value would cost:

$$\frac{\$2.99}{36 \text{ ounces}} = \frac{x \text{ dollars}}{48 \text{ ounces}}$$

When we solve for x, we find that $x = \$3.99$; that is, if the 48-ounce jug cost $3.99, the two jugs would have the same value. Since the 48-ounce jug costs less, it is a better buy.

> ### HISTORY
>
> Many states now require grocery stores to show the unit price below each item. One of the reasons for this law is that many companies realized that people tended to believe that larger packages were cheaper. Even today with unit prices, you can find instances in most stores where the larger amount is not cheaper.

INVESTIGATION **6.2** How Much Money Will the Trip Cost?

Most real-life uses of ratios and rates involve proportions. For example, let's say you are planning a 2,000-mile trip and want to estimate how much money you will spend on gas. How would you do that? Work on this problem on your own and then read on. . . . 🖉

DISCUSSION

As you may have realized, the cost of gas for the trip would depend on two variables: how many miles per gallon your car gets and the cost of gasoline. Let's say your car averages 25 miles per gallon and that you estimate that gas will cost $1.39 per gallon on the trip. Now estimate the cost of gas for the trip and then read on. . . . 🖉

The rate at which your car uses gas is expressed by the ratio 25 miles : 1 gallon. The following proportion enables us to determine how many gallons of gas you will need at that rate of consumption:

$$\frac{25 \text{ miles}}{1 \text{ gallon}} = \frac{2,000 \text{ miles}}{x \text{ gallons}}$$

In other words, what number do we need to divide 2,000 by so that the ratio is still 25 to 1?

We find x by solving the proportion for x: $25x = 2,000$; therefore $x = 80$ gallons.

We can now use another proportion to find the cost of 80 gallons.

$$\frac{\$1.39}{1 \text{ gallon}} = \frac{y}{80 \text{ gallons}}$$

We find y by solving the proportion for y: $y = (\$1.39)(80)$; therefore $y = \$111.20$.

We could have solved the entire problem in one step using dimensional analysis. The units for the answer will be dollars. Therefore, we begin with the amount that is represented by dollars: the cost of gasoline. If we multiply the ratio representing the cost of gasoline by the ratio representing the consumption of gasoline, look what happens:

$$\frac{\$1.39}{\text{gallon}} \times \frac{1 \text{ gallon}}{25 \text{ miles}} \times 2,000 \text{ miles} = \$111.20$$

Rates as Functions

You may recall working with proportional functions in Chapter 2. If you did Exploration 6.3, you explored several different proportional functions. Rates express a functional relationship between two variables. For example, if my car averages 25 miles per gallon, there is a functional relationship between the miles I drive and the gallons of gas my car consumes (see Figure 6.3). In this case, we say that these variables are *directly proportional* to each other. Do you see why?

If we take any two points on the graph in Figure 6.3—for example, the points (1, 25) and (4, 100)—and represent them as ratios—25 miles/1 gallon and 100 miles/4 gallons—the ratios are equal; that is, 25/1 = 100/4. When two ratios are equal, by definition, we have a proportion.

Now that we have worked with ratios and proportions, let us revisit some investigations from previous chapters for which ratios and proportions are appropriate strategies for answering the questions.

FIGURE **6.3**

INVESTIGATION **6.3**   **Reinterpreting Old Problems**

> **A.** In Investigation 5.6, Josh finds that 1/8 of the balloons are blue and that there are 120 more red balloons than blue balloons. How many blue balloons are in the box? In Section 5.2, we explored several different ways to solve this problem. How could you solve this problem using ratios and proportions? Work on this and then read on. . . .

DISCUSSION

If 1/8 of the balloons are blue, then the ratio of blue balloons to red balloons is 1:7. Why is this?

We need to focus on the ratio of blue to red balloons; that is, blue:red = 1:7. If there are 120 more red balloons than blue balloons, we can express this relationship by letting x = the number of blue balloons and $x + 120$ = the number of red balloons. Since the ratio is still 1:7, we have the proportion

$$\frac{x}{x + 120} = \frac{1}{7}$$

Solving the proportion for x, we have

$$7x = x + 120$$

from which we find that $x = 20$.

Thus, there are 20 blue balloons and 140 red balloons.

B. In Section 5.2, Investigation 5.3, Jose paid $6 for a 3/4-pound box of chocolates. What is the price of 1 pound (at this rate)?

DISCUSSION

Many students find this problem challenging as a fraction problem but can solve it more easily if they use decimals and proportions:

$$\frac{\$6}{0.75 \text{ pound}} = \frac{x \text{ dollars}}{1 \text{ pound}}$$

C. In Investigation 5.3, Marvin has 23 yards of cloth to make costumes for the play. Each costume requires $3\frac{1}{4}$ yards of material. How many costumes can he make?

DISCUSSION

In Section 5.3, we solved this problem by interpreting it as division (repeated subtraction). However, it can also be interpreted as a proportion. In this case, 3.75 yards can be seen as the unit, that is, the number of yards needed for 1 costume.

$$\frac{1 \text{ costume}}{3.75 \text{ yards}} = \frac{x \text{ costumes}}{23 \text{ yards}}$$

INVESTIGATION **6.4**   **Using Estimation with Ratios**

The following investigations consist of problem-solving situations that can be answered with an estimate (rather than an exact answer). Assume that you have no calculator or pencil and paper.

A. It took Rene 24 minutes to go 15 miles from Hingham to Marshfield. What was Rene's average speed for the trip? What is your first impression (5-second estimate)? What is your best estimate? Can you get the "exact" answer? Why is the "exact" answer probably not exact? Work on these questions and then read on. . . .

DISCUSSION

The problem can be represented as the following proportion: 15 miles is to 24 minutes as x miles is to 60 minutes (that is, one hour).

$$\frac{15 \text{ miles}}{24 \text{ minutes}} = \frac{x \text{ miles}}{60 \text{ minutes}}$$

STRATEGY 1: Use equivalent fractions

We can see that 15/24 is just under 16/24, which is equivalent to 2/3, and 2/3 of 60 = 40. Thus, a quick estimate (if you connect this question to equivalent fractions) is "slightly under 40 miles per hour."

STRATEGY 2: Use the missing factor model of division

We can get a decent estimate by asking: 24 times what is equal to 60? This strategy is related to the compatible numbers strategy we have used before; it would not have been so straightforward had the number of minutes been, say, 22.

Since 24 times $2\frac{1}{2}$ is equal to 60, we now have to determine 15 times $2\frac{1}{2}$, but that is relatively simple using multiplication as repeated addition: $15 + 15 + 7\frac{1}{2} = 37\frac{1}{2}$, which is the exact answer — well, sort of.

The exact answer of $37\frac{1}{2}$ miles per hour is itself an approximation. Why is this? The 24 minutes and 15 miles are rounded numbers. In this case, the "exact" numbers were 23 minutes and 45 seconds and 15.2 miles. Even if we now computed Rene's "exact" average speed, that is,

$$\frac{15.2}{23.75} = \frac{x}{60}$$

and solved for $x = 38.4$ miles, the term *average speed* is itself a mental construct, not something that exists in an observable sense. At times Rene was going 55 miles per hour; at times Rene was going 20 miles per hour. We will study the concept of average in more detail in Chapter 7.

> **B.** It is Christmas time, and virtually every store in town is selling wrapping paper. If Zoe doesn't care about looks and just wants the cheapest, which should she buy? Work on this and then read on. . . .

- Store A: 36 square feet for 88¢.
- Store B: 50 square feet for $1.79.
- Store C: 150 square feet for $2.99.

DISCUSSION

If we divide the cost (in pennies) by the square feet, the resulting ratio will tell us the cost per square foot. The ratio that is the smallest number will represent the cheapest paper. Try this on your own and then read on. . . .

In this case, if the prices are not terribly close, you may need only one run-through.

- Store A: 88/36 = more than 2, that is, more than 2¢ per square foot.
- Store B: 179/50 = more than 3, that is, more than 3¢ per square foot.
- Store C: 300/150 = 2¢ per square foot. We can use 300 instead of the exact 299¢ because 1¢ makes virtually no difference in this case. There is no need to do more arithmetic here because store C clearly has the "best" ratio.

> **C.** Let's say Ellie bought a new car on August 16. On November 1 the odometer read 2650. Ellie's insurance company gives a discount if she puts less than 10,000 miles per year on the car. Will she qualify? Work on this and then read on. . . .

DISCUSSION

Since the time between August 16 and November 1 is very close to $2\frac{1}{2}$ months, we can represent this problem by the following proportion:

$$\frac{2{,}650 \text{ miles}}{2\frac{1}{2} \text{ months}} = \frac{x \text{ miles}}{12 \text{ months}}$$

We can once again obtain a quick estimate by using the idea of equivalent fractions: What multiple of $2\frac{1}{2}$ will be closest to 12? A bit of mental arithmetic yields the realization that $2\frac{1}{2} \times 5 = 12\frac{1}{2}$. Therefore, the estimated miles per year will be 2,650 × 5. How can you calculate that amount mentally?

Since 2,650 × 10 = 26,500, 2,650 × 5 will be half that amount, or 13,250. At this rate, she will travel about 13,250 miles in just over 12 months, and won't qualify for the discount.

Another quick estimate can be obtained by connecting to compatible numbers: 2,650 miles is just over 2,500 miles, which is 1/4 of 10,000 miles. So, if she had traveled 2,500 miles in 3 months, she would be on target to travel 10,000 miles in 12 months. Since she has traveled more than 2,500 miles in less than 3 months, her ratio of miles:months is higher than 2,500 miles:3 months.

Real-Life Applications

The next three investigations are not quite as simple and tidy as the previous ones and require a careful application of concepts we have studied thus far. I find that most real-life applications of proportion are more like the following investigations than like the previous ones. Just a reminder: Work on these actively—that is, get out a pencil and paper and a calculator and work on them yourself, as opposed to just reading what I have written. By doing so, you will not only deepen your understanding of proportional reasoning but also improve your computational ability, including estimation and mental math.

INVESTIGATION 6.5 Is the School on Target?

An all-female college first began admitting men three years ago. Its goal for this, the third year, is to have a 2:1 ratio of females to males in the incoming freshman class. The admissions department has just reported a problem. When the college sent out letters of acceptance to this year's freshman class, the ratio of females to males was 2:1. However, the ratio of females to males in the 1,000 students who indicated that they will be coming this fall is 7:3. If the college still wants to meet the 2:1 goal, how many more males will it need to accept to reduce the ratio of females to males to 2:1? Try to solve this problem on your own and then read on. . . . 🖎

DISCUSSION

The desired ratio of females to males is 2:1. If the ratio of females to males among the 1,000 incoming freshmen is 7:3, that means that there are 700 women and 300 men. One way of representing the dilemma is to let x be the number of additional males the college needs to admit.

In other words, if the college admits x more males, the ratio of females to males will be 700:(300 + x), and this ratio needs to be equal to 2:1. Since the two ratios are equal, we have the following proportion:

$$\frac{700}{300 + x} = \frac{2}{1}$$

We find that $x = 50$.

This problem could also have been solved using common sense. A ratio of 2 females to 1 male can be interpreted as wanting the number of males to be one-half the number of females. Since 350 is half of 700, the college needs a total of 350 males—that is, 50 more males than it has presently accepted.

INVESTIGATION **6.6** **Transferring Credits**

> **I** attended the University of Tennessee in my freshman year and then transferred to the University of Arizona. At that time Tennessee ran on a quarter system (the academic year consisted of three 10-week quarters and then summer school), and Arizona followed the more common fall and spring semesters, each being about 15 weeks long. At the University of Tennessee, I took 15 credits in the first quarter, 15 in the second, and 19 in the third, giving me a total of 49 credits for the year. When I transferred to Arizona, how many semester-hour credits did my 49 quarter-hour credits convert into?

DISCUSSION

STRATEGY 1: "See" the implied proportion

If we see that two ratios must be equal, we can immediately create a proportion: 49 quarter-hour credits is to x semester-hour credits as 3 quarters is to 2 semesters.

$$\frac{49}{x} = \frac{3}{2}$$

$$3x = 98$$

$x = 32\frac{2}{3}$ semester-hour credits

STRATEGY 2: Solve a simpler problem

We can solve a simpler problem and then generalize. If I had taken 16 quarter-hours for each of the three quarters, then that would be equivalent to taking 16 semester-hours for each of two semesters. That is, 48 quarter-hours is equivalent to 32 semester-hours. This means that a conversion ratio is 48:32, which simplifies to 3:2. This can be stated in fractions as saying that we have to multiply the quarter-hour credits by 2/3 to get the semester-hour credits, because 2/3 of 48 is 32. In this case, 2/3 of 49 is $32\frac{2}{3}$.

INVESTIGATION **6.7** **Stuck Behind a Truck**

> **O**ne day I was driving to see a student teacher who was teaching in a nearby town. I was late, and I got stuck behind a truck. The speed limit was 45 miles per hour, but I was stuck for 5 miles behind the truck, which went only 20 miles per hour. How much time did I lose?

DISCUSSION

As is true with many problems, we need to define the question. In this case, I am assuming that I would have averaged 45 miles per hour as opposed to 20 miles per hour for those 5 miles.

STRATEGY 1: Use ratios

At the rate of 20 miles per hour (that is, 20 miles in 60 minutes), I would go 10 miles in 30 minutes or 5 miles in 15 minutes.

At the rate of 45 miles per hour (had I not been stuck behind the truck), I would go 5 miles in 1/9 of an hour. Why is this? If we round 1/9 to the nearest tenth of an hour, we have 0.1 hour and 0.1 hour $\times$ 60 minutes per hour = 6 minutes.

Instead of taking 6 minutes, it took me 15 minutes, so I lost about 9 minutes.

STRATEGY 2: Set up proportions

$$\frac{45 \text{ miles}}{60 \text{ minutes}} = \frac{5 \text{ miles}}{x \text{ minutes}}$$

$$x = 6.7 \text{ minutes}$$

$$\frac{20 \text{ miles}}{60 \text{ minutes}} = \frac{5 \text{ miles}}{x \text{ minutes}}$$

$$x = 15 \text{ minutes}$$

Thus, I lost 15 − 6.7 = 8.3 minutes, or about $8\frac{1}{3}$ minutes.

INVESTIGATION 6.8   Electric Bill—What Do All Those Numbers Mean?

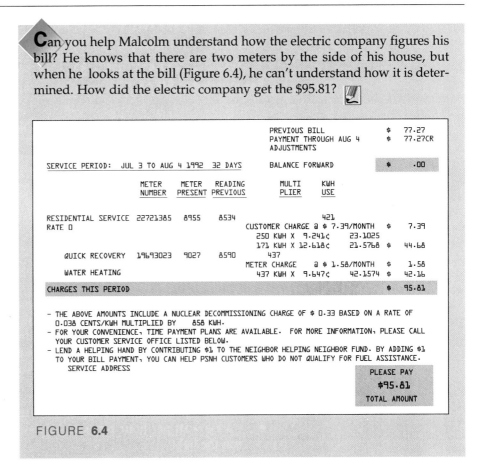

FIGURE **6.4**

DISCUSSION

First, let's see where the $95.81 comes from: $7.39 + $44.68 + $1.58 + $42.16. Do you understand what each of the four numbers represents or where each came from? Think and read on. . . .

- The $7.39 represents the "customer charge." What does that mean?

- The $44.68 is actually a sum: $23.10 + $21.58. We will explore it further in just a bit.

- The $1.58 represents the meter charge. What does that mean?
- The $42.16 is the charge for the electricity used to make hot water.

The math involved in the $44.68 is interesting:

$$250 \text{ KWH} \times 9.241¢ \quad 23.1025$$
$$171 \text{ KWH} \times 12.618¢ \quad 21.5768 \quad \$44.68$$

At this point, could you explain in meaningful terms how the $44.68 is obtained? If so, try it. If not, read on.

The electric company counts one's usage of electricity in kilowatt-hours.[5] They charged Malcolm's first 250 kilowatt-hours at the rate of 9.241¢ per kilowatt-hour. After that, the rate went up to 12.618¢ per kilowatt-hour. Malcolm gets hot water from an electric hot-water heater. The company charges him yet another rate for the electricity used by the hot-water heater: 9.647¢ per kilowatt-hour. It's the same kind of electricity. For reasons not known to me, the company charges different rates for "regular" electricity and electricity for hot-water heaters.

Going back to the figure on page 291, the electric company has actually shown us its computations:

$$250 \text{ KWH} \times 9.241¢/\text{kWh} \quad \$23.1025$$
Similarly, $\quad 171 \text{ KWH} \times 12.618¢/\text{kWh} \quad \$21.5768$

When we add $23.1025 + $21.5768, we get $44.6793, which the company has rounded to $44.68.

INVESTIGATION 6.9 How Much Does That Extra Light Cost?

Let's say that you are considering the installation of a 300-watt outdoor security light for your home. By how much will your electric bill increase?

DISCUSSION

In order to answer this question, what assumptions do we need to make? What data do we need?

Let us assume that the light will be on an average of 12 hours per day over the course of a year—less than 12 in the summer, and more than 12 in the winter. We also need to know how much electricity costs. For this problem, use the rate of 12.325¢/kWh. See if you can do the problem on your own now, and then read on. . . .

STRATEGY 1: Multiply step by step

- 0.3 kilowatt per hour times 12.325 cents/kWh = 3.6975 cents per hour to run the light.
- 3.6975 cents per hour times 12 hours per day = 44.37 cents per day to run the light.
- 44.37 cents per day times 365 days per year = 16195.05 cents per year to run the light.

Note: This problem illustrates the need to constantly make sure that each step makes sense. Many of my students give me an answer of $16,195.05. How-

---

[5] A kilowatt is 1,000 watts. For example, if you run a lamp with a 100-watt light bulb for 10 hours, you have used 1,000 watt-hours or 1 kilowatt-hour.

ever, the number 16195.05 refers to cents, not dollars. How do you convert cents to dollars?

STRATEGY 2: Use dimensional analysis

By aligning the rates correctly, we can solve the problem in one step:

$$\frac{0.3 \cancel{kW}}{\cancel{hour}} \times \frac{12.325 \cancel{cents}}{\cancel{kW}} \times \frac{12 \cancel{hours}}{\cancel{day}} \times \frac{365 \cancel{days}}{year} \times \frac{\$1}{100 \cancel{cents}} = \frac{\$161.9505}{year}$$

Instead of doing each computation separately, what we do on the calculator is simply

$$.3 \; \otimes \; 12.325 \; \otimes \; 12 \; \otimes \; 365 \; \oslash \; 100 \; \ominus$$

What appears on the calculator is 161.9505. Dimensional analysis tells us that the meaning of this number is dollars per year.

Dimensional Analysis Explained

Dimensional analysis was first introduced in Chapter 1. Can you now justify this method?

The justification lies in the concept of equivalent fractions and rates. Usually, we think of finding equivalent fractions by multiplying the numerator and denominator by the same number. However, we can generalize this notion of equal number to equal amount. When we use the light bulb, we are using electricity at the rate of 300 watts per hour, that is, 0.3 kilowatt/hour. Since the electric company charges us 12.325 cents per kilowatt-hour, we can determine the cost of 1 hour of usage of this light bulb with a proportion:

$$\frac{12.325 \text{ cents}}{1 \text{ kWh}} = \frac{x \text{ cents}}{0.3 \text{ kWh}}$$

Solving the proportion for x, we find $x = 3.6975$ cents. That is, this represents the cost to run the light bulb one hour.

When using dimensional analysis, we are treating the units as if they were numbers:

$$\frac{0.3 \text{ kW}}{\text{hour}} \times \frac{12.325 \text{ cents}}{\text{kW}}$$

Our initial problem.

$$= \frac{0.3}{1} \times \frac{\text{kW}}{\text{hour}} \times \frac{12.325}{1} \times \frac{\text{cents}}{\text{kW}}$$

Our knowledge of multiplication of fractions tells us that this is an equivalent representation.

$$= \frac{0.3}{1} \times \frac{12.325}{1} \times \frac{\text{kW}}{\text{kW}} \times \frac{\text{cents}}{\text{hour}}$$

The commutative and associative properties tell us that we can change the order.

$$= \frac{3.6975}{1} \times \frac{\text{kW}}{\text{kW}} \times \frac{\text{cents}}{\text{hour}}$$

Our knowledge of multiplication of fractions tells us that we have the amount 3.6975.

$$= \frac{3.6975}{1} \times 1 \times \frac{\text{cents}}{\text{hour}}$$

Any amount divided by itself is equal to 1.

$$= \frac{3.6975}{1} \times \frac{\text{cents}}{\text{hour}}$$

The identity property of multiplication tells us that when we multiply an amount by 1, the value is unchanged.

$$= \frac{3.6975 \text{ cents}}{\text{hour}}$$

Our knowledge of multiplication of fractions tells us that this is an equivalent representation.

Of course, when we use dimensional analysis, we simply compute and "cancel" units when appropriate.

Summary

In this section, we have explored the last interpretation of fractions that was introduced in Section 5.2: fraction as ratio. We have seen that not all ratios can be expressed as fractions—only those that are given in part-whole terms or can be translated into part-whole terms. We have seen that rates are a special kind of ratio, one that cannot be expressed in fractional terms. Rates also express a functional relationship between two variables.

In this section, we have made explicit the difference between additive and multiplicative comparisons. If you did Exploration 6.5, you probably realized how tempting it was to use additive comparisons to compare slopes. Like fractions, ratios and rates signify multiplicative relationships between two amounts. When two ratios are equal (or when two rates are equal), we have a proportion. Thus, the concept of a proportion connects to the notion of equivalent fractions, which we studied in Chapter 5. In the next section, we will build the concept of percent upon the concept of proportion.

We have examined several real-life applications of ratios, rates, and proportions. In doing so, we found that it is critical to make sure that the computations make sense. We have given names to two methods that students often invent: the factor of change method and the unit-rate method. Dimensional analysis is one tool that helps us to solve proportion problems. Finally, we have seen that many estimation problems involve proportions.

EXERCISES 6.1

Exercises 1–16 present you with fairly straightforward ratio and proportion situations. In each problem, first obtain a rough estimate (5 to 10 seconds, entirely in your head), then obtain a refined estimate (30 or so seconds, with a minimum of paper and pencil) or the "exact" answer mentally. Then explain how you obtained the rough estimate and the refined estimate (or exact answer). Finally, explain whether the exact answer is, itself, actually exact or an estimate.

1. A quart (32 ounces) container of yogurt contains 920 calories. Approximately how many calories would there be in a 5-ounce serving?

2. **a.** If the Dow Jones Industrial Average in the stock market began the day at 2700 and lost 180 points, how much would a proportional fall be if the stock market began the day at 1000?

   b. If the stock market was at 2700 and rose 75 points, how much would a proportional rise be if the stock market began the day at 1000?

3. An advertisement says that 5 out of 8 dentists recommended the new zigzag toothbrush. If 264 dentists were interviewed, how many recommended the toothbrush?

4. An intravenous solution needs 2 liters (l) of glucose mixed with 7 units of blood. How much glucose is needed for 40 units of blood?

5. An employee making $24,000 was given a raise of $1,000. If all employees were given proportional raises,

   a. How much of a raise would an employee making $18,000 receive?

   b. How much of a raise would an employee making $30,000 receive?

   c. How much of a raise would an employee making $23,450 receive?

6. If $1\frac{3}{4}$ cups of flour are required to make 30 cookies, how many cups of flour (to the nearest 1/4 cup) are required for 96 cookies?

7. In the summer of 1991, Israel airlifted 14,000 Ethiopian Jews to Israel as immigrants. If the United States were to receive a proportional number of refugees at one time, how many would we receive? The population of Israel is approximately 4.4 million, and that of the United States is 270 million.

8. **a.** On one map, 1/3 inch represents 18 miles. If two cities are $2\frac{1}{2}$ inches apart on the map, what is the actual distance between them?

   b. On another map 1 inch represents 65 miles. Los Angeles is about 1,000 miles from Portland. How many inches apart would Portland and Los Angeles be on this map?

9. You can use proportions to estimate the height of a tree. John is 6 feet tall, and his shadow is $10\frac{1}{2}$ feet long. How high is a tree whose shadow is 90 feet long?

10. Jane finds that she can read 36 pages of a book in 40 minutes. At this rate, how long, to the nearest minute, will it take her to finish a book of 473 pages?

11. The other day Janet was using the rowing machine in the Fitness Center. Her goal was to row 2,200 meters in

10 minutes. At exactly 7 minutes, she saw that she had rowed 1,560 meters. Is she going to make her goal if she continues at this rate?

12. Sheila and Dora worked $3\frac{1}{2}$ hours and $4\frac{1}{2}$ hours, respectively, on a programming project. They were paid $176 for the project. How much did each earn?

13. A photograph was 3 inches high and 5 inches wide. If it is enlarged to be 7 inches high, how wide will it be (to the nearest 1/4 inch)?

14. The recommended dosage for a particular medication is 6.8 milligrams (mg) per pound of body weight per day, not to exceed 1,000 mg per day. For a 125-pound patient, about what would you expect the doctor to recommend for a daily dosage?

15. A car and a train both begin at the same time and are moving at constant speeds, but the train is moving faster. For every 2 miles that the car travels, the train travels 3 miles.
    a. How far will the train have traveled when the car has traveled 30 miles?
    b. How far will the car have traveled when the train has traveled 40 miles?

16. What is the average speed in each of the situations below?
    a. You travel 11 miles in 16 minutes.
    b. You travel 31 miles in 39 minutes.
    c. You travel 85 miles in 90 minutes.
    d. On a bicycle you travel $12\frac{1}{2}$ miles in 45 minutes.
    e. On a bicycle you travel $3\frac{3}{4}$ miles in $10\frac{1}{2}$ minutes.

17. Make up and solve a real-life problem that lends itself to needing a rough or refined estimate.

Exercises 18–37 are nonroutine, multistep problems. If it is possible to estimate the answer, do so and briefly explain how you obtained your estimate. If you feel that making an estimate is not practical, describe what measures you took to ensure that your answer is reasonable.

18. a. If you are traveling 65 miles per hour, how fast are you traveling in kilometers per hour, to the nearest whole number? (Fifty miles per hour is equivalent to 80 kilometers per hour.)
    b. If you are traveling 35 kilometers per hour, how fast are you traveling in miles per hour, to the nearest whole number?

19. It was reported that Ross Perot spent approximately $40 million of his own money in the 1992 presidential election. His total worth is reported to be approximately $4 billion. If your total worth were $50,000 and you spent the same fraction of your worth on an election as Perot did, how much money would you have spent?

20. In a healthy person, the ratio of red blood cells to other blood cells should be about 1 to 5,000. Amy just got back a lab report which showed 300 red blood cells out of 230,000 blood cells. Is her red blood cell count low, high, or normal?

21. A car travels 60 miles per hour, and a plane travels 15 miles per minute. How far does the car travel when the plane travels 600 miles?

22. On a TV game show, a contestant makes $700 for every correct answer but loses $500 for every wrong answer. After answering 24 questions, Sarah broke even. How many questions did she answer correctly?

23. Five cups of a certain flour weigh 1 pound, and 1 cup of cornstarch weighs 1/4 pound. If the ratio of flour to cornstarch in a mixture is 2:1, how much would 1 cup of the mixture weigh?

24. This is a problem given to students in Baghdad over 2,000 years ago. Two men sat down to eat, one with five loaves, and the other with three, all the loaves having the same value. Just as they were about to begin, a third man came along and proposed to eat with them, promising to pay eight cents for his part of the meal. If they ate equally and consumed all the bread, how should the eight cents be divided?

25. In the women's downhill during the Olympics, the difference between first place and second place was 0.04 second. If the two skiers had been racing side by side, what would have been the distance between the two at the finish line? Assume that they were going 60 mph at the end of the race.

26. Convert each of the following figures to miles per hour.
    a. The world record (as of 1993) for the men's 100 meters was 9.86 seconds, held by Carl Lewis. What was his average speed over the course of that race?
    b. The world record (as of 1993) for the men's 10,000 meters was 27:08.23 by Artuor Barrios of Mexico. What was his average speed over the course of that race?
    c. The world record (as of 1993) for the women's 100 meters freestyle swimming was 54.48 seconds by Jenny Thompson. What was her average speed over the course of that race?

27. In the *Guinness Book of World Records*, the record for handshaking is 16,615 in 7 hours and 25 minutes. How many is this per minute? The person shook one hand every ___ seconds.

28. At a certain college, the ratio of men to women is $9:4$. If there are presently 360 women, how many additional women would it take to reduce the ratio of men to women to $2:1$?

29. At a certain college, there are 7 men for every 5 women. If there are 420 more men than women, what is the total enrollment?

30. Yosha is working on a small project that is due in 2 days. She has spent $4\frac{1}{2}$ hours on it and figures that she is about 3/4 done. How many more hours will she need to spend?

31. A painting crew of 4 takes 5 days to do an apartment building. There are 40 apartment buildings in their current project.

a. If the foreman wants to do the project in 20 days, how many people should he hire? What assumptions do you make in order to solve this problem?

b. A crew of 3 could do one building in ___ days.

32. Ginger wants to fill her new swimming pool. She has two pumps; the large pump takes 40 minutes to fill the pool, and the small pump takes 60 minutes. How long would it take to fill the pool if both pumps are working?

33. The ratio of physicians to inhabitants of the United States is 1 to 549. The ratio of prison inmates to inhabitants of the United States is 1 to 497. Are there more physicians or prison inmates in the United States? Approximately how many are there of each?

34. Here are the directions from an oatmeal container:

Servings	1	2	3
Water or milk	3/4 cup	1 2/3 cup	2 1/3 cup
Cereal	1/2 cup	1 cup	1 1/2 cup
Salt (optional)	Dash	1/8 tsp	1/8 tsp

a. The proportions are not the same. Explain why not.

b. What amount of each ingredient would you use to make 10 servings? Explain your work.

35. A recipe for chocolate chip cookies is:

$1\frac{1}{4}$ cups flour

$\frac{1}{2}$ cup sugar

$\frac{1}{2}$ teaspoon salt

$\frac{1}{2}$ cup butter

6 oz chocolate chips

1 teaspoon vanilla extract

1 egg

$\frac{1}{2}$ teaspoon baking powder

The recipe makes 4 dozen cookies.

a. How much of each ingredient would you need if you wanted to make 10 dozen cookies?

b. Unlike in the oatmeal problem, it is essential in this case that certain ingredients be in the "correct proportion." Explain what that phrase means.

36. An advertisement says that 5 out of 8 doctors recommended one brand of aspirin over another. In actuality, 325 doctors were interviewed, and 199 of the doctors recommended the first brand over the other. Is the advertisement accurate? Explain your response.

37. If the ratio of boys to girls in a class is 3 to 8, will the ratio of boys to girls stay the same, become greater, or become smaller if 2 boys and 2 girls are added to the class? Justify your response.

Problems 38–44 require you to make some assumptions in order to determine an answer. Describe and justify the assumptions you make in determining your answer.

38. A worker estimates that she spends 75 minutes a day at the copying machine. How many hours would this be per year?

39. Two persons have the same yearly income, but one gets paid every other week, while the other gets paid twice a month. Which paycheck is larger?

40. One morning I was listening to National Public Radio, which was conducting its annual pledge drive. The announcer said, "Our goal this morning (from 6 A.M. to 9 A.M.) is to get 40 new pledges. We've received 15 pledges so far, so we're on track." I was puzzled because it was 7:30.

a. Explain why the announcer was inaccurate from a mathematical perspective.

b. Assuming that the announcer was aware that the math wasn't quite right, explain why he might have made that statement.

41. Ursula and Brad are going to buy Christmas wrapping paper. Their choices are a jumbo roll containing 200 square feet for $3.99 or a jumbo package containing 8 different rolls (each containing 25 square feet) for $3.99. Ursula says that even though the ratios are the same in both cases, the former is a better buy. Brad says that they're the same deal because you get the same amount of wrapping paper for the same amount of money. What do you think?

42. Sonja claims that she was 20 minutes late to work because she got stuck behind a truck the whole way. Is this plausible? If not, explain why. If so, make up some numbers to support your conclusion.

43. Determine the cost of flying from your nearest airport to two different cities. If we consider the fares as rates, that is, cost per mile, are the two rates proportional? If not, why do you think they are not proportional?

44. You are in charge of designing a 6-week summer school program at your college. Some classes will meet every day, and others will meet three times per week. How long will the every day classes be? How long will the three times a week classes be?

SECTION 6.2 **PERCENTS**

You first learned percents in the sixth or seventh grade, and you see them every day in the newspaper. Yet the confident use of percents as a tool eludes most adult Americans. The concept of percents is not as much one of the big ideas of arithmetic as it is a tool that rests upon many big ideas of arithmetic. In this section, you will see how percents rest upon the notion of fractions (in terms of part/whole relationships) and proportions (in terms of equivalent ratios or equivalent fractions). You will learn to translate freely among percents, fractions, and decimals.

The Origin of Percent

The word *percent* literally means per hundred, and comes directly from the Latin *per centum*.

There are direct and immediate connections between percent, equivalent fractions, and proportions. For example, let's say that a student correctly answered 12 out of 16 questions on a quiz. To determine the student's score as a percentage, we are asking, what fraction with a denominator of 100 is equivalent to 12/16? This question can be stated as a proportion:

$$\frac{12}{16} = \frac{x}{100}$$

That is, what value of x makes $x/100$ and 12/16 equivalent fractions?

HISTORY

The concept of percent is related to societies' need to compute interest, profit and loss, and taxes.

When the Roman emperor Augustus levied a tax on all goods sold at auction . . . the rate was 1/100 . . . . In the Middle Ages, as larger denominations of money came to be used, 100 became a common base for computations. Italian manuscripts of the 15th century contained such expressions as "20p100,"

"x p cento," and "vi p c°" to indicate 20 percent, 10 percent, and 6 percent. . . . The percent sign, %, has probably evolved from a symbol introduced in an anonymous Italian manuscript of 1425. Instead of "per 100," "P100," or "P cento" which were common at that time, this author used P° . By about 1650 the ° had become ° ̸ so per ° ̸ was often used. Finally the per was dropped, leaving ° ̸ or %.[6]

Uses of Percent

We use percents for a variety of purposes:

- To communicate—for example, we hear on the news that a fire is 30% contained.

- To make sense of situations—a manufacturer may say that the germination rate of a grass seed is 80%.

- To make decisions—should I buy a house if the interest rate is down to 7.5%?

- To compare—in one high school of 345 there were 12 dropouts, and in another high school of 567 there were 17 dropouts; which school has the lower dropout rate?

Let us use this basic understanding of percents to solve a few problems and then look at commonalities and differences among those problems.

[6] *Historical Topics for the Mathematics Classroom: 31st Yearbook* (Reston, VA.: NCTM, 1969), p. 147.

INVESTIGATION **6.10** Who's the Better Free-Throw Shooter?

You are the coach of the girls' basketball team at a local middle school. It is the third game of the season, the game is tied, and there are only 5 seconds left on the clock. The referee has called a technical foul on the other team. You get to choose any one of your girls to take the shot. Based only on their free-throw shooting thus far this season, whom would you pick?

- Becky has made 6 of 9 free throws.
- Rachel has made 12 of 17 free throws.

DISCUSSION

STRATEGY 1: Use fractions

Represent the players' free-throw shooting as fractions.

$$6/9 = 2/3$$

Since 12/18 is also equal to 2/3, we can see that 12 baskets in only 17 shots is a better percentage. Thus, Rachel is doing better.

STRATEGY 2: Make a proportion

Some students feel more comfortable with proportions. How would you describe why this proportion will tell us the answer?

$$\frac{2}{3} = \frac{x}{17}$$

In this case, x represents how many baskets Rachel must have made in order to have the same ratio as Becky. When we solve for x, we get $x = 11.3$. Since Rachel has made 12 out of 17, which is better than 11.3, she is doing better than Becky.

STRATEGY 3: Convert fractions to decimals or percents

$$\frac{6}{9} \approx .67 = 67\% \quad \text{while} \quad \frac{12}{17} \approx .71 = 71\%$$

In real-life, what factors other than the players' free-throw percentages might a coach consider before making the decision?

> **LEARNING**
>
> When Investigation 6.10 is given to middle school students, many will pick Becky, saying that she has missed fewer shots. Do you see why? What is their misconception?

INVESTIGATION **6.11** Understanding a Newspaper Article

A newspaper story reports that 8% of the 7,968 students at Midvale College work full-time. How many students work full-time? First try to estimate the number of students and then determine the exact answer.

DISCUSSION

STRATEGY 1: Use 10% as a benchmark

A very rough estimate: 8% is close to 10%, which is 1/10, a fraction that we can do mental multiplication with rather simply. If we round 7,968 to 8,000, then 1/10 of 8,000 is 800.

STRATEGY 2: Use 1% as a benchmark

We could mentally find 1% and use simpler numbers to build up to 8%:

> 1% of 7,968 is about 80.
>
> 8% of 8,000 is 80 × 8 = 640.

STRATEGY 3: Find a close unit fraction

We can get a slightly more accurate estimate by using 1/12 for 8%. Do you see why?

In this case, we can use the compatible numbers strategy from Chapter 3.

$$\frac{7,968}{12} \approx \frac{8,400}{12} = 700$$

When we compare this to 7,200/12 = 600, we conclude that the actual number of students working full-time is between 600 and 700.

STRATEGY 4: Break the problem into parts

We could also adapt the decomposition strategy developed for whole numbers in Chapter 3.

> 10% of 8,000 is 800.
>
> 5% of 8,000 is 400.

Since 8% is between 5% and 10% (a little bit closer to 10%), we can conclude that 8% of 8,000 is a little more than 600.

Converting among percents, decimals, and fractions   When we estimate the answers to percent problems, it is helpful to know the basic conversions among percents, fractions, and decimals. Table 6.3 shows some of the more commonly used conversions.

TABLE 6.3

Fraction	Decimal	Percent
1/2	0.5	50%
1/3	0.333. . . or $0.\overline{3}$	$33\frac{1}{3}\%$
1/4	0.25	25%
1/5	0.2	20%
1/10	0.1	10%
1/100	0.01	1%

With this in mind, let us examine different ways to determine the "exact" number of students working full-time at Midvale College.

STRATEGY 1: Connect to the meaning of percent

We can represent the ratio of students working full-time to the total number of students as a fraction, that is,

$$\frac{\text{\# working full–time}}{\text{Total \# of students}} = \frac{8}{100}$$

If we let x represent the number of students working full-time, we have the following:

$$\frac{x}{7,968} = \frac{8}{100}$$

Now we can solve for x.

8% of 7,968 $= 0.08 \times 7,968 = 637.44$

About 637 students work full-time.

STRATEGY 3: **Use a diagram**

Figure 6.5 shows 8%. How can you use this diagram to solve the problem?

If the whole square represents the total student population, that means that 100 boxes represent 7,968 students. The shaded area represents that fraction (percent) of the student body that works full-time.

To solve the problem using this diagram, we need to know the value of 8 boxes. If

100 boxes $= 7,968$

then

1 box $= 79.68$

so

8 boxes $= 79.68 \times 8 = 637.44$

FIGURE **6.5**

An answer of 637.44 or even 637 is too precise; it is an example of what I call pseudo-precision. Why is this? Think before reading on. . . .

When the college reports that 8% of its students work full-time, if it is using mathematics appropriately, it is saying that the percent of the students who work full-time is closer to 8% than it is to 7% or 9%. That is, when the person in the college determined that 8% of the students work full-time, he or she took the number of students who work full-time and divided by the total number of students, and the number that appeared on the calculator was closer to 0.08 than it was to 0.07 or 0.09.

In other words, the actual number of students who work full-time is between 7.5% of 7,968 and 8.5% of 7,968. That is, the actual number is between 598 and 677. Do you see why?

We have just found that any number of full-time students between 598 and 677 will round to 8% of 7,968. Since we know only that 8% was reported, it would be more accurate to say not that 637 students work full-time, but rather that the number of students who work full-time is between 598 and 677, or 637 ± 40.

INVESTIGATION **6.12** Buying a House

The Benanders are going to buy a house. Before giving a family a mortgage to buy a home, banks generally require that the total monthly payment (including property taxes) be no more than 28% of the family's gross monthly income. What must the Benanders' monthly income be in order to buy a home on which the monthly payment will be $800?

This is not an easy question. Please think about it, grapple with it, apply your understanding of percent and your problem-solving toolbox, and then read on. . . .

DISCUSSION

STRATEGY 1: **Use guess–check–revise**

One way of paraphrasing the problem is to say that if the bank computes 28% of the Benanders' monthly pay, this number must be at least $800 or the bank will turn them down. In other words, the bank takes their monthly income and multiplies it by 0.28. If the product is greater than $800, they qualify.

For many students, this line of reasoning leads to guess–check–revise.

TABLE 6.4

Guess	Computation	Analysis
$3,000	$3,000 × 0.28 = $840	Too much. Guess less.
$2,900	$2,900 × 0.28 = $812	Too much. When the guess went down by $100, the payment went down by $28. [What is the connection to ratios here?] If the next guess is $50 less, the payment will be $14 less, which will be too low (798).
		So make a guess of $40 less.
$2,860	$2,860 × 0.28 = $800.80	

It would take several more trials to get the exact answer, and that is one limitation of guess–check–revise: It is not practical when you need an exact answer. However, unlike the electric company in Investigation 6.8, when determining eligibility, the bank is not interested in 3 decimal places. Banks have some flexibility; that is, if you are "close" to 28% and there are other factors in your favor (such as job stability, a promotion due, or an inheritance), then you are likely to qualify.

STRATEGY 2: Rewrite the problem as an equation

Another set of students paraphrases the problem something like this:

28% of their salary must be at least 800.

Changing the wording to be more "mathematical," we have

28% of what is $800?

The jump to an equation now is not as great:

0.28 times x = 800, where x = their monthly salary

That is, if $0.28x = 800$, solve for x.

STRATEGY 3: Use a diagram

We can also represent this problem with a diagram. Even if you "understand" how to get the answer, can you explain the "why" of Figure 6.6? Try to do so before reading on. . . .

In Figure 6.6, the whole box represents their monthly income and the shaded area represents 28% of their income.

If we look at the problem from a part:whole perspective,

$$\frac{\text{Part}}{\text{Whole}} = \frac{28 \text{ boxes}}{100 \text{ boxes}} = \frac{\$800}{\text{total income}}$$

We can also interpret the figure in the following way:

If 28 boxes has a value of 800, then 100 boxes has a value of what?

If 28 boxes	represents a value of	$800, then
1 box	represents a value of	$28.571428 (Why is this?)
100 boxes	represents a value of	$2,857.14

FIGURE **6.6**

Connections Between Percent and Other Mathematical Topics

How would you represent the three previous investigations in terms of part/whole relationships? How would you interpret them in terms of proportions?

One of the keys to seeing the interconnectedness of all three problems is to realize that in percent problems there are 2 parts and 2 wholes.

For example, in Investigation 6.10, the 9 shots Becky attempted is the whole and 6 is the part she made. When we determine that this part/whole relationship is equivalent to 67%, we are saying that this is equivalent to 67 parts in a whole of 100 [Figure 6.7(a)].

To determine 8% of 7,968 in Investigation 6.11, we need to find the part out of the whole of 7,968 that is equivalent to 8 parts out of 100 [Figure 6.7(b)].

In Investigation 6.12, to determine the Benanders' monthly payment, we ask, 800 is 28% of what whole [Figure 6.7(c)]?

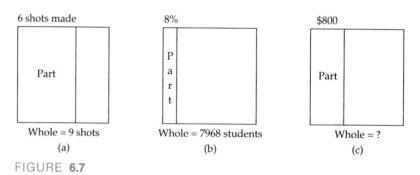

FIGURE **6.7**

If we now examine these problems in terms of proportions, in each case 100 represents the whole. From this perspective, we can see that the differences among the 3 problems have to do with what part or whole is missing.

$$\frac{\text{Part}}{\text{Whole}} \qquad \frac{6}{9} = \frac{x}{100} \qquad \frac{x}{7,968} = \frac{8}{100} \qquad \frac{800}{x} = \frac{28}{100}$$

Now that we have investigated some of the basic aspects of percents, the following investigations can serve both as stretching problems and as a self-assessment of how well you "own" the concept (that is, how well you can apply your knowledge to nonroutine problems). If you did Exploration 6.6, you grappled with understanding and justifying different ways of solving percent problems.

INVESTIGATION 6.13 Sale?

Jorge is excited. He just saw in the newspaper that Showroom Appliances is celebrating 20 years in business by offering 20% off on all merchandise. He just went there yesterday to buy a television set that was regularly priced at $260. What is the sale price of the television?

DISCUSSION

Probably the most common solution I see to this problem looks like this:

$0.20 \times \$260 = \$52$

$\$260 - \$52 = \$208$

Jorge will pay $208.
However, Randi says that she solved the problem in one step:

$$0.80 \times \$260 = \$208$$

Do you understand why Randi did this? How would you explain it to someone else? Please reflect on these questions before reading on. . . . 🖋️

One way to get beyond the "what" of this shortcut and into the "why" is to represent this problem with a diagram. In Figure 6.8, if the whole box represents $260 (the original price) what do the two shaded areas represent (that is, 20 boxes and 80 boxes)? Think before reading on. . . . 🖋️

FIGURE **6.8**

The 20-box shaded region represents the **discount** , that is, the amount by which the store will reduce the price, or how much Jorge will save.

The 80 boxes therefore represents the **sale price** of the television. Since it is the sale price that we are looking for, we do not need to find 20% of the price and subtract it from the original price; we can determine the sale price directly.

We can show that the two procedures are mathematically equivalent:

$$260 - 0.20(260) = 260(1 - 0.20)$$ We are using the distributive property.
$$= 260(0.80)$$ Since $1 - 0.20 = 0.80$

Thus,

$$260 - 0.20(260) = 260(0.80)$$

Percent Change

Many problems involving percents in real life are not simple problems like the ones we have investigated thus far, but rather involve change; such comparisons are called percent increase, percent decrease, percent change, percent error, percent faster or slower, percent more or less, and so forth.

We need to be able to understand change in order to intelligently interpret the changes in our society—in employment, the economy, AIDS, and other areas. *On the Shoulders of Giants: New Approaches to Numeracy*[7] is a book that was written by mathematicians to help people to see the "big ideas" of mathematics. The six chapter titles are: pattern, dimension, quantity, uncertainty, shape, and change. In one sense, the authors are saying that *this* is what mathematics is about, not just formulas and rules. Do you feel the presence of these six ideas in the work we have been doing thus far? Percent is one of many mathematical tools that we have that can help us to better understand and make sense of change.

This concept of percent change or difference is one of the more elusive concepts to own. I find that more students rent this concept of percent change than almost any other concept in the course. Therefore, it is even more imperative that you enter this section owning the knowledge in the previous discussions and that you engage in the investigations in this section and in the explorations. Explorations 6.7 and 6.8 require you to make sense of percent change and to examine ways of determining percent change.

[7] Lynn Steen (ed.), *On the Shoulders of Giants: New Approaches to Numeracy* (Washington, D.C.: National Academy Press, 1990).

INVESTIGATION **6.14** **What Is a Fair Raise?**

> **L**et's say I am the president of a small company, Bassarear's Bagels, that has done very well in the last year. I have decided that I want to share my good fortune with my hard-working and devoted employees. I announce that I will be giving a $1 an hour raise to everyone. Two days later I become aware of some grumbling. A number of employees are complaining that this is not fair. I am stunned. To me, giving everyone the same raise is the epitome of fairness. Why are some employees grumbling? How would you explain this to me if you were one of my dissatisfied employees? Think and then read on. . . .

DISCUSSION

When I do this investigation with my own students, I receive many different (reasonable) reasons for the complaints:

- Workers with more seniority should receive "bigger" raises.
- Full-time workers should receive "bigger" raises.
- Hard-working workers should receive "bigger" raises.
- This raise is not fair to the people making more money.

For the concept of percent increase, I want to focus on the last reason. Why would a higher-paid employee feel that my raise was not fair to him or her? Imagine you are such an employee. How might you help me to see your point? Think and read on. . . .

Let's say the janitor is making $4 an hour and the manager of one of the stores is making $12 an hour. From a proportional perspective, the janitor is pretty happy because $1 an hour represents 1/4 of her salary. The manager, however, is not very happy, because $1 represents only 1/12 of her salary. From the proportional perspective, a "fair" raise would be one in which the ratio of raise : present salary would be equal for everyone; that is, all the raises would be proportional.

Additive versus multiplicative increases   The chart below shows the difference between adding the *same* amount to each person's wage (an additive increase) and multiplying each person's wage by the *same* amount (a proportional increase).

Original salary	Add the same amount	Multiply by the same amount
4	4 + 1 = 5	4 (1.25) = 5
12	12 + 1 = 13	12(1.25) = 15

What if I were to be convinced that I should not add the same amount to each person's salary, but rather should multiply each person's salary by the same amount? How would I announce that to the company in terms of percent? Think and read on. . . .

If we multiply the janitor's salary by 1.25, we are in effect increasing her salary by 1/4. That is,

$$4(1.25) = 4 + 0.25(4) = 4 + 1 = 5$$

If we multiply the manager's salary by 1.25, we are in effect increasing her salary by 1/4. That is,

$$12(1.25) = 12 + 0.25(12) = 12 + 3 = 15$$

Since 1/4 is equivalent to 25/100, we say that both employees have received a 25% raise; that is, their salaries are 25% greater than they were before.

In order to better understand the difference between additive and multiplicative changes, look at Figure 6.9, which shows the before and after salaries using both methods. What do you notice?

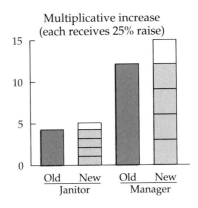

FIGURE **6.9**

In the additive case, "equal" means the same amount; that is, they both receive a $1 increase. In the proportional case, "equal" means that the ratio "raise : salary" is equal, that is, 1 : 4.

As I hope you are seeing, the idea of "equality" is as complex in mathematics as it is in history and political science. It is also important to know that not everyone would agree that the 25% raise is fair. Many people interpret this scenario as "the rich getting richer" because the difference between the janitor's and the manager's hourly pay was $8 and is now $10.

Now let us investigate a problem that is near and dear to the hearts, or at least the pocketbooks, of most students.

INVESTIGATION **6.15** How Much Did the Bookstore Pay for the Textbook?

When college bookstores purchase textbooks, they generally sell the books for 20 to 25 percent more than they paid for them. In other words, their markup is between 20 and 25 percent. Let's say that you paid $65 for a textbook and your bookstore marked up the price by 25%. How much did the bookstore pay for the textbook? Work on this problem before reading on. . . .

DISCUSSION

STRATEGY 1: Act it out

Let's say you are working in the bookstore. You would take the price of the book (which we don't know at this point) and find 25% of that number, and then you would add that to the price of the book. This sum would be $65. We can solve the problem using guess–check–revise or by forming an equation.

STRATEGY 2: Use guess–check–revise

TABLE 6.5

Guess	Work	Reflection
40	$0.25(40) + 40 = 50$	Too low.
50	$0.25(50) + 50 = 62.50$	Increasing the guess by 10 increases the sum by 12.50.
53	$0.25(53) + 53 = 66.25$	Too high.
52	$0.25(52) + 52 = 65$	Done!

STRATEGY 3: Form an equation

If we let x = the price the bookstore paid for the book, many students can "see" the equation emerging from acting it out. The bookstore employee finds 25% of x and then adds this amount to the amount the bookstore paid for the book; this sum must be $65.

That is,

$$.25x + x = 65$$
$$1.25x = 65$$
$$x = 52$$

Virtually every day I see percents described in the context of a variety of situations. One of the difficulties many people have is translating percent ideas into words. The following situation is one of many instances of the need to translate.

Percents Less than 1 or Greater than 100

In real life, we frequently encounter percents greater than 100% or less than 1%. Researchers and teachers know that when students do not thoroughly understand the concept of percents, the success rate with such problems goes down dramatically.

INVESTIGATION 6.16   The Copying Machine

Clark Elementary School has decided to buy a new copying machine. One of the selling points of the new machine is that the manufacturer advertised that the school can expect about 2 paper jams per 1,000 copies. After six months, the faculty wanted to see how the copier was actually doing. They had run 42,164 copies and had encountered 96 paper jams. Think about the following questions and then read on. . . .

A. What do you think? Is the school averaging about 2 paper jams per 1,000 copies? Do you think the ratio of paper jams at Clark is consistent with the advertised paper jam rate?

B. Represent the advertised paper jam rate as a ratio, a fraction, a decimal, and a percent.

C. Which one would you use if you were writing the ad for the copier?

D. How do you think the manufacturer determined the figure of 2 paper jams per 1,000 copies?

DISCUSSION

A. One way (of several) to answer this question is to set up the following proportion:

$$\frac{96}{42,164} = \frac{x}{1,000}$$

Could you explain this proportion to someone who didn't understand it? What does the x mean?

Solving for x, we find $x \approx 2.3$, which means that Clark is averaging about 2.3 paper jams per 1,000 copies. Since the paper jam rate for Clark is closer to 2 jams per 1,000 than to 3, we would conclude that the copier is acting as advertised.

B. All of the following are mathematically equivalent to a paper jam rate of 2 per 1,000:

1 in every 500 copies will jam.

1/500 of the copies will jam.

0.2% of the copies will jam.

One-fifth of one percent of the copies will jam.

C. As an advertiser, I think I would say that the paper jam rate is one-fifth of one percent. This sounds smaller than 2 copies per 1,000. However, I also know that most people will understand 2 copies per 1,000 much better than one-fifth of one percent.

D. The manufacturer probably divided the total number of jams by the total number of copies. I would hope that this was done with many different copiers rather than just one copier, and I would hope that these copiers were not all brand new. The ratio that resulted from this calculation was closer to 2 per 1,000 than to 1 per 1,000 or 3 per 1,000.

INVESTIGATION 6.17 132% Increase?

In 1990, I read in a newspaper that "the percent increase since 1975 in births by Cesarean section in the United States is 132." The article went on to say that 640,000 Cesarean sections had been done in 1975. I immediately wondered how many had been done in 1990, and that is the question I want you to answer now. Think and then read on. . . .

A. Before you solve the problem, try to make a rough or refined estimate.

B. Then solve the problem.

DISCUSSION

A. *A rough estimate:* Since a 100% increase is double the original number, the number of Cesarean sections more than doubled. So the answer will be more than 1,280,000 Cesarean births in 1990.

A refined estimate:

An increase of 132% = original amount + 100% + 32% (about 1/3)

600,000 + 600,000 + 200,000 = 1,400,000 Cesarean births in 1990

B. STRATEGY 1: Break the problem into parts

A 132% increase can be broken into a 100% increase and a 32% increase.
A 100% increase is equivalent to doubling, which gives us 1,280,000.
A 32% increase is 0.32(640,000) = 204,000.
Therefore a 132% increase brings us to 1,484,800 Cesarean births in 1990.

STRATEGY 2: Connect to a similar, simpler problem

For example, if the problem had said that there had been a 25% increase, many students would have found the answer by multiplying 640,000 by 1.25. Do you see why?

If a 25% increase is determined by multiplying by 1.25, what would we do to determine a 132% increase? Think and then read on. . . .

We would multiply 640,000 by 2.32.

One of the subtleties of estimating is to know when a rough estimate is fine and when a more accurate (refined) estimate is called for. What do you think in this case?

Without an estimate, many students arrive at the wrong answer of 844,800 because they multiply 640,000 by 1.32 or they add 32% of 640,000 to 640,000. In this case, even a very rough estimate serves many students nicely: It tells them that the number of Cesarean births in 1990 must be at least 1.2 million. Students who do a very rough estimate and then obtain an actual answer of 844,800 see a contradiction between the estimate and the computed answer that causes them to go back and reexamine their work. This is one of the many useful aspects of estimating.

Interest

One of the ways in which almost everyone encounters percents is with interest—when you buy a car, when you buy a house, and when you don't pay off your entire credit card balance at the end of the month, you pay interest on the amount that you owe.

Most people have a very limited understanding of the consequences of interest. Let's say you buy a house for $110,000 and make a down payment of $10,000. You go to the bank and take out a 30-year mortgage for $100,000, and you are told that your monthly payment will be $767. Multiply this monthly payment by 360 (there are 360 months in 30 years) to determine how much you actually pay for the house (the $100,000 you borrowed plus all the interest). Then read on. . . .

No, you did not mispunch the calculator. Yes, you really will pay that much for the house!

Let us examine how interest is determined, first in a simple case and then in some instances that are more realistic. There are several variables that will affect how much interest you receive (on an investment) or pay (on a loan): the original amount, called the principal (P), the annual interest rate (r), specified in percent, and the time of the loan (t), specified in years.

Although simple interest is not common, a good starting point for understanding how interest is determined is the case of simple interest—when the principal does not change over the course of the loan. For example, let's say that Jenna borrows $2,000 from a relative and agrees to repay the loan after 1 year at the rate of 6%. At the end of the year, she pays $2,000 + 6% of $2,000; that is, $2,000 + $120 = $2,120.

More commonly, interest is compounded; that is, the interest is determined at specified intervals and added to the principal at those times. For example, if Jenna's relative had specified that the loan be compounded semiannually, to determine how much Jenna would owe at the end of the year, the interest would be determined every 6 months and added to the principal. Thus, after 6 months, she would owe $2,000 + 0.03(2,000) = $2,060. Why is this?

Since the annual interest rate is 6%, the semiannual rate is 1/2 of 6%, or 3%, because 6 months is 1/2 year. After the next 6 months, we determine how much she owes: $2,060 + 0.03(2,060) = 2,060 + $61.80 = $2,121.80. In this particular case, a one-year loan compounded only semiannually, the difference between simple and compound interest is not huge. However, on most deposits and loans, the interest is compounded daily; that is, the annual interest rate is divided by 365.

In the following investigation, we will develop the formula for determining compound interest. In the second investigation, we will examine a very relevant situation.

INVESTIGATION **6.18** Saving for College

When Emily was born, her grandparents decided to contribute toward her college education by opening a savings account for $1,000. If they added no other money, and if the account earned 6% compounded annually, how much money will there be in the account after 18 years?

DISCUSSION

This is a nonroutine, multistep problem. Therefore, let us go one step at a time.

After 1 year How much money would there be in the account after 1 year? Do this and then read on. . . .

There are several different methods students will use.

We can find 6% of $1,000 and then add that to 1,000; that is, $1,000 + .06($1,000) = $1,060. Or, as we have seen earlier in this chapter, we can obtain $1,060 in one step: $1,000(1.06) = $1,060. Do you see why?

This connection between procedures is important because in order to understand this problem, you need to be able to understand the second procedure; the first one is too cumbersome.

After 3 years Now determine how much money would be in the account after 3 years and then read on. . . .

$1,000(1.06) = $1,060 after 1 year

$1,060(1.06) = $1,123.60 after 2 years

$1,123.60(1.06) = $1,191.02 after 3 years

Let us stop and analyze this strategy. In the first step, we multiplied 1,000 by 1.06 to get 1,060. In the second step, many students clear the calculator and then multiply 1,060 by 1.06. Then, in the third step, they clear the calculator and then multiply 1,123.60 by 1.06. If we examine this carefully, we can see a shortcut. See if you can find it yourself before reading on. . . .

We could simply do this on the calculator:

$$1,000 \ \otimes \ 1.06 \ \otimes \ 1.06 \ \otimes \ 1.06$$

Do you see why? If you don't believe this, do it on the calculator to see that it does work. Then try to explain why it works before reading on. . . . 🖉

We can represent what we have learned as

$$\$1,191.02 = 1,000(1.06)(1.06)(1.06)$$

We can now use our knowledge of exponents to say

$$\$1,191.02 = 1,000(1.06)^3$$

The third, and most efficient, method for finding the amount after three years uses this knowledge. How would we enter the last expression in a scientific calculator? Try it before reading on. . . .

Simply enter $1,000 \times 1.06 \ y^x \ 3$ to get the same answer.

Before we move on to solve the original question, this is a good time to understand the basic formula for use with interest. Look at how we determined the value (amount) in the bank after three years. Try to represent that procedure with a formula using the interest symbols introduced above and then read on. . . . . 🖉

$$\text{The money after 3 years} = (1,000)(1.06)^3$$
$$= 1,000(1 + 0.06)^3$$

That is,

$$A = P(1 + r)^t$$

After 18 years This discovery makes the original problem much less tedious to solve.

STRATEGY 1: Use the y^x button
The most straightforward solution is to use the y^x button on your calculator:

$$1,000 \ \otimes \ 1.06 \ \ (y^x) \ \ 18 = \$2,854.34$$

STRATEGY 2: Use the memory key
If your calculator lacks an exponentiation key, you could use the memory key M+ by doing the following:
First, activate the memory by pressing 1.06 and then M+.
Now press $1,000 \times MR =$ (you should see 1,060, that is, the amount after one year).
To get the amount for each succeeding year, you simply press $\times$ MR that many times.

$$\overbrace{\text{That is, you press } 1,000 \times MR \times MR \times MR \cdots \times MR =}^{\text{18 times}}$$

STRATEGY 3: Use a spreadsheet
A spreadsheet (on a computer) can also be used. When you open the spreadsheet, the columns are marked with letters—A, B, C, and so on—and the rows are marked with numbers. In column A, we enter the numbers 0 through 18 (see Figure 6.10). In column B, we enter 1,000 into the first row, signifying the amount we have at the beginning.

	A	B
1	0	1000
2	1	
3	2	
4	3	
5	4	
.	.	
.	.	
.	.	
.	.	
.	.	
.	.	
.	.	
19	18	

FIGURE **6.10**

In the B2 cell, we now enter "= B1*1.06"; that is, we tell the computer to multiply the amount in the B1 cell by 1.06.

Now, we highlight the B column from row 2 through row 18 and select "Fill down." This command essentially tells the computer to repeat the computation—that is, to multiply the previous amount by 1.06. After we do this, the computer will display the amount at the end of each year!

The advantage of the spreadsheet is that we can play the "what if" game: what if they had started with $3,000, what if the interest rate had been 7%, and so on.

INVESTIGATION **6.19** **How Much Does that Credit Card Cost You?**

Most adults in the United States have credit cards. Usually, credit cards require a minimum monthly payment each month. If the customer is not able to pay the entire balance (for example, after a vacation or after Christmas), the customer pays at least this minimum amount; then a fee called a finance charge is determined by the credit card company, based on the interest rate the company is charging.

Let's say George found himself in just that situation. His VISA bill has come in, and the balance is $761.34. He decides he can pay $61.34. If the bank issuing the VISA card determines the finance charge at the annual rate of 18%, called the APR (annual percentage rate), what will his finance charge be? Think and then read on. . . .

DISCUSSION
Since the balance is compounded monthly, the bank will determine George's finance charge by multiplying his unpaid balance ($700) by 0.015. Do you see where the 1.5% comes from?

To find the monthly rate, we divide the yearly rate by 12 (months): 18%/ 12 = 1.5%, and 1.5% = 0.015.

Thus, George's finance charge will be $700(0.015) = $10.50.

Summary

In this section, we began with the basic concept of percent, a part expressed as a hundredth, and then we connected this to the concepts of equivalent fractions and proportions. This simple notion of percent, though, needed to be refined when dealing with percents greater than 100, with percent increase and decrease, and with nonroutine problems. This need for a richer concept of percent was also underscored in the explorations.

In examining percent problems, you saw applications of percents in several areas, including interest. You also saw the importance of estimating—sometimes because the question calls for an estimate instead of an exact answer, and sometimes because estimation helps you to check your solution or your reasoning.

EXERCISES 6.2

1. For each of the following questions, estimate first, and briefly explain how you determined your estimate. Then determine the actual answer. Compare your estimate to the actual answer. If your estimate was close, move on; if not, you might want to reread part of the section and/or consult with a friend or the instructor.

   a. What is 4% of 450?
   b. What is 23% of 85?
   c. What is 83% of $1,460?
   d. What is 3.2% of 1,700?
   e. What is 0.25% of 345?
   f. What is 120% of 200?
   g. 1,200 is what percent of 1,500?
   h. 30 is what percent of 35?
   i. 56 is what percent of 657?
   j. 1.2 is what percent of 4.6?
   k. 75 is what percent of 400?
   l. 175 is what percent of 120?
   m. What is 3% more than 45?
   n. What is 20% more than 400?
   o. What is 16% more than 6.2?
   p. What is 100% more than 35?
   q. What is 10% less than 36?
   r. What is 3% less than 45?
   s. What is 1.2% less than 1,200?
   t. What is 80% less than 800?

In Exercises 2–15, first estimate the answer and briefly describe how you determined the estimate. Then determine the actual answer.

2. Missy Adams's gross pay is $1,500 per paycheck. If her total payroll deductions are $340, her take-home pay is what percent of her gross pay?

3. All three second grade teachers at Uphill Elementary School asked their students how many have pets at home. The response was that 23 out of 65 of the students have pets. What percent of the students have pets?

4. A victim won damages of $2.4 million from a company. If the lawyer's fee was 35%, how much did the lawyer get?

5. If 30% of the patients in a hospital have heart problems and there are 210 patients with heart problems, how many patients are there in the hospital?

6. Last year Mr. Rich paid $27,000 in income taxes, because he was taxed at the rate of 38% of his net income. What was his net income?

7. a. Between 1980 and 1987, the price of an average house in Keene increased from $42,000 to $97,000. What is the percent increase (rounded to the nearest whole number) in the average selling price?

   b. What is the percent increase for a house that sells for $60,000 and then later for $75,349?

   c. What is the percent increase for a house that sells for $71,450 and then later for $102,500?

   d. What is the percent increase for a house that sells for $62,000 and then later for $144,000?

8. Two dresses are on sale. The first was selling for $119 and is being marked down 40%. The second was selling for $79.99 and is being discounted by 20%. Which dress costs less now?

9. At birth a baby weighed 8 pounds 4 ounces. Two days later, the baby weighed 7 pounds 12 ounces. What percent of its weight had it lost? This weight loss is normal—part of the adjustment to the living outside the mother's womb. If a 160-pound adult lost the same proportion of its weight in 2 days, how much weight would the adult have lost?

10. *The Unofficial U.S. Census* reports that 34,177,500 of America's 139,500,000 cars are washed at least once each week, and that 6,556,500 cars are never washed. Assuming that these numbers are relatively accurate:

    a. What percent of cars are washed each week?

    b. What percent of cars are never washed?

11. In 1990, about 248 million people lived in the United States, and the world population was about 5.13 billion. Approximately what percent of the world population lived in the United States?

12. A 1991 news story said that 16% of the elderly are served by the Medicare prescription program, in which they receive assistance when their monthly prescription bill exceeds a certain amount. The story went on to say that about 5 million people are served by the program. What is the total number of elderly people in the United States?

13. It has been estimated that 0.8% of Americans are homeless. Now 0.8% is a small percentage, but there are approximately 270 million people in the United States, and 270 million is a large number. Approximately how many Americans are homeless?

14. In 1988 only 900,000 of the 2.6 million eligible voters aged 18 to 24 actually voted. What percent voted?

15. In an up-and-coming town, housing prices rose an average of 115% in five years. If a home cost $42,000 five years ago, how much would that home cost now?

Exercises 16–22 are nonroutine and/or multistep problems. If it is possible to make an estimate, do so and briefly explain how you obtained your estimate. If you feel that an estimate is not practical, describe what measures you took to ensure that your answer is reasonable.

16. A store reduced the price of a computer by 20% and sold it for $1,760. How much did the computer originally sell for?

17. Janice Brady borrowed $4,200 to buy a new car. If she pays the loan back in one year at 8.2% interest, how much will she actually pay for the car? (Assume simple interest.)

18. A store collected $53 in sales tax alone in one day. If the sales tax is 5.5%, how much did they sell that day?

19. John paid $330 for a new mountain bicycle to sell in his shop. He wants to price it so that he can offer a 10% discount and still make 20% profit. At what price should he mark the bike?

20. A teacher was hired at a salary of $18,200 and is to receive a raise of 5.5% after her first year and 4% after her second year. What should her salary be after the two-year period?

21. Your optimal exercise heart rate for cardiovascular benefits is calculated as follows: Subtract your age from 220 and then find 80% of the difference. Find the optimal heart rate for a 50-year-old and for a 20-year-old. The optimal rate for the 20-year-old is ___ % greater than the optimal rate for a 50-year-old.

22. A city budget is $21.43 million. The city council voted to increase the budget by 4.4%. What is the new budget, rounded to the nearest $1,000?

23. In the 1980s, the company that built the Seabrook nuclear reactor in New Hampshire went bankrupt. When Northeast Utilities bought the company out, the agreement was that Northeast could raise electricity rates at least 5.5% each year for the next seven years.

    a. If the Jones family paid an average of $83.00 per month for electricity last year and the rate rises 5.5% each year, what will they pay after seven years?

    b. If the Jones family's income is $40,000 this year and rises at a rate of 5.5% each year, what will be their income after seven years?

24. The owners of High Hopes Apple Farm have a crop of approximately 1,000 bushels of apples. They can have the apples picked by a regular labor crew for $2.50 per bushel and then sell the apples for $5.00 per bushel. Or they can let the public pick the apples at $4.00 per bushel. Which way will provide more income? One factor that they need to take into account is that when the public picks their own apples, the owners will lose about 20% of the crop from waste (eaten and dropped apples).

25. How long will it take $1,000 at 6% simple interest to double?

26. Arthur was not able to get his income taxes ready by April 15. The penalty for late returns is assessed at a 20% annual rate of interest. Arthur filed his income taxes on June 20. He owed $2,000 plus the penalty. How much did he owe?

27. Selena recently bought a computer, which she paid for with her VISA card. The computer cost $2,137. When her VISA bill came the next month, the total balance was $2,534. If she paid only the minimum $20, how much was her finance charge if the APR on her VISA card is 19.6%?

28. Several years ago, newspapers reported that the average unpaid balance on VISA cards was about $1,500. Let's say that you are an average consumer, that your VISA card charges you at the rate of 18% per year, and that each month for one year, you have an unpaid balance of exactly $1,500.

    a. How much will your finance charges add up to for the year?

    b. How much money would you save if you switched to a credit card that charged only an 8% annual interest rate?

29. A *USA Today* article reported that "Senior high school principals now average $61,768 a year. Their counterparts make $57,504 in junior high and $53,856 in elementary schools. The average U.S. teacher made $33,041 in 1990–91."

    a. Compare the average salaries in percent greater language; that is, compare all salaries to the $33,041 figure.

    b. Compare the average salaries in percent less language; that is, compare all salaries to the $61,768 figure.

30. Express 0.5% as a ratio in simplest terms. For example, 40% can be expressed as 40 out of 100, and in simplest terms as 2 out of 5.

31. Let's say that tests on a new vaccine show that less than 0.5% of all children have a serious reaction to the drug.

    a. Gerry is not very mathematically literate. Help her to understand mathematically what this means.

    b. What additional information would you like to have in order to help you decide whether or not to have your child take the vaccine?

32. The figures below are disease rates for heart disease and cancer (per 100,000 people).

	1960	1988
Heart disease	286.2	166.3
Cancer	125.8	132.7

    a. Describe the change in the rates of heart disease and cancer since 1960, using percent language.

    b. Compare the 1988 rates for heart disease and cancer, using percent language.

33. Let's say you read that the rate of inflation in the United States last year was 5%, and the rate of inflation in another country was 400%. Compare the two inflation rates in the way that will let the greatest number of readers relate to your statement.

34. A road sign says "7% grade." What does that mean?

35. The U.S. Bureau of the Census reported that there were 35.7 million Americans living below poverty level in 1991, 14.2 percent of the population. The U.S. Bureau of the Census also gives figures for persons living "below 125% of poverty level." They reported that 47.5 million persons, or 18.9 percent of the population were in this category.

 a. If the poverty level for a nonfarm family of four in 1991 was $13,924, what would be the cutoff for a family of four "below 125% of the poverty level"?

 b. Why do you think they came up with the reference point of "below 125% of the poverty level"?

36. First Bank Expressline made the following claim in an advertisement. The bank was offering 9.46% interest on the monthly unpaid balance. The chart below showed how much money a consumer with a $3,500 balance would save by switching to First Bank's credit card. Is the ad valid?

	Current APR	Expressline Savings
First Bank Expressline	9.46%	
Citibank	19.8%	$361.90
Discover	19.8%	$361.90
Sears	18.0%	$298.90
GM Card	16.4%	$242.90

37. Below are the infant mortality rates of 7 countries in 1993 and the predicted rates for 2000. *Infant mortality rate* is defined as the number of deaths of children under 1 year of age per 1,000 live births in a calendar year.

Country	1993	2000	Change 1993-2000	Estimated % change	Actual % change
United States	8.4	6.6			
Cuba	10.5	9.2			
Egypt	78.3	65.7			
Haiti	109.5	102.2			
Japan	4.3	4.1			
Mexico	28.8	20.7			
Somalia	162.7	87.1			

 a. Fill in the third, fourth, and fifth columns. You need not show your work for the third column. You need to briefly explain each of your estimates. If you use a calculator for the fifth column, briefly explain the procedure you used.

 b. If you were writing a story on changes in infant mortality and you could choose either the "Change" or the "Percent Change" column, which would you choose? Why?

 c. Convert Somalia's 1993 infant mortality rate to percent language. That is, *x* percent of children in Somalia die before the age of 1.

 d. Joanne still does not understand what "infant mortality rate" means. Translate the formal description, given at the beginning of this problem, to more understandable language.

Problems 38–45 require you to make some assumptions in order to determine an answer. Describe and justify the assumptions you make in determining your answer.

38. Let's say that you read in the newspaper that last year's rate of inflation was 7.2%.

 a. If your grocery bill averaged $325 per month last year, about how much would you expect your grocery bill to be this year?

 b. Let's say you received a $1,200 raise, from $23,400 to $24,600. Did your raise keep you ahead of the game, or are you falling behind?

39. There was a proposal in New Hampshire in 1991 to reduce the definition of "drunk driving" from an alcohol blood content of 0.1 to 0.08. Some saw this as a little drop and some saw it as a big drop. What do you think? Explain why some might consider this a little drop and others might consider it a big drop. What do you think?

40. A recent news article stated that in 1986, women were paid only 64¢ for every dollar paid to men. Transform this statement to the following form: Men were paid ___% more than women.

41. Refer back to Investigation 6.11. Jane still doesn't understand the problem. Roberto tries to help her make sense of the problem by saying that the 8% means that if we were to select 100 students at the college, 8 of them would be working full-time. What do you think?

42. Annie has just received a 5% raise from her current wage of $9.80 per hour.

 a. What is her new wage?

 b. What would this amount to over a year?

 c. What assumptions did you make in order to answer part (b)?

 d. What if the raise had been 5.4%?

43. Jack is building an office building. The local building code says that the window area in the building can be no more than 20% of the floor area.

 a. If the two-story building will contain 12 offices and have 3,000 square feet of floor space, what is the maximum area of window area allowed?

 b. About how many windows would that be?

44. The table at the top of page 315 lists the annual percent changes in consumer prices.

	ANNUAL PERCENT CHANGE		
Country	**1987—88**	**1988—89**	**1989—90**
United States	4.0	4.8	5.4
Brazil	682.3	1,287	2,938
Canada	4.0	5.0	4.8
Egypt	17.7	21.3	16.8
Japan	0.7	2.3	3.1
Mexico	114.2	20.0	26.7
Peru	667.0	3,399	7,482

a. Anders has trouble understanding percent changes over 100. Explain Peru's percent change of 667 to Anders.

b. Approximately how much would you spend in the United States in 1990 to buy items that cost you $100 in 1987?

c. Approximately how much would you spend in Brazil in 1990 to buy items that cost you $100 in 1987?

d. Approximately how much would you spend in Japan in 1990 to buy items that cost you $100 in 1987?

e. Approximately how much would you spend in Mexico in 1990 to buy items that cost you $100 in 1987?

45. If Jonah puts $25,000 in the bank at 8% interest compounded quarterly (four times a year), how much will his investment be worth in 20 years?

46. If Liam puts $10,000 in the bank at 5% interest compounded quarterly (four times a year), how much will his investment be worth in 5 years?

CHAPTER SUMMARY

1. When we compare amounts, we can do so in additive or multiplicative ways. Both have value. In many cases, one is more appropriate.

2. Ratios, proportions, and percents involve multiplicative relationships between numbers.

3. Ratios are both like and unlike fractions. Ratios can be expressed in fraction notation, but many ratios involve part-to-part or whole-to-whole relationships. Not all such ratios can be translated into fraction language. Rates never can.

4. Percent, seen only as what part of 100, is too limiting. For example, a 132% increase expresses a relationship between an original and a new amount.

Basic Concepts

Uncertainty: Data and Chance

We have spent a considerable amount of time examining operations with numbers and different ways to represent amounts. We can add, subtract, multiply, and divide amounts; we can represent amounts and relationships between amounts with whole numbers, negative numbers, fractions, decimals, and percents. In this chapter, we will focus on another way in which we use numbers—to understand and deal with uncertainty.

In this world, nothing can be said to be certain except death and taxes.

by BENJAMIN FRANKLIN

We expend a lot of energy trying to understand the uncertainty and chance in our lives. Let us consider a few examples of uncertainty and chance. What do the examples below have in common? Think and then read on. . . .

- A newspaper takes an opinion poll to determine which candidate people prefer.
- The government collects information to determine the rate of inflation.
- Scientists collect samples of air to determine the extent of air pollution.
- Researchers collect data to understand the AIDS epidemic.
- Colleges collect data in order to determine how to weight admission factors such as high school GPA, SAT scores, recommendations, and so on.
- A company conducts market research to determine how much it should charge for a new product.
- A weather forecaster makes predictions based on analyses of data.
- Peter collects and analyzes information to determine which car is the best buy.

317

■ You want to know what are your chances of getting a teaching job after graduation.

As you can see from these examples, we collect data for a variety of reasons: to make predictions, to make decisions, to answer questions, and to better understand aspects of our life.

All of the examples above have two things in common: They all involve **uncertainty**, and collecting and analyzing data increases the chances that the decision or prediction will be a good one despite this uncertainty.

We often refer to that field of mathematics that focuses on collecting and interpreting data as statistics and that branch of mathematics that focuses on determining the chance of something happening as probability. However, as you may have discovered from the Chapter 7 explorations, much of our interpretation of data involves chance, and much of our understanding of chance involves collecting and analyzing data. This is one of the reasons I have chosen to have you examine these ideas within one chapter rather than in two separate chapters called "Statistics" and "Probability." Furthermore, just as you found that the words *carrying* and *borrowing* mask the essential connectedness of these two procedures, so too the terms *statistics* and *probability* tend to mask the essential connectedness of these two fields.

For example, when we say that the average annual snowfall in Buffalo, New York, is 92.2 inches,[1] that does not mean that you should expect 92.2 inches of snow in Buffalo this year (or 92 or 90 inches, for that matter). There are variations in any phenomenon; this number represents an average from data collected over 42 winters. We cannot say with certainty that we will get 92 inches of snow this year. We cannot even say with certainty that Buffalo will get between 82 and 102 inches this year. However, the average gives us an idea of what we might expect. In this sense, it tells us that when we look at the snowfall data for Buffalo, this amount is more common—it is in the middle of the data that have been collected.

Similarly, when we say that the chance of flipping a coin and getting tails is 50%, this does not mean that we will get 5 tails if we flip a coin 10 times. Even with this event, with less variation than snowfall in Buffalo, there is variation and a lack of certainty. I have flipped many coins (I was particularly fascinated by this and the dice probabilities as a youngster). I have occasionally gotten only 2 tails out of 10 throws, and it is statistically possible, though improbable, to flip a coin 10 times and have 0 tails.

In everyday life, *uncertain* has several connotations: not known or established, not determined, not having sure knowledge, and subject to change.[2] In one sense, our study of statistics and probability is meant to make our conclusions about phenomena that are not certain to occur more reliable and trustworthy while at the same time recognizing the truth of Benjamin Franklin's statement.

Data Interpretation and Chance in Society

Collecting, organizing, describing, displaying, and interpreting data, as well as making decisions and predictions on the basis of that information, are skills that are increasingly important in a society based on technology and communication.

(*Curriculum Standards*, p. 54)

[1] *Information Please* (Boston: Houghton Mifflin, 1993), p. 392.
[2] *American Heritage Dictionary of the English Language*, 3d ed. (Boston: Houghton Mifflin, 1996), p. 1942.

Understanding uncertainty is a crucial skill that all citizens need, yet few have. There is much evidence that many students understand the fundamental ideas of statistics and probability even less well than they understand other ideas in the elementary school classroom. Not surprisingly, misuse of statistics—by politicians, special interest groups, entrepreneurs, and others—is pervasive. Sometimes the misuse is deliberate—for example, to manipulate decisions and opinion. However, often the misinterpretation of data occurs either out of ignorance or because the problem is very complex.

At the same time, investigating situations involving uncertainty can be some of the most exciting and informative work that you (and your students) will do in mathematics classrooms. Toward this end, I find that students need to experience statistics and probability more directly, and so the investigations have been fashioned with that in mind. The NCTM also urges more hands-on work with all aspects of what we call statistical analysis:

> Teachers should have a variety of experiences in the collection, organization, representation, analysis, and interpretation of data. Key statistical concepts for all teachers include measures of central tendency, measures of variation (range, standard deviation, interquartile range, and outliers), and general distributions. Representations of data should include various types of graphs, including bar, line, circle, and pictographs as well as line plots, stem-and-leaf plots, box plots, histograms, and scatter plots.
>
> (*Professional Standards,* p. 136)

There is another point about examining concepts in statistics and probability that is important to note: language. As you recall, the NCTM strongly emphasizes language in mathematics (Curriculum Standard 2). Many students report being intimidated by the language of mathematics. I hope you are coming to realize in this book that mathematical language can actually make mathematical ideas easier to understand and grasp. For example, the terms *digit* and *place* make it easier to discuss numeration, computation algorithms, and estimation strategies. There are a number of words used in this chapter that are used in everyday life, but that have a slightly different or more precise meaning in mathematics—for example, uncertainty, population, sampling, reliability, combination, and event. To get too technical is to lose readers; to stay too informal is to cause confusion. Therefore, I have made an attempt to stay away from either extreme.

SECTION 7.1

REPRESENTING AND INTERPRETING DATA

WHAT DO YOU THINK?

- How can the way a set of data is represented affect the way it is interpreted?
- How can the decisions about what data to collect affect the information learned from those data?
- Consider a representation or description of data that you have recently encountered. Was it accurate? How could you tell?

In this first section of the chapter, we will examine different methods for describing and interpreting data. In the course of this work, most of you will learn more about events outside the classroom, too.

In each of the investigations in this section, you will initially be presented with a set of data or a graph. You will be asked to record your initial impressions and conclusions. You will also be asked to note questions you have about the data or the graph. We will discuss two kinds of questions: (1) questions about aspects of the data or graph that you don't understand, and (2) questions about the reliability and validity of the data—two issues that also come up repeatedly in this chapter's explorations. Questions about reliability ask whether two people collecting the data would get the same numbers. Questions about validity ask if the methods used to collect the data are sound. Addressing all the questions that people have is beyond the scope of this book; therefore, the discussion of the data and graphs will focus on the questions that seem most important. Another reason for emphasizing questions is to encourage you to develop a critical mind when examining any data or graph.[3]

INVESTIGATION **7.1** Viceocassette Recorders

Although videocassette recorders (VCRs) are almost everywhere now, they are a relatively recent invention. In this first investigation, we will examine two commonly used graphs and some of the problems involved in making them. Take a minute to examine the data in Table 7.1. First, describe the growth of VCRs, as mathematically as possible, as if you were talking to someone on the phone. Please be more precise than, "Wow, they sure got popular fast." Second, describe any questions you have about the data. Then read on. . . .

TABLE 7.1

Year	U.S. households with VCRs ('000s)
1978	200
1979	400
1980	840
1981	1,440
1982	2,530
1983	4,580
1984	8,880
1985	17,600
1986	30,920
1987	42,560
1988	51,930
1989	58,400
1990	66,940

Source: *The Universal Almanac 1992*, John W. Wright, General Editor. (Andrews and McMeel [A Universal Press Syndicate Company], Kansas City), p. 253.

DISCUSSION

At the most basic level, Table 7.1 shows that the number of U.S. households with VCRs increased every year. At a slightly more sophisticated level, using our knowledge of multiplication and estimation, we can say that the number of households with VCRs just about doubled every year until 1987.

Possible questions about this table include: What does ('000s) mean? What has happened since 1990? Since the table starts in 1978, does that mean that that was the year in which VCRs were first sold? Who collected the data, and how did they get these numbers?

Many people wonder what ('000s) means. This is a convention that graph makers use when dealing with large numbers. There are two equivalent ways to "decode" this symbol: "write three zeros after each number in the table to get the actual numbers" or "each number is in the thousands; thus 200 means two hundred thousand." Recall our discussions about the choice of unit in Chap-

---

[3] Note that *critical* here does not refer to criticizing, but rather to critical in the sense of "characterized by careful, exact evaluation and judgment" [*The American Heritage College Dictionary*, 3d ed. (Boston: Houghton Mifflin, 1996), p. 443]. Reproduced by permission.

ter 5. From this perspective, '000 means that the graph makers chose 1,000 instead of 1 as the unit.

Graphing these data   Now let us examine how a graph can help us to see the data better. What kind of graph do you think might best describe these data?[4] Make your own graph with graph paper first, before reading on. . . . 🖎

Look at the two graphs in Figure 7.1 and address the following questions: What do they tell us about the growth of VCRs? Are both graphs "correct," or is one "better" than the other? Summarize the pros and cons of each graph. Then read on. . . . 🖎

U.S. Households with VCRs

U.S. Households with VCRs

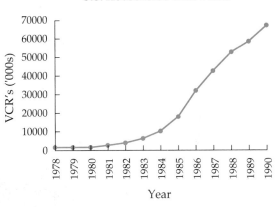

FIGURE **7.1**

Both of these graphs are valid ways to represent these data. Many people prefer **bar graphs** to **line graphs,** finding the former easier to understand. The primary advantage of the line graph has to do with slope. If you recall from algebra, in a linear equation, the slope is constant, and so a straight line indicates constant growth. However, when the slope keeps increasing, that indicates that the rate of growth is increasing, and we refer to such growth as exponential. The line graph more clearly shows that the rate of increase started to slow down in 1986.

Finally, let us recall the discussion at the beginning of the chapter about uses of data. Other than satisfying curiosity, what use might these data and these graphs serve? Think and read on. . . . 🖎

An individual deciding to invest in the stock market would probably be less interested in an area whose growth was slowing down rather than picking up. Someone doing a report on the growth of the home entertainment industry might want to see how and when the VCR market grew.

INVESTIGATION **7.2** World Population

Graphs can also serve an educational purpose by helping us to "see" numbers better. For example, most people know that more people live in Asia than in any other region of the world. Let us examine how graphs can help us to understand world population in a new light. Take a minute to examine the data in Table 7.2. As before, first describe what the data tell

[4] The word *data* is the plural of the word *datum.* Therefore, it is correct to say that "data *are* used" and "the data *support* the following conclusion."

you and then describe any questions you have about the data. Then read on. . . . 🖎

TABLE 7.2

World population, by region (1990)

Africa	647,518,000
Asia	3,108,475,000
North America	275,880,000
Latin America	448,096,000
Europe	497,740,000
Former USSR	287,990,000
Oceania	26,476,000

Source: *Universal Almanac 1992*, pp. 317–318.

DISCUSSION

There are many conclusions that we can draw from these data. Two are that the population of Asia is much greater than that of any other region, and that the population of Africa is more than double the population of North America.

There are many possible questions that people can ask about these data: Why did the people who made this table divide the world into these regions? What do they mean by Latin America (for example, does this include Central America or the Caribbean)? How did they get these numbers? How accurate are the numbers?

Changing units   Many people report being overwhelmed by all the numbers. People who make tables take this into account by changing the unit used to report the figures. For example, look at Table 7.3, giving the same data. Can you see more from this table?

TABLE 7.3

Region	Population (millions)
Africa	648
Asia	3,108
North America	276
Latin America	448
Europe	498
Former USSR	288
Oceania	26

Recalling our discussions of unit in Chapter 5, we can say that the second table uses 1 million persons as the unit instead of 1 person. Many people find that relative comparisons are easier to make when the unit is larger. For example, many people can more easily see that the population of Africa is almost 400 million more than that of North America, or that there are more than twice as many people in Africa as in North America.

Graphing these data   Let us now consider how we might display these data. Make your own graph(s) first, before reading on. . . . 🖎

Now look at the two graphs in Figure 7.2. What do they tell us about the population of different regions? Are both graphs "correct," or is one "better" than the other? Summarize the pros and cons of each graph. Does your graph resemble one of these, or did you do something different?

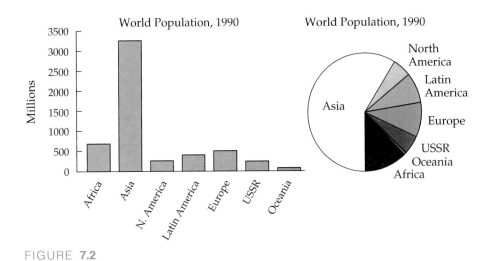

FIGURE **7.2**

In this case, a line graph would not be appropriate. In general, a line graph is used when we want to look at changes in data over time. However, a bar graph is still appropriate, and is commonly used when our independent variable consists of categories rather than numbers. In this case, a circle graph is also appropriate. Let us first compare the pros and cons of bar and circle graphs and then discuss the construction of circle graphs.

The main advantage of the bar graph is that we don't lose any data; for example, from the bar graph, we can see that the population of Asia is more than 3 billion, whereas in the circle graph, we lose the numbers. The main advantage of the circle graph has to do with fractions and parts of wholes. That is, we can quickly estimate what fraction of the entire world's people come from each region (for example, we can see that over half of the world's people live in Asia), whereas the relative proportions have to be deduced from the bar graph.

Constructing a circle graph Before reading on, first make a (rough) circle graph for these data freehand, that is, without a protractor. Then make a precise circle graph with a protractor. Then read on. . . .

In order to make a circle graph, we have to know what proportion (or percent) of the whole is represented by each group. To do that, we first have to find the entire population and then determine percentages, as in Table 7.4 on page 324. As always, I strongly suggest that you read this section actively — that you do the computations (either on a calculator or on a spreadsheet) and make a circle graph on your own paper.

Once we know the percent for each region, we can construct a rough circle graph. If you haven't done so yet, do so now before reading on. Note your reasoning, for there is no single "right" way.

TABLE 7.4

	Population (millions)	Percent	Degrees
Africa	648	12%	44°
Asia	3,108	59%	211°
North America	276	5%	19°
Latin America	448	8%	30°
Europe	498	9%	34°
Former USSR	288	5%	20°
Oceania	26	1%	2°
Total	5,292	99%	360°

Since the percentages have been rounded to the nearest whole number, the sum here is 99%.

To make a rough circle graph, we make use of proportional reasoning; that is, we look at the relative amounts. For example, if we recall that 25% is equivalent to 1/4, we can see that Africa will be about 1/2 of a quarter circle. Similarly, Latin America and Europe will each be about 1/3 of a quarter circle (see Figure 7.3). In one sense, we are using the quarter circle as a unit of measurement. Next, we see that North America and the former USSR are each slightly over 1/2 the size of Europe.

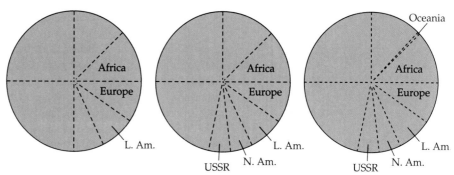

FIGURE **7.3**

The remainder of the circle should be Asia. If our work is accurate, then this should represent 59% of the circle. How might we check our work at this point?

We have one complete quarter circle (25%) and one almost complete quarter circle (23% or 24%), and we have just under half of another quarter circle (12%). The sum of these three numbers is 60, which is pretty close to 59.

In order to make an exact circle graph, we need to know how many degrees each wedge will be. How do we determine this? Work on this yourself before reading on. . . . 🖎

There are several ways to do this. We can make and solve a proportion. That is, if Africa is 12% of the total population, then 12 out of 100 is equal to x out of 360. Alternatively, we can see that we need to calculate 12% of 360. To be even more accurate, we would use the original population figures:

$$\frac{648}{5{,}292} \times 360.$$

In either case, we find that the Africa slice of the circle will be about 44°. We can now use a protractor to determine the size of each slice.

The placement of each slice in a circle graph is a matter of preference. Some people start by drawing a horizontal line to the right of the center of the circle, as I did in Figure 7.3. However, some people start by drawing a vertical line above the center of the circle. Some people prefer to order the slices from largest to smallest, whereas other people prefer to arrange them by geographical proximity—for example, placing North America and Latin America next to each other.

INVESTIGATION 7.3   AIDS

Thus far, we have examined three fundamental kinds of graphs: line graphs, bar graphs, and circle graphs. In the next three investigations, we will examine some of the issues involved in the construction and interpretation of graphs. You may have encountered some of these issues yourself in Explorations 7.1 and 7.2.

Take a minute to think about what you know about the AIDS epidemic. Then look at the data in Table 7.5. Describe your initial conclusions from the data. In other words, what do the data tell us about the epidemic? Think and then read on. . . .

TABLE 7.5   AIDS in the United States

	Cases diagnosed this year	Cases diagnosed to date	Known deaths this year	Known deaths to date
1981	392	392	163	163
1982	1,110	1,502	449	612
1983	2,974	4,476	1,465	2,077
1984	5,994	10,470	3,343	5,420
1985	11,263	21,733	6,623	12,043
1986	18,277	40,010	11,356	23,399
1987	27,172	67,182	15,279	38,678
1988	32,669	99,851	19,602	58,280
1989	36,110	135,961	24,761	83,041
1990	30,704	166,665	22,236	105,277

DISCUSSION

From the first column, we see that the number of new cases diagnosed each year increased every year until 1990. We see that in the earlier years, the number of new cases rose *substantially*. For example, there were almost three times as many cases diagnosed in 1982 as in 1981, and more than twice as many in 1983 as in 1982. We are looking at exponential growth rather than linear growth. When a disease is characterized by exponential growth, we use the word *epidemic*.

Graphing these data   Why might we want to make a graph for these data? Think and then read on. . . .

The graph can help us to visualize the data. For example, if we graph the "Cases diagnosed to date," we can see the growth of the epidemic. It will be helpful if you make your own line graph for these data before reading on. . . .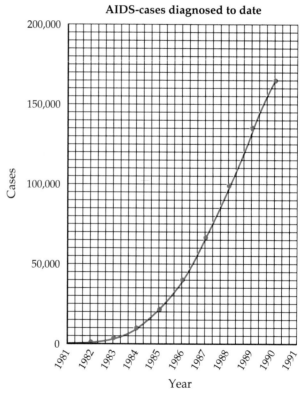

As you made the graph, what difficulties (if any) did you encounter? How did you solve them?

Figure 7.4 shows a line graph for the "Cases diagnosed to date" data. Although a bar graph would not be "wrong," as discussed before, a line graph enables us to better see the change in the data over time, and so it is preferable for these data. One of the problems that many students struggle with is to determine the scale for these data—that is, our unit of measurement for this graph. If you are plotting these data by hand, and you want one sheet of graph paper to contain the data, each vertical interval on a sheet of typical graph paper will need to stand for about 5,000 or 10,000 cases. In Figure 7.4, the scale (unit) is 5,000 cases for each vertical line.

Suppose a classmate who was having difficulty asked you, "How do you know exactly where to put 21,733 (the 1985 figure)?" How would you explain how you made that decision?

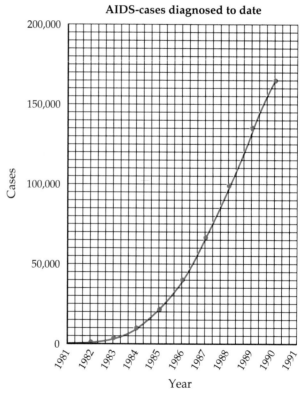

AIDS-cases diagnosed to date

FIGURE **7.4**

Once again proportional reasoning is useful. We can see that 21,733 is between 20,000 and 25,000. More specifically, we are concerned with what part 1,733 is of the whole (5,000). Basic estimation tells us that this point is about 1/3 of the way from 20,000 to 25,000.

A common graphing mistake There are other issues related to scale that need to be addressed. One major mistake that people commonly make is that they choose one unit for part of the graph and then choose another unit for another part of the graph. For example, it is not uncommon for students to make graphs like the one in Figure 7.5. Do you see what the students did? Why is it wrong?

AIDS-cases diagnosed to date

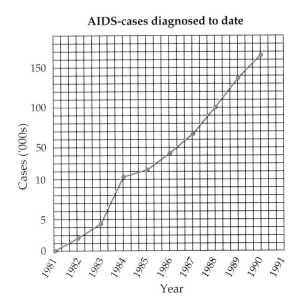

FIGURE **7.5**

What the students did was to have two different vertical units on the same graph. That is, for the first ten vertical intervals, the unit is 1,000 cases; thereafter, the unit is 10,000 cases. The rationale for the different scale is that by doing this, they can place the smaller numbers more accurately. However, changing the unit (or scale) on a graph is not acceptable. Why do you think this is so?

It changes the appearance of the graph dramatically. For example, Figure 7.5 implies that the rate of the epidemic slowed down after 1985, when in fact that was not true.

On the other hand, there is no single "right" answer to what is the "best" unit—for example, 5,000 or 10,000 or 20,000 or 25,000. In general, the smaller the unit, the better we can see trends in the data. However, the smaller the unit, the bigger the graph.

Horizontal spacing This issue of scale and unit also applies to the horizontal spacing. For example, one can choose to have more or less horizontal space between the years, as long as the spacing is constant—that is, as long as each year is the same distance from the previous year. Although there are no rights and wrongs with respect to these decisions, the choice of units *will* alter the graph's appearance. For example, the two graphs in Figure 7.6 represent the same data, and the vertical scale is identical. The difference is that in the graph at the left, the years are closer together. Do you see, though, why both graphs are considered to be correct?

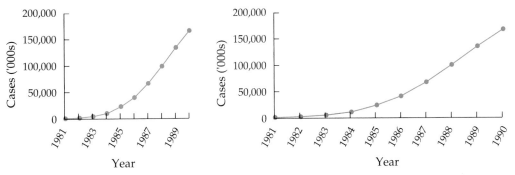

FIGURE **7.6**

Although the two graphs appear to be very different, they are mathematically equivalent. For example, the number of cases in 1985 was double the number of cases in 1984. In both graphs, the point representing 1985 is twice as high as the point representing 1984.

INVESTIGATION 7.4   Life Expectancy Over the Past 70 Years

We frequently use graphs not simply to "see" or analyze one set of data, but to compare two sets of data. Table 7.6 shows average life expectancy in the United States since 1920. What are your first impressions from examining the data? What questions do you have about the data? Think and then read on. . . .

TABLE 7.6 Life Expectancy in the United States		
	Males	**Females**
1920	53.6	54.6
1930	58.1	61.6
1940	60.8	65.2
1950	65.6	71.1
1960	66.6	73.1
1970	67.1	74.7
1980	70.0	77.4
1990	71.5	78.3

DISCUSSION

A quick look shows that the life expectancy for both males and females has increased every decade and that during this time period, the female life expectancy has always been greater than the male life expectancy.

Before graphing these data and examining what a graph can show us, let us stop and think about what the data actually mean. For example, what does 71.5 years (the 1990 number for males) actually mean?

These numbers are actually **predictions** (which represent **probabilities**). The 71.5 means that the authors of the table are *predicting* that if we were to take all the males born in the United States in 1990 and go forward in time to a point when they had all died, the "average" lifetime of these males born in 1990 would be 71.5 years. Some would have lived fewer years — for example, died in childhood — and some would have lived more years, but the average lifetime of all these males would have been 71.5 years. That is, the authors of the table are predicting that 71.5 years is the most probable lifetime.

Graphing these data   From the data, we have a general sense that the life expectancies are getting longer, but a graph would give us a visual sense of the data. What kind of graph do you think would best help us to see both the male and female life expectancies over this time period? Think and then read on. . . .

Although a bar graph would not be wrong, a line graph enables us to see changes over time more clearly. What do you "see" from the graph in Figure 7.7? Describe your reactions before reading on. . . .

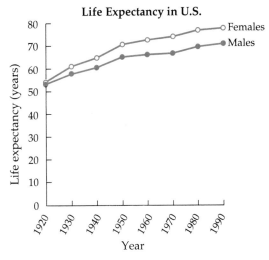

FIGURE **7.7**

We can see that the life expectancies of both males and females were increasing at a faster rate between 1920 and 1950 than they were between 1950 and 1990. However, the data are all crammed into the top part of the graph. To better see trends in the data, we can "zoom" in on the data. In Figure 7.8, the vertical scale begins at 50 years, since all of the data are above 50. What additional conclusions can you draw from this graph?

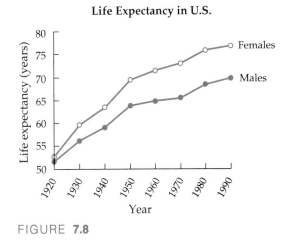

FIGURE **7.8**

We can see that in some decades, the life expectancy of women grew faster than that of men (that is, the line is steeper). We can see that since 1970, the two graphs are more parallel than before, indicating a similar growth rate. From this graph, we can also more accurately estimate the actual numbers. For example, if you did not have the data but only the graph and wanted to estimate the life expectancies in 1990, you could make a more accurate estimate from the Figure 7.8 than from Figure 7.7.

Interpreting Graphs

In everyday life, we generally don't collect data and graph data as much as we interpret other people's graphs of data that they or yet other people have collected. The ability to interpret and to critique graphs is important. As we will find, many times, a graph distorts the data. Sometimes this is intentional on the part of the people making the graph, whereas other times it is unintentional, the result of carelessness or ignorance on the part of the people who made the graph.

In Explorations 7.1 and 7.2, we critically examined data collected by other people and then constructed graphs. In the next three investigations, we will critically examine graphs made by other people. As you read each graph, I encourage you to think about three kinds of questions before you read the discussion. As always, if you write down your responses, you are likely to retain more from your work.

Conclusions What conclusion(s) can I draw from the graph? What is the graph telling me? What do the labels and numbers mean?

Fairness/appropriateness/reasonableness Is the graph fair? Would another graph be more appropriate? Do the data from which the graph was made seem reasonable?

Reliability/validity What questions would I ask of the people who collected the data or made the graphs? Do I need more information to be able to better interpret the data?

Let us begin with a graph that indicates hopeful news.

INVESTIGATION 7.5 Fatal Crashes

Examine the graph in Figure 7.9 and answer each of the three kinds of questions before reading on. . . .

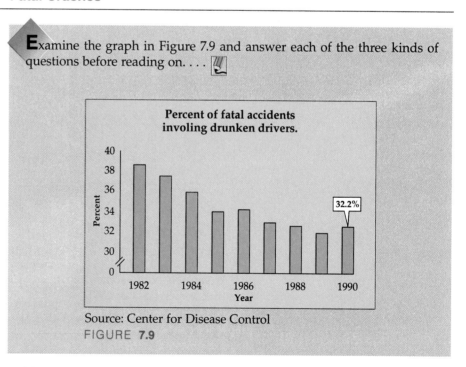

Source: Center for Disease Control
FIGURE **7.9**

DISCUSSION

One student wrote the following: "The percent of fatal car crashes in which the driver was drunk fell dramatically between 1982 and 1990." What do you think of her summary? Think and then read on. . . .

Actually, there are several problems with the student's summary. First, the data don't seem to be restricted to just car crashes. What kinds of "fatal crashes" do you think count in these data? Think and then read on. . . .

Other kinds of fatal crashes include crashes between two motor vehicles (trucks, cars, motorcycles) in which one or both drivers were drunk, single motor vehicle accidents in which the driver was drunk, and possibly accidents in which a motor vehicle hit a pedestrian or a person on a bicycle.

A second problem with the student's summary has to do with what "drunk" means. What do the graph makers mean by "drunk"? How did the people who recorded the data know that a driver was drunk? How were the data gathered? Think and then read on. . . .

It seems reasonable to expect that there are data for every motor vehicle accident in which there was a fatality. However, how did the people who recorded the data determine the number of such accidents in which at least one driver was drunk? Did a sobriety test or a blood test show that the person was drunk? Furthermore, the definition of *drunk* varies from state to state: In some states, a person with a blood alcohol level of 0.08% is considered drunk, whereas in other states the blood alcohol level has to be 0.10%.

Now let us examine the student's use of the word *dramatically* to describe the change in fatalities. Look back at the graph—what does the jagged line just below 30% mean? Think and then read on. . . .

It means that this is a **truncated graph,** that is, the authors of this graph deleted the 0%–30% interval. In the previous investigation, we truncated the life expectancy graph so that we could zoom in on the actual data. Why else might someone want to truncate a graph? Think and then read on. . . .

Sometimes graphs are truncated to save space. However, sometimes they are truncated to distort the data. Let us see how the graph would look if it had not been truncated (see Figure 7.10). How does the decline in the percentage of drunk drivers in fatal accidents look now? Think and then read on. . . .

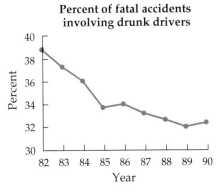

FIGURE **7.10**

As you can see, the decline does not seem so great in the untruncated graph. The actual percent decrease from 39 to 32 is about an 18% decrease (that is, $\frac{39 - 32}{39} = 0.18 = 18\%$).

Which graph would you have picked if you were working for a beer company preparing an advertisement showing that drunk driving is on the decline? What if you were a member of SADD (Students Against Drunk Driving)?

What do the numbers mean? Let us examine two more aspects of this graph. In 1982, the number of fatal crashes involving drunk drivers was about 39%.

Write a sentence describing what that 39 means, as if you were talking to someone who didn't understand, then read on. . . .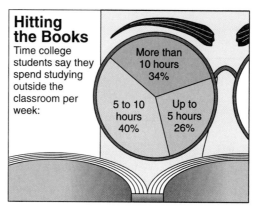

Below are two of many possible responses.

■ In 1982, 39% of all fatal motor vehicle accidents involved a drunk driver.

■ In 1982, of every 100 fatal motor vehicle accidents, 39 involved a drunk driver.

Pseudo-precision   Another aspect of the graph worth examining is the 1990 figure of 32.2%. This figure looks very precise—that is, not 32.1% or 32.3%, but 32.2%. Are the actual data really that precise? Think and then read on. . . .

Let's say there were 253 fatal accidents in a state, and that state reported that drunken drivers were involved in 98 of them. That state could report that 38.7% of the fatal accidents involved drunk drivers. Given the discussion above, how much room for error do you think there is? Think and then read on. . . .

Let's say that we determine that this number might be off by as much as 5. That is, it is possible that the actual number of accidents involving a drunk driver could have been as low as 93 or as high as 103. What would the percentages have been in those cases? Think and then read on. . . .

If the actual number had been 93, the percentage would have been 36.8%; if the actual number had been 103, the percentage would have been 40.7%. Given the possible sources of error in the data—definition of drunk, definition of fatal (does it mean that an injured person dies within 24 hours, 1 week, 1 month?), and likely inconsistency among different states—the 32.3% is another example of pseudo-precision.

Questions   Finally, let us examine additional questions that we might ask. What do you predict has happened since 1990? Do you think the percentage has leveled off or has continued to decline? Where could you go to find out? What other data would you like to see?

I N V E S T I G A T I O N   **7.6**   **Hitting the Books**

Take a few moments to examine the graph below. As in Investigation 7.5 and Explorations 7.1 and 7.2, a critical aspect of this examination is asking yourself questions about conclusions, fairness, and reliability. Write your responses to these questions before reading on. . . .

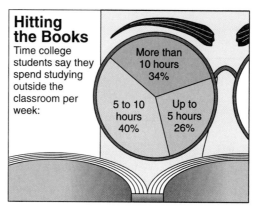

Hitting the Books
Time college students say they spend studying outside the classroom per week:

More than 10 hours 34%

5 to 10 hours 40%

Up to 5 hours 26%

Source: Copyright 1992, *USA Today.* Reprinted with Permission.

FIGURE **7.11**

DISCUSSION

Describing the graph   Critique the following two statements, which represent conclusions that people have made from this graph.

■ Barely one-third of college students study more than 10 hours per week.

■ Most college students average less than two hours a day on homework.

The first conclusion is simply taken straight from the graph: "Barely 1/3" is consistent with 34%. The second statement represents a valid interpretation of the graph, since less than half of the students spend more than 10 hours a week.

What do the data mean?   Now let us look beyond the first impressions to examine what the data mean. If you could meet with the people who collected these data, what questions would you ask? Think and then read on. . . . 🖎

Below are three of many possible questions that we might ask. As you read these questions and consider your own questions, ask yourself if the answers to these questions would make a difference. Then read on. . . . 🖎

■ How did you get the data (take a survey outside the dining commons, have questionnaires filled out in some classes)?

■ What kind of students are included (full-time, a "representative" sample)?

■ What did you ask—for example, did you ask, "About how many hours did you study last week?" or, "Last week, did you spend less than 5 hours studying, between 5 and 10 hours, or more than 10 hours?"

As you may have seen in Exploration 7.3 (Typical Person), the way in which we gather data can make a big difference in how the graph appears. For example, if the questions were asked of students coming out of the dining commons, that means that off-campus students were not asked. And if off-campus students tend to study a lot more or less than on-campus students, this could change the data quite a bit. Similarly, if the data included both part-time and full-time students, the number of hours reported would naturally go down. Why is this? Finally, how we ask the question has an influence on our data. You might want to replicate this study on your own campus and compare the results of asking the question in two different ways.

Choice of graph   The makers of this graph chose a circle graph. What other choices would be appropriate, or is the circle graph the "best" choice? What do you think? 🖎

In this case, it is more a case of personal preference. Circle graphs work well when we are looking at parts of wholes. In this case, the whole represents all students, and the makers of the graph have divided the whole into three subsets. However, a bar graph would not be wrong.

INVESTIGATION **7.7**   **Presence of Parents**

Figure 7.12 presents some very sobering data about the status of American families. However, it is not a simple graph. Take a minute to look at it. Do you understand what it means? If not, focus on just one bar—for example, 1992 "All races"—and think about what you know about percent. Then read on. . . . 🖎

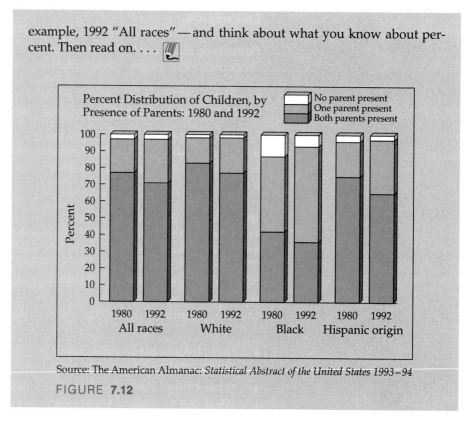

Source: The American Almanac: *Statistical Abstract of the United States 1993–94*

FIGURE **7.12**

DISCUSSION

Let us look at the 1992 "All races" bar to make sure you are interpreting the graph correctly. According to the data, in 1992, about 70% of all children lived with both parents, about 26% or 27% lived with one parent, and about 3% or 4% lived with neither of their parents.

Why did the authors choose this kind of graph, called a stacked bar graph? Think and then read on. . . . 🖎

Since all the data are in percentages, the total height of the bars in each column is equal. This makes it much easier to compare (among white, black, and Hispanic) the percentages of children that live with both parents; in other words, we can make proportional (multiplicative) comparisons. For example, we can say that a black child in 1992 is more than twice as likely to live with neither parent than is a white child, since the "No parent present" segment of the bar for blacks is more than twice as long as the "No parent present" segment for whites.

After examining these bar graphs, one of my students suddenly stopped and said, "Wait a minute, the stacked bar graph combines the advantages of a bar graph and a circle graph." Do you see that? If not, go back and look at the earlier discussion of the advantages of bar and circle graphs. Do you see how this kind of graph retains the advantages of bar graphs and incorporates the advantages of circle graphs?

Summary

What have you learned about how to describe data and interpret graphs? Write your thoughts before reading on. . . . 🖎

We have examined three basic kinds of graphs: line graphs, bar graphs, and circle graphs.

We have learned that in some cases, which graph is made is a matter of preference, and that each graph has certain characteristics that we might want to use:

■ Line graphs enable us to see change over time.

■ Bar graphs enable us to compare the quantity of each category.

■ Circle graphs enable us to see the part each category is of the whole.

We have learned that we need to take care that our graph does not distort the data. For example, we need to be careful when choosing the units for our spacing, both horizontally and vertically, in line graphs and bar graphs.

We have also learned that when interpreting others' graphs, we need to think about what the data mean and how the data were gathered, and we need to realize that some graphs are distorted, either intentionally or out of ignorance or carelessness. At the same time, we have learned that although a truncated graph does indeed distort the data, there are times when it has advantages. We have learned that whether we are making graphs from data collected by other people or interpreting graphs made by other people, it is important to carefully examine the data and the graphs with respect to fairness, appropriateness, reasonableness, reliability and validity. "Students should begin to develop a critical attitude toward information presented in the media and learn to ask relevant questions before making judgments based on that information."[5]

My hope is that the graphs and discussions in this section have inspired many of you to investigate some of these topics further on your own.

[5] Center for Statistical Education and the American Statistical Association, *Teaching Statistics: Guidelines for Elementary Through High School*, Dale Seymour Publications, p. 23.

EXERCISES 7.1

1. The table below is taken from a research project reported in the *International Journal of Educational Research* in 1990. The researchers surveyed hundreds of teachers at four different grade levels in 1977 and in 1985–86. The numbers in the "Male," "Female," and "Missing" columns are percentages.

   a. Select and make an appropriate graph for these data. Justify your choice.

   b. Write a brief summary of this information to accompany the graph.

SEX OF MATHEMATICS TEACHER BY GRADE RANGE

	1977				1985–86			
Grade	Male	Female	Missing	Sample *N*	Male	Female	Missing	Sample *N*
K–3	6	94	0	297	4	93	3	433
4–6	21	76	2	277	20	79	1	246
7–9	54	46	0	550	45	51	4	671
10–12	68	32	0	548	53	46	1	565

Source: Iris R. Weiss, "Perspectives on Research in Mathematics Education," *International Journal of Educational Research*, 14, No. 2 (1990), 140.

2. The following data are taken from a delightful book called *The Unofficial U.S. Census: What the U.S. Census Doesn't Tell You* by Tom Heymann.

   a. Select and make an appropriate graph for these data. Justify your choice.

   b. Write a brief summary to accompany the graph.

NEW YEAR'S RESOLUTION, BY NUMBER
MADE AND LENGTH OF TIME KEPT—
NUMBER MADE: 91,200,000

Length of time keeping resolution	Number keeping
1 week	70,224,000
1 month	50,160,000
6 months	36,480,000
2 years	17,328,000

Source: Tom Heymann, *The Unofficial U.S. Census: What the U.S. Census Doesn't Tell You* (New York: Ballantine Books, 1991), p. 137.

3. It is estimated that 36 million Americans were the victim of a crime last year, but that 22 million of these victims did not report the crime. The following table gives the estimated numbers for the eight most common reasons people gave for not reporting a crime.

Reason for not reporting crime	Number
The crime was not successfully completed	5,676,000
Perceived lack of proof	2,354,000
Private matter	1,606,000
No ID number on lost property	1,518,000
Police would not want to be bothered	1,430,000
Too inconvenient	748,000
Police would not be able to help	594,000
Fear of reprisal	286,000

Source: Tom Heymann, *The Unofficial U.S. Census: What the U.S. Census Doesn't Tell You* (New York: Ballantine Books, 1991), p. 118.

a. Select and make an appropriate graph for these data. Justify your choice.
b. Write a brief summary to accompany the graph.
c. How do you think the author obtained these data?
d. How accurate do you think the data are?
e. What other data would you like to see?

4. The data below are taken from the 1989–1990 National Fire Protection Association survey.

Month	Percent of fires	Time of day	Percent of fires
January	14.1	Midnight–1:59	14.0
February	11.4	2–3:59	15.9
March	10.3	4–5:59	11.4
April	7.8	6–7:59	8.4
May	6.5	8–9:59	7.8
June	5.0	10–11:59	6.5
July	5.4	Noon–1:59	5.4
August	5.2	2–3:59	4.6
September	5.3	4–5:59	4.3
October	7.7	6–7:59	4.8
November	8.7	8–9:59	6.5
December	12.7	10–11:59	10.5

Source: 1989–1990 National Fire Incident Reporting System, National Fire Protection Association survey.

a. Select and make an appropriate graph for the "Month" data. Justify your choice.
b. Write a brief summary to accompany the graph.
c. Why do you think more fires occurred in December, January, February, and March?
d. Select and make an appropriate graph for the "Time of day" data. Justify your choice.
e. Write a brief summary to accompany the graph.
f. Why do you think more fires occurred between 10 P.M. and 6 A.M.?

Exercises 5 and 6 refer to data presented in the *Journal for Research in Mathematics Education* concerning the composition of the over 80,000 members of the National Council of Teachers of Mathematics.

5.

YEARS OF TEACHING EXPERIENCE

Years	Percent
Less than 3	4.6
4–9	13.3
10–19	28.1
Greater than 20	54.0

Source: Mary M. Lindquist, "President's Report: Tides of Change—Teachers at the Helm," *Journal for Research in Mathematics Education*, 24, No. 5 (November 1993), 470.

a. Select and make an appropriate graph for the data. Justify your choice.
b. Some students don't like these categories. Either defend the choice of these four categories for all teachers' experience or suggest and defend a different categorization.

6.

AGE OF THE NCTM MEMBERS

Age	Percent
Less than 30	6.7
30–39	16.6
40–49	47.3
50–59	24.1
60 or over	5.3

Source: Mary M. Lindquist, "President's Report: Tides of Change—Teachers at the Helm," *Journal for Research in Mathematics Education*, 24, No. 5 (November 1993), 470.

a. Select and make an appropriate graph for the data. Justify your choice.
b. If you were in charge of the data, would you have used these age groupings or different ones? Explain your answer.

7. The National Education Association presented the following information concerning single-parent families:

	1980	1992
Male parent only	690,000	1,472,000
Female parent only	6,230,000	9,028,000

Source: *NEA Today,* 12, No. 5 (December 1993), 16.

a. What conclusions can you make about the changes in the relative proportion of fathers and mothers heading single-parent families between 1980 and 1992?

b. Select and make an appropriate graph for the data. Justify your choice.

c. What other conclusions can you draw from these data?

8. The National Education Association reported the highest education attainment levels for adults in the United States in 1990. Select and make an appropriate graph for the data below. Justify your choice.

Category	Percent
Eighth grade or less	10.4
Some high school, no diploma	14.4
High school diploma	30.0
Some college, no degree	18.7
Associate degree	6.2
Bachelor's degree	13.1
Graduate degree	7.2

Source: *NEA Today,* 12, No. 6 (February 1994), 32.

9. The table below gives data on the SAT test.

Type of Test and Characteristic	TEST SCORES			
	1970	1980	1990	1992
Verbal, total	460	424	424	423
Male	459	428	429	428
Female	461	420	419	419
Math, total	488	466	476	476
Male	509	491	499	499
Female	465	443	455	456

Source: *The American Almanac: Statistical Abstract of the United States, 1993–1994,* p. 170.

a. Select and make an appropriate graph for these data. Justify your choice.

b. Write a brief summary to accompany the graph.

c. Describe the trends you see in the data. Predict the scores for 1995.

d. Check out the scores from 1995.

10. The table below shows certain vital statistics for selected countries in 1993.

Country	Birth rate*	Death rate	Expectation of life at birth	Infant mortality rate
United States	15.5	8.7	75.8	8.4
Bangladesh	35.4	11.9	54.7	109.2
Brazil	21.8	8.3	62.7	61.7
Canada	14.5	7.4	78.0	7.0
Cuba	17.1	6.5	76.7	10.5
Egypt	32.2	9.3	60.5	78.3
El Salvador	33.1	6.5	66.5	42.8
Ethiopia	45.4	14.2	52.2	108.8
India	29.1	10.5	58.1	80.5
Japan	10.3	7.2	79.2	4.3
Mexico	27.7	4.8	72.6	28.8
United Kingdom	13.6	10.9	76.5	7.4

Source: *The American Almanac: Statistical Abstract of the United States, 1993–1994,* p. 844.

*Number of births during 1 year per 1,000 persons (based on midyear population).

†Number of deaths during 1 year per 1,000 persons (based on midyear population).

‡Number of deaths of children under 1 year of age per 1,000 live births in a calendar year.

For each of the columns, do the following:

a. Select and make an appropriate graph for these data. Justify your choice.

b. Write a brief summary to accompany the graph.

c. Which rate surprised you the most? Why?

11. The table below gives the average monthly temperatures for Boston and Miami.

Month	Boston	Miami
January	26	68
February	28	69
March	34	70
April	46	73
May	57	76
June	68	78
July	72	80
August	71	81
September	64	78
October	53	76
November	41	71
December	31	68

a. How do you think these numbers were determined? That is, someone in Boston and Miami records the temperatures (high and low and possibly each hour) every day. What was done to those data in order to get the "average monthly temperature" for each month?

b. Select and make an appropriate graph for these data. Justify your choice.

c. Write a brief summary to accompany the graph.

12. The table below shows the U.S. immigration rate by decade, 1820–1990.

U.S. IMMIGRATION RATE BY DECADE, 1820–1990		
Period	Total number ('000s)	Rate per 1,000 U.S. pop.
1820–30	152	1.2
1831–40	599	3.9
1841–50	1,713	8.4
1851–60	2,598	9.3
1861–70	2,315	6.4
1871–80	2,812	6.2
1881–90	5,247	9.2
1891–1900	3,688	5.3
1901–10	8,795	10.4
1911–20	5,736	5.7
1921–30	4,107	3.5
1931–40	528	0.4
1941–50	1,035	0.7
1951–60	2,515	1.5
1961–70	3,322	1.7
1971–80	4,493	2.1
1981–90	7,338	2.9

Source: U.S. Immigration and Naturalization Service, *1990 Statistical Yearbook* (1991).

a. Describe your first impressions from examining these data. Are there any surprises?

b. Make two separate line graphs, one using the total number and one using the rate per 1,000 population. Describe the different impressions conveyed by the two graphs. Which graph do you think gives a "better" comparison of immigration to the United States? Why?

c. What did you learn about mathematics from this exercise?

d. What did you learn about immigration from this exercise?

13. The table below shows the 1990 population and the predicted population in 2025 (in millions) for the following regions. Make graphs to compare these two sets of figures.

Region	1990	2025
Africa	648	1,581
Asia	3,108	4,889
North America	276	333
Latin America	448	760
Europe	498	512
Oceania	26	39

Source: *Universal Almanac 1992*, pp. 317–18.

Exercises 14–26 contain graphs that you are asked to interpret. In each case, also describe any questions you have about the graphs with respect to fairness, reasonableness, appropriateness, validity, and reliability.

Births jump; more mothers working

Here is a look at child-bearing trends across the USA, according to a new Census report released today:

Births climb

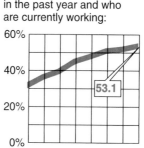

Birth rates by race/ethnic group

Births per 1,000 women age 15 to 44:

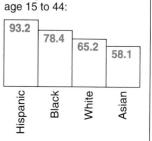

Working mothers with infants

Percentage of women 18-44 who have had a child in the past year and who are currently working:

Older mothers

Births per 1,000 women, by age group:

Source: *USA Today*, December 4, 1991. Copyright © 1991, USA TODAY. Reprinted with permission.

14. Write a one- or two-sentence summary of the "Births climb" graph that a newscaster might read as the graph appeared on the screen.

15. Examine the graph "Birth rates by race/ethnic group."

   a. Compare the birth rates of the four groups in at least two different ways—for example, additive, percent difference, ratios.

   b. Explain what "Births per 1,000 women age 15 to 44" means.

16. Examine the "Working mothers with infants" graph. Summarize the changes in the data between 1976 and 1990.

17. Examine the "Older mothers" graph.

   a. Explain this graph as if you were talking to someone who is completely baffled by the graph. You can assume that this person can read simple graphs.

   b. Summarize the changes in the data between 1980 and 1990.

   c. Which age group had the highest percent increase in birth rate? Explain how you got your answer.

18. The graph below shows who is getting AIDS and at what age.

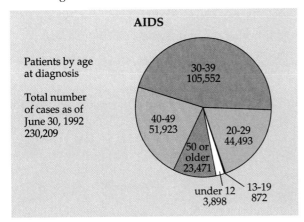

a. Summarize the graph as if for an article to accompany the graph.

b. Why do you think there are more cases among people under 12 than among the 13–19 age group?

c. If you were in charge of writing the article, would you have chosen to represent the data with a bar graph or with another type of graph? Justify your answer.

19. The graph below shows U.S. AIDS patients by race.

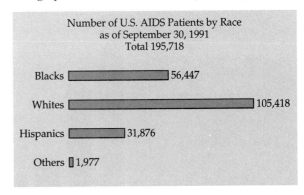

a. Summarize this graph as if for an article to accompany the graph.

b. The number of blacks and Hispanics is disproportionate. Explain what this statement means.

20. Examine the graph below called "Redefiining the American family."

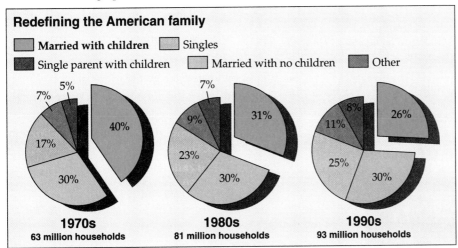

Source: "Redefining the American Family" from *The Boston Globe,* October 4, 1992. Reprinted by permission.

a. Compare the American family in 1970 and 1990, as if you were writing an article to accompany the graph.

b. If you were in charge of writing the article, would you have chosen to represent the data with circle graphs or with another type of graph? Justify your answer.

21. The graph at the right is taken from the book, *Making the Grade in Mathematics.*

a. Summarize the graph as if you were writing a newspaper article to accompany the graph.

b. Describe and explain any questions you have concerning the reliability or validity of the data.

Percentage of time teachers led mathematic classes

Source: Harold W. Stevenson, Max Lummis, Shinying Lee, and James W. Stigler, *Making the Grade in Mathematics: Elementary School Mathematics in the United States, Taiwan, and Japan* (Reston, VA.: NCTM, 1990), p. 16. Reprinted with permission. All rights reserved.

22. Examine the "Drunk Drivers" graph below.

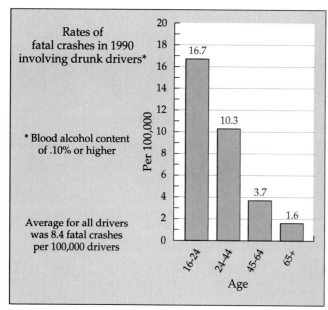

Source: National Highway Transportation Safety Administration.

a. Explain the meaning of the data in the graph (16.7, 10.3, 3.7, and 1.6) as if you were talking to someone who was completely baffled by the graph.

b. Write a sentence comparing the rates of the youngest group to those of the age 45–64 group.

23. Examine the "Birth and death in the USA" graph below.

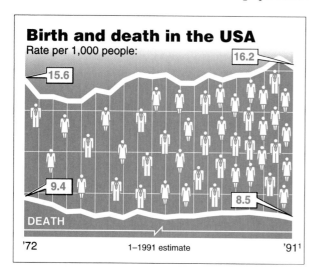

Source: "Birth and death in the USA" by Cliff Vancura from *USA Today* April 15, 1993. Copyright © 1993, USA TODAY. Reprinted with permission.

a. Many magazines and newspapers "dress up" graphs to make them more visually appealing. Summarize the graph by explaining what it tells you. Then discuss the advantage and disadvantage of the "dressing up of the graph."

b. Aaron says that we can use these data to conclude how fast the population is increasing: Just take the difference between births and deaths and then solve

the following proportion:

$$\frac{7.7}{1,000} = \frac{x}{250,000,000}$$

Do you agree or disagree with Aaron? Why?

24. The line graph below shows the proportion of young families who own their own homes.

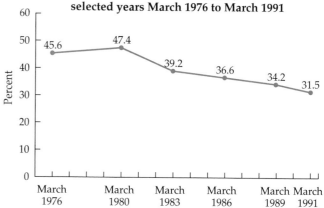

Source: Clifford M. Johnson, Andrew M. Sum, and James D. Weill, *Vanishing Dreams: The Economic Plight of America's Young Families* (Washington, D.C.: Children's Defense Fund, 1992), p. 24. Reprinted with permission.

a. Briefly summarize the graph.

b. Thelma says that the dots should be spaced evenly. What do you think?

25. The graph below shows the percentage of children in poverty in young families.

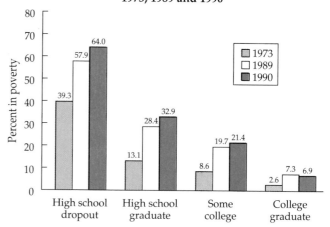

Source: Clifford M. Johnson, Andrew M. Sum, and James D. Weill, *Vanishing Dreams: The Economic Plight of America's Young Families* (Washington, D.C.: Children's Defense Fund, 1992), p. 10. Reprinted with permission.

a. Describe the changes in the poverty rates between 1973 and 1990 as if you were writing a newspaper article to accompany the graph.

b. Describe the relationship between education of the family head and poverty rate in 1990.

26. Examine the graph below. Have things improved or gotten worse between 1973 and 1990? Explain.

**Distribution of 20- to 29-year-old civilian males
by earnings, 1973 and 1990**
(in 1990 dollars)

Yearly earnings

Source: Clifford M. Johnson, Andrew M. Sum, and James D. Weill, *Vanishing Dreams: The Economic Plight of America's Young Families* (Washington, D.C.: Children's Defense Fund, 1992), p. 20. Reprinted with permission.

SECTION **7.2** DISTRIBUTIONS: CENTERS AND SPREADS

WHAT DO YOU THINK?

- What do we mean by average?
- How can there be different averages for the same set of data, depending on which center of a distribution you use?
- How can statistical analysis help us interpret and compare data?

In the previous section, we examined changes in populations over time (AIDS, fatal crashes), and we examined specific subsets of other populations (the world, students studying more than 10 hours). In this section, we will focus on analyzing populations in order to understand the distribution of the data within a population. This focus is consistent with what has been traditionally seen as statistical analysis.

Tools We Will Use

When we are presented with a set of data describing some characteristics of a population (income, height, age, and so on), there are three kinds of mathematical tools that are commonly used to better understand the population: (1) tools to help us determine the center of the population, sometimes called the typical or representative or average; (2) tools to tell us how the data are dispersed or spread, for example, the range of values, the quartiles, and the standard deviation; and (3) words to describe the overall distribution, such as uniform, normal, skewed, and random. These are not esoteric tools that only some people can understand. Rather, they are tools that are based on common sense. It is my hope that this section helps to demystify the word *statistics*. This section is critical because one of the most common uses of statistics is to gather information on a subset (called a sample) of a population in order to make generalizations about the whole population. Many of the examples of data collection and analysis cited at the beginning of the chapter involve sampling—for example, opinion polls, market research, and studies to determine if a vaccine is effective.

Lynn Steen edited a book called *On the Shoulders of Giants: New Approaches to Numeracy,* a book written by mathematicians to help mathematics educators and others realize the vision of the NCTM Standards. As we have seen, a key aspect of this vision is to get people to realize that mathematics is more than just numbers, formulas, and computations. The six chapter titles are especially relevant to this section: Pattern, Dimension, Quantity, Uncertainty, Shape, and Change. Much of the reason for collecting and analyzing data is to deal with *uncertainty* and to understand and predict *changes* in populations; we look for *patterns* and trends in the data; the *shape* of the data tells us much, and certain

HISTORY

The name of the book edited by Steen comes from a quotation from Isaac Newton, who most people think of as the guy who discovered gravity when the apple fell on his head. However, he is also one of the creators of calculus, which he developed to explain his observations in physics. Newton remarked, "If I have seen farther than others, it is because I have stood on the shoulders of giants."

quantities (mean, standard deviation) also tell us much about the data. *This* is what this chapter deals with: uncertainty and change, shapes, patterns, and quantities.

What Is Average?

Let us begin with the concept of average. When you hear the word *average*, what comes to mind? Think and then read on. . . . ✐

Most of my students wind up telling me how to find the mean; that is, "add all the values and divide by how many you have." However, *average* is not a formula; rather, it is one of many concepts that can help us to understand a population.

We see and use references to average all the time—for example, what is your grade point average, what is the average starting salary of a teacher these days? Some of the investigations in Section 7.1 dealt with averages—for example, average life expectancy. Can you think of other examples where you have seen or used the concept of average?

When we stop and think about it, we find that this concept is used frequently. Let me now ask you to reflect on another question: Why do we want to know the average this or the average that? ✐

Mean, Median, Mode

The idea of average was created (by somebodies, somewhere) so that one number or one word would give us a sense of the typical or representative of the data. Depending on the population we are studying and the question we are asking, we may find the "average" by determining the *mean*, the *median*, or the *mode*. Statisticians refer to the mean, median, and mode as **measures of central tendency** of a distribution, although this long term is being replaced simply by **measures of the center**.

In some cases, we want to know the **mean**, which we find by taking the sum of the data and dividing by the number of data. If you took five tests in a course, your instructor would generally determine your average score by using the mean—adding up the scores and dividing by 5. The 1994 *Information Please Almanac*[6] reports that the mean number of people in U.S. households in 1992 was 2.62.

In some cases, we want to know the **median**, which we find by determining the numerical middle of the data. For example, if you determined the height of all the students in your class and ordered the numbers from smallest to greatest, the number in the middle would be the median. If the number of students in the class is an even number, then there is no middle number. In that case, you "split the difference" of the two numbers closest to the middle; technically, you take the mean of those two numbers. The 1993–1994 *American Almanac*[7] reports that the median age in the United States in 1991 was 33.1 years.

In some cases, we want to know the **mode**, which is the datum that appears most often. The mode is often used when the characteristic we are studying is not a number. For example, if you were to collect data on what state the students in your class were born in, the mode would be the state that occurred

---

[6] *1994 Information Please* (Boston: Houghton Mifflin, 1993), p. 827.

[7] *The American Almanac: Statistical Abstract of the United States 1993–1994* (Austin, Tex.: The Reference Press, 1994), p. 15.

most frequently. We often use the word *typical* with mode. For example, the typical professional basketball player is over 6 feet. If you did Exploration 7.3, you defined *typical* for a specific population, you and your classmates in this course. When a newspaper reports that more women in the U.S. work force were employed in administrative support than in any other category, they are saying that when we examine the population of working women and look at the characteristic called "type of job," "administrative support" is the mode.

One of the reasons for determining the average of a set of data is that one number or one phrase tells us much about the data. Sometimes the mean, median, and mode are all candidates to be considered as the representative of the data. In some cases, the mean, median, and mode are very close, but sometimes they are not. Let me connect this notion of representative of a population to a real-life situation. When I was in the Peace Corps in Nepal, the country director told new volunteers that we needed to think about our behavior because we were representatives of the United States. In one sense, the director was referring to average. Because the people we worked with had had little or no previous contact with Americans, whatever we did, they would likely see as typical. If we wore blue jeans or drank alcohol, many people would likely generalize that all (or at least most) Americans wear blue jeans and drink alcohol. This relates directly to the notion of sampling—that is, making generalizations about a whole population based on data from a sample of the population.

Average is only one of several tools we use to better understand a population. Rather than explain the others now, let us move on to some investigations of average and see what we find. Again, this is a modeling of the NCTM problem-solving standard, in which teachers are encouraged to use problem-solving approaches to investigate and understand content. We will examine data for which it makes sense to ask about averages. In the following five investigations, we will examine graphs that can help us to "see" the data. We will discover some tools that help us to describe the center of the data and how the data are dispersed (spread). As in Section 7.1, we will also look critically at the data—what they mean, where they came from, and the like.

INVESTIGATION 7.8   Years of Experience

Let us begin with a relatively simple case and work toward more complex cases. Maplewood Elementary School is preparing its accreditation report. One of the questions on the report asks for the average years of experience of the staff. What do the people who prepare the report need to do to answer this question—that is, what data do they need, and what do they do with the data? Think and then read on. . . .

First, the people who prepare the report need to decide what "years of experience" means. Let's say they decide to interpret this question as the number of years of experience a teacher had at the beginning of the school year. However, they still have to decide what to do about teachers who taught part-time (job sharing) or taught for part of a year (started in January), among other things. Let's say they decide to use whole numbers.

Here are the number of years of experience Maplewood's teachers have:

0, 2, 2, 3, 3, 4, 20, 2, 4, 3, 2

> How might you analyze these data to answer the question on the accreditation report? Take some time to explore this set of data, using knowledge you already have. State your conclusions and then read on. . . .

DISCUSSION

The mean number of years is 4.09 years, which is very close to 4. The median is 3 years. Some people mistakenly conclude that the median is 4. If you are one of these people, remember that the median is the middle number only when the numbers have been arranged from smallest to greatest. It is not the middle number in the original list; do you see why? The mode is 2 years.

In one sense, a case can be made for each of these three numbers as representing the average (typical) teacher. Do you see why?

The mean is the term most people think of when they hear *average*. The median is literally in the middle. One could argue for the mode, because more teachers have 2 years of experience than any other number of years. So what do they write on the report?

They decide to make a bar graph to see if that will help. One teacher makes the graph in Figure 7.13(a), and another makes the graph in Figure 7.13(b). Before we discuss the graphs, a note on interpretation. The numbers on the x axis represent years of experience. The numbers on the y axis represent frequency—that is, how many teachers have that amount of experience. Thus, the first bar tells us that 1 teacher has zero years of experience, the second bar tells us that 4 teachers have two years of experience, and so on.

FIGURE **7.13**

Are both graphs right, or is one better? What do you think?

When we make bar graphs for numerical data, graphs like that in Figure 7.13(a) are frowned upon. Do you see why? In Figure 7.13(a), the numbers are all clumped together. Like the AIDS graph in Investigation 7.3, this distorts the fact that 20 is much further from 4 than 4 is from 3.

As you can see from Figure 7.13(b), the number 20 stands out like the proverbial sore thumb. Data whose values are significantly greater or less than those of other data are referred to as **outliers**. We will explore them more in the next investigation.

The bar graph shows that the overwhelming majority of teachers (9 out of 11) have 2, 3, or 4 years of experience. Since 3 is in the middle of this cluster, the teachers decide that the median (3 years) makes the most sense to report as the average years of experience.

A more efficient way to determine the mean   In this investigation, we could determine the mean of the data by adding all 11 numbers and then dividing by 11. We will use Table 7.7 to examine two easier ways to determine the mean;

this is especially useful as the size of the sample becomes larger. The first column shows all the years for which we have people; that is, there are no teachers with 1 year of experience, none with 5 to 19 years of experience, and none with over 20 years of experience. The second column shows the frequency of each of these numbers. For example, there are 1 teacher with 0 years of experience, 4 teachers with 2 years of experience, and so on. The third column is obtained by multiplying the numbers in the first two columns. Why will multiplying these pairs of numbers help us to determine the mean?

TABLE 7.7

Number of years of experience	Frequency	Product
0	1	0
2	4	8
3	3	9
4	2	8
20	1	20
Sum	11	45

Basically, we are simply applying the repeated addition context of multiplication. Thus, rather than adding all 11 numbers

$$0 + 2 + 2 + 2 + 2 + 3 + 3 + 3 + 4 + 4 + 20$$

we are doing the following:

$$0 + \quad 4(2) \quad + \quad 3(3) \quad + 2(4) + 20$$

In cases of large sets of data, we can reduce the tedium of calculations further by entering the first two columns of data into a spreadsheet program and then "telling" the computer to multiply the rows together and then find the sum of the third column.

These numbers are measurements This investigation brings out another important aspect of statistical analysis. When we are representing a characteristic of a population with a number, we are actually measuring. In this case, the measurement is rather straightforward, although the teachers still had to make some decisions—for example, whether to count partial years and whether to round experience to the nearest year. In many cases, the measurement is not as straightforward and obvious. For example, if we were to graph the SAT scores of the freshman class at your college, what does SAT measure? What does IQ measure? How do we measure productivity?

Let us now focus on a situation in which we have more data.

INVESTIGATION 7.9 Class Sizes in a College

Cost of education is always an issue in the minds of taxpayers. One of the ways to reduce cost is to increase class size. Let's say you are the principal of a small high school and these are the sizes of classes in your school. What would you say is the average class size?

7, 28, 29, 31, 31, 16, 18, 29, 29, 19, 24, 30, 34, 30, 40, 25, 27, 29, 7, 28, 30, 31, 30, 25, 26, 31, 30, 30, 32, 26, 27, 32, 17, 33, 16

DISCUSSION

The mean is 26, the median is 29, and the mode is 30. The school board has decided to use the mean as the average. However, the principal argues that it is not fair to use the mean as the average for these data. Why do you think the principal objected to the mean as the best representative of "average class size?" As before, take some time to consider what analyses you might do of these data. Summarize your observations and conclusions and then read on. . . .

Stem plot This is a good time to demonstrate another graph called a stem plot, which is also a good way to organize the data. The **stem plot**, also referred to as a stem–and–leaf plot, uses the idea of place value. In this case, we look at the tens digits of our data and make a row for each, as shown on the left-hand side of Table 7.8. Now we simply insert each datum into the proper row. For example, 35 is entered into the 3 row as 5, and 28 is entered into the 2 row as 8.

Once this is done, it is a simple task to put the (ones) digits into numerical order. Now examine the stem plot. What does it tell you?

TABLE 7.8

4	0
3	1 1 0 4 0 0 1 0 1 0 0 2 2 3
2	8 9 9 9 4 5 7 9 8 5 6 6 7
1	6 8 9 7 6
0	7 7

4	0
3	0 0 0 0 0 0 1 1 1 1 2 2 3 4
2	4 5 5 6 6 7 7 8 8 9 9 9 9
1	6 6 7 8 9
0	7 7

From one perspective, a stem plot is similar to a bar graph that has been laid on its side. We can quickly determine that there are more classes in the 30s than in any other "decade" and that only two classes have less than 16 students.

Line plot We can also construct a **line plot**. First, we make a scale. Next we place an *x* (or other mark) at the appropriate place for each piece of data. What can you tell about class sizes in the school from the line plot in Figure 7.14? Think and then read on. . . .

FIGURE **7.14**

We can use ordinary English to describe some of our observations:

We can see that the class sizes vary from a low of 7 to a high of 40. The difference between the extreme values is called the *range*. Thus, the range for these data is 33.

We can see that there is a **cluster** of data in the high 20s and low 30s.

There are also **gaps in the data** between 7 and 16, between 19 and 24, and between 34 and 40.

One of the primary advantages of such a graph is that not only can we see the range of the data but we get a much richer sense of how the data are **distributed** or spread out, and we don't lose any information about individual values.

Thus, the line plot helps us to interpret how the numbers are actually distributed. We see that the mean (26) does not seem as fair a representative of the center of this set of data as the median (29) or the mode (30).

Boxplot Finally, let us consider one more graph, which builds on the line plot. The box-and-whisker graph, or **boxplot** (invented by J. W. Tuckey in this century), packs a lot of information into one graph. It is often difficult for students to understand at first. Therefore, I recommend that you read through the description first, just to get an idea, and the second time through actually make the graph along with me.

1. Copy the class sizes onto your paper horizontally and circle the median of the data; in this case, there are 17 values to the right and to the left of the circled 29.

7 7 16 16 17 18 19 24 25 25 26 26 27 27 28 28 29 ㉙ 29 29 30 30 30 30 30 30 31 31 31 31 32 32 33 34 40

2. Find and circle the median of the bottom half of the data, and then find and circle the median of the upper half of the data.

7 7 16 16 17 18 19 24 ㉕ 25 26 26 27 27 28 28 29 ㉙ 29 29 30 30 30 30 30 30 ㉛ 31 31 31 32 32 33 34 40

We call 25 the **first quartile** and 31 the **third quartile** because these two numbers and the median essentially partition the data into four quarters that are (roughly) equal in size. The first quartile lets us know the top of the first quarter, and the third quartile lets us know the top of the third quarter. We use these three numbers plus the low and high data (7 and 40) to make the box plot.

3. Make a scale and mark a dot for each of these 5 numbers at the appropriate spot on the scale, as in Figure 7.15.

FIGURE **7.15**

4. Make the boxes and whiskers, as in Figure 7.16!

FIGURE **7.16**

Stop for a moment and look only at the boxplot. What does it tell you about the sizes of classes in the school? Think and then read on. . . .

■ The largest class (the end of the right whisker) has 40 students.
■ The smallest class (the end of the left whisker) has 7 students.
■ The median class size (the line in the middle of the boxes) is 29.
■ Half of the classes (the two boxes) have between 25 and 31 students.

Let us consider the boxplot from a more general perspective. That is, in general, what do the boxes represent? What do the whiskers represent? Think and then read on. . . .

The left whisker tells us the range of the bottom quarter of the data, and the right whisker tells us the range of the top quarter of the data. In this case, about

1/4 of the classes are between 7 and 25, and about 1/4 of the classes are between 31 and 35. The two boxes tell us where the middle half of the data lie.

Outliers and boxplots Recall the observation in Investigation 7.8 that the number 20, representing the teacher with 20 years of experience, was an outlier. Let us now quantify that term. To determine if a datum is an outlier, we first find the difference between the third and first quartiles. We call this amount the **interquartile range (IQR)**. In one sense, the IQR is like a mini-range—that is, it is the range of the middle half of the data. We multiply the interquartile range by 1.5. If a datum is more than 1.5 IQRs from the first or third quartile, we call it an outlier. (It is important to note that not all statisticians use 1.5; even statisticians do not agree on everything!) Apply this procedure to this example to determine if there are any outliers, and then read on. . . .

The difference between the third quartile and first quartile is 6; $31 - 25 = 6$, and $6(1.5) = 9$. Thus, any number below 16 or above 40 is an outlier, since $25 - 9 = 16$ and $31 + 9 = 40$.

In this case, we see that the class size of 7 is an outlier because it is less than 16, and the class size of 40 is on the verge of being an outlier.

Figure 7.17 illustrates the notion of outliers in this instance. If it is outside the region shown, then it's an outlier.

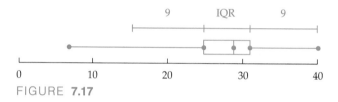

FIGURE **7.17**

Because the boxplot is such a new kind of graph, most students need to do several to get a feel for it. Some readers notice that the line plot and the boxplot look "similar." Explaining their similarities will be left as an exercise. The interested reader is encouraged to make boxplots of some data from the exercises.

In the following investigation, we examine a situation in which we still have quite a few data and they are much more spread out.

INVESTIGATION **7.10** **Average Time to Finish the Exam**

One year, I recorded the time (in minutes) it took each student to do the final examination in my course. Technically, it was a two-hour test, but I told the students that I would stay for three hours. I recorded the time each student took to finish the exam to determine whether or not I should make the exam shorter. The data below list the time in minutes each student took on the exam:

62, 76, 88, 89, 95, 96, 98, 99, 101, 102, 104, 106, 111, 112, 114, 114, 115, 115, 123, 123, 125, 125, 132, 134, 134, 136, 138, 139, 139, 144, 146, 149, 149, 154, 154, 155, 160

What analyses might you do of these data to advise me? Take some time to explore the data, using knowledge that you already have. Summarize what you learned and state your conclusions, and then read on. . . .

DISCUSSION

Examining the spread of the data A stem plot helps us to organize the data (see Table 7.9).

TABLE 7.9

16	0
15	4 4 5
14	4 6 9 9
13	2 4 4 6 8 9 9
12	3 3 5 5
11	1 2 4 4 5 5
10	1 2 4 6
9	5 6 8 9
8	8 9
7	6
6	2

A line plot (Figure 7.18) gives us a sense of the distribution without losing any data, but in this case the range is so great that patterns in the data are not apparent.

FIGURE **7.18**

The stem plot suggests another way of organizing and representing the data. We can group the data using an interval size suggested by the stem plot, 10 minutes. By selecting an interval size, we can make a **grouped frequency table** for the data. The intervals are called **classes**. It is important to note that there is no one "right" interval size. For example, we could choose an interval size of 10 minutes, in which case we have Table 7.10. However, this choice produces 11 classes. Alternatively, we could choose an interval size of 20 minutes, in which case we have Table 7.11, which gives us 6 classes.

TABLE 7.10

Interval	Frequency
60–69	1
70–79	1
80–89	2
90–99	4
100–109	4
110–119	6
120–129	4
130–139	7
140–149	4
150–159	3
160–169	1

TABLE 7.11

Interval	Frequency
60–79	2
80–99	6
100–119	10
120–139	11
140–159	7
160–179	1

From these data, we can make a new kind of graph, a **histogram**, which is a bar graph in which there is no space between the bars. Histograms are commonly used for data in which the data are numbers as opposed to categories. Examine the two histograms in Figure 7.19. What do you see now that you didn't see before? What do they tell you about the data that is similar? What do they tell you about the data that is different? Then read on. . . .

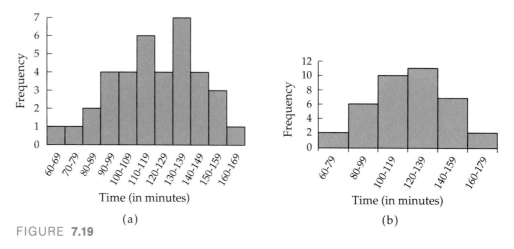

FIGURE **7.19**

The histogram in Figure 7.19(a) indicates that the majority of the times are between 90 and 150 minutes, and it shows two peak intervals: 110–119 and 130–139. The histogram in Figure 7.19(b) indicates that the majority of the times lie between 80 and 159 minutes.

Note that with the second set of grouped frequencies, we could also make a circle graph for the data. This would give a quicker sense of what proportion of the class finished in each of the time intervals. Technically, we could do this with the first set, but a circle graph with 11 slices is a bit much.

Finding the center   If you haven't already done so, estimate the median from the line plot or one of the histograms. Then read on. . . .

From the line plot (Figure 7.18), we can see that there are about as many test lengths above 120 minutes as below. From Figure 7.19(a), we can see that there are roughly as many test lengths above the 120–129 group as there are below. In fact, the median is 123 minutes. In this case, the mean is close, 120 minutes.

The strict interpretation of the mode is relatively meaningless in this case. There are several test lengths that occurred twice, but a frequency of only 2 in a set of 37 hardly makes a number a candidate for typical. Thus, when we make grouped frequency tables, we speak of a **modal class,** that is, the class that occurs most frequently. A look at Figure 7.19(a) reveals two intervals that stand out: the 110–119-minute interval and the 130–139-minute interval. Even though the 130–139 interval has one more time than the other, both of them stand out from the other intervals, and so we can say that this set of data has two modal classes. In such a case, we say that the distribution is **bimodal;** that is, it has two modes.

We can draw several conclusions from the data and the graphs. When given more than two hours, over half the class took the extra time. The "average" time for completion was about two hours, although it is ironic that while the mean and median are both very close to two hours, this is where the actual distribution dipped. I wondered if that was just a coincidence or whether it was related to the traditional time limit. In any case, since over half the class took longer than two hours, I decided to make a shorter exam.

Let us now see how our knowledge can be used by a teacher to analyze the test scores of a whole class.

INVESTIGATION **7.11 Scores on a Test**

Let's say you have a friend, also a teacher, who has just finished grading his students' midterms. The scores are given below.

77, 96, 58, 100, 66, 76, 88, 73, 94, 75, 76, 84, 91, 74, 87, 92, 67

You ask how his students did, but the teacher does not know much mathematics. All he can say is that this is an unusual class. He can see that the scores range from 58 to 100. Take some time to analyze these data. What can you do with the data to help your friend better understand the overall picture of his students' performance? State your conclusions and then read on. . . .

DISCUSSION

Simply from examining the numbers as listed, we can quickly determine that the median score is 77. Either by observation or from a stem plot, we can also see that grades of C and A dominate the data. Thus, grades of C and A are the modal classes for these data. (Recall that when we group the data, we speak of modal classes instead of modes. However, in both cases, the idea is the same: the value or interval that occurs most frequently.)

Look at the histogram and circle graph in Figure 7.20. What do they add to our understanding of the scores?

 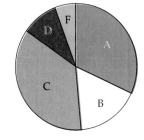

FIGURE **7.20**

From the histogram, we can see that technically the modal class is a grade of C. However, since there is only one more C than A and since these two intervals stand out, we call this distribution of scores bimodal. From the circle graph, we could frame our analysis optimistically (almost half the class got As and Bs) or pessimistically (more than half the class got C or lower).

What do the line plot and boxplot (Figure 7.21) add to our understanding of the distribution of the scores?

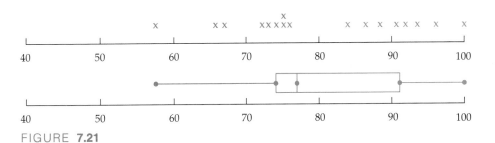

FIGURE **7.21**

The line plot shows two major gaps, one from 58 to 66 and the other from 77 to 84. The line plot also shows a sense of a "top" group and a "bottom" group of the class. From your friend's perspective, this might help him understand why this is an unusual class. If he teaches to the top group, he is likely to lose the bottom group; on the other hand, it he teaches to the bottom group, he is likely to bore the top group.

In this case, since the number of data is small, the boxplot has no advantages over the line plot. From a teaching perspective, an examination of the boxplot is useful, so that you can use it and interpret it when working with larger sets of data. As stated earlier, the boxplot shows us the range. Using the idea that the boxplot partitions the data into four roughly equal groups, we can focus on the two boxes and see that about 1/2 of the students scored between 75 and 90. We can also say that roughly 3/4 of the class scored above 75. Note that the left-hand box is narrower than the right-hand box. The narrowness of the left-hand box indicates a cluster of scores in that range, that is, the mid-70s.

A geometric view of median and mean Thus far we have determined the median (77) and the modal classes (C and A). What about the mean? Let us take this opportunity to develop another perspective for understanding the mean. From a computational perspective, we can compute the mean. From a geometric perspective, the mean is the center of gravity of the data. Imagine the data as weights placed on a seesaw. Where would the point be at which the seesaw would balance? Take a few moments to look at the line plot and estimate the balance point of this set of data. Do you think it will be greater than, equal to, or less than the median of 77? Why? Then read on. . . .

FIGURE **7.22**

If you imagine a seesaw, then you realize that numbers that are further from the center will tip the scale, like a seesaw (see Figure 7.22).

In this set of data, the data won't balance at the median (77). Only one score in the lower half is far from 77, but several scores in the top half are far from 77. Thus, we can see that the mean will be higher than the median. In fact, the mean is 81.

With respect to the center of the data, we can tell your friend that the score of 77 is the median, that the mean score is 80, and that grades of C and A are the modal classes.

With respect to the spread of the data, we can report that the scores range from 58 to 100. Both the line plot and the boxplot can help give the teacher a visual sense of how the scores are spread out.

Thus far, we have used our graphs and our measures of the center and spread to describe and analyze one set of data. Another use of these tools is to compare two sets of data.

I N V E S T I G A T I O N **7.12** **Which Battery Do You Buy?**

Let's say you were going to buy an expensive long-life battery for your portable CD player. Two companies claim that they have developed batteries that will last an average of 40 hours instead of lasting only a few hours. The cost of the batteries is the same. What other information would you want to know before making a decision?

It doesn't matter, you say? What if you had these data:

Battery A: 37, 42, 40, 38, 42, 40, 39, 38, 41, 40, 39, 41, 43, 39, 40, 40, 41

Battery B: 30, 48, 44, 36, 42, 36, 40, 34, 46, 38, 40, 40, 42, 44, 38, 40, 32, 50

> What analyses of these data might you do to inform your decision? Take some time to explore these two sets of data, using knowledge you already have. Summarize what you learned and state your conclusions, and then read on. . . .

DISCUSSION

If you did explore the data, you found that for each set, the mean, median, and mode were 40. In this case, the measures of the center tell us nothing about differences in these two sets of data. This occasionally happens with real-life data and illustrates a point that statisticians make: Measures of the center of a distribution give an incomplete picture of the data. Let us now discuss some graphs that help us to see how the data are spread out. In this case, since we are comparing two sets of data, we can make a back-to-back stem plot (Table 7.12).

TABLE 7.12		

Battery A		Battery B
	5	0
3 2 2 1 1 1 0 0 0 0 0	4	0 0 0 0 2 2 4 4 6 8
9 9 9 8 8 7	3	0 2 4 6 6 8 8

The stem plot enables us to quickly determine the ranges of the two sets of data. We see that the data for Battery B are much more spread out (dispersed) than the data for Battery A:

- The range of the data for Battery A is 6 (37 to 43).
- The range of the data for Battery B is 20 (30 to 50).

If we make line plots (Figure 7.23), what do we see?

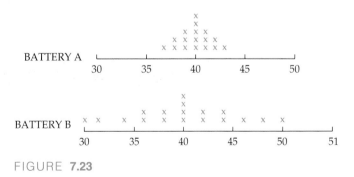

FIGURE **7.23**

Finally, we can make boxplots, which we can stack on top of each other as in Figure 7.24.

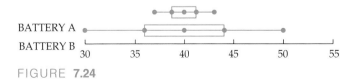

FIGURE **7.24**

Both the line plots and the boxplots indicate that the data for Battery A are more clumped together, whereas the data for Battery B are more spread out.

Shortly we will examine a new concept for measuring how spread out a set of data is. However, before we do that, we need to spend some time looking at some generalized kinds of statements we can make about distributions of data.

Different distributions   There are many ways in which a set of data can be distributed. In this course, we will focus on five distributions: **uniform**, **skewed to the right**, **skewed to the left**, **bimodal**, and **normal**. The graphs in Figure 7.25 represent idealized (smoothed) versions of these distributions. In real life the data are seldom so smooth. Can you think of a scenario for each of these graphs? Try to do so before reading on. . . .

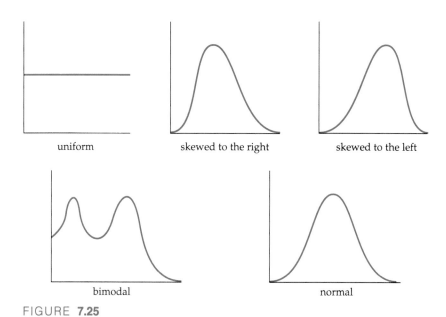

FIGURE **7.25**

HISTORY

As you have discovered in this book, much of what we call elementary mathematics is relatively recent knowledge. So, too, is the idea of looking at distributions of data. In the 1830s a Belgian mathematician, L. A. J. Quetelet, collected measurements of many kinds of data on people, including heights, weights, length of arms, and intelligence. He did this for many people. What he found was that in most of these cases, the graphs were similar. What do you think all the graphs looked like? Think and read on. . . .

All of the distributions were similar to the normal curve.

Some students report having difficulty making sense of the preceding discussion. If this applies to you, the following may be helpful. The distributions shown in Figure 7.25 represent five (of many) ways in which a set of data may be distributed. The line graphs shown can be thought of as evolving from bar graphs (with which most students report being more comfortable). For example, if we collected data on the number of siblings, we would have the bar graph shown at the left in Figure 7.26. If we made a line graph from those data, we would have the line graph shown at the right in Figure 7.26. If you look at the idealized graph, you can see that we can say that these data are skewed to the right. That is, this graph has the characteristics of a "skewed to the right" distribution.

FIGURE **7.26**

Table 7.13 gives one example for each of the five distributions.

TABLE 7.13

Distribution	*x* axis (independent variable)	*y* axis (dependent variable)
Uniform	Months of the year	Temperature in Hawaii
Skewed (right)	Salaries in a factory	Frequency
Skewed (left)	Class sizes in a high school	Frequency
Bimodal	Time to finish an exam	Frequency
Normal	Hours that Battery A lasted	Frequency

What Measures of Central Tendency and Dispersion Tell Us

Investigations 7.8 through 7.12 have focused on three tools that enable us to make statements about a set of data: graphs, measures of the center (mean, median, and mode), and measures of dispersion (range, clusters, gaps, outliers, and interquartile range).

Before moving on, let us take some time to reflect on our understanding of measures of the center and measures of dispersion. We will focus first on measures of the center. For each of the three terms for average, describe the reasons for using it and its disadvantages. Then describe a real-life scenario in which that term would be most appropriate and justify your choice.

TABLE 7.14

	Reasons for using	Disadvantage
Mean	This is the term usually associated with average.	It can give a distorted sense of the middle if there are extreme data (outliers).
	It is often easier to compute with a large set of data.	It might not make sense. For example, what does a mean shoe size of 6.3 mean?
	It is the center of gravity of the data.	
Median	It is not affected by outliers.	It is not always appropriate—for example, for a baseball player's batting average.
	It is the physical center of the data.	
Mode	It shows the most common datum.	It might be far from the center.
	It is easy to determine from a graph.	There might be no modes or more than one mode.

We can make some generalizations about using these terms to describe the center of a set of data:

- If the distribution of the data is skewed, the median will often be more representative than the mean.

- If the data are categories rather than numbers (for example, favorite TV show versus age), there is no mean or median, and so the mode is used to convey the center of the data—that is, the most commonly occurring datum. We might say, for example, that the typical American family eats hot dogs on the Fourth of July; this statement indicates that it has been determined that more families eat hot dogs on the Fourth of July than any other food.

■ If the distribution is symmetric, the mean, median, and mode will be close to one another.

I hope that you have also seen that the average alone gives an incomplete picture of the data. One of the things that graphs do is to give us a sense of the spread of the data. The stem plot, boxplot, line plot, and histogram all enable us to gain a sense of how the data are spread out. Some show clusters, outliers, and gaps in the data better than others.

Thus far, we have found that one measure of the center (the median) is often used together with the boxplot, with the median telling us the middle of the data and the boxplot telling us about the spread of the data. That is, shorter boxes and whiskers indicate that there is a cluster of data, and longer boxes and whiskers indicate that this portion (quarter) of the data is more spread out.

Not surprisingly, there is a measure of spread that works well with the mean. It is called the *standard deviation.* However, most students do not feel comfortable computing it, and few students are able to use it confidently when analyzing data. In order to understand the standard deviation, however, we first need to examine more closely the normal distribution (often referred to as a normal curve) because the standard deviation has most power with a set of data that are normally distributed.

Normal Distribution

A line graph depicting a set of data that are normally distributed is often referred to as a bell-shaped curve; that is, the frequency values are highest in the middle, and the graph is symmetrical. The discussion below is what is referred to as a "thought experiment"; that is, we are not going to use data from an actual situation, but rather we are going to imagine data from an ideal situation. Suppose we have collected data on the heights of all students at a small college. As you have seen from Section 7.1, we could make a histogram from these data. The graph at the left in Figure 7.27 shows how the actual histogram might look in this ideal case; that is, the graph is symmetrical. If we trace a smooth line over the tops of the bars, we have the line graph at the right in Figure 7.27. When normally distributed data are visually depicted, the writers generally show a line graph. For example, in the case of the heights at the college, the figure on the right is a smoothed-out line graph for the heights. However, in actuality the heights have been measured in whole inches, and therefore the histogram on the left is a truer depiction of the data. Thus, whenever you see a "normal" curve, it will help if you realize that this curve is an idealization of a histogram. For example, we say that SAT scores and IQ scores are normally distributed. In each case, the x axis represents the score and the y axis represents the frequency of each score.

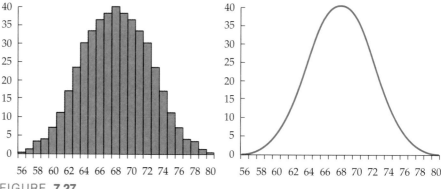

FIGURE **7.27**

There are, of course, variations within kinds of distributions. For example, we would say that both of the graphs in Figure 7.28 represent data that are normally distributed.

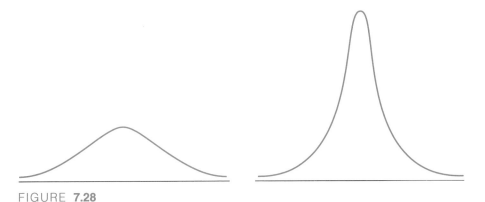

FIGURE **7.28**

FIGURE **7.28**

Now let us examine what standard deviation means and how it helps us to make generalizations from sets of data that are normally distributed. Many of my students have told me that this investigation actually makes the standard deviation make sense! For the time being, if you have had negative experiences with standard deviation, please suspend your judgment and pretend you have never heard of this idea before.

INVESTIGATION **7.13** Understanding Standard Deviation

Up to now, we have relied on graphs to help us get a sense of how spread out the data are. For example, if we make histograms to represent the battery data from Investigation 7.12 (see Figure 7.29), we see that the data for Battery A are more spread out than the data for Battery B.

FIGURE **7.29**

The only number associated with spread has been the range. However, just as we have found that the center of some sets of data can be characterized by a single number (mean, median, or mode), we will develop the idea of one number that can give us a sense of the "spread" of a set of data by revisiting our data on the two batteries in Investigation 7.12. As stated above, we can see that the data for Battery B are more spread out than the data for Battery A. How else might we describe how spread out the data in these two sets are? Think and then read on. . . .

DISCUSSION

One way to do so would be to note how far each number is from the mean and then take the average (mean) of those scores. This would give us an "average distance from the mean." Recall that in both cases, the mean life of the batteries was 40 hours. Determine the "average distance from the mean" for each of the two classes and then read on. . . .

Table 7.15 shows the computations:

TABLE 7.15

BATTERY A		BATTERY B	
Number of hours	**Distance from the mean**	**Number of hours**	**Distance from the mean**
37	3	30	10
38	2	32	8
38	2	34	6
39	1	36	4
39	1	36	4
39	1	38	2
40	0	38	2
40	0	40	0
40	0	40	0
40	0	40	0
40	0	40	0
41	1	42	2
41	1	42	2
41	1	44	4
42	2	44	4
42	2	46	6
43	3	48	8
		50	10
Total distance from the mean	20		72
Average distance	20/17 = 1.2 hours		72/18 = 4.0 hours

If we look at how far each number is from the mean and find the average of those numbers, we can say that for Battery A, the average distance from the mean is 1.2 hours, whereas for Battery B, the average distance is 4.0 hours. Just as the mean, median, and mode are concepts that enable us to give a sense of the middle of the data with a single number, "average distance from the mean" enables us to compare the relative spreads of the data with a single number. Since 4.0 is more than 3 times 1.2, if someone were to tell you that the means from both sets of data were equal but that the average distance from the mean for Battery B was 4.0 hours compared to 1.2 hours for Battery A, this number would instantly tell you that the former set of data is more spread out.

Now the skeptical reader might be wondering, "Is it possible that real mathematicians do something this simple?" or might be wondering, "Why have I never heard the term 'average distance from the mean' before?" The answer to the first question is yes, and we will defer the second question temporarily. What we call the standard deviation is actually quite closely related to the average distance from the mean. For reasons that will be explained very shortly, the computation is slightly more complicated.

Finding the standard deviation To determine the standard deviation, we can use much of the work we did for average distance from the mean. There are two more steps (see Table 7.16).

To determine average distance from mean.	*To determine standard deviation.*
Find the distance from the mean of each datum.	Find the distance from the mean of each datum.
	Square each of these numbers.
Add this column of numbers.	Add this column of numbers.
Divide this sum by the number of data.	Divide this sum by the number of data.
	Take the square root of this number.

TABLE 7.16

		BATTERY A			BATTERY B	
	Score	**Distance from the mean**	**Square of the distance**	**Score**	**Distance from the mean**	**Square of the distance**
	37	3	9	30	10	100
	38	2	4	32	8	64
	38	2	4	34	6	36
	39	1	1	36	4	16
	39	1	1	36	4	16
	39	1	1	38	2	4
	40	0	0	38	2	4
	40	0	0	40	0	0
	40	0	0	40	0	0
	40	0	0	40	0	0
	40	0	0	40	0	0
	41	1	1	42	2	4
	41	1	1	42	2	4
	41	1	1	44	4	16
	42	2	4	44	4	16
	42	2	4	46	6	36
	43	3	9	48	8	64
				50	10	100
Sum		20	40		72	480
Sum/n		Average distance = 1.2	2.35		Average distance = 4.0	26.7
Square root			Standard deviation = 1.53			Standard deviation = 5.16

Now that we have examined the meaning of the standard deviation and developed the procedure for determining it, you are more likely to be able to make sense of the mathematical definition of the standard deviation.

If we have a set of data whose values are denoted $x_1, x_2, x_3, \ldots, x_n$, and the mean of this data is represented as $\bar{x}$, then the standard deviation is

$$\text{Standard deviation} = \sqrt{\frac{(x_1 - \bar{x})^2 + (x_2 - \bar{x})^2 + (x_3 - \bar{x})^2 + \cdots + (x_n - \bar{x})^2}{n}}$$

In this case, the standard deviation for the data for Battery A is 1.53 compared to the standard deviation of 5.16 for Battery B. Like the average distances from the mean, the two standard deviations tell us that the data for Battery B are much more spread out. Once again, the skeptical reader will ask, "If they both give us a sense of spread, why not use the average distance from the mean, since it is easier to understand and compute?"

Using standard deviation The reason that we use the standard deviation has to do with some rather amazing generalizations that we can make about a set of data that is normally distributed. Let us look at those generalizations, make sure you understand them, and then see how we can apply these generalizations.

When a set of data is normally distributed, we can make the following conclusions (see Figure 7.30):

- 68% of the data lie within one standard deviation of the mean.

- 95% of the data lie within two standard deviations of the mean.

- 99.8% of the data lie within three standard deviations of the mean.

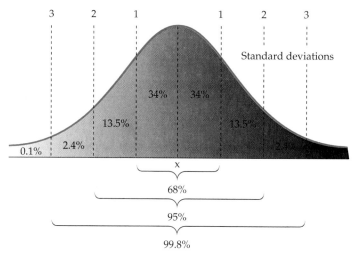

FIGURE **7.30**

Let us apply these conclusions to our data for Battery A. Determine what percent of the data lie within one standard deviation of the mean. Then read on. . . . 🖉

In this case, the mean was 40 hours and the standard deviation was 1.5 hours. Thus, we are looking for how many data points lie between 40 − 1.5 and 40 + 1.5, that is, between 38.5 and 41.5. We find that 10 of the 17 data points lie within this range, and 10/17 is equivalent to 65%. If we look at the data for Battery B, and find how many data points lie within 1 standard deviation of the mean, we are looking for data points that lie between 40 − 5.2 and 40 + 5.2, that is, between 34.8 and 45.2. We find that 12 of the 18 data points lie within this range, and 12/18 is 67%.

What about other distributions? When data are not normally distributed, then these generalizations are not as useful. We can summarize our knowledge of how to use standard deviation by saying the following:

- When data are not normally distributed, the standard deviation is a tool that enables us to describe how spread out the data are or to compare the spreads of two sets of data.

■ When data are normally distributed, then the standard deviation is a unit for measuring dispersion; that is, approximately 68% of the data will lie within 1 standard deviation of the mean, and so on.

It is important to note that these numbers (68%, 95%, and 99.8%) are theoretical figures that are realized when the number of data is very large and when the data are "perfectly" normally distributed. However, even when the number of data is smaller and the distribution is not perfectly normal, we will generally find close to 68% of the data lying within one standard deviation of the mean.

Now that we have examined standard deviation, we can summarize the uses of measures of the center and of spread for different kinds of distributions. In general, the mean and standard deviation are used together to describe the center and spread of a set of data that is normally distributed. In general, the median and quartiles are used together to describe the center and spread of a set of data that is skewed.

Let us now consider some examples from real life that use the concept of standard deviation.

INVESTIGATION 7.14 Analyzing Standardized Test Scores

Let's say that a standardized test has a mean of 250 and a standard deviation of 50. Suppose 2,000 students took the test and their scores were normally distributed. Think about the following questions, then read on. . . .

A. How many students would you expect to score over 350?

B. How many students would you expect to score at least 200?

DISCUSSION

A. Since a score of 350 is two standard deviations above the mean, we conclude that 2.5% of the scores will be over 350 [Figure 7.31(a)]. Then, we simply need to compute 2.5% of 2,000. We can use a calculator, or we can just as quickly do it mentally: 10% of 2,000 is 200, so 5% is 100, and 2.5% is 50.

B. This question is slightly more complex. The answer is that about 1,680 students will score at least 200. If you got this wrong, it is possible that you may understand the procedures but not the concepts related to standard deviation. Figure 7.31(b) illustrates one solution path. If we think of the results of the test in terms of a histogram, we can see that all the shaded bars represent scores over 200. However, when we superimpose this histogram on the graph showing the percent of scores with respect to standard deviations, we find that this means that 84% of the students scored at least 200.

FIGURE **7.31**

MATHEMATICS

When the SAT was first introduced, it was calibrated so that it had a mean of 500 and a standard deviation of 100. Over the past 20 or so years, the average score has declined considerably. In 1994, the Educational Testing Service proposed adjusting the test so that the mean would once again be 500. However, this proposal provoked quite a controversy. Why do you think the ETS made the proposal? Why do you think some people objected? Think about these questions before reading on. . . .

The rationale given by the ETS was that if 500 were the "average" score, then the scores would be more meaningful. That is, if a student's score was above 500, that student would know that the score was above average. Many people objected because such a move would make it appear that scores had not gone down.

The concept of standard deviation is used regularly by industries. Let us examine one such example.

INVESTIGATION 7.15 How Long Should the Tire Be Guaranteed?

A tire company has developed a new tire, and has tested it extensively. The results of the tests showed that the "average" tire lasted 44,000 miles, that the distribution of wearing was normal, and that the standard deviation was 2,500 miles. If the company guarantees that the tire will last 39,000 miles, what percent of the tires are likely to wear out before 39,000 miles and thus be subject to refund?

DISCUSSION

Again, a graph makes the solution to this problem much easier (see Figure 7.32). From the graph, we can conclude that 2.5% of the tires are likely to wear out before 39,000 miles.

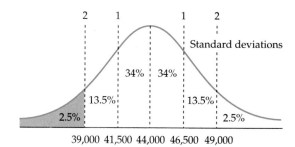

FIGURE **7.32**

What if the company wanted to guarantee 40,000 miles? What percent of the tires are likely to wear out before 40,000 miles? In this case, you cannot get an "exact" answer. What could you do to increase the accuracy of your estimate? This question will be left as an exercise.

Sampling

In this section, we have developed tools that enable us to describe sets of data: measures of the center, measures of the spread, and graphs that can be useful. One of the applications of these tools is in sampling. As stated at the beginning of the chapter, people collect data on samples (opinion polls, product research, samples of a vaccine) and then make generalizations about the whole population. For example, if 55% of our sample favor Candidate *X*, then we believe that about 55% of the whole population will favor Candidate *X*. If 90% of the tires in the sample lasted more than 40,000 miles, then we believe that about 90% of all tires of this model will last more than 40,000 miles.

Engaging in opinion sampling is beyond the scope of this course. However, it is important that you have a basic understanding of this enterprise.

A **sample** is a subset of a population. If our sampling of the population is to give us accurate information, we must try to ensure that the sample is as representative of the total population as possible. This involves developing a method for selecting subjects (whether they be people, fish, or tires) that gives every member of the population an equal chance of being selected. That is, we want our sample to be a **random sample**.

This is easier said than done. A classic example of a sampling error occurred in the 1936 presidential election. The *Literary Digest* sent questionnaires to 10 million voters. Of the 2,266,566 responses, 1,293,669 were for Landon and 972,897 were for Roosevelt. That is, more than 57% were for Landon. In electoral politics, if a candidate receives more than 55% of the vote, this is considered to be a landslide. History shows that, in fact, Roosevelt received 62% of the votes, winning by a landslide. What happened?

Analysis of the sampling process showed two flaws. First, the editors did not send the survey to a random sample of potential voters. They had gotten their sample (that is, the names and addresses) from telephone directories and lists of automobile owners. Second, less than one-fourth of the people responded to the survey. These two factors (the sample not being randomly determined and the response rate being too low) caused their error. Let us focus on the idea of obtaining a random sample. Why wasn't the *Literary Digest* sample a random sample? How could that have biased the data?

In those days, a much smaller fraction of the population owned telephones and/or cars. Therefore, the sample was not representative, but rather was biased toward upper-income voters.

Let's say that a large university wants to survey freshmen to see if they are planning to transfer. There are currently 8,000 freshmen, and the administrators decide to randomly survey 250 of them. How might they do so?

They could put all the students' names in a hat and draw out 250, but this would be very time-consuming. Computers are often used to accomplish the same purpose. For example, we could assign each student a number between 1 and 8,000. We could then have the computer select the numbers 1 through 8,000 in a random fashion. We would then match the first 250 numbers selected by the computer with our code, and these would be the students we would interview.

Sometimes we need a **stratified random sample**, a sample in which there are distinct subsets of the population that need to be proportionally represented. For example, if we are surveying students on campus and 25% of the students are married, we may want to make sure that 25% of our sample are married students. Consider one more example: Let's say that 60% of the voters in a district are white, 30% are black, and 10% are Hispanic. In this case, we will want to make sure that our sample contains these proportions also.

Let us consider a real-life situation involving sampling and apply our knowledge of statistics to better understand the authors' graphs and report.

HISTORY

The beginning of modern statistics can be traced to the work of the Englishman John Graunt (1620–1674), who collected data on births and deaths. In his book *Natural and Political Observations of Mortality*, he presented such findings as: more boys are born than girls, more men than women die violent deaths, and the death rate in urban areas is greater than the death rate in rural areas.

INVESTIGATION **7.16** Comparing Students in Three Countries

Figure 7.33 is taken from a book entitled *Making the Grade in Mathematics: Elementary School Mathematics in the United States, Taiwan, and Japan.* Before reading on, first look at the graph. Take some time to understand what information the authors are trying to present. Then take some time to write down what you think they are saying. Then read on. . . .

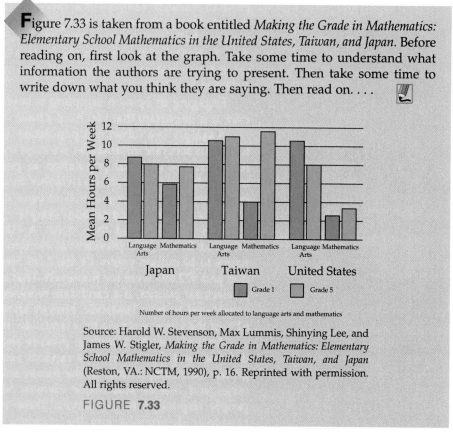

Number of hours per week allocated to language arts and mathematics

Source: Harold W. Stevenson, Max Lummis, Shinying Lee, and James W. Stigler, *Making the Grade in Mathematics: Elementary School Mathematics in the United States, Taiwan, and Japan* (Reston, VA.: NCTM, 1990), p. 16. Reprinted with permission. All rights reserved.

FIGURE **7.33**

DISCUSSION

In their report, the authors state that three cities were selected: Minneapolis (U.S.), Taipei (Taiwan), and Sendai (Japan). They chose "representative samples of ten schools in each city. Within each school, we randomly selected two first- and two fifth-grade classrooms. . . . Thus, our report deals with data from 1440 children (240 first graders and 240 fifth graders in each of the three cities)."[8] The data were collected in the early 1980s.

Note that there are several cases in which the authors needed to ensure that the samples were random. All of these choices could affect the results: the choice of cities, the choice of schools, the choice of classrooms, and the choice of students.

For this investigation, we will focus on the differences among the countries in grade 5 mathematics. How would you summarize the differences? To give this question more context, assume that you are a writer for a national television network. The nightly newscast is going to have a feature story on the differences among the educational systems in these three countries. You are to write the story. At one point, this graph will appear in the background. What do you want the anchor to say? Think and then read on. . . .

[8] Harold W. Stevenson, Max Lummis, Shinying Lee, and James W. Stigler, *Making the Grade in Mathematics: Elementary School Mathematics in the United States, Taiwan, and Japan* (Reston, VA.: NCTM, 1990), p. 2.

First, let us make sure we are interpreting the information validly. The numbers refer to the numbers of hours per week allocated to mathematics. The graph indicates that these are means (as opposed to medians or modes). If we assume that the data are normally distributed, then all three measures will be close. Given the use of computers, it is easier to determine the mean than the median.

Now let us analyze the wording. Does "allocate" mean how much time is scheduled for mathematics, or does it mean how much time is actually spent on mathematics? I was not able to infer from the book exactly how the data for this graph were gathered. My interpretation (from reading the book and consulting the dictionary) is that the hours allocated to mathematics were determined by adding up the time scheduled for mathematics in the teacher's plan book.

Now let us examine the hours allocated to mathematics each week in grade 5 and determine how we might convey that information to other people. Before we can make comparisons, we need to determine the actual times. Before reading on, determine the number of hours per week spent on math in grade 5 in each of the three countries. ✏️

Looking at the graph, we can conclude that in Japan, the number of hours allocated is about 8; in Taiwan, the number of hours is about 12; and in the United States, the number of hours is slightly over 3, or about $3\frac{1}{2}$ hours.

You have several options for how you write the news item:

1. *Simply report the numbers.* "In the ten Japanese schools, almost 8 hours per week was allocated to math in the fifth grade, compared to almost 12 hours per week in the ten Taiwanese schools and about $3\frac{1}{2}$ hours per week in the ten U.S. schools."

2. *Make additive comparisons.* "The Japanese schools allocate about $4\frac{1}{2}$ hours more per week than the U.S. schools, and the Taiwanese schools allocate about $8\frac{1}{2}$ hours more per week than the U.S. schools."

3. *Make multiplicative comparisons.* "The Japanese schools allocate more than twice as many hours per week as the U.S. schools, and the Taiwanese schools allocate more than three times as many hours per week as the U.S. schools."

4. *Make multiplicative comparisons using percent language.* "The Japanese schools allocate about 140% more time than the U.S. schools, and the Taiwanese schools allocate about 225% more time than the U.S. schools."

I hope you have seen that even when examining a reputable study, we need to critically examine and question the data and graphs that we read. Given their understanding of statistical analysis, the authors took pains to make the data as random as possible, and are therefore confident that if they had had more money and had been able to sample more students in more places, those results would have been close to the results that they found.

Weighted Average

We will consider one more concept in this section: *weighted averages.* In our work thus far with the mean, we have encountered situations in which we computed the simple mean. However, there are many situations in which we use what we call **weighted means**. This concept is a bit more complex and requires a strong understanding of the concept of *mean.* Let us investigate some examples.

INVESTIGATION 7.17 Grade Point Average

Table 7.17 gives Ed's semester grades. First estimate his grade point average (GPA), and then compute his actual GPA. Recall that A = 4 points, B = 3 points, C = 2 points, and so on. How can you explain and justify your estimation and computations?

TABLE 7.17

Course	Grade	Credits
Mathematics 151	B	3
Philosophy 205	A	3
Computer Science 100	C	3
Biology 102	A	3

DISCUSSION

One way of estimating is to use the concept of balance; recall the seesaw analogy. Where would the balance point be in this case?

```
C    B    A
x    x    x
          x
```

Clearly it would be between the B and the A. If you place the wedge under the B, the seesaw will not balance there because the two As "weigh" more than the one C. Numerically, we can determine Ed's average by taking the mean of the four grades:

$$\frac{(3 + 4 + 2 + 4)}{4} = 3.25$$

What if the computer course had been only a one-credit course? What would Ed's GPA be now? Think and read on. . . .

Intuitively, many students realize that his GPA will go up, since the low grade is now only worth 1 credit—that is, it doesn't "count as much" as the others. We can capitalize on this intuitive sense by connecting it to the idea of unit, which we have seen is one of the big ideas of mathematics. That is, we can count the B in Mathematics (worth 3 points) three times, the A in Philosophy 3 times, the C in Computer Science only once, and the A in Biology three times: (3 + 3 + 3) + (4 + 4 + 4) + 2 + (4 + 4 + 4) = 35. We divide the sum by 10 (that is, the number of credits he is taking), and so we find that his GPA is 3.5 (see Table 7.18).

We can understand the most efficient procedure for determining GPA by connecting our understanding that multiplication can be seen as repeated addition. We now multiply the numerical equivalent for each grade by the number of credits to get the grade points for each course. Then we add the grade points to get the total number of grade points for the whole semester and divide by the number of credits.

TABLE 7.18

Course	Grade	Numerical equivalent	Credits	Grade points
Mathematics 151	B	3	3	9
Philosophy 205	A	4	3	12
Computer Science 100	C	2	1	2
Biology 102	A	4	3	12
			10	35

INVESTIGATION 7.18   What Does Amy Need to Bring Her GPA Up to 2.5?

Now let us use this knowledge to solve a problem many college students face: determining how their grades in the present semester will affect their overall GPA. At Keene State College, education majors need to have a 2.5 GPA in order to be able to student-teach. You might want to check the policies at your college if you haven't already done so.

Let's say Amy didn't do so well her first three semesters in college (Table 7.19). What GPA will she need this semester (she is taking 16 credits) in order to bring her overall GPA up to 2.5? Once again, estimate first. Then determine the exact answer.

TABLE 7.19

	Credits	GPA
Beginning of the semester	50	2.35
Spring semester	16	?
Total	66	2.50

DISCUSSION

We can use the balance idea again. The 50 credits Amy has already taken will count more than the 16 credits she is taking this semester. Since the ratio of 50 to 16 is approximately 3:1, we can represent the problem by placing 3 weights at 2.35 and the balance point at 2.5 (see Figure 7.34). How far away must this semester's GPA be in order to balance the 2.35?

FIGURE **7.34**

If we combine the idea of ratios and number lines with our "balance sense," we realize that the one weight (representing this semester) will have to be three times as far from 2.50 as is 2.35. Do you see why? If not, go out and play on a seesaw with some friends. Seriously! Therefore, we can estimate that she will need a GPA of about 2.95.

One way to determine the exact answer is to determine how many total grade points she has now (2.35×50) and how many total grade points she needs if she is to have a GPA of 2.5 at the end of the semester (2.5 × 66). The difference of these numbers will tell us how many grade points her 16 credits this semester have to provide.

That is, 2.35 × 50 = 117.5 and 2.5 × 66 = 165. We now divide the difference of 47.5 by 16 (the number of credits she is taking this semester), and we find that she must get a GPA of at least 2.97 to bring her GPA up to at least 2.5. As you can see, the estimate was very close.

Some students understand the solution better with a slightly different phrasing. At this point (50 credits), she has accumulated 50 × 2.35 grade points, or 117.5. At the end of the semester (66 credits), if she is to have a GPA of 2.5, she will need to have accumulated a total of 66 × 2.50 grade points, or 165. What does she need to accumulate this semester? She needs 165 − 117.5 = 47.5 grade points. Now we compute: 47.5 grade points divided by 16 credits = 2.97.

INVESTIGATION 7.19 Course Grades Are Weighted Averages

Another area in which weighted averages are encountered is figuring one's grade in a course. Table 7.20 gives Amy's grades for a course, the weight of each component, and the grading scale for the course. What is her average for the course? Please work on this before reading on. . . .

There are several different ways to determine her average.

TABLE 7.20

Component of course	Weight	Amy's grades
Homework	30%	72, 84, 50, 72, 85, 80
Exams	30%	75, 83, 97, 78
Quizzes	15%	60, 0, 100, 90, 80
Final exam	25%	81

DISCUSSION

We first need to determine her average (mean) for each component. We find that her homework average is 74, her exam average is 83, and her quiz average is 66.

STRATEGY 1: Use accumulated grade points

Using the same idea that we used in determining GPA, we see that the homework counts 30 times, the exams count 30 times, the quizzes count 15 times, and the final exam counts 25 times.

$$\begin{array}{cccc} \text{hw} & \text{exam} & \text{quiz} & \text{final} \\ (30 \times 74) + & (30 \times 83) + & (15 \times 66) + & (25 \times 81) = \\ 2{,}220 \quad + & 2{,}490 \quad + & 990 \quad + & 2{,}025 \quad = 7{,}725 \end{array}$$

What does this 7,725 mean?

It means the total accumulated points. Since the entire course is 100 percent, we have to divide 7,725 by 100, and we get her average of 77.25.

STRATEGY 2: Apply proportional reasoning

Some students realize that what is crucial in the computation is the *proportion* of each component. The ratios of the four components of the course are

$30:30:15:25$, and we can simplify these ratios to $6:6:3:5$. Even though the weight of each component is smaller, the ratios are the same; for example, $30:15 = 6:3$. Can you use this idea to compute her average now? Do so before reading on. . . . ✏️

$$(6 \times 74) + (6 \times 83) + (3 \times 66) + (5 \times 81) = 1{,}545$$

What must we divide 1,545 by to determine her average? Think and read on. . . . ✏️

The sum of the weights is 20, and $1{,}545/20$ gives us 77.25.

The exercises will examine some of the many nuances of determining students' averages.

Summary

In this section, we have investigated a variety of tools that enable us to analyze different sets of data. We have added stem plots, grouped frequency tables, histograms, line plots, and boxplots to our graphing toolbox. We have seen similarities between stem plots and histograms, and similarities between line plots and boxplots. We have seen that when the range of a set of data is great, it is often helpful to select intervals and make a grouped frequency table, from which we can then make a histogram to give us a visual sense of the data.

We have learned about the three candidates for the "center" of a set of data: mean, median, and mode. We have discussed when each of these is an appropriate representation of the center and when it is not. We have found that these numbers, just like people, are not always good representatives! You encountered dilemmas of this nature if you did Exploration 7.3 (Typical Person).

We have also examined different ways to quantify the dispersion (or spread) of a set of data, from simple ideas like range, clusters, gaps, and outliers to more complex ideas like interquartile range and standard deviation. We have seen that the mean and standard deviation can be used together to describe the center and spread of a set of data that is normally distributed, and that the median and quartiles can be used together to describe the center and spread of a set of data that is skewed.

One chapter in a book called *Benchmarks for Scientific Literacy* focuses on the kind of mathematical knowledge especially useful in scientific inquiry. Below is an excerpt from the description of students' need to be able to interpret data:

> One common misunderstanding is the belief that averages are always highly representative of a population; little or no attention is given to the range of variation around averages. . . . Because there is a persistent misconception, even in adults, that means are good representations of whole groups, it is especially important to draw students' attention to the additional questions, "what are the largest and smallest values?" and "how much do the data spread on both sides of the middle?"[9]

We have touched upon the notion of sampling. The actual practice of gathering data on samples of a population in order to make generalizations about the entire population is rather complex. However, we have explored some of the issues that are encountered in this practice. Taking measures to ensure that the sample is as representative of the total population as possible involves

[9] American Association for the Advancement of Science, *Benchmarks for Scientific Literacy* (New York: Oxford University Press, 1993), pp. 226–227.

taking measures to ensure that the samples that are obtained are random samples. In cases where there are distinct subgroups within the population, this often involves stratified random samples.

Finally, we examined the notion of weighted means. We connected the computation of weighted means and simple means, and we connected the concept of both kinds of means—that is, the notion of the balance point of the set of data.

EXERCISES 7.2

1. Suppose an instructor gives the same quiz to two classes. Tell the instructor how the students did in each class and how the classes compare.

   Class 1: 9, 8, 8, 7, 7, 7, 7, 6, 6, 5

   Class 2: 10, 9, 8, 8, 7, 7, 7, 6, 6, 5, 4

2. Suppose the instructor in Investigation 7.11 gave the same test to another class whose scores are given below. Tell the instructor how the students did in each class and how the classes compare.

   Class 2: 96, 94, 93, 92, 89, 85, 85, 85, 83, 80, 79, 77, 77, 77, 75, 74, 74, 68, 67, 65, 65

3. Below are the heights of adults in a college class.
   a. Make a histogram for these data.
   b. Determine the mean and standard deviation.
   c. What percent of the values lie within 1 standard deviation of the mean?

Height (inches)	Frequency
59	1
60	1
61	3
62	8
63	11
64	13
65	17
66	14
67	11
68	7
69	4
70	2
71	1
72	1

4. Below are the ages of students in a Mathematics for Elementary Teachers class:

   18, 18, 18, 19, 19, 19, 19, 19, 19, 20, 20, 20, 21, 21, 21, 21, 21, 21, 23, 24, 24, 26, 27, 37, 42, 43, 46

   a. Use one or more graphs to show the data.
   b. What is the average age? Justify your answer.
   c. Describe the spread of the data.

5. Below are the annual salaries (in thousands of dollars) of workers in Bates Ball Bearing factory:

   12, 12, 13, 13, 13, 16, 16, 16, 16, 18, 18, 18, 21, 21, 21, 26, 26, 28, 31, 51, 51, 75

   a. Use one or more graphs to show the data.
   b. What is the average salary? Justify your answer.
   c. Describe the spread of the data.

6. The teachers at Gates Memorial High School got to talking about cars and how long they keep them. Someone wondered about the average age of the teachers' cars. Below is a graph representing the ages, rounded to the nearest year.

   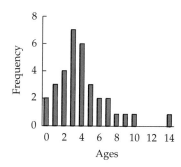

   a. Before computing, predict the mean and the median. Explain your reasoning.
   b. Determine the mean and the median.

7. Willie has an average (mean) of 83.4 on the first 5 exams. What is the least he can score in order to have an average of 85 for all six exams?

8. A student's mean score on five quizzes is 73. What does the student need on the next two quizzes in order to bring her overall average up to 78?

9. If the mean income of 24 people is $28,000, how much is the mean increased by the addition of a single income of $200,000?

10. John's bowling average is 152. The other night, John's scores on the first two games were 132 and 138. What does he need to bowl on the third game in order to maintain his average?

11. In driving to a nearby town, it took Maurice 27 minutes to go 18 miles. What was his average speed?

12. In a special triathlon, Betty swam 1 mile in 25 minutes, biked 25 miles in 45 minutes, and then ran 5 miles in 40 minutes. What was her "average" speed for the race?

13. The scores on a recent exam were

    62, 84, 90, 78, 80, 77, 92, 84, 88, 100

    Determine the mean and median scores. Determine the standard deviation.

14. Lucy took three tests. If her median score was 82, her mean score was 87, and the range was 17, what were her three test scores?

15. The mean of five numbers is 6. If one of the five numbers is removed, the mean becomes 7. What is the value of the number that was removed?

16. On a certain exam, Tony corrected 10 papers and found the mean for his group to be 70. Alice corrected the remaining 20 papers and found that the mean for her group was 80. What is the mean of the combined group of students?

17. Create a set of 10 test scores for which the mean is higher than the median.

18. A student scores 16 points on a 20-point quiz and 35 points on a 50-point quiz. The professor determines her average in the following unconventional way. What do you think of this system?

    $$\frac{16}{20} + \frac{35}{50} = \frac{51}{70}$$

19. I recently read an article in which the following sentence appeared: "The average cost of a car is $14,000." How do you think that number was determined? In your answer, you need to state whether you think that figure represents the mean, median, or mode.

20. How far above or below the average temperature do the numbers need to be in order for people to refer to a month as a hot month or a cold month?

21. The following information comes from the *Universal Almanac, 1994,* which was reporting the results of a 1988 study of 27 major cities by the U.S. Conference of Mayors.

    > The composition of the cities' homeless population was, on average: 49% single men, 34% members of families, 13% single women, and 5% runaway and so-called "throwaway" youth (children rejected by parents). Children—both in families and runaways—account for about 25% of the population; persons considered mentally ill account for about 25%; substance abusers account for 34%. The survey also found that 21% of homeless people are employed in full- or part-time jobs; 26% are veterans.
    >
    > Another study found that the average age of single homeless men and women was between 34 and 37, which is much lower than found in previous decades.[10]

    Discuss the use of the word *average* in this report with respect to what you have learned in this chapter.

22. The median time between divorce and remarriage is 2.2 years for men and 2.5 years for women. Interpret this statement and then translate the fuller statement into English.

23. We found that in a normally distributed set of data, the mean, median, and mode are virtually identical. However, this is not necessarily true for other distributions. What about data whose distribution is skewed to the right? Can you predict the numerical order of the three averages? For example, will the mean be largest, followed by the median, followed by the mode? Or do you think "it depends"? Justify your answer.

24. Explain the similarities between a line plot and a boxplot. You are encouraged but not required to use data from a set of data such as that in Investigation 7.9 or 7.10.

25. There is another way to figure the mean of a set of data. Here's how it works. Let's say we want to find the mean weight of these boxes of fruit: 26, 27, 38, 35, 34, 29. I estimate the average as 30 and then add or subtract the distance of each datum from my estimate. In this case, the arithmetic would be

    $$^-4 + {}^-3 + 8 + 5 + 4 + {}^-1 = +9$$

    Next, 9/5 = 1.8, and so the mean is 31.8.

    a. Explain why this procedure works.

    b. Make up another set of data and use this strategy to determine the mean.

26. Suppose the distribution of heights of a group of 400 children is normal, with a mean of 150 centimeters and a standard deviation of 12 centimeters. About how many of these children are taller than 162 centimeters?

27. The heights of 1,500 boys at West High School were measured, and the mean was found to be 66 inches, with a standard deviation of 2.5 inches. If the heights are approximately normally distributed, 95% of the boys are between ____ and ___ inches tall. About how many of the boys are less than 5 feet tall? *Note:* You cannot get an exact answer here. Any answer will involve some estimating.

28. Let's say a student scored 45 on a math achievement test for which the mean was 36 and the standard deviation was 6. Based on this performance, what score would you predict for her on a standardized test for which the mean is 100 and the standard deviation 15?

29. What happens to the mean and the standard deviation of a set of data when the value of each datum is increased by the same amount?

30. A tire company tested a particular model of super radial tire and found the tires to be normally distributed with respect to wear. The "average" (mean) tire wore

---

[10]John W. Wright, ed., *Universal Almanac 1994* (Kansas City: Andrews and McMeel [A Universal Press Syndicate Company], 1991), p. 215.

out at 59,000 miles, and the standard deviation was 2,500 miles.

a. If 2,000 tires are tested, about how many are likely to wear out before 54,000 miles?

b. What if the company wanted to guarantee 55,000 miles? What percent of the tires are likely to wear out before 55,000 miles? In this case, you cannot get an "exact" answer. What could you do to increase the accuracy of your estimate?

31. A tire company tested another model of tire and found the tires to be normally distributed with respect to wear. The "average" (mean) tire wore out at 46,000 miles, and the standard deviation was 2,400 miles. If 2,000 tires are tested, about how many are likely to wear out before 45,000 miles? You cannot get an exact answer. I want your best estimate. Please use graph paper to help you estimate.

32. Jack and Jill go to different schools. Jack got an 82 on a test with a mean of 60 and a standard deviation of 15. Jill got a 78 on a test with a mean of 60 and a standard deviation of 9. If both tests are graded on a curve, who did better?

33. Wendy took three standardized aptitude tests: English, mathematics, and general information. The table below gives her score, the mean, and the standard deviation for each test. On which test did she do the "best"? Justify your answer.

Test	Wendy's score	Mean	Standard deviation
English	85	75	7.5
Math	63	55	6
General information	104	94	8

34. The following scenarios have been taken from the *Instructor's Course Planner* for the textbook *Children*.[11] In each case, do you think the sample is a random sample or a biased sample? Justify your response.

a. The researchers asked teenage boys about their driving records and habits by going to a movie drive-in, a local bar, the beach, and a baseball park.

b. Parents at a PTA meeting were interviewed about the quality of the local public school system.

c. A telephone survey assessed a community's attitudes toward welfare recipients.

d. Children were asked their opinion of Santa Claus on December 28.

35. Holly is driving through New England. The first 100 miles of her trip were on local roads, and her mean speed for that part of the trip was 40 mph. The next 100 miles of the trip are on an interstate highway. At what speed would she have to travel on the second part of the trip in order to achieve a mean speed of 50 mph for the entire trip?

36. Compute Ed's GPA, to two decimal places, for the semester (A = 4 , B = 3, C = 2).

Course	Grade	Credits
Mathematics	B	3
Elementary Methods	A	6
Computers in School	C	1
Biology	B	4

37. Marcia has a 3.42 GPA after three semesters (47 credits). She had some personal problems during the next semester and did not do as well. Below is a report of her grades. What is her overall GPA now?

Course	Credits	Grade
Eng 232	3	B
Geog 142	3	BC
Chem 125	3	D
ED 202	1	C
ED 262	3	B

38. Perry has a 2.53 GPA after 112 credits. This is his last semester, he is taking 15 credits, and he has senioritis.

a. What is the minimum GPA Perry can get and still graduate with at least a 2.5 GPA?

b. He is taking five 3-credit courses. Give one scenario that will let him "squeak by."

	Grade
Course 1	
Course 2	
Course 3	
Course 4	
Course 5	

39. Joe has a 3.22 GPA after 46 credits. He says that he has a total of 148.12 grade points. Julie says that's impossible. What do you think?

40. Below are Amy's grades for each component of the course, the weight of each component, and the grading scale for the course.

Component of course	Weight	Amy's grades
Attendance/class participation	15%	78
Homework	30%	70, 84, 40, 82, 85, 60
Exams	25%	75, 83, 87, 78
Quizzes (10-point quizzes)	5%	5, 0, 10, 9
Final exam	25%	81

a. What is Amy's overall average for the course?

[11] Allen Keniston and Blaine Peden, *Instructor's Course Planner* for *Children*, by John Santrock, (Dubuque, Iowa: Brown & Benchmark, 1995), p. 36.

b. What would her grade have been if her grade on the homework on which she got a 40 had been an 82?

c. How much did the missed quiz hurt her grade? Assume she would have gotten an 8 instead of the zero.

41. Grace's grades and their relative weight are listed below.

	Weights	Grades
Quiz	15%	76
Homework	30%	83
Exams	30%	82.5
Final exam	25%	

a. Determine Grace's average at the beginning of the final exam.

b. What does Grace need to score on the final to get a B (bottom B is 80%)?

42. Pauline wants to have an idea of her present grade, about halfway through the semester. Based on the data below, how would you figure her grade? What would Pauline's grade be at this time?

	Scores	Relative weight
Homework	72, 80, 65	30%
Exams	68, 83	25%
Quizzes	60, 90	15%

43. Refer to Investigation 7.19, in which we determined Amy's average for the course. One student says that I should not have rounded. For example, her homework average is really 73.83. What do you think? Could rounding, rather than using the exact scores, actually affect the student's grade?

S E C T I O N   **7.3**   **CONCEPTS RELATED TO CHANCE**

▲ The study of probability . . . should not focus on developing formulas or computing the likelihood of events pictured in texts. Students should actively explore situations by experimenting and simulating probability models. . . . Students should talk about their ideas and use the results of their experiments to model situations or predict events.

(Curriculum Standards, p. 109)

If you did one or more of Explorations 7.7 through 7.12, you have conducted experiments and simulations and grappled with the fundamental probability ideas that we will now examine more formally.

Stop for a moment and think of situations in which probability enters into our lives. Then read on. . . . 📝

We make and are affected by probability decisions every day. For example,

■ If you decide to have two children, what is the probability that you will have a boy and a girl?

■ What is the probability that you will get a teaching job after you graduate?

■ If you are independently employed, should you buy health insurance? People's decisions are influenced by their estimate of the probability that they will have a catastrophic illness.

■ If you drive over the speed limit or decide not to put money in the parking meter, what is the probability of your getting a ticket?

■ What is the probability that everyone who buys an airline ticket will actually take the trip? Airlines regularly sell more tickets than they have seats because they know that the probability of this is very low.

These situations all have in common that their results are unknown. Much of our understanding of probability is based on collecting and analyzing data on occurrences of situations that, individually, are random. Analyzing the data helps us to see patterns in these occurrences and to make predictions. For example, since the probability that a 21-year-old male will have an accident is much greater than the probability that a 50-year-old male will have an accident, car insurance rates for 21-year-old males are higher than those for 50-year-old males.

Our work with data that are normally distributed connects to probability; for example, if a tire company's sample of tires lasted an average of 42,000 miles with a standard deviation of 2,000, the company can say that there is an 84% probability that a specific tire will last at least 40,000 miles.

Random phenomena   It is important to note the way in which mathematicians use the word *random*. When mathematicians use the word *random*, we are referring to phenomena that are unpredictable individually but that have regular patterns when considered as a group, or when considered over the long run. Random is not a synonym for *haphazard*, but rather refers to phenomena for which we cannot make individual predictions. The following example nicely illustrates this point. If we drop a coin from a certain height, we can predict the time it will take to reach the ground with a great deal of precision. However, if we flip that coin, we can give only the probability that it will land heads or tails. We do not say that flipping a coin is haphazard, but rather that it is random.[12] When we flip many coins, we find that there are many patterns, as you will find in this section.

In this section, we will investigate both well-defined questions (for example, the probability of tossing 4 heads in a row) and questions that are not as well defined (for example, insurance premiums).

Preliminary Terms and Concepts

We hear probability statements all the time. Let's say you turn on the television and hear the weather forecaster say, "There is a 25% chance of rain tomorrow." What does that statement mean? Write your thoughts before reading on. . . . 🖊

When we make a probability statement, we are giving a numerical value that represents the degree to which we believe that event will or will not happen.

Probabilities can be represented by fractions, decimals, percents, ratios, and odds. The following five statements are equivalent:

- There is a 25% chance of rain tomorrow.

- The probability of rain tomorrow is 1/4 .

- The probability of rain tomorrow is 0.25.

- There is a 1 chance in 4 of rain tomorrow.

- The odds against rain tomorrow are 3 to 1.

Outcomes and events   There are two terms whose definition will make our discussion about probabilities much clearer: outcome and event. Answer the two questions and then read on. . . . 🖊

- If you select a card from a regular deck of playing cards, what is the probability of drawing the queen of spades?

---

[12] David Moore, "Uncertainty" in *On the Shoulders of Giants: New Approaches to Numeracy,* ed. Lynn Steen (Washington, D.C.: National Academy of Sciences, 1990), p. 98.

■ If you select a card from a regular deck of playing cards, what is the probability of drawing any queen?

The probability of drawing the queen of spades is 1/52, and the probability of drawing any queen is 4/52 or 1/13.

We often use notation as a shorthand to express probabilities:

$$P(\text{Q of spades}) = \frac{1}{52} \qquad P(\text{Q}) = \frac{1}{13}$$

We refer to "queen of spades" as an outcome and "any queen" as an event. Let us examine the difference between the two. When we define a situation (in this case, drawing a card from a deck), each possibility is called an **outcome**. The set of all possible outcomes is called the **sample space**. Thus, each outcome is an element of the sample space. Within the sample space, there are many possible subsets, for example the subset consisting of the elements

$E =$ {queen of diamonds, queen of spades, queen of hearts, and queen of clubs}

Any subset of a sample space is called an **event**.

When All Outcomes Are Equally Likely

In this case, we are examining situations in which the probability of each outcome is **equally likely**. When we are examining a situation in which all outcomes are equally likely, we can determine the probability of an event by computing the following ratio, expressed both in probability language and in set language. If all outcomes in a sample space are equally likely, then the probability of event E is given by

$$P(E) = \frac{\text{number of favorable outcomes}}{\text{number of total outcomes}} \qquad P(E) = \frac{\text{number of elements in } E}{\text{number of elements in } S}$$

When All Outcomes Are Not Equally Likely

On many occasions, all outcomes are not equally likely. Consider the spinner in Figure 7.35. In this case, there are four outcomes: 1, 2, 3, 4. However, they are not equally likely. In this case, what is the probability of spinning an odd number?

FIGURE **7.35**

$$P(\text{Odd}) = P(1) + P(3) = \frac{1}{2} + \frac{1}{8} = \frac{5}{8}$$

We can generalize from this example to state the probability of an event when each outcome is not equally likely:

The probability of an event is equal to the sum of the probabilities of all outcomes in that event.

That is, if event E consists of n different outcomes $O_1, O_2, O_3, \ldots, O_n$, then $P(E) = P(O_1) + P(O_2) + P(O_3) + \cdots + P(O_n)$.

Note that this more general definition of probability works with both kinds of situations.

When we speak of the probability of an event happening, at one extreme we have **impossible events**—for example, the probability of a student having a GPA of 4.4. At the other extreme, we have **certain events**—for example, the probability that it will rain this year in Jacksonville, Florida. If an event is impossible, we say that the probability is 0. If it is certain, we say that the probability is 1. Thus, the probability of any event is between 0 and 1.

Theoretical and Experimental Probabilities

When working with probability situations, we distinguish between theoretical probabilities and experimental probabilities. In some situations involving probabilities, we can determine the theoretical probability—for example, the probability of a couple having 5 boys in a row or of rolling doubles 3 times in a row when playing Monopoly. In situations where we can determine the total number of outcomes and we can count the number of outcomes in a specific event, we refer to the probability as the **theoretical probability**. That is, the theoretical probability refers to our expectation, assuming that things turn out ideally. For example, we can say that when we flip a coin, theoretically the probability of its being heads is 1/2.

There are many real-life situations in which it is either impossible or very expensive to determine theoretical probabilities. In those situations, we determine the experimental probability by collecting and analyzing data. For example, manufacturers determine the probabilities that their products will last a certain time by testing some of the models. For example, if 90% of the sampled tires last at least 40,000 miles, the manufacturer will assume that close to 90% of all the tires of that model will last at least 40,000 miles. In this case, we would say that the experimental probability of a tire's lasting at least 40,000 miles is 90%. In situations in which the probability of an outcome or event has been determined by collecting data and determining the fraction of the time in which the outcome or event actually occurred, we refer to that fraction as the **experimental probability**. Some books and authors use the term **empirical probability** instead.

Let us now investigate some situations to deepen our understanding.

INVESTIGATION **7.20**   Probability of Having 2 Boys and 2 Girls

Let's say a couple is planning to begin their family and would like to have 4 children. What is the probability that they will have 2 boys and 2 girls? What do you think? What problem-solving tools might help? Take some time to work on this question before reading on. . . .

DISCUSSION

Three common initial hypotheses are 50%, 20%, and 37.5%. Let us investigate each of these.

Those who answer 50% reason something like this: Each time there is a 50% chance of getting a boy or a girl, so it makes sense that the "balanced" possibility (same number of boys and girls) will take place 50% of the time.

Those who answer 20% reason something like this: There are 5 possibilities (events)—4G0B (that is, 4 girls and 0 boys), 3G1B, 2G2B, 1G3B, 0G4B. Thus, 2G2B is 1 out of 5, which is 20%.

Those who answer 37.5% reason something like the following: There are 16 possible outcomes (BBBB, BBBG, BGBB, and so on), and 6 of the 16 involve 2 boys and 2 girls. Therefore, the probability of having 2 boys and 2 girls = 6/16 = 3/8 = 37.5%.

What do you think now?

Rather than present the answer just yet (presenting the answer too quickly means that more students are more likely to rent the solution rather than own it), let us do a **simulation**. This is what scientists, economists, and mathematicians often do when they are beginning an investigation or when they have different hypotheses: They construct a model of the situation and then run a simulation. How might we run a simulation of this question? Please think for a minute yourself and then read on. . . . 🖊

There are many ways to simulate this scenario:

1. We could write a computer program using a random number generator. That is, we could ask the computer to randomly select among two numbers, for example, 0 and 1, and then translate the 0 to a boy and the 1 to a girl. We could program the computer to generate and translate four numbers at a time and then translate that outcome as 4 boys, 3 boys and 1 girl, 2 boys and 2 girls, and so on.

2. We could roll dice: If we roll a 1, 2, or 3, it's a girl; if we roll a 4, 5, or 6, it's a boy. We could also tape a B on three sides of a die and tape a G on the other three sides. We could then roll one die 4 times, or we could roll 4 dice and arrange them in a line.

3. We could write B and G on the same number of slips of paper and put them in a hat and then take slips out. This would be slower and has one other potential problem. What is it?

    We would need to put the paper back after each draw. For example, we could put a B on 5 pieces and a G on 5 pieces. If we picked a G and didn't put it back, the probability of getting a B would now be 5/9 and the probability of getting a G would be 4/9.

4. We could label a spinner (see Figure 7.36). Every four spins would represent one random outcome, such as BBGG.

FIGURE **7.36**

Your instructor may have you do this simulation in class. If not, do it yourself. As you may have learned from Explorations 7.7 through 7.12, we can use simulations not only to help us determine the experimental probability but also to better understand how to develop the theoretical probability.

With the knowledge gleaned from the simulation, let us now explore how the theoretical probability is determined.

STRATEGY 1: Be systematic and look for patterns

There are many ways to be systematic. Let us examine one way below.

First, the couple could have all girls or all boys: GGGG and BBBB.

Note the use of letters to represent boy and girl rather than spelling them out. This saves time and makes patterns in the data easier to see.

Next, we could determine the different ways in which the couple could have 3 girls and 1 boy. If you did not do the problem this way, stop now and see if you can determine the answer to this particular question. . . .

One way to do this systematically is to see that the boy could be in four different positions: oldest, second, third, youngest. Symbolically, this looks like

B G G G

G B G G

G G B G

G G G B

Do you see a pattern here? How would you describe it?

If you look only at the B, you can see it move diagonally. Do you see that this systematic approach also practically gives us the ways to have 3 boys and a girl?

If you stop and think for a minute, you might realize that since there are four different ways to have 3 girls, there must also be four different ways to have 3 boys. Do you see why? There are many symmetries in probability situations.

Finally, we need to determine how many different ways there are to have 2 boys and 2 girls. Do this first yourself before reading on. . . .

There are a variety of methods you might use to come up with the 6 different ways in which one could have 2 boys and 2 girls. (In probability language, we are saying that the event 2B, 2G consists of 6 outcomes.)

B G B G

G B G B

B G G B

G B B G

B B G G

G G B B

Since 6 of the 16 outcomes have 2 Bs and 2 Gs, the probability we sought is 6/16, or 37.5%.

STRATEGY 2: Make a tree diagram

Figure 7.37 is a tree diagram for this problem; it is a different way to represent and solve the problem. Can you interpret the tree diagram? Do you see why it is called a tree diagram? How is the tree diagram made? How is this similar to other diagrams used in the book?

Now make a table of the 16 outcomes. (The table is not shown—you have to make it!) What patterns do you see in the table? Write the patterns you see and then read on. . . .

There is a pattern in each of the columns. The right column simply alternates between B and G. The next column alternates between 2 Bs and 2 Gs. The third column alternates between 4 Bs and 4 Gs. The last column consists of 8 Bs and 8 Gs.

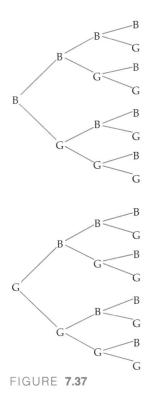

FIGURE **7.37**

Some students see the symmetrical nature of the table. Pair each row in the table in the following way: row 1 and row 16, row 2 and row 15, and so on. Another way of saying this is to fold the table in half and look at the rows that lie on top of each other. Each half is like a mirror image of the other: BBBB and GGGG, BBBG and GGGB, and so on.

Note that this table is not identical to the table that comes from Strategy 1 although they contain the same 16 outcomes. The other table exhibited different patterns. What is important here is that both tables represent a systematic approach to the problem. If a student were to generate the 16 outcomes in a more random fashion, there would probably be fewer patterns and hence a greater probability of missing one or more outcomes.

MATHEMATICS

Blaise Pascal, whom we have encountered before, once said, "Chance favors the prepared mind." A powerful illustration of this occurred one year while my students were investigating this question. Some students noted that since the letters G and B are similar, it was hard to see patterns. One student replaced the Gs with 0 and the Bs with 1. The contrast between 0 and 1 is much greater than that between B and G. The student then listed all 16 outcomes on the board, noting that 0 represented B and 1 represented G. This notation made it easier to discuss patterns and also provoked another discovery. Does Table 7.21 remind you of something you have studied before?

TABLE 7.21
0 0 0 0
0 0 0 1
0 0 1 0
0 0 1 1
0 1 0 0
0 1 0 1
0 1 1 0
0 1 1 1
1 0 0 0
. . .
1 1 1 1

This table is simply the first 16 numbers in base 2!

Let us now examine two related questions for this couple, from which new probability concepts will emerge.

INVESTIGATION **7.21**   Probability of Having 3 Boys and 2 Girls

What if the couple were planning to have 5 children? What is the probability of having 3 boys and 2 girls? Work on this and then read on. . . .

DISCUSSION

There are several different ways to answer this question. You can make a new table, extend the tree diagram, or extend the base 2 counting table and look for outcomes that show two 0s and three 1s or three 0s and two 1s. However, in any of these cases, obtaining the solution is relatively cumbersome. It becomes downright tedious if we extend the question further. For example, what is the probability of having 4 girls and 4 boys?

What is happening here is a classical example of a kind of situation that has contributed to the development of mathematics and science—a representation or a solution that worked well at some point becomes less useful at another point, and so a new approach or method is needed.

Table 7.22 represents another way of solving the problem: by looking at the number of outcomes in different events. I have filled in the fourth row of the table, which shows the frequency of five events in the case of 4 children: 4G0B, 3G1B, 2G2B, 1G3B, 0G4B. Take a few minutes to make sense of the table. If you can make sense of the table, fill in the missing cells. If you don't understand the table, then read on.

TABLE 7.22

NUMBER OF GIRLS							Number of children
6	5	4	3	2	1	0	
							1
							2
							3
		1	4	6	4	1	4
							5

What this table shows is that if you have 4 children, there is 1 way to have 4 girls, there are 4 ways to have 3 girls (and 1 boy), there are 6 ways to have 2 girls (and 2 boys), there are 4 ways to have 1 girl (and 3 boys), and there is 1 way to have no girls (that is, all boys). Do the same for 1 child, 2 children, 3 children, and then 5 children. If you didn't understand the table before, fill out the table now before reading on. . . . 🖉

What patterns do you see? Describe them as if you were talking to someone on the phone. . . . 🖉

There are small (local) patterns; for example,

- The top-right-to-bottom-left diagonal contains only 1s.
- The column representing 0 girls contains only 1s.
- The column representing 1 girl is the counting numbers: 1, 2, 3, 4, 5.

There are also large (global) patterns. For example, there is a connection between each row and the next row. Look at the third row and the fourth row. What do you see? Think and then read on. . . . 🖉

By now you may be smiling because you realize that you have seen this pattern before. Yes, this is simply Pascal's triangle, which you first saw in Investigation 1.6! Connecting this problem to Pascal's triangle makes our work much less tedious. If a couple has five children, what is the probability of 3 girls and 2 boys? Think and then read on . . . . 🖉

The cell representing 3 girls and 2 boys contains 10 outcomes, and there are 32 outcomes in all; therefore, the probability of 3 girls and 2 boys is 10/32, or about 31%. Similarly, the probability of having 2 girls and 3 boys is also 10/32. So now what is the probability that the couple will have 3 girls and 2 boys or 2 girls and 3 boys?

Mutually exclusive events   We can simply add the two probabilities together. The justification for this goes back to set theory. The two events (3B, 2G) and

(2B, 3G) represent disjoint sets. In probability language, we say that they are **mutually exclusive events**.

If events A and B are mutually exclusive, then $P(A \text{ or } B) = P(A) + P(B)$.

There is another global pattern that comes out of the table above. It comes from adding a new column headed "Total number of outcomes." If you have not yet seen this pattern, add that new column and fill in the numbers. What do you see? Think and then read on. . . . 🖉

This column simply can be described most succinctly (in English) as "powers of 2."

INVESTIGATION **7.22** Probability of Having at Least 1 Girl

Let us examine another situation. Let's say a couple is planning to have four children. What is the probability that they will have *at least* one girl? Work on this and then read on. . . . 🖉

DISCUSSION

STRATEGY 1: Refer to the table or tree diagram and count

From the tables you created in Investigation 7.20, count those outcomes in which there is at least 1 girl and divide by 16.

STRATEGY 2: Connect this problem to sets

Let us explore this strategy because it has implications for other probability situations. What if you were asked, "What is the probability of having no girls?" Do you see how the answer to this question enables us to answer the question, What is the probability of having at least 1 girl?

Do you see why the following formula is true: $P(\text{no girls}) + P(\text{at least } 1 \text{ girl}) = 1$?

Consider the sample space for having 4 children, and put the outcomes into two subsets:

$A =$ the set of outcomes containing no girls

$B =$ the set of outcomes containing at least one girl

Complementary events   In this case, all outcomes go into one subset or the other. Not only are the two subsets disjoint, their union is equal to the whole sample space. Since every outcome is in either set A or set B, that means that $A = \bar{B}$. In other words, these are complementary sets. In probability language, we say that these are **complementary events.** Not surprisingly, if we have two events such that event A and event B are complementary, then $p(A) + p(B) = 1$.

If we recall Investigation 7.21, we see that complementary events represent a special kind of mutually exclusive event.

In this case, the probability of A (the probability of having no girls) is much easier to determine than the probability of B (the probability of having at least 1 girl), and we can use basic algebra to transform the equation $p(A) + p(B) = 1$ into the equation $p(B) = 1 - p(A)$. We can now determine the probability of having at least 1 girl:

$$p(B) = 1 - p(A) = 1 - \frac{1}{16} = \frac{15}{16}$$

Let us now make use of our understanding of probability to investigate two related problems.

INVESTIGATION 7.23 50-50 Chance of Passing?

PEANUTS reprinted by permission of United Feature Syndicate. Inc.

FIGURE 7.38

Poor Peppermint Patty. Today there is a true-false quiz with 10 questions. She forgot to read the story on which the questions are based, and so she has to guess at every question (see Figure 7.38). Assuming that she has a 50% chance at each question, what is the probability that she will get 70% or better on the quiz? Think about this and then read on. . . .

HISTORY

The development of probability theory was spurred by gamblers' questions. The great Italian scientist Galileo (1564–1642), who is better known for getting in trouble with the Inquisition by insisting that the earth revolved around the sun, was asked why one is more likely to get a sum of 10 than a sum of 9 when rolling three dice and adding the numbers. The foundations for probability as a mathematical discipline were laid by the work of Blaise Pascal (1623–1662) and Pierre Fermat (1601–1665) as they responded to several questions asked by a professional gambler, Chevalier de Mere. One of those questions was: Why would one lose money by betting (even money) that you would get at least one double 6 when throwing 2 dice 24 times?

Since many people object to students studying gambling theory in school, we will de-emphasize the gambling connections between dice and probability. However, this is not hard because dice are also used in many board games.

DISCUSSION

STRATEGY 1: Make a tree diagram

In order to use a tree diagram for this problem, you would need a very big sheet of paper and a lot of time. However, the tree diagram points to another strategy. What is it?

STRATEGY 2: Be systematic and look for patterns

There is only one way she can get all 10 right. Why is this?

Now, how many ways can she get 9 out of 10 right; that is, how many different outcomes are there for getting 9 questions right? There are several ways to determine the number. Work on this question yourself before reading on. . . .

Some students reason like this: "She could get all but the last one (#10) right, she could get all but #9 right, she could get all but #8 right, and so on." What pattern do you see here?

Some students see the systematic nature of this approach better by looking at, and filling out, the diagram below:

RRRRRRRRRW

RRRRRRRRWR

RRRRRRRWRR

etc.

Regardless of how we saw this problem, we find that there are 10 different ways in which she could get 9 out of 10 correct. More formally, we would say that there are 10 outcomes in the event "9 correct answers."

Now does the following row of Pascal's triangle make sense?

1   10   45   120   210   252   210   120   45   10   1

If not, analyze a 4-item test in which she guesses each time: There is 1 way to get all 4 correct, there are 4 ways to get 3 right, there are 6 ways to get 2 right, and so on. Can you use Pascal's triangle now to determine the probability of Patty's getting a score of 70% or greater? Think and then read on. . . .

If you have understood the application of Pascal's triangle to this problem, you have done the computation

$$\frac{(120 + 45 + 10 + 1)}{1,024} = 0.17$$

Can you express the answer to the problem in a full sentence? Do so and then read on. . . .

There are many valid ways to express the answer. A couple of these are

- "Peppermint Patty has a 17% chance of getting at least 70% right."
- "Peppermint Patty has about a 1 in 6 chance of getting at least 70% right."

Does the answer surprise you? Is it higher or lower than you expected? Many teachers do not believe in true-false tests because they believe that a lucky student can appear to know more than that student really does. Does this investigation make you feel more or less disposed toward true-false tests? What if there were 20 questions and the student guessed at each one? Will the probability of getting at least 70% be greater or less than on a 10-item quiz?

INVESTIGATION 7.24 What Is the Probability of Rolling a 7?

If we roll one die, the probability of each outcome (that is, 1, 2, 3, 4, 5, or 6) is 1/6 (assuming a fair die). Suppose we roll 2 dice and find the sum of the numbers on the dice. What is the probability of rolling a 7? Work on this problem and then read on. . . .

DISCUSSION

There are several ways to be systematic, and there are several ways to represent this problem. Look at each of the following partially completed representations. How would you finish them? Now, complete the tables.

REPRESENTATION 1

Table 7.23 was created by thinking systematically.

TABLE 7.23

1, 1	2, 1	?, ?
1, 2	2, 2	
1, 3	?, ?	
1, 4		
1, 5		
1, 6		

REPRESENTATION 2

Table 7.24 was created by thinking systematically in a slightly different way.

TABLE 7.24		
1, 1	1, 2,	?, ?
2, 1	2, 2	
3, 1	3, ?	
4, 1		
5, 1		
6, 1		

REPRESENTATION 3

Figure 7.39 is yet another tree diagram!

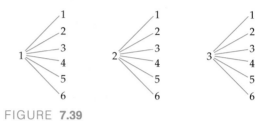

FIGURE **7.39**

In each of these cases, we find that there are 36 distinct possible outcomes. This is a useful time to formally present the **multiplication principle** which can be stated in outcomes or in probabilities:

Stated in number of outcomes   If event A consists of a outcomes and event B consists of b outcomes, the event "A then B" consists of $a \cdot b$ outcomes. In this case, event A is rolling a die and event B is rolling a die; both consist of 6 outcomes. Thus, the event "roll a die and then roll it again" consists of $6 \cdot 6 = 36$ outcomes.

Stated in probabilities   If the probability of event A is x and the probability of event B is y, then the probability of the event "A then B" is $x \cdot y$.

We can now count the number of outcomes that produce a 7 and answer the original question. The probability of rolling a 7 is 6/36, or 1/6.

What if we wanted to know the probability of *each* event, that is, of rolling a 2, a 3, a 4, and so on? How can you use your work on the previous question to answer this question? What patterns do you see in your previous work that would help you to make the table? Describe the patterns you see in your table and then read on. . . . 📖

One way of describing what we find is to say that each time the sum increases, the number of outcomes increases by 1 until we get to (the event) 7. Then the number of outcomes decreases by 1 (for each event) until we get to 12 (see Table 7.25).

TABLE 7.25	
Number (event)	**Frequency**
2	1
3	2
4	3
5	4
6	5
7	6
8	5

TABLE 7.25	*Cont.*
Number (event)	**Frequency**
9	4
10	3
11	2
12	1

INVESTIGATION 7.25 What Is the Probability of Rolling a 13 with 3 Dice?

Let us extend the investigation now to three dice. Suppose we rolled 3 dice and added the 3 numbers; what is the probability of rolling a 13? Work on this question before reading on. . . .

DISCUSSION

First, we can use the multiplication principle to determine the total number of outcomes from rolling 3 dice, that is, the size of the sample space. There are $6 \cdot 6 \cdot 6 = 216$ possible outcomes!

How many of those outcomes produce a 13? Work on this and then read on. . . .

As you work, make note of what problem-solving strategies help you do the problem, help to keep you on track, and help you check your solution. Virtually all solutions to this problem require the solver to be systematic. However, there are different ways to be systematic, and you can use many different representations that will help answer this question. Below are the beginnings of two different strategies.

REPRESENTATION 1

Table 7.26 is a table created by thinking systematically.

TABLE 7.26

661	652	643	553	?
616	625	?	?	
166	562			
	526			
	265			
	256			

REPRESENTATION 2

Table 7.27 is another table created by thinking systematically.

TABLE 7.27

661	562	463	?
652	553	?	
643	544		
634	535		
625	?		
?			

The completed tables are shown at the end of this chapter on page 409. Regardless of the representation used to solve the problem, we find that there are 21 outcomes that produce a sum of 13. Therefore, the probability of rolling a 13 is 21/216, or slightly under 1 in 10.

An alternative strategy is to construct the entire sample space. If you find all 216 outcomes in the sample space, then you can make use of patterns to count the number of outcomes in the event called "sum of the 3 dice equals 13." Making the table is an exercise in thinking about and looking for patterns that some people find fun and others find tedious. If you are in the latter group, you may look at the two different tables, each containing all 216 outcomes, at the end of the chapter. Look for patterns—my students and my children have found hundreds!

INVESTIGATION **7.26** "The Lady or the Tiger"

There is a famous story, written by Frank Stockton, called "The Lady or the Tiger," which I have modified slightly to make an interesting problem. It seems that the king and queen had arranged for their daughter to be married to a prince, but she fell in love with a peasant. When the king discovered this affair, he ordered that the peasant be thrown into a room full of tigers. However, in response to his daughter's pleas, he agreed to have the peasant walk through a maze to one of two rooms (see Figure 7.40). The princess would be waiting in one of the rooms, and the tigers would be in the other room. The princess asked if she could choose the room in which she would wait; the king agreed, for he believed that the chances were equal. If you were the princess, which room would you choose? Think about this and then read on. . . .

FIGURE **7.40**

DISCUSSION

STRATEGY 1: Solve this as a tree diagram

Can you take your understanding of the tree diagrams used in other problems and apply it to this problem? Try to do so now; determine the probabilities of each event (the princess or the tigers), and then read on. . . .

Figure 7.41 shows 6 different doors (1 through 6) that open into two different rooms (A and B). The probability that the peasant will end up in room A = 1/6 + 1/3 + 1/9 = 11/18. Do you see why?

We can see why by breaking this problem into parts. We are assuming, of course, that at each point, there is an equally likely chance that the peasant will take any path. The probability that, at the first junction, he will take the top path is 1/3; and the probability that, at the second junction, he will take the top path is 1/2. Therefore, using the multiplication principle, the probability that he will end up at door number 1 is (1/3)(1/2) = 1/6. We can determine the probabilities of arriving at the other five doors in a similar manner.

Since A and B are complementary events, we can conclude that the probability that he will end in room B is 1 − 11/18, or 7/18. Thus, the princess should choose to wait in room A.

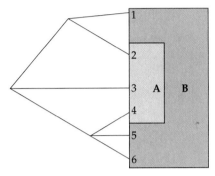

FIGURE **7.41**

STRATEGY 2: Use an area model

At the beginning of the maze, there are three paths. Assuming that each is equally likely to be taken, we can represent them as having the same area (see Figure 7.42).

Figure 7.43 represents the outcomes of each of the paths with respect to the probabilities. Do you understand the diagram? How would you explain it?

The fraction of the area of the diagram contained by the three As represents the probability that the peasant will end up at room A, that is, 1/6 + 1/3 + 1/9 = 11/18. Do you see why?

FIGURE **7.42**

FIGURE **7.43**

This next situation is somewhat different from the previous ones. Let us first explore the problem and then examine what is different about it.

INVESTIGATION 7.27 Gumballs

Josie asks her dad for money to buy 2 gumballs, 1 for her and 1 for her brother. There are only 4 white gumballs and 2 red gumballs left in the machine (see Figure 7.44), and Josie really likes the red ones because they are spicy. What is the probability that she will get at least 1 red gumball? Work on this question and then read on. . . .

FIGURE **7.44**

DISCUSSION

STRATEGY 1: Do a simulation

We need to be careful, for there are ways to go wrong. However, if you write R on two slips of paper and W on four slips of paper and then simulate taking out two gumballs, after a number of trials your experimental probability will be more and more likely to be close to the theoretical probability. Some students find that they don't really understand the problem at first, but after several trials with the simulation, they suddenly understand the problem more clearly and can then go back and determine the theoretical probability.

STRATEGY 2: Use reasoning

One student claims that there are 4 possible outcomes—RR, RW, WR, WW—and so the probability of getting at least one red is 3/4. What do you think?

Plausible as this sounds, it is wrong. The mistake here is similar to the mistake that students often make in the boys and girls problem when they reason that there are five possible ways to have 4 children: 4G0B, 3G1B, 2G2B, 1G3B, and 0G4B. This line of reasoning is valid only if each outcome is just as likely to occur as any other.

If we think back to that problem (or to the dice problems) and look at ways to apply what we learned there to this problem, a tree diagram comes to mind. Explore a tree diagram before reading on. . . . ✎

STRATEGY 3: Make a tree diagram

Figure 7.45 shows one way to represent this problem with a tree diagram. There are 6 trees because there are originally 6 gumballs. Each tree shows the outcomes if that gumball comes out first. That is, if a red gumball comes out first, then there are 5 gumballs left, 1 red and 4 white. However, if a white gumball comes out first, then there are 2 reds and 3 whites left.

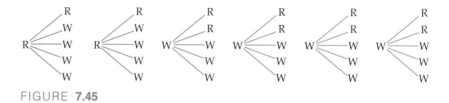

FIGURE **7.45**

From Figure 7.45, we find that there are 30 outcomes and that the event "at least 1 red" occurs 18 times. Thus, the probability of getting at least 1 red gumball is 18/30, or 0.6.

STRATEGY 4: Make a more sophisticated tree diagram

We have seen that many developments in mathematics and the invention of many notations were spurred by a desire to find faster ways to determine answers and more efficient ways to communicate them. In this case, some people look at the tree diagram in Figure 7.45 and say, "There's a simpler way." This simpler tree diagram is shown in Figure 7.46. Study it and try to make sense of it. Can you see the solution contained within the diagram?

FIGURE **7.46**

When we put the money in the machine, the probability of getting a red is 1/3, and the probability of getting a white is 2/3. Let's say we get a red the first time. In this case, the probability of getting a red is now 1/5, and the probability of getting a white is 4/5. Why is this? Similarly, let's say we get a white the first time. In this case, the probability of getting a red is now 2/5, and the probability of getting a white is 3/5.

We can use the multiplication principle to determine the probabilities of each branch of the tree, and we can check our work, since the sum should be 1. Do you see why?

$$P(\text{RR}) = \frac{1}{3}\left(\frac{1}{5}\right) = \frac{1}{15}$$

$$P(\text{RW}) = \frac{1}{3}\left(\frac{4}{5}\right) = \frac{4}{15}$$

$$P(\text{WR}) = \frac{2}{3}\left(\frac{2}{5}\right) = \frac{4}{15}$$

$$P(\text{WW}) = \frac{2}{3}\left(\frac{3}{5}\right) = \frac{6}{15}$$

Since these events are mutually exclusive (why is this?), we can conclude that the probability of getting at least one red is

$$\frac{1}{15} + \frac{4}{15} + \frac{4}{15} = \frac{9}{15} = 0.6$$

Dependent and independent events Now let us return to the question posed at the beginning of the investigation: How is this scenario different from the ones we have explored before? Think and then read on. . . . 🖊

With the gumballs, the probability of obtaining a red or white gumball the second time depended on what happened the first time. In the case of having boys and girls or throwing dice, the probability of the second stage of the activity does not depend on what happened the first; that is, its probability is independent of the first result.

> Two events are **dependent** if the probability of the second event is affected by the outcome of the first event.

> Two events are **independent** if the probability of the second event is not affected at all by the outcome of the first event.

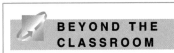
BEYOND THE CLASSROOM

Most states now have lotteries. In one lottery scenario, players pick four numbers between 1 and 50. The state then randomly selects four numbers from the sample space—for example, 2, 5, 23, and 47. In another lottery scenario, the players pick four one-digit numbers between 0 and 9. The state then randomly selects one digit at a time, replacing the selected number before drawing the second number. In this case, 1, 1, 2, 2 is a possible winning combination. The first situation is an example of dependent events, and the second is an example of independent events.

Fair Games

Another application of probability has to do with the idea of fair games and expected value, which has important real-life applications. Let us begin with a simple situation.

INVESTIGATION **7.28** Is This a Fair Game?

FIGURE **7.47**

> **C**onsider the following game for two players. Each person spins the spinner (see Figure 7.47). If the spinner lands on the same animal twice, the first player wins. If it lands on a different animal each time, the second player wins. If you could choose, would you want to be the first or the second player, or doesn't it matter? Think about this and then read on. . . .

DISCUSSION

Can you see similarities between this problem and others we have investigated in this section? If not, look back and try to find connections. Then answer the question and read on. . . .

This problem is similar to the questions about the probability of having boys and girls. Do you see why?

Applying these similarities, we find that there are four equally likely outcomes in this game: (1) cat, cat, (2) dog, dog, (3) cat, dog, and (4), cat, dog. Thus, the theoretical probability of winning is equal for each player.

Using probability language, we say that this is a **fair game**. How would you define "fair game" at this point? Write down your thoughts and then read on. . . .

INVESTIGATION **7.29** What About This Game?

> **A** school is having a carnival to raise funds. In the following game, the player spins the spinner (Figure 7.48) and receives the dollar amount of the number on which the arrow lands. If it costs $2 to play the game, is this a fair game? What do you think?
>
> 5 0
> 2
> 0 2
> 4
>
> FIGURE **7.48**

DISCUSSION

STRATEGY 1: Make a simulation

You could make a spinner like the one in Figure 7.48 and simulate 100 games. If you made approximately $200, the game is probably a fair game. If you didn't have a spinner, how else could you simulate this game?

First, we need to determine the probability of each outcome. That is, $P(0) = 1/2$, $P(2) = 1/4$, $P(4) = 1/8$, $P(5) = 1/8$. So you could make 8 pieces of paper and write 0 on four of them, 2 on two of them, 4 on one of them, and 5 on one of them, and then draw, making sure to put the piece of paper back each time.

STRATEGY 2: Determine the theoretical probabilities

We have spoken of theoretical and experimental probabilities earlier. Can we apply the concept of theoretical probability to theoretical winnings?

We can compute the theoretical winnings per turn using the concept of weighted average (from Section 7.2):

$$0.125(5) + 0.125(4) + 0.25(2) + 0.5(0) = 0.625 + 0.5 + 0.5 = 1.625$$

That is, theoretically, $1/8$ of the time the player will win \$5; $1/8$ of the time, \$4; $1/4$ of the time, \$2; and $1/2$ of the time, nothing. Some students own this solution, while others rent it. If this solution falls into the category of "it sort of makes sense," what might you do to make it "really make sense"? Think and then read on. . . .

One strategy would be to act it out. For example, let's say the person played the game 80 times. Theoretically, how much money will the player win in 80 turns? (Do you see why I chose 80 turns instead of 50 or 100 turns?)

Theoretically, $1/8$ of the time, or ten different times (because 10 is $1/8$ of 80), the player will win \$5, and thus the player will win a total of \$50 on those 10 turns. When we apply this strategy to the \$4 and \$2 outcomes, we find that theoretically the player's total winnings will be \$130. Do you see that this is equivalent to the weighted average we obtained above?

If the player wins \$130 after 80 turns, the winnings are an average of \$1.625 per turn. Referring now to the original question, we find that theoretically, the player will lose money playing this game because it costs \$2 to play the game. It is important to note that we are not saying that the player will lose. The player might be very lucky and play 10 games and win \$50. However, playing a large number of games makes losing money more likely than winning it.

Can you revise your original definition of "fair game" so that it works for Investigations 7.28 and 7.29?

Expected Value

There is a term for the theoretical winnings per turn: **expected value**. The concept of expected value is an aspect of probability that has many real-life applications. For example, car insurance premiums are based on the insurance company's estimate of the probabilities of different groups of people having accidents. Our knowledge of expected value also arose from gambling, as gamblers wanted to make sure that, over time, they would be more likely to make money than lose money. If an experiment (activity) consists of n events, and each event has a specific probability and a specific payoff, we can determine the expected value of that experiment (activity) in the following manner:

Let us denote each event as $E_1, E_2, E_3, \ldots, E_n$.
Let us denote the probability of each event as $P_1, P_2, P_3, \ldots, P_n$.
Let us denote the payoff of each event as $X_1, X_2, X_3, \ldots, X_n$.
The **expected value** $= P_1 \cdot X_1 + P_2 \cdot X_2 + P_3 \cdot X_3 + \cdots + P_n \cdot X_n$

The concept of expected value is used to formally define a fair game. Before reading on, try to describe whether a game is fair or not using the concept of expected value. . . .

A game is **fair** if and only if the expected value of the game equals the cost of playing the game.

Let us now extend the concept of expected value to a real-life application.

INVESTIGATION **7.30** **Insurance Rates**

Let's say that an insurance company is determining the rates for car insurance for the next year. The company has determined that for every 10,000 policyholders:

- 1 is likely to have an accident for which the company will have to pay a $200,000 claim.
- 10 are likely to have an accident for which the company will have to pay a $100,000 claim.
- 20 are likely to have an accident for which the company will have to pay a $50,000 claim.
- 100 are likely to have an accident for which the company will have to pay a $10,000 claim.
- 1,000 are likely to have an accident for which the company will have to pay a $1,000 claim.
- The remainder of the policyholders will have no claims for the year.

Do you understand how the insurance company will use the concept of expected value in determining its rates? If so, determine the expected value of the claims and then read on. . . .

If you don't see the connection between this situation and the others, please go back and reread the previous investigations and the definition of expected value. Do you see connections now?

DISCUSSION

This investigation has many connections to Investigation 7.29, in which each player asks: Will the money I win (take in) be greater than the money that I put in? Since the events did not all have the same probability, it was necessary to use the concept of weighted average, which was developed in Section 7.2.

In order to compute the expected value in the insurance situation, the insurance company wants to get an idea of the "average" payout per customer. This problem is a model of what insurance companies do, not what they actually do. Given the existence of powerful computers, they can use more sophisticated techniques than we are using here. However, this simplified model is useful in understanding the concept of expected value and how it applies to the business world. When we say that 20 people are likely to have an accident for which the insurance company will have to pay $50,000, we are really saying that they expect about 20 out of 10,000 policyholders to have accidents that will cost the company in the neighborhood of $50,000. Thus, even before computing the expected value, there has already been some averaging and approximating.

In order to determine the expected value, the incidence of each event must be converted to probability language. For example, "1 in 10,000 claims will be in the neighborhood of $200,000" translates to "0.0001 probability of a $200,000 claim."

Thus,

$$\text{Expected payout} = 0.0001(200{,}000) + 0.001(100{,}000) + 0.002(50{,}000)$$
$$+ 0.01(10{,}000) + 0.1(1{,}000) = 420$$

What does this 420 mean? Can you explain what it means in one or two sentences, as if you were talking to a fellow student who missed that class and doesn't quite own this concept? Write your rough draft and then read on. . . .

It means that if the accidents occur at the rate and amount that the insurance company is predicting, it will pay out an average of $420 per policy (per year). The actual rate the company charges will be determined by this expected value, the company's overhead (salaries, cost of operations, etc.), and the profit margin.

As before, some students may better understand the problem by determining the expected payoff for the 10,000 policies.

$$\$200,\!000(1) + \$100,\!000(10) + \$50,\!000(20) + \cdots$$

Do you see how this strategy and the previous strategy are connected?

BEYOND THE CLASSROOM

One of my sisters is an insurance agent. As I was consulting with her when writing this material, she told me something that surprised me. I had always thought that insurance companies would ideally like to have as large a percentage of policyholders as possible. That is, if a company had 35% of the market in a city or state, it would strive to keep increasing this percentage to get it higher and higher. However, this is not the case. Can you imagine why an insurance company would not want to have 100% of the policyholders in an area? Think and then read on. . . .

The reason companies don't want to have all the clients has to do with natural disasters. Several major natural disasters have recently brought even some of the big companies to their knees: Hurricane Andrew in 1992 in Florida, the Midwest floods in the summer of 1993, the California earthquake in 1994, and the severe winter of 1995–1996 in the Northeast. In southern California, for example, the total damage from the earthquake came to over $30 billion. Had even the largest insurance company had most of the homeowners' policies in this region, it would have gone bankrupt. Therefore, insurance companies determine the maximum percentage of total policyholders in any particular area that they want to insure.

Having performed several explorations and investigations on probability in this section, you are likely to have found that when we try to make predictions based on a small sample, we may or may not be close to the actual probability. For example, if you perform only 10 trials of having 4 children, you might get 2 boys and 2 girls 50% of the time, but that is not close to the theoretical probability of 3/8. In other words, you have found that if you want to be more confident of your answer, you need to perform more trials. However, this will not necessarily get you closer. For example, you could flip a coin 10 times and find 5 heads, but flip the coin 100 times and find 60 heads. In this case, the experimental probability from the larger sample is not closer to the actual probability. Thus, we *cannot* say that the more trials we perform, the closer we will get to the actual probability. What we *can* say is that as we perform an experiment over and over, the experimental probability will converge on a fixed number. This generalization is called the **Law of Large Numbers.**

Summary

In this section, we have developed some basic language for exploring and describing probability situations. Probabilities can be expressed as rational numbers between 0 and 1 and can be expressed using percents, ratios, and odds. We can discuss probabilities using set language, in which case the set of all possibilities is called the sample space. We distinguish between outcomes, which are elements of the sample space, and events, which are subsets of the sample space.

We have learned other distinctions between different kinds of probability situations.

- In some cases, all outcomes are equally likely; in other cases, this is not true.
- Some events are independent and some are dependent.
- In all situations, we can determine the experimental probability of an event or an outcome by collecting data; in some cases, we can determine theoretical probabilities using different problem-solving tools.

We have examined several rules and formulas that have come out of making sense of situations and understanding connections between probability and other areas, such as sets, weighted average, and our understanding of operations:

- Complementary events: $p(A) + p(B) = 1$
- Mutually exclusive events: $p(A \text{ or } B) = p(A) + p(B)$
- the multiplication principle: If $p(A) = x$ and $p(B) = y$, then $p(A \text{ then } B) = x \cdot y$
- Expected value: $P_1 \cdot X_1 + P_2 \cdot X_2 + P_3 \cdot X_3 + \cdots + P_n \cdot X_n$

We have found that there are many different techniques we can use to solve probability problems: tree diagrams, formulas, area models, and simulation. These techniques work better when they are used with other problem-solving tools: making tables, looking for patterns, being systematic, and using reasoning.

Some real-life situations are similar to ones we have studied here, for example, the probabilities associated with genetics, as in Exploration 7.12. Some real-life situations are more complex than the ones we have discussed here, and additional tools are required to solve those problems.

EXERCISES 7.3

1. **a.** Which of the following would you choose if you were picking 1 ball and wanted black? Justify your choice.

   b. What if you were picking two balls (without replacement) and wanted two black ones?

2. A drawer has 4 red socks and 4 blue socks.

   a. If 2 are drawn, what is the probability of a match?

   b. If 3 are drawn, what is the probability of a match?

   c. What is the probability of having all one color after 4 draws?

3. **a.** Drawing from a regular deck of playing cards, what is the probability of drawing a face card (jack, queen, or king) 3 times in a row? (Assume that jokers are taken out, and assume no replacement.)

   b. How would the probability change if you assumed replacement?

   c. Marla believes that the answer to the second question is $3/13 + 3/13 + 3/13$. Describe how you might convince her that this answer is incorrect.

4. If it snows, there is a 33% chance that schools will close. The weather person says that there is a 25% chance of snow tomorrow. What is the probability that there will be no school tomorrow?

5. The American Lung Association states that approximately 1 out of every 17 deaths in the United States last year was from lung cancer. If there are 34 students in a class, does that mean that 2 people in this class will die from lung cancer?

6. Let's say there is a 15% chance of getting strep if you are exposed to a person with strep. Let's say there is a 50% chance that you were exposed.

a. What is the probability that you will get strep?

b. Let's say each person in your (4-person) family had a 50% chance of being exposed. What is the probability that you will all get strep?

7. Consider the following game: Each person rolls two standard dice and makes a proper fraction with the two numbers.

   ■ If the fraction is in simplest form, the first player wins.

   ■ If the fraction is not in lowest terms, the second player wins.

   ■ If the two numbers are identical, the second player wins.

   Is this a fair game?

8. Consider a pair of pyramid-shaped dice (that is, containing the numbers 1 through 4, rather than 1 through 6 as on regular dice. If you roll two dice at a time, what is the most likely sum and what is the probability of that sum?

9. What are the possible results from rolling two dice and subtracting the number showing on the face of one from that showing on the face of the other in such a way that a nonnegative number is obtained? What result is most likely, and what is its probability?

10. The following experiment consists of rolling a 12-sided die. The outcome set is {1, 2, 3, 4, 5, 6, 7, 8, 9, 10, 11, 12}. What probability would you assign to each of the following outcomes?

    a. An even number turns up.

    b. A prime number turns up.

    c. A divisor of 12 turns up.

    d. What is the most probable event if you roll two such dice and add the numbers? What is its probability?

11. Determine the probability of getting 8 heads in a row when flipping a coin eight times. Give the answer both in decimal form and in ratio form. In decimal form, round the answer to two digits past the string of zeros, and write the decimal you obtained in words. By ratio form, I mean the chance is 1 in ___.

12. If you flip a coin 10 times, what is the probability of getting at least 4 heads?

13. In the board game Monopoly, if you roll three doubles in a row, you go to jail. What is the probability of rolling three doubles in a row? Describe three ways in which you could represent this probability. Then select the one that you think would be most understandable to the general population. For example, if you were writing an article for the daily newspaper about math in society, which representation would you choose and why?

14. When my children were young, they played Junior Monopoly, which uses only one die. One day, Josh rolled a 2, then Emily rolled a 2, then I rolled a 2. Josh and Emily thought this was great fun. What is the probability of rolling three 2s in a row on three tosses of a die?

15. If we look at the last column of Table 7.31 (on page 410) showing the 216 outcomes for three dice, this column starts to look like the handshake column, but it deviates at the seventh row. The number there is 25 instead of 28. Why does this column deviate at this point?

16. Make 2 six-sided dice so that only even sums are possible and each sum is equally likely. Your solution must be other than the trivial solution of "the same odd number on all 12 faces."

17. a. The following dates all have a similar pattern. Describe that pattern.

    $$6/12/72 \qquad 3/25/75 \qquad 5/19/95$$

    b. What is the probability of such a date in the year 1996?

    c. In which year of the century will such dates be most probable?

18. Recall the gumball investigation. What if Josie spent a third quarter? Do you think $P(WWR) = P(WRW) = P(RWW)$? Why or why not?

19. Let's say a four-year-old child sits down at the word processor and strikes four letters at random. What is the probability that the child will spell the word "math"? What assumptions did you make in answering this question? For example, is the probability of striking each key the same; that is, do you assume that they are all equally likely outcomes?

20. A popular Hanukkah game is called Dreidel. Each player begins with a number of pieces of gold (actually chocolate in a round gold-colored wrapper in the shape of a coin). The game consists of spinning a top which has four sides.

    If the top lands on the side labeled gimel, the player gets all the gold in the pot.

    If the top lands on the side labeled shin, the player has to put one coin in the pot.

    If the top lands on the side labeled hay, the player gets half of the gold in the pot.

    If the top lands on the side labeled nun, the player gets nothing.

    a. What is the probability of getting no gimels after 4 turns?

    b. What is the probability of the top landing on each of the four sides on your first four turns?

21. Consider a multiple-choice quiz consisting of 5 questions with 3 possibilities per question. What is the total number of possible outcomes? What does "outcome" mean here?

22. Suppose a person takes a true-false test of 20 questions. If the person guesses at each answer (that is, has a prob-

ability of 50% each time), what is the probability that the person will get at least a 70% on the quiz?

23. Write a program to simulate flipping a coin 1,000 times. Analyze the data, using what you learned about statistics in Section 7.2. For example, are the data normally distributed? Do 68% of the data lie within one standard deviation of the mean? Are the mean, median, and mode identical?

24. If you flipped a coin 6 times, what is the probability that you would have a run of 3 or more heads or tails in a row?

25. Let's say 1,000 people play the carnival game in Investigation 7.29 over the course of the carnival. Theoretically, how much money will the school make from this game?

26. Let's say you wanted to make the carnival game in Investigation 7.29 a fair game. Describe one situation that would be a fair game. Explain why that game would be fair.

27. Write a computer program to simulate the carnival game in Investigation 7.29 and analyze the results.

28. There is a carnival game called chuck-a-luck. The game works this way.

> The player picks a number from 1 to 6. The operator then rolls three dice.
>
> If the player's number comes up all 3 times, the player wins $3.
>
> If the player's number comes up 2 times, the player wins $2.
>
> If the player's number comes up 1 time, the player wins $1.
>
> If the player's number doesn't come up, the player pays the operator $1.
>
> If the game costs $1, is this a fair game?

29. Let's say a state is considering introducing a new lottery game. The state will charge $1 for a ticket. Each week, one person's name will be selected at random. The amount of the person's prize will be determined in the following manner: Five Ping-Pong balls—four white and one black—will be placed in a hopper. The balls will be selected one at a time until all five balls are in a line.

- If the black ball is first, the person wins $1,000,000.
- If the black ball is second, the person wins $100,000.
- If the black ball is third, the person wins $10,000.
- If the black ball is fourth, the person wins $1,000.
- If the black ball is fifth, the person wins $500.

   a. Is this a fair game?
   b. The state expects to sell 250,000 tickets each week. Do you think this game will be a good money raiser? Why or why not?

30. Just as insurance companies use the concept of expected value in determining insurance rates, oil companies use expected value in determining whether or not to drill for oil. Let's say that an oil company is considering drilling for oil in a certain area. The company estimates that it will cost an average of $200,000 to drill each oil well. It has determined that there are three kinds of outcomes: a dry well, a "medium" strike that would produce about $750,000, and a big strike that would produce about $2,500,000. The company has estimated that the probability of a medium strike is 1/5 and the probability of a big strike is 1/25. Should the company drill for oil? Determine the expected value, and then describe your conclusion as if you were talking to a group of speculators who don't understand expected value.

31. Describe a real-life scenario whose occurrence is a probability and whose probability you would be interested in determining.

   a. Define the scenario.
   b. Describe how you might go about determining the probability.
   c. Describe some aspects of the problem that would influence the actual probability.

   I have sketched one scenario below; this would be the beginning of a good response.

   a. The probability I will get a job after I graduate.
   b. Interview professors who work with teacher certification and average their guesses; interview principals in this area and average their guesses; contact those students who got certified at KSC last summer and determine how many got jobs.
   c. Probabilities will differ depending on whether I will only look in this area, what my certification is (early childhood, elementary, middle, etc.), whether I am 22 or 32, and so on.

32. The inspiration for this problem came from one of my Middle School Mathematics Methods students. Let's say you have a bag that contains 10 colored beads. You can pull out one bead at a time and then put it back and then shake up the bag. Let's say you have done this five times and have pulled out a red bead three times, a blue bead, and a green bead. What are the facts and what inferences do you have about the contents of the bag? List and justify your facts and inferences.

33. The inspiration for this problem came from a question asked of me by a parent. Let's say the local middle school has five sixth grade teachers, two of whom are female, four seventh grade mathematics teachers, one of whom is female, and four eighth grade teachers, one of whom is female. Assuming that the students' placement is random, what is the probability that a student will have at least one female mathematics teacher during the student's three years at the school?

COUNTING AND CHANCE

- What does "counting" mean in the context of probability?
- What is the difference between a combination and a permutation?

In many probability problems, simply determining the size of the sample space can be quite tedious. In this section, we will examine some algorithms that can make solving probability problems much easier. As has been the case throughout the book, the goal is not simply to "get" the algorithms, but to understand why they work. There is a reasonable probability that some of you will never use the algorithms developed in this section with your students. However, there is a reasonable probability that all of you who go on to teach elementary mathematics will have your students engage in simpler counting investigations. So what can you expect to get out of this section?

These investigations will help you to apply problem-solving tools to probability concepts. They focus on representing a problem in useful ways and solving a problem by making a similar, simpler problem and then generalizing from the simpler problem to the actual problem. They call on your skills in recognizing patterns and then using those patterns to solve the problem. They build on your ability to communicate and reason mathematically. They encourage you to see connections among probability problems and connections to other problems we have already investigated.

INVESTIGATION 7.31 How Many Ways to Take the Picture?

Let's say your college has a chapter of Kappa Delta Pi, the national education society. Let's say this was a new society in your college, and in the first year there were 9 members. Let's also say that the members decided to have a group picture taken and wanted only one row—that is, they wanted everyone in the first row. In how many different ways can they line up for the picture? Work on this question yourself before reading on. . . .

DISCUSSION

This is one of the many problems in mathematics where many people find that if they see a solution, they see it right away, and if they don't, they're stuck. Even if you were systematic, you could become stuck trying to do this one:

1 2 3 4 5 6 7 8 9

1 2 3 4 5 6 7 9 8

etc.

Stuck, that is, unless you have problem-solving tools. If you are stuck, look at the steps for problem-solving on the inside front cover of the *Explorations* volume. What strategies might help? Then read on. . . .

STRATEGY 1: Make a simpler problem

There are several different strategies that can be successfully applied to this problem. The first one we will discuss is "make a similar, simpler problem and then work up." If you didn't make much progress on your own and you like this method, use it to finish the problem.

Let's see how it works. Let's start with a club with only three members:

123
132
213
231
312
321

This gives us a total of 6 different arrangements. Where did the 6 come from?

Most people see 3 groups of 2, and hence 3×2. Some people can jump to the solution of the original problem from here; others need more data from which to generalize.

If you don't yet feel confident that you can connect this to the original problem, let's try a club with four members. If you haven't done this, try it on your own before reading on . . . . 🖎

1234
1243
1324
1342
1423
1432

This gives us six possibilities in which person number 1 is on the left. Either by reasoning or by working out the other possibilities yourself, you can see that there will be 6 outcomes in which each of the other three members is on the left. This gives us a total of 24 outcomes. Where did the 24 come from?

As before, we have 4 groups, each of which consists of 2 groups of 3. If we put the numbers in order, we have either $4 \times 3 \times 2$ or $2 \times 3 \times 4$.

If you feel that you can jump from here to the solution to the problem, do so. If not, then you can either determine the number of possibilities for a group with 5 members or try another strategy.

STRATEGY 2: Make a tree diagram

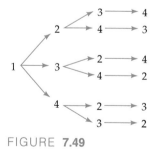

FIGURE **7.49**

In this case, a tree diagram (Figure 7.49) is not terribly helpful for most students. In Section 7.3, we found that a tree diagram was helpful when we were looking at having 2 or 3 or 4 children. However, as the number of children increased, the tree diagram became less helpful and more tedious. I mention this here because many students who struggle in math often think that the better students and the teacher *always* know what to do and *always* pick the "right" strategy, and this is not true. I know many students who have done well in the course who admit that they will frequently find that their first attempt at a challenging problem was not productive and that they needed to try another strategy.

STRATEGY 3: Connect this problem to something familiar
What about the multiplication principle? Many people understand this strategy better if we simultaneously use the "act it out" strategy.

Let's begin with the first person. We have nine possibilities. Once we have that person set, how many choices do we have for the second position? There are eight possibilities. Do you see why? Do you see how to finish the problem using this line of reasoning? Work on it before reading on. . . .

Using this line of reasoning, the number of possibilities will be nine times eight times seven times six and so on, so that the total number of possibilities is:

$$9 \times 8 \times 7 \times 6 \times 5 \times 4 \times 3 \times 2$$

Do you see how the first strategy hinted at this solution?
New terminology will make our discussion of this problem and other probability problems easier. How would you describe the computation above to someone—let's say a friend in class who didn't have this book? Do so and then read on. . . .

One way: "Start with nine, then eight, then seven, and keep reducing the number by one till you can't anymore. Now compute the product."
This kind of computation is common in probability and has a name: factorial. That is, $9 \times 8 \times 7 \times 6 \times 5 \times 4 \times 3 \times 2$ can be written as 9!.
Mathematicians insert a 1 at the end of this product, and define any number n **factorial**, $n!$, as

$$n! = n \times (n-1) \times (n-2) \times \cdots \times 3 \times 2 \times 1$$

Often, the order of the numbers matters; for instance, a lottery ticket reading 1 2 3 4 5 6 7 8 9 is "different" from one reading 1 3 5 7 9 2 4 6 8. We refer to different arrangements of the same numbers as permutations.
If you did Exploration 7.13 (Area Codes and Phone Numbers), you have had some direct experience with a real-life permutation situation.

LANGUAGE
Yes, a factorial contains an exclamation point; maybe the person who discovered this pattern was so surprised or excited that he or she decided to denote this algorithm with an exclamation point!

INVESTIGATION **7.32** **How Many Different Election Outcomes?**

Let's say Kappa Delta Pi has its first election: for president and treasurer. How many possible ways can a president and treasurer be elected from a pool of 9 people? Work on this and then read on. . . .

DISCUSSION

STRATEGY 1: Be systematic, make a table, and look for patterns

TABLE 7.28		
1, 2	2, 1	
1, 3	2, 3	
1, 4	2, 4	
1, 5	2, 5	etc.
1, 6	2, 6	
1, 7	2, 7	
1, 8	2, 8	
1, 9	2, 9	

Note that the numbers in Table 7.28 represent possible outcomes. For example, 1, 2 represents the outcome "person 1 as president and person 2 as treasurer." Why is {2, 1} not simply a duplicate of {1, 2}? Why did we skip {2, 2}? Can you finish from here?

STRATEGY 2: Make a tree diagram
Some students find a tree diagram (Figure 7.50) very helpful. Can you finish from here?

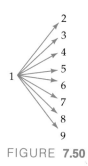

FIGURE **7.50**

STRATEGY 3: Connect to previous problems
We can use the multiplication principle again. Do you see how?

There are 9 different possibilities for president (each member), but only 8 possibilities for treasurer (assuming that no one will be both president and treasurer).

Without too much difficulty, most students can see this as 8 groups of 9, or 9 × 8.

This is "sort of like" the beginning of factorial.

Electing three officers   Now let's see how confident you are about this idea. What if the group decided to have a president, a treasurer, and a secretary? How many different outcomes are there for this scenario? Work on this and then read on. . . .

Each of the three strategies from before still applies (see Figure 7.51).

FIGURE **7.51**

The total number is $9 \cdot 8 \cdot 7$.

Number of different subsets This question (about president, treasurer, secretary) is more complex than the question in Investigation 7.31 about the picture. Instead of looking at all the possible permutations of a set of specified size, which we did in the picture investigation, we are now asking how many different *subsets* of specified size can we make from a set of a given size. In this situation, the outcome "1 2 3" is considered to be different from the outcome "1 3 2." Do you see why?

Using symbols, we say that our election question seeks the number of different subsets of size r that we can make from a set of size n. We can also refer to this amount as "the number of permutations of n things taken r at a time." The shorthand for this situation is $_nP_r$. (*Note:* Some books use the following notation P_r^n.)

In the case of the different possibilities for president and treasurer, we were looking for $_9P_2$.

In the case of the different possibilities for president, treasurer, and secretary, we were looking for $_9P_3$.

Can you now generalize a formula for the number of permutations of a subset of size r from a set of size n? Try to do so and then read on. . . .

The generalization is

$$_nP_r = n(n-1) \cdots (n-r+1)$$

If this makes sense, great. If not, substitute 9 for n and 2 (and then 3) for r so that it makes sense.

Some authors prefer a different formula, one that helps the learner to see how many terms to include and/or what the last term is. This formula rests on the following observation:

$$9 \cdot 8 \cdot 7 = \frac{9!}{6!}$$

(Active readers will make sure that they believe this equivalence!) In this situation, 6 is the number of people who will not be elected. This observation leads to an alternative formula:

$$_nP_r = \frac{n!}{(n-r)!}$$

INVESTIGATION **7.33** How Many Outcomes This Time?

Suppose Kappa Delta Pi decided to elect two members to send to the national convention. How many possible outcomes are there now? Think and then read on. . . .

DISCUSSION

Do you understand why this is not the same as the problem with the president and treasurer? If so, explain why. If not, think and then read on. . . .

Combinations   Using the notation of the investigation with the president and treasurer, the outcomes {1, 2} and {2, 1} represent different outcomes. In the first outcome, student 1 is the president and student 2 is the treasurer, whereas in the second outcome, student 2 is the president and student 1 the treasurer. However, delegates {1, 2} and {2, 1} represent the same outcome. Mathematically, we distinguish between permutations and combinations. In probability situations in which order matters, we speak of permutations; when order doesn't matter, we speak of combinations. For example, if outcomes "*abc*" and "*bac*" are considered to be different, we are in a permutation situation; if they are considered to be the same, we are in a combination situation.

Using symbols, we can write the number of combinations of n things taken r at a time as $_nC_r$.

Now let us discuss the solution to how many outcomes there are for this question.

First, we will be systematic and look for patterns (see Table 7.29).

TABLE 7.29			
1, 2	2, 3	3, 4	
1, 3	2, 4	3, 5	
1, 4	2, 5	3, 6	
1, 5	2, 6	3, 7	etc.
1, 6	2, 7	3, 8	
1, 7	2, 8	3, 9	
1, 8	2, 9		
1, 9			

Can you finish the problem? Does this problem remind you of a problem or a pattern that we have encountered before? Think before reading on. . . .

If you thought about the handshake problem (Exploration 1.1) or the sum of the first 100 numbers (Investigation 1.5), you are right.

We find that there are 36 different outcomes; that is, $8 + 7 + 6 + 5 + 4 + 3 + 2 + 1$. We would like to be able to generalize this procedure so that we can use it in a variety of situations; for example, what if we had a set of 20 elements (instead of 9) and we wanted all outcomes consisting of 3 elements at a time (instead of 2)? One way to determine the general procedure is to analyze the results of the simpler problems. Thus, we will explore where the 36 come from. Work on this before reading on. . . .

From one perspective, we can see that 36 comes from $8 + 7 + 6 + 5 + 4 + 3 + 2 + 1$. Thus, we could generalize that if there were 20 members and we wanted all outcomes of two at a time, there would be $19 + 18 + 17 + \cdots + 3 + 2 + 1$. What if we wanted all possible outcomes of three at a time? In order to develop a procedure that will work in more situations, we have to look more deeply. What other ways do you see to determine the 36? Think before reading on. . . .

Using the algorithm developed in Exploration 1.1 (The Handshakes Problem), we can say that

$$_9C_2 = \frac{9(8)}{2} = 36$$

Now this should look similar to the permutation algorithm:

$$_9P_2 = 9(8) = 72$$

Why do we divide by 2? Think about this before reading on. . . .

Since each combination is connected to two permutations, we can see that in this case, the number of combinations will be half the number of permutations.

Do you feel able to make a hypothesis for the general combination algorithm, $_nC_r$? If so, make it and then read on. . . .

If not, work through the next problem and then try to make a hypothesis.

If 3 people go to the convention What if 3 people could go to convention? How many different combinations are there? Complete Table 7.30 before reading on. What patterns do you see that could help you to complete the table or help you to determine the total?

TABLE 7.30

1 2 3	1 3 4	1 4 5	1 5 6	1 6 7	1 7 8	1 8 9
1 2 4	1 3 5	1 4 6	1 5 7	1 6 8	1 7 9	
1 2 5	1 3 6	1 4 7	1 5 8	1 6 9		
1 2 6	1 3 7	1 4 8	1 5 9			
1 2 7	1 3 8	1 4 9				
1 2 8	1 3 9					
1 2 9						
2 3 4	2 4 5	2 5 6	2 6 7	2 7 8	2 8 9	
2 3 5	2 4 6	2 5 7	2 6 8	2 7 9		
2 3 6	2 4 7	2 5 8	2 6 9			
2 3 7	2 4 8	2 5 9				
2 3 8	2 4 9					
2 3 9						
3 4 5	3 5 6	3 6 7	3 7 8	3 8 9		
3 4 6	3 5 7	3 6 8	3 7 9			
3 4 7	3 5 8	3 6 9				
3 4 8	3 5 9					
3 4 9						

In the first set of outcomes, where person number 1 is first, we have 28 total outcomes, and this number is the sum of the sequence $7 + 6 + 5 + 4 + 3 + 2 + 1$. In a similar fashion, the number of outcomes in the second set is equal to $6 + 5 + 4 + 3 + 2 + 1 = 21$. From these patterns, it is reasonable to conclude that we can continue in this manner. Doing so, we find that there are 84 different outcomes for this situation; that is, $28 + 21 + 15 + 10 + 6 + 3 + 1$. Stated in everyday language, we say that there are 84 possible ways to send 3 people to the convention.

Determining a way of connecting this 84 to a formula that we can use is not obvious, but there are connections. What do you think? Can you generalize from the handshakes problem in Exploration 1.1? Work on this before reading on. . . . 🖊

There are many possible paths that will let us see the general procedure. Let us take one path.

First, let us summarize what we know:

> We know that $_9P_2 = 9 \cdot 8 = 72$ and $_9C_2 = 9 \cdot 8/2$, and that there is a similarity between these two.
>
> We know that $_9P_3 = 9 \cdot 8 \cdot 7 = 504$.
>
> Therefore, we might suspect that $_9C_3$ might be something like $9 \cdot 8 \cdot 7/x$.
>
> But we know that $_9C_3 = 84$. So we can make an equation and solve for x. That is, $_9C_3 = 84 = 9 \cdot 8 \cdot 7/x$.

Solving the equation, we find that $x = 6$. This still prompts the question, why do we divide by 6? What do you think? Work on this before reading on. . . . 🖊

In this case, each combination outcome is connected to six permutation outcomes.

$$
\left.
\begin{array}{l}
1\ 2\ 3 \\
1\ 3\ 2 \\
2\ 3\ 1 \\
2\ 1\ 3 \\
3\ 1\ 2 \\
3\ 2\ 1
\end{array}
\right\} \quad 1\ 2\ 3
$$

Can you make the leap? Do you see a pattern?

$$_9C_2 = \frac{9 \cdot 8}{2}$$

$$_9C_3 = \frac{9 \cdot 8 \cdot 7}{6} = \frac{9 \cdot 8 \cdot 7}{1 \cdot 2 \cdot 3}$$

$_nC_r = ?$ What do you think?

$$_nC_r = \frac{n \cdot (n-1) \cdots (n-r+1)}{r!} = \frac{_nP_r}{r!} = \frac{n!}{(n-r)!\,r!}$$

I N V E S T I G A T I O N **7.34 Pick a Card, Any Card!**

Consider a standard deck of playing cards. Pick two cards. What is the probability of getting two queens? Can we use any of the algorithms? Can you explain why one of the algorithms applies or why none of them apply? Work on this problem and then read on. . . . 🖊

DISCUSSION

This is a combination (not a permutation) problem. Do you see why?

$$_{52}C_2 = \frac{52 \cdot 51}{2} = 1,326$$

Does this mean that the probability is 1/1,326? What do you think?

The answer to this question is not 1/1,326. The number 1,326 means that there are 1,326 different possible combinations. Since we want to know the probability of getting two queens, we also have to determine how many of those 1,326 combinations involve two queens. What do you think? Do this now before reading on. . . .

One strategy is to list them systematically—for example, SD, SH, SC, HD, HC, DC. Another strategy is to use the appropriate combination algorithm appropriately. Do you see how $_4C_2$ applies to this part of the problem?

In either case, we find that there are 6 different combinations that involve 2 queens.

Thus, we find that the probability of a queen is

$$\frac{6}{26 \cdot 51} = \frac{1}{13 \cdot 17} = \frac{1}{221}$$

INVESTIGATION **7.35** So You Think You're Going to Win the Lottery?

Since 1980, the number of states with lotteries has increased considerably. What factor(s) do you think might have led to the increase in states having lotteries?

During the 1980s, federal aid to states and cities shrank considerably. Many states "solved" this problem by establishing or increasing lotteries and designating the profits from the lottery for expenses such as education. The state lotteries have been called voluntary taxes. Can you see why?

Let's begin with a rather straightforward lottery in which players select four digits. The winning number is commonly selected in the following fashion: 10 Ping-Pong balls (each with a digit 0 through 9 written on it) are placed in a hopper. One Ping-Pong ball is selected. That digit now goes in the first place. That Ping-Pong ball is put back in the hopper, and the process is repeated three times.

What is the probability of picking a winning number? Work on this and then read on. . . .

DISCUSSION

STRATEGY 1: Connect to the multiplication principle

Each time, there are 10 possibilities; thus, the sample space is $10 \times 10 \times 10 \times 10$. Since all outcomes are equally likely, the probability of any outcome is 1/10,000.

STRATEGY 2: Act it out

What are some possible winning numbers?

[13] *Utne Reader*, November/December 1993, p. 19.

Possibilities include 1234, 4612—in fact, any number from 0000 to 9999. How many combinations is that?

Can you extend this problem or think of similar problems?

INVESTIGATION **7.36** Connecting These Algorithms to Other Problems

In Chapter 6, we learned that we could apply our ratio and proportion knowledge to find simpler ways to solve problems that we had previously solved in Chapter 5. Let us reflect on what we have learned here and then revisit some problems we have already solved to see when the algorithms we have developed in this section apply to those problems.

For each of the following, do you think we could have used the permutation or combination algorithms to answer the question? Write your thoughts before reading on. . . .

A. If we want to know the probability of having 2 boys and 2 girls, as in Investigation 7.20, can we use $_6P_2$ or $_6C_2$?

B. If we want to know how many different outcomes there are when rolling two dice and finding the sum, as we did in Investigation 7.24, can we use $_6P_2$ or $_6C_2$?

C. Consider the gumball problem, Investigation 7.27. Suppose we denote each ball by a number and then draw one ball and then draw a second ball. How many different outcomes are possible? Can we use $_6P_2$ or $_6C_2$?

DISCUSSION

A. In the boys and girls problem, since BBGG is seen as a different outcome from GGBB, we are looking at permutations rather than combinations.

However, in the case of the boys and girls, we are saying that in each case, we have two choices. Thus, the multiplication principle rather than the permutation algorithm applies.

B. In the case of the dice, once again we are looking at permutations rather than combinations. Why is this?

Some students find that the dice question is very similar to asking for the number of permutations of 6 objects taken 2 at a time. However, $_6P_2 = 6 \times 5 = 30$, and we know that the number of outcomes for 2 dice is 36 rather than 30. Does this mean that, as we found above, that the permutation algorithm does not apply here either? Think and then read on. . . .

Since we are looking at a set of 6 elements and taking 2 at a time, the $_6P_2$ algorithm will give us the number of outcomes in which the first and second elements are different. If we add this number to the 6 outcomes in which the numbers on the dice are the same, we do get 36 outcomes. Exploration 7.15 examines traditional Native American "dice" games.

C. If we label the gumballs 1, 2, 3, 4, 5, and 6 and draw them as stated before, both the multiplication principle and the permutation algorithm apply. Do you see why? Think before reading on. . . .

According to the multiplication principle, there are 6 possibilities on the first draw and 5 possibilities on the second draw, so that there are $6 \times 5 = 30$ different outcomes in the sample space. According to the permutation algorithm, we are considering all permutations of 6 elements taken 2 at a time. Since there is no replacement, there is no possibility of getting the same number twice (as there was with the dice). Therefore, $_6P_2 = 30$ also applies.

Summary

In this section, we have examined a number of situations known as counting situations. That is, we have looked for patterns and order in those situations in order to find easier ways to count the number of outcomes in the sample space. Many children find such counting problems to be interesting. We learned the difference between combinations and permutations, and we examined how the formulas work.

Once again, it is important to emphasize that the algorithms themselves are useless if you do not understand what they mean. I strongly believe that there is too much blind application of algorithms in our schools. I see this regularly in schools that I visit, and I see many of my students doing this also, either out of math phobia or out of apathy. It is my hope that over time, more and more students and teachers will strive to make sense of situations in which mathematics applies.

EXERCISES 7.4

1. In how many ways can the following students' names be displayed on a poster: Amy, Betty, Carl, Ed, Frank, Gisela?

2. In how many ways can the names of 4 candidates be listed on a ballot for an election?

3. Find the number of different ways in which 4 flags can be displayed on a flagpole, one above the other, if 10 different flags are available.

4. Mrs. Olson has 7 brands of cat food and 3 cats, each of which receives 1 can per day. In how many different ways can she serve the cats on any day, assuming that no 2 cats get the same brand?

5. Those students who celebrate Christmas and come from large families may find this problem to be familiar. Let's say that a family of 5 decides that instead of each person buying a present for each other person in the family, all the family members will put their names in a hat. Each person then takes one name out of the hat and buys a present for that person. What is the probability of every family member getting his or her own name?

6. Several years ago I received as a gift a book of different animals. However, the picture of each animal's body had been cut into three pieces, and the pages of the book enabled me to make different combinations of animals. The name of the book was *Por-gua-can* because the head was a porcupine's, the torso was an iguana's, and the feet were a pelican's. There were 9 animals. How many different animal combinations are possible?

7. The German club has 12 members. In how many different ways can a subset of 3 members be selected to go on a field trip?

8. A basketball team has 9 players.
   a. How many different starting lineups are possible?
   b. How many different starting lineups are possible if the star must be in the lineup?

9. Let's say you went out for ice cream. The store had 9 different flavors, and you wanted a triple-decker ice cream cone. How many different triple-decker ice cream cones are possible at this store?

10. Janine's boss has allowed her to have a flexible schedule. Her boss says she can pick whatever 5 days a week she will work.
   a. How many different work combinations can be made?
   b. How many give her consecutive days off?
   c. How many choices give her Wednesday off?

11. This unfortunate event happened to me when my two children were little. Each of them had a friend over for lunch. After lunch, we had popsicles for dessert. There were 9 popsicles in the freezer and 3 flavors: 3 grape, 3 cherry, and 3 orange. What is the probability that each child will get the popsicle that child wants?

12. Let's say a company has 10 members on its management team, 7 men and 3 women. There is a conference in Hawaii, and the company has decided to send 3 people.

If the selection of the 3 people to go to Hawaii is determined by lottery, what is the probability that at least 1 woman will be selected?

13. You and a friend are at Paul and Elizabeth's Restaurant for a night of fine dining. You can choose among 2 appetizers, 4 main dishes, and 3 desserts.

Appetizer: soup or salad

Main dish: fish, chicken, beef, vegetarian

Dessert: chocolate cake, apple pie, ice cream

   a. How many possible different dinners are there?

   b. If there are 3 choices of salad dressing and 4 choices of ice cream, how many possible dinner combinations are there?

14. If you pick a card from a regular deck of cards, what is the probability of getting a face card 3 times in a row? Assume that the face card is put back in after each draw, so that you are selecting from a full deck each time.

15. If you select 2 cards from a deck, what is the probability of getting 2 matching cards (2 kings, 2 fives, and so on)?

16. If you select 5 cards from a deck, what is the probability that you will get 4 of a kind? 3 of a kind? 2 of a kind?

17. Recall Investigation 7.35. Suppose the Ping-Pong ball was not replaced. Now what is the probability?

18. Explain why these two formulas are equivalent.

$$ _nP_r = \frac{n!}{(n-r)!} \quad \text{and} \quad _nP_r = n(n-1)\cdots(n-r+1) $$

19. What do you think will be the value of $_nP_n$?

20. Little Caesar's pizza had a commercial on television that said that you could buy one pizza and get another one free, with up to 5 toppings per pizza. The dialogue on the commercial went something like this. The older person said, "5 toppings per pizza; that's 10 different pizzas to choose from." The little guy then said, "No, it's 1,048,576 combinations." What do you think?

21. Interview a nearby automobile dealership. Ask the people responsible for ordering how they determine which cars to order to have on hand. Compare the selection process for a small dealership that can stock only 5 Plymouth Voyager minivans with that for a large dealership that can stock 50 Plymouth Voyager minivans.

22. a. How many possible words can be spelled using the letters from the word *mathematics*?

   b. What word can you find with the highest ratio of actual (possible) words to the theoretical number of words?

CHAPTER SUMMARY

1. There are many ways to represent data. In some cases, what graph to use is a matter of preference; in other cases, different graphs are more appropriate than others.

2. Different graphs can give different impressions of a set of data.

3. Graphs can be constructed to distort the impression a reader might have!

4. When examining data that others have gathered, we need to examine the data carefully, especially thinking about the reliability and validity of the data.

5. When interpreting graphs that others have made, we need to examine the graph carefully, asking if it is fair, appropriate, or distorted.

6. The terms *mean*, *median*, and *mode* each represent an "average." Each of the three terms has a conceptual base:

   ■ The mean is the center of gravity of a set of data.

   ■ The median is the numerical middle of the set of data.

   ■ The mode is the datum that occurs most often.

7. In some distributions, the mean, median, and mode are equal. In others, they may be very different, and some may not even be appropriate. In those cases, we need to examine which measure is the best representative for average.

8. Averages are not always highly representative of a population. In most cases, when we are examining a population, we need to have more information about the population, depending on the questions we are asking. We may want to know the center of the data, or we may want to know about the spread of the data, in which case knowing the extreme values, the range, and the standard deviation is important.

9. When a set of data is normally distributed, we can make powerful generalizations and predictions about that set of data.

Basic Concepts

Section 7.1: Representing and Interpreting Data

Completed probability tables for Investigation 7.25, p. 385

TABLE 7.26

6 6 1	6 5 2	6 4 3	5 5 3	4 4 5
6 1 6	6 2 5	6 3 4	5 3 5	4 5 4
1 6 6	5 6 2	3 6 4	3 5 5	5 4 4
	5 2 6	3 4 6		
	2 5 6	4 6 3		
	2 6 5	4 3 6		

TABLE 7.27

6 6 1	5 6 2	4 6 3	3 6 4	2 6 5	1 6 6
6 5 2	5 5 3	4 5 4	3 5 5	2 5 6	
6 4 3	5 4 4	4 4 5	3 4 6		
6 3 4	5 3 5	436			
6 2 5	5 2 6				
6 1 6					

Two different representations of the sample space of rolling 3 dice

---

Note: The first column is simply to make communication easier; for example, we can talk about patterns in rows 19 to 24.

TABLE 7.31

1	1 1 1	2 1 1	3 1 1	4 1 1	5 1 1	6 1 1
2	1 1 2	2 1 2	3 1 2	4 1 2	5 1 2	6 1 2
3	1 1 3	2 1 3	3 1 3	4 1 3	5 1 3	6 1 3
4	1 1 4	2 1 4	3 1 4	4 1 4	5 1 4	6 1 4
5	1 1 5	2 1 5	3 1 5	4 1 5	5 1 5	6 1 5
6	1 1 6	2 1 6	3 1 6	4 1 6	5 1 6	6 1 6
7	1 2 1	2 2 1	3 2 1	4 2 1	5 2 1	6 2 1
8	1 2 2	2 2 2	3 2 2	4 2 2	5 2 2	6 2 2
9	1 2 3	2 2 3	3 2 3	4 2 3	5 2 3	6 2 3
10	1 2 4	2 2 4	3 2 4	4 2 4	5 2 4	6 2 4
11	1 2 5	2 2 5	3 2 5	4 2 5	5 2 5	6 2 5
12	1 2 6	2 2 6	3 2 6	4 2 6	5 2 6	6 2 6
13	1 3 1	2 3 1	3 3 1	4 3 1	5 3 1	6 3 1
14	1 3 2	2 3 2	3 3 2	4 3 2	5 3 2	6 3 2
15	1 3 3	2 3 3	3 3 3	4 3 3	5 3 3	6 3 3
16	1 3 4	2 3 4	3 3 4	4 3 4	5 3 4	6 3 4
17	1 3 5	2 3 5	3 3 5	4 3 5	5 3 5	6 3 5
18	1 3 6	2 3 6	3 3 6	4 3 6	5 3 6	6 3 6
19	1 4 1	2 4 1	3 4 1	4 4 1	5 4 1	6 4 1
20	1 4 2	2 4 2	3 4 2	4 4 2	5 4 2	6 4 2
21	1 4 3	2 4 3	3 4 3	4 4 3	5 4 3	6 4 3
22	1 4 4	2 4 4	3 4 4	4 4 4	5 4 4	6 4 4
23	1 4 5	2 4 5	3 4 5	4 4 5	5 4 5	6 4 5
24	1 4 6	2 4 6	3 4 6	4 4 6	5 4 6	6 4 6
25	1 5 1	2 5 1	3 5 1	4 5 1	5 5 1	6 5 1
26	1 5 2	2 5 2	3 5 2	4 5 2	5 5 2	6 5 2
27	1 5 3	2 5 3	3 5 3	4 5 3	5 5 3	6 5 3
28	1 5 4	2 5 4	3 5 4	4 5 4	5 5 4	6 5 4
29	1 5 5	2 5 5	3 5 5	4 5 5	5 5 5	6 5 5
30	1 5 6	2 5 6	3 5 6	4 5 6	5 5 6	6 5 6
31	1 6 1	2 6 1	3 6 1	4 6 1	5 6 1	6 6 1
32	1 6 2	2 6 2	3 6 2	4 6 2	5 6 2	6 6 2
33	1 6 3	2 6 3	3 6 3	4 6 3	5 6 3	6 6 3
34	1 6 4	2 6 4	3 6 4	4 6 4	5 6 4	6 6 4
35	1 6 5	2 6 5	3 6 5	4 6 5	5 6 5	6 6 5
36	1 6 6	2 6 6	3 6 6	4 6 6	5 6 6	6 6 6

TABLE 7.32

	3	4	5	6	7	8	9	10	11	12	13	14	15	16	17	18
1	111	112	113	114	115	116	126	136	146	156	166	266	366	466	566	666
2		121	122	123	124	125	135	145	155	165	256	356	456	556	656	
3		211	131	132	133	134	144	154	164	246	265	365	465	565	665	
4			212	141	142	143	153	163	236	255	346	446	546	646		
5			221	213	151	152	162	226	245	264	355	455	555	655		
6			311	222	214	161	216	235	254	336	364	464	564	664		
7				231	223	215	225	244	263	345	436	536	636			
8				312	232	224	234	253	326	354	445	545	645			
9				321	241	233	243	262	335	363	454	554	654			
10				411	313	242	252	316	344	426	463	563	663			
11					322	251	261	325	353	435	526	626				
12					331	314	315	334	362	444	535	635				
13					412	323	324	343	416	453	544	644				
14					421	332	333	352	425	462	553	653				
15					511	341	342	361	434	516	562	662				
16						413	351	415	443	525	616					
17						422	414	424	452	534	625					
18						431	423	433	461	543	634					
19						512	432	442	515	552	643					
20						521	441	451	524	561	652					
21						611	513	514	533	615	661					
22							522	523	542	624						
23							531	532	551	633						
24							612	541	614	642						
25							621	613	623	651						
26								622	632							
27								631	641							

Geometry as Shape

In the next three chapters, we will focus on three aspects of geometry: shapes, transformations, and measurement. Look at the pictures in Figure 8.1. What do you see?

FIGURE 8.1   Three natural spirals: (a) leaves of the sago palm, (b) horns of a mountain sheep, (c) the chambered nautilus.

We see a shape that is called a spiral occurring in different parts of the world: in a plant and on two different animals. How is this shape formed? Why is this shape formed in these situations — that is, what purpose or function does this shape serve? These are questions that mathematicians, biologists, physicists, and others have asked and answered. Essential to answering these questions is a deep understanding of these shapes, which also involves understanding their measures.

It is very possible that the study of geometry is as old as the study of numbers. Geometry is an important part of human life, both from an aesthetic and from a practical perspective. Geometry helps explain why some paintings, sculptures, and shapes, and even some music, appeal to more people than others. Geometry helps us to determine which shapes are more useful than others, and which are stronger than others. In Chapter 1, we saw that patterns is a theme that runs through all of mathematical thinking. In the next three chapters, we will examine the patterns that arise from shapes. In one sense, shapes are patterns. "Geometric patterns can serve as relatively simple models of many kinds of phenomena, and their study is possible and desirable at all levels."[1]

As you will soon discover, our understanding of geometry has been strongly influenced by people who lived in Greece over two thousand years ago who sought to go beyond merely observing patterns to proving *why* they are so. In doing so, they defined many of the words that we use to describe shapes. However, shape itself is an undefined term in the sense that even today we do not have a precise definition for this idea.

> We know that shapes may be alike in some ways and different in others. A football is not a basketball, but both are smooth closed surfaces; a triangle is not a square, but both are polygons. . . . We know that shapes can change and yet be in some way the same: our shadows are always *our* shadows, even though they change in size and contour throughout the day.[2]

The goals of Chapters 8 through 10 are basic: We will discover similarities and differences among shapes, analyze the components of shapes, and examine shapes from different perspectives. Our tools will include classification (looking for patterns among shapes: similarities and differences), analysis, and representation (such as diagrams or looking at the same shape from different perspectives). We will also look for connections between other mathematical knowledge and what we learn about geometry. Finally, we will continue to develop and refine the problem-solving tools that were introduced in Chapter 1.

Read the NCTM Standards concerning geometry from the cover of the book. What do you notice? Think before reading on. . . .

I hope you realize that learning geometry is not just memorizing the names of a lot of figures or just doing proofs. If you have done some of the Chapter 8 explorations, you recognized many of the things mentioned in the Standards: comparing and classifying figures, predicting, developing spatial sense, understanding and applying geometric properties, and developing an appreciation of the importance of geometry both in everyday life and in business.

[1] Branko Grünbaum, cited in Marjorie Senechal, *On the Shoulders of Giants: New Approaches to Numeracy,* Lynn A. Steen, ed. (Washington, D.C.: National Academy Press, 1990), p. 139.

[2] Marjorie Senechal, in *On the Shoulders of Giants: New Approaches to Numeracy,* Lynn A. Steen, ed. (Washington, D.C.: National Academy Press, 1990), p. 140.

Geometry and Spatial Thinking

It is important to note that "school geometry" is only one of many subsets of a much larger set called spatial thinking. Let us examine some of the other subsets so that you can have a better sense of the larger goal and vision of geometry in school mathematics.

One aspect of spatial thinking is hand-eye coordination. Most young children are still very much in the process of developing this ability. There are many activities in the field of geometry that can help children to develop this ability, such as copying shapes that the teacher or other students have made with pattern blocks, geoboards (such as those at the end of the *Exploration* volume), or other manipulatives.

Another important spatial thinking ability is called **figure-ground perception**, the ability to identify a figure against a complex background. One example that most of my students remember from elementary school is a picture for which the directions ask, "Can you find the 12 monkeys hidden in this picture?" The activity is far more than just a fun exercise. This ability to discriminate what you are looking for from extraneous lines or information is important in many professions.

Another important ability is called **perceptual constancy**, the ability to recognize figures and objects when they are not in their familiar orientation. For example, many students see the triangle on the left in Figure 8.2 as an isosceles triangle, but will say that the triangle on the right is not an isosceles triangle. Similarly, other students will see that the triangle on the right is an obtuse triangle but fail to see that the triangle on the left is also an obtuse triangle. In fact, the two triangles are congruent.

FIGURE **8.2**

Visual discrimination is the ability to find similarities and differences between or among objects. You have probably seen tasks developing this ability in *Sesame Street*, commercial activity books and schoolbooks. For example, five similar objects are shown, and the student is asked to pick the two that are identical.

Visual memory has to do with a person's ability to accurately describe or draw an object that is no longer in view. In Section 8.2, there will be an investigation that asks you to look at an object for only a few seconds and then try to draw that object from memory.

These are but a few of the many kinds of abilities that come under the larger heading of spatial thinking and that are important in everyday life and crucial in many occupations. Douglas Clements and Michael Battista state that "much of the thinking required in higher mathematics is spatial in nature,"[3] and they note that Einstein said that he thought not so much in words as in images. Ultimately, we want students to realize that virtually all fields of mathematics have spatial aspects and applications.

---

[3] Douglas H. Clements and Michael T. Battista, "Geometry and Spatial Reasoning," in *Handbook of Research on Mathematics Teaching and Learning*, ed. Douglas A. Grouws (New York: Macmillan, 1992), p. 442.

The van Hiele Levels of Geometric Thinking

Two Dutch educators, Pierre and Dina van Hiele-Geldorf, were concerned with how geometry was generally taught. In the late 1950s, they developed what is now known as the van Hiele model. Ignored for many years in the United States, it is now gaining more prominence. Let us look and see what the van Hiele model says about learning geometry. The van Hieles found that there are levels, or stages, in the development of a person's understanding of geometric ideas and concepts. Each level describes the sophistication of the learner's thinking tools for learning geometric ideas. The following descriptions are meant as an introduction and overview; the complete model is rather sophisticated and worth more attention.

FIGURE **8.3**

Level 1: Visual (recognition)   At this level, the person's primary thinking tool is direct visual observation. A student at this level can recognize and name figures, but does so more by focusing globally — for example, "This is a square because it looks like one." Although students at this level may be made aware of the various properties of geometric objects (for example, that a square has four equal sides), such awareness can be overridden by other factors. For example, if we turn a square on its side, as in Figure 8.3, the student may insist that it is no longer a square but is now a diamond.

Level 2: Analysis   At this level, the person can go beyond mere appearance and recognize and describe shapes by their properties, such as a square's four right angles, equal sides, parallel opposite sides, and so on. However, a student at this level does not spontaneously and regularly look at *relationships* between figures. A student who argues that a figure is not a rectangle because it is a square is showing level 2 thinking.

Level 3: Relationships   At this level, the student can start to *consistently* use more abstract reasoning processes. The student can now classify figures more powerfully; for example, the student can now see that squares are a special kind (subset) of rectangles. Students at this level can begin to harness the power of "if-then" reasoning and are able to follow and make informal proofs. However, they are not yet able to really appreciate the need for formal, axiomatic geometry.

Level 4: Formal proof   This is the level of high school geometry — axioms, definitions, postulates, theorems, and so on. Students thinking at this level can understand and appreciate the need for a more rigorous system of logic and are able to work with abstract statements and make conclusions based on logic rather than just on intuition.

Level 5: Mathematical systems   This is the level of college geometry. At this level, students are able to successfully focus on the systems themselves, not just on the deductions in the given system.

It is important to reemphasize that these are not descriptions of *what* students know, but rather of the ascending levels of *how* they are able to think, that is, the kinds of thinking tools they can use to learn geometry. It is expected that by the end of middle school, students are able to think at level 3 and are "ready" for level 4 tasks and investigations.

The NCTM supports this notion of building formal knowledge from investigations that are at a level appropriate for the learner: "Geometry should focus on intuitive, 'common sense' investigations of geometric concepts in such a way that general properties emerge and are used as the basis for conjectures and deductions. Later, observations and deductions can be studied more formally as part of a mathematical system" (*Professional Standards*, p. 137).

BASIC CONCEPTS OF GEOMETRY

WHAT DO YOU THINK?

- Why do we not define terms like point, line, and plane?
- What does the name we give a line (or angle) tell us about it?
- Why are there 360 degrees in a circle?

Early geometry   Archaeologists tell us that over 5,000 years ago, the Egyptians and Babylonians had given names to many geometric figures and had discovered many geometric relationships. By 3000 B.C., the Egyptians had developed rather sophisticated understandings about geometry. For example, the relationship between the lengths of the three sides of a right triangle ($a^2 + b^2 = c^2$) had been known to the Egyptians at least 1,500 years before and to the Chinese for at least 1,000 years.[4] They used this knowledge in many ways—for example, to make the pyramids and to redraw boundaries each year after the Nile river flooded the fields. The ancient Greek historian, Herodotus, wrote:

> Seostris . . . made a division of the soil of Egypt among the inhabitants. . . . If the river carried away any portion of a man's lot . . . the king sent persons to examine, and determine by measurements the exact extent of the loss. . . . From this practice, I think, geometry first came to be known in Egypt, whence it passed into Greece.[5]

However, our records indicate that the Egyptians' knowledge was intuitive and inductive. Before deductive reasoning was developed, they could not be sure of their conclusions, and in fact many of their formulas were wrong, such as those for the area of a circle and the volume of some solids.

Geometry as a mathematical system   Modern mathematics was born in ancient Greece, for it was the Greeks who pushed mathematics from the mainly empirical level to the deductive level. It was Thales (who lived in the sixth century B.C.) first and then his student Pythagoras and his students who not only asked *how* and *what* but also asked *why*. These early Greeks were not content to know that $a^2 + b^2 = c^2$ *seemed* to be true for all right triangles; they were driven to be able to prove that it *must* be true. This change in thinking (analogous to moving from van Hiele level 3 to level 4) "symbolizes the circumstances under which the foundations not only of modern mathematics but also of modern science and philosophy were established."[6] It is not surprising that the word *geometry* comes from two Greek words: *geo*, meaning "earth," and *metria*, meaning "measurement."

Over many hundreds of years of exploration, the Greeks came to invent what we call mathematical systems. About 300 B.C. a Greek mathematician, Euclid, published *The Elements*, a set of 13 books that essentially organized what the Greeks had learned about mathematics up to that time. It contained over 600 theorems resting upon 10 fundamental postulates. *The Elements* were viewed by most mathematicians as a model of deductive reasoning for nearly 2,000 years.

Although a formal treatment of geometry is not the focus of this chapter, I believe that an awareness of mathematical systems and their value in modern society is important. It is essential that your future students develop a good mathematical foundation in elementary school (van Hiele levels 1, 2, and 3) so that they can build confidently on this knowledge in high school and beyond. Geometry is only one of many modern mathematical systems. Some others are matrix algebra, abstract algebra, analysis, differential equations, probability, statistics, and chaos theory.

This notion of mathematical systems has taken thousands of years to develop and is one of the primary reasons for the explosion of science and technolo-

[4] H.A. Freebury, *A History of Mathematics* (New York: Macmillan, 1961), p. 35.
[5] Quoted in Julian L. Coolidge, *A History of Geometrical Methods* (New York: Dover, 1963), pp. 8–9.
[6] Dirk J. Struik, *A Concise History of Mathematics* (New York: Dover, 1948), p. 41.

gy in the past 400 years. The truth of any mathematical system rests upon certain terms that are left undefined and certain ideas whose truth is assumed (postulates). This is because we cannot define every term that we use. The futility of such an approach is humorously treated in the B.C. cartoon in Figure 8.4.

Source: By permission of Johnny Hart and Creators Syndicate.

FIGURE 8.4

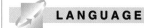

LANGUAGE

A convention among mathematicians is to use capital letters to refer to points and lowercase letters to refer to lines and planes.

Before we examine basic geometric definitions and concepts, let us briefly describe three fundamental undefined terms. In everyday life, we refer to the starting point of a race or a point on a map. Geometrically, a **point** has no dimension (length or width), but it does have a location. In everyday life, we refer to lines on a paper and lines of longitude. Geometrically, a **line** is straight and extends infinitely in two directions. We can also think of a line as an infinite collection of points that indicate a straight path. In everyday life, we refer to planes when we talk about floors and countertops. Geometrically, a **plane** is considered to be a flat surface that extends infinitely in all directions.

INVESTIGATION 8.1   Point, Line, and Plane

The purpose of this investigation is to have you come to appreciate the kind of thinking the Greeks started. You may find it helpful to use the point of your pencil or pen to represent a *point*, a ruler (or other object with a straight edge) to represent a *line*, and a piece of posterboard to represent a *plane*. By cutting slits in the posterboard, as shown in Figure 8.5, you can more concretely investigate the questions asked below.

FIGURE 8.5

Points and lines

A. Draw a point on a piece of paper. How many different lines can you draw that go through that point?

B. Draw two points on a piece of paper. How many different lines can you draw that go through both points?

C. Draw three points on a piece of paper. How many different lines can you draw that go through all three points?

If you answer any of the questions, "it depends," can you be more specific? Write down your responses before reading on. . . .

FIGURE **8.6**

FIGURE **8.7**

FIGURE **8.8**

FIGURE **8.9**

FIGURE **8.10**

DISCUSSION

A. An infinite number of lines will go through any point (see Figure 8.6).

B. Only one line will go through any two points. That is, if we draw *any* two points, there will always be one and *only* one line that contains those two points (see Figure 8.7).

This powerful, but generally partially understood, conclusion is often stated as: **Two points determine a line.** Do you understand the equivalence of the two statements?

C. How many lines we can draw through three points depends on the points. If the three points are on a line, then we can draw only one line (see Figure 8.8). However, if the three points are not on a line, then three points will determine three lines (see Figure 8.9).

This leads us to our first true definition: **Collinear** points are points that lie on the same line. As we have just seen, any two points are collinear.

On the other hand, if three (or more) points do not lie on a single line, then those points are said to be **noncollinear.** In Figure 8.9, points *A*, *B*, and *C* are collinear points, whereas points *A*, *B*, and *D* are noncollinear points.

There is a common misconception about collinear points that needs to be addressed. Draw a point on a line and place your pencil somewhere above the desk. If the point on the paper is point *A* and the tip of the pencil is point *B* (see Figure 8.10), are points *A* and *B* collinear? Think before reading on. . . .

Yes; *any* two points are said to be collinear. Even if a line is not already drawn, if it is *possible* to draw such a line, then the points are collinear.

Part 3 of Exploration 8.4 addresses similar issues.

Planes

A. Now draw a point on a piece of paper. How many different planes can go through that point?

B. Draw two points on a piece of paper. How many different planes can go through both points?

C. Draw three points on a piece of paper. How many different planes can go through all three points?

If you answer any of the questions, "it depends," can you be more specific? Write down your responses before reading on. . . .

DISCUSSION

A. An infinite number of planes will go through any one point.

B. An infinite number of planes will go through any two points.

C. The answer for three points depends on where you put the points. If we draw three noncollinear points, there is only one plane that will contain all three points. Do you see why? Think and then read on. . . . 🖉

FIGURE **8.11**

FIGURE **8.12**

One of the best ways to demonstrate this requires three people. First, draw one point on a sheet of paper. Next, the first person puts a pencil in the air (tip up). Then the second person puts another pencil in the air (tip up), making sure only that the three points are noncollinear. Now the third person takes a model of a plane (cardboard or a hard-cover book). How many different planes contain all three points?

When two or more points lie on the same plane, they are said to be **coplanar** points. As you have just seen, any two or three points are coplanar, because we can always find one plane that will contain them (see Figure 8.11).

There is another way to see this concept concretely. Make a model of a three-legged stool like the one shown in Figure 8.12. You can be creative; for example, use three pencils, some glue and a piece of cardboard. Put the model on a flat surface. Make a model of a four-legged stool like the one shown and put it on a flat surface. What do you notice? Think before reading on. . . . 🖉

The three-legged stool will never rock. Many four-legged stools will. Why? How would you explain why to a friend who is not in this course?

Since the three points at the bottom of the stool are not collinear, there is only one plane that will contain them. However, the four points at the bottom of the four-legged stool may or may not all lie on the same plane. Thus, we have a famous property: **Three noncollinear points determine a plane.**

Line Segments and Rays

In most everyday situations, we don't work with lines; instead, we work with line segments and rays.

> We define a **line segment** to be a subset of a line that contains two points of the line (which we call the **endpoints**) and all points between those two points.

> We define a **ray** as the subset of a line that contains a specific point (the endpoint) and all the points on the line that are on the same side of that point.

Table 8.1 shows the difference between a line, a line segment, and a ray.

TABLE 8.1

Term	Diagram	Notation
Line		$\overleftrightarrow{AB}$ or $\overleftrightarrow{BA}$
Line segment		$\overline{AB}$ or $\overline{BA}$
Ray		$\overrightarrow{AB}$ but not $\overrightarrow{BA}$

The notation to represent lines, line segments, and rays is a convention that has evolved. The conventional way to denote a line is by using two points on the line and a double arrow above the two letters. In Table 8.1, it would not be incorrect to refer to the line as $\overleftrightarrow{ABC}$, but it would be unconventional, like offering to shake someone's hand with your left hand.

The conventional way to denote a line segment is to use two letters, representing the endpoints, and a bar above the two letters.

Naming rays requires careful thought, for there is unconventional and then there is incorrect! For example, $\overrightarrow{AB} \neq \overrightarrow{BA}$. Why is this? The convention for naming a ray is to use two letters, the first of which is the endpoint of the ray. The second letter can be any other point on the ray and indicates the direction of the ray. For example, in Figure 8.13, we can speak of $\overrightarrow{DA}$, which is different from $\overrightarrow{AD}$. On the other hand, $\overrightarrow{DA}$ and $\overrightarrow{DM}$ are considered to be the same ray. Why is this?

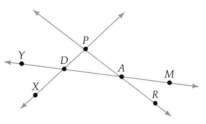

FIGURE **8.13**

Kinds of Lines

As you saw if you worked on Exploration 8.3, there are many possible ways in which two or more lines may be related to each other. For example, they may **intersect**, as in Figure 8.14. Two lines are said to intersect if they have exactly one point in common.

FIGURE **8.14**

If two intersecting lines form right angles, they are said to be **perpendicular**. (See Figure 8.15.)

If three or more lines intersect at a single point (that is, have a point in common), they are said to be **concurrent** lines. (See Figure 8.15.)

As you know, not all lines intersect. If two lines lie in the same plane and never intersect, they are said to be **parallel** lines. (See Figure 8.15.)

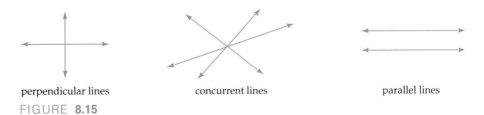

perpendicular lines   concurrent lines   parallel lines

FIGURE **8.15**

There is a fourth possibility: two lines that do not intersect because they do not lie in the same plane. Such lines are called skew lines. For example, in Figure 8.16, $\overleftrightarrow{AD}$ and $\overleftrightarrow{EF}$ are skew lines.

FIGURE **8.16**

Angles

When two or more lines intersect, many different kinds of *angles* are formed. How would you define an angle in your own words? Try to do so before moving on. . . .

A common mathematical definition is that an angle consists of the union of two rays that have a common endpoint, which we call the vertex of the angle. Each of the rays is called a side of the angle (see Figure 8.17).

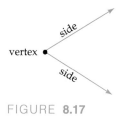

FIGURE **8.17**

Does this make sense, or is it just more mathematical jargon? Is your definition consistent with this one? Think before reading on. . . .

An angle partitions a plane into three disjoint regions: the angle itself, the interior of the angle, and the exterior of the angle (see Figure 8.18).

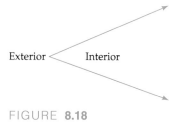

FIGURE **8.18**

Now that we have defined angles, let us examine how they are named. Before reading on, though, make sure that you are actively thinking while reading. What do you know about naming angles? Write down what you know before reading on. . . .

Naming Angles

We often refer to an angle by using its vertex. For example, we can call the angle at the left in Figure 8.19 angle *A*. We can also refer to angles by using a numbering system. In the diagram at the right in Figure 8.19, we can talk about angle 1, angle 2, angle 3, and angle 4.

FIGURE **8.19**

Both ways of referring to angles have limitations. Look at Figure 8.20. If someone asks you to look at angle *A*, what are the possibilities? How might we resolve this dilemma? Think before reading on. . . .

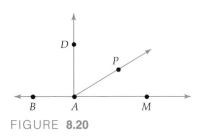

FIGURE **8.20**

One way out of this dilemma is to use the symbol ∡ and three letters to name an angle. The order of the three letters is important. We start with a point on one side of the angle, then give the vertex, and then give a point on the other side of the angle (see Figure 8.21). These three points determine an angle in much the same way that three noncollinear points determine a plane.

Thus, in Figure 8.20, we can distinguish between ∡*DAM*, ∡*PAD*, and ∡*PAM*.

∡*PAM* = ∡*MAP*. Do you see why?

∡*DAM* ≠ ∡*ADM*. Do you see why?

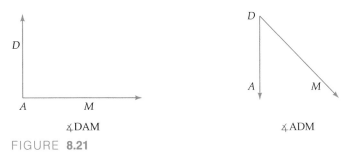

∡DAM   ∡ADM

FIGURE **8.21**

Measuring Angles

We measure angles by how "open" they are, and the tool we use is a **protractor**. The most common unit of measurement for angles is a **degree**.

HISTORY

You may recall that there are 360 degrees in a circle. Do you know where the 360 comes from?

It comes from the Babylonians who, for reasons unknown to us, decided (over 3,000 years ago) to divide a circle into 360 parts. We know that 360 was an important number for them, perhaps because there are approximately 360 days in a year.

When the French converted measures of length, mass, and other quantities to the metric system, why

didn't they convert measures of a circle? We know that the French attempt to metrify the week (10 days in a week and 10 hours in a day) failed. Perhaps the 24-hour day and 7-day week were just too deeply ingrained, and perhaps this was also true with angles. Actually, 360 has advantages over 100. Consider some common angles—for example, 60° and 45°. If there were 100 degrees in a circle, what would these angles be?

Although protractors come in a variety of styles, the correct use of all protractors requires the following:

1. The vertex of the angle must lie at the center of the protractor, which is not always the center of the bottom edge of the protractor (as shown in Figure 8.22).

2. One ray of the angle must lie directly under the line that goes through a 0 point of the protractor (which is not always labeled).

3. The measure of the angle is read by looking at the number corresponding to where the other ray of the angle crosses the same number line at the edge of the protractor, as the 0 mark.

In the right-hand figure, the protractor has been moved in order to measure an angle, neither of whose vertices are parallel to the bottom of the page. Measure the two angles and then check your measurements below or with a friend.

FIGURE **8.22**

The measure of the angle at the left is 63 degrees, and the measure of the angle at the right is 126 degrees.

For the most part, the level of precision of measuring angles in this course will consist of rounding the measure to the nearest whole number. However, an angle can be divided into 60 minutes (denoted by '), and a minute can be divided into 60 seconds (denoted by "). Can you think of a situation in which this kind of precision would be necessary? For example, an angle of 0 degrees and 1 minute is 1/21,600 of a circle, too small to show on a piece of paper.

Classifying Angles

We have names for different kinds of angles. We can classify angles with respect to an angle whose measure is one-fourth of a circle, that is, 90 degrees. This is a **right** angle. Just as 1/2 is a reference fraction, a right angle is a reference angle.

An angle whose measure is less than 90 degrees is called an **acute** angle.

An angle whose measure is greater than 90 degrees but less than 180 degrees is called an **obtuse** angle.

If angles are seen from a static perspective, these terms are often sufficient, but angles can also be seen from the dynamic perspective of *turns*. For example, someone might be told to open a valve "one-quarter of a turn," or 90 degrees. A half turn would be 180 degrees, a full turn would be 360 degrees, and one and a half turns would be 540 degrees. It sometimes makes sense to speak of angles with measures of 180 degrees or greater.

An angle whose measure is 180 degrees is called a **straight** angle.

An angle whose measure is greater than 180 degrees is called a **reflex** angle. Determine the measure of the reflex angle in Figure 8.23. You might want to compare notes with another student because there is more than one way to do it.

FIGURE **8.23**

The measure of the angle is 225°. One way to determine the measure is to extend the horizontal ray to the right and measure the resulting acute angle and add 180 to the measure of the acute angle. Another way is to measure the obtuse angle and then subtract it from 360. Do you understand both ways? Did you determine the measure in a third way?

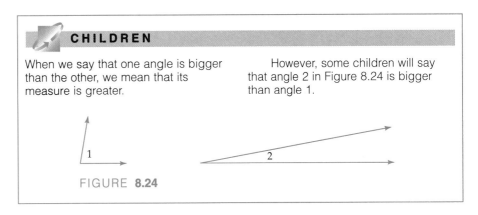

CHILDREN

When we say that one angle is bigger than the other, we mean that its measure is greater.

However, some children will say that angle 2 in Figure 8.24 is bigger than angle 1.

FIGURE **8.24**

Sometimes the relative location of two angles is important. For example, we speak of adjacent angles. What do you think adjacent angles are? Can you draw two adjacent angles? Can you write a definition? If you do, give it to someone who doesn't know the term and see if that person understands the term in the way that you meant it. Then read on. . . .

Adjacent means "next to," but more specifically, two angles are adjacent if and only if they have the same vertex and share a side.

Thus, in Figure 8.25, $\angle DAP$ and $\angle PAM$ are adjacent angles. There are other adjacent angles in the diagram. How many pairs of adjacent angles can you find in the diagram?

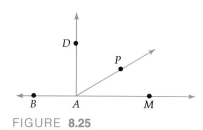

FIGURE **8.25**

We sometimes speak of complementary and supplementary angles.

If the sum of the measures of two angles is 90 degrees, we call them com-plementary angles.

If the sum of the measures of two angles is 180 degrees, we call them sup-plementary angles.

In Figure 8.25, $\angle DAP$ and $\angle PAM$ are complementary, and $\angle BAP$ and $\angle PAM$ are supplementary. It is important to note that angles do not have to be adjacent angles in order to be complementary or supplementary.

Look at Figure 8.26. Which pairs of angles appear to be equal? Could you justify their being equal or prove why they are equal?

What other relationships between pairs of angles do you see?

FIGURE **8.26**

Whenever two lines intersect, four angles are formed. The angles that are opposite each other—for example, $\angle 1$ and $\angle 7$ in Figure 8.26—are called ver-tical angles. How would you define vertical angles formally? This will be left as an exercise.

At a van Hiele level 1 perspective, it certainly seems reasonable that verti-cal angles are always equal. An example of a level 4 activity would be a formal proof. Though this text is not emphasizing proofs, I believe a few proofs are helpful so that the elementary teacher can see what the various levels look like. How might we prove that the vertical angles *must* be equal? Think about this before reading on. . . .

A key to the proof is to realize that each pair of adjacent angles in Fig-ure 8.26 is supplementary. For example, $\angle 1$ and $\angle 2$ are supplementary. Do you see why? If you didn't see this, can you now see how we might show that $\angle 2$ and $\angle 8$ must be equal?

If you see the relationships, the proof is fairly straightforward:

Statement	Justification
$m\angle 1 + m\angle 2 = 180$	Together they form a straight angle.
$m\angle 7 + m\angle 2 = 180$	Together they form a straight angle.
$m\angle 1 + m\angle 2 = m\angle 7 + m\angle 2$	Transitive property; both sums are equal to 180.
$m\angle 1 = m\angle 7$	Algebra—we subtracted the same amount from both sides.

Again, it is this type of thinking (level 4) that made what the Greeks did over 2,000 years ago so different from what had been done before.

Summary

In this section, we have focused on the building-block language and concepts of Euclidean geometry: point, line, and plane. Line segments can intersect and join together to make plane figures, also called two-dimensional figures, which we shall explore in Section 8.2. We have examined different subsets of lines (line segments and rays) and different kinds of lines (parallel, perpendicular, concurrent, and skew). Plane figures can intersect to make space figures, also called three-dimensional figures, which we will explore in Section 8.3.

We have examined the different kinds of angles that can be formed by intersecting lines. We can classify angles by their measure: acute, right, obtuse, straight, and reflex. We can also classify angles by their relationship to other angles: complementary, supplementary, and vertical.

EXERCISES 8.1

1. Name all the possible different rays that can be formed from the three points below.

$$A \qquad B \qquad C$$

2. How many different rays can be formed from four collinear points?

3. Sketch four lines such that three are concurrent and two are parallel.

4. Sketch a pair of angles whose intersection is
   a. exactly two points or explain why this is not possible.
   b. exactly three points or explain why this is not possible.
   c. exactly four points or explain why this is not possible.

5. True or false? If true, briefly explain why. If false, provide a counterexample.
   a. If two distinct lines do not intersect, then they are parallel.
   b. If two lines are parallel, then they lie in the same plane.
   c. If two lines intersect, then they lie in the same plane.
   d. If two planes have a point in common, then they have infinitely many points in common.
   e. If a line is perpendicular to a plane, then it is perpendicular to all lines in that plane.
   f. If a plane contains a line segment, then it contains the line of which the segment is a subset.
   g. If three lines are concurrent, then they are also coplanar.
   h. If two planes intersect, the intersection is either a point or a line.
   i. Three different planes can have at most one point in common.
   j. Two distinct planes either intersect or are parallel.
   k. Two intersecting lines determine one and only one plane.
   l. Vertical angles can be supplementary.

6. When two lines in a plane intersect, four distinct regions are formed.

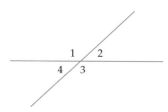

a. If three lines intersect in a plane, what is the maximum number of regions that can be formed?

b. If four lines intersect in a plane, what is the maximum number of regions that can be formed?

c. If five lines intersect in a plane, what is the maximum number of regions that can be formed?

d. If *n* lines intersect in a plane, what is the maximum number of regions that can be formed?

7. Estimate the measure of the following angles. Describe your reasoning process. Then measure the angles with a protractor and determine your percent error.

(a)   (b)

(c)   (d)

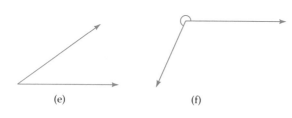

(e)   (f)

8. Make at least five more angles. Then estimate their measure, determine their measure, and determine your percent error. Then graph your percent error for the angles in Exercises 7 and 8. If you note that the percent error seems to be decreasing, can you articulate any thinking processes that you are developing that are making your estimates more accurate?

9. Using only a straightedge and reasoning, try to make angles with the following measures. Then describe your reasoning process. After making each angle, check your work with a protractor and determine the percent error.

a. 30°   b. 45°   c. 150°   d. 300°   e. 67°

10. In the figure below, $\overleftrightarrow{AB}$ and $\overleftrightarrow{BC}$ are perpendicular lines.

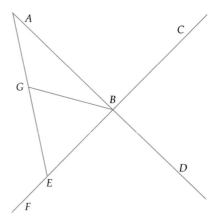

a. Name two complementary angles.

b. Name two supplementary angles.

c. Name two vertical angles.

d. Name two adjacent angles.

11. Refer to the cube pictured below, and use symbols such as $\overline{AB}$ to name the following:

a. Two parallel line segments

b. Two line segments that do not lie in the same plane

c. Two intersecting line segments

d. Three concurrent line segments that do not lie in a single plane

e. Two skew line segments

f. A pair of supplementary angles

g. A pair of perpendicular line segments

h. Are points *A*, *B*, and *H* coplanar points? Why or why not?

12. This exercise focuses on communication. For each of the following terms, suppose a friend in the class has come to you and told you that the term just doesn't make sense. Describe how you would help that person to make sense of the term. Your description must include your own definition of the term.

a. Collinear points   b. Concurrent lines

c. Adjacent angle   d. Skew lines

13. **a.** Find the sum of the following two angles: 45°32′ and 73°57′.

   b. Write 18°45′ in decimal form, to two decimal places.

   c. Express 128°24′ in decimal form, to two decimal places.

14. Clock problems.

   a. How many times a day will the minute hand be directly on top of the hour hand?

   b. What times could it be when the two hands make a 90-degree angle?

   c. What angle do the hands make at 7 o'clock?

   d. What angle do the hands make at 3:30?

   e. What angle do the hands make at 2:06?

   f. Make up and answer a problem like these. Then swap problems with a friend, and have the friend check your work and you check the friend's work.

15. How many different pairs of vertical angles are formed by three concurrent lines?

16. Dot-matrix printers, television screens, and college marching bands all create pictures from dots. For example, the diagram below shows three ways in which the letter U might be formed on a dot-matrix printer.

   a. Using a 5 by 5 grid, make designs for each of the (capital) letters of the alphabet.

   b. The diagram below shows two different arrangements of band members that form the letter U. Determine the minimum number of band members necessary to spell MSU on a field.

   c. Determine the minimum number of band members necessary to spell your college's initials on a field.

17. Draw a Venn diagram to show the relationships between intersecting, perpendicular, parallel, concurrent, and skew lines. Let U be the set of all lines. Explain your diagram.

18. Construct two rays AB and CD for which $\overrightarrow{AB} \cap \overrightarrow{CD}$ is a set containing one point and $\overline{AB} \cap \overline{CD} = \varnothing$.

19. Define vertical angles formally.

20. In this exercise, our universal set will be the 26 capital letters of the alphabet. Separate the letters into two or more groups so that each group is alike in some way. Describe each subset and give it a name. If you know of a mathematical term that fits the description, use it; if you don't, then be creative. In how many different ways can you arrange the letters into subsets? For each classification, remember to describe the subset, give it a name, and list the members of that subset.

SECTION ◆ 8.2

TWO-DIMENSIONAL FIGURES

WHAT DO YOU THINK?

- In what ways are triangles and quadrilaterals different? In what ways are they similar?

- How are circles and polygons related?

- Can every polygon be broken down into triangles? Why or why not?

- Why do we use two words to name different triangles, but only one word to name different quadrilaterals?

Think of geometric figures that people generally find pleasing, such as those in Figure 8.27 on page 430. What words would you use to explain why these objects are interesting or appealing? When you look at the various objects and pictures, what similarities do you see between certain objects and shapes, for example, triangles or hexagons?

When we discuss similarities and differences in my class, many geometric terms emerge in the discussion. Some students talk about similar shapes—for example, hexagons in honeycombs and snowflakes, squares in some pictures, and triangles in others. Some students observe that many of the shapes are symmetrical. In explaining similarities, some students talk about the angles, the length of sides, or the fact that some figures look similar. Many students observe that even the more complex shapes can be seen as being constructed from simpler shapes, such as triangles and quadrilaterals.

In this section, we will learn more about geometric figures and shapes, and you will learn and discover some of the secrets of the patterns in the objects you have seen. During this time, you will learn quite a bit of vocabulary and many of the properties that make these patterns possible. In Chapter 9, we will examine how shapes can be put together to make interesting designs you have seen, such as those in quilts, plants and animals, and buildings.

FIGURE **8.27**

(a) (b) (c) (d)

(e)

Source: Le Roy H. Appleton, *American Indian Design & Decoration* (Dover, NY: 1950)

(f)

INVESTIGATION **8.2** Classifying Figures

Before we examine and classify important two-dimensional shapes, we need to first investigate the kinds of possible two-dimensional shapes. Classify the 13 shapes in Figure 8.28 into two or more groups so that each group has a common characteristic. Do this in as many different ways as you can, then read on. . . .

FIGURE **8.28**

DISCUSSION

If you did Exploration 8.5, you have some direct experience with classifying figures. In this investigation, one possibility is to put all the figures that have curved lines into one group (subset) and those composed only of straight lines into another. One of the figures has both straight and curved lines. It could be in a third subset, all by itself. Note that we leave "curved" as an undefined term.

Curved

Straight

Curved and straight

Another way to group the figures is according to whether they have an opening.

Opening

No openings

Among those that do not have an opening (that is, that are closed), we can make two distinct subsets: Those that intersect themselves and those that don't.

Intersect

Do not intersect

Those figures that do not have an opening are called closed curves. We can state this a bit more formally by saying that a curve is closed if it can be drawn by starting and ending at the same point. Figures that do not intersect themselves are called simple curves.

- Draw a simple closed curve.

- Draw a simple open curve.

- Draw a nonsimple closed curve.

- Draw a nonsimple open curve.

Exchange figures with another student. Do each of you agree that each of the other's drawings matches the description? If so, move on. If not, take some time to discuss your differences.

Any simple closed curve partitions the plane into three disjoint regions: the curve itself, the interior of the curve, and the exterior of the curve (see Figure 8.29). This seems obvious, but there is actually a theorem called the **Jordan curve theorem** that proves this.

LANGUAGE

What other words might you use to describe the intersecting and not intersecting subsets?

Some students use the phrase "trace over," and others talk about figures that "run over themselves" or "cross themselves." Other students talk about the set of figures that contain two smaller regions within each figure.

CHILDREN

Using the terms developed in this investigation, how would you classify dot-to-dot pictures?

FIGURE **8.29**

In this book, we will focus on figures that are simple, closed curves. It is important to note that curves that are open and curves that are not simple are also interesting and have real-life applications. It's just that we can't investigate all mathematical topics in this book. In elementary school, students generally encounter two kinds of simple, closed figures: polygons and circles.

CHILDREN

One way in which children can learn mathematical ideas is by copying figures. The drawings in Figure 8.30 represent common attempts by four-year-olds to copy a circle, a square, and a triangle. What do you notice?

The drawings show that what the children notice is that all are simple, closed curves. What they do not seem to notice are other attributes that seem so obvious to us: the number of sides,

the size of the angles, and so on. (This discussion connects to a field of mathematics called *topology*, one of the many fields of mathematics that we will not study in this text.) These same children as six-year-olds (with no "training") will generally copy the figures fairly accurately. Their minds are developing at a rapid rate at this period of their lives.

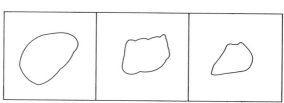

Richard W. Copeland, *How Children Learn Mathematics*, 3rd edition (Prentice-Hall, NJ: © 1976). Reprinted by permission.

FIGURE **8.30**

Polygons

A **polygon** is defined as a simple, closed curve composed only of line segments. Thus, the simple, closed curve in Figure 8.29(a) is not a polygon, whereas the simple, closed curve in Figure 8.29(b) (which looks like the state of Nevada) is a polygon.

The word *polygon* has Greek origins: *poly-*, meaning "many," and *-gon*, meaning "sides." You are already familiar with many kinds of polygons. Just as we found in Chapter 2 that the names we give numbers have an interesting history, so do the names we give to polygons. The most basic naming classification involves the number of sides (see Table 8.2).

TABLE 8.2	
Number of sides	Name
3 sides	Triangle
4 sides	Quadrilateral
5 sides	Pentagon
6 sides	Hexagon
7 sides	Heptagon
8 sides	Octagon
n sides	n-gon

On any polygon, the point at which two sides meet is called a **vertex**, the plural of which is **vertices**.

Congruence

As you have seen from Explorations 8.6 and 8.7, questions sometimes arise about whether two figures are "the same" or not. Such observations and questions deal with the idea of congruence.

At an informal level, we can say that two figures are congruent iff they have the same shape and size. An informal test of congruence is to see if you can exactly superimpose one figure on top of the other. This is closely connected to how children initially encounter the concept and is related to the dictionary definition: "coinciding exactly when superimposed."[7] That is, if one figure can be superimposed over another so that it fits perfectly, then the two figures are congruent. (Henry Ford literally changed our world by thinking to make cars out of sets of congruent parts rather than one at a time. For example, the left front fender of a 1997 Dodge Caravan in Minnesota is congruent to the left front fender of any other 1997 Dodge Caravan.)

Formally, we say that two polygons are **congruent** iff all pairs of corresponding parts are congruent. In other words, in order for us to conclude that two polygons are congruent, two conditions have to be met: (1) Each corresponding pair of angles must have the same measure, and (2) each corresponding pair of sides must have the same length. We use the symbol $\cong$ to denote congruence.

For example, in Figure 8.31, triangle *CAT* and triangle *DOG* are congruent iff $\angle C \cong \angle D$, $\angle A \cong \angle O$, $\angle T \cong \angle G$, $\overline{CA} \cong \overline{DO}$, $\overline{AT} \cong \overline{OG}$, and $\overline{TC} \cong \overline{GD}$.

FIGURE **8.31**

The notions of congruent and equal are related concepts. We use the term *congruence* when referring to having the same shape, and we use the term *equal* when referring to having the same numerical value. Thus, we do not say that two triangles are equal; we say that they are congruent. Similarly, when we look at line segments and angles of polygons, we speak of congruent line segments and congruent angles. However, when we look at the numerical value of the line segments and angles, we say that the lengths of two line segments are equal and that the measures of two angles are equal.

[7] Houghton Mifflin Company, *The American Heritage Dictionary of the English Language*, © 1996. Reprinted by permission.

BEYOND THE CLASSROOM

When do we need congruence in everyday life or in work situations? Take a few minutes to think about this before reading on. . . .

Congruence is important in manufacturing; for example, the success of assembly-line production depends on being able to produce parts that are congruent. One of the differences between a decent quilt and an excellent one is being able to ensure that all the squares are congruent. This is quite difficult when using complex designs. Most of the manipulatives teachers use with schoolchildren (Pattern Blocks, unifix cubes, Cuisenaire rods, and fraction bars) have congruent sets of pieces.

INVESTIGATION 8.3 Re-creating Shapes from Memory

For this investigation, you will want to have a pencil and an eraser.

A. Turn to page 461. Keep the book open for about 1 second and then draw Figure 8.75 from memory.

Check the picture again for 1 second. If your drawing was incomplete or inaccurate, change your drawing so that it is accurate. Check the picture again for 1 second. Keep doing this until your drawing is complete and accurate.

Now go back and try to describe your thinking processes as you tried to re-create the figure. From an information processing perspective, your eyes did not simply receive the image from the paper, and your knowledge of geometry helped determine *how* you saw the picture. What did you hear yourself saying to help you remember the picture? Compare your thinking processes with another student. Then read on. . . .

DISCUSSION

Some students see a diamond and 4 right triangles. Other students see a large square in which the midpoints of the sides have been connected to make a new square inside the first square. Yet other students see four right triangles that have been connected by "flipping" or rotating them.

B. Now look at Figure 8.76 (on page 461) for several seconds. Then try to draw it from memory. As before, check the picture again for a couple of seconds. If your drawing was incomplete or inaccurate, fix it. Keep doing this until your drawing is complete and accurate. Then go back and try to describe your thinking processes as you tried to re-create the figure.

DISCUSSION

This figure was more complex. Some students see a whole design and try to remember it.

Some decompose the design into four black triangles and four rectangles as shown in Figure 8.32.

The figure can also be seen as being composed of 9 squares, which can also be seen in Figure 8.32. The four corner squares have been cut to make congruent right triangles. Each of the other four squares on the border has been cut into two congruent rectangles.

Some students re-create this figure by seeing a whole square and then looking at what was cut out (see Figure 8.33). That is, they saw that they needed to cut out each corner, and they saw that they needed to cut out a rectangle on the middle of each side. Finally, they remembered to cut out a square in the center.

When I did this exercise myself, I saw a "square race track" with a similar pattern on each corner (Figure 8.34).

This is a famous quilting pattern called the Churn Dash. When people made their own butter, the cream was poured into a pail called a churn. Then the churner rolled a special pole back and forth with his or her hands. At the end of the pole was a wooden piece called a dash, which was shaped like the figure you saw. If you make many copies of this pattern and put them together, you can see what a Churn Dash quilt looks like.

There are several implications for teaching from this investigation. How a person re-creates the figure is related to the person's spatial thinking preferences and abilities. Different people "see" different objects. That is, not everyone sees the same figure. Although there are differences in how people re-create the figure, very few people can re-create the figure without doing some kind of decomposing, that is, without breaking the pattern into smaller parts. Being able to do this depends partly on spatial skills and partly on being able to use various geometric ideas (congruent, triangle, square, rectangle) at least at an intuitive level.

While some people manage to live happy, productive lives at the lowest van Hiele level, an understanding of basic geometric figures and relationships among them is often helpful in everyday life (for example, in home repair projects and quilting) and in many occupations. Now that your interest in geometric figures has been piqued by this investigation and the pictures at the beginning of the section, let us examine the characteristics and properties of basic geometric shapes.

FIGURE **8.32**

FIGURE **8.33**

FIGURE **8.34**

Triangles

There are many kinds of triangles. As before, you will probably better understand the names and be able to apply your knowledge of triangles if you actively engage in the following investigation.

INVESTIGATION **8.4**   Classifying Triangles

You will find nine triangles in Figure 8.35 at the top of page 436. Copy them and cut them out, and then separate them into two or more subsets so that each subset has a common characteristic. Can you come up with a name for each subset? What names might children give to different subsets? Do this in as many different ways as you can before reading on. . . .

FIGURE **8.35**

DISCUSSION

STRATEGY 1: Consider sides

One way to classify triangles is by the length of their sides: all three sides having equal length, two sides having equal length, no sides having equal length. There are special names for these three kinds of triangles.

- If all three sides have the same length, then we say that the triangle is **equilateral**.

- If at least two sides have the same length, then we say that the triangle is **isosceles**.

- If all three sides have different lengths—that is, no two sides have the same length—then we say that the triangle is **scalene**.

Which of the triangles in Figure 8.35 are scalene? which are isosceles? which are equilateral?

STRATEGY 2: Consider angles

We can also classify triangles by the relative size of the angles—that is, whether they are right, acute, or obtuse angles. This leads to three kinds of triangles: right triangles, obtuse triangles, and acute triangles.

- We define a **right** triangle as a triangle that has one right angle.
- We define an **obtuse** triangle as a triangle that has one obtuse angle.
- We define an **acute** triangle as a triangle that has three acute angles.

Many students see a pattern: A right triangle has 1 right angle, an obtuse triangle has 1 obtuse angle, yet an acute triangle has 3 acute angles. What was the pattern? Why doesn't it hold? Think before reading on. . . .

The key to this comes from looking at the triangles from a different perspective: Every right triangle has 2 acute angles, and every obtuse triangle has 2 acute angles; thus a triangle having more than 2 acute angles will be a different kind of triangle. This perspective is represented in Table 8.3. Does it help you to better understand the three definitions given above?

TABLE 8.3

First angle	Second angle	Third angle	Name of triangle	
Acute	Acute	Right	Right triangle	
Acute	Acute	Obtuse	Obtuse triangle	
Acute	Acute	Acute	Acute triangle	

STRATEGY 3: Consider angles and sides

This naming of triangles goes even further. What name would you give to the triangle in Figure 8.36?

FIGURE **8.36**

This triangle is both a right triangle and an isosceles triangle, and thus it is called a right isosceles triangle or an isosceles right triangle. How many possible combinations are there, using both classification systems? Work on this before reading on. . . .

There are many strategies for answering this question. First of all, we find that there are nine possible combinations (see Figure 8.37). We can use the idea of Cartesian product to determine all nine. That is, if set S represents triangles classified by side, $S = \{$Equilateral, Isosceles, Scalene$\}$, and set A represents triangles classified by angle, $A = \{$Acute, Right, Obtuse$\}$, then $S \times A$ represents the nine possible combinations.

FIGURE **8.37**

MATHEMATICS

Did you notice the geometric balance in Figure 8.37, which represents the Cartesian product of the two sets of triangles?

However, not all nine combinations are possible. For example, any equilateral triangle must also be an acute triangle. Why is this? So "equilateral acute" is a redundant combination. However, it is possible to have scalene triangles that are acute, right, and obtuse. Similarly, we can have isosceles triangles that are acute, right, and obtuse.

Name the two triangles in Figure 8.38. Then read on. . . .

FIGURE **8.38**

Both are obtuse, isosceles triangles. The orientation on the left is the standard orientation for isosceles triangles. Any time we position a triangle so that one side is horizontal, we call that side the **base.** As stated at the beginning of the chapter, students often see only one aspect of a triangle; for example, they see the triangle at the left as isosceles but not also obtuse, and they see the triangle at the right as obtuse but not also isosceles.

Special Line Segments in Triangles

There are four special line segments that have enjoyed tremendous influence in Euclidean geometry: angle bisector, median, altitude, and perpendicular bisector. These line segments are explored in more depth in Exploration 8.9.

An **angle bisector** is a line segment that bisects an angle of a triangle.

In triangle ABC (Figure 8.39), $\overline{AD}$ is an angle bisector. Hence, $m\angle BAD = m\angle DAC$.

FIGURE **8.39**

A **median** is a line segment that connects a vertex to the midpoint of the opposite side.

In triangle SAT (Figure 8.40), $\overline{TR}$ is a median. Hence, $SR = RA$.

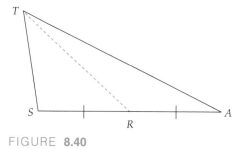

FIGURE **8.40**

An **altitude** is a perpendicular line segment that connects a vertex to the side opposite that vertex. In some cases, as in $\triangle SAT$ below, we need to extend the opposite side to construct the altitude.

In triangle ABC (Figure 8.41), $\overline{BF}$ is an altitude. Hence, $m\angle BFA = m\angle BFC = 90°$.

In triangle STA, $\overline{TP}$ is an altitude. Hence, $m\angle TPA = 90°$.

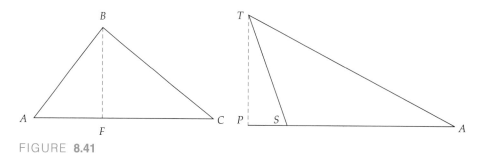

FIGURE **8.41**

Many students have trouble with the idea of an altitude being outside the triangle. This happens when we have an obtuse triangle oriented with one side of the obtuse angle as the base of the triangle. If you are having trouble connecting the definition of altitude in these situations, I recommend the following: Trace the triangle and cut it out. Stand it up so that $\overline{SA}$ is on the plane of your desk and T is above that plane. Now draw a line from T that goes "straight down." What do you notice?

If triangle STA were large enough so that you could stand with your head at point T, the length of line segment $\overline{TP}$ would tell you how tall you were!

A **perpendicular bisector** is a line that goes through the midpoint of a side and is perpendicular to that side. In triangle PEN (Figure 8.42), $\overleftrightarrow{MX}$ is a perpendicular bisector of side $\overline{PN}$, because M is the midpoint of $\overline{PN}$ and $\overleftrightarrow{MX}$ is perpendicular to $\overline{PN}$.

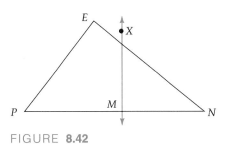

FIGURE **8.42**

Triangle Properties

You probably remember that the sum of the measures of the angles in any triangle is 180 degrees. How could you convince someone who does not know that?

This is a case in which the van Hiele levels are instructive. A level 2 activity would be to have the students measure and add the angles in several triangles. If their measuring was relatively accurate, one or more students would see the pattern and offer a hypothesis that the sum is always 180.

An example of a level 3 activity, which I recommend if you have never done it, is to cut off the three corners of a triangle as in Figure 8.43 and then put the three corners together. What do you see?

FIGURE **8.43**

An example of a level 4 activity would be a formal proof.

We now turn our attention to polygons having four sides, that is, quadrilaterals.

Quadrilaterals

Do you recall Investigation 2.1, where we classified quadrilaterals in order to develop the idea of subsets? You may wish to refresh your memory by reviewing that investigation before reading on.

In this book, we will define the following kinds of quadrilaterals:

- A trapezoid (Figure 8.44) is defined as a quadrilateral with exactly one pair of parallel sides.

FIGURE **8.44**

- A parallelogram (Figure 8.45) is defined as a quadrilateral in which both pairs of opposite sides are parallel.

FIGURE **8.45**

- A kite (Figure 8.46) is defined as a quadrilateral in which two pairs of adjacent sides are congruent.

FIGURE **8.46**

- A rhombus (Figure 8.47) is defined as a quadrilateral in which all sides are congruent.

FIGURE **8.47**

- A rectangle (Figure 8.48) is defined as a quadrilateral in which all angles are congruent.

FIGURE **8.48**

- A square (Figure 8.49) is defined as a quadrilateral in which all four sides are congruent and in which all four angles are congruent.

FIGURE **8.49**

Diagonals One characteristic of all polygons with more than three sides is that they have diagonals. The more sides in the polygon, the more diagonals. This term is probably familiar to most readers. However, before reading the definition of diagonal below, stop and try to define the term yourself so that it works for all polygons, not just squares and other quadrilaterals. Then read on. . . .

A diagonal is a line segment that joins two nonadjacent vertices in a polygon.

Figure 8.50 shows two different diagonals. One of the exercises will ask you to find patterns to determine the number of diagonals in any polygon.

FIGURE **8.50**

Angles in quadrilaterals We know that the sum of the measures of the angles of any triangle is 180°. Will the sum of the measures of the four angles of *any* quadrilateral also be equal to one number, or will there be different numbers for different quadrilaterals? What do you think? What could you do to check your hypothesis? Once you believe that your hypothesis is true, how could you prove it? Think before reading on. . . .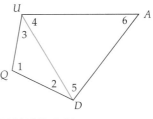

It turns out that for any quadrilateral, the sum of the measures of the four angles is 360°. The following discussion is an informal presentation of one proof. If we draw a generic quadrilateral *QUAD* and one diagonal, as in Figure 8.51, what do you notice that might be related to this proof?

FIGURE **8.51**

If you see two triangles and *connect* this to our knowledge that the sum of the measures of the angles of a triangle is 180°, you have the key to the proof. That is, you can conclude that the sum of all six angles must be 360 degrees. However, these six angles are equivalent to the four angles of the quadrilateral!

Relationships Among Quadrilaterals

If you did Exploration 8.10 (Quadrilaterals), you found that we can view the set of quadrilaterals in much the same way we view a family tree showing the various ways in which individuals are related to others. Figure 8.52 shows one of many ways to represent this family tree for quadrilaterals. Take a few moments to think about this diagram and to connect it to what you know about these different kinds of quadrilaterals. Write a brief description. Does it make sense? Does it prompt new discoveries in your mind?

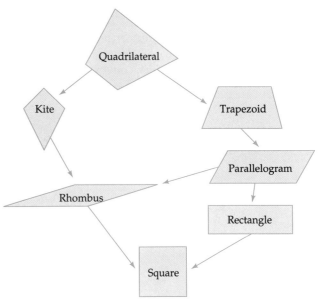

FIGURE **8.52**

One way to interpret this diagram is to say that any figure contains all of the properties and characteristics of the ones above it. The "quadrilateral" at the top represents those quadrilaterals that have no equal sides, no equal angles, and no parallel sides; this is analogous to the scalene triangle. The kite and the trapezoid represent two constraints that we can make: two pairs of congruent, adjacent sides or one pair of sides parallel. If we take a kite and require all four sides to be congruent, we have a rhombus. If we take a trapezoid and require *both* pairs of opposite sides to be parallel, we have a parallelogram. If we require the angles in a parallelogram to be right angles, we have a rectangle. If we require all four sides of a parallelogram to be congruent, we have a rhombus. Both the rhombus and the rectangle can be transformed into squares with one modification—requiring the rhombus to have right angles or the rectangle to have congruent sides. Exploration 8.10 enables you to explore these relationships further. A key point is to begin to see connections and relationships among figures. Many students find in this course, that their picture of geometry changes from looking like a list of definitions and properties to looking more like a network with connections among the various figures. This quadrilateral family tree can also help students to realize why mathematics teachers say that a square is a rectangle and it is a rhombus: It has all the properties of each! In everyday language, we say that a square is a special kind of rhombus and a special kind of rectangle. In mathematical language, we say that the set of squares is a subset of the set of rhombuses and a subset of the set of rectangles. The Venn diagram in Figure 8.53 illustrates this relationship.

FIGURE **8.53**

Convex Polygons

Another concept that emerges with polygons having four or more sides is the idea of convex. Before reading on, look at the two sets of polygons in Figure 8.54, convex and concave (not convex). Try to write a definition for convex. Then read on. . . .

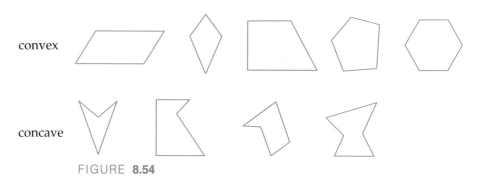

FIGURE **8.54**

For many students, defining convex is much like defining balls and strikes in baseball. As one umpire once said, "I knows it when I sees it." Many students focus on the word *concave* and say that the figure has at least one part that is caved in. Such a description is acceptable at level 1 on the van Hiele model, but we need a definition that is not as vague as "caved in."

Examine the following definition to see if it makes sense. Think before reading on. . . .

> A polygon is convex iff the line segment connecting any two points in the polygonal region lies entirely within the region.
>
> If a polygon is not convex, it is called concave.

Looking at diagonals is an easy way to test for concave and convex. If *any* diagonal lies outside the region, then the polygon is concave. In polygon *ABCDE* in Figure 8.55, the diagonal *AD* lies outside the region.

FIGURE **8.55**

Other Polygons

Although most of the polygons we encounter in everyday life are triangles and quadrilaterals, there are many kinds of polygons with more than four sides. Stop for a moment and think of examples, both natural and human-made objects. Then read on. . . .

All of the figures in Figure 8.56 are polygons.

- The stop sign is an octagon—an eight-sided polygon.
- The Pentagon in Washington has five sides.
- The common nut has a hexagonal shape—a six-sided polygon.

FIGURE **8.56**

Let us examine a few important aspects of polygons with more than four sides.

First, we distinguish between regular and nonregular polygons. What do you think a regular pentagon or a regular hexagon is? How might we define it? Think about this and write down your thoughts before reading on. . . .

> A **regular polygon** is one in which all sides have the same length and all interior angles have the same measure.

What do we call a regular quadrilateral? What about a regular triangle? Is it possible for a regular polygon to be concave? Think about these questions before reading on. . . .

A regular quadrilateral is called a square. A regular triangle is called an equilateral triangle. A regular polygon cannot be concave.

We found that the sum of the degrees of the interior angles of any triangle is 180, and the sum for any quadrilateral is 360. What do you think is the sum of the interior angles of a pentagon? Can you explain your reasoning? Can you find a pattern in this progression that will enable you to predict the sum of the interior angles of any polygon—for example, one with 10 sides or with 100 sides? Work on this before reading on. . . .

TABLE 8.4

Sides	Sum	Reasoning
3	180	
4	360	Increases by 180 each time
5	540	
6	720	

From Table 8.4, many students can see that the sum increases by 180 each time, but cannot come up with the general case. The solution to this question comes from connecting the problem-solving tool of making a table to the seeing of patterns to seeing "increases by 180" as equivalent to "these are multiples of 180." We can represent this equivalent representation in a fourth column that contains 180, $2 \cdot 180$, $3 \cdot 180$, and so on. What do you see now? Then read on. . . .

The number we multiply 180 by is 2 less than the number of sides in the polygon. Therefore, the sum of the angles of a polygon having n sides will be equal to $(n - 2)180$.

Curved Figures

There is one more class of two-dimensional geometric figures that we need to discuss: those that are composed not of line segments but of curved lines.

How many words do you know that describe shapes that have curved lines in them? Think and then read on. . . .

We have many curved geometric figures—for example, circle, semicircle, spiral, parabola, ellipse, hyperbola, and crescent (see Figure 8.57).

FIGURE **8.57**

Before we define terms that we use in relation to circles, we need to stop for a moment to discuss language. Although most students are not perplexed when I use the phrase "curved lines" to describe the common characteristic of the figures in Figure 8.57, many mathematicians flinch at this language. To them, the term *line,* although undefined, implicitly means *straight,* which is also undefined; therefore to speak of curved lines would be a contradiction. However, dictionaries by their very nature attempt to define terms. Below are the first two of thirty-five senses one dictionary uses to define line.[8]

1. The path traced by a moving point.
2.a. A thin continuous mark, as that made by a pen, pencil, or brush applied to a surface.

With respect to the dictionary definition, to use the term "curved line" makes sense. As a mathematics educator preparing future elementary teachers I'm concerned that many people find that the language and notation used in mathematics just doesn't connect well to how they think. I find that most of my students learn mathematics (and other subjects) best if we discuss ideas in a way that makes sense and then build from those understandings the more formal, precise terms and theorems that we need. This concept further relates to the van Hiele model.

In this course, we will focus on the simplest of all curved geometric figures: the circle. Stop for a moment to think about circles. How would you define a circle? Try to do so before reading on. . . .

A circle is the set of points in a plane that are all the same distance from a given point, the center.

You are probably familiar with the following basic vocabulary for circles.

In Figure 8.58, C is the *center* of the circle.

The line segment $\overline{CA}$ is called a *radius,* the plural of which is *radii.*

The line segment $\overline{AB}$ is called a *diameter.*

The line segment $\overline{XY}$ is called a *chord.*

The line $\overleftrightarrow{PQ}$, which intersects the circle only at point D, is called a *tangent.*

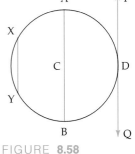

FIGURE **8.58**

An *arc* is any curved line that lies on the circle. We use two letters to denote an arc if the arc is less than half of the circle. However, for larger arcs, we use three letters. Do you see why?

We need this to distinguish between the arc at the left ($\overset{\frown}{AD}$) in Figure 8.59 and the arc at the right ($\overset{\frown}{ABD}$), as both of them have points A and D as endpoints.

---

[8] *The American Heritage Dictionary of the English Language* 1992 ed.

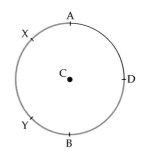

FIGURE **8.59**

Based on these descriptions and your previous experience with circles, try to write a definition for each of these terms. Then compare your definitions with the ones below. . . . 🖎

A **radius** of a circle is any line segment that connects a point on the circle to the center.

A **diameter** of a circle is any line segment that connects two points of the circle and also goes through the center of the circle.

A **chord** is any line segment that connects two points of the circle. Thus, a diameter is also a chord.

A **tangent** line intersects a circle at exactly one point.

An **arc** is a subset of a circle.

Summary

Look back over this section and the related explorations that you did. What did you learn? In this section, we have examined basic building-block terms, concepts, and properties that are necessary if we are to explore and understand shapes in two dimensions. You now better understand why we have so many names for different triangles and quadrilaterals. More importantly, you can see the relationships among triangles and among quadrilaterals, so that terms like right isosceles triangle make sense and the statement that "a square is also a rectangle" makes sense. Knowing the terms and, more importantly, the properties and relationships gives us the background to understand the structures of three-dimensional shapes (in Section 8.3) and the many intricate two-dimensional designs we find in quilts and art (in Chapter 9).

EXERCISES 8.2

1. Consider the figure at the right. You are given the following information:

   △*ABC* is an isosceles triangle.

   △*ADE* is a right triangle.

   ∡*BAE* = 51°

   ∡*BCA* = 62°

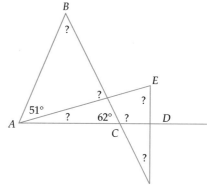

Determine the measures of the angles that have question marks.

2. Given that:

$\overline{AD} \parallel \overline{HE}$

$\overline{BH} \parallel \overline{CG}$

$\overline{HE} \perp \overline{DE}$

$\triangle CJD$ is an isosceles triangle.

$\angle ABH = 126°$

Find the measures of angles 1, 2, 3, 4 and 5.

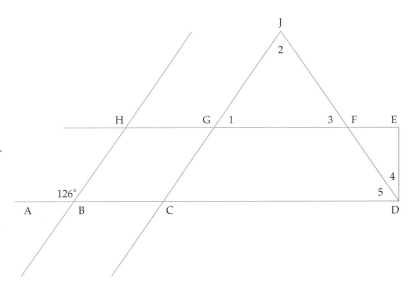

3. The definition of a regular polygon states that all sides have the same length and all interior angles have the same measure. Why is the second part of the definition necessary — that is, why can't we just say that a polygon is a regular polygon if all the sides are the same length?

4. For each of the figures below, write "polygon" or "not a polygon." If it is a polygon, also write "convex" or "concave."

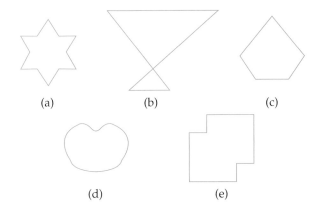

(a)   (b)   (c)

(d)   (e)

5. Describe all the geometric shapes you see in the quilt designs below:

a.

b.

c.

Source: Jinny Beyer, *The Quilter's Album of Blocks and Borders* (McLean, VA.: EPM Publications, Inc., 1986), pp. 96, 117. Reprinted with permission.

6. Draw each of the following or briefly explain why such a figure is impossible.

a. An isosceles trapezoid

b. A concave quadrilateral

c. A curve that is simple and closed but not convex

d. A nonsimple closed curve

e. A concave equilateral hexagon

f. A concave pentagon having three collinear vertices

g. A hexagon that has 3 acute angles and 3 obtuse angles

h. A pentagon that has 3 right angles and 1 acute angle

7. For the following questions, if the answer is yes, draw a picture; if it is no, briefly explain why not.

a. Can a right triangle also be an isosceles triangle?

b. Can a quadrilateral have 3 obtuse angles?

c. Can a rhombus have 4 acute angles?

d. Can a square also be a rectangle?

8. Express the relationship between scalene, isosceles, and equilateral triangles with a Venn diagram.

9. Make a family tree to represent the relationships among different kinds of triangles.

10. Explain why it is impossible to have a triangle whose three sides are 6 cm, 8 cm, and 15 cm.

11. Is this figure a kite? Why or why not?

12. Describe all quadrilaterals that meet these characteristics. If there is more than one, say so.
    a. A quadrilateral with opposite sides parallel
    b. A quadrilateral with 4 right angles
    c. A quadrilateral with all sides equal
    d. A quadrilateral in which the diagonals bisect each other
    e. A quadrilateral in which the diagonals are congruent
    f. A quadrilateral in which adjacent angles are congruent
    g. A quadrilateral in which opposite angles are equal
    h. A quadrilateral in which no sides are parallel
    i. A quadrilateral with 4 congruent sides and 2 pairs of congruent angles
    j. A quadrilateral with 4 congruent angles and 2 pairs of congruent sides

13. Show that the family tree for quadrilaterals also holds for the characteristics of the diagonals.

14. Draw a Venn diagram to illustrate the relationship between squares, rectangles, and rhombuses.

15. In this section, we found that we could name some quadrilaterals in terms of their "ancestors." For example, we could say that a rhombus is a parallelogram with four equal sides. What other quadrilaterals could we describe in terms of their ancestors?

16. Write directions for each of the figures below. To assess the accuracy and clarity of your directions, your instructor will do exactly what you say. Before turning in your directions, you might want to have a friend, not in this class, try to draw these figures using only your directions.

    a.   b.

c.

d.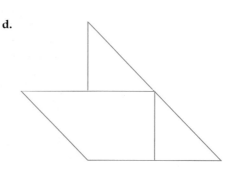

17. Just as we can speak about interior angles of polygons, we can speak about exterior angles. We simply need to define them. Take any regular polygon and select one interior angle. Extend one side of the angle outside the polygon. The exterior angle has the same vertex as the interior angle and shares a common side.
    a. Are these directions sufficient? That is, is there only one possible angle that can be made following these directions?
    b. Draw and label the exterior angle of a triangle. What is the measure of the exterior angle?
    c. Draw and label the exterior angle of a quadrilateral. What is the measure of the exterior angle?
    d. Draw and label the exterior angle of a hexagon. What is the measure of the exterior angle?
    e. What is the measure of each exterior angle of a regular polygon with n sides?

18. a. Sketch a pair of parallelograms whose intersection is exactly three points.
    b. Sketch a pair of parallelograms whose intersection is exactly four points.
    c. Sketch a pair of parallelograms whose intersection is exactly five points.
    d. Describe the maximum number of points of intersection that two parallelograms can have and sketch your answer.

19. How can you draw three line segments within an equilateral triangle so that you form a regular hexagon? (See triangle at top of page 449.)

20. a. Draw any square. Find the midpoint of each side. Connect the midpoints to make a new quadrilateral. What do you observe? Can you prove your generalization?

b. Draw any rectangle. Find the midpoint of each side. Connect the midpoints to make a new quadrilateral. What do you observe? Can you prove your generalization?

c. Draw *any* quadrilateral. Find the midpoint of each side. Connect the midpoints to make a new quadrilateral. What do you observe? Can you prove your generalization?

21. The diagram below shows a square that has been cut so that we now have 6 smaller squares. The more general statement of this problem is: Can you find a way to cut a square into x smaller squares?

a. For which of the following x's can you find a solution?

b. For which of the following x's can you find more than one solution?

c. If you cannot find a solution, make an argument that this is impossible.

d. Summarize strategies that you used and/or patterns that you saw that helped. For example, did you find strategies that you could modify to enable you to cut the square into a different number of smaller squares?

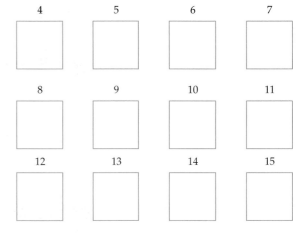

SECTION   8.3   **THREE-DIMENSIONAL FIGURES**

Just as we discovered patterns and relationships among many two-dimensional objects, so too there are many patterns and relationships among three-dimensional figures, also called space figures. With respect to practical matters, understanding the geometry of human-made objects helps us to make them work better and, in the case of objects like bridges, overpasses, and airplanes, to make them work more safely. Geometry also helps us to understand natural phenomena better—for example, why certain animals have the shapes they have. An understanding of shapes has many applications in science. For example, many carcinogens are virtually identical in size and shape to other compounds, and thus they fool the body into thinking they are not harmful. The silicon chip has the same structure as the diamond, except that there are silicon atoms instead of carbon atoms at these positions.[9] With respect to aesthetics, geometry helps us to understand why some shapes are so appealing to people and to understand patterns within those shapes (see Figure 8.60).

---

[9]Marjorie Senechal, *On the Shoulders of Giants,* p. 173.

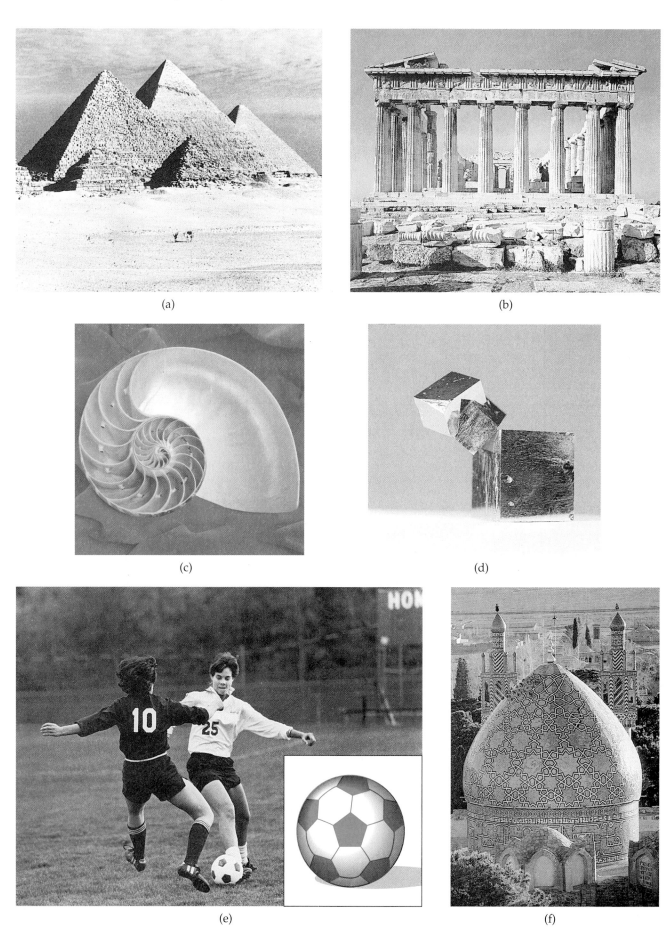

(a)

(b)

(c)

(d)

(e)

(f)

FIGURE **8.60**

INVESTIGATION 8.5   Connecting Polygons to Polyhedra

Just as we examined families (subsets) of triangles and quadrilaterals, we will now investigate families of three-dimensional geometric figures (see Figure 8.61). If you did Exploration 8.12, you grappled with describing and classifying three-dimensional figures.

FIGURE **8.61**

Let us explore the connection between polygons and *polyhedra,* which will be loosely defined (for now) as three-dimensional figures made up of polygons.

The second column of Table 8.5 describes several attributes of polygons, which we investigated in Section 8.2. Which of these attributes do you think hold for polyhedra or can be modified to describe different kinds of polyhedra? Fill in as much of the third column as you can. The questions below are given to help you focus on the connections between how we see and define two- and three-dimensional figures. After you have completed as much of the third column as possible, compare your hypotheses with another student. Then read on. . . .

- If a polygon is defined as a simple, closed curve, is there an analogous definition for a polyhedron?
- All polygons have vertices, line segments, and angles. Do these terms work for describing component parts of polyhedra? Do we also need new terms?
- Can we classify polyhedra by the number of sides?
- If there are regular polyhedra, how might they be defined?
- If there are convex polyhedra, how might they be defined?

TABLE 8.5

	Polygons (two-dimensional)	Polyhedra (three-dimensional)
What they are	Simple, closed curves	
Definition	Union of line segments	

Component parts	Vertices	
	Line segments	
	Angles	
	Other?	
Classification	By number of sides	
	Regular vs. not regular	
	Convex vs. concave	

DISCUSSION

In Section 8.2, we began with simple closed curves that partitioned a plane (two dimensions) into three disjoint sets: the curve, inside, and outside.

Though we will not rigorously define simple closed surfaces, we can say that they partition space (three dimensions) into three disjoint sets: the surface itself, inside, and outside (see Figure 8.62).

We will use the term **space figure** to describe any three-dimensional object.

We will use the term **polyhedron** (the plural is **polyhedra**) to describe those simple closed surfaces that are composed of polygonal regions.

We will use the term **solid** to describe the union of any space figure and its interior.

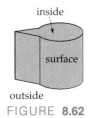

inside

surface

outside

FIGURE **8.62**

Component parts   Just as the component parts of polygons have special names, so do those of polyhedra.

Each of the separate polygonal regions of a polyhedron is called a **face**; for example, square *ABFE* is a face of the cube in Figure 8.63.

The sides of each of the faces are called **edges**; for example, $\overline{AB}$ is an edge of the cube in Figure 8.63.

The **vertices** of the polyhedron are simply the vertices of the polygonal regions that form the polyhedron; for example, *E* and *F* are vertices of the cube in Figure 8.63.

FIGURE **8.63**

Convex and concave   Just as polygons can be convex or concave, so can polyhedra. Before reading the definition of a convex polyhedron, think back to the definition of a convex polygon and see if you can modify that definition for three-dimensional objects. Then read on. . . . 🖊

A polyhedron is **convex** iff any line segment connecting two points of the polyhedron is either on the surface or in the interior of the polyhedron (see Figure 8.64).

FIGURE **8.64**

Families of Polyhedra

Now let us investigate some of the families of polyhedra, which you may have explored in Exploration 8.12. Take a few minutes to examine the figures in Figure 8.65. How are these figures alike? How are they different? Write your thoughts in your notebook before reading on. . . .

FIGURE **8.65**

One characteristic of several quadrilateral families we explored in Section 8.2 has to do with parallel sides. All of the polyhedra in Figure 8.65 have a parallel aspect. Can you see it? How would you describe it?

We use the word prism to describe all polyhedra that have at least one pair of parallel faces.

Do you see that all of the polyhedra in Figure 8.65 have at least one pair of parallel faces?

The parallel faces are called the bases of the prism. The two bases must be congruent polygons.

The other faces are called lateral faces.

What one shape can be used to describe the lateral faces of *all* prisms? In other words, all lateral faces of all prisms are _____. Think and read on. . . .

In all prisms, the lateral faces are parallelograms. In some cases, all of the lateral faces are rectangles. How would you describe the differences between those prisms whose lateral faces are parallelograms and those whose lateral faces are rectangles?

In the latter case, the plane of the base and the plane of the lateral faces are perpendicular (see Figure 8.66). We could also say that the *dihedral* angle formed by either base and any face is a right angle. (A dihedral angle is simply a three-dimensional angle, that is, an angle whose vertex is a line and whose sides are planes.)

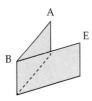

FIGURE **8.66**

Thus, we can define a **right prism** as a prism in which the lateral faces are rectangles. Alternatively, we could define a right prism as a prism in which the angle formed by either base and any lateral face is a right dihedral angle.

A prism that is not a right prism is an **oblique prism** (see Figure 8.67).

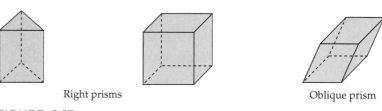

Right prisms   Oblique prism

FIGURE **8.67**

Long before they study formal geometry, many children know the names for two special kinds of prisms.

Though this is not a term mathematicians use, what we call a **box** is actually a prism in which all six faces are rectangles. If all six faces are squares, we call the figure a **cube** (see Figure 8.68).

Cube   Rectangular prism

FIGURE **8.68**

Pyramids

Let us consider now another family of polyhedra. You may recognize the polyhedra in Figure 8.69 as pyramids. How might we define that term? Make your own definition and then read on. . . .

FIGURE **8.69**

We use the word **pyramid** to describe those polyhedra whose base is a polygon and whose sides are triangles that have a common vertex. That common vertex is called the **apex** of the pyramid.

An alternative way to think of a pyramid is to start with any polygon and a point above the plane of the polygon. Now connect that point to each vertex of the polygon.

Most of the pyramids you have seen in pictures (or in person, if you are lucky) have square bases. However, the base can be any polygon. A pyramid is named according to its base: triangular pyramid, square pyramid, etc.

Regular Polyhedra

In Section 8.2, we discussed regular polygons. How might we define a regular polyhedron? Try to do so before reading on. . . .

One of the ways we classified polygons was by the number of sides: triangles, quadrilaterals, pentagons, hexagons, etc. We could speak of a regular hexagon and a nonregular hexagon. However, that doesn't work with polyhedra. Do you see why?

We define a **regular polyhedron** as a convex polyhedron in which the faces are congruent regular polygons and in which the number of edges that meet at each vertex is the same.

Stop! Does that definition make sense? I find that the concept of a regular polyhedron is one of the more abstract in the book. What does it mean to say that "the number of edges that meet at each vertex is the same"? If you are still not sure, read on, but then go back and check to see if this definition jibes with that of regular polyhedra.

Which of the prisms and pyramids we have discussed so far do you think might be regular polyhedra? Think before reading on. . . .

A cube is a regular polyhedron. A triangular pyramid composed of equilateral triangles is a regular polyhedron and has a special name, **tetrahedron**. The origin of the name is Greek: *tetra* ("four") and *hedron* ("face").

A fact that surprises many people is that there are not a large number of regular polyhedra. In fact, there are only five regular polyhedra: the tetrahedron, the cube, the **octahedron** (with 8 triangular faces), the **dodecahedron** (with 12 pentagonal faces), and the **icosahedron** (with 20 triangular faces) (see Figure 8.70). The solids made from the regular polyhedra are called Platonic solids after the Greek philosopher Plato.

Tetrahedron

Octahedron

Cube

Icosahedron

Dodecahedron

Source: The five regular solids drawn by Johannes Kepler in *Harmonices Mundi, Book II,* 1619.
FIGURE **8.70**

[10] H.A. Freebury, *A History of Mathematics* (New York: Macmillan, 1961), p. 36, H.A. Eves, *An Introduction to the History of Mathematics* (New York: Holt, Rinehart and Winston, 1969), p. 68.

BEYOND THE CLASSROOM

These regular polyhedra occur in nature:

- Crystals of salt and of pyrite have been found in the shape of a cube.

- Crystals of chrome alum have been found in the shape of a tetrahedron.

- Crystals of pyrite have been found in the shape of an octahedron.

- Skeletons of microscopic sea animals have been found in the shape of a dodecahedron and in the shape of an icosahedron (see Figure 8.71). Honest, I didn't make this up![11]

Many viruses have icosahedral shapes. (An example is the Polyoma virus)

Here is the packing of spheres in an icosahedron

Source: Radiolarians—*Kunstformen der Natur*, Vols. 1–10, Ernst Häckel des Bibliographischen Instituts, Leipzig, Germany, 1899–1904; Polyoma virus–Drawn after K. W. Adolph, D. L. D. Caspar, C. J. Hollingshed, E. E. Lattman, W. C. Phillips, and W. T. Murakami, *Science*, Vol. 203, p. 1117, 1979; Packing of spheres—Drawn after A. L. Mackey, *Acta Crystallographica*, Vol. 15, p. 916, 1962 as seen in *Symmetry: A Unifying Concept*, 1994.

FIGURE **8.71**

Cylinders, Cones, Spheres

In Section 8.2, we defined one of many two-dimensional geometric figures that was not a polygon: the circle. There are three kinds of space figures that are not polyhedra that we will examine next.

Consider the cylinders in Figure 8.72. What family of polyhedra are they connected to?

FIGURE **8.72**

Like prisms, cylinders have a pair of bases that are parallel. How would you define a cylinder? Please try to do so before reading on. The point here is not to find the "right" definition or to be picky, but rather to emphasize the role of language in mathematics.

[11] Historical Topics for the Mathematics Classroom: Thirty-first yearbook, NCTM (Reston, VA.: NCTM, 1969), p. 220.

We can define a cylinder by connecting cylinders to prisms and saying that a **cylinder** is a prism in which the bases are circles. Each of the circles is a *base* of the cylinder.

We can also define a cylinder as a simple closed surface that is bounded by two congruent circles that lie in parallel planes.

Earlier, we talked about right prisms. A cylinder is a **right cylinder** iff the center of the upper circle is directly above the center of the lower circle. If a cylinder is not a right cylinder, it is called an **oblique cylinder.**

Consider the cones in Figure 8.73. What family of polyhedra are they connected to?

FIGURE **8.73**

Like a pyramid, a cone has a base and a point, called an apex. How would you define a cone? Please try to do so before reading on. . . .

We can define a **cone** by relating cones to pyramids and saying that a cone is a pyramid in which the base is a circle.

If the vertex of the cone lies directly above the center of the base, then we call it a **right cone.** If a cone is not a right cone, it is called an **oblique cone.**

In everyday life, we generally experience only right cones and right cylinders. Therefore, in this book, we will use the terms **cones** and **cylinders** unless we are referring to oblique cones or cylinders.

Finally, consider the sphere. Can you apply the earlier definition of a circle to define sphere? Try to do so before reading on. . . .

A **sphere** is the set of points in space equidistant from a given point, which is called the **center.**

How would you define the radius and diameter of a sphere? Try to do so before reading on. . . .

Any line segment joining the center of the sphere to a point on the surface is called a *radius.*

Any line segment whose endpoints lie on the surface of the sphere and that contains the center is called a *diameter.*

Summary

In this section, we have named and classified the basic kinds of three-dimensional geometric figures. From the investigations and explorations, you can see that a variety of seemingly different figures are actually prisms. You have seen that prisms and cylinders are closely related. You have seen that pyramids and cones are closely related. We will take advantage of these similarities when we examine formulas for surface areas and volumes of figures in Chapter 10. In Explorations 8.11 and 8.13, you explored some relationships between two-dimensional and three-dimensional figures.

EXERCISES 8.3

1. Given the tetrahedron below, name the following:

   a. A face

   b. A vertex

   c. An edge

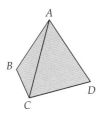

2. Name the figures below.

3. Which of the polyhedra below are convex?

4. Draw a nonconvex rectangular or pentagonal prism.

5. We defined a regular polyhedron as a convex polyhedron in which the faces are congruent regular polygons and in which the number of edges that meet at each vertex is the same. Carlos says that instead of saying that the number of edges that meet at each vertex is the same, we could have said that the number of faces that meet at each vertex is the same. What do you think? Support your choice.

6. Can you make a pyramid in which the triangular faces are not all congruent?

7. Write a definition of *diagonal* for polyhedra.

8. There is a relationship between the number of diagonals and the base of a prism. That is, triangular prisms have a certain number of diagonals, square prisms have a certain number of diagonals, and so on.

   Determine this relationship so that you can answer the following question: How many diagonals does a prism have whose base is a regular polygon with *n* sides? [Your instructor may or may not give you hints for this problem. If not, I suggest looking at the 4 Steps

for Problem Solving on the inside front cover of the *Explorations* volume.]

9. Consider a prism whose base is a regular *n*-gon, that is, a regular polygon with *n* sides. How many vertices would such a prism have? How many faces? How many edges? You may want to start with a triangular prism, square prism, pentagonal prism, and so on, and look for patterns.

10. Consider a pyramid whose base is a regular *n*-gon, that is, a regular polygon with *n* sides. How many vertices would such a pyramid have? How many faces? How many edges?

11. **a.** Describe the relationship between the number of vertices of an *n*-gon prism and an *n*-gon pyramid.

    b. Describe the relationship between the number of faces of an *n*-gon prism and an *n*-gon pyramid.

    c. Describe the relationship between the number of edges of an *n*-gon prism and an *n*-gon pyramid.

12. At the center of every tissue of toilet paper is a cardboard cylinder. Find and examine one of these cylinders. You can see a curved line running along the face of the cylinder.

    a. If you cut the cylinder along this line, what would the unfolded shape look like? Predict the shape and explain your reasoning.

    b. Why do you think these cylinders are manufactured this way instead of having a vertical cut?

13. Is there one geometric shape that describes *all* the sides of (right) pyramids? If there is, name it and justify your answer. If there is more than one shape, describe the shapes and justify your response.

14. Look at the figures below. For each, (a) describe how to make it, then (b) describe another way.

15. Below are the top, front, and side views of two buildings created with only cubes. For each building, answer the following:

    (i) Without making the building, predict how many cubes it will have. Explain your prediction.

    (ii) Predict the left-hand view. Explain your prediction.

    (iii) Insert numbers into the top view showing how high the building will be at each spot.

(iv) Draw a picture of the building using the dot paper at the end of the *Explorations* volume.

a.

Top	Front	Right-side

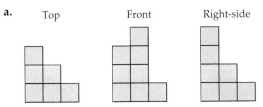

16. Look at the shape shown below. Let's say you wanted to describe that figure to someone on the phone so that that person could make the shape. What might you say?

17. Which of the nets below is a possible net for a cereal box?

18. Which of the nets below is a possible net for an oatmeal box (which has the shape of a cylinder)?

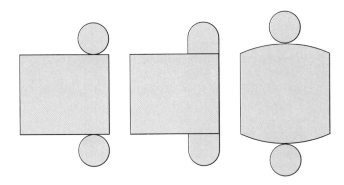

19. As a child, I was given a puzzle called the Soma cubes, which consists of six different pieces constructed from four cubes and one piece constructed from three cubes. At the top of the next column are diagrams of the seven pieces. In order to do this problem, you need to find a set or make a set.

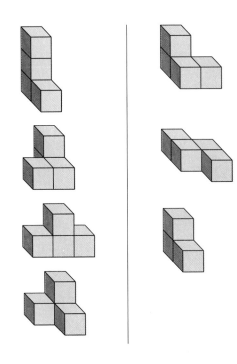

a. The figure below can be made from two pieces. Describe any thoughts that helped you solve this problem. Figure out a way to communicate your solution. That is, I need to know not only which pieces but how they were put together.

b. The figure below can be made from three pieces. Describe any thoughts that helped you solve this problem. Figure out a way to communicate your solution. That is, I need to know not only which pieces but how they were put together.

c. The figure at the top of page 460 can be made from three pieces. Describe any thoughts that helped you solve this problem. Figure out a way to communicate your solution. That is, I need to know not only which pieces but how they were put together.

20. Below are drawings of several polyhedra. Draw the top, front, and side views for the polyhedra.

21. How would you make the octahedral dice shown below?

22. Using paperboard and an exacto knife, make an oblique triangular prism.

Part 1:

a. Describe your attempts (my first one did not work either).

b. Describe what you learned during the construction.

c. Describe the relationships among the three lateral faces.

Part 2:

a. Predict how to make an oblique rectangular prism with stiff paper. Describe the relationships among the four faces. Explain your prediction.

b. Make an oblique rectangular prism. If your prediction was accurate, great. If your prediction was not accurate, describe where your prediction was inaccurate and explain the reasoning behind the part(s) of your prediction that were inaccurate.

c. Draw a net for an oblique rectangular prism.

Part 3:

a. Predict the relationship among the five lateral faces of an oblique pentagonal prism.

b. Predict the relationship among the five lateral faces of an oblique hexagonal prism.

CHAPTER SUMMARY

1. School geometry is a subset of spatial thinking.

2. Important spatial thinking abilities include eye-motor coordination, figure-ground perception, perceptual constancy, visual discrimination, and visual memory.

3. The van Hiele levels of geometric thinking help us to understand the development of understanding of geometric ideas.

4. Our current knowledge of geometry took thousands of years to develop and is the result of intuitive thinking, inductive thinking, and deductive thinking.

5. The Greeks were the first people to develop mathematical systems, that is, a coherent system of mathematical ideas.

6. Geometric ideas are related to sets; for example, a line segment is a set of points.

7. Geometric ideas are related to functions; for example, the sum of the interior angles of a polygon = $(n - 2)180$.

8. Geometric figures can be classified in many ways, and these classifications are useful. For example, many seemingly different figures are all prisms because two faces are parallel.

Basic Concepts

Section 8.1 Basic Concepts of Geometry

figure-ground perception **415**
perceptual constancy **415**
visual discrimination **415**
visual memory **415**
Point, line, plane, on, and between are undefined terms. **418**
Sets of points may be collinear or noncollinear. **419**
Sets of points may be coplanar or not; lines may be coplanar or not. **420**

$\longleftrightarrow$
line **420** $\underline{\quad\quad}$ line segment **420**
$\longrightarrow$
ray **420**   • endpoint **420**
intersect **421**
Relationships between lines: perpendicular, parallel, concurrent, skew **421**
Angles have vertices and sides. **422**
Angles have an interior and an exterior. **422**

Naming angles:

with one letter, one number, three letters **423**

Measuring angles:

protractor **424**   degree **424**

Kinds of angles

right *425*   acute *425*
obtuse *425*   straight *425*
reflex *425*   adjacent *426*
complementary *426* supplementary *426*
vertical *426*

Section 8.2 Two-Dimensional Figures

Kinds of lines and curves

closed curves *431*   simple curves *431*
Any simple closed curve partitions the plane into 3
    disjoint regions. *431*
polygon *432*   base *438*
vertex (vertices) *433* sides *433*
congruent *433*

Classifying triangles

By length of sides: equilateral, isosceles, scalene.
    436
By size of angle: right triangle, obtuse triangle,
    acute triangle *436*

Special line segments in triangles

angle bisector *438*   median *438*
altitude *438*   perpendicular bisector
                              439

Quadrilaterals

trapezoid *440*   parallelogram *440*
kite *440*   rhombus *440*
rectangle *440*   square *440*

Polygons

convex or concave *443*   regular polygon *444*
diagonal *440*

Properties

The sum of the measures of the angles of a convex
    polygon = 180(*n* − 2). *444*

Circles

circle *445*   radius (radii) *446*
diameter *446*   chord *446*
tangent *446*   arc *446*

Section 8.3 Three Dimensional Figures

space figure *452*   polyhedron *452*
polyhedra *452*   solids *452*

Parts

face *452*   edge *452*
vertex *452*

Classifying

convex *452*   concave *452*

Polyhedra

prism *453*   box *454*
base *453*   cube *454*
lateral face *453*
dihedral *453*
right prism *454*
oblique prism *454*

Pyramid

pyramid *454*
apex *454*

Regular polyhedra

tetrahedron *455*   icosahedron *455*
octahedron *455*
dodecahedron *455*

Cylinders, Cones, Spheres

cylinder *457*
oblique cylinder *457*
right cylinder *457*
right cone *457*
obliquecone *457*
sphere *457*
center *457*

Figures to accompany Investigation 8.3, p. 434

FIGURE **8.75**   FIGURE **8.76**

Geometry as Transforming Shapes

- ▶ **9.1 Translations, Reflections, and Rotations**
- ▶ **9.2 Symmetry**
- ▶ **9.3 Similarity**

Look at the pictures in Figures 9.1 to 9.3. As you do, recall Investigation 8.3, where you drew the churn dash. Different people will see different things. What do *you* see? Note your ideas before reading on. If possible, check your observations with another student.

FIGURE **9.1**

FIGURE **9.2**

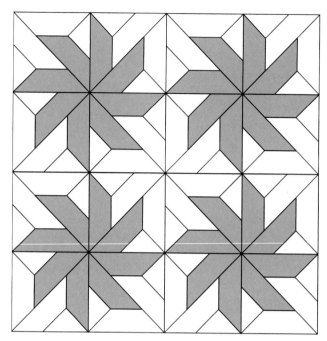

FIGURE **9.3**

In Figure 9.1, focus on the butterflies. Though the butterflies are in different positions and of different sizes, they all have the same shape. This is true for each of the animals pictured. The arrangement of the animals is not random, but intentional. If you focus only on the butterflies, what do you notice? From one perspective, we can say that every butterfly has a twin, and each butterfly can be moved from its position to its twin's position by flipping, turning, or sliding, or a combination of these moves.

Figure 9.2 shows an Islamic design composed entirely of two shapes: an 8-pointed star and a 16-sided polygon. What do you notice about the relationships between the 8-pointed stars? about the relationships between the 16-gons? If we focus on the 8-pointed stars, each star can be moved to the position of a nearby star by sliding it—either horizontally, vertically, or diagonally. Each 16-gon can be moved to the position of a nearby 16-gon by turning it.

Figure 9.3 illustrates one of many parquet floor designs. Most people see pinwheels composed of 8 congruent trapezoids. Some people see these embedded in squares. Other people see congruent pinwheels of a different color. Others see white pinwheels composed of 4 white isosceles triangles. Each dark pinwheel can be moved to the position of a nearby light pinwheel by sliding it. Each trapezoid in a pinwheel can be moved to the position of an adjacent trapezoid by a turn.

These three figures illustrate two kinds of ways in which we can make designs from figures. We can make exact copies of a figure and move it to different positions by slides, flips, and turns. We call these congruence transformations because the figures are congruent to each other. Only their position has changed. We can also make bigger or smaller copies of a figure but keep the shape the same. We call these similarity transformations because although the size changes, the shapes remain similar.

Four Transformations

In Chapter 8, we focused on properties of two- and three-dimensional shapes and relationships among shapes. In this chapter, we will focus on what is called transformational geometry, and we will focus only on two-dimensional figures. That is, we will investigate various operations that transform a two-dimensional figure—changing the position of the figure or changing the size of the figure. Figure 9.4 illustrates the four transformations we will investigate. In each case, what name might you give to the operation that has been done on the figure at the left to create the figure on the right? How might you give directions for making the figure at the right? In what ways are the figures in each pair alike, and in what ways are they different? Think and then read on. . . .

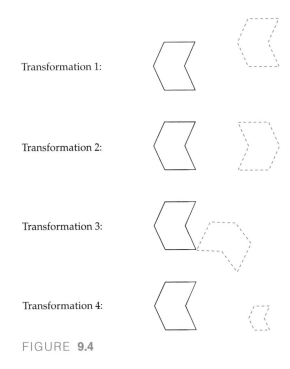

FIGURE **9.4**

- Transformation 1 is often called a **slide** by students and is called a *translation mapping* by mathematicians.

- Transformation 2 is often called a **flip** by students and is called a *reflection mapping* by mathematicians.

- Transformation 3 is often called a **turn** by students and is called a *rotation mapping* by mathematicians.

- Transformation 4 is often called **reducing** or **shrinking** by students and is called a *similarity mapping* by mathematicians.

Mapping   Before we move on, let us understand this new context for the word **mapping**. Recall our discussion in Chapter 8 in which we said that we could think of a line as a set of an infinite number of points. If we consider a line as a set of points, we can describe the operation of transforming the first figure to the second figure in such a way that each point in the first figure maps onto a specific point in the second figure. Therefore, the operation meets the criteria of a function. Why is this? When both the input and output sets of a function are points, we often find it more convenient to use the term *mapping* instead of *function*. That is, we can talk of a figure being mapped onto another figure. This language may feel a bit awkward at first. Over the course of this chapter, you will probably see that the term *mapping* actually works well for this family (subset) of functions.

In the first section, we will discuss what we call congruence mappings—that is, those mappings in which the original figure and the new figure are congruent to each other. We will then connect these mappings to art, to see how designs embody these mappings. In the third section, we will discuss what we call similarity mappings—that is, those mappings in which the original figure and the new figure are not the same size but have the same shape.

In elementary school, we want students to explore these important ideas of congruence and similarity in different ways, so that when they investigate these ideas more formally in high school, they will have had concrete but also substantive interactions with them. Although we will investigate transformations at a more sophisticated level than do elementary school children, these concepts are important ones, and they are ones that most children enjoy exploring.

"Explorations of flips, slides, turns, stretchers, and shrinkers will illuminate the concepts of congruence and similarity" (*Curriculum Standards,* p. 114).

SECTION **9.1**

TRANSLATIONS, REFLECTIONS, AND ROTATIONS

WHAT DO YOU THINK?

- How are translations, reflections, and rotations related?
- How might you describe the translation, reflection, or rotation of a three-dimensional figure in space?
- How are the operations translation, reflection, and rotation like the operations addition, subtraction, multiplication, and division?

At this point, you have an informal understanding of slides, flips, and turns. In the next few pages, we will examine these transformations more precisely. This precision is needed in order to create aesthetically pleasing designs, such as those found in art, quilts, tiles, or wall coverings. This precision is also needed in order to understand naturally occurring structures, both those that are visible to the eye (honeycombs, snowflakes, and nautilus shells) and those at the molecular level. The following investigations will all be driven by this question: How can we describe what we have to do to move an object from here to there on a plane? If you read these investigations actively, you will probably get stuck at times, frustrated at times, and excited at times. It is important to keep two things in mind. First, much of the knowledge presented in this book represents hundreds and sometimes thousands of years of investigation. Second, the struggle for precision has often led scientists and mathematicians to see new patterns, unanticipated connections, and new properties.

Translations

When you see the word *translation,* you probably think of translating from one language to another: The translator replaces English words with Spanish, for example, but the meaning of the phrase remains the same. In geometry, a translation involves moving an object along a straight line and not turning it.

Each of the designs in Figure 9.5 shows translations. Figure 9.5(a) is from the Native American Yuchi tribe and depicts storm clouds. Figure 9.5(b) shows a quilt border called Orange Peel. Figure 9.5(c) shows a papercutting, which is a common elementary school activity. As noted above, a translation is a special kind of congruence mapping. In each of the designs, we have congruent figures in the design, and we can imagine picking up part of the figure, moving it in a straight line, and then putting it back down on top of another congruent part of the figure.

(a)

(b)

(c)

Source: (a) Le Roy H. Appleton, *American Indian Design and Decoration* (New York: Dover Publications, 1971), Plate 15 (in insert). (b) Jinny Beyer, *The Quilter's Album of Blocks & Borders* (McLean, VA.: EPM Publications, Inc., 1986), p. 185.

FIGURE **9.5**

Do you see the translations in these designs? Based on what you see, how would you describe translations? The following investigation looks at translations in some depth.

INVESTIGATION **9.1** **Understanding Translations**

You may have already worked with translations in Exploration 9.3. In order to make intricate designs, we often need to be precise in describing the translation. For example, let's say you were talking on the phone to a friend and you wanted to describe the translation of the triangle *CAT* in Figure 9.6 from its original location to its new location. The original triangle is *CAT*; its translation image is *C'A'T'*. How would you do this? You may assume that you and your friend have any resources you need: scissors, ruler, compass, graph paper, etc. Think and then read on. . . . 📖

Note: There are many valid descriptions.

FIGURE **9.6**

DISCUSSION

One common response is to say that we slide the triangle from one location to the other. The mathematical word for slide is *translation,* and we talk about a figure and its **image**. There are many different ways to describe a translation. Each of these descriptions represents different perspectives and preferences concerning how to communicate what has happened to triangle *CAT*. Some of the perspectives are easier to describe if we draw the two triangles on graph paper (see Figure 9.7 on page 468). What they all have in common is the realization that when we translate a figure, every point on the figure moves the same distance and in the same direction.

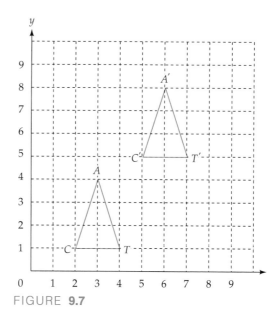

FIGURE **9.7**

DESCRIPTION 1: Use "taxicab language"

Just as we could ask a cabbie to "go three blocks east and four blocks north," we could say that each point has been moved 3 units to the right and 4 units up. For example, copy triangle *CAT* onto another sheet of paper and cut it out. Then place it on the paper above and move the whole triangle, first 3 units to the right and then 4 units toward the top of the paper.

DESCRIPTION 2: Invent new notation

We can use notation to express this same idea more succinctly:

$$(x, y) \rightarrow (x + 3, y + 4)$$

If we understand the idea of translation, then this notation gives the directions "go 3 units to the right and 4 units toward the top of the page" very succinctly.

DESCRIPTION 3: Specify the distance and the angle

We could say that the figure has been moved a distance of 5 units at about a 54-degree angle from the *x*-axis (see Figure 9.8). That is, *C* and *C'* are 5 units apart; the distance between any point on triangle *CAT* and the corresponding point on triangle *C'A'T'* is 5 units. Similarly, the angle formed by the rays *CC'* and *CT* is equal to approximately 54 degrees. I encourage you to check this for yourself with a ruler and a protractor.

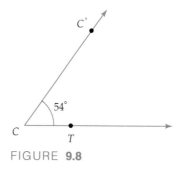

FIGURE **9.8**

DESCRIPTION 4: Use vectors

Another alternative is to use a vector. By definition, a **vector** has a length and a direction. For example, the instructions for the translation could be shown by drawing one vector, as in Figure 9.9.

FIGURE **9.9**

We will formally define **translation** as a transformation on a plane determined by moving each point in the figure the same distance in the same direction.

Properties of Translations

Now let us determine some of the properties of translations. We know from Chapter 8 that two points determine a line. Therefore, if we connect each vertex in the triangle *TAR* to its image, *T'A'R'*, we have three line segments, *TT'*, *AA'*, and *RR'* (see Figure 9.10). What relationship do you notice among these line segments?

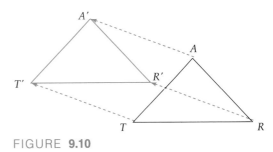

FIGURE **9.10**

The three line segments are all congruent (same length) and all parallel (same direction). How might this make the task of drawing the translation image easier? Think and then read on. . . .

Translate the rectangle in Figure 9.11, using the translation arrow shown.

FIGURE **9.11**

We can draw four lines, each going through a vertex, that are parallel to the translation arrow. If we copy the length of the arrow using a compass, we can quickly mark off the same lengths on the lines to determine the vertices of *M'A'T'H'* (see Figure 9.12).

FIGURE **9.12**

 MATHEMATICS

Too many people see little connectedness between various mathematical topics. It is important that you realize the similarities between the operations in this chapter (translation, reflection, and rotation) and the operations in Chapter 3 (addition, subtraction, multiplication, and division). In this chapter, we operate on figures: We move a figure to a new position in a certain way; in Chapter 3, we operated on numbers: We combined two numbers in a certain way. In both situations, we are often decomposing (a figure or a number) to make the operation easier to perform. For example, when translating triangle *CAT*, we can either decompose the translation into a horizontal component (3 units right) and a vertical unit (4 units toward the top) or decompose the translation into a distance (5 units) and a direction (54-degree angle). Similarly, when multiplying 15 · 12 mentally, we can decompose this operation into 15 · 10 and 15 · 2, or we can decompose it into 15 · 6 and 15 · 6. When investigating reflections and rotations, it will be helpful if you can see them as operations that can be decomposed, just as you discovered in Chapter 3 that addition, subtraction, multiplication, and division were indeed operations on numbers and that we could decompose the numbers to make the operation easier.

Reflections

Like translations, reflections may be accomplished in a variety of ways. (See Exploration 9.1 for more work with reflections.) One of the simplest is by folding paper. Trace the triangle and the line below from Figure 9.13 onto a blank sheet of paper, and then fold the paper at the line.

FIGURE **9.13**

Now trace over the figure. This is like making a carbon copy of the figure. When you fold the paper on the line, each point on the triangle coincides with its image on the reflected triangle. Do you think we need to trace the whole figure? What do you think is the minimum tracing needed?

If you trace the points *F*, *O*, and *X*, you will have the points *F'*, *O'*, and *X'*, because we know that three noncollinear points determine a triangle.

INVESTIGATION **9.2**   **Understanding Reflections**

Figure 9.14 shows a trapezoid that has been reflected (flipped) in three different ways. In each case, bold lines denote the original figure and dotted lines denote the flipped image.

A. Find the line of reflection in each case.

B. Can you discover a rule that would allow us to find the line of reflection in all cases? Can you describe an algorithm for determining the line of reflection? Stop, think, and write.

DISCUSSION

You can just read on and find the rule, or you can experience the kind of mathematical thinking that so many men and women and children have found very exciting.

A. You may find it helpful to start by tracing these figures on tracing paper and finding the line (by folding the paper) that makes the original figure coincide with its reflected image. Do you see what is happening? Try making figures of your own on paper; fold the paper and then trace the reflection image of the figure you drew. Do this several times. Play the "what-if" and "is it possible" games: What if the line of reflection went through the figure? Is it possible to have the line of reflection go right through the figure? Islamic artists, M. C. Escher, and many others have discovered so much by playing these two games.

FIGURE **9.14**

Paper folding is one of many ways to draw reflections. What other ways can you think of?

B. *Properties of reflections.* What is true for all reflections is that if we connect any point on the original figure with the corresponding point on the reflected figure, the line of reflection is the perpendicular bisector of that line segment. See Figure 9.15. That is, $A'X = XA$, and AA' and line l are perpendicular.

FIGURE **9.15**

This realization leads to a more formal definition of reflection. A **reflection** is a transformation that maps a figure so that a line, the **line of reflection**, is the perpendicular bisector of every line segment joining a point on the figure and the corresponding point on the reflected figure.

INVESTIGATION **9.3**   **Understanding Rotations**

This investigation uncovers ways in which we can describe rotations. In both of the diagrams in Figure 9.16, a triangle has been rotated. Can you describe how we can get each triangle from its original position to its new position? In order to describe any rotation precisely, what do we need? Stop, think, and then read on. . . . 🖋

FIGURE **9.16**

DISCUSSION

As with the concept of reflection, you might want to explore this yourself. You can do this by drawing a figure on a piece of paper and then tracing it on another piece of paper. Line up the two pieces of paper so that the top figure lies on the bottom figure, place your pencil or pen point on the paper at some point, and then rotate the bottom sheet of paper. Draw the rotation image by tracing over the image you see from the bottom sheet. This is easier if the top sheet is a sheet of tracing paper, but it works well with regular blank paper, too.

In order to rotate any figure (in a plane), we need to select a *center of rotation* (that is, a point that does not move), and we need to decide how much to rotate the figure. "How much" is determined by specifying an angle.

In the case of the first rotation in Figure 9.16, the center of rotation is the point that is the bottom right vertex of the triangle, and the degree of rotation is 90 degrees clockwise. If you trace the figure, place your pencil on the point, and turn the paper 90 degrees, the figure will now be in the new position.

In the second case, the location of the center of rotation is not immediately obvious. If you take any two corresponding points on the two triangles and connect them, the center of rotation will be on the perpendicular bisector of this line segment.

Formally, we say that a **rotation** is a transformation on a plane determined by holding one point fixed and rotating the plane (in our case, the paper) about this point by a certain number of degrees in a certain direction. The fixed point is called the **center of rotation**.

These three transformations — translation, reflection, and rotation — are known as congruence transformations because the images are congruent to the original figure. As you may have seen in Exploration 9.2 (Tessellations), and as you will see in the explorations in the next section, many art designs involve one or more of these transformations. Let us now examine some of the relationships among these three transformations.

INVESTIGATION **9.4**   **Letters of the Alphabet**

In one particular kind of reading disability, children get the letters *b, d, p,* and *q* confused. How can we use transformations to describe their mistake? That is, which letters can be mapped onto which other letters by a translation, a reflection, or a rotation? Write down your thoughts and then read on. . . .

b d p q

DISCUSSION

■ If we reflect *b* across a vertical line, its reflection image looks like a *d*.

■ If we reflect *b* across a horizontal line, its reflection image looks like a *p*.

■ If we reflect *d* across a horizontal line, its reflection image looks like a *q*.

■ If we rotate *b* 180 degrees, its rotation image looks like a *q*.

■ If we rotate *d* 180 degrees, its rotation image looks like a *p*.

If we do only this much thinking, we have made a connection between these letters and geometric transformations. However, there is more, and this is where notation (to represent these operations) and tables (which often show patterns more clearly) come in. As we have stated before, all mathematical notation has two characteristics: It has been invented, and (most) people agree to use *this* particular notation. (Recall that the notation for representing decimals is not universal, even today.) In order to more succinctly represent the discoveries noted above, I have invented the following notation: I will use a capital R to represent a rotation, a capital L to represent a reflection, and a 0 to represent no transformation. I will use lowercase letters to refer to the kind of reflection or rotation; for example, h = horizontal line, 90 refers to a 90-degree rotation.

Fill in the rest of Table 9.1. What patterns do you see?

TABLE 9.1

	b	*d*	*p*	*q*
b	0	L_v	L_h	R_{180}
d	L_v			
p				
q				

If you compare this table to an addition or multiplication table from Chapter 3, you will see many similarities. Mathematically, many operations work in similar ways. In Chapter 3, we investigated operations that work on numbers. Here we are investigating operations that work on shapes. A field of mathematics that focuses on relationships between various operations is abstract algebra. Discoveries in abstract algebra have had applications in science.

Combining Slides, Flips, and Turns

Now that we understand these three basic transformations of the plane, let us examine combinations of these transformations. If you have been playing the "what-if" game, you may have already thought about this and even investigated it yourself. For example, what if you reflect a figure and then rotate it? As with so many aspects of mathematics, you might expect there to be patterns in the combinations.

Let us do one brief activity that will help you to understand a property of combinations of transformations. Trace Figure 9.17 on a sheet of paper and translate the figure 2 inches in a direction directly above its original position.

The translation vector is shown at the left. Then reflect the translated image across the line *l*. What do you get?

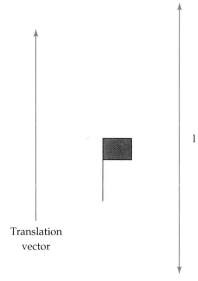

Translation
vector

FIGURE **9.17**

What if you reverse the order—that is, first reflect the flag over the line and then move it 2 inches north? Will the flag wind up in the same space? In other words, are these operations commutative? First predict the answer and note your justification, then check it out.

It turns out that a translation followed by a reflection is equivalent to a reflection followed by a translation. We call any combination of transformations a **composite transformation**.

There is a special name for the combination of reflection and translation: **glide reflection**.

Look at Figure 9.18 taken from a woodcut by M. C. Escher. Do you see the glide reflections? How would you explain them?

FIGURE **9.18**

Any black bird can be mapped onto any white bird by translating the bird and then reflecting the translated image across a line. Of course, to do it exactly, we would need to specify the translation vector (direction and distance) and the reflection line (direction and distance from the translated image of the black bird).

At this point, there are lots of possible "what-if" and "is it possible" questions. Which ones come to your mind? Think before reading on. . . .

Such questions include the following:

1. Are all combinations of these transformations commutative? That is, if you do any two transformations, will you get the same result regardless of the order?

2. How many possible combinations are there?

3. Look back at the transformations we did with the letters *b*, *d*, *p*, and *q*. If you reflect *b* across a horizontal line and then reflect its image across a vertical line, this is equivalent to rotating the *b* 180 degrees. In other words, two reflections (across vertical and horizontal lines) are equivalent to a rotation (of 180 degrees). Is this true for other transformations? For example, is some combination of translation and rotation equivalent to a reflection across a line?

These and many other questions have led to many discoveries, one of which has been used by artists and has been proved by mathematicians: If two congruent figures lie on the same plane, one figure can be moved to the position of the other figure by some combination of translation, reflection, and/or rotation.

This theorem can be stated more formally as: **Given two congruent figures on the same plane, one can be mapped onto the other by some combination of transformations**.

Congruence

In Chapter 8 and Exploration 9.5, we discussed and worked with different concepts of congruence. At the most basic level, we can say that two figures are congruent if they coincide when we superimpose one over the other — in other words, when we move one figure (by translation, reflection, or rotation) so that its image coincides with the other figure. Now that we know that we can move any figure to any position through some combination of transformations (the theorem just cited), we can use this theorem to give a more general definition of congruence:

Two figures are **congruent** iff there is a translation, reflection, rotation, or composite mapping that maps one figure onto another.

Tessellations

For thousands of years, people have chosen to cover surfaces (for example, floors, walls, tables, beds, or roads) with patterns. We will use transformational geometry to examine one kind of covering, called tessellations. Look at the pictures in Figure 9.19, all of which are examples of tessellations. From these pictures, what do you think tessellation means? That is, a pattern that tessellates is one in which . . .

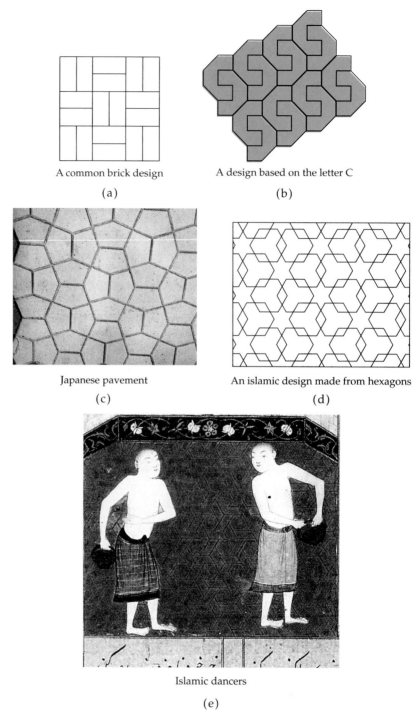

A common brick design

(a)

A design based on the letter C

(b)

Japanese pavement

(c)

An islamic design made from hexagons

(d)

Islamic dancers

(e)

FIGURE **9.19**

In preparing for this book, I read more than 10 authors' descriptions of tessellation. It was interesting to note that none of the definitions were identical, unlike the definition of isosceles triangle in 10 different books! However, all of the definitions had two elements in common: There can be no gaps, and there can be no overlap. We will say that a figure or a combination of figures **tessellates** the plane if a regular repetition of the figure or figures covers the plane so that there are no gaps and no overlapping of figures. Look back at the five designs. Do you see that all of these designs qualify as tessellations? However, only certain geometric figures and combinations of figures will tessellate, and mathematics holds the clue to why.

One common difficulty that people encounter when first making sense of this definition has to do with the borders. When discussing tessellations, we will not be concerned with whether the borders are smooth or straight. For example, if we were covering a floor with square tiles, unless both the length and the width of the floor were equal to a multiple of the length of the tile, the person laying the floor would have to cut the square to fit the edge of the room. Thus, when we say that a pattern tessellates, we are talking not about the edges of the design, but about the design itself.

We will investigate some basic ideas related to two-dimensional tessellations here. Explorations 9.2 and 9.3 carry these ideas further.

INVESTIGATION **9.5** **Which Triangles Tessellate?**

One starting point for investigating tessellations is to ask, which figures will tessellate? We will begin with the triangle (see Figure 9.20). What triangles tessellate? Just a reminder that you will learn more if you really do think before reading on. . . .

Note your first thoughts as predictions. Then make copies of some figures and test your ideas. One simple way to do so is to fold a piece of paper in half, then in half again, and then in half again. Now if you make a triangle and then cut the figure, you will have 8 copies of the triangle.

FIGURE **9.20**

DISCUSSION

Many students are surprised to find that all triangles tessellate! Did you predict this? If not, make some copies of different triangles and confirm this fact. Then come back to the text. Now that you realize that all triangles tessellate, can you justify this—that is, explain why? Work on this question before reading on. . . .

Let us begin with a scalene triangle, shown in Figure 9.21(a). I have labeled the three angles of the triangle. If we rotate the triangle 180 degrees (or reflect it vertically and then horizontally), we can join the triangle and its image together [see Figure 9.21(b)]. You may sense that the combining of the triangles creates a parallelogram, and it can be proved that the result is indeed a parallelogram. If we take this parallelogram and translate it, we now have four triangles [see Figure 9.21(c)]. Figure 9.21(d) shows that we can extend this pattern in all directions infinitely.

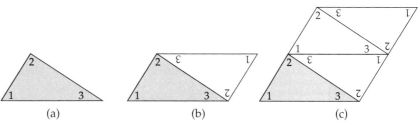

(a)   (b)   (c)

FIGURE **9.21**

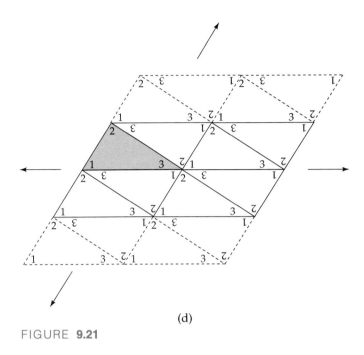

(d)

FIGURE **9.21**

Our eyes tell us that it "looks as if" the triangle tessellates. We will now take some time to confirm what our eyes tell us. Again, this is not a formal geometry course, so we will not give a two-column proof, but rather a more informal justification. Figure 9.22 below repeats Figure 9.21(c), but with some vertices labeled to make communication easier. We can see that we have angles ∡1, ∡3, and ∡2 meeting at vertex B.

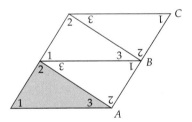

FIGURE **9.22**

However, we know from Chapter 8 that the sum of the angles of any triangle is 180 degrees, and therefore ∡ABC = 180. However, this means that $\overleftrightarrow{AC}$ is a straight line. Looking back at Figure 9.21(d), we can see that there will be six angles at any vertex (∡1, ∡2, ∡3, ∡1, ∡2, ∡3), and the sum of these six angles is 360. As you might be thinking, 360 is an important number; that is, one complete revolution about a point is 360 degrees. Thus, we can see that we can repeat this triangle so that there are no gaps or overlap, and so the triangle tessellates.

In a similar fashion, we can show that any quadrilateral also tessellates the plane. Does this surprise you? If so, make a number of different quadrilaterals to convince yourself that, indeed, *any* quadrilateral does tessellate. Justification of this will be left as an exercise.

INVESTIGATION **9.6** **Which Regular Polygons Tessellate?**

Another common starting point for understanding tessellations is to examine that subset of all polygons called regular polygons—that is, polygons in which all sides are the same length and all angles have the same measure. Which regular polygons will tessellate? Work on this before reading on. You might want to use Figure 9.23 as a template to make copies, or you might choose to apply your understanding of the properties of regular polygons. In either case, do some thinking on your own before reading on. . . .

FIGURE **9.23**

DISCUSSION

It turns out that only three regular polygons tessellate: the equilateral triangle, the square, and the regular hexagon. Note that an equilateral triangle is a regular triangle and a square is a regular quadrilateral. The reason has to do with the sum of the angles.

Whether or not you concluded that these three are the only regular polygons that tessellate, take a few minutes to see if you can justify this conclusion—that is, explain why it is true. Then read on. . . .

If you recall from Chapter 8, the sum of the angles of any polygon = $(n - 2)180$. From this formula, we can find the measure of each interior angle of regular polygons, shown in Table 9.2. Can you see how these numbers help us to understand why only three regular polygons tessellate? Think before reading on. . . .

TABLE 9.2

Figure	Sum of angles	Measure of each interior angle
Equilateral triangle	180	60
Square	360	90
Regular pentagon	540	108
Regular hexagon	720	120
Regular octagon	1,080	135

Table 9.3 helps us to understand why the equilateral triangle, square, and regular hexagon tessellate, but no other regular polygons will. If we place three pentagons at a common vertex, the sum of those angles is 324. This is not quite 360; however, there is not enough room to place a fourth pentagon at that

vertex (see Figure 9.24). Similarly, if we place two octagons at a common vertex, the sum of the two angles is 270, and there is not enough room to place a third octagon at that vertex.

TABLE 9.3		
Figure	**Number of angles at common vertex**	**Sum of those angles**
Equilateral triangle	6 angles	360
Square	4 angles	360
Regular pentagon	3 angles	324
Regular pentagon	4 angles	432
Regular hexagon	3 angles	360
Regular octagon	2 angles	270
Regular octagon	3 angles	405

FIGURE **9.24**

If you are playing the "what-if" game in your mind, you may have realized that $270 + 90 = 360$ and conjectured that a combination of octagons and squares *will* tessellate. This is true, as Figure 9.25 illustrates. There are many combinations of regular polygons that will tessellate, in fact, infinitely many! Mathematicians have names for certain subsets. One that we will consider here is the semiregular tessellation—a tesselation of two or more regular polygons that are arranged so that the same polygons appear in the same order around each vertex point. The tessellation in Figure 9.25(a) is a semiregular tessellation because the two figures are a square and a regular octagon. The tessellation in Figure 9.25(b) is not a semiregular tessellation because the two figures are a square and a nonregular octagon. As you can see, by varying the lengths of the sides of the octagons (that is, the ratio of the noncongruent sides), we can change the appearance of the tessellation.

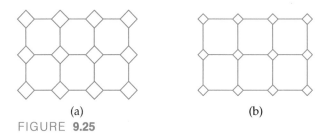

(a)   (b)

FIGURE **9.25**

Explorations 9.2 and 9.3 involve many interesting ways to extend your understanding of tessellations.

INVESTIGATION **9.7**   **Transformations and Art**

Transformations have a lot to do with the patterns we see in tiles, quilts, and other art, especially Islamic art and the work of M. C. Escher. Look at the two patterns in Figure 9.26, which we have seen before. Do you see translations, reflections, and/or rotations in these figures? Write your thoughts and then read on. . . .

parquet   churn dash
FIGURE **9.26**

DISCUSSION

In the parquet pattern, we can see that each light trapezoid can be mapped onto a dark trapezoid through a translation along a diagonal line. Each light trapezoid can also be mapped onto a dark trapezoid through a 90-degree rotation. Furthermore, if we rotate the figure 90 degrees (clockwise or counterclockwise), the figure maps onto itself. If you don't see this, make a copy of the figure, superimpose the figure on the figure in the book, and rotate it.

From another perspective, you can see that the "pinwheel" part of the parquet pattern can be generated by taking only one-quarter of the pinwheel (that is, two adjacent trapezoids) and rotating that portion 90 degrees three times (see Figure 9.27).

FIGURE **9.27**

In the churn dash pattern, each of the dark triangles can be mapped onto each of the other dark triangles across a line of reflection. This is also true for the white triangles. If we rotate the churn dash 90 degrees, with the center of rotation being the center of the figure, it maps onto itself. Furthermore, the churn dash, like the parquet pattern, can be generated by taking one-quarter of the figure and rotating it 90 degrees (clockwise or counterclockwise) three times (see Figure 9.28).

FIGURE **9.28**

INVESTIGATION **9.8** **Generating Pictures Through Transformations**

As you are seeing, translations, reflections, and rotations are actions that we can perform on a figure. Let us investigate how a tessellation figure is composed. Figure 9.29 shows one of my favorite tessellation figures, one that appears in many Islamic designs. Let's say this was a jigsaw puzzle and all the pieces were congruent. How would you put the puzzle together? I have numbered some of the pieces to make communication simpler. Make your own plan before reading on. . . .

DISCUSSION

A quick glance at this tessellation shows us that each of the figures are congruent, and we have learned that if we have two congruent figures on the same plane, they can be mapped onto each other by some combination of translation, reflection, and rotation. Also each of the figures has line symmetry. As we look for patterns within this design, we notice that each figure has two reflections. For example, if we reflect figure 8 across a horizontal line that passes through the top vertex of the figure, we get figure 2. On the other hand, if we reflect figure 8 across a horizontal line that passes through the bottom vertex of the figure, we get figure 14. If we decompose this picture into pairs of figures, we start to unlock the puzzle. Consider the following three pairs: figures 1 and 7, figures 4 and 5, and figures 2 and 8. If we consider these six figures as a unit, we can create the entire design by translating this block of figures, either horizontally or vertically.

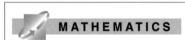

Recall our discussion of unit in Chapter 5. We will also discuss unit in the next chapter when we discuss measurement. One of the goals of this course is for you to see that unit is not just "inch, foot, ounce, etc." What do you think "unit" means?

Source: Dale Seymour and Jill Britton, *Introduction to Tessellations* (Palo Alto, Calif.: Dale Seymour Publications, 1989). Used by permission.

FIGURE **9.29**

Summary

In this section, we have examined three fundamental ways in which we can transform a geometric figure: translation, reflection, and rotation. We have glimpsed the application of this knowledge in tessellations and in art. We have uncovered connections among these transformations—for example, two specific reflections are equivalent to a specific rotation.

There are other connections that are important to note. Many, many people do not see the connectedness of mathematical concepts, and this is unfortunate, because that connectedness is where much of the power of mathematical application comes from.

It is easy for students to see translations, reflections, and rotations as essentially different processes. The explorations of tessellations show that these transformations are in fact very connected! We have consistently used the words *transformation* and *mapping* to underscore the connectedness of these three operations—that is, they are all transformations, they are all mappings, and they are all operations. Recall the connection developed in Investigation 9.4: We can talk of operations on numbers, and we can talk about operations on figures. There are many similarities between the operations of addition, subtraction, multiplication, and division and the operations of translate, reflect, and rotate. There is one more connection: All of these operations (addition, subtraction, multiplication, division, translation, reflection, and rotation) are functions. Do you see why?

In each case, we can specify the operation by matching any input with a unique output.

These investigations of geometric transformations of two-dimensional figures in a plane can be extended. What if we examined transformations of geometric figures into different planes? What if we examined transformations of three-dimensional objects? These investigations occupy the attention of many mathematicians and have applications in other fields. Scientists in many fields are benefiting from a deeper mathematical analysis of three-dimensional tessellations. For example, the way in which atoms are packed helps to determine the properties of a compound.

EXERCISES 9.1

1. Below is a figure and a translation vector. Determine the translation. Describe at least two ways to describe the translation other than providing the vector.

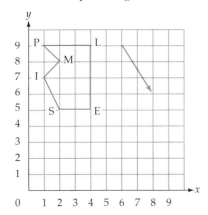

2. Below is a figure and a translation vector. Without using pencil or pen, determine whether the image overlaps the original figure or not. Explain your reasoning.

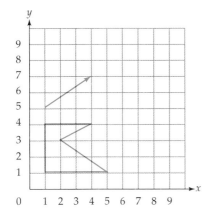

3. Find the image of the kite reflected across line *r*.

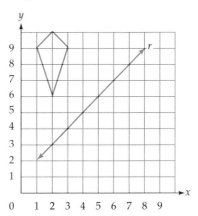

4. The figure below shows quadrilateral *ABCD* and a line of reflection. Determine the coordinates of *A'*, *B'*, *C'*, and *D'* using only reasoning (that is, without folding). Explain your reasoning.

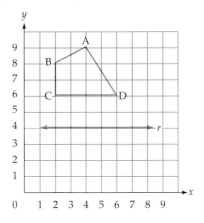

5. The figure below shows a figure and its image. Without folding, sketch the approximate location of the line of reflection. Explain your reasoning.

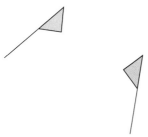

6. Without actually doing the reflection, predict the cases in which the two images are reflections of each other across the line. Explain your reasoning.

7. Determine the rotation image of triangle *MAT* if the triangle is rotated 90 degrees clockwise about point *A*.

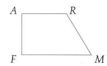

8. Determine the rotation image of trapezoid *FARM* if the figure is rotated 90 degrees counterclockwise about point *F*.

9. Determine the rotation image of the figure below if it is rotated 180 degrees clockwise about point *A*. Explain your reasoning.

10. **a.** Determine the coordinates of the vertices of the rotation image of trapezoid *ABCD* below if it is rotated 90 degrees clockwise about vertex *A*. Explain your reasoning.

   b. Determine the coordinates of the vertices of the rotation image of trapezoid *ABCD* below if it is rotated

90 degrees clockwise about point *X*. Explain your reasoning.

c. Determine the coordinates of the vertices of the rotation image of trapezoid *ABCD* below if it is rotated 90 degrees clockwise about point *Y*. Explain your reasoning.

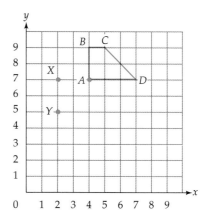

Exercises 11 and 12 involve various composite transformations. In each case:

a. First predict the relative location and sketch the image of the figure after the transformations. Explain your reasoning.

b. Perform the two transformations. If your prediction was correct, great. If not, explain the error in your reasoning. Explain also your plans for "correcting" that error.

c. Predict whether the doubly transformed image will be the same if you do the transformations in the opposite order. Then do the two transformations. If your prediction was correct, great. If not, explain the error in your reasoning. Explain also your plans for "correcting" that error.

11. First transformation: translation ⟶

Second transformation: reflect the figure across line *l*.

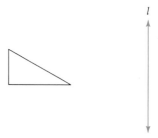

12.

First transformation: translation ↓

Second transformation: reflection across line *l*

b. Predict whether the reflection of the trapezoid across line *m* and then across line *l* will give you the same image. Explain your reasoning.

c. Test your conjecture, and correct it if necessary.

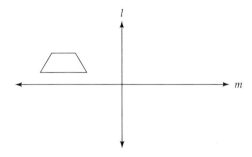

13. Under what circumstances will a glide reflection (translation then reflection) be commutative, that is, when will the translation followed by a reflection produce an image that coincides with the reflection followed by the translation? Explain your reasoning.

14. a. Determine the location of the image of the trapezoid below after it is reflected across line *l* and its reflection image is then reflected across line *m*.

b. Predict whether the reflection of the trapezoid across line *m* and then across line *l* will give you the same image. Explain your reasoning.

c. Test your conjecture, and correct it if necessary.

15. a. Determine the location of the image of the rectangle below after it is reflected across line *l* and its reflection image is then reflected across line *m*.

b. Predict whether the reflection of the rectangle across line *m* and then across line *l* will give you the same image. Explain your reasoning.

c. Test your conjecture, and correct it if necessary.

16. a. Determine the location of the image of the trapezoid after it is reflected across line *l* and its reflection image is then reflected across line *m*.

17. a. Rotate △*DIG* 90° clockwise about point *D*. Then reflect the rotated image across line *l*.

b. Is there another transformation or composition mapping that will produce the same effect?

18. Consider parallelogram *STRU*, whose diagonals intersect at *M*.

a. Describe a transformation that would map $\overline{ST}$ onto $\overline{RU}$.

b. Describe a transformation that would map ∡*SRU* onto ∡*TSR*.

c. If we reflect $\overline{UM}$ across line $\overleftrightarrow{SR}$, will the image be $\overline{MT}$? If so, explain why. If not, explain why not.

19. Consider isosceles triangle *PRO*, where *M* is the midpoint of *PR*.

a. Describe a transformation that would map $\overline{PR}$ onto $\overline{OR}$.

b. What transformation would map △*PMR* onto △*OMR*?

20. a. Describe a single or composite transformation that will map △SRO onto △OTS.

   b. Describe a single or composite transformation that will map △SRO onto △RST.

   c. Describe a single or composite transformation that will map △SRO onto △TOR.

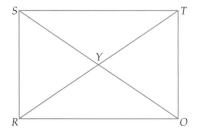

21. The figure below shows triangle *CAT*, which has been reflected across line *m*.

   a. What relationships do you see between the coordinates of the vertices in △CAT and those of its reflection image △C′A′T′?

   b. What generalizations can you make from this exercise? You may want to gather more evidence on your own—that is, make and reflect different figures.

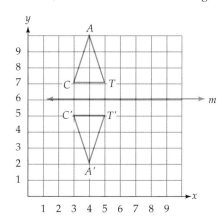

22. Consider the concave quadrilateral *BENT* and its image *B′E′N′T′*. Under what circumstances will *B′E′N′T′* be the reflection of *BENT* across line *m*?

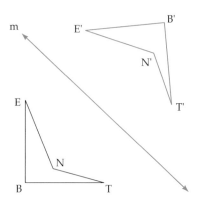

23. Look back to Figure 9.19 on page 476. For each of the figures, describe any translations, reflections, and rotations within the figure. For translations, supply a vector or other means of communicating the translation; for reflections, describe the line(s) of reflection; for rotations, describe the angle of rotation.

   a. Figure 9.19(b)

   b. Figure 9.19(d)

   c. Figure 9.19(e)

   d. Figure 9.19(f)

24. Follow the directions in Exercise 23 for Figure 9.2 on page 463.

25. Follow the directions in Exercise 23 for the quilt patterns below.

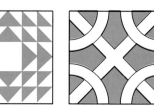

Baby Blocks   Broken Windows   Cross Roads

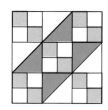

Pinwheel   Tulip Basket   Underground Railroad

26. Follow the directions in Exercise 23 for the Islamic designs below.

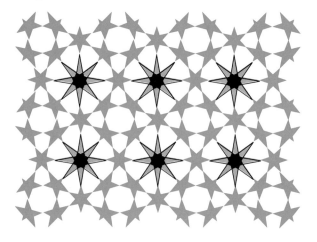

Source: Dale Seymour and Jill Britton, *Introduction to Tessellations* (Palo Alto, Calif.: Dale Seymour Publications, 1989), p. 8. Used by permission.

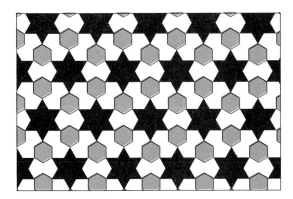

Source: Dale Seymour and Jill Britton, *Introduction to Tessellations* (Palo Alto, Calif.: Dale Seymour Publications, 1989), p. 176. Used by permission.

27. Make the quilt blocks below using a computer software program. Describe how you used transformations to do so. In each case, you do not have to draw the whole block. That is, you can make a part of the block and then finish the block by translating, rotation, and/or reflecting part(s) of the pattern.

   a. Baby Blocks (see Exercise 25)

   b. Broken Windows (see Exercise 25)

   c. Pinwheet (see Exercise 25)

   d. Snail's Trail   **e.** Does and Darts   **f.** May Basket

28. Look at the tessellation at the top of the next column, a hexagon that has been decomposed into six congruent hexagons called chevrons.

   a. Can you identify two chevrons in which the one is a translation of another? Describe the translation.

   b. Can you identify two chevrons in which the one is a reflection of another? Describe the reflection.

   c. Can you identify two chevrons in which the one is a rotation of another? Describe the rotation.

   d. Can you identify two chevrons in which the one is a glide reflection of another? Describe the glide reflection.

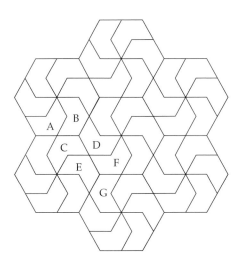

29. Which of the following figures tessellate? If you believe a figure tessellates, you need to show why. If you believe a figure does not tessellate, you need to explain why not.

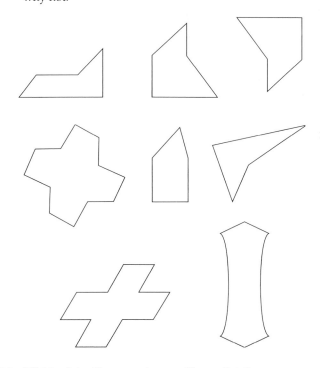

30. Which of the 12 pentominoes will tessellate?

31. You have learned that a regular hexagon will tessellate. Below are two conjectures. There are three parts to what you turn in: your response: true or false; your justification of your response; your work — that is, the hexagons that you made up and tested to see whether they tessellated or not.

   a. If a hexagon has line or rotation symmetry, then it must tessellate.

   b. All convex hexagons will tessellate.

32. Under what conditions will a pentagon tessellate? There are three parts to what you turn in: Your conclusion in the following form: If a pentagon has the following characteristics (listed), then it will tessellate; your justification of your conclusion; your work—that is, the pentagons that you made up and tested to see whether they tessellated or not.

33. Earlier in the book, we discussed palindromes; for example, 1331 is a palindrome. There are word palindromes too. Some close friends of mine, math educators too, named their children HANNAH and AVIVA. We can make a new subset of palindromes, called reflection palindromes, that are legible when reflected. For example, if we reflect 1331 across a vertical line, it will read 𝟏𝟑𝟑𝟏, and if we reflect 1331 across a horizontal line, it will read 𝟏𝟑𝟑𝟏. But if we reflect AVIVA across a vertical line, we still have AVIVA. Explore different palindromes and reflections. Describe the characteristics of palindromes (both number and letter) that will be legible after reflections across horizontal lines, legible after reflections across vertical lines, and legible after reflections across either lines.

34. **a.** If we reflect the angle formed by 3 o'clock through a vertical line through the center of the clock, what will be the time?

    b. If we rotate the angle formed by 3 o'clock 90 degrees clockwise, what will be the time?

    c. Make up and solve a similar problem.

35. We can use reflections to create polygons by folding paper. For example, start with the following figure: two perpendicular line segments. If we make a vertical fold in the paper and trace the image of the two perpendicular line segments, we get the figure in the third picture. If we then make a horizontal fold in the paper and trace that figure's image, we get a rectangle.

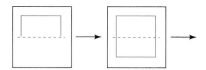

    a. Write directions for making a square from two folds.

    b. Write directions for making a parallelogram from two folds.

    c. Write directions for making an equilateral triangle. There is more than one way.

    d. Write directions for making a hexagon from folding. There is more than one way.

36. The table below is a base 10 multiplication table in which only the ones digit is given. For example, since 8 times 2 = 16, only the 6 is shown.

1	1	2	3	4	5	6	7	8	9	10
1	1	2	3	4	5	6	7	8	9	0
2	2	4	6	8	0	2	4	6	8	0
3	3	6	9	2	5	8	1	4	7	0
4	4	8	2	6	0	4	8	2	6	0
5	5	0	5	0	5	0	5	0	5	0
6	6	2	8	4	0	6	2	8	4	0
7	7	4	1	8	5	2	9	6	3	0
8	8	6	4	2	0	8	6	4	2	0
9	9	8	7	6	5	4	3	2	1	0
10	0	0	0	0	0	0	0	0	0	0

    a. Describe translations, reflections, and rotations within this table. For example, the first half of the 2s row (2, 4, 6, 8, 0) can be translated (5 boxes horizontally). Without transformation language, we would say the first half of the 2s row is the same as the second half of the 2s row. For the purposes of this exercise, consider only the location of the digit, not its spatial orientation.

    b. Make a multiplication table for base 12 in which only the ones digit of the product is given. Describe the transformations that can map one row or column onto another row or column. What similarities and differences do you see between the two tables?

37. The object of the game below is to move the arrow from the top-left corner to the bottom-right corner, using transformations. The only restriction is that you cannot go back to a square once occupied.

    a. Describe how to move the arrow from the top-left corner to the bottom-right corner in as few moves as possible.

    b. Describe how to move the arrow from the top-left corner to the bottom-right corner in as few moves as possible, with the additional restriction that each move has to be to a square that has at least one point in common with the square in which the figure resides.

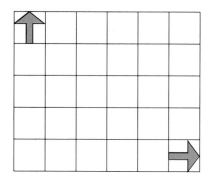

SYMMETRY

"Symmetry, as wide or as narrow as you may define its meaning, is one idea by which humanity through the ages has tried to comprehend and create order, beauty, and perfection."[1]

Symmetry pervades our lives, and many people find symmetrical figures appealing. We see symmetry in both natural objects and human-made objects—snowflakes, starfish, flags, logos, quilts, and many kinds of art, to name but a few. Look at Figure 9.30. Each of its elements is a well-known symbol or figure. For each of them, write what it is about that figure that is visually appealing or that attracts your attention. Describe the symmetry within each figure. Then read on. . . . 📝

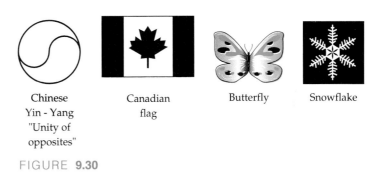

Chinese Yin - Yang "Unity of opposites"

Canadian flag

Butterfly

Snowflake

FIGURE **9.30**

I think it is very possible that the first mathematical acts of human beings had to do not with numbers but with symmetry. As we saw in Chapter 2, many cultures survived even into the twentieth century without numbers or with very primitive number systems. However, to my knowledge, the archaeological records of virtually every culture show symmetry in some of that culture's artifacts: its baskets, its pottery, the artifacts created for celebrations and rituals. I can think of virtually no religious symbols that do not have symmetries within them.

Let us then investigate this aspect of mathematics more deeply, to better understand what we mean by the term *symmetry* and what kinds of symmetries there are. We will investigate three kinds of symmetry: translational, reflection, and rotational.

Kinds of Symmetry

One of the main goals of this book is for students to come to appreciate the interconnectedness of mathematics, as opposed to seeing mathematics as a collection of different topics. The concept of symmetry is closely connected to the concept of congruence. Think of the concept of congruence and think of your "working definition" of symmetry. How are the two related or connected? Please think about this and note your thoughts before reading on. . . . 📝

We speak of congruence when we compare two or more figures: They are congruent if we can pick up one and superimpose it onto the other. Symmetry has to do with congruence *within* a figure. If we can pick up part of a figure and, by a translation, reflection, or rotation, move it so that it can be superimposed over another part of that figure, then the figure will have some kind of

[1] Hermann Weyl, *Symmetry* (Princeton, N.J.: Princeton University Press, 1952), p. 5.

symmetry. Thus, we can think of symmetry as a congruence relationship within a figure.

Translational Symmetry

Based on our work with translations in Section 9.1, what do you think translational symmetry will mean? Can you describe it? Do any of the quilt blocks from Exploration 9.6 have translational symmetry? Can you create a figure that you think will have translational symmetry? Try to do so before reading on. . . .

Translations have to do with movement, and our conception of symmetry relates to congruence within a figure. Although the notion of **translational symmetry** is fairly straightforward, communicating what it is with words is often difficult. Therefore, let us begin with this notion: If a figure has translational symmetry, we can pick up part of the figure and put it down onto itself, and thus the figure can be repeated as long as we like. For example, each of the patterns in Figure 9.5 on page 000 has translational symmetry. That is, we can generate the pattern by picking up and moving (in a straight line) part of the pattern. Technically, translational symmetry exists only for infinite patterns. That is, a figure (which is finite) by definition cannot have translational symmetry. However, practically, we find translations used in borders—on buildings, on quilts and bedspreads, on walls, and in many other places. Thus, when asking about translational symmetry, we are asking if the *pattern* has translational symmetry.

The Japanese pavement pattern in Figure 9.19(c) (page 476) has translational symmetry. Do you see why?

If we consider the four pavement stones shown in Figure 9.31 as our unit, we can make a row by translating this pattern. Then by translating this row, we can make other rows both above and below this row.

More formally, we can say that if we can generate an entire figure by translating a part of the figure so that the translated image coincides with another part of the figure, then the figure has translational symmetry. More succinctly, if we can translate a figure so that it maps onto itself, then that figure has translational symmetry.

If you did Exploration 9.2 (Tessellations) and/or Exploration 9.6 (Quilts), do you see connections to translational symmetry? Many tessellations have translational symmetry. Many quilts have translational symmetry because they are made by putting quilt blocks together.

Reflection Symmetry

Based on our work with reflections in Section 9.1, what do you think reflection symmetry will mean? Can you describe it? Look at some of the figures from Section 9.1. If you did Exploration 9.2 (Tessellations) or Exploration 9.6 (Quilts), you might want to refer to some of the figures in those explorations. Can you create a figure that you think will have reflection symmetry? Try to do so before reading on. . . .

In order to create a reflection image, we used a line: A figure is a reflection image of another figure if we can fold a paper on the line and the first figure can be superimposed onto the second figure.

If we adapt this language to one figure instead of two figures, we can say that if there is a line (called a **line of symmetry**) that can be drawn through a

FIGURE **9.31**

figure such that if we fold the paper on the line, the two halves of the figure are superimposed on each other, then the figure has **reflection symmetry**.

Many of the geometric shapes we investigated in Chapter 8 have reflection symmetry. Describe the line symmetries you see in the equilateral triangle, the isosceles triangle, and the scalene triangle in Figure 9.32. Then read on....

FIGURE **9.32**

We find that the equilateral triangle has three lines of symmetry, the isosceles triangle has one line, and the scalene triangle has none (see Figure 9.33).

  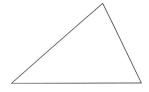

FIGURE **9.33**

INVESTIGATION **9.9** Reflection Symmetry in Quadrilaterals

> **W**hat about quadrilaterals? Which ones have reflection symmetry, and how many lines of symmetry are there in each? Draw different quadrilaterals—trapezoid, parallelogram, kite, rhombus, rectangle, square, and concave quadrilaterals. Work on this before reading on....

DISCUSSION

A kite has one line of symmetry, a rhombus has two lines, a rectangle has two lines, and a square has four lines of symmetry.

In Section 8.2, we created a family tree for quadrilaterals. Each descendant had all the properties of its ancestor plus at least one more property. Will that same family tree hold for lines of symmetry? This will be left as an exercise.

Rotational Symmetry

Based on our work with rotations in Section 9.1, what do you think rotational symmetry will mean? Can you describe it? Can you create a figure that you think will have rotational symmetry? Try to do so before reading on....

In order to create a rotation image, we rotated the paper around a point. A figure is a rotation image of another figure if we can rotate the paper a certain amount so that the first figure can be superimposed on the second figure.

If we adapt this language to one figure instead of two figures, we can say that if there is a point around which we can rotate the figure so that a rotation of some degrees will cause the figure to superimpose on itself, then the figure has **rotational symmetry**.

INVESTIGATION **9.10** **Rotational Symmetry in Triangles and Quadrilaterals**

Let us examine some polygons (see Figure 9.34). Which of them have rotational symmetry? How would you describe the rotational symmetry? Think and then read on. . . .

FIGURE **9.34**

DISCUSSION

Triangles If we rotate an equilateral triangle (see Figure 9.35) 120 degrees clockwise through the center of the triangle, the rotated triangle will fit perfectly (map) onto itself. If we rotate it another 120 degrees (making a total of 240 degrees), it will map onto itself again. Thus, we say that an equilateral triangle has 120- and 240-degree rotational symmetry. It is the only triangle that has rotational symmetry.

FIGURE **9.35**

Quadrilaterals The square (Figure 9.36) has 90-degree, 180-degree, and 270-degree rotational symmetry.

FIGURE **9.36**

The kite and trapezoid have no rotational symmetry.

The parallelogram, rhombus, and rectangle each have 180-degree rotational symmetry (see Figure 9.37).

FIGURE **9.37**

Hexagons If we examine the hexagon, we can see that it clearly has rotational symmetry. There are several ways to describe its rotational symmetry. One way is to turn the hexagon through its center and realize that six identical rotations will bring it back to its starting point. Since there are 360 degrees in a circle, each of the rotations must be 60 degrees. Thus, we say that a regular hexagon has the following rotational symmetry: 60-degree, 120-degree, 180-degree, 240-degree, and 300-degree.

Point symmetry   As you may have already observed, many figures have 180-degree rotational symmetry but no other rotational symmetry. A figure has 180-degree rotational symmetry if it looks the same when you turn the paper upside down. This particular kind of rotational symmetry is called point symmetry.

360-degree rotational symmetry?   One last note on rotational symmetry: When I ask my students to tell me whether or not a figure has rotational symmetry, many of them will say that a figure has 360-degree rotational symmetry. What does it mean to say that a figure has 360-degree rotational symmetry? Think and read on. . . .

To say that a figure has 360-degree rotational symmetry means that if we turn it completely around, it will look the same. However, this is true for any figure. Since any figure has 360-degree rotational symmetry, we do not use this when describing the rotational symmetries of a figure.

Figures with Multiple Symmetries

We have now examined the three kinds of symmetry separately. As you may have already realized, many figures and objects have more than one kind of symmetry. Let us explore this idea a bit further with the capital letters of the alphabet.

INVESTIGATION **9.11**   **Letters of the Alphabet and Symmetry**

Examine the letters of the alphabet. Which letters have rotational symmetry? What kind(s) of rotational symmetry? Which letters have reflection symmetry? What kind(s) of reflection symmetry? Work on this and then read on. . . .

A B C D E F G H I J K L M N O P Q R S T U V W X Y Z

DISCUSSION

When we examine the letters in terms of reflection symmetry, we find that there are three kinds of lines of reflections: vertical, horizontal, and diagonal.

The following letters have vertical line symmetry: A, H, I, M, O, T, U, V, W, X, Y. I thought it interesting that over half of the letters with vertical line symmetry occur at the end of the alphabet.

The following letters have horizontal line symmetry: B, C, D, E, H, I, K, O, X. Here we have the opposite phenomenon: four consecutive letters near the beginning of the alphabet.

Three letters have diagonal line symmetry (depending on how they are drawn): O, Q, and X.

The following letters have point symmetry: H, I, N, O, S, X, Z.

Tessellations and Symmetry

In Section 9.1 we examined how we could construct a tessellation pattern using translations, reflections, and rotations. Now let us examine some tessellations in terms of symmetries.

Look back to the simple brick tessellation in Figure 9.19(a) (page 000). Describe the symmetries in this pattern and then read on. . . . 🖎

First, let us examine the construction of the figure. Each brick, ☐ or ▭, can be translated to different parts of the figure. From another perspective, ☐☐ can be seen as the unit of construction, because we can construct the pattern by translations and rotations of this unit.

As discussed earlier in this section, the figure, by definition, does not have translational symmetry. However, the pattern does have translational symmetry. Why is this? If we think of this brick pattern as extending indefinitely in all directions, we can see that we can take one row and slide that row in a diagonal line to make the row above or below it. This figure has vertical and horizontal line symmetry because we can map (superimpose) the figure onto itself by a horizontal line through the center in the middle row and by a vertical line through the center in the middle column. The only kind of rotational symmetry in this figure is point symmetry, or 180-degree rotational symmetry. That is, if we rotate the figure 180 degrees (turn it upside down), we can superimpose this image on the figure itself.

Symmetry for Three-Dimensional Objects

Thus far we have examined symmetry with two-dimensional figures. However, we see symmetry in many three-dimensional figures. Buildings often have symmetry; think of the Taj Mahal or the U.S. Capitol building. Everyday objects such as forks, nuts and bolts, and windows have symmetry. Many natural forms, including starfish, honeycombs, pyrite, and crystals, are also symmetrical.

Let us briefly examine symmetry of three-dimensional objects. We will focus on reflection and rotational symmetry.

When we defined reflection symmetry with two-dimensional figures, we used a line. Therefore, it should make sense that when we define reflection symmetry with three-dimensional figures, we will use a plane. Since we have added one more dimension to the figure (two to three), we add one more dimension to the instrument of reflection (one to two).

If there is a plane that can be drawn through a three-dimensional figure so that one half of the figure is a mirror image of the other, then the figure has reflection symmetry. The plane is called the **plane of symmetry**.

Similarly, when we defined rotational symmetry with two-dimensional figures, we used a point (a one-dimensional object). We define rotational symmetry with three-dimensional figures using a line (a two-dimensional object).

If there is a line that can be drawn, around which a three-dimensional figure can be rotated so that it coincides with itself, then the figure has rotational symmetry. The line about which the figure is rotated is called the **axis of symmetry**.

Figure 9.38 shows two three-dimensional objects that have reflection and/or rotational symmetry. In each case, determine and try to describe the plane(s) of symmetry and the axis (or axes) of symmetry. Then read on. . . . 🖎

Equilateral

Nightstand

The prism has 120-degree rotational symmetry about its axis, the line connecting the centers of the two bases. The prism has one plane of symmetry, a horizontal plane. The nightstand has one plane of symmetry, a vertical plane.

Summary

We have found that each of the transformations from Section 9.1 leads to a type of symmetry—translational, reflectional, and rotational. One of the more important goals is for you to see symmetry as a movement—as a verb, rather than a noun. When we see symmetry in an object, we do so by moving that object or parts of that object in our minds. Perhaps that is why symmetry is so appealing: It requires activeness on the part of our minds to appreciate it. When we find that an object has symmetry, we are using the notion of congruence; that is, we have found that we can move the figure (or part of the figure) and superimpose the figure on itself. We have seen that symmetry has many applications in the world of art (quilts, mosaics), in everyday life (wallpaper and tiles), and in science (symmetry at the atomic level). We have seen that symmetry helps us to better understand how and why tessellations work.

Finally, we have introduced the notion of three-dimensional symmetry, which has many important applications in everyday life and in science. I have talked with scientists about the usefulness of symmetry in their fields. A chemist told me that molecules of similar symmetry will give similar spectra and that advances in our mathematical understanding of symmetry have helped organic chemists to better understand the structure of organic compounds. At a molecular level, the atomic structure of various elements and compounds determines how they will be packed together. As Marjorie Senechal has written, "if all we learn about symmetry is to identify it, we miss the whole point. Symmetry is an effect, not a cause."[2]

[2]Marjorie Senechal, *On the Shoulders of Giants* p. 153.

EXERCISES 9.2

1. Describe the rotational and reflectional symmetries in the figures below.

a.

b.

c.

d.

2. Describe the rotational and reflectional symmetries in the figures below.

a.

Maple leaf
Canada

b.

"Life"
Ancient Egypt

c.

"Unity is Strength"
Ghana

3. Describe the rotational and reflectional symmetries in the flags below.

a.

Barbados

b.

Switzerland

c.

Korea

4. Describe the rotational and reflectional symmetries in the corporate logo below.

a.

Chevrolet

Source: Courtesy of Chevrolet Motor Division, General Motors Corporation.

5. Describe the rotational and reflectional symmetries in the quilt patterns below.

a. Churn Dash

b. Eight-Point Star

c. Baby's Blocks

d. Diamonds in the Sky

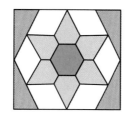

6. Describe at least three symmetries in the quilt below, which is called Cake Stand.

7. **a.** Describe the rotational and reflectional symmetries of the tangram pieces.

   b. Make a design that has symmetry with some or all of the tangram pieces. Explain the symmetry.

8. Classify the pentominoes by the kind(s) of symmetry that they have. Explain the different subsets.

9. Describe the rotational and reflectional symmetries of the ten digits in base 10.

10. Look back on the classification of the letters of the alphabet according to their symmetries. Represent those symmetries with a Venn diagram.

11. Recall the family tree for the properties of quadrilaterals in Chapter 8. When we look at the symmetries of the quadrilaterals in the family tree, will that same family tree still hold true? That is, does each descendant quadrilateral have the same symmetries as its ancestor plus at least one more symmetry? Justify your answer.

12. Tell whether the statements below are true or false. If a statement is true, explain why. If it is false, provide a counterexample.

    a. If a figure has rotational symmetry, it must also have reflection symmetry.

b. If a figure has point symmetry, it must also have rotational symmetry.

c. If a figure does not have point symmetry, it cannot have reflectional symmetry.

13. Create a figure (not one copied from this book) that has the symmetry described below. In each case, describe your thought processes, including ideas that did not pan out.

   a. 60-degree rotational symmetry

b. 120-degree rotational symmetry

c. 90-degree rotational symmetry

d. Two lines of symmetry

e. Three lines of symmetry

f. At least one line of symmetry and some kind of rotational symmetry

g. Reflectional symmetry but not rotational symmetry

h. Rotational symmetry and exactly one line of reflection

14. Describe the rotational and reflectional symmetries in the Navajo designs as they are drawn below. Then, imagining them to extend to the right and left indefinitely, describe any translational symmetries.

15. Make the designs using computer software. Describe how you made the designs.

16. Describe the symmetries—rotational, reflectional, and translational—in the Navajo rugs shown below.

17. Give instructions for making the patterns below as if you were talking to someone on the phone. Use symmetries when possible.

a.

Shoo fly

b.

Amish design

c.

Star

18. Design a flag that has
   a. Rotational symmetry
   b. Reflectional symmetry
   c. Rotational symmetry but no reflectional symmetry
   d. Reflectional symmetry but no rotational symmetry

19. Examine a deck of cards and separate them into subsets that have the same kinds of symmetry.

20. The word "HIDE" has one (horizontal) line of symmetry. This means that if we flip the word over, it will still spell HIDE. Find another word that has horizontal symmetry.

21. The word "WITH" has one (vertical) line of symmetry if we write it vertically. Find another word that has vertical symmetry.

W

I

T

H

22. Find a two-dimensional or three-dimensional figure on campus or from your home that has some symmetries. Sketch the figure and describe the symmetries.

23. Find examples of children's toys that have symmetries.

24. Describe the symmetries in a nut and the reason why it might have these symmetries.

SECTION   **9.3**   **SIMILARITY**

WHAT DO YOU THINK?

- What does it mean to say that two figures or two objects are similar?

- Are an object and its shadow similar? Why or why not?

In Section 9.1, we explored several transformations that let us change the position of an object but preserve its size and shape. That is, all of the images were congruent to the original figure. In this section, we will investigate a transformation in which the size of the figure is changed but the shape is not; we will call these transformations **similarity transformations** or **similarity mappings**.

In mathematics, the term *similar* has a very specific meaning. I believe that if you participate in the development of the idea, rather than just having the mathematical definition presented to you, you will come to own the concept and the related properties. Therefore, the opening question is: What does it

You have used the concept
"similar" since you were young.
"Similarity seems to be a very
fundamental concept.
Preschoolers understand that
miniature animals, doll clothes,
and play houses are all small
versions of familiar things. The
fact that even such young
children know what these tiny
objects are supposed to
represent shows that they
intuitively understand change of
scale. Building and taking apart
scale models of towers,
bridges, houses, shapes of any
kind give the child—of any
age—a firm grasp of this
idea."[3]

mean to say that two figures or two objects are similar? Can you think of real-life objects that are similar? Think and then read on. . . .

A response that many students articulate in one way or another is that two objects that are similar are different in size but look the same.

One of the more common everyday uses of *similar* is in photocopying, when enlarging or reducing a figure. Also, children (and adults) build scale models, which are mathematically similar (see Figure 9.39).

FIGURE **9.39**

INVESTIGATION **9.12** Developing an Understanding of Similarity in Mathematics

The purpose of this investigation and Explorations 9.8 to 9.11 is to help you construct an understanding of similarity that goes deeper than "one more definition or formula to memorize." As you do the investigations and explorations, the notion of similarity as a transformation—that is, as a verb—is critical. One of the most common applications of similarity beyond the classroom involves enlarging or shrinking a figure (as in photocopying) or an object (as in scale models).

Let us begin our investigation of similarity by using the notion of *enlarging* and *reducing* on a copy machine. When a photocopier enlarges or reduces a diagram or picture, the enlargement or reduction is similar to the original. Connecting to our statement that similarity is a transformation, each of the figures in the left column of Figure 9.40 has been transformed by a similarity mapping to the figure on the right. Most people would agree that each pair is similar.

[3] Marjorie Senechal, *On the Shoulders of Giants* pp. 141–142.

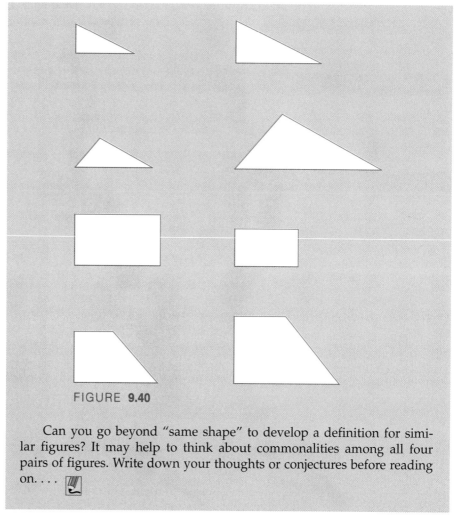

FIGURE **9.40**

Can you go beyond "same shape" to develop a definition for similar figures? It may help to think about commonalities among all four pairs of figures. Write down your thoughts or conjectures before reading on. . . .

DISCUSSION

As in our investigation of transformations and symmetry, a "hands-on" approach can be quite instructive. Trace the figures and cut them out or make a photocopy of the page and cut out the eight figures. Place the original on top of the enlargement, so that two sides of the smaller figure lie on top of the corresponding sides of the larger figure, as shown in Figure 9.41.

Now what do you notice? Does this activity match your definition, does it contradict it, or does it give you some new ideas? If one of the latter is true, revise your definition of similarity. Then read on. . . .

FIGURE **9.41**

Angles   In Chapter 8, we defined two polygons as being congruent iff all corresponding angles were congruent and all corresponding sides were congruent. What relationships do you notice between angles and sides of the similar figures that might enable us to define two polygons being similar? Write down your present hypothesis before reading on. . . .

It can be easily determined that in each of the four cases in Figure 9.40, the corresponding angles of the similar figures are equal. If you worked with the Pattern Blocks in Exploration 9.8, the tangrams in Exploration 9.9, the geoboards in Exploration 9.10, or the reptiles in Exploration 9.12, you may have come to the same conclusion. You can confirm this relationship either with a protractor or by placing the smaller figure on top of the larger one and verifying by inspection.

Sides What about the sides? Obviously, the sides are not congruent. What relationship do they have? Think about this before reading on. . . .

One observation is that if both figures are aligned as shown, then corresponding sides are parallel. Another possible observation involves the lengths. Measure the lengths of corresponding sides. Do you notice anything? Do this before reading on. . . .

It turns out that the lengths of corresponding sides are proportional. What does that mean? Can you explain that statement to someone who doesn't understand it? If you don't understand it yourself, go back and review the discussion of proportion in Chapter 6 before reading on. . . .

When we say that the lengths of corresponding sides are proportional, this means that if we find the ratio of the lengths of two corresponding sides, the ratio of the lengths of every other pair of corresponding sides will be the same number.

These observations lead us to a definition of similarity:

> Two polygons are **similar** iff corresponding angles are congruent and corresponding sides are proportional.

We use the symbol ~ to denote similarity. For example, in Figure 9.42, $\triangle ABC \sim \triangle XYZ$.

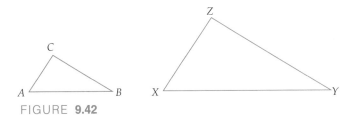

FIGURE **9.42**

INVESTIGATION 9.13   **Making Similar Drawings**

The notion of enlarging and shrinking animals and humans has fascinated people for ages. *Gulliver's Travels* by Jonathan Swift is an ageless classic. Movies dealing with this include *King Kong, Honey, I Shrunk the Kids,* and many grade B science fiction movies (not to imply that the former two were models of excellence). Knowing that a figure can be blown up and shrunk by making corresponding angles equal and corresponding sides proportional is fine if you have a simple polygon, but this process can be very cumbersome if you have a more complex figure. Consider the two pictures in Figure 9.43 (a simple sailboat and a shark) and do a 50 percent enlargement—that is, make the base of the new sailboat

50 percent longer than the one in Figure 9.43 and the length of the new shark 50 percent greater than the length of the shark in Figure 9.43.

How might you apply our definition of similarity to draw larger pictures of each of these figures? Work on this yourself before reading on. . . . 🖎

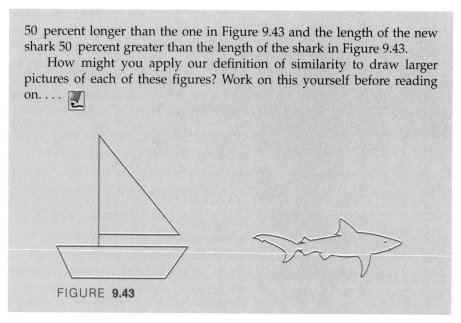

FIGURE **9.43**

DISCUSSION

There are several possibilities. We will investigate two, both involving graph paper. What if we placed these figures over a grid—either traced them onto the graph paper or placed a sheet of transparent graph paper over the figures (see Figure 9.44)? How would this help?

Focus on the figure We have two choices. First, we can draw the similar but bigger figure on the same kind of graph paper but make each line 50 percent longer. For example, the bottom of the sailboat is 12 units long in Figure 9.44, and so it would be 18 units long in the new picture. This works fine with horizontal and vertical lines, but what about the diagonal lines on the sailboat and the curved lines on the shark?

For example, we could measure the length of the diagonal line going up from the bottom of the sailboat, points *A* and *B*, and we could measure the length of the curve from one point of the shark to another point, marked *C* and *D* in Figure 9.44. But how would that help? Think about it, because the answer involves applying our understanding of similarity. Then read on. . . . 🖎

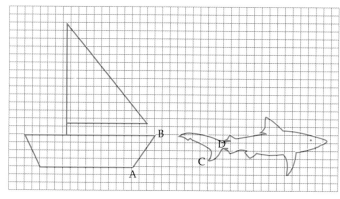

FIGURE **9.44**

Since the angles must be the same in similar figures, we can measure the angle and the distance. We keep the angle the same but make the distance

50 percent longer. We can accomplish the same goal, in a simpler fashion, however, by connecting the idea of slope. That is, to get from A to B, we go 3 units to the right and 4 units up. If we increase these figures by 50 percent (go 4.5 units to the right and 6 units up), we will have the same angle on our bigger sailboat, and the distance will be 50 percent longer. Check it out! We use the same idea for the shark.

Focus on the paper Another strategy would be to use a piece of graph paper with the distance between the lines 50 percent longer. Then we could use the same number when counting on the bigger grid; for example, to get from A to B on the sailboat, we would move 3 units to the right and 4 units up. We can copy the shark grid by grid also. We are essentially checking to see that each grid is "similar," and this can be done in more than one way. For example, look at the top left-hand square in both pictures in Figure 9.45. In both cases, we start at the top left-hand corner, and we meet the right side of the square about one-fourth of the way down. To check our work, we use proportional reasoning. How do we do this?

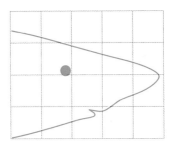

FIGURE **9.45**

The line that we draw divides the square into two regions. We visually check to see if the ratio of the larger to the smaller region is the same in both cases. Figure 9.46 shows a case in which the artist would decide that it "wasn't right" and would do it over.

FIGURE **9.46**

If you worked on Exploration 9.13, did you use any of these strategies in creating variations on the Spool quilt block? Did you use different strategies that you might apply to the shark drawing?

Summary

In this section, we have investigated the idea of similarity so that your thinking about this concept could move up the van Hiele scale — that is, beyond "similarity means they look alike." We have also looked at how some ways to draw similar figures connect to the concept of similarity. The *Explorations* volume contains other ways to look at the idea of similarity.

In this chapter, we have investigated only a small subset of the field of transformational geometry. Another field, called topology, examines transformations in which one shape can be turned into another shape by stretching, shrinking, bending, and/or twisting, but without making any cuts or tears in the figure. Thus, a square and a triangle are topologically equivalent. Recall the research showing that young children are not able to copy a square and a triangle accurately. Mathematically, we say that young children intuitively understand topological mappings before they understand congruence mappings. Other applications of topology include understanding networks and maps.

EXERCISES 9.3

1. In each case below, the two polygons are similar. Find the length of the side labeled x.

2. The two triangles **below** are similar, but they have gotten mixed up. Determine the corresponding parts and explain how you did so.

3. The figure at the right below has been created from four triangles that are congruent to the triangle at the left. Are the two triangles similar? Explain why or why not.

4. For each of the questions below, answer yes or no. In either case, justify your response.
   a. Are all isosceles triangles similar?
   b. Are all equilateral triangles similar?
   c. Are all squares similar?
   d. Are all rhombuses similar?
   e. Are congruent polygons similar?

5. Gerald has a photo that is 8×11 and a frame that is 4×6.
   a. Explain to him why we cannot reduce the photo so that it will fit perfectly in the frame.

   b. Explain to him his options for cutting so that the reduced photo will fit.

6. When we use an overhead projector in a classroom, is the image on the screen similar to the object on the overhead projector?

7. Below is a map of Utah. If the actual distance across the bottom of Utah is 275 miles, determine the scale of the map. That is, 1 inch = x miles, or 1 cm = x miles.

8. The diagram below shows how we can find the distance across a lake using the principle of similar triangles.

   a. Explain how points C, B, and A would be determined, as if you were talking to someone who understands the idea of similar triangles but has never heard of this method before.
   b. Explain why $\triangle ABC \sim \triangle EDC$.
   c. If $AB = 324$ feet, $BC = 103$ feet, and $CD = 212$ feet, what is the distance across the pond?

9. Explain how you could use shadows and similarity to find the height of a building.

10. A common standard setting for enlarging on a copy machine is 121 percent. What does this mean?

11. Find a quilt block that contains similar figures. Explain why the figures are similar.

12. Find a tessellation pattern that contains similar figures. Explain why the figures are similar.

CHAPTER SUMMARY

1. Both congruence and similarity are kinds of transformations.

2. Congruence can be defined in Euclidean terms (the classical definition) and in terms of congruence mappings.

3. There are different ways to perform and describe different transformations. Which one(s) we use depends partly on preference and partly on purpose.

4. Translations, reflections, and rotations are congruence transformations—the figure is moved, but its shape and size are not changed.

5. The geometric transformations of translation, reflection, and rotation are operations, with many similarities to the operations of addition, subtraction, multiplication, and division.

6. Symmetry has to do with congruence within a figure.

7. There are many symmetries in geometric figures: translational, reflectional, and rotational. Many figures have more than one kind of symmetry.

Basic Concepts

10

Geometry as Measurement

W̲hat do you think of when you hear the term *measurement?* In what ways do you use measurement, and in what ways are you measured?

We measure and are measured all the time. When we ask how much or how many, we are often asking a question requiring a direct or indirect measurement:

■ How much time will it take?

■ How far is it from here to there?

■ How much paint do we need to paint the house?

Long before they start school, children are fascinated by measurement, and some of their measurement questions leave parents confused, too:

The child asks, "How long until we get there?" The parent says, "One hour." The child asks, "Is that long?"

Or the parent divides the candy bar into two pieces (measures), and one child says, "His half is bigger than mine."

By the end of this chapter, you will come to understand that measurement is far more than just an examination of the quantities we use in everyday life, such as length, area, volume, or time. You will want to refer to the NCTM measurement standards before you have your children investigate this topic.

◢ Among the important ideas in measurement are:

■ There are many attributes that we measure.

■ The number associated with a measurement is meaningless unless we know the unit (feet, square feet, pounds, and so on).

■ Our answer depends on the degree of accuracy required in a particular situation.

■ The measurer needs to select appropriate tools and units (such as centimeters for the length of a pencil and kilometers for the distance between two towns).

   # SYSTEMS OF MEASUREMENT

WHAT DO YOU THINK?

■ What does it mean to measure?

■ What are some difficulties we encounter when measuring?

■ When do we need our measurements to be precise, and when it is acceptable to just have a "rough" measurement?

■ How do we measure heights of mountains?

Visualize yourself measuring different things—for example, how far to your parents' house, how much paint you would need to buy to paint a house, how much a package weighs. We might want several measures of something. Consider a room. If we wanted to stencil the top of the wall around the room, we would want to know the room's perimeter. If we wanted to paint the room, we would want to know its surface area. If we wanted to store a bunch of stuff in the room, we would want to know its volume. Think of the process of measuring in each of these situations. What is common to each of them? Think and then read on. . . . 🖉

In each case, we must:

1. Identify what we want to measure—that is, identify the *attribute* we want to measure.

2. Select or determine the *unit* we will use to tell us how much.

3. Determine the amount we have in terms of the units we have chosen.

Keep these three aspects in mind as you read the text and do the explorations.

Development of Measurement Systems

Measuring is probably one of human beings' earliest forms of mathematical activity. In the following pages, we will examine the development of the units and systems of measurement people commonly use in everyday life.

Time   One of the first quantities that people measured was time. Many thousands of years ago, people developed ways to determine the number of days in a year. Why do you think they wanted to know this? Think before reading on. . . . 🖉

There are many reasons, such as wanting to know when to celebrate certain rituals, when to hunt, or when to plant. Early divisions of the day were probably marked by three significant times: sunrise, midday, and sunset. Later, midnight became significant too. We say that 1 day = 24 hours, 1 hour = 60 minutes, and 1 minute = 60 seconds. However, this has not always been so. Where do you think 24 and 60 came from? Think and then read on. . . . 🖉

Over 3,000 years ago, the Babylonians divided the day into 12 hours and the night into 12 hours. However, the length of an hour depended on the time of year; that is, in the winter, a day hour was shorter than a night hour. At some point, the Greeks decided to divide the entire day into 24 equal parts, but it was not until around 1330 that the hour was standardized—that is, that an hour in January and an hour in June were equal, and an hour in Stockholm and an hour in Venice were equal.

For centuries, people used the sundial to measure the passage of time. The earliest known sundial comes from Egypt and dates from about 1500 B.C. The sundial, of course, has several limitations: It is not useful on cloudy days or at night, and it is not useful for small amounts of time. An early attempt to address this limitation was the water clock. The first water clock came from

LANGUAGE

The origins of our words for the days of the week can be traced to the Babylonians and correspond to the seven "planets" they had identified: Sun, Moon, Mars, Mercury, Jupiter, Venus, and Saturn. Which ones do you recognize? What might have happened to the names of the other days?

Egypt and dates from about 1400 B.C., and the first evidence of an hourglass is from ancient Rome in about 300 B.C. Columbus used a sand clock to measure time on his voyage.[1] It was not until the 1700s that the mechanical watch (with springs) was both accurate enough and inexpensive enough to be used outside of scientific experiments. The present definition of a second is the duration of 9,192,631,770 periods of the cesium-133 atom![2] Believe it or not, there are actually machines that can count these periods. The ability to accurately measure time intervals of one-millionth of a second is crucial in fields like particle physics.

Length The history of the various units that different peoples have selected to measure length (see Figure 10.1) is quite fascinating, even to those who are not "math people."

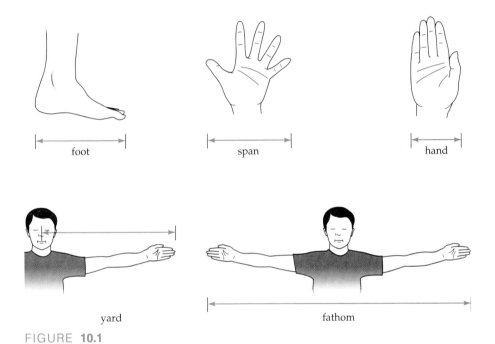

FIGURE **10.1**

The earliest recorded linear unit of measurement was the cubit, the distance from the point of the elbow to the outstretched tip of the middle finger. The word *cubit* is derived from the Latin *cubitum*, meaning "elbow."

CHILDREN

Virtually all mathematics textbooks now have young children first measure lengths with nonstandard units. For example, they might ask students to find how long the desk is in terms of paper clips. Why do you think teachers are being encouraged to start with nonstandard units?

There are several reasons for doing this. First, it helps to keep the focus of the students' thinking on the attribute that is being measured and

learned. If you did Exploration 10.2, you may have seen this concept in action. For example, it is much simpler (conceptually) to line up and count paper clips than it is to line up and count units on a ruler. Second, the answers can be more understandable to the children—for example, the length of the soccer field in terms of footsteps or the number of body lengths of one student in the class.

---

[1] Daniel Boorstin, *The Discovers* (New York: Random House, 1983), p. 34.

[2] H. Arthur Klein, *The World of Measurements* (New York: Simon and Schuster, 1974), p. 163.

In the language of King Henry I (1496), the word for yard literally meant "stick." Thus our term *yardstick* is redundant. This is similar to speaking of the river that flows along the border between Texas and Mexico as the Rio Grande River. In Spanish, Rio Grande literally means "big river."

It should not be surprising that the foot was one of the units of measurement in ancient times. The Roman writer Plutarch stated that the foot was based on the actual length of Hercules' foot. It is likely that the French foot was originally the actual measurement of the length of King Charlemagne's foot.[3] In the tenth century, King Edgar I decreed that the yard would be the distance from the tip of *his* nose to the tip of the middle finger of *his* outstretched arm. The reason behind the decree was a desire to regulate trade in textiles, so that one yard of cloth would be approximately the same in all parts of England.

The Romans divided 1 foot into 12 units (*unciae*, from which our word *inch* comes). The Roman pace consisted of 5 feet—that is, the distance of a left step and a right step—and their mile (*milia passuum*) was 1,000 paces. Do you see a connection between their mile and our mile? When Alexander the Great conquered the known world, he had professional pacers to measure how far his army had traveled so that their maps would be accurate. These pacers were trained to make each step virtually the same length regardless of terrain: flat, uphill, or downhill.

Weight   Two ancient units for weight were the barleycorn and the seed of the carob plant (from which comes the word *carat* for the measure used to weigh gold and diamonds). Over the centuries, three different systems of weights evolved: the avoirdupois system for everyday use, the troy system to weigh precious metals and gems, and the apothecaries' system for very small amounts. However, conversion was confusing. For example, in the troy system, there were 12 ounces in a pound, whereas in the avoirdupois system, there were 16 ounces in a pound!

Volume and capacity   Over time, two related systems of measure for what we call volume evolved, depending on whether the thing being measured was dry or wet. For dry volume, some basic units were the ounce, pint, quart, peck, and bushel. For liquid volume, there were a host of units. Thomas Jefferson almost certainly memorized the following ditty, which was commonly used in the eighteenth century to teach schoolchildren the units:

> Two mouthfuls are a jigger; two jiggers are a jack; two jacks are a jill; two jills are a cup; two cups are a pint; two pints are a quart; two quarts are a pottle; two pottles are a gallon; two gallons are a pail; two pails are a peck; two pecks are a bushel; two bushels are a strike; two strikes are a coomb; two coombs are a cask; two casks are a barrel; two barrels are a hogshead; two hogsheads are a pipe; two pipes are a tun—and there my story is done![4]

Which measures do you recognize?

The familiar nursery rhyme Jack and Jill was written as a protest against King Charles of England's taxation of jack(pots) of liquor. King Charles not only lost his crown, he lost his head! (He was beheaded.)

Temperature   In 1714, a German instrument maker named Gabriel Fahrenheit made the first mercury thermometer. He designated the lowest temperature he could create in the laboratory as 0° and the normal temperature of the body as 98°. On his scale, the freezing point of water is 32° and the boiling point of water is 212°.

Let us now examine the metric system, with an emphasis on understanding its structure.

---

[3] Terry A. Richardson, *A Guide to Metrics* (Ann Arbor, Mich.: Prakken Publications, 1978), p. 2.

[4] S. Carl Hirsch, *Meter Means Measure: The Story of the Metric System* (New York: Viking Press, 1973), p. 29.

The Metric System

The idea of a system of measures based on powers of 10, which is what the **metric system** is, was first proposed in 1670 by Gabriel Mouton, from Lyons, France. Over the next 100 years, many scientists and nonscientists made various proposals for a uniform system of measurement. Before the development of the metric system, there were literally hundreds of systems of measurement in Europe alone. What is particularly important is that they were not uniform, so that a bushel in one location was not the same as a bushel in another location. These differences were often used by the rich to exploit the poor, who obviously resented this. One of the first acts of the French government after the French Revolution in 1789 was to develop a uniform system of measurement so that the rich could not cheat the poor. In 1793, the French Academy of Sciences proposed a new metric system for *all* units of measurement.

The United States has not officially adopted the metric system, and its adoption is not imminent. (Our system is called the **U.S. customary system.**) However, metric units are finding their way into everyday life — for example, some gas stations sell gasoline by the liter, some road markers now give distances in kilometers as well as miles, and most soda is now sold by the liter. Furthermore, international travel is so common that many Americans encounter the metric system in their travels (even to Canada and Mexico), and most industries that compete in international markets have gone metric, since most of the rest of the world uses the metric system. Thus, it is helpful to have a rough idea of the metric system.

There is one feature of the metric system that it is helpful to know before we examine the different units. Once the French had determined the unit, whether it was meter, liter, or gram, they used Greek prefixes for *multiples* of this unit and Latin prefixes for *fractions* of this unit.

Several of these prefixes show up in familiar words; for example, a millennium is 1,000 years, a century is 100 years, and a decade is 10 years.

Table 10.1 shows the metric prefixes and their relationship to the basic metric units. Note that in everyday life, we rarely use *deci-*, *deca-*, or *hecto-*.

TABLE 10.1

Prefix	Milli	Centi	Deci	Deca	Hecto	Kilo
Relationship to the basic unit	1/1,000	1/100	1/10	10	100	1,000
Example	milliliter	centimeter				kilogram

Metric Length

The standard unit of length in the metric system is the **meter**, which was defined (most likely after much debate) as one ten-millionth of the length of the line that starts at the equator and goes to the North Pole through Barcelona, Paris, and Dunkirk. In other words, this distance was decreed to be 10 million meters, and the meter was the length that was one ten-millionth of that distance. How they decided upon 10 million and how they knew the exact distance to the North Pole is an interesting story in itself! The most commonly used metric units of length are, from largest to smallest, *kilometer, meter, centimeter,* and *millimeter*. Most yardsticks and rulers sold in the United States have inches and feet on one side and metric measurements on the other.

Becoming Comfortable with Metric Measurements

What if you heard that someone is 182 centimeters tall and weighs 80 kilo-grams? Most Americans can easily visualize 6 feet and 176 pounds, the U.S. customary equivalents of the metric measures given in the first sentence, but are less comfortable with measurements given in metric units. We will address this need by providing some reference measures and conversion ratios.

The diagrams in Figure 10.2 give approximations for a meter, a centimeter, and a millimeter.

1 m   1 cm   1 mm

FIGURE **10.2**

Some common conversion ratios are 1 meter ≈ 39 inches, 1 mile ≈ 1.6 kilo-meters, and 1 inch ≈ 2.5 centimeters.

I N V E S T I G A T I O N **10.1** Developing Metric Sense

Try to do these problems yourself. Then read on. . . .

A. Insert the decimal point in the proper place.

■ The diameter of a penny is 19 centimeters.

■ The length of a page of notebook paper is 279 centimeters.

■ The common adult height of an elephant is about 39 meters.

B. If the speed limit says 90 kilometers per hour, what is the speed in miles per hour?

DISCUSSION

A. The diameter of a penny is 1.9 centimeters.

■ The length of a page of notebook paper is 27.9 centimeters.

■ The common adult height of an elephant is about 3.9 meters.

B. We can use dimensional analysis (introduced in Chapter 1 and discussed in Chapter 5) to convert this speed to miles per hour. We can also use rea-soning to deduce that we need to divide 90 by 1.6.

$$\frac{90 \text{ kilometers}}{\text{hour}} \times \frac{1 \text{ mile}}{1.6 \text{ kilometers}} \approx \frac{56 \text{ miles}}{\text{hour}}$$

Metric Volume

The metric system was designed so that we use the same units to measure vol-ume (dry) and capacity (liquid). The standard metric unit for volume is the

1 cubic
centimeter (cm³)

1 liter equals

FIGURE **10.3**

liter. A liter is approximately 34 ounces, or slightly more than a quart. The liter is also defined to be the volume of a cube whose sides are 10 centimeters. Thus, 1 liter is equivalent to 1,000 cubic centimeters, abbreviated as cm^3 (see Figure 10.3).

However, a milliliter is also 1/1,000th of a liter. Therefore, we have the equivalence between liquid and dry measures: $1 \ cm^3 = 1$ ml. Most canned goods give the amount in milliliters. If a can contains 240 ml, how many liters is that? Do this before reading on. . . .

Since there are 1,000 ml in a liter, we must divide by 1,000. Therefore, 240 ml = 0.24 liter, about one-fourth of a liter.

The creators of the metric system not only worked to connect liquid and dry measures, they also connected volume and mass. They defined a kilogram to be the mass of one liter of pure water at a certain temperature.

Metric Mass

The standard of mass in the metric system is the **gram.** Technically, mass and weight refer to different attributes. **Weight** refers to the force that gravity exerts on an object, and **mass** refers to the amount of matter that makes up the object. If you went to the moon, you would weigh about one-sixth as much as you do on Earth, but your mass would be the same. Because the Earth is much larger than the moon, the force of gravity on your body is much greater on Earth. You may recall hearing that because the force of gravity is less on the moon, we could jump six times as high on the moon as we can on the Earth.

Some metric units of mass — kilogram, gram, and microgram — are encountered more often than others. One kilogram is approximately equal to 2.2 pounds. Where do you see metric mass in everyday life in the United States? Think before reading on. . . .

The net weight on most canned goods is generally given in both ounces and grams. This is one of the few places where one might see metric units for mass used in the United States at present. Some scales also have weights in metric units.

Metric Temperature

FIGURE **10.4**

In 1742, a Swedish astronomer named Anders Celsius proposed a modification in the units of measurement that the Fahrenheit system used. He proposed that the reference points be the freezing point of water (0°) and the boiling point of water (100°) (see Figure 10.4). This *Celsius* system was also called the *centigrade* system (that is, 100 grades).

Time and Angles

As mentioned earlier, the French Academy of Sciences recommended that *all* known measures be based on powers of 10. Thus, they recommended changing the calendar so that there would be 10 months in a year, 10 days in a week, and 10 hours in a day. They also proposed that there be 400 degrees in a circle, which would mean that a right angle had 100 degrees. As you know, not all of these proposals survived! When Napoleon came to power, he repealed the law making metric measure compulsory. Although the French continued to use metric units for length, volume, and weight, they (happily) threw out the metric system for time and returned to the more familiar 7-day week, 24-hour day, 60-minute hour, and 60-second minute.

Measurement of Other Quantities

The quantities that we have examined in this section—length, volume, mass, time, and temperature—represent only a small subset of the quantities measured in our world. What other things do we measure? Why do we need to measure them? What are some of the units used to measure those things? What instruments are used? Think about things that we measure and make a table like Table 10.2 for those things you can think of. Do this before reading on. . . . 📖

TABLE 10.2

What do we measure?	Why?	Units	Instruments
Noise	To study noise levels that can cause hearing damage	Decibels	Audiometer

The following is only a partial list: speed (miles per hour), fuel consumption (miles per gallon), light intensity (candela), electric current (amperes), efficiency (production per unit of time), density (amount per unit volume), and infant mortality (deaths per 1,000 live births).

Precision

There is another aspect of measurement that requires some attention. Virtually all measurements are approximations. For example, if you ask for the dimensions of a room, you might be told that it is 14 feet by 11 feet. If you ask for more accuracy—let's say you are buying a rug—you might be told that it is 14 feet 2 inches by 10 feet 11 inches.

The precision of our measurement depends on the reason we are measuring. Sometimes we want to measure amounts with much precision, and sometimes less precision is quite acceptable. For example, when selling cloth, clerks generally measure the length roughly and then add an extra couple of inches. However, if you go to a candy store or buy meat, the amount is generally weighed to the nearest tenth of an ounce, and cylinders in cars need to be accurate to the nearest thousandth of an inch. See also Explorations 10.1, 10.2, and 10.3.

Though many people use the words **precise** and **accurate** synonymously, the two concepts are not identical. A measurement can be very precise (for example, 34.628 meters) but be inaccurate (if the measurer made a mistake). Similarly, a measurement can be not very precise (for example, $16\frac{1}{2}$ feet) but be very accurate (that is, the actual distance is closer to $16\frac{1}{2}$ feet than to 16 feet or 17 feet).

Greatest possible error We can quantify the amount of precision in our measurement, and we use two terms to do so. First, we can determine the **greatest possible error (GPE)**. If you were to measure the width of a sheet of paper to the nearest millimeter, what would you get? Do so before reading on if you have a ruler close at hand. . . . 📖

It is 21.6 centimeters or 216 millimeters. That is, my reporting of 216 millimeters means that I believe the true width is closer to 216 millimeters than to

215 millimeters or 217 millimeters. What do you think the greatest possible error would be in this case? That is, if someone were to measure the width of the paper to the nearest hundredth of a centimeter, what would be the biggest difference between my measurement and the most precise measurement? Think and then read on. . . . 🖎

The greatest possible error would be 0.5 millimeter—that is, one-half the unit that I used to measure.

Relative error The relative error tells us the percent error of the greatest possible error. The following example illustrates this concept. A measurement of 300 centimeters and a measurement of 3 centimeters both have the same greatest possible error, 0.5 centimeter, but 0.5 centimeter is a much bigger part of 3 centimeters than it is of 300 centimeters. What is the relative error in these two cases (3 centimeters and 300 centimeters)? Do this before reading on. . . . 🖎

The relative error in the former case is

$$\frac{0.5 \text{ centimeter}}{3 \text{ centimeters}} \times 100 = 17\%$$

The relative error in the latter case is

$$\frac{0.5 \text{ centimeter}}{300 \text{ centimeters}} \times 100 = 0.2\%$$

Measurement as a Function

At a very basic level, measuring tells how much of something there is. From another perspective, measurement is the act of assigning numbers to amounts. The number refers to a specified unit. Do you realize that the operation of measuring an amount is a function? If you do, describe how it fits. If not, go back and review the discussion of functions in Chapter 2, then write your thoughts before reading on. . . . 🖎

In order for an operation to qualify as a function, each element of the input set must be mapped onto exactly one element of the output set. As we found in Chapter 2, the two sets need not be sets of numbers. When we measure, we take the amount to be measured (the input element) and determine the number that corresponds to that amount. Though you need not know that measuring represents a functional relationship between two sets, this is simply one more example of the underlying connectedness and relatedness of so many seemingly different mathematical ideas and topics.

Summary

In this section, we have explored what it means to measure an object, and we have realized that many objects have several attributes that can be measured—for example, weight, surface area, and volume. We have also examined where many of the units came from, both U.S. customary and metric. We have noted that many, if not most, of the numbers we use represent measurements. We have learned that most measurements are approximations and that there is a difference between precision and accuracy. Finally, we considered measurement from a functional perspective.

EXERCISES 10.1

1. Select the unit below that you would use to express the following. Briefly explain your choice.

   Length: millimeters, centimeters, meters, kilometers
   Volume: milliliters, liters
   Mass: milligrams, grams, kilograms

   a. Your height
   b. Your weight
   c. The length of a butterfly
   d. How much fluid there is in a drinking cup
   e. The mass of a fingernail
   f. The volume of a thimble

2. Fill in the blanks:

   a. 500 m = ____ km
   b. 4.5 cm = ____ mm
   c. 670 mL = ____ L
   d. 3.6 L = ____ mL
   e. 450 g = ____ kg
   f. 35 kg = ____ g
   g. 24 mg = ____ g

3. There are about 5 billion people on earth. If they all lined up and held hands, how long a line would they form?

4. The lengths of most older U.S. swimming pools are multiples of yards, generally 25 yards. However, newer pools are 25 or 50 meters long. Suppose an American swimmer is practicing for a 400-meter race. Eight lengths of the pool is 400 yards, which is "close" to 400 meters. How close is it? That is, how much shorter is 400 yards than 400 meters? First, predict the amount, using only mental math. Explain how you got your prediction and how you did the operations in your head. Then determine the amount (to the nearest yard).

5. Alan and Bill are going to have a 400-meter race, but Alan gets a head start because he is slower. Their best times of the season are 75 seconds and 82 seconds. How much (distance) of a head start should Alan get?

6. Let's say your estimate of a length was 100 feet and the actual length was 105 feet. Clearly this would not be "as big" a difference as that between an estimate of 10 feet and an actual length of 15 feet, although both estimates were "off" by 5 feet. Compare the accuracy of the estimates in such a way that we can see from the language that the first estimate was much closer than the other.

7. To determine the relatinship between miles and kilometers, if we use the conversion 39.37 inches = 1 yard, we find that 1 kilometer is approximately equal to 0.62 mile. What if we use the conversion 2.54 centimeters = 1 inch? How far apart are the answers (1 kilometer = x miles) using the different conversions?

8. When examining the relationship between kilometers and miles, we now have two conversion formulas:

1 kilometer = 0.62 mile and 1 mile = 1.6 kilometers. What relationship do 0.62 and 1.6 have?

9. The Biblical Goliath was said to be six cubits and one span tall (1 Samuel 17:4). How tall do you think he was in feet and inches? Explain both your reasoning and your calculations.

10. Suppose you were King Henry I (1496), who declared that from henceforth, one yard would be equal to the distance from his nose to his forefinger. How long would a yard be, based on your body?

11. The table below compares the relative lengths of one foot in various countries in 1788.

A Comparison of the American foot with the feet of other Countries.		
The American foot being divided into 1000 parts, or into 12 inches, the feet of several other Countries will be as follow.		
	Parts	*Inch.lin.points*
America	— 1000	— — — 12 0 0 *dec.*
London	— 1000	— — — 12 0 0
Antwerp	— 946	— — — 11 4 1, 32
Bologna	— 1204	— — — 14 5 2, 25
Bremen	— 964	— — — 11 6 4, 89
Cologne	— 954	— — — 11 5 2, 25
Copenhagen	— 965	— — — 11 6 5, 76
PIKE'S "ARITHMETICK," 1788 Early difficulties with weights and measures.		

Source: Louis Karpinski, *The History of Arithmetic* (New York: Russel & Russel, Inc., 1965), p. 159. Reprinted with permission of Scribner, a Division of Simon & Schuster

   a. Explain the meaning of the column entitled "Parts," as if you were talking to a fifth grader who didn't understand.
   b. Make a graph for the column entitled "Parts."
   c. Describe the variation among the various feet.
   d. What do you think the second column means?
   e. Are the numbers in the two columns proportional? How did you determine your answer to this question?

12. If the United States did go metric:

   a. What would you propose as the size of a standard sheet of paper? Justify your choice.
   b. What would you propose as the two standard sizes for soft drinks to replace 12 ounces and 16 ounces?
   c. Instead of buying a pound of butter, what would we buy?

13. If you filled up your car's gas tank and it took 48.3 liters, approximately how many gallons is that?

   a. Use mental math and estimation to determine approximately how many gallons of gas this amount is equivalent to.

b. By how much would your conversion be off if you used 1 liter ≈ 1 quart instead of the more precise 1 liter ≈ 34 ounces conversion?

14. The average human heart pumps about 60 milliliters of blood for each beat.

    a. About how many liters of blood does your heart pump each day?

    b. Do you think a reasonable degree of precision for this question would be to report the answer to the nearest 100 liters, 10 liters, 1 liter, or 1 milliliter? Explain your reasoning.

    c. About how many gallons is this?

15. Suppose we measured the passage of time during the day as the Babylonians did. Compare the length of a daytime hour on the longest day of the year to the length of a daytime hour on the shortest day of the year where you live. Part of this question has to do with resourcefulness, an important trait for teachers to develop—where can you go to get the information needed to answer this question?

16. Which is greater, an increase of 5° Fahrenheit or an increase of 5° Celsius? Justify your answer.

17. A train is traveling 60 miles per hour and is about to enter a tunnel that is 1,200 feet long. How long will it take the train to completely pass through the tunnel? What additional information do you need in order to solve this problem?

18. **a.** One way to determine the speed of the current of a river is to measure how long it takes a leaf to pass under a bridge. For example, let's say it takes a leaf 9 seconds to pass under a bridge that is 35 feet wide. What is the speed of the current in miles per hour?

    b. How might we determine the speed of the current if we are in a boat?

19. Two cups are half full. Cup A holds coffee. Cup B holds milk. One teaspoon of coffee is taken from cup A to cup B. Then one teaspoon of the mixture is taken from cup B to cup A. The two cups now have the same amount of liquid. Is there more coffee in cup A than milk in cup B, the same amount of coffee in A as there is milk in B, or less coffee in A than milk in B? Explain your reasoning.

20. Let's say that a 12-ounce cup of coffee is 20 percent milk. If you add 6 ounces of coffee, what is the percentage of milk in the new mixture?

21. Let's say that train B goes 20 percent further than train A in 20 percent less time, and that train A's average speed is 60 miles per hour. What is train B's average speed?

22. **a.** Determine the following dimensions for your body: height, wrist, neck, leg, arm, foot.

    b. Determine the following ratios: height : foot, height : leg, neck : wrist, height : arm.

c. Before determining the ratios for the entire class, predict which will ratio have the most variation, and which the least variation. Explain your reasoning.

d. Gather the class data. Decide on a way to determine the variation and to compare the variation.

23. Will the ratio of the heights of an adult and a child be equivalent to the ratio of the lengths of their feet? If it will be, explain why you think so. If not, predict which ratio will be greater and why. Gather some data. Do the data support your predictions? Explain.

24. You will need a scale for these problems.

    a. Buy several bananas. Compare the price per pound that you paid and the price per pound of what you actually eat. If there are enough data, graph the actual price for the entire class. Before you do so, predict the shape of the distribution: normal, uniform, and so on.

    b. Do the same for peanuts.

    c. Buy several oranges of two types, one type with a thick skin and one type with a thin skin. Compare the ratios for both kinds of oranges.

25. Before they wash their faces, most people run the tap until the water is hot. How much water is wasted waiting for the water to get hot?

    a. With a partner, determine a plan for answering this question.

    b. Determine the amount of water (in U.S. customary units) wasted at the place you live.

    c. Describe the relative precision of your answer. For example, if you say 3 quarts, is your answer to the nearest quart?

    d. Graph the class data.

    e. Let's say the average for the United States is close to the average in this class and that 200 million people in the United States wash their faces every day. How many gallons of water are wasted?

26. You will need a dropper for this problem. Let's say you have a leaky faucet that drips every 6 seconds. How much water is wasted in one day? Explain the assumptions that you made and describe your solution path.

27. Take a sheet of blank paper. Tear it in half. Place one half on top of the other. Tear these two sheets in half. Place one half (two sheets) on top of the other. Assume for the purposes of this problem that you were able to continue this process for a total of 20 times. What would be the height of the stack of paper?

28. Select a trip in your part of the country for which there is not one obvious shortest way.

    a. Determine which way is shortest by using a map. Explain your work.

    b. Have at least one person try more than one way to determine the actual distance and the actual time it took in each case.

    c. Is the shorter way faster?

d. Describe the possible sources of error in part (a).

e. Determine the average speed for each route.

f. Based on the data you have, which way would you go, or do you need more data?

29. a. Measure your classroom in meters and then make a scale model of your classroom so that 1 centimeter on your model represents 1 meter.

b. Measure your classroom in feet and inches and then make a scale model of your classroom so that 1 inch on your model represents 1 foot.

c. Are the computations in both problems about the same, or are the computations for the metric-scale map easier? Explain.

30. In *The History of Arithmetic,* Louis Karpinski describes the Babylonian system of measure:

3 lines = 1 sossus

10 sossus = 1 palm

3 palms = 1 small ell (cubit)

5 palms = 1 large ell

6 large ells = 30 palms = 1 large seed

60 palms = 1 gar

60 gar = 1 ush

30 ush = 1 kask

The Babylonian palm was equal to approximately 4 of our inches.

a. Compare the Babylonian kask to a metric length.

b. Describe the connections between their choice of units and their numeration system.

c. The cubic palm (called a ka) was used as a unit of capacity. Compare the cubic palm to the liter.

d. The weight of one ka of water was the unit of weight and was called one mina. Thus, the units of length and weight were connected. In analyzing the Babylonian system, Louis Karpinski notes the parallels between the ancient Babylonian system and the modern metric system, noting that both systems established a connection between linear and cubic measure and a unit of weight. He further states that the parallel is "one of the most striking [parallels] to be found in the development of scientific ideas."[5] Explain Karpinski's praise for the Babylonian system as if you were talking to someone who is clueless.

31. Is the relation "the perimeter of" a function? Justify your answer.

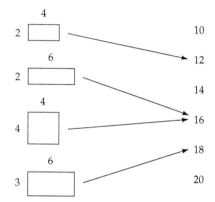

SECTION ◆ 10.2 **PERIMETER AND AREA**

WHAT DO YOU THINK?

▪ Can two shapes with different perimeters have the same area? Why or why not?

▪ Is the relationship between a surface and its area a function? Why or why not?

▪ What does pi mean?

In this section, we will investigate the concepts of perimeter and area, both for geometric figures for which there are formulas and for irregularly shaped objects. It may surprise you that many students do not understand these concepts well. For example, consider the data in Table 10.3 concerning questions reported in the *Results from the Fourth Mathematics Assessment.*[6]

TABLE 10.3

	PERCENT CORRECT	
Question	Grade 3	Grade 7
What is the perimeter of the rectangle below?	17	46

[6] Mary M. Lindquist ed., *Results from the Fourth Mathematics Assessment* (Reston, Va.: NCTM, 1989), p. 40.

| | PERCENT CORRECT | |
Question	Grade 3	Grade 7
What is the area of this rectangle?	20	56
What is the area of this rectangle?	5	46

The NCTM Standards stress that teachers should not just help students better understand how to perform the procedures for determining perimeters and areas. Rather, if the students develop these formulas through problem-solving and reasoning, if they are required to express their understanding in words also (not just in formulas), and if they can see connections among the formulas, *then* performance on these and more challenging problems will increase dramatically.

Perimeter

Let us begin first with the concept of **perimeter**, essentially the distance around an object. Many practical applications of perimeter involve surrounding an object — for example, fencing a yard or running a baseboard around the base of a room. We will first look at distances around circles.

Circumference and π

When we determine the distances around figures and objects, sometimes the path is not a straight line, but rather is a circle. You may remember a formula involving the distance around a circle, or the **circumference**, and that it involves π. You may have constructed a definition of π in Exploration 10.9. Before reading on, take a few moments to think about what π means. That is, the value of π is 3.14 (to two decimal places), but what does π *mean?* For example, where did the number 3.14 come from? How is this number related to the circumference or diameter or radius of a circle (not the formula, but a description of the relationship)? Write your thoughts before reading on. . . .

In one sense, π is a ratio — that is, π is the ratio of the circumference to the diameter of *any* circle. If we could precisely measure the circumference and diameter of any circle and then divide the circumference of the circle by its diameter, we would *always* get π. If we call the circumference C and the diameter d, we have $\pi = C/d$.

Thus, we have the formulas

$$C = \pi d \quad \text{and} \quad C = 2\pi r$$

FIGURE **10.5**

FIGURE **10.5**

In Figure 10.5, C is the center of the circle, $\overline{AC}$, $\overline{BC}$, and $\overline{DC}$ are radii (plural of radius), and $\overline{AD}$ is a diameter.

There is another way to think about π. Imagine placing a string around the circumference of the circle in Figure 10.5 and then straightening out that string. If the diameter of the circle is d, then the length of the string is $3.14d$. That is, if we unwrap the circumference, its length will always be 3.14 times the length of the diameter.

Let us now examine one application of these formulas.

INVESTIGATION **10.2**   **What Is the Length of the Arc?**

In Figure 10.6, the radius of the circle is 3 centimeters and the measure of angle BOC is 42 degrees. How long is arc BC? Think about this and then read on. . . .

FIGURE **10.6**

DISCUSSION

STRATEGY 1: Make a simpler problem

What if the angle had been 90 degrees? Can you solve that problem? Think before reading on. . . .

If the angle had been 90 degrees, then the arc would simply have been one-fourth of the circumference of the circle. Do you see why? Can you adapt this strategy to solve this problem now? Try to do so yourself before reading on. . . .

Since 42 does not divide 360 evenly, we don't have an easy fraction. However, we can multiply the circumference of the circle by 42/360.

STRATEGY 2: Use a proportion

We could also solve this problem using a proportion. Can you make the proportion? Try to do so before reading on. . . . 📝

Arc $\overset{\frown}{BC}$ is a fraction of the circumference of the circle. Similarly, 42 degrees is a fraction of 360 degrees, the number of degrees in a circle. From the ratio construct of fractions, these two ratios are equal. Why is this?

Since the circumference of the circle is πd, which equals 18.84 inches, we can set up the following proportion, since the two part:whole ratios are equal:

$$\frac{\text{arc } \overset{\frown}{BC}}{18.84 \text{ inches}} = \frac{42°}{360°}$$

When we solve the equation, we find that the length of arc BC is 2.2 inches.

Area

Earlier we stated that perimeter questions generally deal with "how much" it takes to surround or go around an object. In order to answer perimeter questions, we have to select an appropriate unit, and thus the answer takes the form of how many of those units. Area questions generally deal with "how much" it takes to *cover* an object — for example, how much fertilizer to cover a lawn, how much material to cover a bed. In order to answer area questions, we have to select an appropriate unit, and thus the answer takes the form of how many of those units. However, the units for perimeter and area are not the same. For example, if we have a 20-foot by 10-foot garden, we say that we need 60 feet of fence to surround the garden, but we would say that the area of the garden is 200 *square* feet. The need for units and the difference between units for perimeter, area, and volume are generally not well understood by students and therefore are worth emphasizing more than once.

Many people remember or recognize the basic formulas for determining areas, but few people understand why they work or where they came from. Let us investigate them for a bit. You may have encountered these ideas in Explorations 10.6 and 10.7. Understanding of this area will pay dividends when we attempt to solve more complex problems. The simplest case for area involves rectangles and squares.

Just as we have found that average is a number that gives us a sense of the middle of a set of data and standard deviation is a number that gives us a sense of the variation of a set of data, **area** is a number that gives us a sense of the size of something — for example, how much surface that object covers or how much material (cloth, plastic, paint, carpet) it would take to cover that surface. If the geometric figure is a square or a rectangle, we can easily determine the area by multiplying the *base* by the *height*.

Base and height Since most students use the more common terms "length" and "width," let us take a moment to examine what *base* and *height* mean, because they will become important when we investigate other figures for which the terms *length* and *width* are not appropriate.

Any polygon can be rotated so that its bottom side will be parallel to the bottom of the paper. Thus, any side can be taken as the **base** of the polygon. For example, we can rotate the triangle at the left in Figure 10.7 so that any one of its sides is the base. Which one we choose is generally an arbitrary decision. See Figure 10.7.

The height of a polygon is the distance from the side chosen as the base to the point furthest away, measured along a line perpendicular to the base. See Figure 10.7 for an illustration of this notion with triangles.

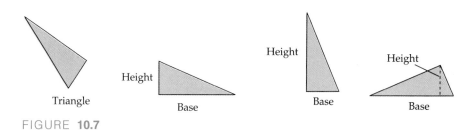

Triangle   Height   Base   Height   Base   Height   Base

FIGURE **10.7**

FIGURE **10.8**

Thinking about area by looking at rectangles Let us focus on some more subtle aspects of the concept of area.

What does it mean to say that one rectangle (or other figure) covers more area than another? Consider the diagrams in Figure 10.8 of two pieces of plastic sheeting that I use to cover two different woodpiles in my back yard. One piece is 10 feet by 3 feet, and the other is 6 feet by 5 feet.

When I ask young children if the sheets are the same size or if one is bigger, they generally say that the 10-foot by 3-foot sheet is bigger. Older children and adults know that the area of both sheets is equal, 30 square feet. We can demonstrate this by covering each figure with 30 squares, each of which is 1 foot by 1 foot (see Figure 10.9).

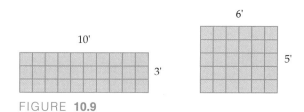

FIGURE **10.9**

Although this may seem very simple and straightforward, many people are at least initially stumped when they try to explain what *area* means when the dimensions of a rectangle are not whole numbers—for example, when a rectangle is 3.5 centimeters by 2.5 centimeters. We say that the area of the rectangle is 8.75 square centimeters, because we know that the area of a rectangle is obtained by multiplying its length by its width. Can you explain what that 8.75 means, as if you were talking to a child who understands that in the previous problem, both sheets of plastic have an area of 30 square feet? Do this before reading on. . . . 🖊

Figure 10.10 shows one way of explaining what it means to say that the area is 8.75 square centimeters: cutting up the rectangle and reassembling the pieces in a certain way. Do you understand this diagram? Did you explain the meaning of the 8.75 square centimeters in another way that also makes sense? Take some time to see if you can understand the diagrams below before you read my explanation. 🖊

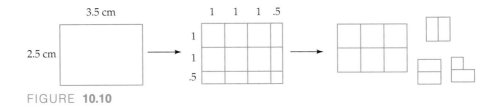

FIGURE **10.10**

We can partition the rectangle in a manner similar to the way we used partitioning in the multiplication of fractions and decimals. That is, we have 6 one-centimeter by one-centimeter squares, and we can combine the remaining pieces to make another 2.75 square centimeters (see Figure 10.10).

Area as a function   From another perspective, once we specify the unit of measurement the relationship between any surface and its area is a functional relationship: For every surface, there is a unique number that we associate with its area. Even when the surface is not a rectangle or the dimensions are not whole numbers, the number that represents the area tells us the equivalent number of square units that this object covers.

Let us now turn our attention to understanding some of the more commonly used formulas for determining the area.

Understanding the area formula for parallelograms   The formulas for many common figures are striking, both in their simplicity and in their connection to one another. It still surprises me that so few people understand why they work. The formula for determining the area of a parallelogram is connected to the formula for determining the area of a rectangle. The diagram at the right in Figure 10.11 illustrates the connection. Can you see it? How would you explain it?

FIGURE **10.11**

If we cut the triangle from the parallelogram and reconnect it at the right-hand side, we have transformed the parallelogram into a rectangle. Since we have not added or subtracted any area, the areas of the parallelogram and the rectangle must be equal. From Figure 10.11, you can see that the base of the parallelogram is congruent to the base of the rectangle and the height of the parallelogram is congruent to the height of the rectangle. Since we know that the areas of the two are equal, we can now state *the area of any parallelogram is equal to the product of its base and its height*; that is, $A = bh$ (see Figure 10.12).

FIGURE **10.12**

Understanding the area formula for triangles We will use what we have learned about parallelograms to develop the formula for the area of triangles. Just as we connected the area of any parallelogram to a rectangle, take a few minutes to see if you can adapt this idea to develop formulas for the areas of triangles. Then read on. . . .

Consider triangle *MAN* (see Figure 10.13). If we make a congruent copy of this triangle and move that triangle into place as shown (that is, by reflecting the original triangle two times), we form a parallelogram. Do you see how we can use the formula for parallelograms to determine the formula for triangles now? See if you can do it on your own before reading on. . . .

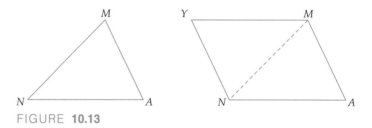

FIGURE **10.13**

The base of the parallelogram and the base of the triangle are identical, and so are the heights.

If the area of the parallelogram = base · height, then (since the area of the two triangles is equal to the area of the parallelogram), *the area of the triangle = $\frac{1}{2}$(base · height)*, or $A = \frac{1}{2}b \cdot h$.

Understanding the area formula for trapezoids Can you now apply what you have learned about the areas of these figures to determine the formula for the area of a trapezoid (see Figure 10.14)? Try to do so before reading on. . . .

FIGURE **10.14**

There are several ways to derive the formula for the area of a trapezoid. We will discuss two that connect to our preceding discussions. First, we can draw a diagonal of the trapezoid, which cuts (decomposes) it into two triangles. We know how to find the areas of these triangles: The areas are $\frac{1}{2}ah$ and $\frac{1}{2}bh$. Since the sum of the areas of the two triangles is equal to the area of the trapezoid, *the area A of the trapezoid is $\frac{1}{2}ah + \frac{1}{2}bh$, or $A = \frac{1}{2}(a + b)h$.* See Figure 10.15.

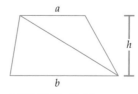

FIGURE **10.15**

Figure 10.16 shows another method for finding the area of a trapezoid. If we construct a congruent trapezoid and connect it (via a translation and a rotation) to the original trapezoid, we have a parallelogram, and the area of the parallelogram is equal to the product of its base and its height; that is, the area is equal to $(a + b)h$. Since the area of the trapezoid is equal to one-half the area of this parallelogram, the area of the trapezoid $= \frac{1}{2}(a + b)h$.

FIGURE **10.16**

Pythagorean Theorem

As we saw in Chapter 8, the relationship between the lengths of the sides of a right triangle was known long before it was proved by Pythagoras. That is, Pythagoras proved that *for any right triangle, the sum of the squares of the lengths of the two sides (say, a and b) is equal to the square of the length of the hypotenuse (say, c)*; that is, $a^2 + b^2 = c^2$ [see Figure 10.17(a)].

It is important to note that for the Greeks, this was not an algebraic relationship, but rather a geometric relationship [see Figure 10.17(b)]. That is, if you make a square whose sides are congruent to the length of side a, a square whose sides are congruent to the length of side b, and a square whose sides are congruent to the length of the hypotenuse c, then the sum of the areas of the two smaller squares will be equal to the area of the larger square.

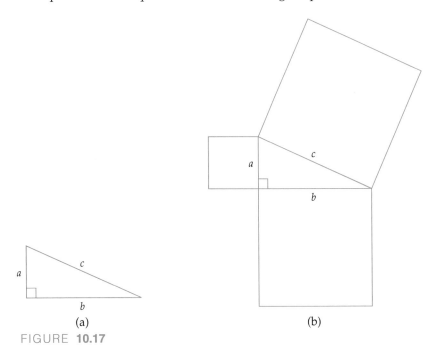

(a)   (b)

FIGURE **10.17**

At the last count, there were over 370 different proofs of the Pythagorean theorem, including one by one of our own presidents, James Garfield. The Pythagorean theorem has many practical applications, such as the one below, where it is used to determine the length of something that we cannot measure directly. The need for the Pythagorean theorem arises both in determining lengths of lines and in determining areas.

INVESTIGATION **10.3** Using the Pythagorean Theorem

We can use the Pythagorean theorem to determine the length of a lake. In Figure 10.18, a right triangle has been created in such a way that the length of the lake is part of the length of one side of the triangle. The lengths of *AB*, *BC*, and *CD* have been measured, since they are on land. The triangle has been carefully made so that all lines are straight lines, so that point *D* lies on side *AC*, and so that angle *C* is 90 degrees. What is the length of the lake? Work on this before reading on. . . .

FIGURE **10.18**

DISCUSSION
Let us discuss two different strategies and then discuss problem-solving.

STRATEGY 1
Let x be the length of the pond. Using the Pythagorean theorem, we have

$$(x + 45)^2 + 30^2 = 92^2$$

We now have a quadratic equation, which we can solve using the *quadratic formula*:

$$x^2 + 90x + 2{,}025 + 900 = 8{,}464$$
$$x^2 + 90x - 5{,}539 = 0$$
$$x \approx 42 \text{ feet}$$

STRATEGY 2
Looking at the problem from a different perspective, we can find the length of the base of the triangle ($\overline{AC}$) rather easily, and then we can subtract 45 feet from the base to find the length of the lake.

$$AC^2 + BC^2 = AB^2$$
$$AC^2 + 900 = 8{,}484$$
$$AC^2 = 7{,}584$$
$$AC \approx 87 \text{ feet (to the nearest whole foot)}$$

Thus, $AD \approx 42$ feet (87−45).

This investigation illustrates the idea of examining a problem from different perspectives. The second solution is quicker and simpler, although the first

MATHEMATICS

The *quadratic formula*, which you may remember from algebra, lets you solve an equation of the form

$$ax^2 + bx + c = 0$$

that is, a quadratic equation. The formula is

$$x = \frac{-b \pm \sqrt{(b^2 - 4ac)}}{2a}$$

solution is not difficult for someone who is adept at algebra. Often in mathematics problems (and in real-world problems too), a problem that at first glance seems very complex and difficult may, when looked at from another perspective, be much simpler than it first appeared.

I N V E S T I G A T I O N **10.4** **Understanding the Area Formula for Circles**

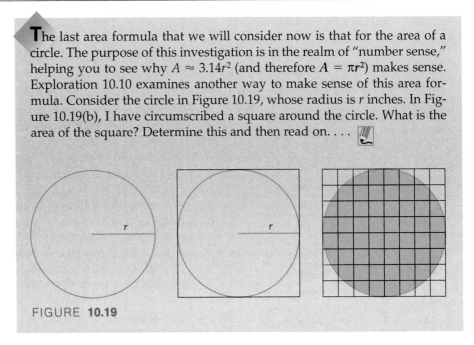

The last area formula that we will consider now is that for the area of a circle. The purpose of this investigation is in the realm of "number sense," helping you to see why $A \approx 3.14r^2$ (and therefore $A = \pi r^2$) makes sense. Exploration 10.10 examines another way to make sense of this area formula. Consider the circle in Figure 10.19, whose radius is r inches. In Figure 10.19(b), I have circumscribed a square around the circle. What is the area of the square? Determine this and then read on. . . .

FIGURE **10.19**

DISCUSSION

If the radius of the circle is r inches, then the length of each side of the square is $2r$, and thus the area of the square is $(2r)(2r) = 4r^2$.

The area of the circle thus is clearly less than 4 times r^2. We can use our spatial sense to estimate that the circle covers about 3/4 as much space as the square and thus approximate the area of the circle as $3r$, or we can place a grid over the figure and determine what proportion of the square is covered by the circle. In this case, we get a more accurate estimate of the area of the circle [see Figure 10.19(c)].

HISTORY

Some of the area formulas we have investigated were known by the Egyptians, Babylonians, Chinese, and other peoples thousands of years ago. We know that both the Egyptians and the Babylonians knew not only the formulas for the area of the square and the rectangle, but also the formula for the area of a trapezoid. They knew the formula for finding the area of a right triangle. There were correct and incorrect formulas for the areas of isosceles triangles. For example, there is an example in the Rhind papyrus (from ancient Egypt) of finding the area of an isosceles triangle by finding half the product of the base and the length of one of the equal sides, instead of the altitude. For the circle, the Babylonians developed the formula $A = C^2/12$ and the Egyptians developed the formula $A = (\frac{8}{9}d)^2$. It will be left as an exercise to see how close their formulas were to the actual formula.

INVESTIGATION **10.5** **A 16-Inch Pizza Versus an 8-Inch Pizza**

Let's say you are going out to have pizza with several friends. You are thinking of getting one large pizza—let's say its diameter is 16 inches. However, some people are vegetarians, and so you decide to get two little pizzas, each of which is 8 inches in diameter. Suddenly someone asks, "Are we getting the same amount of pizza if we get two little pizzas instead of one large one?" What do you think? Please work on this before reading on. . . .

DISCUSSION

This is generally one of the most amazing investigations in this book because so many people are so surprised. To determine the area, we can use the area formulas: If the large pizza has a diameter of 16 inches, it has a radius of 8 inches. Therefore its area is $\pi(8)^2 = 64\pi \approx 201$ square inches.

If the small pizza has a diameter of 8 inches, it has a radius of 4 inches.

Therefore, its area is $\pi(4)^2 = 16\pi$. Therefore, the area of two small pizzas is 32π, or approximately 100.5 square inches.

Amazing, isn't it? Not only are two 8-inch pizzas not equal to one 16-inch pizza, but it takes *four* 8-inch pizzas to have the same area as *one* 16-inch pizza. Some people still don't believe their eyes. If you find this result amazing, draw a circle to represent the large pizza and then figure out how to place the two smaller pizzas inside the circle.

INVESTIGATION **10.6** **How Big Is the Footprint?**

The area of most objects cannot be determined by a formula. For example, biologists and environmentalists want to know the total surface area of the leaves of a tree in order to determine the amount of oxygen the tree produces. What if we wanted to measure the area of another irregularly shaped object, like the footprint in Figure 10.20?

Take some time to think about how you might determine the area and to try out your ideas. Then read on. . . .

FIGURE **10.20**

DISCUSSION

There are many, many possible strategies. Several are briefly described below.

STRATEGY 1: Use graph paper

This is one of the simpler strategies. There are two issues worth pursuing: (1) what to do with the partially filled squares, and (2) the advantages and disadvantages of graph paper with smaller squares.

STRATEGY 2: Draw rectangles and triangles

We can partition the footprint into rectangles and triangles. One advantage of this over the previous strategy is that in this case, one rectangle will account for a large portion of the print. One disadvantage is that there is room for error, depending on how the rectangles and triangles are made. This procedure could also become a bit tedious.

STRATEGY 3: Draw trapezoids

We can partition the footprint into trapezoids. This strategy arises from the realization that trapezoids are easily broken into rectangles and triangles; also, this method involves less computation than the previous method. I can approximate the area of the footprint with four trapezoids.

STRATEGY 4: Find the perimeter

We can trace the figure with string to get the perimeter of the print, then make a rectangle with the string and compute the area of the rectangle. There is a flaw in the reasoning behind this strategy. If you do not see this flaw, revisit this problem after doing the next investigation.

STRATEGY 5: Weigh it

We can trace this print onto a piece of thick posterboard and cut it out. We can then cut out another piece of posterboard in the shape of a rectangle. The ratio of the area of the footprint to the area of the rectangle will be equal to the ratio of the weight of the footprint to the weight of the rectangle. Therefore, we can use the following proportion:

$$\frac{\text{Area of footprint}}{\text{Area of rectangle}} = \frac{\text{weight of footprint}}{\text{weight of rectangle}}$$

INVESTIGATION 10.7   Making a Fence with Maximum Area

Joshua has decided to convert part of his back yard into a garden. He knows from his neighbor's experience that he needs to fence in the garden to keep the animals out. At the hardware store, he buys 200 feet of chicken wire. After he gets home and unrolls the wire, he finds to his surprise that there are many different size gardens that he can make with 200 feet of fencing. He decides that he wants to get the largest garden from 200 feet of fencing. If he wants a garden that is rectangular in shape, what are the dimensions of that garden? Work on this before reading on. . . .

DISCUSSION

STRATEGY 1: Use guess−check−revise

TABLE 10.4

Length	Width	Area	Reasoning
80 feet	20 feet	1,600 square feet	If the perimeter is 200, then $l + w = 100$.
			Reduce the length by 10 and increase the width by 10.
70 feet	30 feet	2,100 square feet	This has more area, so reduce the length by 10 and increase the width by 10.
60 feet	40 feet	2,400 square feet	This has more area, so reduce the length by 10 and increase the width by 10.
50 feet	50 feet	2,500 square feet	Why does this feel like it "should" be the biggest garden?

FIGURE **10.21**

STRATEGY 2: Reason and make a model

A very tactile way to "feel" this investigation is to cut a piece of string and tie the ends together. Now, using your two thumbs and two forefingers, make as skinny a rectangle as you can (see Figure 10.21).

Now slowly move your thumbs and forefingers apart—that is, decrease the length and increase the width. What seems to be happening to the area? Why must it stop increasing when the length and width are equal?

STRATEGY 3: Be creative and adventurous

What if we made the garden in the shape of a circle? Do this before reading on. . . .

Since the circumference of the circle is 200 feet, the radius of the circle will be $r = C/2\pi \approx 200/(2 \cdot 3.14) = 31.8$ feet. Now that we know the radius, we can find the area:

$$A = \pi r^2 \approx 3.14(31.8)^2 = 3,175 \text{ square feet}$$

Compare the area of the circular garden to that of the square garden: The former shape will give Joshua more than 25 percent more area.

Summary

In this section, we examined some measurement ideas and procedures related to perimeter and area. In one sense, perimeter concerns how much is needed to surround an object, and area refers to how much is needed to cover an object. We have learned that π can be viewed both as how many times a diameter can wrap around a circle and as the ratio between a circle's circumference and its diameter. We have explored area formulas (and why they work) for triangles, for certain quadrilaterals, and for circles. We have explored the Pythagorean theorem and an application of this theorem in problem-solving. We have moved beyond more routine applications of perimeter and area to examine how areas of irregularly shaped figures are determined. Finally, we have found that the relationship between perimeter and area is not a simple one. For example, if we double the area of a square, we do not double its perimeter. Similarly, two objects can have the same perimeter and different areas, and two objects can have the same area but different perimeters.

EXERCISES 10.2

1. Determine the perimeter and area of the figures below.

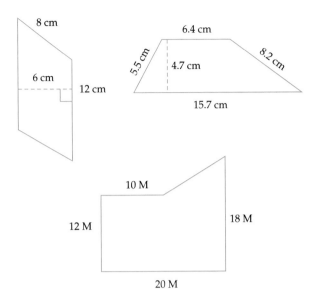

2. Determine the area of each figure below in two different ways.

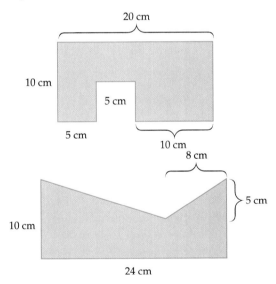

3. Bernice wants to seed her large back yard with grass. Her back yard is in the shape of a rectangle with dimen-sions 120 feet by 80 feet. The seed costs $3.99 for a 1-pound bag, and each bag covers up to 1050 square feet. How much will the seed cost?

4. Kayla wants to spread bark mulch to make a uniform border around a 6-foot by 10-foot shed. She figures that she has enough mulch to cover 40 square feet. How wide should the border be?

5. Let's say a teacher at your school recently bought a bag of fertilizer for her lawn. The directions say that 1 bag will cover 5,000 square feet. The dimensions of her lot are 110 feet by 70 feet. The dimensions of her house (including garage) are 45 feet by 30 feet. The driveway is 17 by 9 feet. The circular garden has a diameter of 15 feet. Did she buy enough fertilizer?

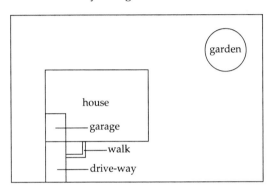

6. A farmer has a fence that encloses a square plot with an area of 36 square meters. If the farmer uses this fence to enclose a circular flower garden, what will the area of the garden be?

7. Let's say we have a square whose sides each measure 10 inches. Determine to two decimal places the dimensions of the square that has twice the area of this square.

8. How many 2-inch by 3-inch by 8-inch bricks will you need to build a (uniformly wide) brick walk with the shape shown in the figure below? (Lay the bricks so that the largest face is up.)

9. Find the area of the triangles below, using a ruler to measure the appropriate lengths.

a.   **b.**

10. Find the length of the base of the right triangle *x* to the nearest tenth of a unit, using the Pythagorean theorem and guess–test–revise. You may not use the square root key on the calculator.

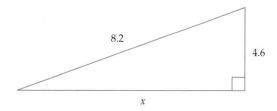

11. A Little Leaguer asks her mother to make her a home plate for a sandlot baseball game. According to her encyclopedia, an official plate is made from a square by making two 12-inch cuts as shown below. What is the length of the side of the original square?

12. How many right triangles with sides 3 inches and 6 inches can be cut from a sheet of paper that is 18 inches by 40 inches?

13. What percent of the quilt square below is gray?

14. The directions on a treasure hunt state: Go 20 feet north, then 30 feet east, then 12 feet north, then 15 feet west, and finally 50 feet north. Let's say you were able to walk directly from the beginning point to the treasure.

    a. Determine how far you would have walked.

    b. This distance is ____ % less than the distance given by the directions.

    c. If you were giving the directions for this shorter distance and the reader had a compass, what direction would you tell the reader to walk?

15. An equilateral triangle whose area was 100 square centimeters was reflected to make a congruent equilateral triangle so that the six smaller triangles are all congruent.

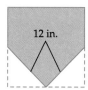

    a. What is the area of each of the little triangles?

b. What is the area of the hexagon in the middle?

16. The steps to the entrance of the school are 40 inches high. The school has decided to make the building wheelchair-accessible. If a city ordinance states that the ramp cannot be steeper than 5°, how long must the ramp be? Solve this without using trigonometry.

17. Some people have an intuitive sense of whether things will fit or not. For example, let's say you have bought a circular table top with a diameter of 7 feet and a thickness of 3 inches, and your doorway is 78 inches by 30 inches. First, predict whether or not the table top will fit. Then determine whether or not it will fit.

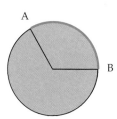

18. Determine the length of the arc $\overset{\frown}{AB}$ if the diameter of the circle is 10 feet and the angle is 128 degrees.

19. If each of the circles has a diameter of 10 meters, what is the area of the region inside the four circles?

20. The figure below is a common representation of the famous yin-yang relationship, which originated in China.

    a. Can you explain how the figure is made?

    b. If the radius of the circle is *r*, what is the length of the curved line in the interior of the circle that separates the white region from the black region?

21. A circular flower bed is 6 meters in diameter and has a circular sidewalk 1 meter wide around it. Find the area of the sidewalk in square meters.

22. Sixteen circles (of equal area) are cut out of a square sheet of tin whose sides are 40 centimeters. What is the area of wasted tin if the circles are made as large as possible?

23. Compare the Babylonian formula for the area of the circle, $A = C^2/12$, and the Egyptian formula, $A = (\frac{8}{9}d)^2$. Which is more accurate? Justify your choice.

24. If possible, determine the perimeter of the figures below. If there is not enough information, explain why.

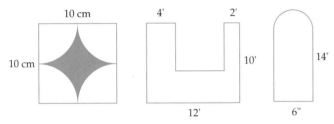

25. If possible, determine the area of the figures below. If there is not enough information, explain why.

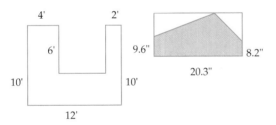

Regular hexagon;
each side is 6cm

26. For each of the problems below, if there is not enough information given for there to be exactly one answer, explain why and provide one more piece of information that would enable us to determine the solution. If there is enough information, solve the problem.

   a. The hypotenuse of a right isosceles triangle is 10 inches. Find the area.

   b. The perimeter of one rectangle is twice the perimeter of another rectangle. The dimensions of the rectangle with the bigger perimeter are 8 inches by 6 inches. Find the dimensions of the smaller rectangle.

   c. The area of a rectangle is 20 centimeters. Find its perimeter.

   d. A farmer is fencing his pasture. The fence posts will be 10 feet apart. The pasture is in the shape of a rectangle whose length is double its width. The farmer needs 54 fence posts. What are the dimensions of the pasture?

27. In Investigation 10.6, we discussed several strategies for finding the area of irregularly shaped figures. Describe a situation for which one of the strategies would be preferable to the others. Make a convincing argument that the particular strategy would indeed be more practical and/or more accurate.

28. Describe how you would find the surface area of the top of each of the following:

29. Make a photocopy of a map of your state and determine the area of your state.

   a. Show and explain your work.

   b. Justify the precision in your answer—for example, the choice of unit and the number of decimal places, if any.

   c. Describe and explain your degree of confidence in your result.

   d. Describe any difficulties you had and how you overcame them.

30. Anne used a grid to determine the area of an irregularly shaped figure, and she determined that the area was 23 square centimeters. Then she realized that she wanted square inches. How can she convert from square centimeters to square inches? There are 2.5 centimeters in 1 inch.

31. Adam is also confused. He wonders why, if you take a rectangle and multiply the length of each side by 1.5, the area of the new rectangle isn't 1.5 times as big as the area of the old rectangle. How would you explain this to him?

32. If a circle has a radius of 5 inches, using the formula, we would say that the area of the circle is approximately 78.5 square inches. A fellow student has come to you and asked, why do we use *square inches* to represent the area of the circle? What does 78.5 square inches mean?

33. a. Suppose a goat was tethered at the middle of a 100-foot-long fence and the length of the rope was 50 feet, as shown in the diagram below. Over how much area could the goat graze? Describe any assumptions you make in order to solve the problem.

   b. What if the point at which the goat was tethered was at the middle of a 50-foot-long fence, as shown in the diagram below? Over how much area could the goat graze? Describe any assumptions you make in order to solve the problem.

50'

Rope

34. Find the length of *x*, to the nearest tenth of a foot. *Note: The figure is not drawn to scale.*

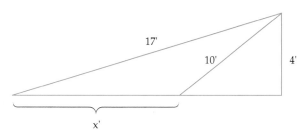

17'

10'

4'

x'

35. Around 240 B.C., Eratosthenes, a Greek mathematician, estimated the circumference of the Earth. His estimate was off by only 1 percent! Let us see what he did. He knew that on a certain day, the sun would be directly overhead at a town called Syene (now called Aswan). However, the sun would not be exactly overhead in Alexandria, which was 5,000 stadia (about 490 miles) north of Syene. Using the figure below, determine how Eratosthenes measured the circumference of the Earth. Explain your reasoning, your assumptions, and your calculations.

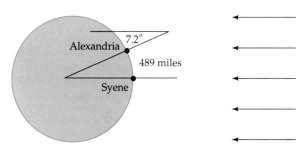

Alexandria 7.2°

489 miles

Syene

36. Suppose a wire that is stretched tightly around the Earth is elongated by 5 meters and then placed back around the Earth. Could a person crawl under the elongated wire?

37. Let us examine three ways to travel from point *A* to point *D* on the cube below. Assume that the cube is 1 meter on each side.

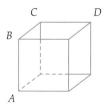

C   D

B

A

a. What would the distance be if you went from *A* to *B* and then from *B* to *C* and then from *C* to *D*?

b. If you had to travel on the surface of the cube, but

didn't have to travel on edges, what is the shortest distance?

c. What if you could go (in space) directly from *A* to *D*? Now what is the shortest distance?

d. Compare the three distances.

38. a. Explain what assumptions you need to make in order to determine the area of the figure below. Then determine the area.

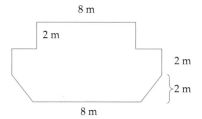

8 m

2 m

2 m

2 m

8 m

b. If the figure below is "similar" to the figure above, explain how you can apply your work from the previous problem to find the area of the figure below.

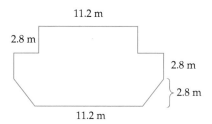

11.2 m

2.8 m

2.8 m

2.8 m

11.2 m

39. In the figure below, we begin with a square whose sides are 10 centimeters. Then we form a new square by joining the midpoints of the first square, and so on.

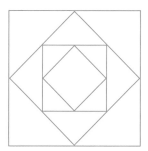

a. Complete the table below.

	1st	2d	3d	4th	5th				
Perimeter									
Area									

b. Describe the relationship you observe between the perimeters of the various squares.

c. Use that relationship to determine the perimeter of the 9th square.

d. Describe the relationship you observe between the areas of the various squares.

e. Use that relationship to determine the area of the 9th square.

40. On a blank sheet of paper, draw from memory:

- A rectangle the size of a dollar bill
- A rectangle the size of a floppy disk
- A circle the size of a penny
- A circle approximating the top view of a soda can

a. Before you check your estimates, predict the relative accuracy of your estimates, from 1 to 4, with 1 denot-ing the drawing that you predict will be "closest" to the actual shape.

b. Determine the actual area of each of your shapes and the actual objects. Describe how you determined which of your measurements was "closest" to the actual measurement.

S E C T I O N ◆ **10.3** ◆   ## SURFACE AREA AND VOLUME

WHAT DO YOU THINK?

- Is the relationship between surface area and volume a functional relationship? Why or why not?
- If we doubled the volume of a room, would its surface area double too?

In Section 10.2, we examined two attributes of two-dimensional objects: perimeter and area. In this section, we will examine two attributes of three-dimensional objects: surface area and volume. We can think of surface area as the area needed to cover all the faces of a three-dimensional object and volume as the amount of space contained within that object.

Understanding the Surface Area of Prisms

Very simply, the *surface area of a prism is equal to the sum of the areas of all of its faces.* Thus, to determine the surface area, we need to be able to determine the dimensions of each face. Let us consider a rectangular prism first. Determine the surface area of the rectangular prism in Figure 10.22 and then read on. It may help to first draw a net of that prism, which is shown at the right.

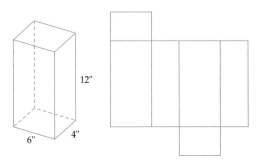

FIGURE **10.22**

There are patterns in this prism that make its surface area easier to determine. You can see that the bottom and top bases are congruent; similarly, the front and back faces are congruent, and the right and left faces are congruent. Thus,

Surface area of the prism = 2(24 in²) + 2(72 in²) + 2(48 in²) = 288 in²

With a concrete example under our belts, let us now investigate the surface area of prisms whose bases are regular polygons. We will use this thinking to develop the general formulas for the surface areas and volumes of some basic three-dimensional geometric figures. Most readers find it necessary to read this material more than once and to read actively, with pencil in hand. After all, I am presenting you a summary of something that took hundreds of years of effort by some of the brightest people of their time!

What do we know about the different surfaces of prisms that would make the task easier? Look at the three diagrams in Figure 10.23, showing three prisms and their nets. What do you see? Think before reading on. . . .

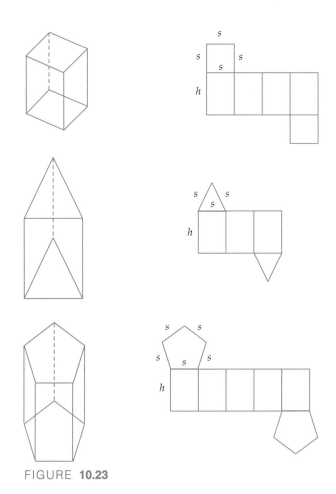

FIGURE **10.23**

If you constructed nets in Exploration 10.15, you saw that each prism has a bottom and a top base that are congruent. Therefore, the areas of the top and bottom bases will be equal. Similarly, the lateral surfaces (sides) of all these prisms are congruent; therefore, their areas will be equal. The number of lateral surfaces is equal to the number of sides of the base. If we let this number be *n*, we can state a generic formula for *the surface area of all prisms whose bases are regular polygons:*

Surface area = 2 times the area of one base + n *times the area of one lateral face*

Since the area of the base will not be the same in all cases, we can let *B* stand for the area of the base. Since the area of each of the lateral faces is equal to the side *s* times the height *h* (Figure 10.23), or *s · h*, we can now present a general formula:

Surface area of an n*-gon prism =* 2B + nsh

We can further simplify the formula by noting that *ns* is equal to the perimeter *p* of the base. Thus, an alternative representation of this formula (one that will be more useful later) is

Surface area of a prism = 2B + *ph*

Understanding the Surface Area of Cylinders

FIGURE **10.24**

Just as we saw a relationship between cylinders and prisms when we first examined them in Chapter 8, there is a relationship between the formulas for the surface areas of cylinders and prisms. In other words, the formulas for the surface areas of cylinders and prisms are connected. How do you think we might determine the surface area of a cylinder (see Figure 10.24)? Even if you can't figure out the whole formula, write down what you do know. Then read on. . . . 🖎

DISCUSSION

One of the connections between prisms and cylinders is that both have two congruent bases. Thus, to find the surface area of a cylinder, we have to find the area of one base and multiply that by 2. What about the lateral surface area? How do you think we might find that? If you are not sure, find a cylinder. (Use an empty toilet paper tube or paper towel tube, or wrap a piece of paper around a soup can or soda can.) What is the shape of the lateral face? Do this yourself before reading on. . . . 🖎

Yes, it is a rectangle! The height of the rectangle is equal to the height of the cylinder. What about the length of the base of the rectangle? How is it connected to the cylinder's base? Think and then read on. . . . 🖎

The length of the base of the rectangle is equal to the circumference of the circle! See Figure 10.25. With this knowledge, see if you can now discover the formula for the surface area of any cylinder in terms of the radius of the cylinder and the height of the cylinder. Then read on. . . . 🖎

lateral face

FIGURE **10.25**

- The area of the base is πr^2, and since we have two bases, the area of the two bases is $2\pi r^2$.

- The area of the rectangle = (the circumference of the circle) times (the height of the cylinder); that is, the area of the rectangle = $2\pi rh$.

Thus, **the surface area of a cylinder = $2\pi r^2 + 2\pi rh$**

Understanding the Surface Area of Pyramids

Whether we have a triangular pyramid, a square pyramid, or whatever, we have a base, and we have as many lateral faces as we have sides of the base. We will develop the formula for pyramids in which the apex is directly above the center of the base so that the lateral faces will be congruent triangles. Can you determine the surface area of the pyramid in Figure 10.26, if s represents the length of each side of the base and l is the slant height of the pyramid—that is, the altitude of each of the lateral faces? Try to do so before reading on. . . . 🖎

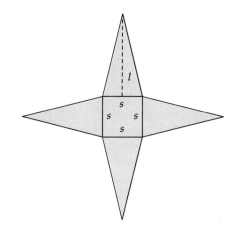

FIGURE **10.26**

The surface area of the pyramid above $= s^2 + 4\left(\dfrac{1}{2}sl\right) = s^2 + 2sl$

In order to determine the general formula, we need to make two substitutions. First, as before, we will let B represent the area of the base of the pyramid. Second, the perimeter of the base of the pyramid in the formula above is equal to $4s$. Since we have a $2s$ in the second part of the formula, we have, in essence, one-half of the perimeter. Thus, we will substitute $\frac{1}{2}p$ for $2s$. It will soon become apparent why we want to make this substitution. Thus, substituting B for s^2 and $\frac{1}{2}p$ for $2s$, we have

Surface area of a pyramid $= B + \dfrac{1}{2}pl$

Understanding the Surface Area of Cones

Just as we saw connections between the surface areas of prisms and cylinders, there are connections between the surface areas of pyramids and cones. Both objects have bases, and both have slant heights (see Figure 10.27). If we model the formula for the surface area of a cone after that of a pyramid, we have

The surface area of a pyramid $= B + \dfrac{1}{2}$(perimeter)(slant height)

Thus,

The surface area of a cone $= B + \dfrac{1}{2}$(perimeter)(slant height)

What do we know about B, the area of the base of the cone? What is the equivalent of $\frac{1}{2}p$? What do you think?

All cones have a circular base, and so the area of the base B is equal to πr^2. The perimeter (circumference) of a circle is $2\pi r$; thus, the value of $\frac{1}{2}p$ for the cone is πr.

Therefore, we can say that

Surface area of any cone $= \pi r^2 + \pi rl$

Volume

In Section 10.2, we connected the terms *perimeter* and *surround*, and we connected the terms *area* and *cover*. With respect to volume, we can say that vol-

FIGURE **10.27**

ume deals with how much it will take to *fill* an object. Exploration 10.16 also helps you to understand basic volume concepts and formulas.

Understanding the Volumes of Prisms

FIGURE **10.28**

Let us first develop the formula for the volume of a rectangular prism (more commonly known as a box). Imagine a box whose base is 4 centimeters by 3 centimeters and whose height is 2 centimeters (see Figure 10.28). If we were to fill that box with little cubes, each with dimensions 1 centimeter by 1 centimeter by 1 centimeter — that is, with a volume of 1 cubic centimeter — how many little cubes would it take?

It would take 24 little cubes — that is, $4 \cdot 3 \cdot 2$. Therefore, it makes sense to say that *we can determine the volume of a rectangular prism by multiplying its length, its width, and its height: $V = l \cdot w \cdot h$.*

Volume of an oblique prism   What about an oblique prism? What if the two prisms in Figure 10.29 have the same height and the same base? Will they have the same volume, or will their volume be different? What do you think?

FIGURE **10.29**

An analogy that is helpful is to think of a stack of paper. We can arrange the stack of paper to look like each of the diagrams in Figure 10.30. However, we still have the same volume of paper. This principle was first articulated by an Italian mathematician, Bonaventura Cavalieri, in the early seventeenth century. Cavalieri proved that two solids with congruent bases and the same height will have the same volume if the following condition is true: Each cross section that is parallel to the plane of the bases has the same area for each solid.

FIGURE **10.30**

Thus, we can say that the volume of any prism can be determined by multiplying the area of its base by its height.

Understanding the Volumes of Cylinders

What about cylinders? Can you connect what we have learned about determining the volume of prisms to determining the volume of cylinders? Think and then read on. . . .

The following discussion does not constitute a proof of the formula for determining the volume of a cylinder. Rather, it is designed to help you make sense of the formula. Recall the sentence in NCTM Curriculum Standard 3: Students should "believe that mathematics makes sense" (*Curriculum Standards,* p. 29).

In Section 10.2, we used our understanding of the area of a square to shape our understanding of the area of a circle. We will do something similar here. Consider the cylinder at the left in Figure 10.31. We can approximate the volume of the cylinder by breaking it down into a number of prisms — in this case, five prisms, as shown in the middle figure. Recall Investigation 10.6 (How Big Is the Footprint?) and Exploration 10.13 (Irregular Areas). We know that the volume of each of the prisms is *Bh.* Thus, if we denote the area of the bases of the prisms as B_1, B_2, B_3, and so on, we can say that the volume of the figure in the middle diagram is $B_1h + B_2h + B_3h + B_4h + B_5h = (B_1 + B_2 + B_3 + B_4 + B_5)h$. That is, the volume of this object is equal to the product of the height and the total area of the bases. Thus, it makes sense to conclude that the volume of a cylinder is equal to the product of the height and the total area of the bases. By breaking the cylinder into smaller and smaller prisms, as in the figure at the right, we can come closer and closer to the actual volume, just as we can closely approximate the area of a circle by covering it with a grid with smaller and smaller squares.

FIGURE **10.31**

Finally, just as we applied Cavalieri's principle to state the formula for finding the volume of any prism, not just right prisms, so too we can apply Cavalieri's principle to state the formula for finding the volume of any cylinder, not just right cylinders:

$$V = Bh \qquad \textit{where B represents the area of the base}$$

Understanding the Volumes of Pyramids

Let's look at pyramids. The formula is difficult for most people to develop, but it becomes much more understandable with concrete models.

We will illustrate the formula using a cube. It so happens that three congruent pyramids will fit inside the cube. Most people need to see this to believe it, and Figure 10.32 provides the necessary information to make three congruent pyramids that can be joined together to make a cube.

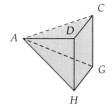

FIGURE **10.32**

At this moment, let us examine the implications of this relationship for determining the volume of a pyramid. Based on this information, what do you predict will be the formula for the volume of a pyramid? Think before reading on. . . . 🖎

If three congruent pyramids can be fit into the cube, and the bases of the pyramids are congruent to the base of the cube, this means that the volume of the pyramid is one-third the volume of the cube, and that *the formula for finding the volume of a pyramid is*

$$V = \frac{1}{3}Bh \qquad \textit{where B is the area of the base (any face) of the cube}$$

Understanding the Volumes of Cones

FIGURE **10.33**

What about cones? Knowing the formula for the surface area of a pyramid and thinking of the similarities between pyramids and cones, can you hypothesize a formula for the volume of a cone with radius r, height h, and slant height l (see Figure 10.33)? Try to do so before reading on. . . . 🖎

We can deduce that just as the volume of a pyramid is one-third the volume of a prism with the same base and height, the volume of a cone must be one-third the volume of a cylinder with the same base and height:

$$\textit{Volume of a cone is } V = \frac{1}{3}Bh$$

INVESTIGATION **10.8** Are Their Pictures Misleading?

FIGURE **10.34**

More and more newspapers, magazines, and brochures that companies put out are using graphs to display data in a way that will catch the reader's eye. The hypothetical example below illustrates the dangers. Let's say that Yummy Soda sold twice as much soda as Good Soda last year. The graph in Figure 10.34 is a pictorial representation of the sales of the two sodas that Yummy included in an ad. Why do you think Good Soda might object to the graph and actually file a lawsuit for unfair advertising? Write down your thoughts before reading on. . . . 🖎

DISCUSSION

If the reader looks at this as simply a "cute" bar graph, the height of the Yummy bar is twice the height of the Good bar. However, the diameter of the base of the Yummy can is twice the diameter of the base of the Good can, causing the Yummy can to look more than twice as big as the Good can. What is the ratio of the volumes of the two cans? Determine this before reading on. . . . 🖎

One solution is to take the actual dimensions:

■ The Good Soda can has a radius of 1 millimeter and a height of 10 millimeters.

■ The Yummy Soda can has a radius of 2 millimeters and a height of 20 millimeters.

Using the volume formula for cylinders, $V = \pi r^2 h$, we have

- Volume of Good Soda can = 10π
- Volume of Yummy Soda can = 80π

That is, the Yummy Soda can has 8 times the volume of the Good Soda can.

Note: Do you see why we used π instead of using a decimal approximation? We also could have used the ratios; that is,

Volume of Good Soda can = $\pi r^2 h$

Volume of Yummy Soda can = $\pi(2r)^2(2h) = 8\pi r^2 h$

In either case, we find that the graph gives a visual impression that Yummy Soda is selling much more than twice as much as Good Soda.

Determining the Volumes of Irregularly Shaped Objects

In Section 10.2, we acknowledged that formulas have limited usefulness in real life. Often we need to find the area of an irregularly shaped figure. Similarly, we often need to find the volume of a solid for which the formulas do not apply. How can we do this? Think about this before reading on. . . .

This is actually a very challenging problem that stumped ancient mathematician-scientists for quite some time. One way of addressing this question was developed by one of the greatest mathematicians of all times, Archimedes, who lived in the city of Syracuse, located in modern Italy, over 2,000 years ago.

Archimedes was summoned by the king, who suspected that the goldsmith who had made his crown had not made it of solid gold, but had mixed some silver in it. He wanted Archimedes to determine whether the crown was pure gold without having to cut into it.

Poor Archimedes. In those days, one did not disappoint kings. In fact, it was not unusual for disappointed kings to banish or even execute advisors who failed to solve their problems.

Archimedes knew that silver was only about half as dense as gold. (We determine the density of an object by dividing its mass by its volume—for example, grams per cubic centimeter.) Archimedes was aware of the formula volume $\times$ density = mass (for example, $cm^3 \times g/cm^3 = g$). Thus, if he could determine the volume of the crown, he would be able to solve the problem. But how was he to find the volume of the crown accurately?

Some time later, possibly that same day, Archimedes was taking a bath when the solution suddenly came to him: He could determine the volume of the crown by submerging it in water, because two objects with the same volume will displace the same amount of water. Legend has it that he became so excited that he ran outside, still naked, shouting "Eureka," which means, in Greek, "I have found it!"

How did this discovery enable him to determine if the crown was counterfeit?

Now that he knew a way to determine the volume with some precision, he could use this number and the density of gold in the formula given above to determine how much the crown would weigh if it were pure gold. (It turns out that the goldsmith had indeed cheated the king!)

INVESTIGATION 10.9 Finding the Volume of a Hollow Box

8 m

10 m

12 m

FIGURE **10.35**

Imagine a large object that will be used to hold water or other materials (see Figure 10.35). The outer dimensions are 12 meters by 10 meters by 8 meters. The walls are 1 meter thick, and so is the floor. What is the volume of the container in cubic meters? For example, if we were to make this object from concrete, we would need to know how much concrete to order. Work on this until you determine the volume or become stuck. Then read on. . . .

DISCUSSION

STRATEGY 1: Break the problem into parts

Just as a rectangular prism has six surfaces, a prism with no top will have five surfaces. Let us identify them and then determine the dimensions of each of them: bottom, front, right side, left side, back. If you did not think of this strategy, seeing if you can use it to determine the volume will be a useful exercise of your problem-solving tools. If you used a different strategy, do you get the same answer using this strategy? Work on this before reading on. . . .

The volume of the bottom will be

$$12 \text{ m} \cdot 10 \text{ m} \cdot 1 \text{ m} = 120 \text{ m}^3$$

The front and back sides are congruent, and the volume of each will be

$$12 \text{ m} \cdot 7 \text{ m} \cdot 1 \text{ m} = 84 \text{ m}^3$$

(Do you see why it is not 8 m? If not, make a model of the container.)
The right and left sides are congruent, and the volume of each will be

$$8 \text{ m} \cdot 7 \text{ m} \cdot 1 \text{ m} = 56 \text{ m}^3$$

(Do you understand these dimensions? If not, make a model.)

STRATEGY 2: See the problem from a different perspective

For example, determine what the volume would be if the container were not hollow. Then determine the volume of the hollow region. Then subtract! Do you understand this strategy?
Volume of the whole region:

$$12 \text{ m} \cdot 10 \text{ m} \cdot 8 \text{ m} = 960 \text{ m}^3$$

Volume of the hollow:

$$10 \text{ m} \cdot 8 \text{ m} \cdot 7 \text{ m} = 560 \text{ m}^3$$

What is the difference between the two? Does this answer match the answer from Strategy 1? Exploration 10.17 provides more opportunities to apply your understanding of volume concepts.
Again it is important to note that this discussion illustrated only two of several possible ways to solve this problem.

INVESTIGATION **10.10** Surface Area and Volume

In Section 10.2, we discovered that perimeter and area are not related in a simple way; for example, if you double the perimeter, that doesn't necessarily mean that you double the area. Let us investigate the relationship between surface area and volume. As you can imagine, there are many applications of this relationship in fields outside mathematics!

Consider a set of 8 small cubes, each of whose dimensions are 1 centimeter by 1 centimeter by 1 centimeter (see Figure 10.36).

FIGURE **10.36**

What arrangement of those cubes will have the smallest surface area?

What arrangement of those cubes will have the largest surface area?

Work on these questions before reading on. . . .

DISCUSSION

There are two aspects of this question that are not well defined. First, some students, applying this idea to real-life applications like melting ice, consider the "surface area" to be the amount of surface exposed. Thus, they do not count the base. Other students imagine having to paint the whole arrangement, and thus count the base. In this investigation, when we say "surface area," we will mean the latter.

The second part of the question that is not well defined is "arrangement." In this investigation, in order for something to count as an arrangement, at least one entire face of each cube will have to cover an entire face of another cube. Thus, simply putting the six cubes down on the table so that they are all disjoined does not count as an "arrangement" as I am defining this problem. With these two aspects of the problem now well-defined, solve the problem before reading on. . . .

Arranging the cubes into a large cube will create the smallest surface area (see Figure 10.37). If you didn't find this, make them into a cube (or draw a diagram) and determine the surface area.

FIGURE **10.37**

Since all six faces of the cube are congruent, we can multiply the area of one face (4 cm²) by 6 (the number of faces), to get 24 cm².

The largest surface area is obtained by arranging the six cubes in a line (see Figure 10.38). If you didn't find this, please determine the surface area. If you did, you may want to compare your solution path with that of another student. Then read on. . . . 🖎

FIGURE **10.38**

STRATEGY 1: See this arrangement as a prism with six sides

The surface area of the front, top, back, and bottom is 32 cm².
The surface area of the two bases (the two sides in this diagram) is 2 cm².
Thus, the total surface area is 34 cm².

STRATEGY 2: See this arrangement as two end cubes and six cubes in the middle

The surface area of the six cubes in the middle is 24 cm².
The surface area of the two cubes on the end is 10 cm².
Thus, the total surface area is 34 cm².

Summary

If this section has been successful, the various formulas for surface area and volume make sense. In order to make sense of these formulas, we used some strategies like the ones we used to make sense of area formulas in Section 10.2 (breaking a figure into parts) and built on previous knowledge. Connections were an important aspect of making sense of these formulas. That is, the formulas for finding the surface area and volume of prisms are fairly straightforward. By seeing how prisms and cylinders are similar, we could then use the prism formulas to understand the cylinder formulas. Similarly, we connected the volume of a pyramid to the volume of a cube in order to understand the formula for the volume of a pyramid. After we developed the formula for finding the surface area of a pyramid, seeing how pyramids and cones are similar enabled us to make sense of the formula for the surface area of a cone. Understanding the formulas and having a good problem-solving toolbox then enabled us to solve nonroutine problems. Finally, we examined the relationship between surface area and volume, realizing as we did so that this relationship, like that of perimeter and area, is not simple.

EXERCISES 10.3

1. Determine the surface area and volume of each of the following:

   a. ∡*ABC* is a right angle.
     AB = 10 inches, *BC* = 12 inches
     AD = 3 feet

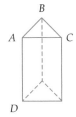

   b. The base is a square.

c. The diameter is 5 feet 6 inches.
The height is 11 feet 3 inches.

2. **a.** Determine the surface area and volume of the watering trough below. The length of the trough is 16 feet, the two ends of the trough are isosceles triangles whose base is 2 feet, and the height is 1 foot.

b. Determine the surface area of the inside of the room below and the volume of the room. The base of the room is in the shape of an isosceles trapezoid. The longer base is 12 feet 4 inches, and the shorter base is 8 feet 9 inches. Both slant sides are 13 feet. The height of the room is 9 feet.

c. The base of the pyramid is a square. The slant height of the pyramid is 18 feet.

3. **a.** Determine the surface area and volume of the swimming pool below.

b. Determine how many gallons of water the pool will hold.

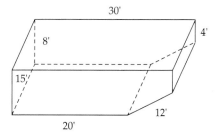

4. Before we had children, my wife and I went camping in a pup tent, shown below at the left. After having two children, we bought a much bigger tent, like the one in the middle. Since the determination of the volume of that tent is rather complex, let us assume that the big tent was actually a square pyramid with a height of 8 feet.

a. How much bigger is the new tent than the old tent? First, predict the answer and explain the reasoning behind your prediction. Then do the computations.

b. Compare the amount of material needed to make each tent. First, predict the answer and explain the reasoning behind your prediction. Then do the computations.

c. Using what you have learned about two- and three-dimensional figures in the last three chapters, describe your hypotheses for how you might determine the actual volume of the middle tent. The height of the truncated pyramid is 6 feet, and the height of the small pyramid at the top is 2 feet.

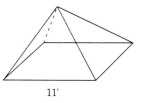

5. The napkin ring pictured is to be resilvered. How many square millimeters of surface area must be covered?

6. This past year the local elementary school has bought 50 boxes of paper, each box containing 10 reams. Each ream contains 500 sheets of paper. There are two shelves in the copy room, each 12 inches wide and 5 feet long. The second shelf is 2 feet above the first shelf and 3 feet below the ceiling. Assuming that the shelves are sturdy, how many sheets of paper can be stored on the shelves? What percent of the yearly purchase is this?

7. The U.S. federal debt, at the time of the writing of this book, was $4.8 trillion. One way to get a sense of the enormousness of that number is to imagine how much space 4.8 trillion one-dollar bills would occupy. Determine the space. Then recommend a denomination that would enable a semitrailer to haul that much money.

8. The planned Three Gorges Dam in China will require approximately 950 million cubic feet of concrete. Do something with this number to make it more understandable. For example, it would be equivalent to a block 1 mile long, 1 mile wide, and x feet high.

9. The Great Pyramid was build around 2600 B.C. and is considered to be one of the "Seven Wonders of the

World." It was built for Pharaoh Khufu. The pyramid was made from about 2.3 million stone blocks, whose total weight was about 6 million tons! It has been estimated that it took 100,000 workers about 30 years to make it, and we believe they hauled the blocks only during the three months of the year when the Nile was flooded—that is, when the farmers weren't farming. The pyramid has a square base, and each side is 768 feet. The height of the pyramid is 481 feet.

a. Compare the volume of the pyramid to the volume of the building in which you are taking this course.

b. Compare the volume of the pyramid to the volume of a building 100 feet high covering a football field (120 yards long and 55 yards wide).

c. Compare the Great Pyramid to the Transamerica Pyramid in San Francisco. The height and base of the Transamerica Pyramid are 870 feet and 117 feet, respectively.

d. When I was researching this book, one of the books I read said that the height of each of the triangular faces of the pyramid was 232 meters. Is that figure compatible with the height of the pyramid given here, 481 feet?

e. Many books have been written about many of the "coincidental" measurements of the pyramid. For example, it is said that the area of one of the triangular faces of the pyramid is equal to the square of the height of the pyramid. Are these two dimensions equal?

10. Joe has 8 blocks of ice, each measuring 30 centimeters by 30 centimeters by 30 centimeters.

a. How should he stack them if he wants them to melt as slowly as possible?

b. How should he stack them if he wants them to melt as quickly as possible?

c. What if the blocks were 50 centimeters by 50 centimeters by 50 centimeters? What would be the ratio of exposed surface area between the slowest and the fastest scenarios?

11. Let's say a company is manufacturing juice boxes that are rectangular prisms with dimensions 4 inches by 3 inches by 4 inches. The company has a warehouse whose dimensions are 40 feet by 30 feet by 20 feet. If the company makes 200,000 juice boxes, will it be able to store all the juice boxes in the warehouse?

12. Sharon has 150 cassettes and has decided to make a wooden shelf to hold them. The space between cassettes needs to be only 2 millimeters. Design a shelf that will hold at least 200 cassettes.

13. Given 8 cubes, each with dimensions of 1 centimeter by 1 centimeter by 1 centimeter, can you find arrangements that will have surface areas for every whole number between the minimum and maximum that were found in Investigation 10.10—that is, between 24 square centimeters and 34 square centimeters?

14. One inch is about 2.54 times as long as a centimeter. We could say that it takes just over $2\frac{1}{2}$ centimeters to make an inch.

a. Predict how many cubic centimeters it would take to fill a container that was one cubic inch. Explain your reasoning.

b. Determine the actual ratio.

c. Assess your prediction, both in terms of percent error and in terms of reasoning.

15. Consider two cubes. The smaller cube measures 4 inches on a side, and the larger cube measures 10 inches on a side. What is the ratio of the surface areas of the two cubes? What is the ratio of the volumes of the two cubes?

16. Consider the two similar rectangular prisms below (not drawn to scale). The dimensions of the smaller prism are 3 inches by 2 inches by 4 inches, and the dimensions of the larger prism are 9 inches by 6 inches by 12 inches. That is, the ratio of their sides is 3:1.

a. Predict the ratio of their surface areas and explain your reasoning. Then determine the actual ratio of the surface areas. If your prediction was off, explain the error in your prediction.

b. Predict the ratio of their volumes and explain your reasoning. Then determine the actual ratio of the volumes. If your prediction was off, explain the error in your prediction.

17. When my children were younger, we bought a set of dominoes. A complete set had every possible combination of numbers from 0 (represented by a blank) to 9 on each domino. For example:

a. How many dominoes are in a complete set?

b. If each domino is 1 inch × 2 inches × 3/8 inch, design a carrying case that would hold all of them.

18. This problem is taken from a book called *Measurement Investigations: Book One*.[7] I have noticed that "flats" of berries and "flats" of young plants are not cubical in shape, but rather are rectangular prisms (see the picture below).

Suppose you wanted a flat that would hold 4,000 cubic centimeters of strawberries. What would be the dimensions of the prism that would require the least amount of cardboard to make?

19. **a.** The cake pictured below has been cut into three equal pieces. One more person comes. How can you make one cut in the cake so that each of four persons will get the same amount of cake?

b. The cake pictured below has been cut into *n* equal pieces. One more person comes. How can you make one cut in the cake so that each of *n* + 1 persons will get the same amount of cake?

20. Below are three possible floor plans for a new office building. Each plan has almost exactly the same amount of floor space.

a. Analyze the advantages and disadvantages of each of these designs.

b. If each building were made of bricks, compare the relative amount of bricks needed for each.

c. If the outside walls of each building were 10 feet tall and one gallon of paint covers approximately 500 square feet, determine the amount of paint that would be needed to paint each building.

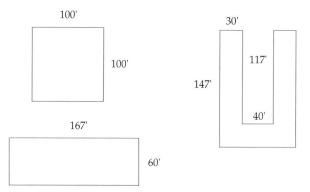

21. Each American produces about 3.5 kilograms of solid waste (garbage) a day. If 1 cubic meter of garbage weighs 90 kilograms, what would be the size of the waste produced each day by:

a. The population of your college

b. The people in your state

c. The people in the United States

In each case, describe the assumptions you made in order to answer the question.

22. Many automobile commercials have stressed that the new model being advertised has more carrying capacity.

a. How might you determine the carrying capacity of two similar automobiles?

b. Select two comparable automobiles and determine the carrying capacity of each. Look up the carrying capacity given by the manufacturers. Do you agree with their amounts? If not, do you think one of the figures is erroneous, or do you think the term was defined differently?

23. This problem has been adapted from *Measurement Investigations; Book One*[8]. When a boat or ship sinks, the Red Cross recommends that people huddle together to stay warm. Let's say three adults huddle together to keep warm. Determine a way to answer the following question: What is the ratio of body surface area exposed to the cold water when floating alone (in a life jacket) as opposed to when huddling?

[7] Randall Souviney, Murray Britt, Salvi Garguilo, and Peter Hughes, *Measurement Investigations: Book One* (Palo Alto, Calif.: Dale Seymour Publications, 1988), p. 10. Reprinted by permission.

[8] Ibid.

24. Analyze the following graph for its accuracy. First, predict whether you think it is accurate or not and explain your reasoning. Then do the measuring and calculating and explain your interpretation of the numbers. Then assess your prediction. If the prediction and the reasoning behind it were accurate, great. If either the prediction or the reasoning behind it was not accurate, explain the errors in the prediction.

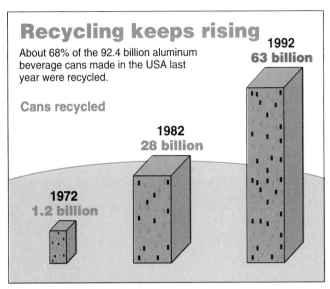

Source: The Aluminum Association, Can Manufacturers Institute, Institute of Scrap Recycling Industries. USA TODAY research. Adapted from an original graph by Sam Ward © 1993 USA TODAY. Reprinted with permission.

25. Make a net for a soccer ball. Describe your process. For example, how did you determine how many faces the soccer ball had and how to put them together? Describe any discoveries, conjectures, and questions that came from this exploration.

26. Take a standard 8 1/2- by 11-inch sheet of paper and determine how to cut and fold the paper so that you could make a rectangular prism with no top that would contain the greatest volume.

27. Predict how many feet of floor space there are in the building in which you are taking this class. If it is a large building, your instructor may wish to have you determine the floor space in a specific subset of the whole building. As accurately as you can, determine the actual floor space.

CHAPTER SUMMARY

1. To measure an object means to assign a number to some attribute of the object.

2. Two objects do not have to be congruent to have the same measure. For example, two objects can have different shapes but have the same volume.

3. In order to measure, we must decide on a unit.

4. All units are conventions, as opposed to absolutes.

5. Virtually all measurements are approximations.

6. On some occasions, we cannot directly measure an attribute and must rely on indirect measurement.

7. Different attributes of an object—perimeter and area, and surface area and volume—are not related in simple ways.

Basic Concepts

Section 10.1: Systems of Measurement
metric system *511*
U.S. customary system *511*
meter *511*

liter *000*, gram *513*
weight, mass *513*
precise *514*   accurate *514*
greatest possible error (GPE) *514*
relative error *515*

Section 10.2: Perimeter and Area
perimeter *519*, circumference *519*
π *519*   area, base, height *521*
Pythagorean theorem *525*
Understanding the area formulas for
    parallelograms *523*, triangles *524*, trapezoids *524*, and circles *527*
Areas of irregularly shaped figures *526*
Relationships between perimeter and area *530*

Section 10.3: Surface Area and Volume
Understanding the surface area formulas for
    prisms *535*, cylinders *537*, pyramids *537*, and cones *538*

Constructions

The Greeks were fascinated by the challenge of what we call construction problems. **Constructions** involve making geometric figures using only a compass and a straightedge — in other words, without a protractor or ruler.

Consider these three famous constructions, which were first attempted over 2,000 years ago:

1. Construct an angle whose measure is one-third the measure of a given angle; this is often called the trisect.

2. Construct a square whose area is equal to the area of a given circle.

3. Given the face of a cube, construct the face of a cube whose volume is exactly double the volume of the first cube.

Some of the greatest mathematicians in the world grappled with these constructions. It was not until the early 1800s that the brilliant French mathematician Evariste Galois proved that they are indeed impossible.

To the modern student, these problems may seem silly or pointless. However, the pursuit of some of the more difficult constructions is directly responsible for some major discoveries in mathematics, including the theory of equations and group theory.[1]

A reasonable question that many of my students ask is, so why do constructions now? There are several reasons. First, there is rich opportunity for problem-solving, reasoning, and making connections. Another is that many students who struggle with computational mathematics love constructions. A third is that it can be fun, and some very pretty figures can be constructed.

In this appendix, we will cover some basic constructions. The exercises offer some interesting challenges that call upon you to apply your reasoning and problem-solving tools.

---

[1] Vivian Shaw Groza, *A Survey of Mathematics: Elementary Concepts and Their Historical Development* (New York: Holt, Rinehart and Winston, 1968), p. 149.

Construction 1 Copying a Line Segment

The first construction we will consider is simply copying a line segment. We need this when constructing congruent triangles and other polygons. If you have a given line segment, how could you make another line segment that was the same length using only a compass and a straightedge? Think before reading on. . . .

This is a fairly straightforward construction.

Let $\overline{AB}$ be the given line segment.

Begin by drawing another segment, and call one endpoint X.

Open the compass so that the point lies on A and the pencil point[1] lies on B.

Without changing the opening of the compass, place the point of the compass on X and make a mark with the pencil of the compass. Call that point Y.

$$\overline{AB} \cong \overline{XY}$$

Construction 2 Copying a Triangle when Three Sides Are Given

We can apply this construction to **copy any triangle.** From the definition of congruent triangles, in order to know for sure that two triangles are congruent, we need to verify that all six pairs of corresponding parts — three pairs of sides and three pairs of angles — are congruent. Do we need all six? Let us see what the following construction tells us.

Let ABC be the given triangle.

Copy line segment $\overline{AC}$ and label it $\overline{XY}$.

Open the compass so that the point lies on A and the pencil point lies on B.

With the same opening and the point on X, draw an arc.

Open the compass so that the point lies on C and the pencil point lies on B.

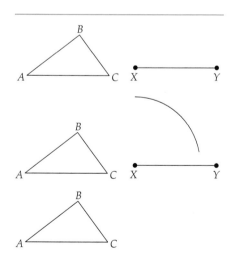

[1] Language note: We will refer to the point of the compass that writes as the *pencil point* and the other point simply as *the point*.

With the same opening and the point on Y, draw an arc. Call the point at which this arc intersects the other arc point Z.

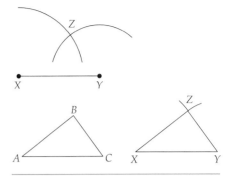

Connect points X and Z. Connect points Y and Z.

$$\triangle ABC \cong \triangle XYZ$$

Thus, we made a copy of $\triangle ABC$ by making $\overline{XY} \cong \overline{AC}$, $\overline{ZY} \cong \overline{BC}$, and $\overline{XZ} \cong \overline{AB}$.

It turns out that if the three sides are congruent, the two triangles must be congruent. This is known in geometry as the side–side–side congruence property (SSS).

Thus, we have discovered that we can make triangles without having to know that all six pairs of corresponding parts are congruent!

Construction 3   Copying an Angle

Sometimes we need to copy an angle. How might we do that? What do you think?

Let angle A be the given angle.

Begin by drawing a line segment and labeling one endpoint O.

With the point of the compass on point A, draw an arc that intersects each side of the angle. Call those points B and C.

Now place the point of the compass on point O and draw an arc with the same radius so that it intersects the line segment. Call that intersection point P.

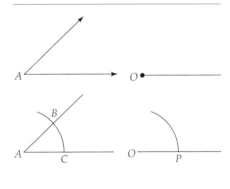

Open the compass so that the point lies on C and the pencil point lies on B.

Keeping the compass at the same setting place the point of the compass on point P and draw an arc that intersects the arc you drew before. Call the point of intersection of the two arcs T.

Connect points O and T.

$$\angle BAC \cong \angle TOP$$

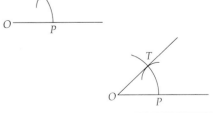

Construction 4 Copying a Triangle when Two Sides and the Angle Between Are Given

We just found that if all three pairs of corresponding sides are congruent, two triangles must also be congruent. What if we knew that two pairs of corresponding sides were congruent and that the angles between these pairs of sides were congruent? Must the two triangles be congruent? If so, this would be known as the SAS property. That is, if you copy two sides and the angle between them, *must* the two triangles be congruent?

For example, suppose △ABC is the given triangle. If we construct △XYZ so that $\overline{AB} \cong \overline{XY}$, $\overline{AC} \cong \overline{XZ}$, and ∡A ≅ ∡X, must the copied triangle be congruent to △ABC? What do you think? Try this yourself before reading on. . . . 🖉

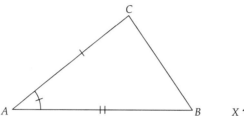

Note: The marks on the triangles are visual aids to represent the congruent pairs. That is, sides $\overline{AC}$ and $\overline{XZ}$ have one mark, sides $\overline{AB}$ and $\overline{XY}$ have two marks, and angles A and X each have one mark.

First, we copy $\overline{AB}$ so that $\overline{XY} \cong \overline{AB}$.

Then we copy angle A so that ∡X ≅ ∡A.

Next we copy $\overline{AC}$ so that $\overline{XZ} \cong \overline{AC}$.

The only thing remaining is to connect Y and Z.

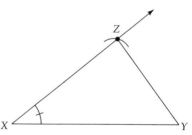

It turns out that if we copy two sides of a triangle and the angle between them, the new triangle must be congruent to the first triangle. Therefore, the side–angle–side congruence property (SAS), proposed above, holds true.

Construction 5 Copying a Triangle when Two Sides and an Angle That Is Not Between Those Sides Are Given

What if we knew that two pairs of corresponding sides were congruent and that an angle that was not between these pairs of sides was congruent? Must the two triangles be congruent? If so, this would be known as the SSA property. That is, if you copy two sides and an angle not between them, *must* the two triangles be congruent? For example, suppose △ABC is the given triangle. What if we copy ∡A, $\overline{AC}$, and $\overline{CB}$? What do you think? Try this yourself before reading on. . . .

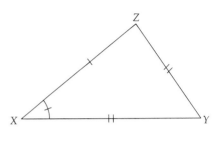

We can begin by copying ∡A so that ∡A ≅ ∡X.

Then we can copy $\overline{AC}$ so that $\overline{XZ}$ ≅ $\overline{AC}$.

Finally, we can copy $\overline{BC}$ so that $\overline{YZ}$ ≅ $\overline{BC}$.

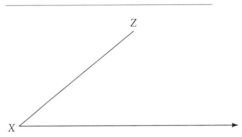

However, with the point of the compass on Z, we find that the arc crosses $\overline{XY}$ at two points.

What does this mean?

It means, unfortunately, that the SSA property does not hold water. Why is this?

If we compare △ABC to △XY$_2$Z,

$\overline{AC}$ ≅ $\overline{XZ}$

$\overline{BC}$ ≅ $\overline{Y_2Z}$

and ∡A ≅ ∡Z

If we compare △ABC to △XY$_1$Z,

$\overline{AC}$ ≅ $\overline{XZ}$

$\overline{BC}$ ≅ $\overline{Y_1Z}$

and ∡A ≅ ∡Z

That is, we have constructed two different triangles from two sides and a nonincluded angle of the given triangle.

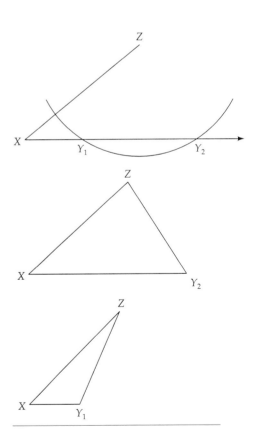

Thus, we have seen that there is not an SSA triangle congruence property. What about ASA? What about AAS? These will be left as exercises.

In order to make some of the more elaborate designs found in the exercises, we need several more constructions.

Construction 6 Bisecting a Given Line Segment

Some constructions require us to bisect a line segment. How might we do that?

Let $\overline{TP}$ be the given segment.

With the point of the compass on T, make an arc above and below the line segment. *Note:* The length of the compass opening must be greater than half the length of the line segment. Why is this?

Now place the point of the compass on P and make an arc above and below the line segment.

If you made the arcs large enough, they will intersect at two points. Call those points A and B.

Place the straightedge so that it contains points A and B. The point at which the straightedge intersects $\overline{TP}$ will be the midpoint of $\overline{TP}$. That point is called M in the diagram.

Furthermore, $\overleftrightarrow{AB}$ is perpendicular to $\overleftrightarrow{TP}$. Do you see why?

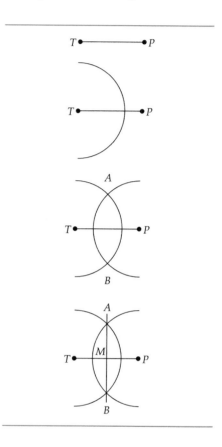

Construction 7 Bisecting an Angle

Sometimes we need to be able to bisect an angle. Let A be the given angle.

With the point of the compass on point A, draw an arc that intersects each side of the angle. Call those points B and C.

With the point of the compass on point B, draw an arc.

With the point of the compass on point C, draw an arc with the same radius. Call the point at which the two arcs intersect point P.

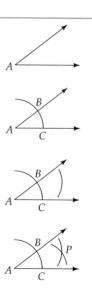

Draw ray $\overrightarrow{AP}$.

Angle A has now been bisected. Thus,

$$m\angle BAP = m\angle PAC$$

Can you prove that the angle has been bisected — that is, that $m\angle BAP = m\angle PAC$? Think about it before reading on. . . .

$\overline{AB} \cong \overline{AC}$	Constructed that way
$\overline{BP} \cong \overline{CP}$	Constructed that way
$\overline{AP} \cong \overline{AP}$	Any segment is congruent to itself.
$\triangle ABP \cong \triangle ACP$	SSS
$m\angle BAP = m\angle PAC$	They are corresponding angles of congruent triangles.

Construction 8 Constructing a Perpendicular to a Given Line Segment Through a Given Point

Sometimes we have a line segment and we want to make a right angle — for example, when constructing a right triangle or a square. In that case, we want to construct a line segment perpendicular to a given line segment through a given point.

Begin with a line segment and a point P that lies on the line segment.

Place the point of the compass on point P and draw an arc so that it intersects the line segment on either side of P.

Call those points of intersection A and B.

Open the compass wider and with the point of the compass on point A, draw an arc above the line segment.

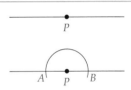

Place the point of the compass on point B, keeping the same setting, and draw an arc above the line segment. Call the point of intersection X.

Connect points X and P.

$$\overline{XP} \perp \overline{AB}$$

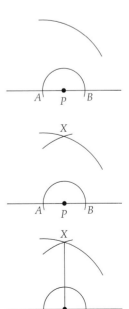

Construction 9   Constructing a Perpendicular from a Point to a Line

In some cases, we have a point and we want to connect that point to a line segment so that perpendicular lines are formed. In that case, we want to construct a perpendicular from a point to a line.

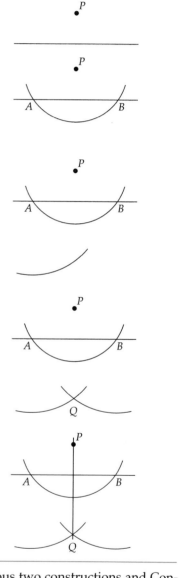

Begin with a line and a point not on the line.

Open the compass so that its radius is great enough so that with one point of the compass on P, an arc will intersect the line segment at two points, which we will call A and B. Draw arc AB.

Now open the compass so that its radius is appreciably greater than half the distance from A to B.

Place the point of the compass on point A and draw an arc below the line segment.

Place the point of the compass on point B and draw an arc below the line segment. If the previous arc was long enough, the two arcs will intersect. Call the intersection point Q.

Connect points P and Q.

$$\overline{AB} \perp \overline{PQ}$$

Do you see connections between the previous two constructions and Construction 6?

Construction 10   Constructing a Square

Earlier we discovered several postulates that enable us to construct triangles or to copy a given triangle. We now have enough tools to construct a square.

There are many ways to construct a square.

For example, we could start with line segment $\overline{AB}$. We could construct $\overline{AC}$ perpendicular to $\overline{AB}$ and having the same length.

Then we could construct $\overline{CD}$ perpendicular to $\overline{AC}$ and having the same length.

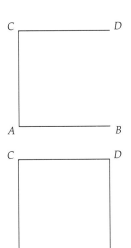

Then we could connect D and B.

However, there are many other ways to construct a square—easier ones, too. Try to develop a way to construct a square yourself before reading on. . . .

ANOTHER WAY TO CONSTRUCT A SQUARE

One construction would be to start with a line segment $\overline{PQ}$ and construct a perpendicular bisector as we did in Construction 9. Call the intersection point T.

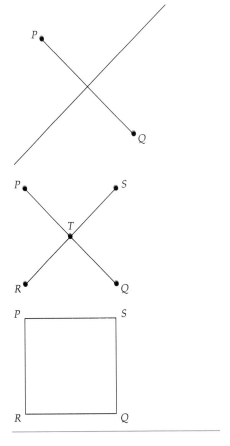

Then open the compass to the desired length, that is, the length of $\overline{PT}$.

Mark points R and S so that $\overline{PT}$, $\overline{ST}$, $\overline{QT}$, and $\overline{RT}$ are all congruent.

Connect points $PSQR$, and voilà, you have a square.

Do you see why this is a square?

How many other ways can you find to construct a square?

Johann says this isn't quite "legal." He says that this technique won't work if you have to construct a square congruent to a given square, let's say square *ABCD* above. What do you think? Will this technique work? If it does not work directly, can it be adapted, or is Johann right?

Construction 11   Inscribing an Equilateral Triangle

Many of the elaborate constructions found in the exercises begin by inscribing a figure in a circle. The three constructions below enable us to inscribe an equilateral triangle in a circle, a square in a circle, and a hexagon in a circle.

Draw a circle and call the center C.

Make a diameter and call the two endpoints A and B.

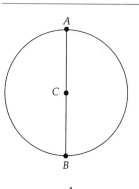

Open the compass so that its opening is equal to the radius of the circle.

Place the point of the compass on point B and draw an arc that intersects the circle in two places. Call those points D and E.

If you now connect points A, D, and E, you have an equilateral triangle.

The proof that this indeed is an equilateral triangle will be left as an exercise.

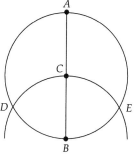

Construction 12   Inscribing a Square

Draw a circle and call the center C.

Make a diameter and call the two endpoints A and B.

Construct another diameter that is perpendicular to $\overline{AB}$. (That is, construct the perpendicular bisector of $\overline{AB}$.) Call this diameter $\overline{EF}$.

Connect the points to make square AEBF.

The proof that this indeed is a square will be left as an exercise.

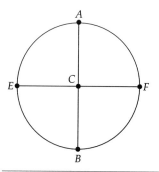

Construction 13 Inscribing a Hexagon

Draw a circle and call the center C. Make a diameter and call the two endpoints A and B.

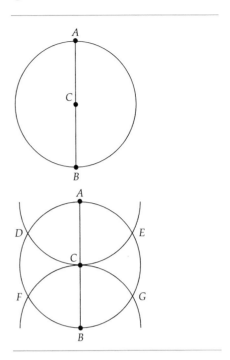

Open the compass so that its opening is equal to the radius of the circle.

Place the point of the compass on point A and draw an arc that intersects the circle in two places. Call those points D and E.

Place one point of the compass on point B and draw an arc that intersects the circle in two places. Call those points F and G.

Connect the points to make hexagon *ADFBGE*.

The proof that this is a regular hexagon will be left as an exercise.

Construction 14 Construct This Figure

Now we have the tools to construct the following figure, the figures in the exercises, and a whole world of other figures that you can create. This construction not only serves to continue to develop your problem-solving and reasoning skills, but will also serve as an assessment of your understanding of the constructions we have developed. If you own the constructions that we have studied so far, you will be better able to apply that knowledge to new problems that are not just like the ones we have done before.

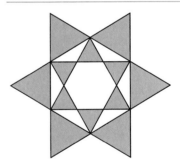

Can you figure out how to make this figure using only your compass and straightedge? Try to do so before reading on. . . . 🖎

Construct a regular hexagon, but do not connect the points to make a hexagon.

Instead, connect points *BDF* and points *ACE* to make two equilateral triangles.

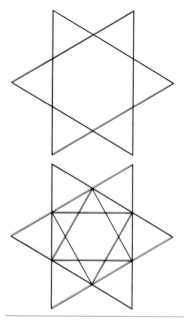

Within the hexagon in the middle of the figure, connect points so as to make two equilateral triangles.

If you now shade in the appropriate regions, you will have the desired figure.

EXERCISES

1. There are three more congruence properties for triangles: ASA, AAS (that is, two pairs of angles are congruent and one pair of sides not between the two angles is congruent), and HL (that is, with right triangles, the two hypotenuses are congruent and one pair of legs is congruent).

   a. Justify the ASA property for triangles.

   b. Justify the AAS property for triangles

   c. Justify the HL property for triangles.

2. Justify the following constructions:

   a. Construction of a perpendicular bisector

   b. Construction of a perpendicular from a point not on a line

   c. Inscribing an equilateral triangle in a circle

   d. Inscribing a square in a circle

3. In Chapter 8, an isosceles triangle was defined as a triangle having at least two congruent sides. It was also mentioned that it can be proved that the base angles of isosceles triangles are equal. Prove that now. *Note:* There is more than one possible way to do so.

4. **a.** Draw a scalene triangle. Construct the midpoints and connect them to form a triangle. Is there a relationship between this new triangle and the original one?

   b. Construct an isosceles triangle. Construct the midpoints and connect them to form a triangle. Is there a relationship between this new triangle and the original one?

   c. Construct an equilateral triangle. Construct the midpoints and connect them to form a triangle. Is there a

   relationship between this new triangle and the original one?

   d. Construct a right triangle. Construct the midpoints and connect them to form a triangle. Is there a relationship between this new triangle and the original one?

5. **a.** Do you think there is an SSSS congruence property for quadrilaterals? Write your initial response and justification.

   b. Design and test a way to prove or refute this hypothesis. Justify your assertion.

6. Draw a variety of different quadrilaterals. In each quadrilateral, construct the midpoints of the two sides and then connect the midpoints to create a new quadrilateral inside the original one.

   What generalizations and conclusions can you make about the quadrilateral formed by connecting the midpoints of various quadrilaterals? For example, if the given quadrilateral is convex, must the new one also be convex? If the given quadrilateral is a rectangle, must the new quadrilateral be a rectangle?

7. Using your ruler, first draw line segments of the following lengths: 3 inches, 4 inches, 5 inches, 6 inches, and 8 inches. Then use the compass and straightedge to construct the following triangles.

   a. 3 inches, 4 inches, and 5 inches

   b. 3 inches, 4 inches, and 6 inches

   c. 3 inches, 4 inches, and 8 inches

   d. Describe your conclusions from these constructions.

8. There are many applications of congruent triangles in real life. For example, we can use congruent triangles to

determine the distance across a lake. Explain and justify one such method. *Note:* There is more than one possible way to do so.

9. Can you construct the following figures? If you can, do it and explain how you did it. If you can't, explain why it is not possible.

   a.

   b.

   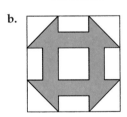

10. Make the following designs.[2] After you have figured out how to do so, write the directions for doing so. (Before turning in your directions, you might want to give them to a fellow student and see if that student can follow your directions.) Justify the construction.

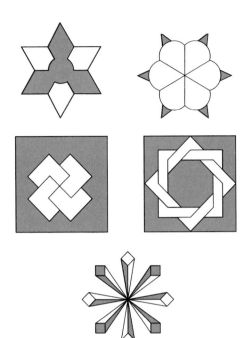

11. How might you find the center of the circle below? You are encouraged to try constructions, but you are not limited to constructions. How many different ways can you find? Justify each way.

    You may want to trace or construct circles on a sheet of paper and experiment.

12. In this section, we learned how to inscribe geometric figures within a circle. What if we *began* with the figure and circumscribed a circle around the figure?

    a. Determine a method for circumscribing a circle around an equilateral triangle.

    b. Determine a method for circumscribing a circle around any triangle or explain why you think it is not possible.

    c. Determine a method for circumscribing a circle around a square.

    d. Determine a method for circumscribing a circle around a rectangle.

    e. Determine a method for circumscribing a circle around a parallelogram.

[2] Dale Seymour and Reuben Schadler, *Creative Constructions* (Palo Alto, Calif.: Creative Publications, 1974).

f. Determine a method for circumscribing a circle around any quadrilateral or explain why you think it is not possible.

13. There are many ways to construct tangrams.

a. Begin with a square sheet of paper and make a tangram by only folding. Then write the directions and justify each step.

b. Using only a compass and a straightedge, construct a tangram. Then write the directions and justify each step.

c. Using a graphics program on a computer, create a program. Then write the directions and justify each step.

d. Write a LOGO program that will make the tangram square with the seven pieces.

LOGO

Your mathematics education differs in many ways from that of your grand-parents, and I firmly believe that the mathematics education of children 20 years from now will differ even more. One of the reasons for this profound difference will be technology. The potential for using calculators and computers to help people learn mathematics is extraordinary.

Computers are almost everywhere today, but this was not always so. Although I am not so old (I started teaching in 1973), my first substantive interaction with computers was in 1984, when I bought one for graduate school. I was terrified! But now I don't know how I would teach without them. However, it's a different story with my children. When they were still preschoolers, I bought them some software and was amazed at how quickly they caught on. I was even more amazed when I came into my home office one day and found 4-year-old Emily playing on my computer by herself. She had figured out how to turn it on, get into her program, quit her program, and play with my programs! Many of your students will be as comfortable with computers as my children are, and most children will quickly learn to use computers as long as they sense your enthusiasm and confidence.

It has been over 20 years since computers first started finding their way into schools. While they have had many positive effects, there have been as many misuses and abuses of computers as there have been positive uses. Toward this end, NCTM issued a position statement on the use of computers in the learning and teaching of mathematics. You will examine the whole statement in your Methods course later. At this point, we will focus on one part that is relevant to this course:

> Teachers should plan for students' use of technology in both learning and doing mathematics. A development of ideas is to be made with the transition from concrete experiences to abstract mathematical ideas,

focusing on the exploration and discovery of new mathematical concepts, and problem solving processes.[1]

LOGO

The computer language most often used in elementary schools and the one I find the most exciting is called LOGO. It was developed in the 1960s by a team of researchers at MIT under the direction of Seymour Papert. Papert was strongly influenced by Jean Piaget, a man about whom you will probably read more in your education courses than about any other theorist. One of Piaget's fascinations was how children are able "to build complex knowledge out of simple components."[2] Papert wanted to create a computer language that would reflect Piaget's views of how children learn.

Work on LOGO began with a mechanical device, called a turtle, that children could move around by issuing commands through a control box. The turtle had a pen under its center so that children could literally see the results of their commands. Ultimately, these ideas moved from a mechanical turtle to a simulated turtle that appears on a computer screen. There are many resources that give both the history of LOGO and how to use it, and the interested reader is encouraged to consult them. For now, let's get started.

Getting Started

If you have never worked with LOGO before, open the program and type the following commands:[3]

FD 50 RT 90 FD 50 RT 90

You can press RETURN or ENTER after each command, or you can type all four commands and then press RETURN.

Let us decode these commands. FD 50 means "go forward 50 units." Different LOGO programs have different units, so FD 50 will not necessarily make congruent line segments with different versions. On the other hand, RT 90 will have the same effect regardless of the LOGO program, because it means "turn right 90 degrees," and all LOGO programs accept 360 degrees as one complete revolution.

You should see this on the screen, with the turtle at the top and pointing down.

On your own, enter the commands you think will complete this figure to make a square. You may want to press HT at the end so that the computer will hide the turtle.

If you added the following commands, you will see a square:

FD 50 RT 90 FD 50 RT 90

Table B.1 gives the basic commands that we will use in this course, although your instructor may add more.[4]

---

[1] From the NCTM Position Statement "The Use of Technology in the Learning and Teaching of Mathematics," in the *1995–96 Handbook: NCTM Goals, Leaders, and Positions* (Reston, Va.: NCTM, 1995), p. 24.

[2] Earl Babbie, *Apple Logo for Teachers* (Belmont, Calif.: Wadsworth, 1984), p. 4.

[3] You must have a space between these commands. For example, you will receive an error message if you type FD50. Sometimes a space is essential, sometimes it is optional, and sometimes no space is essential.

[4] Some LOGO versions will have slightly different commands.

TABLE B.1

Function	Command	Abbreviation
Move the turtle forward	FORWARD	FD
Move the turtle backward	BACK	BK
Turn the turtle to its right	RIGHT	RT
Turn the turtle to its left	LEFT	LT
Lift the pen so that the turtle will not leave a trail	PEN UP	PU
Put the pen back down	PEN DOWN	PD
Hide the turtle so that you can see the picture	HIDE TURTLE	HT
Show the turtle so that you can see where it is	SHOW TURTLE	ST
Return the turtle to the center of the screen	HOME	
Clear the screen	CLEAR SCREEN	CS

The REPEAT Command

We have just seen how to make a square by typing in eight separate commands. The square is one of the most basic geometric figures, so imagine how many commands it would take to have the turtle make other geometric figures. Fortunately, there is a command called REPEAT that can greatly reduce the number of commands needed. Let us examine how it works.

If we analyze our eight commands to make a square, we can see that we are simply writing "FD 50 RT 90" four times. Enter the following command into your computer now.[5]

    REPEAT 4 [FD 50 RT 90]

In one sense, the REPEAT command is like the distributive property — for example, 4[5 + 3]. This kind of repetition is called iteration, which is one of the big ideas of programming languages.

Defining Procedures

Now make another square, this one 80 units on each side.
As you may have found, you could simply type

    REPEAT 4[FD 80 RT 90]

There are two procedures that can make our work in LOGO even simpler. First, any series of operations that we want to use several times can be named using the command "TO."

Enter the following:

    TO SQUARE
    REPEAT 4 [FD 80 RT 90]
    END

Second, the "END" tells the computer that the end of this procedure has been reached. You need END when you have a number of procedures in a row. Without it, the computer has no way of knowing when you are finished with one procedure. Some current software versions of LOGO will automatically type in "END" when you are finished.

[5] You must leave a space between REPEAT and 4. However, the space between 4 and the open bracket [is optional.

Just as we save computer files, we can save a LOGO program by giving it a name. For example, if you want to make this square tomorrow, you won't have to type REPEAT 4 [FD 80 RT 90]. However, if we want a square of a different size, we need to delete 80 and insert our new length. The next procedure addresses this need.

Defining Procedures with Variables

The following procedure uses the concept of variable and defines a general procedure for making any square.[6] Type the following program into your computer:

```
TO SQUARE :S
REPEAT 4 [FD :S RT 90]
END
```

To make a square with side 95 units in length, we simply enter SQUARE 95. Try it.

At this point, you have enough information to work with all the LOGO material in this appendix. The following Investigation gives you a little more practice, which most people need before launching out on their own.

INVESTIGATION **B.1** **Making Rectangles**

How would you define a LOGO procedure to draw a rectangle whose length is 80 units and width is 40 units? Think and then read on. . . .

DISCUSSION

Using our knowledge of LOGO and geometry, we find that the following commands will make one-half of a rectangle:

```
FD 40 RT 90 FD 80 RT 90
```

Thus, we can make a complete rectangle by typing

```
REPEAT 2 [FD 40 RT 90 FD 80 RT 90]
```

We can define a procedure for making rectangles by using the idea of variables. In contrast to the SQUARE procedure, we need two variables to define a rectangle: L for length and W for width (some people prefer L1 and L2).

```
TO RECTANGLE :L :W
REPEAT 2[FD :L RT 90 FD :W RT 90]
END
```

We can then make the 80-unit by 40-unit rectangle by typing RECTANGLE 80 40.

Some people prefer to define rectangle as RECT because it's a shorter command to type.

Now use this knowledge to make Figure B.1.

---

[6] In this case, there must be a space between SQUARE, and :, and there must be no space between : and S.

FIGURE **B.1**

This can be made by the following command:

REPEAT 4[RECTANGLE 40 80 RT 90]

INVESTIGATION **B.2** **Making Geometric Figures**

Can you make Figure B.2? Think and then read on. . . .

FIGURE **B.2**

DISCUSSION

This figure exemplifies another positive aspect of LOGO (and many other computer languages): It honors the notion that not everyone thinks in the same way. Have you ever had a teacher who showed his or her way to solve a problem and insisted that you do it that way? I had several such teachers, and it almost ruined me!

Below are three different ways to make the figure above. There are many others, too!

REPEAT 4 [FD 40 RT 90]
REPEAT 4 [FD 40 LT 90] FD 40
REPEAT 4 [FD 40 RT 90]

RECTANGLE 40 80
LT 90 BK 80
RECTANGLE 40 80

RECTANGLE 80 40
LT 90 BK 40
RECTANGLE 80 40

LOGO's Interactive Nature

One of the best aspects of working with LOGO is that students get immediate feedback. If you make a mistake in writing the program, the computer tells you. For example, with LOGO you either get feedback like "I don't know how to

FD50," or the screen shows the figure that is made from your directions. In either case, you can analyze what you did wrong and fix it as opposed to getting a poor grade, telling you that you did it wrong.

In this introduction, it is hoped that not only have you learned about LOGO, but you have also learned a little geometry. In order to solve "good" problems and make figures using LOGO, students must apply their knowledge of geometry and find underlying connections in geometry. If my goals for your work with LOGO are realized, in working with LOGO, you will see the following outcomes in yourself:

- You will be more positively disposed toward mathematics.
- You will learn more about geometry, have a better understanding of certain geometric concepts, and see more connections among concepts.
- Your problem-solving toolbox will be stronger.
- Your logical and analytical thinking abilities will be enhanced.
- Your spatial visualization abilities will be enhanced.

Exploring LOGO

Below are seven Explorations that will enable you to use LOGO to apply your understanding of geometry and to refine your ability to make and test predictions.

EXPLORATION B.1   **Making Letters**

1.   Each of the following sets of commands will create one letter of the alphabet.
    a. Predict the letter that will occur, and then type the commands to find out.

        FD 80 RT 90 FD 40 BK 80
        FD 40 BK 80 FD 40 RT 90 FD 40 LT 90 FD 40 BK 80
        RT 20 FD 80 LT 40 BK 80 FD 40 LT 70 FD 28
        FD 80 LT 20 BK 85 RT 40 FD 85 LT 20 BK 85

    b. At this point, you may want to define each procedure—that is, TO "LETTER" for each letter.

2.   Now use PU, PD, and HOME to spell a word with these four letters on your screen.

The HOME position of the turtle is in the center of your screen. To move the turtle so that you can spell this word, your first command will need to be something like[7]

    PU LT 90 FD 120 RT 90 PD

If we look at the commands in turn, the computer "hears" this:

---

[7] The actual numbers will vary depending on which version of LOGO you are using.

PU	Lift the pen up.
LT 90	Turn 90 degrees to the left.
FD 120	Move forward 120.
RT 90	Turn 90 degrees to the right (that is, return to the initial heading).
PD	Put the pen down (so that you are ready to work).

3. As you may have realized, not all the letters are the same height, and the procedures used to define the letters did not have them all beginning at the bottom of the letter. Fix the procedures used to define each letter so that all the letters are the same size and all begin at the bottom of the letter. You will be finished when you can get the computer to print your word so that it appears just as it would on a typewriter.

4. Spell another word.

EXPLORATION B.2 **Triangles**

1. Commonalities among all triangle procedures. The following program makes an equilateral triangle:

   REPEAT 3 [FD 50 RT 120]

   Most people are at least initially puzzled by the fact that we make an equilateral triangle (whose angles are all 60 degrees) by telling the turtle to move forward and then right 120 degrees three times.

   a. Can you explain why this is so? Discuss your ideas in your group and write your first draft of your response.

   b. After the class discussion, define and execute the following procedures:

      TO TRI1 FD 50 RT 75 FD 60 RT 146 FD 86 RT 139 FD 40 HT END
      TO TRI2 FD 50 RT 100 FD 60 RT 135 FD 70 RT 125 END
      TO TRI3 FD 50 RT 90 FD 120 RT 157 FD 130 HT END

   c. Now try to explain the connection between the procedure necessary to make triangles with LOGO and the fact that the sum of the angles of any triangle is 180 degrees.

2. Making triangles that appear in the classic position.

   a. Modify the REPEAT 3 [FD 50 RT 120] procedure to produce an equilateral triangle with the base parallel to the bottom of the page.

3. Understanding right triangles. Now let us examine how we can use knowledge of geometry to make right triangles. Make the following triangle on your computer:

EXPLORATION B.3 **Investigating Parallelograms**

PART 1: **Properties of parallelograms**

This exploration both requires you to apply your understanding of quadrilaterals and will result in a deeper understanding of the properties of quadrilaterals.

1. Construct several parallelograms with LOGO. Save your procedures — for example, PARA1, PARA2, and so on. Compare your procedures with your partner(s).

2. A parallelogram is defined as a quadrilateral in which both pairs of opposite sides are parallel. What additional properties do you think all parallelograms have, based on your observations on the results of your group's procedures?

3. Write a procedure that will enable you to make any parallelogram. *Note:* First you must think of how many variables you need. For example, a square needed only one variable, whereas a rectangle needed two variables (L for length and W for width).

PART 2: **Predicting outcomes**

In this part, you will try to make predictions and then generalizations. Given the initial variables, can you predict the shape and orientation of the resultant parallelogram? For example, the two parallelograms below are congruent but in different orientations.

1. Using the following procedure, make a variety of parallelograms.

    TO PARA :M :N :A
    REPEAT 2 [FD :M RT :A FD :N RT 180 - :A]
    END

  a. Sketch the relative shape and orientation of the parallelogram that will appear. That is, predict the shape and orientation.

   b. Run the procedure to check your prediction.

   c. If your prediction was close, fine. If not, analyze your prediction and what appeared on the screen and describe what you learned so that your next prediction may be more accurate.

2. Make up examples of your own to further explore the relationships between the lengths of the sides and angles and the resulting parallelogam.

3. Describe hypotheses that emerged from your explorations. Justify them.

4. What kind of quadrilaterals can be made with the PARA procedure? Be as specific as possible. For example, when the first two numbers after PARA are equal and the third number is 90, a square will be made.

EXPLORATION B.4   **Regular Polygons**

A regular polygon is defined as a convex polygon in which all sides have the same length and all angles have the same measure. We have learned how to use LOGO to make a regular triangle and a regular quadrilateral, more commonly known as an equilateral triangle and a square.

1. Write a program that can be used to make a regular pentagon and then a regular hexagon. Describe what you learned from this step.

2. Now write a procedure that will make a regular polygon with n sides. Explain why your procedure works as if you were talking to someone who missed this class.

EXPLORATION B.5   **Circles**

The following investigation is one of my favorites.

1. Develop a procedure that will make a circle. Summarize your rationale/thinking.

2. Enter the procedure given by your instructor. Why does it work?

EXPLORATION B.6 **Polygons and Stars**

Earlier, you developed a procedure that will create regular polygons. Below is another one.

```
TO POLY :N :S :A
REPEAT :N [FD :S RT :A]
END
```

Now experiment with different values for S, A, and N and see what you can find.

1. Summarize your findings and then compare notes with your partner(s).

2. Write a set of rules that will enable the reader to predict which commands will produce polygons, which will produce stars, and which will produce circles. For those commands that produce stars, write directions for predicting the number of points on the star; for example, POLY 9 60 200 will make a 9-pointed star.

3. In some cases, different commands produce the same star. Explain why.

EXPLORATION B.7 **Polyspirals**

The following famous LOGO program produces polygonal spirals that often look like flowers. For example, try POLYSPI 20 190 HT.

```
TO POLYSPI :L :T
IF :L > 300
 [STOP]
FD :L
RT :T
POLYSPI (:L + 3) :T
END
```

1. Experiment with different values of L and T. Describe your findings. Explain them.

2. Explain what roles the "300" and the "3" play.

EXERCISES

1. Complete this procedure so that it makes a trapezoid:

   LT 90 FD 100 RT 43 FD 50

2. Complete this procedure so that it makes a parallelogram:

   LT 90 FD 80 RT 45 FD 70

3. Make the following staircases.

4. Make the following right triangle in different orientations.

5. Make the pointed stars below.

6. Make the following concentric squares and equilateral triangles.

7. Make a net that will fold into a cube.

8. Make these figures:

    a.   **b.**   **c.**

    d. A flower

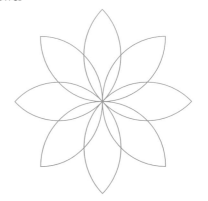

9. The following procedure will make a quadrilateral:

    TO QUAD :M :N :A
    REPEAT 2 [FD :M RT :A FD :N RT 180 - :A]
    END

    Modify the QUAD procedure so that the longest side of the quadrilateral will be parallel to the bottom of the paper.

LESSON
3

Catch of the Day

Purpose Children continue their study of living things as they measure with nonstandard units the lengths of paper fish.

Activity 1: Measuring Length

DRAWING TO LEARN

How long should we make our fish?

Management: Individuals (15–20 minutes)
Materials: Giant Math Activity Pad page 20, paper clips, construction paper, markers, crayons, scissors, stickers

1 Revisit Giant Math Activity Pad page 20. Draw children's attention to the water. *What animals and plants might live in water?*

2 Help children to chain together three to eight paper clips. Let them try to make paper fish the same length as their chains. They can decorate the fish with colorful patterns.

3 Have each child hold up his or her fish. *About how many paper clips long is this fish?* Record estimates on the chalkboard. Let the child hold up the paper-clip chain next to the fish and count the clips out loud. *How close were our estimates? Do our estimates improve with practice?*

My fish is about five paper clips long.

Variation
Materials: Use interlocking cubes instead of paper clips to measure the fish.

Ongoing Assessment
Can the child tell how long the fish are in paper-clip units?
Follow-up: If a child needs more practice measuring with nonstandard units, use the variation.

Journal Opportunity

Let children draw pictures and use invented spelling to describe what they did to make and measure their fish. They might want to tape more paper fish to their pages.

Students Acquiring English

Give children additional practice measuring with their paper-clip chains. Let pairs find classroom objects to measure and talk about. They can share what they find out with others.

Grade 1

Activity 2: Predicting Symmetry

Can we predict a design?

Management: Pairs (20–30 minutes)
Materials: Construction paper, hole punches, crayons

Invite children to predict the number and location of holes you punch in folded construction paper.

1 Fold a sheet of paper in half and punch several holes through both halves. Open the sheet to display the resulting pattern. *How many holes are there? Where are the holes? Is the design symmetrical? Why?*

2 Fold another sheet of paper in half, open it up, and punch holes in only one half.

3 *Where would the matching holes be if you had punched through both halves?* Let a volunteer mark his or her predictions with a crayon.

4 Refold the paper, and punch through the original holes. *How many holes will there be?* Open up the paper to see how close the predictions were.

5 Now have the children work in pairs. One child punches holes in half of a sheet of paper that has a fold line in the center. The other child marks where the symmetrical holes should be and then folds the paper and punches through the original holes to check.

Ongoing Assessment
Can the child accurately predict the placement of the holes?
Follow-up: The children will have opportunities to use visual-spatial reasoning in later modules.

Hey, I guessed right!

Portfolio Opportunity

Invite the children to decorate the covers of their portfolios with symmetrical designs. Add a date to the cover.

Extension

Have the children consider this question: How many holes will there be if one side has 2 and we punch the same amount on the other side? (4) What about for 3, 4, and 5? (6, 8, 10)

Alternate Strategy

Punch or cut holes in felt shapes and have the children feel with their fingers where the holes are. Then fold the shapes and have them feel where the holes should be.

Activity Options

LESSON
9

Measuring with Jars

Purpose Children use jars, bottles, and other containers to explore volume and to sort objects with overlapping attributes.

Activity 1: Measuring Capacity

Which holds more?

Management: Whole group (25–35 minutes)
Materials: Jars and bottles, and water, sand, or tiny seeds
Vocabulary: empty, full, holds more, holds less

- Assemble some jars and bottles from the classroom collection. *What originally came in this container? In this one? What else could you use these jars for?*
- Ask volunteers to place the jars and bottles in a row from shortest to tallest. Select two: for example, a tall, narrow olive jar and a short, wide jam jar.
  Which jar is taller? Which jar do you think holds more? How can we find out?
- As one possible solution, let children try filling one jar with sand, water, or tiny seeds and then pouring the contents into the other.
- Use basic capacity words, such as *empty, full, holds more, holds less,* and *equals* to describe what happened.
- Repeat with other pairs of jars and bottles and then set the materials out for independent exploration.

Variation
Procedure: Pairs of children choose two different-sized jars and try to guess which holds more. They then check by filling one jar and pouring its contents into the other. Label the jar that holds more and compare the result with their estimate.

Ongoing Assessment
- What words does the child use to describe differences in capacity?
- What reasoning does she or he use in judging comparative capacity?
Follow-up: Children will have further opportunities to explore volume in Activity 2 on page 139.

It's overflowing so it must hold less!

Journal Opportunity

Invite children to use invented spelling to write stories about collections or other things they keep in jars.

Music Connection

Sing the song "There's a Hole in the Bucket." **What could you carry in a bucket with a hole?**

Cultural Connection

Encourage children to bring in jars and other containers from their own homes. Invite them to share what the original contents of the jar or container were. You might have children guess what they think different jars might have originally held.

Adding

Part B: Let's play Recycling 8s.

Management: Pairs

- To begin, Player A holds up the rectangular folded worksheet in his or her hands so that the two flaps with the words *Paper* and *Glass* read right-side up and the number sentences are hidden in the fold.
- Player A then inserts his or her thumbs under the flaps in front and index fingers under the flaps in back, pushing them into the corners above each word and then bringing the corners together to form a point.
- Player B picks a word from an outside flap. Player A spells out the chosen word, opening the folded worksheet forward and then sideways for each letter in the word. For example, if *Glass*, a five-letter word, is chosen, Player A opens the worksheet five times.
- Player B then picks one of the four number sentences showing, for example 8 + 5. Player A solves the sentence out loud and opens the worksheet that number of times (13).
- Player A checks the answer by lifting the flap. If the answer is correct, the two players switch roles.

Activity 2: Identifying Attributes

What would a box look like if you laid it flat?

Management: Whole class (20–30 minutes)
Materials: Cardboard boxes, scissors, chart paper, crayons
Vocabulary: net

- Have children share their responses to the question above. Then cut down the edges of a box to show how its faces form a solid. *What can you learn about a solid by looking at its sides laid flat? How could you tell what a box would look like flat without taking it apart?*
- Have children trace all the faces of a geometric solid on paper. Tell them they are making nets. You may need to direct the children to trace one face and then flip the solid and trace another face. *How can you tell if you've traced all the faces?*
- Have some children share their nets. Others can guess which shape was used to make the net. *Are all nets for the same shape alike? Why? Which solids make similar nets? Why?* Post the children's nets on a bulletin board.

Variation
Procedure: Give the children nets printed on construction paper and have them create boxes from them.

Ongoing Investigation

Have the children label objects in the classroom with proper geometric names. Leave this as a permanent display and a resource. Challenge the students to find rarely seen solids such as pyramids.

Extension

Invite children to bring in small, light cardboard boxes, perhaps from cereal or soap. Direct them to use their boxes to make nets. Then have children cut apart their boxes. **Does your net look like your flattened box? Why or why not?**

Alternate Strategy

Children who have difficulty with spatial relationships can first cut apart a box so that all sides lie flat. Then they can trace the flattened box to make a net.

Lesson 9 *continued*

Exercises and Problems

Tiles and Designs

Students look at Italian and Egyptian mosaic and tile patterns and investigate symmetry, congruence, polygons, and line segments.

▶ **Problem Solving Tip**
Students may find that creating a chart or diagram to help them with these exercises and problems will lead to a swifter, surer solution. Refer them to Problem Solving Strategies, Organize Information, on pages 388–389, in the Tool Kit.

Did **Y**ou **K**now**?**
The earliest use of mosaics dates back as far as 3,000 B.C.; Mosaic flooring was in widespread use by about 300 B.C.

From *The World Book Encyclopedia*

Exercises and Problems

Tiles and Designs

1. Possible answers: one line: trapezoid; two lines: rectangle; three lines: triangle; four lines: square

Use your Tracing Tool to help you answer the questions.

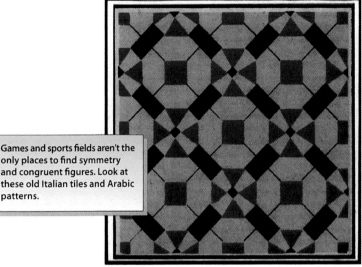

Games and sports fields aren't the only places to find symmetry and congruent figures. Look at these old Italian tiles and Arabic patterns.

Italian

1 Which figures in this tile pattern have one line of symmetry? two? three? four? See above.

2 Find five line segments in the design. Find three lines of symmetry in the design. Can you find more? Answers will vary.

3 Find two congruent squares in the pattern. Do you think all the squares are congruent? Why? Answers will vary; no; they may have sides of different lengths.

378 Module 8: Puzzles, Shapes, and Games

Teaching Options

Geometry Connection

Students can connect slides, flips, and turns with the patterns they see. Have students create and sketch a shape. Then have them use that shape to create a pattern using slides, flips, and turns. Students should write a description of their pattern.

Social Studies Connection

Students might enjoy gathering and sharing tile patterns, mosaics, and designs from other countries. Have them play a show-and-tell in which they point out the lines of symmetry, polygons, and other geometric elements.

Grade 3

4. Possible answer: Triangles, squares, pentagons; 3, 4, 5
5. Triangles, squares, and pentagons; their respective sides and angles are congruent.
6. Yes; the acute angles of the triangles; the obtuse angle of the pentagon, the hexagon, and the octagon

Italian

Arabic

4 Find three different kinds of figures in the design above. If you do not know the names of the figures, tell the number of sides. See above.

5 Which figures are congruent? Explain. See above.

6 Find right angles in the pattern. Do you see angles smaller than right angles? larger? Where? See above.

7 List all of the shapes in the pattern above. Triangle, square, pentagon, hexagon, octagon

8 Are the black and orange figures above congruent? How do you know? Yes; their respective sides and angles are congruent.

9 Would you use a flip, slide, or turn to place figure *A* on top of figure *B*? How would you move figure *A* on top of figure *C*? Slide and turn; slide

10 How many lines of symmetry do the blue and orange figures have? Find one line of symmetry for the entire pattern. Describe it. 2; possible answer: Lengthwise from the midpoint of the top horizontal line to the midpoint of the bottom horizontal line

Section D: Congruence and Symmetry **379**

Extension

Some students might be interested in exploring symmetry with three-dimensional objects. Suggest some objects such as balls, cones, and irregular pyramids. Ask students which ones could be split to produce two identical halves.

Cooperative Learning Tip

Have students discuss and answer the questions for the Exercises and Problems in small cooperative groups. This will enable students to share ideas and suggestions about the patterns and mosaics pictured.

Lesson 6 *continued*

Exercises and Problems

Combinations

 These pages give students an opportunity to play a game of chance and keep track of the probabilities as they play.

Drawing to Learn

Marking their predictions on a number line allows students to connect the predictions they make in this game to the predictions they made in other activities in this module. Using a number line also offers them an occasion to apply a mathematical tool to a real-life game.

▶ **Using the Tool Kit**

Drawing can help students convey information in an exciting way. Refer students to Drawing to Learn, Drawing to Share, on page 407 of the Tool Kit.

Did **Y**ou **K**now?

A game of chance played by the Klamath Indians of Oregon is called *shakla*. Four long sticks are arranged under a blanket. One player guesses the arrangement. If the player guesses correctly, the player wins points .

From *Games of the North American Indians* by Stewart Culin

Exercises and Problems

Combinations

Women of the Twana nation in the state of Washington play a game with beaver teeth. They toss teeth that have carvings on one side. Scoring depends on how the teeth land. You can play this game with your partner, using coins or "beaver teeth" you make from cardboard.

Predict

1 Suppose you want only one out of four pennies to show heads. Is the probability of that happening closer to 0 or 1? Explain.
0, because the probability is $\frac{1}{4}$, which is closer to 0 than to 1

2 Will the chance of tossing one tail be the same as tossing one head? How do you know?
See below.

3 In how many different combinations could the four coins land? 5

4 Sketch the combinations. 4 heads, 3 heads and 1 tail, 2 heads and 2 tails, 1 head and 3 tails, 4 tails

Play

5 Toss four coins 20 times. Record the results of each trial. Display students' data.

    a. Write ratios to compare the number of times each combination was tossed to the total number of trials.

    b. Repeat for 20 more trials. What is the new ratio for each combination in 20 trials?

Module 8: Lucky Summer
2. Yes, because out of the 16 possible outcomes, 4 are 1 head and 3 tails and 4 are 1 tail and 3 heads.

Teaching Options

Cultural Connection

Native American games of chance are of two kinds. In the first kind of game, players randomly throw marked objects. The objects stand for a number or numbers that count toward a sum. In the second kind of game, players guess the locations of concealed objects, worth varying point values.

Computer Opportunity

Invite students to explore probabilities of combinations with *MathKeys.* They can use the coins, spinners, or Number Machine in *Unlocking Probability Vol. II.* Ask students to explain how the bar graph in *Unlocking Probability Vol. II* represents the probability of each combination occurring.

Grade 4

7. Responses should be appropriate to, and reflective of, students' process.

Think

6 Which combination did you toss most often?
See students' data.

7 Why did that happen?
See above.

Possible answer:

$\frac{1}{16}$: 4 heads, 4 tails

$\frac{1}{4}$: 3 heads, 3 tails

$\frac{3}{8}$: 2 heads, 2 tails

8 Draw a number line. Mark 0, $\frac{1}{2}$, and 1. Mark where you think the probability of tossing each combination should be. Use your ratios to help you.
See above right.

9 Explain why you placed each combination where you did. Responses should be appropriate to, and reflective of, students' process.

10 Which combination of coins should be worth the most points? Why do you think so?
Possible answer: The least likely ones (4 heads or 4 tails)

Calculator Tip

If students want to figure scores for the game, they can assign a point value to each combination. Then, encourage students to use their calculators to total the points they scored with their tosses.

▶ **Ongoing Assessment**
Check students' ratios for Exercise 5. The ratios should be written as the number of times a combination was tossed over the total number of tosses.

Follow-up Strategy Students who have difficulty working with four coins may start with one or two coins.

3. Reflecting and Sharing

Journal Opportunity
Have students explain why some combinations occur more frequently than others and how that frequency affects probability.

Section Assessment
An Observation Checklist (**Assessment Master 52**) is available in *Assessment Options*.

Additional Practice and Homework Options

- Extra Practice, p. 439(b)
- Activity Worksheet 74
- Skill Worksheets 185–186
- Alternate Strategy Worksheet 62
- Math to Go 40
- Gameboard Masters 8A–8B

End of Lesson 6

Investigation

Paper Towel Olympics

1 – 2 days
1 2 3 4 5

Purpose
Students will apply knowledge of metric measurements in a problem solving situation and analyze data expressed in metric measures.

Materials
- *pan*
- *three different brands of paper towels*
- *metric measuring beaker*
- *centimeter ruler*
- *gram weights*

Calculator access assumed

1. Getting Started

Are all paper towels created equal? Students might discuss what factors would differentiate them, such as thickness or paper quality.

2. Facilitating Investigations

You might suggest that drying the pan and measuring cup between repeats could improve the accuracy of results. Remind students that they need to record their results so they can analyze the data. Discuss the information they need and the best format.

Investigate! Investigate! Investigate! Investigate! Investigate! Investigate! Investigate!

Investigation

Paper Towel Olympics

Which brand of paper towels is best? How much water do paper towels hold? Do some brands hold more than others? Choose three different brands to investigate. Find out which deserves the gold medal.

1 How much water does each towel hold? Pour a thin layer of water into a pan. How many milliliters of water are in the pan? Place a towel in the pan. Soak it, and remove it. How much water is left in the pan? How much did the towel hold? Repeat this with each brand.

262   Module 5: Faster, Higher, Stronger

Investigate! Investigate! Investigate! Investigate! Investigate! Investigate! Investigate!

Teaching Options

Cultural Connection

According to the *1993 Information Please Almanac,* paper was invented in China around 100 BC. You might suggest that interested students investigate to find out how the Chinese made their paper.

Cooperative Learning Tip

You may want students to do this investigation in groups. Each group should have a materials handler who collects all the materials the group needs and takes responsibility for putting items away at the end of the activity.

Grade 5

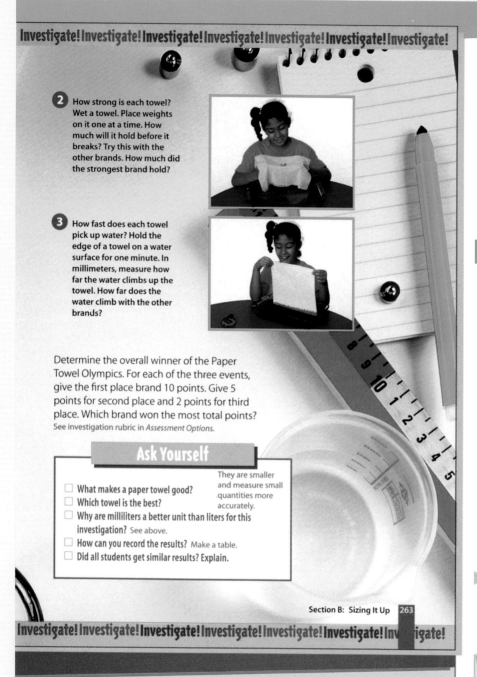

2 How strong is each towel? Wet a towel. Place weights on it one at a time. How much will it hold before it breaks? Try this with the other brands. How much did the strongest brand hold?

3 How fast does each towel pick up water? Hold the edge of a towel on a water surface for one minute. In millimeters, measure how far the water climbs up the towel. How far does the water climb with the other brands?

Determine the overall winner of the Paper Towel Olympics. For each of the three events, give the first place brand 10 points. Give 5 points for second place and 2 points for third place. Which brand won the most total points? See investigation rubric in *Assessment Options*.

Ask Yourself

☐ What makes a paper towel good?
☐ Which towel is the best?
☐ Why are milliliters a better unit than liters for this investigation? See above.
☐ How can you record the results? Make a table.
☐ Did all students get similar results? Explain.

They are smaller and measure small quantities more accurately.

Section B: Sizing It Up 263

Drawing to Learn

You might suggest that students draw a graph to show the comparisons of the three brands of paper towels they have investigated.

3. Reflecting and Sharing

Talk About It

After students complete their investigations, have them discuss the results.

- *"How did you measure the water left in the pan in the first experiment?"* Possible answer: I used a cup marked in milliliters.

- *"What unit of measure did you use to express the results of the second investigation?"* Grams

- *"How were you able to measure how far the water climbs up the towel?"* Possible answer: I measured from the edge of the paper to the highest point the water reached.

▶ **Ongoing Assessment**

A complete scoring rubric for this investigation is available in *Assessment Options*.

Portfolio Opportunity

Students might want to place the results of this investigation in their portfolios.

Computer Opportunity

Have student groups record the results of their experiments in a graphing program. Suggest they create a bar graph. Ask them to explain how it represents the data. Combine all group data on the computer to create a class graph. Have the groups explain how their graph is similar to the class graph.

Students Acquiring English

Students may need some help recording the result of each experiment. They may also need assistance in translating the Ask Yourself questions. Allow ample time for students to formulate their responses.

Building Polygons

Purpose
Students use ratios and polygons to make scale drawings.

Vocabulary
- *polygons*
- *quadrilaterals*

Materials
- *Drawing to Learn: Geometry Tool or protractor Tracing Tool or grid paper*
- *construction paper*
- *ruler*
- *scissors*
- *crayons or markers*
- *MathKeys: Unlocking Geometry Vol. II software*
- *Activity Worksheet 58*
- *Skill Worksheets 181–184*
- *Alternate Strategy Worksheet 46*

Calculator access assumed

1. Getting Started

Students use triangles to make other polygons. You may want to review various polygons.

2. Facilitating Activities

Cut and Combine

Encourage students to think about each figure as combinations of triangles.

Building Polygons

Now use triangles to build **polygons**—closed figures made entirely of line segments.

What You'll Need
- *drawing paper*
- *scissors*

Activity 1 Cut and Combine

With Your Group Combine triangles to make **quadrilaterals**, or four-sided polygons. The six shapes at the bottom of this page are quadrilaterals.
See students' drawings and other work.

1 Fold a sheet of paper in half. Cut out a triangle along the folded edge. Then unfold the triangle.

2 What kind of quadrilateral do you have? What can you say about the two triangles that make it up?
Type of quadrilateral varies depending on triangle used; they are congruent.

3 Cut across the fold line. Arrange the triangles into other quadrilaterals. Record your results.

4 Repeat steps 1–3 with another triangle. What generalizations can you make about the triangles that make up quadrilaterals? Describe your quadrilaterals.
Check student's answers.

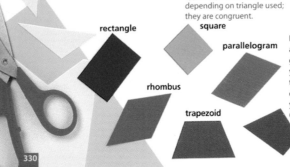

rectangle

square

parallelogram

rhombus

trapezoid

quadrilateral

330

Teaching Options

Math Minute

Have students write each decimal as a fraction.

1. 0.66 2. 3.75 3. 0.1 4. 2.8

1. $\frac{2}{3}$; 2. $3\frac{3}{4}$; 3. $\frac{1}{10}$; 4. $2\frac{4}{5}$

Students Acquiring English

You may want to have students use tangram pieces to learn the names of different polygons. Say a name, display it on an index card, and have students construct the polygon using the pieces. A trapezoid is made with two triangles and a square, for example.

Grade 5

ACTIVITY 2 More Than Four

With Your Group Measure the angles in a quadrilateral. Add them up. Record the number. Do the same with a pentagon and a hexagon. What pattern do you see? See below.

Total Number of Degrees in Regular Polygons

Shape	sides	total degrees
Triangle	3	180
Quadri	4	?
Pentagon	5	?
Hexagon	6	?

Quadrilateral: 360°; pentagon: 540°, hexagon: 720°; for each additional side, add 180°.

ACTIVITY 3 Venning Shapes

With Your Group Look at the Venn diagram below. The outside shape stands for all quadrilaterals. What do the inside shapes stand for?
Parallelograms, rectangles, squares

Draw a quadrilateral that is not a parallelogram.

Draw a parallelogram that is not a rectangle.

Why are trapezoids and parallelograms separate? Trapezoids are not parallelograms.

Which part of the diagram stands for figures that do not have two sets of parallel sides?
Quadrilaterals and trapezoids

Why are squares shown inside rectangles and parallelograms?
See below.

Quadrilaterals

Parallelograms

Rectangles

Squares

Trapezoids

Squares are special types of rectangles and parallelograms.

What You'll Need
- *Geometry Tool or protractor*
- *ruler*

What do you know about expressions that can help you find the pattern? First describe the pattern in words. Then use numbers and a variable. For instance, start with n × 180. See above.

What You'll Need
- *Geometry Tool or protractor*
- *ruler*

Section C: Scale Drawing **331**

Vocabulary Strategy
Many students confuse rhombuses and trapezoids. You might help students remember that a rhombus is a parallelogram by mentioning that both words contain the letter *m*.

ACTIVITY 2 More Than Four

Students should recall that the number of degrees in the angles of a triangle is 180. Students should discover that each time they add a side to a figure, the total number of degrees in the angles increases by 180°.

Problem Solving Tip
Some students may not see the pattern as the number of sides increases. You may want to have students find the difference between the number of degrees in each figure and record their data in a chart.

ACTIVITY 3 Venning Shapes

You may want to ask students questions to help them interpret the Venn diagram.

- *"Are all trapezoids quadrilaterals?"* Yes.

- *"Are all quadrilaterals trapezoids?"* No, trapezoids are a subset.

- *"How does the Venn diagram tell you this?"* The trapezoid section is within the quadrilateral section but the quadrilateral section is not within the trapezoid section.

Lesson 7 continues . . .

Computer Opportunity

Have students make quadrilaterals with *MathKeys: Unlocking Geometry Vol. II*. Students can use the electronic grid or pattern blocks to build their own quadrilaterals. Ask students to find out how many quadrilaterals they can form. In the Notepad, have them categorize and describe each shape. You may want to print out students' drawings to publish a geometry resource book for the class.

Literature Connection

One part of Norton Juster's book *The Phantom Tollbooth* features Mr. Dodecahedron, a three-dimensional twelve-sided figure. You may wish to read the story aloud to students.

Investigation

Circles and Paths

Purpose
Students analyze patterns created by using circles and points on the circle. They analyze the relationship between the number of points on the circle and the number of points they use to make their patterns.

Materials
- *compass*
- *Drawing to Learn: Fraction Tool or protractor and ruler*
- *MathKeys: Unlocking Geometry Vol. II software*

1. Getting Started

Review the number of degrees in a circle. Also review how to mark equidistant points on a circle with a compass.

2. Facilitating Investigations

Students should discover that their patterns involve the common factors of the total number of points and the number of points skipped each time. If these numbers share no common factor, there is only one path. For numbers with a common factor, the number of paths is the GCF of the two numbers.

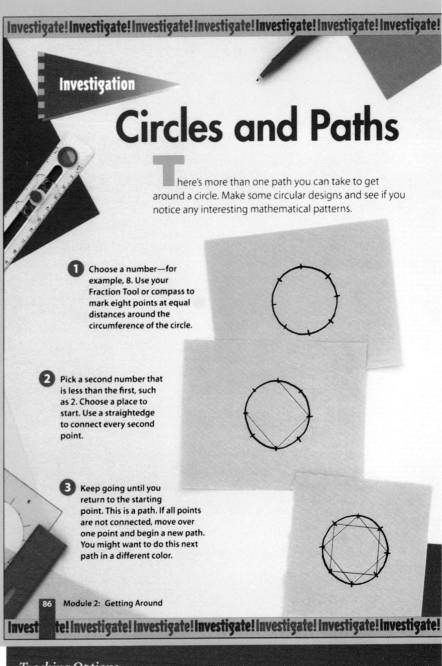

Investigate! Investigate! Investigate! Investigate! Investigate! Investigate! Investigate!

Investigation

Circles and Paths

There's more than one path you can take to get around a circle. Make some circular designs and see if you notice any interesting mathematical patterns.

1 Choose a number—for example, 8. Use your Fraction Tool or compass to mark eight points at equal distances around the circumference of the circle.

2 Pick a second number that is less than the first, such as 2. Choose a place to start. Use a straightedge to connect every second point.

3 Keep going until you return to the starting point. This is a path. If all points are not connected, move over one point and begin a new path. You might want to do this next path in a different color.

86   Module 2: Getting Around

Investigate! Investigate! Investigate! Investigate! Investigate! Investigate! Investigate!

Teaching Options

Science Connection

Some spiders use circles and paths for their webs. Once the spider has spun the boundaries of the web, it spins an inner and an outer spiral. Interested students might do research and report to the class on different types of spider webs.

Grade 6

See investigation rubric in *Assessment Options*.

4 How many paths are in your circle? Make a chart like the one on this page to show your results. Describe your design. What do you notice about the paths and the number of points you used to create the design? Explain.

5 Now try using other numbers to create different designs. Review your explanation. Does it apply to your new designs?

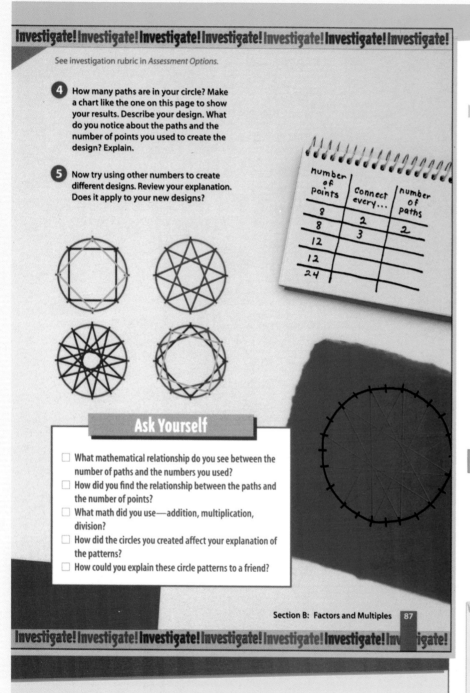

number of points	connect every...	number of paths
8		
8	2	2
12	3	
12		
24		

Ask Yourself

☐ What mathematical relationship do you see between the number of paths and the numbers you used?

☐ How did you find the relationship between the paths and the number of points?

☐ What math did you use—addition, multiplication, division?

☐ How did the circles you created affect your explanation of the patterns?

☐ How could you explain these circle patterns to a friend?

Section B: Factors and Multiples **87**

▶ **Ongoing Assessment**

Can students clearly explain how the paths and numbers relate? Although the patterns on the circles show the greatest common factor of two numbers, students may find other relationships as well.

A complete scoring rubric for this investigation is available in *Assessment Options*.

Follow-up Strategy   Students who have problems creating circles may trace the ones on these two pages. Ask students if they can predict how many paths will occur in a 64-pointed circle counting every 20 points (4 paths with 16 points in each).

3. Reflecting and Sharing

Talk About It

Ask students to share and discuss their explanations with the class. You may want to ask students to think about how they worked through this activity.

Portfolio Opportunity

Students may want to add their circles and explanations to their portfolios.

Geometry Connection

Students may connect the shapes they create with their paths to the number of degrees in a circle. You may wish to suggest the use of a protractor to measure the inscribed angles. Have students describe any relationships.

Extension

Suggest that students start with one point on the circle and connect it to every other point. Ask them to describe the patterns these paths create. Have them also tell how these paths differ from those in the investigation.

Lesson 7 *continued*

2. Facilitating Activities

ᴬᶜᵀᴵᵛᴵᵀʸ 1 Around and About

Students might use pattern blocks to model slides, flips, and turns as they write definitions.

ᴬᶜᵀᴵᵛᴵᵀʸ 2 In Perfect Balance

Students choosing the first option may wish to trace the buildings' outlines on notebook paper, then draw lines of symmetry. For option 2, suggest students label points on their diagrams, then refer to examples of symmetry in their notes.

▶ Questioning Strategy

Help students recall what they know about symmetry.

- *"Where would you draw a line to show two symmetrical halves of the Taj Mahal?"* From the top of the tower to the base of the Taj Mahal.

- *"Is each door and window symmetrical? Explain."* Yes; a vertical line through the center of each forms two matching halves.

- *"How can you make sure you have found a line of symmetry?"* Possible answer: Trace, then fold along the presumed line of symmetry.

Drawing to Learn

 Have students make diagrams to show symmetry of each shape in their Dictionary of Shapes.

What You'll Need
- *Tracing Tool or ruler*

DRAWING TO LEARN

How many lines of symmetry can you find on a square? on a regular octagon or a circle? How can you use what you know about symmetry to add to your definitions of polygons? Possible answer: 4; 8; an infinite number; a regular polygon has as many lines of symmetry as sides.

In the early 1600s in what is now northern India, Mumtaz Mahal died. Her husband, the Mogul Emperor Shah Jahan, had the Taj Mahal built as his and her burial place.

ᴬᶜᵀᴵᵛᴵᵀʸ 2 In Perfect Balance

With Your Partner The Taj Mahal uses flips to create symmetry. You know a **line of symmetry** divides a figure into two congruent halves. Choose one of these two activities to complete.

1. Make a diagram to show what you find.

2. Design a building that uses symmetry in its face and its floor plan. Describe how you used slides and flips to create symmetry and list all the ways in which your building is symmetrical. See students' drawings for 1–2.

Floor plan of the Taj Mahal

Possible answers: Length of each side; diagonals; interior angles at each corner of floor plan

Which angles and lines are congruent? Use your Tracing Tool or ruler to tell.

Do slides and turns also show symmetry? Explain. Yes; each is a duplicate of the original shape.

Teaching Options

Computer Opportunity

Challenge students to use the electronic pattern blocks in *MathKeys: Unlocking Geometry Vol. II* software to design a rug or quilt square. They can flip, slide, and rotate the blocks to make designs. Encourage students to combine pattern blocks to make larger shapes. Invite them to use the Notepad to describe the symmetry of their pattern.

Extension

Ask students to study the symmetry of the structure of their choice. They might select a well-known building or a structure in their neighborhood. Invite students to draw a diagram of the building and list the ways it is symmetrical.

Grade 6

▶ ³ **Round and Round**

With Your Partner An architect needs to describe the **angle of rotation**, or number of degrees a shape is turned, so someone else can follow the plan.

1 Trace an equilateral triangle. Label its vertexes. Rotate and trace the triangle. Line up the edges as you go until you meet your original shape. What shape did you make? Hexagon

2 Estimate how far the triangle was turned each time. Use your protractor to check your answer. 60°

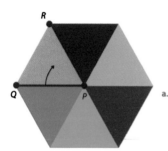

a. Which color panel is a 180° turn of the yellow panel around point *P*? Explain how you know.

Red; it moved 60° each time
3 × 60° = 180°

b. Which color panel shows a 240° turn of the yellow panel around point *P*?
Dark green;
4 × 60° = 240°

c. Which kind of triangle could you rotate to make an octagon? How far would you need to rotate it each time?
Isosceles; 45°

With Your Partner Draw your own tile pattern using turns of 90°, 180°, and 270°.

What You'll Need
- *Tracing Tool or tracing paper*
- *Geometry Tool or protractor and ruler*
- *crayons or markers*

Architect R. Buckminster Fuller designed geodesic domes like the one above. The domes use polygons for the faces. Fuller designed the one that housed the United States exhibit at Expo 67 in Montreal in 1967.

You know there are 360° in a circle. How could you use this information to find the angle of rotation, or turn, of a regular polygon? Divide 360° by the number of sides.

Section C: Beautiful Math **379**

▶ ³ **Round and Round**

 15–30 min

Students might make stencils, trace pattern blocks, or use their Geometry Tool to show turns.

▶ **Questioning Strategy**
Help students relate the activity to polygons.

- *"Why is it important to know that there are 360° in a circle when finding the angle of rotation?"* Possible answer: Because if you keep rotating the figure, you make a circle; 360° divided by the number of turns gives you the angle of rotation.

- *"How can you decide which angle measurements could be rotated to make regular polygons?"* Any measure, such as 10, 20, 45, or 60, that is a factor of 360

▶ **Ongoing Assessment**
Students should be able to figure out the angle of rotation within any polygon.

Follow-up Strategy Have students cut out an isosceles triangle and rotate it around the vertex between the two congruent sides. Then ask them to divide 360° by the number of turns.

- *"What is the angle of rotation? Is the repeated angle a factor of 360°?"* Possible answers: 90°, yes; 36°, yes

Combination Classes

Younger students might use manipulatives to help them find the angle of rotation. In addition, isometric dot paper or grid paper might help some students draw repeated shapes more quickly.

Cultural **Connection**

Islamic buildings are often covered in tile patterns. Ask students to do research on tile patterns in different countries. You might suggest they begin by looking up the Great Mosque of of Córdoba and the Alhambra in Granada, Spain.

Lesson 7 continues . . .

Section C: **Beautiful Math** **379**

Grade 1

Activity 2: Predicting Symmetry

Can we predict a design?

Management: Pairs (20–30 minutes)
Materials: Construction paper, hole punches, crayons

Invite children to predict the number and location of holes you punch in folded construction paper.

1 Fold a sheet of paper in half and punch several holes through both halves. Open the sheet to display the resulting pattern. *How many holes are there? Where are the holes? Is the design symmetrical? Why?*

2 Fold another sheet of paper in half, open it up, and punch holes in only one half.

3 *Where would the matching holes be if you had punched through both halves?* Let a volunteer mark his or her predictions with a crayon.

4 Refold the paper, and punch through the original holes. *How many holes will there be?* Open up the paper to see how close the predictions were.

5 Now have the children work in pairs. One child punches holes in half of a sheet of paper that has a fold line in the center. The other child marks where the symmetrical holes should be and then folds the paper and punches through the original holes to check.

Ongoing Assessment
Can the child accurately predict the placement of the holes?
Follow-up: The children will have opportunities to use visual-spatial reasoning in later modules.

Hey, I guessed right!

Portfolio Opportunity

Invite the children to decorate the covers of their portfolios with symmetrical designs. Add a date to the cover.

Extension

Have the children consider this question: How many holes will there be if one side has 2 and we punch the same amount on the other side? (4) What about for 3, 4, and 5? (6, 8, 10)

Alternate Strategy

Punch or cut holes in felt shapes and have the children feel with their fingers where the holes are. Then fold the shapes and have them feel where the holes should be.

Activity Options

LESSON
3

Catch of the Day

Purpose Children continue their study of living things as they measure with nonstandard units the lengths of paper fish.

Activity 1: Measuring Length *DRAWING TO LEARN*

How long should we make our fish?

Management: Individuals (15–20 minutes)
Materials: Giant Math Activity Pad page 20, paper clips, construction paper, markers, crayons, scissors, stickers

1 Revisit Giant Math Activity Pad page 20. Draw children's attention to the water. *What animals and plants might live in water?*

2 Help children to chain together three to eight paper clips. Let them try to make paper fish the same length as their chains. They can decorate the fish with colorful patterns.

3 Have each child hold up his or her fish. *About how many paper clips long is this fish?* Record estimates on the chalkboard. Let the child hold up the paper-clip chain next to the fish and count the clips out loud. *How close were our estimates? Do our estimates improve with practice?*

My fish is about five paper clips long.

Variation
Materials: Use interlocking cubes instead of paper clips to measure the fish.

Ongoing Assessment
Can the child tell how long the fish are in paper-clip units?
Follow-up: If a child needs more practice measuring with nonstandard units, use the variation.

Journal Opportunity

Let children draw pictures and use invented spelling to describe what they did to make and measure their fish. They might want to tape more paper fish to their pages.

Students Acquiring English

Give children additional practice measuring with their paper-clip chains. Let pairs find classroom objects to measure and talk about. They can share what they find out with others.

NCTM *Standards*

T his appendix includes the NCTM Curriculum Standards for Grades K–4 and 5–8, as they appear in *Curriculum and Evaluation Standards for School Mathematics*, published in 1989 by the National Council of Teachers of Mathematics. It also includes selected teaching standards from *Professional Standards for Teaching Mathematics*, published in 1991 by the NCTM.

NCTM Curriculum Standards for Grades K–4[1]

▇ Standard 1: Mathematics as Problem Solving

In grades K–4, the study of mathematics should emphasize problem solving so that students can—

- use problem-solving approaches to investigate and understand mathematical content;
- formulate problems from everyday and mathematical situations;
- develop and apply strategies to solve a wide variety of problems;
- verify and interpret results with respect to the original problem;
- acquire confidence in using mathematics meaningfully.

▇ Standard 2: Mathematics as Communication

In grades K–4, the study of mathematics should include numerous opportunities for communication so that students can—

- relate physical materials, pictures, and diagrams to mathematical ideas;

---

[1] NCTM, *Curriculum & Evaluation Standards for School Mathematics: Executive Summary* (Reston, VA: NCTM, © 1989). Reprinted with permission.

- reflect on and clarify their thinking about mathematical ideas and situations;
- relate their everyday language to mathematical language and symbols;
- realize that representing, discussing, reading, writing, and listening to mathematics are a vital part of learning and using mathematics.

Standard 3: Mathematics as Reasoning

In grades K–4, the study of mathematics should emphasize reasoning so that students can—

- draw logical conclusions about mathematics;
- use models, known facts, properties, and relationships to explain their thinking;
- justify their answers and solution processes;
- use patterns and relationships to analyze mathematical situations;
- believe that mathematics makes sense.

Standard 4: Mathematical Connections

In grades K–4, the study of mathematics should include opportunities to make connections so that students can—

- link conceptual and procedural knowledge;
- relate various representations of concepts or procedures to one another;
- recognize relationships among different topics in mathematics;
- use mathematics in other curriculum areas;
- use mathematics in their daily lives.

Standard 5: Estimation

In grades K–4, the curriculum should include estimation so that students can—

- explore estimation strategies;
- recognize when an estimate is appropriate;
- determine the reasonableness of results;
- apply estimation in working with quantities, measurement, computation, and problem solving.

Standard 6: Number Sense and Numeration

In grades K–4, the mathematics curriculum should include whole number concepts and skills so that students can—

- construct number meanings through real-world experiences and the use of physical materials;
- understand our numeration system by relating counting, grouping, and place-value concepts;
- develop number sense;
- interpret the multiple uses of numbers encountered in the real world.

Standard 7: Concepts of Whole Number Operations

In grades K–4, the mathematics curriculum should include concepts of addition, subtraction, multiplication, and division of whole numbers so that students can—

- develop meaning for the operations by modeling and discussing a rich variety of problem situations;
- relate the mathematical language and symbolism of operations to problem situations and informal language;
- recognize that a wide variety of problem structures can be represented by a single operation;
- develop operation sense.

Standard 8: Whole Number Computation

In grades K–4, the mathematics curriculum should develop whole number computation so that students can—

- model, explain, and develop reasonable proficiency with basic facts and algorithms;
- use a variety of mental computation and estimation techniques;
- use calculators in appropriate computational situations;
- select and use computation techniques appropriate to specific problems and determine whether the results are reasonable.

Standard 9: Geometry and Spatial Sense

In grades K–4, the mathematics curriculum should include two- and three-dimensional geometry so that students can—

- describe, model, draw, and classify shapes;
- investigate and predict the results of combining, subdividing, and changing shapes;
- develop spatial sense;
- relate geometric ideas to number and measurement ideas;
- recognize and appreciate geometry in their world.

Standard 10: Measurement

In grades K–4, the mathematics curriculum should include measurement so that students can—

- understand the attributes of length, capacity, weight, mass, area, volume, time, temperature, and angle;
- develop the process of measuring and concepts related to units of measurement;
- make and use estimates of measurement;
- make and use measurements in problem and everyday situations.

Standard 11: Statistics and Probability

In grades K–4, the mathematics curriculum should include experiences with data analysis and probability so that students can—

- collect, organize, and describe data;
- construct, read, and interpret displays of data;
- formulate and solve problems that involve collecting and analyzing data;
- explore concepts of chance.

■ Standard 12: Fractions and Decimals

In grades K–4, the mathematics curriculum should include fractions and decimals so that students can—

- develop concepts of fractions, mixed numbers, and decimals;
- develop number sense for fractions and decimals;
- use models to relate fractions to decimals and to find equivalent fractions;
- use models to explore operations on fractions and decimals;
- apply fractions and decimals to problem situations.

■ Standard 13: Patterns and Relationships

In grades K–4, the mathematics curriculum should include the study of patterns and relationships so that students can—

- recognize, describe, extend, and create a wide variety of patterns;
- represent and describe mathematical relationships;
- explore the use of variables and open sentences to express relationships.

NCTM Curriculum Standards for Grades 5–8[2]

■ Standard 1: Mathematics as Problem Solving

In grades 5–8, the mathematics curriculum should include numerous and varied experiences with problem solving as a method of inquiry and application so that students can—

- use problem-solving approaches to investigate and understand mathematical content;
- formulate problems from situations within and outside mathematics;
- develop and apply a variety of strategies to solve problems, with emphasis on multistep and nonroutine problems;
- verify and interpret results with respect to the original problem situation;
- generalize solutions and strategies to new problem situations;
- acquire confidence in using mathematics meaningfully.

■ Standard 2: Mathematics as Communication

In grades 5–8, the study of mathematics should include opportunities to communicate so that students can—

- model situations using oral, written, concrete, pictorial, graphical, and algebraic methods;

[2] NCTM, *Curriculum & Evaluation Standards for School Mathematics: Executive Summary* (Reston, VA: NCTM, © 1989). Reprinted with permission.

- reflect on and clarify their own thinking about mathematical ideas and situations;
- develop common understandings of mathematical ideas, including the role of definitions;
- use the skills of reading, listening, and viewing to interpret and evaluate mathematical ideas;
- discuss mathematical ideas and make conjectures and convincing arguments;
- appreciate the value of mathematical notation and its role in the development of mathematical ideas.

Standard 3: Mathematics as Reasoning

In grades 5–8, reasoning shall permeate the mathematics curriculum so that students can—

- recognize and apply deductive and inductive reasoning;
- understand and apply reasoning processes, with special attention to spatial reasoning and reasoning with proportions and graphs;
- make and evaluate mathematical conjectures and arguments;
- validate their own thinking;
- appreciate the pervasive use and power of reasoning as a part of mathematics.

Standard 4: Mathematical Connections

In grades 5–8, the mathematics curriculum should include the investigation of mathematical connections so that students can—

- see mathematics as an integrated whole;
- explore problems and describe results using graphical, numerical, physical, algebraic, and verbal mathematical models or representations;
- use a mathematical idea to further their understanding of other mathematical ideas;
- apply mathematical thinking and modeling to solve problems that arise in other disciplines, such as art, music, psychology, science, and business;
- value the role of mathematics in our culture and society.

Standard 5: Number and Number Relationships

In grades 5–8, the mathematics curriculum should include the continued development of number and number relationships so that students can—

- understand, represent, and use numbers in a variety of equivalent forms (integer, fraction, decimal, percent, exponential, and scientific notation) in real-world and mathematical problem situations;
- develop number sense for whole numbers, fractions, decimals, integers, and rational numbers;
- understand and apply ratios, proportions, and percents in a wide variety of situations;
- investigate relationships among fractions, decimals, and percents;
- represent numerical relationships in one- and two-dimensional graphs.

Standard 6: Number Systems and Number Theory

In grades 5–8, the mathematics curriculum should include the study of number systems and number theory so that students can—

■ understand and appreciate the need for numbers beyond the whole numbers;

■ develop and use order relations for whole numbers, fractions, decimals, integers, and rational numbers;

■ extend their understanding of whole number operations to fractions, decimals, integers, and rational numbers;

■ understand how the basic arithmetic operations are related to one another;

■ develop and apply number theory concepts (e.g., primes, factors, and multiples) in real-world and mathematical problem situations.

Standard 7: Computation and Estimation

In grades 5–8, the mathematics curriculum should develop the concepts underlying computation and estimation in various contexts so that students can—

■ compute with whole numbers, fractions, decimals, integers, and rational numbers;

■ develop, analyze, and explain procedures for computation and techniques for estimation;

■ develop, analyze, and explain methods for solving proportions;

■ select and use an appropriate method for computing from among mental arithmetic, paper-and-pencil, calculator, and computer methods;

■ use computation, estimation, and proportions to solve problems;

■ use estimation to check the reasonableness of results.

Standard 8: Patterns and Functions

In grades 5–8, the mathematics curriculum should include explorations of patterns and functions so that students can—

■ describe, extend, analyze, and create a wide variety of patterns;

■ describe and represent relationships with tables, graphs, and rules;

■ analyze functional relationships to explain how a change in one quantity results in a change in another;

■ use patterns and functions to represent and solve problems.

Standard 9: Algebra

In grades 5–8, the mathematics curriculum should include explorations of algebraic concepts and processes so that students can—

■ understand the concepts of variable, expression, and equation;

■ represent situations and number patterns with tables, graphs, verbal rules, and equations and explore the interrelationships of these representations;

■ analyze tables and graphs to identify properties and relationships;

■ develop confidence in solving linear equations using concrete, informal, and formal methods;

- investigate inequalities and nonlinear equations informally;
- apply algebraic methods to solve a variety of real-world and mathematical problems.

Standard 10: Statistics

In grades 5–8, the mathematics curriculum should include exploration of statistics in real-world situations so that students can—

- systematically collect, organize, and describe data;
- construct, read, and interpret tables, charts, and graphs;
- make inferences and convincing arguments that are based on data analysis;
- evaluate arguments that are based on data analysis;
- develop an appreciation for statistical methods as powerful means for decision making.

Standard 11: Probability

In grades 5–8, the mathematics curriculum should include explorations of probability in real-world situations so that students can—

- model situations by devising and carrying out experiments or simulations to determine probabilities;
- model situations by constructing a sample space to determine probabilities;
- appreciate the power of using a probability model by comparing experimental results with mathematical expectations;
- make predictions that are based on experimental or theoretical probabilities;
- develop an appreciation for the pervasive use of probability in the real world.

Standard 12: Geometry

In grades 5–8, the mathematics curriculum should include the study of the geometry of one, two, and three dimensions in a variety of situations so that students can—

- identify, describe, compare, and classify geometric figures;
- visualize and represent geometric figures with special attention to developing spatial sense;
- explore transformations of geometric figures;
- represent and solve problems using geometric models;
- understand and apply geometric properties and relationships;
- develop and appreciation of geometry as a means of describing the physical world.

Standard 13: Measurement

In grades 5–8, the mathematics curriculum should include extensive concrete experiences using measurement so that students can—

- extend their understanding of the process of measurement;

- estimate, make, and use measurements to describe and compare phenomena;

- select appropriate units and tools to measure to the degree of accuracy required in a particular situation;

- understand the structure and use of systems of measurement;

- extend their understanding of the concepts of perimeter, area, volume, angle measure, capacity, and weight and mass;

- develop the concepts of rates and other derived and indirect measurements;

- develop formulas and procedures for determining measures to solve problems.

Selections from Standards for the Professional Development of Teachers of Mathematics[3]

■ Standard 2: Knowing Mathematics and School Mathematics

The education of teachers of mathematics should develop their knowledge of the content and discourse of mathematics, including —

- mathematical concepts and procedures and the connections among them;

- multiple representations of mathematical concepts and procedures;

- ways to reason mathematically, solve problems, and communicate mathematics effectively at different levels of formality;

and, in addition, develop their perspectives on —

- the nature of mathematics, the contributions of different cultures toward the development of mathematics, and the role of mathematics in culture and society;

- the changes in the nature of mathematics and the way we teach, learn, and do mathematics resulting from the availability of technology;

- school mathematics within the discipline of mathematics;

- the changing nature of school mathematics, its relationships to other school subjects, and its applications in society.

■ Standard 3: Knowing Students as Learners of Mathematics

The preservice and continuing education of teachers of mathematics should provide multiple perspectives on students as learners of mathematics by developing teachers' knowledge of —

- research on how students learn mathematics;

- the effects of students' age, abilities, interests, and experience on learning mathematics;

- the influences of students' linguistic, ethnic, racial, and socioeconomic backgrounds and gender on learning mathematics;

- ways to affirm and support full participation and continued study of mathematics by all students.

---

[3] NCTM, *Professional Standards for Teaching Mathematics* (Reston, VA: NCTM, © 1991), pp. 132, 144. Reprinted with permission.

ANSWERS TO SELECTED EXERCISES

Chapter 1 Exercises, page 33

1. 30 pigs and 139 chickens
3. 17 bottles filled; $1\frac{2}{3}$ (or about 1.7) oz left over perfume/jug; jug size of 11 oz or a multiple of 11 oz
4. $162   **6.** 10,440 handshakes
9. b. ⌐   **d.** 162   **f.** 16
13. 100 $5 tickets and 500 $2 tickets   **15.** $704
20. 7 economy models   **22.** $4.98 per hour

24. 73,500 apples   **28.** 4 times
35. a. 12 ways
36. a. Words: The sum of the first n terms is equal to one less than the $(n + 2)$nd term.
Notation: $A_1 + A_2 + A_3 + \cdots + A_n = (A_{n+2}) - 1$
39. January 12   **44.** 84 rectangles

Exercises 2.1, page 52

1. a. $0 \notin \varnothing$ or $0 \notin \{\}$ **b.** $3 \notin B$
2. a. $D \not\subseteq E$ **b.** $A \subseteq U$
3. a. {e, l, m, n, t, a, r, y} and {x | x is a letter in the word "elementary"}
   c. {2, 3, 5, 7, 11, 13, 17, 19, 23, 29, 31, 37, 41, 43, 47, 53, 59, 61, 67, 71, 73, 79, 83, 89, 97}; {x | x is a prime number less than 100}
4. b. is not well defined, because the "countries in Europe" are constantly changing and may be defined in various geopolitical terms.
6. b. $\subset$ {3} is a subset of the set
   c. $\in$ {1} is an element of this set of sets
   e. $\not\subset$ {ab} is neither a subset nor an element
   f. $\subset$ the null set is a subset of every set
7. a. 64
   b. A set with n elements has 2^n subsets.
13. a.

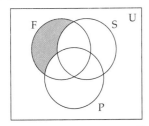

$F \cap (\overline{S \cup P})$ or $F \cap \overline{S} \cap \overline{P}$
   c.

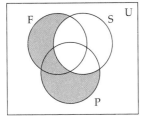

Nonsmokers who are either female or have health problems

   e. $\overline{F} \cap (S \cap P)$
   Males who smoke and have a health problem.
15. b. All numbers that don't evenly divide 12, 15, or 20; $\overline{A \cup B \cup C}$ or $\overline{A} \cap \overline{B} \cap \overline{C}$
   d. All numbers except 1 and 3

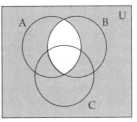

16. a. Students who have at least one cat and at least one dog.

d. $D \cap \overline{C}$

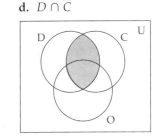

   g. $\overline{D \cup C \cup O}$ or $\overline{D} \cap \overline{C} \cap \overline{O}$
   Students who have no pets.
17. The circles enable us to easily represent visually all the possible subsets. The diagram is not equivalent because there is no region corresponding to elements that are in all three sets.
18.

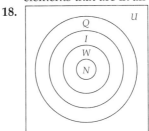

22. b. Technically, this subset represents a lesson in which the students use concrete materials, but not in a lab approach and not in small groups. Pedagogically this doesn't make sense.

Exercises 2.2, page 66

1. Yes. The number of small pieces is a function of the length of the long wire.
4. **a.** 7 buses.
b.

School Buses for Field Trip

6. 164.9 cm
8. **a.** The set of odd numbers.

c.

d. $f(x) = 2x - 1$ **e.** Yes. Answers will vary.
f. Not true. $x = y^2$ is a formula, but y is not a function of x.
9. **a.** 12, 27, $3(n - 1)$ or $3n - 3$
12. No. Two students could spend the same amount of time and get different grades.
13. **a.** $T_n^2 - T_{n-1}^2$ **b.** It is a function.
15. It would be less expensive to rent a car for a week.
16. **c.** Both are functions.
18. **a.** \$3,400   **b.** \$800   **c.** In $6\frac{1}{4}$ years.

Exercises 2.3, page 82

2. **a.** 3,031   **c.** 1,666   **f.** 1,262
3.

	Egyptian	Roman
a. 312	𓎉𓎉𓎉∩||	CCCXII
c. 6000	𓆼𓆼𓆼𓆼𓆼𓆼	MMMMMM

	Babylonian
a. 312	𒁹𒁹𒁹𒁹𒁹 𒌋𒁹𒁹
c. 6000	𒁹 𒌋𒌋𒌋𒌋

5. **a.**

b.

6. **a.** $300 + 40 + 5$ **7.** **a.** 4,859
8. **a.** $500 + 10 + 10 + 5 + 1 + 1 = 527$
c. H H H △ △ △ △ \|\|\|\|\|\|\|
9. **a.** 32,570   **c.** ⫴ ☰ T
10. **c.** $(3 \times 400) + (0 \times 20) + (7 \times 1) = 1,207$
d. ⚏
11. **a.** 40_5 **g.** 130_5 **12.** **e.** 1001_2 **g.** 113_4
13. **b.** $(5 \times 6) + (5 \times 1) = 35$
d. $(2 \times 125) + (1 \times 25) + (4 \times 1) = 279$
14. **a.** 134_5 **c.** 1011100_2 **g.** 112_6

Exercises 3.1, page 108

4. **a.**

$$\begin{array}{r} 543 \\ -317 \\ \hline 23 \end{array} \qquad \begin{array}{r} 5\,4\,\overset{1}{3} \\ -3\,1\,7 \\ \hline 2\,3 \end{array} \qquad \begin{array}{r} 5\,4\,\overset{1}{3} \\ -3\,1\,7 \\ \hline 2\,\cancel{3}\,6 \\ {\scriptstyle 2} \end{array}$$

8. 5 hundreds + 10 tens + 13 ones
= 5 hundreds + 11 tens + 3 ones
= 6 hundreds + 1 ten + 3 ones
= 613

9. **a.** After adding $6 + 8 = 14$, the student wrote the 1 in the ones place, carried the 4, and added it to $3 + 2$.
10. **a.** The greatest sum, 1,593, is obtained when the 7 and 8 are in the hundreds places, the 3 and 6 are in the tens places, and the 1 and 2 are in the ones places.
12. $N = 9$, $P = 2$

13. 372
168   There are many solutions
459
———
999

15. a. $a - b \neq b - a$, because $b - a = -(a - b)$.
19. a. The student subtracted $8 - 6$. Some students automatically subtract the smaller number from the larger number, even if it changes the order of the numbers in the problem.

e. The student changed the zero in the ones place to 10, but didn't rename the 7 in the tens place as 6.
20. a. $876 - 123 = 753$
21. There are many possibilities. Two are shown here: $968 - 734$, $946 - 712$.
22. a. $7 - 5 = 2$
c. $3 + 4 = 7$
e. $3 \cdot 2 = 6$ (repeated addition)
25. Adam: 55 pounds, Ben: 50 pounds, third boy: 65 pounds

Exercises 3.2, page 136

3. c. 20
5. $\{(1, a), (1, b), (2, a), (2, b), (3, a), (3, b)\}$
12. a. ⓐ 25   17
50   8
100   4 $400 + 25 = 425$
200   2
④⓪⓪ 400   1

13. a. $45^2 - 9^2 = 2{,}025 - 81 = 1{,}944$
15. a. The 1 being carried represents 10. It is carried so that it can be added with the other values in the tens column.
17. a. Set up the numbers as shown below.

Find the four partial products and place them in the appropriate places: the ones digit in the lower spot and the tens digit in the higher spot of each cell. *Note:* If the product of the two numbers is less than 10, you can either leave the top cell blank or place a 0 in that spot.

To find the product, find the sum of the numbers on each of the diagonal rows. If the sum of any diagonal row is above 10, carry the digit in the tens place to the next place.

19. a. 8×6: The student wrote down the tens digit and carried the ones digit.
c. 2×46: The student wrote the product in the tens and ones places, even though the 2 represents 20.
20. a. $530 \cdot 71 = 37{,}630$
22. a. 55,999,999,944
$999{,}999{,}999 \cdot 56 = (1{,}000{,}000{,}000 - 1)56$
$= 56{,}000{,}000{,}000 - 56$

27. a. $3 \cdot 2 = 6$ (repeated addition)
30. a. The student didn't use zero as a place holder in the quotient to indicate that 2 (in the tens place) divided by 7 is less than 1 (ten).
31. a. $2\overline{)974} = 487$
33. $x = 7$ and $y = 13$, or vice versa
34. a. 14 buses
35. 60 cans of juice, assuming 8 oz/glass; $53.40
37. 25¢   **39.** 11 cartons
40. 160 tapes   **41.** 700 rolls
42. 2,190,000 gizmos   **45.** The letter a.
46. a. 4,950 cubes   **48. a.** 36 squares
49.

a.

a	b	$a + b$	$a \cdot b$
65	66	131	4,290
234	766	1,000	179,244
1,208	72	1,280	6,976

b.

a	b	$a + b$	$a \div b$
19	1	20	19

d.

a	b	$a \cdot b$	$a \div b$
10	2	20	5

50. a. $74 \cdot 86 = 6{,}364$
e. $1{,}530 = 31 \cdot 48 + 42$
54. Alike: the sum (product) of any row, any column, and both diagonals are identical.
Difference: in a multiplication magic square, it seems that the numbers in the square don't all need to be different.

Exercises 3.3, page 156

1. Answers will vary. One possibility for each is given below.
a. $47 + 53 = 100$ (compatible numbers). Now add 2 more to get 102.

c. $150 + 15 = 165$
e. $575 + 125 = 700$. Now add 3 to get 703.
g. $340 + 16 = 356$
i. $387 + 24 = 400 + 11 = 411$. Then $411 + 53 = 464$.

2. Answers will vary. One possibility for each is given below.
   a. Leading digit: 1,173
   c. Leading digit and rounding: 146,000
   e. Compatible numbers and rounding: 2,700
   g. Leading digit and rounding: 1,400,000,000.
3. a. 37   56   74
   c. 24   47   97
   e. 185 153 274
4. Answers will vary. One possibility for each is given below.
   a. Add 1 to each number: $88 - 30 = 58$.
   c. $34 + 50 = 84$; the answer is 48.
   e. $206 + 300 = 506$; the answer is 296.
   g. $475 + 25 = 500$; add 125 more; the answer is 150.
   i. Add one to each number $507 - 30$; count backwards by tens; 507, 497, 487, 477.
5. Answers will vary. One possibility for each is given below.
   a. Leading digit: 2,100
   c. 28 to 30 is 2, 30 to 73 is 43; an estimate is 45,000.
   e. 285 to 300 is 15, to 413 is 113 more. $113 + 15 = 128$; estimate is 128,000.
   g. Rounding: about 1,200,000
6. a. 475 764   c. 382 723
7. Answers will vary. One possibility for each is given below.
   a. $16 \times 16 = 32 \times 8 = 64 \times 4 = 256$
   c. $66 \times 10 = 660$, so $66 \times 5 = 330$
   e. $6 \times 3 = 18$, so $60 \times 30 = 1,800$
   g. $35 \times 10 = 350$, $35 \times 2 = 70$; answer is $350 + 70 = 420$.
   i. Double 736 twice: 1,472, then 2,944

8. Answers will vary. One possibility for each is given below.
   a. $40 \times 70 = 2,800$
   c. $\begin{array}{r} 60 + 2 \\ 80 + 3 \\ \hline \end{array}$
      $4,800 + 200 + 200 = 5,200$
   e. $30,000 \times 50 = 1,500,000$
9. b is wrong.
10. $34 \times 65 = 2,210$
13. b. A reasonable estimate is 4,200.
15. a. $587 \times 40 = 23,480$
       $587 \times 305 = 179,035$
24. Rough: 500
    Refined: 670
26. Rough: Just under $50,000
    Refined: $45,000
29. Rough: $90
    Refined: $103
32. Rough: 8,000 days
    Refined: 7,300 days
34. about 8 years
37. 3,600 miles. Answers on cost will vary depending on price of gas and miles per gallon that the car gets.
39. $240
47. Answers may vary. 3 million crimes per year would mean about 17,000 crimes per school day (dividing by 180 school days per year). If we divide 17,000 by 50 states, that's about 340 crimes per day per state. That still seems high, so the term *crime* must be broad: It must include such things as vandalism and minor assault. Does it mean "crimes reported to police"?

Exercises 4.1, page 177

3. a. 1, 3, 7, 9 or 1, 3, 5, 11
6. a. 7, 7, 5, 1, 1   7, 5, 5, 3, 1   5, 5, 5, 5, 1
       7, 7, 3, 3, 1   7, 5, 3, 3, 3   5, 5, 5, 3, 3
8. a.

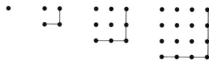

9. b. $8 \cdot 10 = 9^2 - 1^2$
10. b. $123,456,789 \cdot 8 + 9 = 987,654,321$
11. a. 30 and 15   b. 36 and 12
13. a. $37 \times 3 \times 1 = 111$; $37 \times 3 \times 2 = 222$; $37 \times 3 \times 3 = 333$. The digits in the product are the multiple of 3 that appears in the problem.
19. 467,712   21. 301 cards

26. c. The last two digits must be 00, 25, 50, 75.
27. a. True   c. False   e. True
28. a. True   c. True
29. a. The sum of three consecutive numbers will always be divisible by 3 and by the middle number in the sequence. $x + (x + 1) + (x + 2) = 3x + 3$
31. a. Yes   32. a. 1
34. a.

Exercises 4.2, page 187

1. a. $2 \times 2 \times 23$
   b. $2 \times 2 \times 2 \times 2 \times 3 \times 3$
   c. $2 \times 2 \times 7 \times 7$
   d. $2 \times 2 \times 2 \times 3 \times 3 \times 7$

2. a. Prime   b. Prime
   c. Composite: 19×23
4. 1951; 1973; 1987; 1993; 1997; 1999
5. 24

6. Answers may vary: 313, 317, 373
9. a. 2,520
10. a. 1,369; factors: 1, 37, 1,369

13. a. 2, 4, 5, 10, 20, 25, 50
14. a. 3, 7, and 1

Exercises 4.3, page 200

1. a. 15   **b.** 9   **c.** 1   **d.** 27   **e.** 3
2. a. 3
3. a. 60   **b.** 150   **c.** 132
4. a. 300
6. a. 5; 200   **b.** 36; 216   **c.** 84; 1,260
8. 143

10. 224 mm × 224 mm; 28 dominoes
12. a. a is a factor of b, and b is a multiple of a.
   c. a
13. a. True   **c.** False; GCF(12, 18) = 6   **e.** True
15. The box is 120 cm × 120 cm × 120 cm.

Exercises 5.1, page 213

1. a. $^-218$ **c.** 19   **e.** 14   **g.** 7   **i.** 221
2. a. 238   **c.** $^-417$ **e.** 213
3. $^-35$ **5.** $^-5°$ Celsius   **7.** $^-5°$
10. a. 20 mph wind speed
   b. 180 mph maximum speed with no wind
12. 19 hours   **14.** 3761 B.C.
16. All numbers are estimates from the graph.
   a. The lowest trade balance was during 1986. It was

approximately $^-150$.
   b. $^-80$
   c. The biggest decline was in 1983; approximately $^-50$.
20. a. Always positive.   **c.** Always positive.
21. a. Always positive.   **c.** Always positive.
22. 176 pounds

Exercises 5.2, page 227

3. a.   **c.**

   e.

   $\frac{2}{3}$ 1

   g. 7/10 is one possibility.
5. *Note:* Answers will vary. The figure shows one valid representation for each part of 3/5.

7. a. 5/8   **c.** 9/10   **e.** 7/9   **g.** 29/30
11. a. $a/b > a/c$ **c.** $b/c > a/c$
13. 1/10 of your blood

15. a. 1/3   **b.** 1/9
17. Approximately 3/5
19. Approximately 2/3
21.

Religion	Fraction
Christianity	1/3
Islam	1/6
Hinduism	1/8
Buddhism	1/16
Judaism	1/300

23. a. $5/16 \approx 1/3$ **c.** $199/307 \approx 2/3$
25. The new fraction is larger than the original fraction.
27. 1/2 of the plants survived.
30. a. 7/12
   c. Yes. Copper and zinc have different prices.
31. a. The 1/125th shutter speed means that the shutter is open 4 times as long.

Exercises 5.3, page 248

1. a. $80\frac{17}{24}$ **b.** $-2\frac{23}{120}$ **c.** $23\frac{13}{20}$ **d.** $191\frac{11}{16}$
   e. $-3\frac{7}{12}$ **f.** $66\frac{7}{24}$ **g.** 99   **h.** 135
   i. $13\frac{1}{2}$
2. a. 13 3/8   **d.** 19 2/5   **g.** 44
3. a. Less than 10
   c. Greater than 2
   e. Greater than 20
5. Estimate: 4 ounces
   Exact answer: $4\frac{23}{64}$ ounces
7. Estimate: 72 inches

   Exact answer: $73\frac{1}{2}$ inches
9. Estimate: 90 million people
   Exact answer: 2/3 × 136,800,000 = 91,200,000
12. Estimate: Maybe yes, maybe no. It will be close.
   Exact answer: Yes, exactly.
14. 120 freshmen women.
16. a. $\frac{1}{2}^{10}$ or 1/1,024 of the germs remain.
   b. 19,531 germs (theoretically). 1/1,024 × 20,000,000 = 2 × 10⁷ ÷ 1,024. A better answer might be to say approximately 1/1,000 of 20 million ≈ 20,000 germs.

18. 5/12 are single.
20. The person who eats 1 piece eats 1/8 of the total. The person who eats 2 pieces eats 2/8 = 1/4 of the total. The other two each eat 5/16 of the total.
22. 415,220; 1,245,660
24. a. 4 pressings; 6 pressings
27. $\dfrac{bc^2 - bd}{ac}$
28. a. One way: 26 × 11 ÷ 12
33. $\dfrac{9\frac{1}{4}}{3\frac{3}{4}} = \dfrac{9 + \frac{1}{4}}{3 + \frac{3}{4}} \neq \dfrac{9}{3} + \dfrac{\frac{1}{4}}{\frac{3}{4}}$. Rather, $\dfrac{9\frac{1}{4}}{3\frac{3}{4}} = \dfrac{9}{3\frac{3}{4}} + \dfrac{\frac{1}{4}}{3\frac{3}{4}}$.

35. a. They added the denominator.
　　c. They cross-multiplied, one numerator by the other denominator.
38. $\dfrac{5}{9} + \dfrac{3}{7}$
42. $\dfrac{7}{8} \div \dfrac{1}{9}$ if you assumed proper fractions; $\dfrac{8}{2} \div \dfrac{1}{9}$ if you did not.

Exercises 5.4, page 274

1. a. 0.075　　**c.** 0.03　　**e.** 1/200
2. b.

0　　　　.5　　　　1

3. a. 0.4　　**c.** 0.05
4. a. 0.0084, 0.058, 0.56, 0.6
6. a.

2.9　3.0　3.1　3.2　3.3　3.4　3.5　3.6　3.7　3.8

7. $24,440,000 or $24.44 million
10. a. 160　　**c.** 0.8　　**e.** 0.425　　**g.** 0.24
11. a. 1.23456789×10^8　　**c.** 5.6×10^{-10}
12. a. 4.182×10^{18}　　**c.** 1.53×10^{-17}
13. 0.00075 cm
15. a. $1.84467441 \times 10^{19}$
17. a. The right answer is $108. There are several ways to get $1,080. One is 24 × 45.

19. a. Answers and justifications will vary. The range of temperatures in Fahrenheit is 97.16° (for 36.2°C) to 99.5° (for 37.5°C). The mean (average) of these temperatures is 98.33°F.
20. 102 is how many vials can be completely filled, and .4 is the fraction of another vial that can be filled.
24. a. 32.7 miles per gallon
　　b. $18.22
　　c. Her average speed was 405.6 miles/11 hours = 36.9 miles per hour. Also acceptable is 405.6/10.5 = 38.6 miles per hour. This is her average speed while the car was moving.
26. 845 items; $1.21
28. 21,735.3 dominoes per minute, which is 362.3 dominoes per second
30. 27.7¢/day
32. a. Option (b)
　　b. 30 checks
34. a. 2,550 dots　　**b.** 2.805×10^4 dots
37. At his current job he makes approximately $19,000. Not taking into consideration benefits, the work environment, and other factors, the annual salary of $24,000 seems better.
39. a. 72°F　　**c.** 38°C

Exercises 6.1, page 294

1. 143.75 calories. Answer is an estimate.
3. 165 dentists. Answer is an estimate.
5. a. $750; this is an exact answer.
　　c. $977.08; this answer is rounded to two decimal places.
7. 860,000 people. Answer is an estimate (rounded to two significant figures).
9. Approximately 51 feet, 5 inches.
11. Yes; at this rate she will row 2,228.6 meters in 10 minutes, which exceeds her goal.
13. 11 3/4 inches. This is an approximate answer.
15. a. 45 miles. This is an approximate answer.
18. a. 104 km/h.　　**19.** $500

21. 40 miles.　　**22.** 10 questions
24. The man with five loaves should get 7 cents, and the man with three should get 1 cent.
25. 3.5 feet
26. a. 22.7 miles per hour
27. 37 handshakes per minute, which is one handshake in less than 2 seconds
29. 2,520 students
30. $1\frac{1}{2}$ hours more
33. More prison inmates. For a U.S. population of 270,000,000, there are approximately 492,000 physicians and 543,000 prison inmates.

36. 199/325 = 61.2% and 5/8 = 62.5%. These percents are close enough to say that the advertisement is accurate.

39. The person who gets paid once a month will have a larger paycheck.

40. a. In order to get 40 pledges in 3 hours, they would need 20 pledges by 7:30.

b. Two lines of reasoning are appropriate: One is that the announcer may have felt that it would turn people off to say that they were behind; the other is that the announcer might realize that they will get more callers from 7:30 to 9 than from 6 to 7:30, and so they would catch up then.

Exercises 6.2, page 312

1. a. 18   **c.** 1,211.8   **e.** 0.8625   **g.** 80%
i. 8.52%   **k.** 18.8%   **m.** 46.35   **o.** 7.192
q. 32.4   **s.** 1,185.6

3. 35%   **5.** 700 patients

7. a. 131%   **c.** 43%

9. Approximately 6%   **11.** 5%

13. Approximately 2,160,000 (2.16 million) Americans are homeless.

15. Approximately $90,300   **17.** $4,544.40

19. $440   **21.** 18%

24. Having the public pick apples will provide more income.

25. 16 years and 8 months   **27.** $41.06

29. a. The average elementary principal makes an average of 63% more than the average teacher, the average junior high principal makes 74% more, and the average senior high principal makes 87% more.
b. The average junior high principal makes 7% less than the average senior high principal, the average elementary principal makes 13% less, and the average teacher makes 47% less.

31. a. 5 out of 1,000, or 1 out of 200, children will have a severe reaction.

33. In the United States, inflation caused prices to rise 5%, so a $10 item would cost $10.50. In a country with a 400% inflation rate, a $10 item would cost $40 a year later. The value of the item hasn't changed, but the value of the currency used to purchase the item has diminished.

35. a. $17,405
37. a.

Country	Change 1993–2000	Estimated % Change	Actual % Change
United States	1.8	1/5 = 20%	−21.4%
Cuba	1.3	1/9 ≈ 11%	−12.4%
Egypt	12.6	1/6 ≈ 17%	−16.1%
Haiti	7.3	1/15 ≈ 7%	−6.7%
Japan	0.2	1/20 = 5%	−4.7%
Mexico	8.1	1/4 = 25%	−28.1%
Somalia	75.6	1/2 = 50%	−46.5%

39. Answers will vary. It is a 20% drop, but only 0.02 change in blood alcohol content.

41. This interpretation represents an interesting misconception. If we selected 100 students at random, we might or might not find that 8 of them were working full-time. The 8% means that if we take the fraction of students that are working full-time and convert that fraction to a fraction whose denominator is 100, that fraction will be closer to 8/100 than to 7/100 or 9/100.

43. a. 600 square feet of window space
b. It depends on the size of the windows. If the windows are 5 feet × 4 feet, it would be 30 windows.

45. $121,885.98

Exercises 7.1, page 335

Note: In cases where students are asked to explain the graph or to describe questions about reliability, validity, and so on, there are many possible valid ways to answer those questions. Because of space limitations, only one possible response is given here.

1.

Sex of Teacher by Grade Range in 1977 (Male/Female)

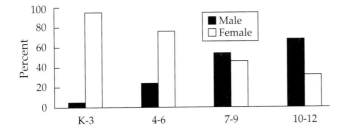

Sex of Teacher by Grade Range in 1985-86 (Male/Female)

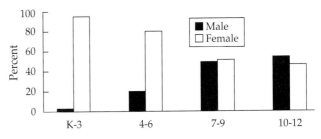

a. Bar graphs work well for these data, although circle graphs are also possibilities.
b. In 1985–86, in the teachers' surveys, the ratio of females to males decreases as the students get older. While 90% of K–3 teachers are female, the

percentages in other grades are 76% in grades 4–6, 46% in grades 7–9, and 32% in grades 10–12. Over the past 10 years, there has been virtually no change in the female:male ratio in grades K–6, the percentage of females in grades 7–9 has risen from 46% to 51%, and the percentage of females in grades 10–12 has risen even more sharply, from 32% to 46%.

3. **a.** A bar graph would work well.
    b. Answers will vary. The most commonly given reason for not reporting a crime was that the crime was not successfully completed. Other common reasons given were lack of proof, that it was considered a private matter, that the stolen property did not have ID numbers, and that the victims thought that the police did not want to be bothered.
    c. The data probably come from a survey.
    d. Without more information, their accuracy is questionable. The reported reasons may not be people's real reasons.
    e. Possibilities include correlating the type of crime with the reason for not reporting it and describing the sampling techniques used in the survey.

5. **a.** A circle graph would work well. A bar graph is also reasonable.
    b. Answers will vary. These categories represent less experienced teachers, two middle ranges of experienced teachers, and long-time teachers, but the time intervals are not evenly distributed.

7. **a.** Answers will vary. In 1980, 90% of the single-parent households were headed by women; and 10% were headed by men. By 1992, these figures had shifted so that 86% of the single-parent households were headed by women, and 14% were headed by men.
    b. Circle graphs would be effective.

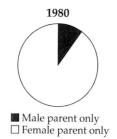

1980

■ Male parent only
☐ Female parent only

1992

■ Male parent only
☐ Female parent only

c. Answers will vary. There was about a 50% increase in single-parent households from 1980 and 1992, from almost 7 million to over 10.5 million. Single-parent households headed by men more than doubled during these years.

9. **a.** Line graphs would work well.
    b. Answers will vary. From 1970 to 1980, SAT scores declined by about 8% in verbal and 4% in math. Females' scores dropped more than males' scores in both categories. Since 1980, the verbal scores have remained constant. The math scores increased by about 2% in the 1980s, with females

increasing their scores more than males.
    c. It seems likely that verbal scores will be relatively unchanged and that math scores will be between 2 and 5 points higher.
    d. Answers will vary.

11.

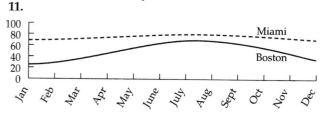

a. Answers will vary. Students could ask a meteorologist for more information.
    b. Line graphs or bar graphs would work well.
    c. Answers will vary. The temperature in Miami ranges from an average of around 70 degrees in the winter to an average of around 80 degrees in the summer. The temperature in Boston is affected more greatly by the seasons. The average temperature ranges from 26 degrees in January to 72 degrees in July, with gradual shifts throughout the year.

13. Bar or circle graphs would work well.

15. **a.** Answers will vary. For every 1,000 women aged 15–44, Hispanic women had 18 more births than white women. The birth rate for Hispanic women aged 15–44 was 43% higher than the birth rate for white women aged 15–44.
    b. It means how many babies were born for every 1,000 women in this age range.

17. **a.** This graph compares the rates at which women in different age groups had babies in 1980 and 1990. The rates are expressed as the number of women who had babies for every 1,000 women in that group.
    b. In three of the five groups, the rate went up. In two of the groups, the rate went down slightly. The greatest rate increases were for women in their thirties.
    c. The rate for the 30–34 group went from 60 to about 81, a 35% increase. The rate for the 35–39 group went from about 26 to about 38, a 46% increase. However, the numbers can only be approximated from the graph.

19. **a.** A possible response: A little more than half the AIDS patients are white, about one-third are black, and about one-sixth are Hispanic.
    b. Disproportionate by definition means that two ratios are not equal:

$$\frac{\text{Number of blacks with AIDS}}{\text{Number of blacks in the Unite\ States}} > \frac{\text{number of whites with AIDS}}{\text{number of whites in the United States}}$$

21. **a.** In 5th grade, the percentage of time that teachers lead the class varies from about 85% in Taiwan to about 70% in Japan to about 50% in the United States.
    b. It is not clear what "teachers led mathematics class" means. Does it mean standing in the front, does it mean whole class instruction? It is not

stated where the data come from: one fifth grade class in each country or many.
23. **a.** Answers will vary.
     b. $x = 1,925,000$, which tells us that in 1991, almost 2 million more people were born than died in the United States. However, this is not the only variable affecting population increase: Immigration is another big one.
25. **a.** A possible response: In 1990, almost two-thirds of high school dropouts lived in poverty, compared with two-fifths in 1973. Two and a half times more families where the head of the family had only a high school diploma were living in poverty in 1990 than in 1973. The poverty rates for families in which the head of the family attended college also increased.
     b. The lower the level of education of the family head, the greater the likelihood that the family will be living in poverty.

Exercises 7.2, page 370

1. The classes had the same mode, median, and mean. The range of the first class was 4 (5 to 9). The range of the second class was 6 (4 to 10).
3. **b.** Mean: 65.15; standard deviation: 2.43   **c.** 68%
5. **a.** Grouped frequency bar graph, histogram, or circle graph is appropriate.
     b. Since the distribution is skewed, the mean, median, and mode are not convergent. The median is 18. The mode is 16. The mean is 24.2.
     c. The range is from 12 to 75; the data are skewed to the right; 51 and 75 are outliers.
7. 93   9. $6,880
11. 40 miles per hour
13. Mean: 83.5; median: 84; standard deviation: 9.77
15. 2   17. Answers will vary.
21. Answers will vary. My guess is that the numbers from all the cities supplying data were totaled. Thus, of the total number of homeless people, 49% were single men, and so on.

23. The mode will have the smallest value, the median will have the middle value, and the mean will have the highest value.
25. **a.** The estimated mean becomes a reference point from which all the scores are measured. The mean of the differences tells you how far your estimated mean is from the actual mean.
     b. Answers will vary.
27. 61, 71; 1% or 15 boys
29. The mean will increase by that amount. The standard deviation will not be affected.
31. Without z-scores, one can only approximate the area under the curve. Approximately 34%, or 680 tires, will wear out before 45,000 miles.
33. Math   35. 66 2/3 miles per hour   37. 3.19
39. Julie is right.
41. **a.** 81.4   **b.** 76
43. Rounding scores generally has an insignificant effect on the final grade.

Exercises 7.3, page 394

1. **a.** The probability of picking a black is the same in each case.
     b. Pick from 6 blacks and 2 whites.
3. **a.** $11/1,105 \approx 0.01$
     b. $27/2,197$
     c. $3/13 + 3/13 + 3/13$ would be the probability of drawing a face card the first time *or* the second time *or* the third time.
5. No. The class is not a representative sample of the people who died last year.
7. No, it is not a fair game.
9. Possible results: 0, 1, 2, 3, 4, 5. Most likely difference: 1. Probability that the difference is 1: $10/36 = 5/18$.
11. 1 in 256; $1/256 = 0.0039$, or thirty-nine ten-thousandths.

14. $1/216$
16. Answers will vary. One die must have the same number on all its faces. The other die could have 1, 1, 3, 3, 5, 5 or three of one odd number and three of another.
18. Yes, $P(WWR) = P(WRW) = P(RWW) = 1/5$
20. **a.** $1/256$ **b.** $3/32$
22. 0.6%   24. $8/10 = 0.8$
26. Many solutions are possible. If the shape of the spinner remains the same, one possibility is $\$6(1/8) + \$4(1/8) + \$2(1/8) + \$2(1/8) + \$1(1/4) + \$0(1/4)$.
28. No. The player can only win half of the cost of playing the game.

Exercises 7.4, page 407

1. 720   3. 5,040   5. 1/5   7. 220
9. If the flavors were scooped in any order, there would be 84 possibilities. If you specified the order of the flavors, there would be 504 possibilities.

11. $\frac{26}{27}\%$ 13. **a.** 24   **b.** 96
15. 3/51   17. 1/5,040   19. ${}_nP_n = n!$
22. **a.** 11! or 39,916,800 possible words
     b. Answers will vary.

Exercises 8.1, page 427

1. $\overrightarrow{AC}$; $\overrightarrow{BC}$; $\overrightarrow{CA}$; $\overrightarrow{BA}$

3.

4. a.

b.

c.

5. a. False.   **c.** True.   **e.** True.   **g.** False.
i. False.   **k.** True.   **l.** True.

7. Estimates will vary.   **a.** 45°   **c.** 125°

11. Several answers are possible. Examples are given.
  a. $\overline{AB}$ and $\overline{DC}$
  c. $\overline{AB}$ and $\overline{AD}$
  e. $\overline{AB}$ and $\overline{EH}$
  g. All intersecting line segments are perpendicular.

13. a. 119°29'

14. a. 24 times   **c.** 150° (and 210°)

Exercises 8.2, page 446

1.

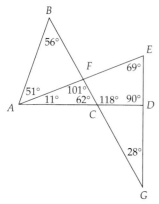

4. a. Concave polygon
  c. Convex polygon
  e. Concave polygon

5. a. Square, rectangle, right isosceles triangle (two different sizes), 9-gon

6. Answers will vary. These are some examples.

  a.

  c.

  e.   **g.**

angles 2, 4 and 6 are acute

10. 15 cm is too long for the third side. No matter what angle is formed between the 6 cm and 8 cm sides, the distance between the endpoints of these sides,

which is the length of the third side, will be less than 14 cm.

12. a. Parallelogram, rhombus, rectangle, square
  c. Square, rhombus
  e. Rectangle, square, isosceles trapezoid
  g. Parallelogram, rhombus, rectangle, square
  i. Rhombus

14.

18. a.

  c.

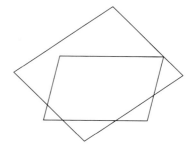

Exercises 8.3, page 458

1. Answers will vary. Several correct answers.
   a. △*ABC*   **c.** $\overline{AB}$
2. **a.** Octagonal prism   **c.** Rectangular prism
3. **a.** Concave
6. Yes. If all the edges of the base are of different lengths, then the triangular faces will not be congruent.
8. $n(n-3)$ diagonals.
10. $n+1$ vertices; $n+1$ faces; $2n$ edges
13. The base can be any polygon. The other faces are isosceles triangles.
15. **a.** **(i)** The figure will have 7 cubes.
    (ii) The left-hand view will be a reflection of the right-hand view.

(iii)   **(iv)**

17. The first one   18. The first one
20. **a.**

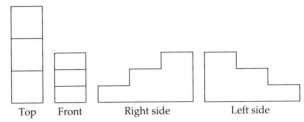

Top   Front   Right side   Left side

Exercises 9.1, page 483

1. Each point of the figure has been moved 2 units to the right and 3 units down.

   Also, the figure has been moved approximately 3.6 units along a vector that makes a 55-degree angle with the *x*-axis. See diagram.

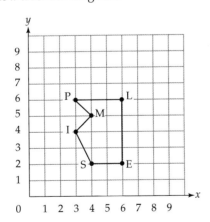

3. See diagram.

6. **a.** Yes, each of the letters will look the same when reflected across a vertical line.
8. See diagram. (The original figure is shown for reference purposes.)

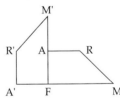

10.

	Point *A′*	Point *B′*	Point *C′*	Point *D′*
a.	(4, 7)	(6, 7)	(6, 6)	(4, 4)
c.	(4, 3)	(6, 3)	(6, 2)	(4, 0)

12. **a.** Answers will vary.
    b. See diagram.

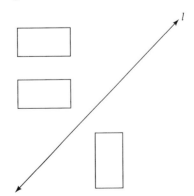

(The original figure is shown for reference purposes.) Numbers indicate the order of the transformations. ② is the final image.

c. See diagram.

The image from translating and then reflecting does not coincide with the image from reflecting and then translating.

14. a. See diagram.

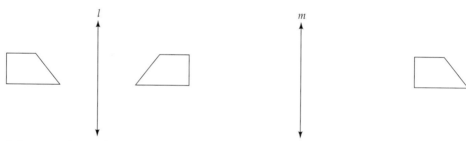

(The original figure is shown for reference purposes.)
b. Answers will vary.
c. See diagram.

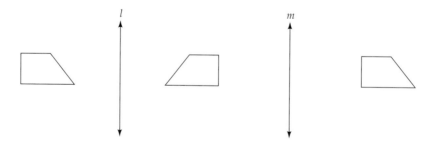

The trapezoid shown is the image produced by reflecting across line *l* and then across line *m*. The image produced by reflecting across line *m* and then line *l* is off the page (to the left).

16. a. See diagram.

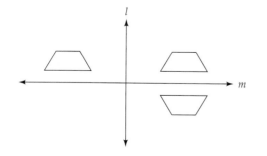

(The original figure is shown for reference purposes.)
b. Answers will vary.
c. The double reflection produces the same image, no matter what the order.
18. a. Translate *ST* along the vector *SU*.
b. Rotate the figure 180 degrees about point *M*.
c. No; in order for the image of *UM* to be *MT*, *UM* would need to be perpendicular to *SR*, which would be the case only if *STRU* were a square.
20. a. Rotate △*SRO* 180 degrees around point *Y*.

23. Answers will vary.
    a. One response: The C-shaped figure is rotated 180 degrees (or reflected vertically) and translated to form an interlocking unit.
    c. The figure consists of hexagons and parallelograms. Each hexagon can be translated to coincide with any other hexagon. One way to describe the parallelogram transformations is to consider the six parallelograms that surround each hexagon as a unit. This unit can be translated to coincide with any other parallelogram unit.
25. Answers will vary.
    Baby Blocks: If we see the figure as composed of rhombuses, each rhombus can be mapped onto a neighboring rhombus by a 60-degree rotation. If we see the figures as hexagons (comprising three different-colored rhombuses), each hexagon can be translated onto any other hexagon.
    Cross Roads: There are horizontal, vertical, and diagonal lines of reflection through the center of the design, and it can be rotated 90, 180, or 270 degrees onto itself.
28. a. *A* and *F*. The chevron is translated from the lower left position of one hexagon to the lower left position of an adjacent hexagon. The vector of translation makes a -30-degree angle with the horizontal.
    c. *A* and *C* (and *D* and *E*) are 180-degree rotations of each other about their points of intersection. *B*, *C*, and *D* (and *E*, *F*, and *G*) are 120-degree rotations of each other about the points where the three chevrons in each cluster intersect.
34. a. 9 o'clock

Exercises 9.2, page 495

1. a. 60-, 120-, 180-, 240-, and 300-degree rotational symmetry
   c. Horizontal and vertical line symmetry
3. a. Vertical line symmetry
   c. No symmetry because of the line segments
4. a. Vertical line symmetry
   c. 180-degree rotational symmetry
5. a. Horizontal, vertical, and diagonal line symmetry; 90-, 180-, and 270-degree rotational symmetry
   c. The figure as a whole has no symmetry.
7. a. Each of the right isosceles triangles has one line of symmetry.
   The parallelogram has point symmetry.
   The square has vertical, horizontal, and two diagonal lines of symmetry; it also has 90-, 180-, and 270-degree rotational symmetry.
9. Answers may vary, according to how the digits are written.
   1—horizontal line symmetry, 180-degree rotational symmetry

2—no symmetry
3—horizontal line symmetry
4—no symmetry
5—no symmetry
6—no symmetry
7—no symmetry
8—horizontal and vertical line symmetry; 180-degree rotational symmetry
9—no symmetry
0—horizontal and vertical line symmetry; 180-degree rotational symmetry
12. a. False   b. True   c. False
14. a. The diamond-shaped unit is translated horizontally; horizontal and vertical line symmetry; 180-degree rotational symmetry.
16. a. Horizontal and vertical line symmetry; 180-degree rotational symmetry

Exercises 9.3, page 504

1. a. 13.5 cm
3. Yes; the angles are the same, and the sides of the figure to the right are twice as long as the sides of the smaller triangle.
4. a. No; different isosceles triangles can have different angles.
   c. Yes; all squares have four 90-degree angles and proportionate sides.

   e. Yes; corresponding sides and angles of congruent polygons are congruent.
6. Yes, in general, but it may be distorted by the angles of the mirrors.
8. c. 666.87 ft
10. The length and width of the document are enlarged by 21 percent. The copy is 121 percent the size of the original.

Exercises 10.1, page 516

1. Answers may vary.
   a. centimeters or meters
   c. millimeters or centimeters
   e. milligrams

2. a. 0.5   c. 0.670   e. 0.450   g. 0.024
5. About 35 meters. If we use their best times, Alan would be 7 seconds behind when Bill crosses the

finish line. At Alan's pace (400 meters/82 seconds), he will run about 35 meters in 7 seconds.

7. The difference in conversions is less than an inch.

11. **a.** The makers of the table essentially set the American/London foot as the unit, with 1,000 parts; the other numbers in this column enable us to see the length of other "foots" in relation to the American/London foot. By setting the unit foot as 1,000 parts, they were able to avoid decimals.

13. **b.** 48.3 liters × 34 oz/liter × 1 gallon/128 oz = 12.83 gallons; or by approximation, 48.3 liters × 1 quart/1 liter × 1 liter/4 quarts = 12.08 gallon. The difference would be about 3/4 gallon.

16. 5° Celsius, because each degree Celsius is equivalent to 1.8 degrees Fahrenheit.

18. 35 ft/9 sec × 1 mi/5280 ft × 60 sec/1 min × 60 min/1 hr = 2.65 miles per hour

20. $13\frac{1}{3}$%. 20% of 12 oz = 2.4 oz. 2.4 oz milk/18 oz coffee × 100 = $13\frac{1}{3}$%.

27. 100 meters! The height depends on the thickness of the paper. Multiply the thickness by the number of sheets of paper; 2^{20} = 1,048,567 sheets of paper. I measured the height of 2,000 sheets of paper (4 reams) and got 190 millimeters. This ratio is equivalent to 0.095 millimeter per sheet.

30. **a.** 1 kask is about 11 kilometers. 1 kask × 30 ush/kask × 60 gar/ush × 60 palm/gar × 4 in/palm × 2.54 cm/in × 1 m/100 cm × 1 km/1000 m = 10.97 km.

Exercises 10.2, page 531

1. **b.** P = 35.8 centimeters; A = 51.9 square centimeters

2. Solution paths will vary.
   a. $A = (5 \times 10) + (5 \times 5) + (10 \times 10) = 50 + 25 + 100 = 175$ square centimeters
   $A = (20 \times 10) - (5 \times 5) = 200 - 25 = 175$ square centimeters

3. $330.37. 9600 sq. ft./145 sq. ft. per bag × $4.99 per bag = $330.37.

5. No. The area to be fertilized is 6,020 square feet, which is greater than 5,000 square feet.

7. 14.14 inches. The lengths of the sides of a square with an area of 200 sq. in. is $\sqrt{200} = 10\sqrt{2} \approx 10 \times 1.414 \approx 14.14$.

9. **a.** Approximately 1.3 square inches

10. 6.8   **12.** 78 triangles

15. **a.** 11.1 square centimeters = 100 sq. cm./9 small triangles.

18. Approximately 11.2 feet

20. **b.** πr

22. Approximately 343 square centimeters

24. **a.** 10π

25. **a.** 80 square feet

26. **a.** 25 square inches   **b.** Not possible

33. $1,250\pi$ square feet   **34.** 7.4 feet

37. **a.** 3 meters
    b. About 2.24 meters
    c. About 1.73 meters
    d. The longest distance is along the edges of the cube; the shortest distance is directly through the cube.

38. **a.** Need to assume that the lengths of the shorter sides that are not marked are all 2 meters and that the angles that look like right angles are right angles. Area is 60 square meters.

Exercises 10.3, page 545

1. **a.** $S.A.$ = 1,474 square inches
   V = 2,160 cubic inches

2. **a.** $S.A.$ = 47 square feet
   V = 16 cubic feet
   c. $S.A.$ = 1,980 square feet

4. **a.** Predictions and explanations will vary.
   Volume of new tent ≈ 322.7 cubic feet
   Volume of old tent = 31.5 cubic feet
   The new tent is 291 cubic feet larger than the old tent.

6. 108,500 sheets (equivalent to 217 boxes)

8. 34 feet

10. **a.** Stack them in two layers with each layer a square, 2 × 2.
    c. Slowest melting: Exposed surface : enclosed surface = 3 : 2

Fastest melting: Exposed surface : enclosed surface = 34 : 7

14. **a.** Prediction: 15 cubic centimeters
    b. 16.387 cubic centimeters

16. **a.** $S.A.$ of small prism : $S.A.$ of large prism = 1 : 9
    The surface area is 3 times larger in two dimensions.
    b. Volume of small prism : volume of large prism = 1 : 27
    The volume is 3 times larger in three dimensions.

17. **a.** 55 dominoes

19. **a.** The cut should be one-fourth of the way from the end.